D1573164

Placenames of France

ALSO BY ADRIAN ROOM
AND FROM McFARLAND

Dictionary of Pseudonyms: 11,000 Assumed
Names and Their Origins, 4th ed. (2004)

Encyclopedia of Corporate Names Worldwide (2002)

A Dictionary of Music Titles: The Origins of the
Names and Titles of 3,500 Musical Compositions (2000)

A Dictionary of Art Titles: The Origins of the
Names and Titles of 3,000 Works of Art (2000)

Placenames of the World: Origins and Meanings of
the Names for Over 5,000 Natural Features, Countries,
Capitals, Territories, Cities and Historic Sites (1997)

Literally Entitled: A Dictionary of the Origins of
the Titles of Over 1,300 Major Literary Works
of the Nineteenth and Twentieth Centuries (1996)

Placenames of Russia and the Former Soviet Union:
Origins and Meanings of the Names for Over 2,000
Natural Features, Towns, Regions and Countries (1996)

African Placenames: Origins and Meanings
of the Names for Over 2,000 Natural Features,
Towns, Cities, Provinces and Countries (1994)

The Naming of Animals: An Appellative Reference to Domestic,
Work and Show Animals Real and Fictional (1993)

Corporate Eponymy: A Biographical Dictionary of the
Persons Behind the Names of Major American,
British, European and Asian Businesses (1992)

A Dictionary of Pseudonyms and Their Origins,
with Stories of Name Changes, 2d ed. (1989)

Naming Names: Stories of Pseudonyms and
Name Changes with a Who's Who (1981)

Placenames of France

Over 4,000 Towns,
Villages, Natural Features,
Regions and Departments

Adrian Room

McFarland & Company, Inc., Publishers
Jefferson, North Carolina, and London

LIBRARY OF CONGRESS CATALOGUING-IN-PUBLICATION DATA

Room, Adrian.
Placenames of France : Over 4,000 towns, villages,
natural features, regions and departments / Adrian Room.
p.   cm.
Includes bibliographical references.

ISBN 0-7864-2052-9 (illustrated case binding : 50# alkaline paper)

1. France — Gazetteers.   2. Names, Geographical — France.
3. France — Dictionaries.   I. Title: Place names of France.   II. Title.
DC14.R76   2004   914.4'003 — dc22   2004013460
British Library cataloguing data are available

Cover images ©2004 Digital Vision

McFarland & Company, Inc., Publishers
Box 611, Jefferson, North Carolina 28640
www.mcfarlandpub.com

Contents

Introduction

This new dictionary gives the origins of the names of just over 4,000 places in France, from natural features such as rivers, lakes, islands, and mountains to inhabited sites such as cities, towns, and villages. Modern and historic administrative regions are also covered, from the old provinces such as Normandy, Brittany, Burgundy, and Provence itself to present-day departments such as Calvados, Indre-et-Loire, and Seine-Maritime. The placenames of Corsica are included, as this island belongs directly to France and is geographically close to it. As such, it usually appears in gazetteers, tourist guides, and maps of France. Names in the two principalities of Monaco and Andorra are likewise entered.

Since, for many people, French history and culture are encapsulated in the history and culture of Paris, two of the five Appendices are devoted to the capital and its names: one to its famed features and tourist attractions (the Louvre, the Champs-Élysées, the Eiffel Tower, the Arc de Triomphe, the Pont Neuf, Montmartre), the other to the Métro with its evocatively named subway stations (Richelieu-Drouot, Maubert-Mutualité, Franklin D. Roosevelt, Porte des Lilas, Filles du Calvaire).

In some ways the history of the placenames of France matches that of the British Isles, spanning a period from pre-Celtic times to the present.

The chronology can be conveniently divided into seven stages, reflecting the various peoples who have settled in the land and the languages that they spoke.

(1) *Greek names: 6th century BC.* Greeks settled on the Mediterranean seaboard of France and their presence is preserved in such names as *Antibes*, *Marseille* and *Nice*, the last from the Greek word for "victory."

(2) *Celtic names: 5th century BC.* These are the oldest names found generally in France, mainly preserved in rivers and mountains, such as the *Isère* ("holy river") and the *Jura* ("wooded height"). They may in some cases be pre–Celtic or, more specifically, Gaulish, from the people who inhabited the region from at least the 6th century BC. Many Gaulish tribes gave the names of towns and cities today, as the *Bituriges* of *Bourges* or the *Parisii* of *Paris*. Geographically, Celtic names are most densely present in Brittany, just as in Britain they are in Wales (the French for which is *Pays de Galles*).

(3) *Gallo-Roman names: 1st century AD.* These are the most numerous names throughout Fance, testifying to the importance of Roman urban civilization, introduced into what was still known as Gaul from 121 BC. (The northern and central regions of

the land were conquered and subdued by Julius Caesar in the mid–1st century BC.) Cities such as *Orléans* (Latin *Aurelianum*) and *Grenoble* (*Gratianopolis*) bear the names of Roman rulers, while Roman baths gave the name of such places as *Aix-en-Provence* and *Bagnères-de-Bigorre*. There was a cult of the Roman goddess Venus at *Port-Vendres*, a Roman camp at *Castres*, and springs or fountains at the various places named *Fontenay*, while Latin names of trees gave the names of such places as *Fayence* (*fagus*, "beech") and *Rouvroy* (*robur*, "oak").

(4) *Germanic names: 5th century AD*. Throughout the Roman period, Gaul was subjected to repeated invasion by Germanic peoples such as the Franks (who gave the name of modern France), Burgundians, and Visigoths, and their presence is preserved today in such names as *La Fère* and *Ham*, this last evoking the *-ham* that ends so many English (and hence a number of American) placenames. Placenames in the northeast of France, near the borders with Belgium and Germany, are the most obvious witness to such names.

(5) *Norman names: 9th century AD*. Whereas the Greeks and Romans invaded Gaul from the south, and the Franks from the east, the Normans came (as their name implies) from the north, as a Scandinavian people. The names they bestowed are thus today found mainly in the north of France, in such places as *Caudebec* ("cold stream") and *Yvetot* ("Ivo's farm").

(6) *Religious names: 11th century*. Following the reign of Charlemagne (747–814), King of the Franks and Christian Emperor of the West, and throughout the whole of the medieval period, Christianity left its imprint in many placenames, both in religious words such as Latin *monasteriolum*, "little monastery," as at *Montreuil*, and in the omnipresent saints' names, such as *Saint-Jean* ("St. John"), *Saint-Martin* ("St. Martin"), and *Saint-Pierre* ("St. Peter"), sometimes preceded by *Dom-*, as *Domrémy*, "St. Remigius." John, Martin, and Peter are the three saints most frequently found in placenames, while others are *Saint-André* ("St. Andrew"), *Saint-Albin* ("St. Alban"), *Saint-Denis* ("St. Denis"), *Saint-Germain* ("St. Germanus"), *Saint-Hilaire* ("St. Hilary"), *Saint-Julien* ("St. Julian"), *Saint-Laurent* ("St. Lawrence"), and *Saint-Michel* ("St. Michael"). Names of female saints are less common, although *Saint-Marie* ("St. Mary") is quite widespread, as is to be expected in a predominantly Roman Catholic country.

(7) *Modern names: 16th century*. France has a reasonable representation of modern placenames, whether that of a famous person, as *Richelieu*, of an aristocratic residence, such as *Bouc-Bel-Air*, of a historic event, for example a battle, such as *Malakoff*, or in some way commemorative, as *Lorient* (after the French East India Company).

A more detailed listing of common words or elements in French placenames will be found in Appendix 5, page 322.

Mention of common words or elements is a reminder that France has an unusually high proportion of identical placenames, most of which are distinguished from one another by the addition of a suffix, sometimes quite cumbersome or lengthy in nature, giving a full name of four or more elements. Saints' names of this type include *Saint-Jean-du-Corail-des-Bois*, *Saint-Martin-de-Bienfaite-la-Cressonnière*, and *Saint-Quentin-*

la-Motte-Croix-au-Bailly. (Compound names like these are always written with hyphenated elements.)

Aside from the numerous saints' names, common names, as listed in the 2003 *Touring Atlas France* (see Bibliography, page 327), include (with 20 or more entries): *Beaulieu*
(22), *Beaumont* (44), *Bourg* (33), *Castelnau* (24), *La Chapelle* (175), *Château* (34),
Châteauneuf (32), *Châtillon* (33), *Courcelles* (32), *Ferrières* (22), *Fontaine* (64), *Fontenay* (28), *Labastide* (29), *Le Mesnil* (57), *Mont* (52), *Montigny* (46), *Montreuil* (30),
Neuilly (24), *(La) Neuville* (66), *Notre-Dame* (35), *Le Plessis* (22), *Pont* (65), *La Roche*
(25), *Savigny* (25), *Val* (21), *Vaux* (40), *Verneuil* (18), *(La) Ville* (45), *(La) Villeneuve*
(88), *Villers* (112), *Villiers* (48). (The meanings of all of these can be found in the Dictionary.) But such names, found with or without a distinguishing suffix, often form a
combining element with that suffix. For every name *Mont* with hyphenated suffix there
are thus dozens of combining *Mont* names, such as *Montfort*, plus the *Montigny* and
Montreuil names entered in their own right. The *Atlas* lists over 800 *Mont* or *Mont*-
related names, making the element one of the most frequently found, and testifying to
the country's prominent hill and mountain districts, from the Armorican Massif of the
northwest, Ardennes of the northeast, Alps of the southeast, and Pyrenees of the southwest, to the extensive highland of the Massif Central.

It is the "manmade" rather than natural names that predominate, however, and of
the 30 types instanced above, two thirds relate directly to buildings or structures: towns,
castles, chapels, churches, and bridges among them. (It will be noted that *église*, the actual word for "church," is conspicuously absent. This is because it is usually implied by
a saint's name.)

Not all of the names in France are obviously French. In those parts of the country where other languages are spoken, or which border other European countries, the
names refect the local tongue. In Brittany one thus has Breton names. In the northeast,
near Belgium, and the east, bordering on Germany, there are Flemish and German
names. There are not so many Italian placenames in the southeast, bordering on Italy,
but the presence of Basque and Spanish names in the southwest is readily apparent.
There are also the regional variations, such as the Provençal names of the south.

A word should be said about the department names. France is divided into 95 departments named and numbered alphabetically from 01 *Ain* to 95 *Val-d'Oise*. (Department 20 is now Corsica's two departments B1 and B2.) The names are mostly those of
rivers, such as 27 *Eure* or 80 *Somme*. In some cases two river names are joined by *et*,
"and," as 35 *Indre-et-Vilaine* or 82 *Tarn-et-Garonne*. In others a river name is prefixed
or suffixed by some defining word, such as 43 *Haute-Loire* or 76 *Seine-Maritime*. Sometimes a mountain name serves, as 39 *Jura* or 88 *Vosges*. Names derived neither from rivers
nor mountains include 21 *Côte-d'Or*, 22 *Côtes-d'Armor*, 29 *Finistère*, 40 *Landes*, 50
Manche, 56 *Morbihan*, 59 *Nord*, 62 *Pas-de-Calais*, 73 *Savoie*, 75 *Paris*, 85 *Vendée*, and
90 *Territoire de Belfort*, this last having a slightly different historical background. Readers unfamiliar with department names should exercise caution, as there are confusing
similarities. A distinction thus needs to be made between 04 *Alpes-de-Haute-Provence*,
05 *Hautes-Alpes*, and 05 *Alpes-Maritimes*, while 10 *Aube* and 11 *Aude*, 42 *Loire* and 45

Loiret, are subtly similar. The name of the Seine River occurs in four departments: 76 *Seine-Maritime*, 77 *Seine-et-Marne*, 92 *Hauts-de-Seine*, and 93 *Seine-Saint-Denis*. (The *Hauts* of 92 is a noun, unlike the adjectival *Hautes* of 05.)

Some of these department names have replaced earlier names as a result of demographic changes or euphemistic amelioration. Thus *Seine-Inférieure*, meaning simply "Lower Seine," but supposedly implying inferiority, is now *Seine-Maritime*, "Seaside Seine," while *Basses-Pyrénées*, "Lower Pyrenees," has now been elevated to *Pyrénées-Atlantiques*. (All such former names are cross-referred to the present names in the Dictionary.)

Form of Entries

The entries themselves are arranged alphabetically and have a consistent order of presentation: first the name, then a description of the named place and its location (usually by department), then its origin or etymology. Where a placename derives from a river name, the latter's own origin is included, if known. Similarly, where a name is based on a saint's name (there are around 350 such entries), an attempt is made to identify the saint in question. Historical forms of a name are often given, including those of Roman towns, together with the date or century of their recording.

Entries for names of non-French origin often give the local form of the name, as *Quimper* in Brittany, whose Breton name is *Kemper*, but names are not actually entered under such local forms. Similarly, where a place is near a national border, and is known by a native form of the name across that border, the foreign form is often given. Thus *Cernay*, near the German border, is known in Germany itself as *Sennheim*. (In this instance the French form of the name probably originated from the German.)

Where a place is usually known in the English-speaking world by the English form of its name, the place is cross-referred to the French form. Thus *Dunkirk* is referred to *Dunkerque* and *Brittany* to *Bretagne*. But the English forms are used in the entries themselves, so that *Brest* is described as a "Brittany city." (The noun form of the region name is preferred, to denote the geographical location of the place, rather than adjectival "Breton," which relates specifically to language or culture.)

Cross-references are made in **bold**, so that the entry for *Quercy* has a reference to **Cahors**.

A number of entries refer to "the associative suffix *-acum*." This Gallo-Roman ending indicates that the person named in the entry either owned the place or gave his or her name to it. Thus the Roman called *Callus* had some sort of connection with the place *Callac*, and the Gaul known as *Renos* gave his name to *Renage*. This *-acum* is also found in names outside France, so that York, England, was originally *Eboracum*, "place associated with Eburos."

The five appendices at the back of the book each have their explanatory preamble. A Bibliography concludes the work.

It is hoped that this dictionary, believed to be the first of its kind in English, will provide an illuminating insight into the placenames of one of the most venerable and vibrant countries of Europe.

Adrian Room
Summer, 2004

The Dictionary

Aa. *River, northern France.* The river derives its name from the Germanic root *aha*, meaning simply "water."

Abbeville. *Town, Somme.* The name was recorded in the 11th century as *Abbatis villa*, from Latin *abbas*, "abbot," and *villa*, "village," denoting its dependence on St. Riquier's abbey here (see **Saint-Riquier**).

Ablon-sur-Seine. *Town, Val-de-Marne.* The Paris suburb, on the **Seine** River, derives its name from the Germanic personal name *Abilo*.

Abondance. *Resort village, Haute-Savoie.* The name was recorded in the 12th century as *Abundantia*, Latin for "fullness," "plenty," denoting a fertile location.

Abreschwiller. *Village, Moselle.* The name was recorded in the 11th century as *Elberswylre*, from the Germanic personal name *Albheri* and Latin *villare*, "farmstead." The village is not far from the border with Germany, where it is known as *Alberschweiler*.

Les Abrets. *Village, Isère.* The name derives from Latin *arbor*, "tree," and the collective suffix *-etum*.

Abscon. *Village, Nord.* The name was recorded in the 12th century as *Asconium*, a derivative of Germanic *ask*, "ash tree."

Achenheim. *Village, Bas-Rhin.* The name probably represents the Germanic personal name *Askin*, from *ask*, "ash tree," and *heim*, "abode."

Achères. *Town, Yvelines.* The name derives from Latin *apiariae*, "apiaries," denoting a suitable place for keeping bees.

Achicourt. *Town, Pas-de-Calais.* The suburb of Arras derives its name from the Germanic personal name *Haric* and the associative suffix *-iacum*, followed by Latin *cortem*, accusative of *cors*, "estate."

Acigné. *Town, Ille-et-Vilaine.* The name was recorded in the 14th century as *Accigneium*, from the Roman personal name *Accinius*, from *Accius*, and the associative suffix *-acum*.

Adour. *River, southwest France.* The river was known to the Romans as *Aturus*, from a pre-Celtic root probably meaning simply "water." See also **Aire-sur-l'Adour**.

Agde. *Town, Hérault.* The name was recorded by Pliny in the 1st century AD as *Agatha*, from Greek *agatha*, the feminine form of *agathos*, "good," implying a propitious future.

Agen. *Town, Lot-et-Garonne.* The name was recorded by Ptolemy in the 2d century AD as *Aginnum*, from Gaulish *aginno*, "height," or *aganno*, "rock." It was the capital of the historic region of *Agenais*.

Agincourt *see* **Azincourt**

Agneaux. *Town, Manche.* The name of the suburb of Saint-Lô was recorded in the 11th century as *Agnels*, from Latin *agnellus*, "lamb," denoting a sheep farm here.

Ahun. *Village, Creuse.* The name was recorded in the 4th century as *Acitodunum*, from the Gaulish personal name *Agedo* and *dunon*, "fort."

L'Aigle. *Town, Orne*. The name was recorded in the 12th century as *Aquila*, Latin for "eagle," and until recently was spelled *Laigle*, with *L'*, "the," prefixed to French *aigle*, "eagle." "The town of L'Aigle is said to take its name from an eagle's nest that was found on the site where its castle, now demolished, was built. The natives of the town bear the nickname of 'Aiglons', or little eagles" [*AA Road Book of France*, p.258].

Aigrefeuille-d'Aunis. *Town, Charente-Maritime*. The name derives from Latin *acrifolium*, "holly." The addition locates the town in **Aunis**.

Aiguebelette-le-Lac. *Resort area, Savoie*. The name is a diminutive form of nearby **Aiguebelle**. The addition refers to the lake (*lac*) here of the same name.

Aiguebelle. *Resort village, Savoie*. The name was recorded in the 11th century as *Aquabella*, from Latin *aqua*, "water," and *bella*, "beautiful," referring to the valley of the Arc River here, which joins the Isère River nearby.

Aigueperse. *Village, Puy-de-Dôme*. The name was recorded in the 11th century as *Aqua sparsa*, from Latin *aqua*, "water," and *sparsa*, "scattered," "spread," denoting a dry area, with no local river.

Aigues-Mortes. *Town, Gard*. The name was recorded in the 13th century as *Aquae mortuae*, from Latin *aqua*, "water," and *mortua*, "dead," "stagnant," referring to the location amidst lagoons and salt pools in the Rhône estuary The town was founded as a seaport in the 13th century by Louis IX but is now silted up.

Aiguille du Midi *see* **Midi, Aiguille du**

Aiguilles. *Village, Hautes-Alpes*. The name derives from Latin *acucula*, "needle," denoting the pointed mountain peaks here in the Alps.

Aiguillon. *Town, Lot-et-Garonne*. The name was recorded in the 13th century as *Aculeo*, from Latin *acucula*, "needle," and the diminutive suffix *-one*.

L'Aiguillon-sur-Mer. *Village, Vendée*. The name has the same origin as **Aiguillon**, referring to the nearby headland *Pointe de l'Aiguille*, "needle point."

Aigurande. *Village, Indre*. The name has the same Celtic or pre-Celtic origin as **Ingrandes**. Aigurande lies between the sources of the Lavaud and Vauvre rivers.

Aillant-sur-Tholon. *Village, Yonne*. The name is of Celtic origin, from an element of unknown meaning with a suffix *-ent*. The village is on the *Tholon* River.

Ailly-sur-Noye. *Village, Somme*. The name derives from the Roman personal name *Allius* and the associative suffix *-acum*. The addition locates the village on the *Noye* River.

Ailly-sur-Somme. *Village, Somme*. The name shares the origin of **Ailly-sur-Noye**, but here the village is on the **Somme** River.

Aimargues. *Village, Gard*. The name was recorded in the 9th century as *Armasanicae*, from the Roman personal name *Armatius* and the suffix *-anica*.

Aime. *Village, Savoie*. The name was recorded in the 2d century as *Axima*, from the name of a local god *Aximo*.

Ain. *Department, eastern France*. The name is that of the river here, from Latin *Idanus*, from pre-Latin *inn*, "water," which also gave the name of the *Inn* River that rises in Switzerland and flows through Austria to Germany.

Ainhoa. *Village, Pyrénées-Atlantiques*. The village has a Basque name, from *aïn*, "beautiful," and a second element of unknown meaning.

Airaines. *Village, Somme*. The name was recorded in the 12th century as *Arenae*, from Latin *arena*, "sand."

Aire-sur-l'Adour. *Town, Landes*. The name was recorded in the 6th century as *Atora*, an early name of the **Adour** River, on which the town lies. It thus has the river name twice.

Aire-sur-la-Lys. *Town, Pas-de-Calais.* The name, recorded in the 9th century as *Aria*, comes from Latin *area*, "space," "courtyard," "garden," "house." The second part of the name, locating the town on the *Lys* River, distinguishes it from **Aire-sur-l'Adour**.

Airvault. *Village, Deux-Sèvres.* The name was recorded in the 10th century as *Aurea vallis*, from Old French *oire* (Latin *aureus*), "golden," and *vau* (Latin *vallis*), "valley." **Vallauris** and **Valloire** have names of identical meaning.

Aisne. *Department, northern France.* The name is that of the river here, recorded by Caesar in the 1st century BC as *Axona*, from pre-Latin *ax*, "river," and the river suffix *-ona*.

Les Aix-d'Angillon. *Village, Cher.* The name was recorded in the 11th century as *Aiae*, from Germanic *haga*, "hedge." The addition is properly *dan Gilon*, from *dan*, a form of Latin *dominus*, "lord," and the personal name *Gilon*.

Aix-en-Provence. *City, Bouches-du-Rhône.* The town was founded in 123 BC by Caius Sextius Calvinus and originally named for him as *Aquae Sextiae*, with Latin *aquae*, the plural of *aqua*, "water," referring to the Rhône here. The present name represents Latin *aquis*, the ablative (locative) plural of *aqua*. The addition locates the town in **Provence**.

Aixe-sur-Vienne. *Town, Haute-Vienne.* The name was recorded early as *Axia*, perhaps from the personal name *Axius*. The town is on the **Vienne** River.

Aix-les-Bains. *Resort town, Savoie.* The name derives from Latin *aquis*, as for **Aix-en-Provence**. The addition ("the baths") refers to the sulfur baths here, famous in Roman times.

Aix-Noulette, *Village, Pas-de-Calais.* The name was recorded in the 13th century as *Ais*, from Latin *aquis*, as for **Aix-en-Provence**. The addition was recorded in the 12th century as *Noellet*, from Latin *nauda*, "marshy place," blending with the suffix *-itta*.

Aizenay. *Town, Vendée.* The name represents *Asinacum*, from Latin *asinus*, "ass," perhaps used as a nickname, and the associative suffix *-acum*.

Ajaccio. *City, Corse-du-Sud.* The Corsican capital, in the southwest of the island, probably takes its name from pre-Low Latin *adjacium*, "halt," "resting place," referring to its site on the Mediterranean coast. A derivation in the name of the Greek mythical hero *Ajax* is also possible.

Albens. *Village, Savoie.* The name was recorded in the 2d century as *Albinenses*, from pre-Celtic *alba*, "hill," and the Gaulish suffix *-ennum*.

Albert. *Town, Somme.* The original name of the town was recorded in the 9th century as *Encra*, from the *Ancre* River here. The present name is that of Charles d'*Albert*, duke of Luynes, who was granted the marquisate here in 1617. See also *Luynes*.

Albertville. *Town, Savoie.* The town is named for Charles *Albert* (Carlo Alberto) of Savoy (1798-1849), king of Sardinia-Piedmont, who combined the villages of L'Hôpital and Conflans here in 1834.

Albi. *City, Tarn.* The name was recorded in the 5th century as *civitas Albigensium*, with Latin *civitas*, "city," prefixed to the Roman personal name *Albius* or pre-Celtic root *alb*, "hill," and a suffix of uncertain meaning.

Albigeois. *Historic region, southern France.* The region centered on **Albi**.

Albigny-sur-Saône. *Village, Rhône.* The name derives from the Roman personal name *Albinius* and the associative suffix *-acum*. The village lies by the **Saône** River.

Albon. *Village, Drôme.* The original form of the name, recorded in the 6th century, was *Epauna*, from Gaulish *epos*, "horse." This later became *Albon*, as if from the Roman personal name *Albus* and the suffix *-one*.

Albret. *Region, southwestern France.* The name of the former duchy is a corruption of *Lebret*, from Latin *Leporetum*, "region abounding in hares," from *lepus, leporis,* "hare."

Alby-sur-Chéron. *Village, Haute-Savoie.* The name was recorded in the 14th century as *Albiacum*, from the Roman personal name *Albius*, and the associative suffix *-acum*. The addition locates the village on the *Chéron* River.

Alençon. *City, Orne.* The name was recorded early as *Alencione*, from the Gaulish personal name *Alantius* and the suffix *-onem*.

Aléria. *Village, Haute-Corse.* The name of the village, in eastern Corsica, was recorded by Pliny in the 1st century AD as *Aleria*, from a pre-Latin word of unknown meaning.

Alès. *City, Gard.* The city, known until 1926 as *Alais*, takes its name from Merovingian *Alesto*, with a root of unknown meaning and the pre-Latin suffix *-est*.

Alet-les-Bains. *Village, Aude.* The name was recorded in the 9th century as *Electus*, Latin for "chosen," perhaps originally a personal name. The addition ("the baths") refers to the mineral springs here.

Alfortville *see* **Maisons-Alfort**

Algrange. *Town, Moselle.* The name was recorded in the 9th century as *Alkerengis*, from the Germanic personal name *Alker* and the suffix *-ing*.

Alincthun. *Village, Pas-de-Calais.* The name was recorded in the 12th century as *Alinthun*, from the Germanic personal name *Alo*, the connective particle *-ing-*, meaning "named after," and Old Saxon *tūn*, "farm." The name thus corresponds exactly to English *Allington*.

Alise-Sainte-Reine. *Village, Côte-d'Or.* The name of the Roman settlement here, recorded by Caesar in the 1st century BC, was *Alesia*, probably from Gaulish *alisia*, "cliff." The addition names the 3d-century martyr *St. Regina* of Autun.

Allaire. *Village, Morbihan.* The name derives from the Roman personal name *Hilarius*.

Allanche. *Resort village, Cantal.* The name was recorded in the 14th century as *Alancha*, from pre-Latin *al*, of uncertain meaning, and the Gaulish suffix *-anca*.

Allassac. *Village, Corrèze.* The name was recorded in the 13th century as *Allassacum*, from the Gaulish personal name *Alacius* and the associative suffix *-acum*.

Allauch. *Town, Bouches-du-Rhône.* The suburb of Marseille derives its name from the Roman personal name *Alaudius*, from Latin *alauda*, "lark."

Allemont. *Village, Isère.* The name was recorded in the 9th century as *Alemo*, from the Germanic personal name *Alamunt*.

Allennes-les-Marais. *Village, Nord.* The name derives from the Germanic personal name *Allin*. The addition means "the marshes."

Allevard. *Resort town, Isère.* The name was recorded in the 8th century as *Aravardus*, from the Germanic personal name *Araward*.

Allier. *Department, central France.* The name is that of the river here, recorded by Caesar in the 1st century BC as *Elaver* and by Apollinaris Sidonius in the 5th century AD as *Elaris*, representing the river root *el*, as probably for **Aube**, and the double suffix *-av* and *-er*.

Allonnes. *Town, Sarthe.* The suburb of Le Mans has a name recorded early as *Alaona* or *Aulana*, from the Gaulish personal name *Alauna* or *Alonna*, that of a god of wells and springs whose own name means "shining one." Allonnes is on the Sarthe River.

Allos. *Resort village, Alpes-de-Haute-Provence.* The name was recorded in the 11th century as *Alodes*, from *Aluntium*, the name of a settlement in Sicily in Roman times. The first part of this is of uncertain origin, but the suffix is pre-Latin *-unt*. The resort is now usually known as *Val-d'Allos*, from its location in the valley of this name.

Allouagne. *Village, Pas-de-Calais.* The location here was recorded in the 11th century as *silva Aslonias*, from Latin *silva*, "wood," and a name probably from Germanic *ask*, "ash tree," and a suffix of obscure origin.

Aloxe-Corton. *Village, Côte-d'Or.* The name was recorded in the 9th century as *Alussa*, probably from the Gaulish personal name *Alussius*, from *Alus*. *Corton* was originally a separate place.

Alpe-d'Huez. *Resort village, Isère.* The ski resort, high in the Oisan **Alps**, is based on the village of *Huez*. Its own name has an obscure, pre-Latin root and the pre-Latin suffix *-esius*.

Alpes-de-Haute-Provence. *Department, southeastern France.* The department has a name translating as "Alps of Upper Provence," referring to its location within the Provence **Alps** in the northern part of **Provence**. Until 1970 it was known as *Basses-Alpes* ("Lower Alps"), but this name was changed because of its suggestion of "inferiority."

Alpes-Maritimes. *Department, southeastern France.* The department has a name translating as "Maritime Alps," referring to its location in the lower part of the French **Alps** with the Mediterranean forming its southern border.

Alps. *Mountains, southeastern France.* The European mountain system, called in French *Alpes*, has a pre-Celtic name probably based on Indoeuropean *alp* or *alb*, "height."

Alsace. *Region, northeastern France.* Known to the Romans as *Alsatia*, the name of the present administrative region may derive from Gaulish *alisia*, "cliff." The Gauls, coming from what is now southern Germany, would have been impressed by the cliffs of the Vosges mountains here. Another possible source is in Gaulish *aliso*, "alder,"

or even in *Illzas*, an old name of the *Ill*, a tributary of the Rhine. The German name of Alsace is *Elsaß*.

Altkirch. *Town, Haut-Rhin.* Altkirch is near the German border and has a German name meaning "old church" (German *alt*, "old," and *Kirche*, "church").

Ambarès-et-Lagrave. *Town, Gironde.* The name combines two places. *Ambarès* derives its name from the Gaulish personal name *Ambarrus* and the suffix *-ensem*. *Lagrave* comes from pre-Latin *grava*, "stone," "pebble," denoting a stony or gravelly place.

Ambazac. *Town, Haute-Vienne.* The name was recorded in the 9th century as *Ambaciacinus*, from the Gaulish personal name *Ambatius*, as perhaps for **Amboise**, and the associative suffix *-acum*.

Ambérieu-en-Bugey. *Town, Ain.* The name was recorded in the 9th century as *Ambariacus*, from the Gaulish personal name *Ambarrius* and the associative suffix *-acum*. The addition locates the town in the region of **Bugey**.

Ambert. *Town, Puy-de-Dôme.* The town's Latin name was *Amberitus*, from Gaulish *ambe*, "river," and *ritu-*, "ford," referring to the Dore River here.

Ambès. *Village, Gironde.* The name derives from Gaulish *ambe*, "river," and the suffix *-ensem*. Ambès is on a tongue of land between the Garonne and Dordogne rivers.

Ambilly. *Town, Haute-Savoie.* The name derives from the Roman personal name *Ambillus* and the associative suffix *-acum*.

Ambleteuse. *Resort village, Pas-de-Calais.* The name, recorded in the 8th century as *Amfleat*, derives from Old English *flēot*, "bay," and Germanic *hof*, "farm." *Am-* is obscure.

Amboise. *Town, Indre-et-Loire.* The Romans knew the town as *Ambacia*, a name perhaps from Gaulish *ambe*, "river," referring to the Loire here, or from the Gaulish personal name *Ambatius*.

Ambrières-les-Vallées. *Village, Mayenne.* The name was recorded in the 11th century as *Ambreras*, either from the Gaulish personal name *Ambarrus* or more likely from Low Latin *amera*, "willow," and the suffix *-aria*. The addition ("the valleys") appeared relatively recently. The village is on the Varenne River.

Ambronay. *Village, Ain.* The name was recorded in the 10th century as *Ambroniacus*, from the personal name *Ambronus*, from the *Ambrones*, a Germanic tribe, and the associative suffix *-acum*.

Amélie-les-Bains-Palalda. *Resort town, Pyrénées-Orientales.* The resort, with its thermal springs, was originally known as *Arles-les-Bains*, from pre-Indoeuropean *arel*, "mountain," as for **Arles**, and French *les bains*, "the baths." In 1840 it was renamed for Marie-*Amélie* de Bourbon (1782-1866), queen of Louis-Philippe. *Palalda* is the old town above the Tech River here, its name coming from Latin *palatium*, "palace," and the personal name *Danus*.

Amfreville-la-Mi-Voie. *Village, Seine-Maritime.* The name was recorded in the 11th century as *Ansfredi villa*, from the Germanic personal name *Ansfrid* and Latin *villa*, "estate." The addition means "halfway," for a midway point on the Seine, distinguishing the village from *Amfreville-la-Campagne* ("the country"), *Amfreville-les-Champs* ("the fields"), and *Amfreville-sous-les-Monts* ("near the hills"), all in Eure.

Amiens. *City, Somme.* The city's Roman name was *Ambianum*, from the *Ambiani*, a Gaulish tribe, whose own name is from Gaulish *ambe*, "river," referring to the Somme River here. Until the 4th century AD, the settlement was known as *Samarobriva*, from *Samara*, the pre-Latin name of the **Somme**, and Gaulish *briua*, "bridge."

Amilly. *Town, Loiret.* The name derives from the Roman personal name *Amilius*, from *Amius*, and the associative suffix *-acum*.

Amnéville. *Town, Moselle.* The name was recorded in the 11th century as *Amerelli villa*, from the Germanic personal name *Amino* and the associative suffix *-iacum*, with Latin *villa*, "estate." When in German hands (1870–1918, 1939–44), Amnéville was known as *Stahlheim*, "steel town," for its metalworks. From the 1980s these were replaced by a thriving leisure industry, with a thermal establishment and a zoo, so that the town is now often known as *Amnéville-les-Thermes*.

Amphion-les-Bains. *Resort town, Haute-Savoie.* The name of the resort on Lake Geneva is associated with *Amphion*, the son of Zeus and Antiope in Greek mythology. The addition ("the baths") refers to the spa and bathing facilities here.

Amplepuis. *Town, Rhône.* The name was recorded in the 11th century as *Amploputeus*, from Latin *amplus*, "ample," and *puteus*, "well." The reference is to the abundant springs here in the Beaujolais hill range.

Ancenis. *Town, Atlantique.* The name was recorded in the 12th century as *Anciensis*, from the Roman personal name *Antianus* and the associative suffix *-acum*.

Ancerville. *Village, Meuse.* The name, recorded in the 12th century as now, derives from the Germanic personal name *Ansher* and Latin *villa*, "estate."

Ancy-le-Franc. *Village, Yonne.* The name was recorded in the 8th century as *Anciacum*, from the Roman personal name *Ansius* or *Antius* and the associative suffix *-acum*. The addition (*franc*, "free") denotes the community's exemption from feudal taxes.

Les Andelys. *Town, Eure.* The town represents the twin communities *Le Grand-Andely* and *Le Petit-Andely*. Hence its plural name, from the Roman name *Andeliacum*, itself from the Gaulish personal name *Andala* and the associative suffix *-acum*.

Andernos-les-Bains. *Resort town, Gironde.* The name derives from the Gaulish personal name *Andernus* and the Aquitanian suffix *-ossum*. The addition ("the baths") refers to the bathing facilities here.

Andlau. *Village, Bas-Rhin.* The name is that of the river here, a small tributary of the Ill, recorded in the 13th century as *Andela*. An alternate name is *Andlau-au-Val* ("in the valley").

Andorra. *Principality, southwestern France.* The Pyrenean principality, under the joint suzerainty of the president of France and the bishop of Urgel (Spain), may derive its name from Navarrese *andurrial*, "terrain covered in bushes." Its capital is *Andorra-la-Vella* (Catalan, "the old"), Spanish *Andorra-la-Vieja*, French *Andorre-la-Vieille*.

Andrésy. *Town, Yvelines.* The name was recorded in the 8th century as *Ondresiacum*, from the Germanic personal name *Underich* and the associative suffix *-iacum*.

Andrézieux-Bouthéon. *Town, Loire.* The name is properly that of two separate places. The first was recorded in the 10th century as *Undresiacum*, with an origin as for **Andrésy.** The second was recorded in the 11th century as *Botedonus*. It is obscure in origin but may combine a Gaulish personal name *Bodius* and *dunon*, "hill," "height."

Anduze. *Village, Gard.* The name, recorded early as *Andusia*, appears to represent pre-Latin *and*, of unknown origin, and the suffix *-usia*.

Anet. *Village, Eure-et-Loir.* The name was recorded in the 12th century as *Anetum*, from Gaulish *ana*, "marsh," and the diminutive suffix *-ittum*.

Angers. *City, Maine-et-Loire.* The city's earlier name was *Andecavis*, from the *Andecavi*, a Gaulish tribe, whose own name is of uncertain origin. The Gaulish name of the settlement is unknown. The Romans knew it as *Juliomagus*, "Julius's market," for *Julius* Caesar, and Gaulish *magos*, "market." (Compare *Caesaromagus* as the Roman name of **Beauvais.**)

Angerville. *Village, Essonne.* The name probably derives from the Germanic personal name *Ansgar* and Latin *villa*, "estate."

Les Angles. *Town, Gard.* The name represents Latin *angulus*, "angle," denoting a settlement built in a corner of land.

Angles-sur-l'Anglin. *Village, Vienne.* Both parts of the name derive from the *Anglin* River here, recorded in the 11th century as *Engle*. For a similar name, see **Aire-sur-l'Adour.**

Anglet. *Town, Pyrénées-Atlantiques.* The name was recorded in the 12th century as *Angles*, from Latin *angulus*, "angle," meaning a corner of land, and the diminutive suffix *-ittum*.

Angoulême. *City, Charente.* The name was recorded in the 6th century as *Ecolisma*, from pre-Latin *ekol*, of uncertain origin, and the Gaulish superlative suffix *-isama*, related to Latin *-issimus*.

Angoulins. *Village, Charente-Maritime.* The name probably derives from the Germanic personal name *Agolenus*.

Angoumois. *Region, western France.* The former province takes its name from **Angoulême**, its historic capital.

Angres. *Town, Pas-de-Calais.* The suburb of Liévin has a name recorded in the 11th century as *Ancra*, probably representing an old river name related to that of the *Ancre*, which gave the original name of **Albert.**

Aniane. *Village, Hérault.* The name was recorded in the 8th century as *Anianum*, from the Roman personal name *Annius* and the suffix *-anum*.

Aniche. *Town, Nord.* The name was recorded in the 11th century as *Enich*, from the Germanic personal name *Annico*.

Anjou. *Historic region, northwestern France.* The name comes from the *Andecavi*, the Gaulish tribe who gave the name of **Angers**, their capital here.

Annay. *Town, Pas-de-Calais.* The name

was recorded in the 10th century as *Aldnais*, from Latin *alnus*, "alder," and the collective suffix *-etum*.

Annecy. *Resort city, Haute-Savoie*. The name was recorded in the 9th century as *Anericiacum*, from the Germanic personal name *Anerik* and the Latin associative suffix, of Gaulish origin, *-iacum*. This is the first mention of the name, replacing earlier *Boutae*, the name of the Gallo-Roman settlement here.

Annecy-le-Vieux. *Town, Haute-Savoie*. The suburb of **Annecy**, 1½ miles from the city center, derives its name from the Germanic personal name *Anerik* and the associative suffix *-iacum*. The addition ("the old") implies an earlier settlement.

Annemasse. *Town, Haute-Savoie*. The name has its origin in the Gaulish personal name *Adnamatius*, with Latin *villa*, "estate," "village," understood.

Anneyron. *Village, Drôme*. The name was recorded in the 9th century as *villa Anarioni*, from Latin *villa*, "estate," and the Roman personal name *Annarius*, from *Annius*, with the suffix *-onem*.

Annezin. *Town, Pas-de-Calais*. The suburb of Béthune has a name recorded in the 12th century as *Anasin*, from the Roman personal name *Anacius*, a variant of *Anicius*, and the suffix *-inum*.

Annœullin. *Town, Nord*. The name was recorded in the 12th century as *Ennelin*, from the Germanic personal name *Annolenus*.

Annonay. *Town, Ardèche*. The name was recorded early as *Anonacus*, from the Roman personal name *Anno, Annonis*, and the associative suffix *-acum*.

Annot. *Resort village, Alpes-de-Haute-Provence*. The name was recorded in the 11th century as *Anoth*, from Gaulish *ana*, "marsh," and the suffix *-ottum*.

Anse. *Town, Rhône*. The name was recorded in the 4th century as *Asa Paulina*, with the first word either from the Roman

personal name *Ansius* or *Antius* or, more likely, from Latin *ansa*, "handle," "loop," here used figuratively of the bend in the Saône river near which the town lies.

Antibes. *City and port, Alpes-Maritimes*. The city was founded in the 4th century BC as the Greek colony *Antipolis*, "city opposite," from *anti*, "opposite," and *polis*, "city," denoting its location across the Baie des Anges from Nice.

Antony. *Town, Hauts-de-Seine*. The Paris suburb has a name recorded in the 9th century as *Antoniacum*, from the Roman personal name *Antonius* and the associative suffix *-acum*.

Anzin. *Town, Nord*. The suburb of Valenciennes derives its name from the Germanic personal name *Anso* and the suffix *-ing*.

Appoigny. *Village, Yonne*. The name was recorded in the 9th century as *Apognaicum*, from the Roman personal name *Apponius* and the associative suffix *-acum*.

Apt. *Town, Vaucluse*. The name was recorded by Pliny in the 1st century AD as *Apta Julia*, from a pre-Latin mountain name and the Roman personal name *Julius*.

Aquitaine. *Region, southwestern France*. Known to the Romans as *Aquitania*, the present administrative region derives its name from Latin *aqua*, "water," referring to its location between the Pyrenees and the Garonne River, and a suffix that presumably means "country."

Aragnouet. *Village, Hautes-Pyrénées*. The name derives from Gascon *aragnou*, "sloe," and the collective suffix *-et*.

Aramon. *Village, Gard*. The name was recorded in the 11th century as *Aramonum*, perhaps from the Germanic personal name *Aramund*.

Arbent. *Village, Ain*. The name represents pre-Celtic *alba*, "hill," "fort," "settlement," and the suffix *-incum*.

Arbois. *Town, Jura*. The name is of obscure origin. It may derive from a Gallo-

Roman personal name *Arvenius* and an Aquitanian suffix *-ossa* or from a form of pre-Latin *alba*, "hill."

L'Arbresle. *Town, Rhône.* The name was recorded in the 13th century as *ecclesia Arbrelle*, from Latin *ecclesia*, "church," and *arbores*, "trees," with the diminutive suffix *-ella.*

Arc. *Village, Haute-Saône.* The name derives from Latin *arcus*, "arch," referring to a bridge over the Saône River here. The village is also known as *Arc-lès-Gray*, from *lès*, "near," and the name of nearby **Gray.**

Arcachon. *Resort town, Gironde.* The name is recorded early as *Arcaisso*, containing the pre-Latin element *cass* found in the names of several Gaulish tribes, such as the *Veliocasses*, whose name may mean "curly-haired ones," from *uelio-*, "better," and *-casses*, "hair."

Arc-en-Barrois. *Village, Haute-Marne.* The name was recorded in the 12th century as *Arcus*, from Latin *arcus*, "arch" (of a bridge), here over the Aujon River. The addition distinguishes this Arc from others by locating it in **Barrois.** (Joan of Arc's family probably took their name from this Arc, although she herself was never actually known as "d'Arc," and on the first day of her trial she stated that she did not know her family name. She was thus referred to as just *Jehanne* or *Jehanne la Pucelle.* See **Domrémy-la-Pucelle.**)

Arcis-sur-Aube. *Village, Aube.* The name was recorded in the 4th centuiry as *Artiaca*, from the Roman personal name *Arcius* or *Arsius*, or the Gaulish name *Artius* (from *artos*, "bear"), and the associative suffix *-acum.* This addition locates the village on the **Aube** River.

Les Arcs. *Town, Var.* The name was recorded in the 11th century as *Archos*, from Latin *arcus*, "arch" (of a bridge). Les Arcs is near the Argens River.

Arcueil. *Town, Val-de-Marne.* The name was recorded in the 11th century as *Arcolei*, from Latin *arcus*, "arch" (of a bridge) and Gaulish *ialon*, "clearing," "settlement." The bridge would have been over the Bièvre River here.

Arcy-sur-Cure. *Village, Yonne.* The name was recorded in the 12th century as *Arsiacum*, from the Roman personal name *Arcius* or *Arsius*, or the Gaulish personal name *Artius* (from *artos*, "bear"), and the associative suffix *-acum.* The village is on the *Cure* River.

Ardèche. *Department, southeastern France.* The name is that of the river here, recorded by the Romans as *Ardesco*, perhaps from the river root *ar* or from Gaulish *arduo-*, "high," as probably for the **Ardennes**, with the suffix *-esc.*

Ardennes. *Department, northeastern France.* The wooded plateau that extends over parts of southeastern Belgium and northern Luxembourg, as well as northern France, probably derives its name from Gaulish *arduo-*, "high," and the suffix *-unna*, although an alternate theory takes it from *ar duenn*, "land of forests," from *are*, "before," "beside," and *deruos*, "oak." There was also a Celtic goddess *Arduina*, whose cult was active until the 14th century.

Ardentes. *Village, Indre.* The name was recorded in the 11th century as *Ardentia*, perhaps from the Roman personal name *Ardentius*, a derivative of Latin *ardens*, "burning," possibly by way of a nickname.

Ardres. *Village, Pas-de-Calais.* The name was recorded in the 11th century as *Arda*, from Dutch *aard*, "field."

Argelès-Gazost. *Resort town, Hautes-Pyrénées.* The first part of the name is of unknown origin, though some have derived it either from Occitan *argelas*, a type of prickly gorse, or Latin *argilla*, "clay." The second part is of pre-Latin origin and equally obscure, with the pre-Latin suffix *-ostum.*

Argelès-sur-Mer. *Resort town, Pyrénées-Orientales.* The name, recorded in the 13th century as *Argilers*, has the same uncertain origin as **Aregelès-Gazost**. The town is not quite "on sea," as the addition implies, but is near the Mediterranean. The actual beach is at nearby *Argelès-Plage*.

Argences. *Village, Calvados*. The name derives from the Roman personal name *Argentius*.

Argentan. *Town, Orne*. The name, recorded in the 11th century as *ecclesia Argentoni*, with Latin *ecclesia*, "church," "religious community," derives from Gaulish *arganton*, "silver," a borrowing from Latin *argentum*, presumably referring to silver mines formerly here.

Argentat. *Town, Corrèze*. The name represents Latin *argentum*, "silver," and the suffix *-ate*.

Argenteuil. *City, Oise*. The name was recorded in the 7th century as *Argentogilum*, from the Gaulish personal name *Argentius*, from *arganton* (see **Argentan**), and *ialon*, "clearing."

L'Argentière-la-Bessée. *Village, Hautes-Alpes*. The name was recorded in the 13th century as *castrum Argenterie*, from Latin *castrum*, "fort," and *argentum*, "silver." Silver-bearing ore was mined here from the 12th through 19th centuries. The addition names nearby *La Bessée*, from Low Latin *bettia*, "birch wood," from Gaulish *betua*, "birch."

Argenton-Château. *Village, Deux-Sèvres*. The name was recorded in the 11th century as *Argentus*, from the Gaulish personal name *Argantius*, from *arganton*, "silver." The addition refers to the former castle (*château*) here.

Argenton-sur-Creuse. *Town, Indre*. The name was recorded in the 4th century as *Argantomago*, from the Gaulish personal name *Argantius*, from *arganton*, "silver," and *magos*, "field," "market." The addition refers to the **Creuse** River here.

Argentré. *Village, Mayenne*. The name was recorded in the 9th century as *Argentratus*, from the Gaulish personal name *Ar-gantius* (from *arganton*, "silver"), and *rate*, "fort."

Argentré-du-Plessis. *Village, Ille-et-Vilaine*. The origin of the name is as for **Argentré**. The addition derives from Old French *plaissié*, "enclosure of plashed branches."

Argent-sur-Sauldre. *Village, Cher*. The name was recorded in the 11th century as *Argentum*, from Latin *argentum*, "silver," meaning a place where the metal was found or mined. The addition locates the village on the *Grande Sauldre* River.

Argonne. *Region, northeastern France*. The name of the wooded plateau was recorded in the 10th century as *sylva Arguennensis*, from Latin *silva*, "wood," and probably a variant form of the name of the **Ardennes**.

Ariège. *Department, southern France*. The name is that of the river here, recorded early as *Aregia*, based on the river root *ar*, as for **Ardèche**.

Arlanc. *Village, Puy-de-Dôme*. The name was recorded in the 10th century as *Arlinco*, from pre-Indoeuropean *ar-el*, "mountain," as for **Arles**.

Arles. *City, Bouches-du-Rhône*. The city was known to the Romans as *Arelatum* or *Arelate*, probably from pre-Indoeuropean *ar-el*, "mountain," and the suffix *-ate*. An alternate origin takes the name from Gaulish *are*, "by," a borrowing from Greek *para*, and *late*, "marsh," from Greek *platus*, "flat." A derivation in French *large autel*, "broad altar," from Latin *ara lata*, is simply popular etymology.

Arles-sur-Tech. *Village, Pyrénées-Orientales*. The origin of the name is as for **Arles**, from which the village is distinguished by its location on the *Tech* River.

Arleux. *Village, Nord*. The name was recorded in the 12th century as *Allues*, from Germanic *alod*, "allodium," meaning an estate not subject to a feudal superior.

Armagnac. *Region, southwestern France*.

The region's Latin name was *pagus Armeni-acensis*, from *pagus*, "country," and a family name *Armenia* of uncertain origin.

Armentières. *Town, Nord*. The name derives from Latin *armentum*, "cattle," and the suffix *-aria*, meaning a place where cattle were raised, otherwise a stock farm.

Armorica *see* **Armorique**

Armorique. *Region, northwestern France*. The name for what is now *Brittany* (see **Bretagne**) derives from Gaulish *Aremorica*, from *are*, "beside," "by," and *mori*, "sea." The name has an alternate form *Armor*, as for the department **Côtes-d'Armor**.

Arnac-Pompadour. *Village, Corrèze*. The name was recorded early as *Artonacus*, from the Gaulish personal name *Artonos* (from *artos*, "bear") and the associative suffix *-acum*. The addition refers to the 15th-century château here which Louis XV gave to the Marquise de *Pompadour*, who took her title from it. Its own name perhaps derives from pre-Latin *pomp*, "hill," "height."

Arnage. *Town, Sarthe*. The suburb of Le Mans has a name recorded in the 11th century as *Anegia*, probably from a Latin word *arenaticum*, from *arena*, "sand."

Arnay-le-Duc. *Village, Côte-d'Or*. The name was recorded in the 12th century as *Arnetum*, either from the Gaulish personal name *Arnos* and the associative suffix *-acum* or, perhaps more likely, from Old Provençal *arn*, the name of a thorny shrub of the genus *Paliurus*, and the collective suffix *-etum*. The addition refers to the duke who was the local lord.

Arnouville-lès-Gonesse. *Town, Val-d'Oise*. The name was recorded in the 11th century as *Ermenovilla*, from the Germanic personal name *Irminold* and Latin *villa*, "estate." (**Hermenonville**, Oise, has a name of identical origin.) The addition locates the town near *(lès)* **Gonesse**, now an outer suburb of Paris.

Arpajon. *Town, Essonne*. The original name of the settlement, as recorded in the

11th century, was *Castra*, from Latin *castra*, "camp." In 1720 a marquisate was erected here for Louis de Sévérac, marquis of **Arpajon-sur-Cère**, Cantal, and the place adopted that name.

Arpajon-sur-Cère. *Town, Cantal*. The name probably derives from a Gaulish personal name *Arepaius* and the suffix *-onem*. The addition of the river name *Cère* distinguishes the town from **Arpajon**, Essonne, which adopted the name in the 18th century.

Arques. *Town, Pas-de-Calais*. The suburb of Saint-Omer has a name recorded in the 7th century as *Arkae*, from Latin *arca*, "arch" (of a bridge). Arques is on the Aa River.

Arques-la-Bataille. *Village, Seine-Maritime*. The name, recorded in the 11th century as *Archis*, has the same origin as that of **Arques**. The addition ("the battle") refers to Henry IV's defeat of the Catholic League under the duke of Mayenne in 1589.

Arras. *City, Pas-de-Calais*. The present name derives from the Gaulish tribe known as the *Atrebates*, from *treb-*, "habitation," related to Latin *tribus*, "tribe." The city's earlier name, recorded by Caesar in the 1st century BC, was *Nemetocenna*, from Gaulish *nemeton*, "sacred temple," and (perhaps) the personal name *Cenna*. A later Gallo-Roman name, with this same Gaulish word and the tribal name, was *Nemetacum Atrebatum*. Arras is the historic capital of **Artois**.

Arreau. *Village, Hautes-Pyrénées*. The name derives from the Basque (Aquitanian) root *harr*, "stone," "rock," with the pre-Latin suffix *-evum*.

Arrée, Monts d'. *Region, northwestern France*. The hilly region of Brittany has the Breton name *Menez Arre*, from *menez*, "mountain," and *Arre*, from pre-Indoeuropean *ar*, "mountain."

Arromanches. *Resort village, Calvados*. The name was recorded in the 13th century as *Aremance*, from a word or element of obscure origin and the suffix *-antia*. The resort is also known as *Arromanches-les-Bains* ("the baths") for its bathing facilities.

Ars-sur-Moselle. *Town, Moselle*. The name was recorded in the 9th century as *Arx*, from Latin *arcus*, "arch" (of a bridge), here over the **Moselle**, where several arches remain of the Roman aqueduct that crossed the river.

Artigues-près-Bordeaux.   *Town, Gironde*. The name, of pre-Latin origin, probably derives from Aquitanian *artica*, "fallow land." The addition locates the town near (*près*) **Bordeaux**.

Artix. *Village, Pyrénées-Atlantiques*. The name was recorded in the 13th century as *Artits*, from an Aquitanian root of uncertain origin and a pre-Latin suffix of some kind.

Artois. *Historic region, northern France*. The region takes its name from the *Atrebates*, the Gaulish people who gave the name of **Arras**, their capital.

Arudy. *Village, Pyrénées-Atlantiques*. The name was recorded in the 13th century as *Aruri*, from Basque *harr*, "rock," and *ur*, "water."

Arve. *River, southeastern France*. The Arve takes its name from the river root *ar*, as for **Ardèche**.

Asfeld. *Village, Ardennes*. The original name of the settlement was *Écry*, recorded in the 8th century as *Erchreco villa*, probably from a Germanic personal name *Ercanrik*, with Latin *villa*, "estate." In 1671 the community was bought by Jean-Jacques III of Mesmes, count of *Avaux*, to expand his nearby estate, and renamed *Avaux-la-Ville*. After his death, in 1726, his two daughters were authorized by the king to partition the estate and dispose of it. It took its present name in 1728, when the residue of the original estate was bought by Claude-François Bidal, baron d'*Asfeld*, and was erected into a marquisate on his ennoblement as marquis.

Asnelles. *Resort village, Calvados*. The name was recorded in the 11th century as *Anerias*, from Latin *asinus*, "ass," and the suffix *-ella*, denoting a place where asses were bred. The resort is also known as *Asnelles-sur-Mer*, for its location on the English Channel.

Asnières-sur-Seine. *Town, Hauts-de-Seine*. The name of the Paris suburb was recorded in the 12th century as *Asnerias*, from Latin *asinus*, "ass," and the suffix *-aria*, giving a sense "place where asses are bred." The addition locates the town on the **Seine** River.

Aspet. *Village, Haute-Garonne*. The name apparently comprises a pre-Latin element *asp* of uncertain origin and meaning and a suffix *-etum* or *-ittum*.

Aspres-sur-Buëch. *Village, Hautes-Alpes*. The name derives from Latin *asper*, "rough," "rocky," here used as a noun, so meaning "rocky height." The village is on the *Buëch* River.

Athis-de-l'Orne. *Village, Orne*. The name was recorded in the 14th century as *Athies*, from Gaulish *attegia*, "hut," "cabin," denoting a rustic Gaulish house rather than a Roman *casa*. The addition of the name of the **Orne** River distinguishes the place from **Athis-Mons**.

Athis-Mons. *Town, Essonne*. The name of the Paris suburb, recorded in the 12th century as *Attiis*, has the same origin as that of **Athis-de-l'Orne**, here with Latin *mons*, "mount."

Attigny. *Village, Ardennes*. The name derives from the Roman personal name *Attinius*, from *Attinus*, and the associative suffix *-acum*.

Aubagne. *Town, Bouches-du-Rhône*. The name was recorded in the 11th century as *villa Albanea*, from Latin *villa*, "village," and the Roman personal name *Albanius*.

Aube. *Department, northeastern France*. The name is that of the river here, probably from the river root *al* or *el*, as for **Allier** and

Ardèche, influenced by Latin *albus*, "white."

Aubenas. *Town, Ardèche*. The name was recorded in the 10th century as *Albenate*, from pre-Celtic *alba*, "hill," and the double suffix *-enn* and *-ate*. Aubenas lies on a hill overlooking the Ardèche River.

Auberchicourt. *Town, Nord*. The name arose in two stages, and at first comprised the Germanic personal name *Odberht* and the associative suffix *-iacum*, giving the *Auberchi-* of the present name. Latin *cortem*, accusative of *cors*, "estate," was added later.

Aubergenville. *Town, Yvelines*. The name, popularly said to represent *auberge-en-ville*, "village inn," was recorded in the 12th century as *Bargenvilla*, from the Germanic female personal name *Autberga* and Latin *villa*, "estate," "village."

Aubervilliers. *City, Seine-Saint-Denis*. The Paris suburb has a name recorded in the 11th century as *Albertivillare*, from the Germanic personal name *Adalberht*, "Albert," and Latin *villare*, "farmstead."

Aubeterre-sur-Dronne. *Village, Charente*. The name derives from Latin *alba terra*, "white earth." "Aubeterre ... owes its name to the amphitheatre of chalk cliffs against which it is built, high above the river Dronne" [Young, p.214].

Aubevoye. *Village, Eure*. The name was recorded in the 11th century as *Albavia*, from Latin *alba*, "white," and *via*, "way."

Aubière. *Town, Puy-de-Dôme*. The name represents Latin *alba*, "white poplar," and the suffix *-aria*.

Aubignan. *Village, Vaucluse*. The name was recorded in the 10th century as *Albegnano*, from the Roman personal name *Albinius* and the suffix *-anum*.

Aubigny-sur-Nère. *Town, Cher*. The name was recorded in the 8th century as *Albiniacus*, from the Roman personal name *Albinius* and the associative suffix *-acum*. The addition locates the town on the *Nère* River.

Aubin. *Town, Aveyron*. The name was recorded in the 10th century as *Albinio*, from the Roman personal name *Albinus*.

Auboué. *Village, Meurthe-et-Moselle*. The name was recorded in the 12th century as *Banvadus*, apparently representing Latin *bonus vadus*, "good ford," meaning one easy to use, here over the Orne River. The initial *Au-* of the name probably represents French *au*, "at the."

Aubusson. *Town, Creuse*. The name was recorded in the 12th century as *Albuso*, from the Roman personal name *Albucius* and the suffix *-onem*.

Auby. *Town, Nord*. The name was recorded in the 12th century as *Albi*, from the Roman personal name *Albius* and the associative suffix *-acum*.

Aucamville. *Village, Haute-Garonne*. The name derives from the Germanic female personal name *Auka* (from Gothic *aukan*, "to increase") and Latin *villa*, "estate."

Auch. *City, Gers*. The name of the original settlement here was recorded in the 1st century AD as *Elimberrum*, from Basque *ili*, "town," and *berri*, "new." In the 4th century the town adopted a name from the Aquitanian tribe known as the *Auscii*, from Basque *euskal*, "Basque." Their capital was at *Elusa*, modern **Eauze**.

Auchel. *Town, Pas-de-Calais*. The name, recorded in the 11th century as *Alceel*, is a diminutive form of the name of **Auchy-les-Mines**.

Auchy-les-Mines. *Town, Pas-de-Calais*. The name was recorded in the 12th century as *Alcis*, from the Roman personal name *Alcius* and the associative suffix *-acum*. The original full name was *Auchy-lès-La Bassée*, after nearby **La Bassée**. The addition to the present name refers to the former coal mines here.

Aude. *Department, southern France*. The name is that of the river here, recorded by Pliny in the 1st century AD as *Atax, Atacis*, itself of uncertain origin.

Audenge. *Village, Gironde*. The name probably derives from the Germanic personal name *Aldo* and the suffix *-ing*, but could represent the Germanic female personal name *Aldinga*.

Audierne. *Resort village and port, Finistère*. The name of the Brittany village is a French form of its Breton name *Gwaien*, recorded in the 15th century as *Goezian*, from the Breton saint *Gwedian*. The French form itself may represent *au Gwedian*, "to Gwedian."

Audincourt. *Town, Doubs*. The name was recorded in the 12th century as *Adincourt*, from the Germanic personal name *Adwin* and Latin *cortem*, accusative of *cors*, "estate."

Audincthun. *Village, Pas-de-Calais*. The name derives from the Germanic personal name *Odo*, the connective particle *-ing-*, meaning "named after," and Old Saxon *tūn*, "farm." Many names in the northwest of Pas-de-Calais testify to an early Saxon settlement.

Audruicq. *Town, Pas-de-Calais*. The name was recorded in the 12th century as *Ouderwich*, from Germanic *oud*, "old," and *wich*, "district."

Audun-le-Roman. *Village, Meurthe-et-Moselle*. The name was recorded in the 7th century as *villa Adtantina*, from Latin *villa*, "estate," and a name probably representing Latin *aquae ductus*, "aqueduct," with a change to the ending. The addition, referring to a region where a Roman (Latin) language was spoken, distinguishes the village from **Audun-le-Tiche**.

Audun-le-Tiche. *Town, Moselle*. The name, recorded in the 14th century as *Audieux*, has the same origin as **Audun-le-Roman**, the addition here referring to a region where a Germanic language was spoken. (*Tiche* relates to English *Teutonic* and to German *deutsch*, "German.")

Aulnat. *Town, Puy-de-Dôme*. The suburb of Clermont-Ferrand has a name recorded in the 11th century as *Alnaco*, from Latin *alnus*, "alder," and the associative suffix *-acum*.

Aulnay-de-Saintonge. *Village, Charente-Maritime*. The name was recorded in the 4th century as *Aunedonacum*, from the Gaulish personal name *Aunedo* and the associative suffix *-acum*. The addition locates the village in **Saintonge**.

Aulnay-sous-Bois. *Town, Seine-Saint-Denis*. The name was recorded in the 13th century as *Alnetum*, from Latin *alnus*, "alder," and the collective suffix *-etum*. The addition ("by the wood") distinguishes the town from other places of the same name

Aulnoye-Aymeries. *Town, Nord*. The first part of the name represents Latin *alnus*, "alder," and the suffix *-eta*. The second part, originally the name of a separate place, derives from the Germanic personal name *Aimar* and the associative suffix *-iacum*.

Aulnoy-lez-Valenciennes. *Town, Nord*. The name was recorded in the 11th century as *Alnetum*, as for **Aulnoye-Aymeries**. The addition locates the town near (*lez*) **Valenciennes**.

Aulus-les-Bains. *Hamlet, Ariège*. The name probably derives from the Roman personal name *Aulus* and the suffix *-ucium*. The addition ("the baths") refers to the mineral springs here.

Aumale. *Village, Seine-Maritime*. The name was recorded in the 11th century as *Albamarula*, from Latin *alba*, "white," and Gaulish *marga*, "marl."

Aunay-sur-Odon. *Village, Calvados*. The name derives from Latin *alnus*, "alder," and the collective suffix *-etum*. The addition locates the village on the *Odon* River.

Auneau. *Village, Eure-et-Loir*. The name was recorded in the 12th century as *Auneellum*, from *alnetellum*, a diminutive form of Latin *alnus*, "alder."

Auneuil. *Village, Oise*. The name was recorded in the 11th century as *Aneolium*, from Latin *alnus*, "alder," and Gaulish *ialon*, "clearing."

Aunis. *Historic region, west central France.* The former province was known to the Romans as *Castrum Alionis*, the old name of *Châtelaillon*, now *Châtelaillon-Plage* (French *plage*, "beach"), Charente-Maritime, its own name deriving from Latin *castrum*, "fort," and the Germanic personal name *Agilo*.

Auray. *Town, Morbihan.* The name of the Brittany town was recorded in the 11th century as *Alrae*, probably from the Breton personal name *Herlé*.

Aurec-sur-Loire. *Town, Haute-Loire.* The name was recorded in the 11th century as *Auriacum*, from the Roman personal name *Aurius* and the associative suffix *-acum*. The addition locates the town on the **Loire** River.

Aureilhan. *Town, Hautes-Pyrénées.* The suburb of Tarbes takes its name from the Roman personal name *Aurelius* and the suffix *-anum*.

Aurignac. *Village Haute-Garonne.* The name derives from the Roman personal name *Orinius* and the associative suffix *-acum*.

Aurillac. *Town, Cantal.* The name was recorded in the 10th century as *Aureliacum*, from the Roman personal name *Aurelius* and the associative suffix *-acum*. Compare the name of **Orly**.

Auriol. *Town, Bouches-du-Rhône.* The name was recorded in the 10th century as *villa Auriolo*, from Latin *villa*, "estate," and *aureolus*, "(golden) oriole."

Auris. *Village, Isère.* The name was recorded in the 12th century as *Aureis*, either from Latin *aura*, "wind," and the suffix *-eium*, or from the Roman personal name *Auricius*. Auris stands high in the Dauphiné Alps.

Aussillon. *Town, Tarn.* The suburb of Mazamet derives its name from the Roman personal name *Aucilius* and the suffix *-onem*.

Aussois. *Resort village, Savoie.* The name perhaps derives from the Germanic female personal name *Alseda*, a shortened form of *Adalsinda*.

Aussonne. *Town, Haute-Garonne.* The name probably derives from the pre-Celtic river name *aliso* and the river suffix *-onna*.

Auterive. *Town, Haute-Garonne.* The name represents Latin *alta ripa*, "high bank," referring to the town's location on the Ariège River. Compare the name of **Hauterives**.

Auteuil. *Town, Oise.* The name of the Paris district was recorded in the 11th century as *Altoil*, from Latin *altus*, "high," and Gaulish *ialon*, "clearing," "village." The church here is on relatively elevated ground by comparison with the woods that covered nearby Billancourt.

Autrans. *Resort village, Isère.* The name was recorded in the 11th century as *Austran*, from the Germanic personal name *Austhramm*.

Autun. *Town, Saône-et-Loire.* The name was recorded in the 1st century AD as *Augustodunum*, "fort of Augustus," from the Roman emperor *Augustus* and Gaulish *dunon*, "fort," "hill." The Roman settlement replaced the former Celtic *oppidum* (fortress town) of **Bibracte**, 13 miles to the east. "Augustodunum — 'Augustusville' — if we can go to America for our parallel — is located on a new site, down in a river plain, so much more convenient" [C.E. Stevens, "Roman Gaul," in Wallace-Hadrill and Mc-Manners, p.25].

Autunois. *Region, central France.* The small region is centered on the town of **Autun** and is named for it.

Auvergne. *Region, south central France.* The present administrative region takes its name from the *Arverni*, a Gaulish tribe whose own name probably means "dwellers in the land of alders," from Gaulish *are*, "by," "at," and *uerna*, "alder."

Auvers-sur-Oise. *Town, Val-d'Oise.* The name, recorded in the 9th century as *Alvernis*, represents Gaulish *Alvernus*, either a family name or from *are*, "before," and *uerna*, "alder." The addition locates the town on the **Oise** River.

Auxerre. *City, Yonne.* The name was recorded in the 4th century as *Autessiodurum*, from the Gaulish personal name *Autessios* and *duron*, "gate," "house," "fort."

Auxi-le-Château. *Village, Pas-de-Calais.* The name was recorded in the 8th century as *Auciacus*, from the Roman personal name *Alcius* and the associative suffix -*acum*. The addition refers to the (now ruined) 12th-century château here.

Auxonne. *Town, Côte-d'Or.* The name probably derives from the pre-Celtic river name *aliso* and the suffix -*onna*. Auxonne is on the Saône River.

Avallon. *Town, Yonne.* The name was recorded in the 4th century as *Aballo*, from Gaulish *aballo-*, "apple," denoting an orchard, and the suffix -*one*. The name is identical to that of *Avalon*, the English isle of Arthurian legend identified with Glastonbury, Somerset.

Avenay-Val-d'Or. *Village, Marne.* The name was recorded in the 9th century as *Avenniacum*, from the Roman personal name *Avenus* and the associative suffix -*acum*. The addition, meaning "golden valley," refers to the vineyards here. See also **Orvault.**

Les Avenières. *Village, Isère.* The name was recorded in the 14th century as *castellania Avenerarium*, from Latin *avena*, "oats," or in a tranferred sense "poor land" (on which oats will grow), and the suffix -*arium*. Latin *castellania* is "district belonging to a castle."

Avesnes-sur-Helpe. *Town, Nord.* The name was recorded in the 11th century as *Avennatis*, of uncertain origin. The addition locates the town on the *Helpe* River, with a Germanic name of equally obscure meaning.

Aveyron. *Department, southern France.* The name is that of the river here, known to the Romans as *Avario, Avarionis*, from Indoeuropean *ab* or *av*, "water."

Avignon. *City, Vaucluse.* The name was recorded in the 1st century AD as *Avennio*, from proto-Indoeuropean *ab*, "watercourse," referring to the Rhône River, and the suffix -*onem*.

Avion. *Town, Pas-de-Calais.* The suburb of Lens has a name recorded in the 12th century as *Aviuns*, probably from the Roman personal name *Avius* and the suffix -*onem*.

Avioth. *Hamlet, Meuse.* The name was recorded in the 13th century as *Aviot*, from the Roman personal name *Avius* and the diminutive suffix -*ot*.

Avize. *Village, Marne.* The name was recorded in the 12th century as *Avizia*, from *Avitia*, the adjectival form of the Roman personal name *Avitius*, with Latin *villa*, "estate," understood.

Avoine. *Village, Indre-et-Loire.* The name derives from Latin *avena*, "oats," or in a transferred sense "poor land" (where oats will grow).

Avord. *Village, Cher.* The name was recorded in the 12th century as *Avor*, from a pre-Latin root *av* of uncertain origin (perhaps meaning "water") and probably Gaulish *ritu-*, "ford."

Avranches. *Town, Manche.* The town takes its name from the *Abricates* or *Abrincatui*, the small Gaulish tribe whose capital it was. The meaning of their own name is uncertain.

Avrieux. *Village, Savoie.* The name was recorded in the 12th century as *Aprilis*, from either the Roman family name *Aprilis* or the personal name *Aprius*, a derivative of *Aper*, and the associative suffix -*acum*.

Avrillé. *Town, Maine-et-Loire.* The suburb of Angers derives its name from the Roman personal name *Aprilius* and the associative suffix -*acum*.

Ax-les-Thermes. *Resort village, Ariège.* The name derives from Latin *aquis*, the ablative (locative) plural of *aqua*, "water," referring to the sulfur springs here. The addition ("the thermal baths") has an identical reference.

Ay. *Town, Marne.* The name was recorded in the 9th century as *Ageius*, from the Gaulish personal name *Adius*, *Aius*, or *Agius*, and the associative suffix *-acum*.

Azay-le-Rideau. *Village, Indre-et-Loire.* The name was recorded in the 11th century as *Asiacus*, from the Roman personal name *Asius* or *Atius* and the associative suffix *-acum*. The addition names the local lord, *Rideau*.

Azincourt. *Village, Pas-de-Calais.* The site of the battle of Agincourt, the English victory over the French in 1415, was recorded in the 12th century as *Aisincurt*, from the Germanic personal name *Aizo* and Latin *cortem*, accusative of *cors*, "estate."

Baccarat. *Town, Meurthe-et-Moselle.* The name is an adoption (and adaption) of Germany's *Bacharach*, west of Wiesbaden, itself of pre-Latin and possibly Celtic origin. The transfer appears to have been made after the 8th century. The two towns are around 120 miles apart.

Badonwiller. *Village, Meurthe-et-Moselle.* The name derives from the Germanic personal name *Baldo* and Latin *villare*, "farmstead."

Bages. *Village, Pyrénées-Orientales.* The name derives from the Roman personal name *Bagia*, with Latin *villa*, "estate," understood.

Bagnères-de-Bigorre. *Resort town, Hautes-Pyrénées.* The town, in the region of **Bigorre**, has a name recorded in the 13th century as *Banneriae*, from Latin *balneum*, "bath," referring to its mineral springs, and the suffix *-aria*. Its earlier Roman name was *Aquae Convenarum*.

Bagnères-de-Luchon. *Resort town, Haute-Garonne.* The name is as for **Bagnères-de-Bigorre**, referring to the local sulfur springs. The addition names *Ilixone*, the pagan goddess of the springs, from Basque *ili*, "town."

Bagneux. *Town, Hauts-de-Seine.* The name of the Paris suburb was recorded in the 9th century as *Balneolum*, a derivative of Latin *balneum*, "bath."

Bagnoles-de-l'Orne. *Resort village, Orne.* The name derives from Latin *balneolum*, from *balneum*, "bath." The village is a noted thermal resort in **Orne**.

Bagnolet. *Town, Seine-Saint-Denis.* The name of the Paris suburb was recorded in the 13th century as *Baignoletum*, from a diminutive of Latin *balneola*, a feminine form of *balneolum*, a derivative of *balneum*, "bath."

Bagnols-les-Bains. *Village, Lozère.* The original name of the settlement, recorded in the Roman period, was *Aquae Calidae*, Latin for "hot waters," referring to the thermal baths here. The present name represents Latin *balneolum*, "bath," with an addition ("the baths") referring to the same mineral springs.

Bagnols-sur-Cèze. *Town, Gard.* The name, recorded in the 12th century as *Baniolas*, has the same origin as **Bagnols-les-Bains**. The addition locates the town near the *Cèze* River.

Baignes-Sainte-Radegonde. *Village, Charente.* The name was recorded in the 11th century as *Beania*, perhaps a popular form of the biblical name *Bethania*. The second part of the name is a dedication to the Germanic princess *St. Radegund*, 6th-century queen of the Franks, wife of Clotaire I.

Baillargues. *Town, Hérault.* The name was recorded in the 9th century as *Bajanicis*, giving a form *Ballianicum*, from the Roman personal name *Ballius* and the double suffix *-anicum*.

Bailleul. *Town, Nord.* The name was recorded in the 11th century as *Bailgiole*, from the Roman personal name *Ballius* and Gaulish *ialon*, "clearing."

Bailly. *Town, Yvelines.* The name represents the Roman personal name *Ballius* and the associative suffix *-acum*.

Bain-de-Bretagne. *Town, Ille-et-Vilaine.* The town derives its name from Latin *balneum*, "bath." The addition locates it in *Brittany* (**Bretagne**).

Bains-les-Bains. *Resort village, Vosges.* The resort derives its name from Latin *balneum*, "bath," referring to the thermal springs here. The addition ("the baths") repeats the reference.

Baisieux. *Town, Nord.* The name, recorded in the 12th century as *Baiseu*, is of uncertain origin, although a source has been proposed in conjectural Gaulish *bacivum*, "orchard," from *baca*, "berry," and the suffix *-ivum*.

Baixas. *Village, Pyrénées-Orientales.* The name represents the Roman personal name *Baccius* or *Bassius* and the suffix *-anum*.

Balan. *Town, Ain.* The name was probably originally *Baladunum*, from an element *bal* meaning "escarpment" and Gaulish *dunon*, "fort."

Balaruc-les-Bains. *Resort town, Hérault.* The name, recorded in the 10th century as *Balarug*, is of uncertain origin and meaning. The addition ("the baths") refers to the hot mineral springs here.

Balinghem. *Village, Pas-de-Calais.* The name derives from the Germanic personal name *Bavilo* and an element corresponding to the Old English *-ingham* frequently found in England, meaning "homestead called after [the named person]."

Ballancourt-sur-Essonne. *Town, Essonne.* The name was recorded in the 12th century as *Berlencurt*, from the Germanic female personal name *Berila* and Latin *cortem*, accusative of *cors*, "estate." The addition to the name locates the town on (or by) the **Essonne** River.

Ballan-Miré. *Town, Indre-et-Loire.* The name of the present suburb of Tours was recorded in the 5th century in the locative case as *Balatedine*. The origin of this is uncertain. The second part of the name, originally that of a separate place, represents the Roman personal name *Matrius* and the associative suffix *-acum*.

Balleroy. *Village, Calvados.* The name was recorded in the 12th century as *Balaré*, from the Gaulish personal name *Balaros* and the associative suffix *-acum*.

Le Ballon d'Alsace. *Mountain, eastern France.* The rounded summit of the southern Vosges is named for its location in **Alsace**. French *ballon*, meaning a round-topped mountain, is not the same as *ballon*, "ball," but an adoption of German *Belchen*, perhaps understood as *Bällchen*, "little ball." The German name for the summit is thus *Elsaßer Belchen*.

Balma. *Town, Haute-Garonne.* The suburb of Toulouse derives its name from pre-Latin *balma*, "cave," "hole at the foot of a rock."

La Balme-de-Sillingy. *Village, Haute-Savoie.* The name has the same origin as **Balma.** The addition refers to nearby *Sillingy*, with a name from the Germanic personal name *Silinga*, the name of a Vandal tribe, and the associative suffix *-iacum*.

Bandol. *Resort town, Var.* The name, of obscure origin, was recorded in the 11th century as *Bendoroi*. A possible source in pre-Indoeuropean *ben-d*, "rock," has been proposed.

Bannalec. *Town, Finistère.* The name of the Brittany town was recorded in the 11th century as *Banadluc*, from Breton *banadloc*, "place where broom grows."

Le Ban-Saint-Martin. *Town, Moselle.* The name derives from French *ban*, a word of Germanic origin used for a feudal administrative district, and a dedication to *St. Martin*.

Banyuls-sur-Mer. *Resort town, Pyrénées-Orientales.* The name was recorded in the 10th century as *Bagnules*, from Latin *balneolum*, a derivative of *balneum*, "bath."

Bapaume. *Town, Pas-de-Calais.* The name represents French *bat paumes*, "beat palms," denoting a gesture of despair at the barrenness of the soil here.

Baraqueville. *Village, Aveyron*. The name derives from French *baraque*, "hut," "shed," and *ville*, "town," denoting a settlement of poor dwellings, otherwise a shanty town.

Barbazan. *Resort village, Haute-Garonne*. The name derives from *Barbatia*, the adjectival form of the Roman personal name *Barbatius* (with Latin *villa*, "estate," understood) and the suffix *-anum*.

Barbazan-Debat. *Village, Hautes-Pyrénées*. The name is as for **Barbazan**. The addition means "below" (*de bas*), comparing the village to nearby *Barbazan-Dessus* ("above").

Barbentane. *Village, Bouches-du-Rhône*. The name was recorded in the 12th century as *Berbentana*, from the Roman personal name *Barbus* and a double suffix *-ent* and *-ana*.

Barberaz. *Town, Savoie*. The name represents *Barbaria*, the adjectival form of the Roman personal name *Barbarius*, with Latin *villa*, "estate," understood.

Barbezieux-Saint-Hilaire. *Town, Charente*. The name was recorded in the 11th century as *Berbezil*, from Latin *vervecile*, "sheepfold." The addition represents a dedication to *St. Hilary* (see **Saint-Hilaire**).

Barbizon. *Village, Seine-et-Marne*. The name was recorded in the 9th century as *Barbitione*, from the Roman personal name *Barbatius* and the suffix *-onem*.

Barby. *Village, Savoie*. The name derives from the Roman personal name *Balbius* and the associative suffix *-acum*.

Barcelonnette. *Resort town, Alpes-de-Haute-Provence*. Recorded in the late 12th or early 13th century as *Barcilona*, the name is probably a diminutive form of *Barcelona*, the Spanish city. The date makes it unlikely that the name represents the title of Raymond Bérenger, count of Provence and *Barcelona*, said to have founded the town in 1231.

Barentin. *Town, Seine-Maritime*. The name may derive from the Roman personal name *Barus* and a double suffix *-ent* and *-inum*.

Barenton. *Village, Manche*. The name has the same possible origin as **Barentin** but with a double suffix *-ent* and *-onem*.

Barfleur. *Village, Manche*. The name was recorded in the 12th century as *Barbeflet*, from Old Scandinavian *barmr*, "corner," "angle," and Old English *flēot*, "inlet," referring either to the inlet here, lying at an angle to the shoreline, or to the location of Barfleur and its inlet on the northeastern tip of the Cotentin Peninsula.

Barjac. *Village, Gard*. The name derives from the Gaulish personal name *Bargius* and the associative suffix *-acum*.

Barjols. *Village, Var*. The name was recorded in the 11th century as *Barjols*, from pre-Gaulish *bar-g*, "mountain," and the suffix *-eolum*. Barjols lies in the foothills of the Maritime Alps.

Bar-le-Duc. *Town, Meuse*. The name was recorded in the 6th century as *Castrum Barrum*, from Latin *castrum*, "fort," and pre-Celtic *barr*, "summit," "height," referring to the hill on which the town stands. It was the capital of the medieval countship of Bar, but in 1354 the countship became a dukedom. Hence the addition to the name, from French *duc*, "duke."

Barlin. *Town, Pas-de-Calais*. The name probably derives from the Germanic personal name *Barila* and the suffix *-ing*, although it could also represent *Basilinum*, from the Graeco-Roman personal name *Basilius* and the suffix *-inum*.

Barneville-Carteret. *Resort village, Manche*. The resort actually consists of three villages: the old town *Barneville*, from a Scandinavian personal name *Biarn* and Latin *villa*, "village," the more modern *Barneville-Plage*, with a beach (*plage*), and *Carteret*, or *Carteret-le-Cap*, with a name of uncertain origin. (Latin *quartarius*, "rocky quarter," and a suffix *-etum* has been proposed, or a pre-Indoeuropean root *kar*, "rock," with an obscure suffix and *-etum*.)

Le Barp. *Village, Gironde*. The name, recorded in the 13th century as *Barbo*, is of uncertain origin. It may represent a form of the Roman or Germanic personal name *Barbo*. The article *le*, "the," may have been added as if to prefix Gascon *barb*, French *barbeau*, "barbel."

Barr. *Town, Bas-Rhin*. The name derives from pre-Celtic *barr*, "height." Barr stands at the foot of the Vosges mountains.

Barrême. *Village, Alpes-de-Haute-Provence*. The name was recorded in the 13th century as *Barrema*, from Occitan *bàrri*, "rampart," and the pre-Latin suffix *-ema*.

Barrois. *Region, northeastern France*. The name of the former duchy derives from Latin *Barrum*, from pre-Celtic *barr*, "summit," "height." **Bar-le-Duc** is an important town.

Le Barroux. *Village, Vaucluse*. The name was recorded in the 12th century as *Albarussum*, from Italo-Celtic *alb*, "height," and the double pre-Latin suffix *-ar* and *-ossum*. The initial *Al-* of this was taken as French *au*, "to the," and was dropped as if not part of the name. French *le* was then prefixed to the shortened form.

Barsac. *Village, Gironde*. The name, recorded in the 13th century as now, derives from the Gaulish personal name *Barcios*, a variant of *Bercius*, and the associative suffix *-acum*.

Bar-sur-Aube. *Town, Aube*. The name was recorded early as *Barrisii castrum*, from pre-Gaulish *barro-*, "summit," "height," and Latin *castrum*, "fort." The addition locates the town on the **Aube** River.

Le Bar-sur-Loup. *Village, Alpes-Maritimes*. The name, of the same origin as **Bar-sur-Aube**, is distinguished by the addition of the local river name *Loup*.

Bar-sur-Seine. *Town, Aube*. The name, recorded in the 9th century as *Barris castro*, has the same origin as **Bar-sur-Aube**, from which it is differentiated by the name of the **Seine** River.

La Barthe-de-Neste. *Village, Hautes-Pyrénées*. The name was recorded in the 12th century as *Barta*, from Gascon (and Languedoc) *barto*, "copse," "thicket," a word of pre-Latin origin. The addition names the *Neste* River here.

Bas-en-Basset. *Village, Haute-Loire*. The name was recorded in the 10th century as *territorium Bassense*, from Low Latin *bassus*, "low," denoting a place lower than the surrounding region. The name thus effectively has "low" twice.

Basque, Pays. *Region, southwestern France*. The region, not to be confused with the *Basque Country* of northern Spain, known also in French as *Pays Basque*, in Spanish as *País Basco* and in Basque as *Euskadi*, take its name from the *Basques* who are its indigenous inhabitants. Their name, a French form of Latin *Vasco, Vasconis*, contains the *sk* element thought to denote a seafaring people, found also in the names of the *Etruscans* of Tuscany, the *Siculi* of Sicily, and the *Gascons* of **Gascogne**.

Basque Region *see* **Basque, Pays**

Bas-Rhin. *Department, northeastern France*. The name translates as "Lower Rhine." The department borders a lower stretch of the **Rhine** than that bounding neighboring **Haut-Rhin**.

La Bassée. *Town, Nord*. The name derives from French *bas*, "low," denoting land lower than the surrounding terrain.

Basse-Goulaine. *Town, Loire-Atlantique*. The basic name, recorded in the 13th century as *Goulena*, probably derives from French *goule* in the sense "neck" (of a bottle), referring to the channeling of superfluous water from the marshes here. The first part of the name ("low") distinguishes the town, now a suburb of Nantes, from nearby *Haute-Goulaine*, on higher ground, with a castle.

Basse-Normandie. *Region, northwestern France*. The name means "Lower Normandy," describing the region's "inferior" status, with Caen as the local capital, in relation to neighboring **Haute-Normandie**, which included Rouen as the capital of *Normandy* (see **Normandie**) overall.

Bassens. *Town, Gironde.* The suburb of Bordeaux has a name recorded in the 13th century as *Bassenxs*, from the Germanic personal name *Basso* and the suffix *-ing.*

Basses-Alpes *see* **Alpes-de-Haute-Provence**

Basses-Pyrénées *see* **Pyrénées-Atlantiques**

Bastelicaccia. *Village, Corse-du-Sud.* The name of the village, in southwestern Corsica, perhaps derives from the Latin root *bast-*, "to build," as for **Bastia**, and the suffix *-acea.*

Bastia. *City and port, Haute-Corse.* The city, in the extreme north of Corsica, derives its name from Low Latin *bastita*, "built," meaning a fortified place. Bastia was founded in 1313.

La Bastide-Clairence. *Village, Pyrénées-Atlantiques.* The village arose as a *bastide* (walled or fortified town) in the 14th century, with a name recorded then in a Spanish form as *La Bastida nueva de Clarenza*. (*Bastide* itself comes from Provençal *bastida*, "built (place).") The distinguishing addition *Clairence* may represent the Roman personal name *Clarentius.*

La Bâthie. *Village, Savoie.* The name, recorded in the 13th century as *Bastia*, derives from Latin *bastita*, "fortified place."

Les Batignolles *see* Appendix 4.

Batilly. *Village, Meurthe-et-Moselle.* The name was recorded in the 13th century as *Bateilly*, from the Roman personal name *Battilius*, a form of *Battius*, and the associative suffix *-acum.*

Batz-sur-Mer. *Resort village, Loire-Atlantique.* The name, of uncertain origin and meaning, was recorded in the 9th century as *Baf.*

Baud. *Town, Morbihan.* The name,

recorded in the 13th century as *Baut*, is of uncertain origin and meaning.

Baugé. *Town, Maine-et-Loire.* The name was recorded in the 11th century as *Balgiacum* or *Balgium*, from the Roman personal name *Balbius* (from *balbus*, "stammerer") and the associative suffix *-acum.*

La Baule-Escoublac. *Resort town, Loire-Atlantique.* The first part of the name may derive from Latin *betulla*, "birch," or from the source of French *bauler*, "to howl" (of the wind), the former referring to the predominant trees here, the latter to the town's exposed site on the Bay of Biscay. The second part of the name, that of the original settlement here, represents the Gaulish personal name *Scopilus* and the associative suffix *-acum.*

Baume-les-Dames. *Town, Doubs.* The name represents pre-Latin *balma*, "cave." The addition ("the ladies") refers to the nuns in the convent here, as distinct from the monks at *Baume-les-Messieurs* ("the gentlemen"), Jura, some 55 miles to the southwest.

Baume-les-Messieurs *see* **Baume-les-Dames**

Bauvin. *Town, Nord.* The name probably derives from the Germanic personal name *Baldwin.*

Les Baux-de-Provence. *Town, Bouches-du-Rhône.* The name was recorded in the 10th century as *Balcium*, from Low Latin *balteus*, from pre-Celtic *bal*, "steep place." Les Baux is situated on a mountain spur, amidst sheer escarpments and declivities.

Bavans. *Town, Doubs.* The name was recorded in the 12th century as *Bavens*, from the Germanic personal name *Bavo* and the suffix *-ing.*

Bavay. *Town, Nord.* The name was recorded in the 4th century as *Bagacum*, from Gaulish *bagos*, "beech," and the associative suffix *-acum*, here denoting a plural ("place of beeches").

Bavilliers. *Town, Belfort.* The name was recorded in the 14th century as *Bavelier*, from the Germanic personal name *Baso* and Latin *villa*, "farmstead."

Bayeux. *Town, Calvados.* The name was recorded in the 5th century as *Baiocas*, from the Gaulish tribe *Baiocasses* or *Badiocasses*, with a name meaning "blond ones," from *badios*, "yellow," "fair," and *-casses*, "hair." The town's original Roman name was *Augustodurum*, "fort of Augustus," from the emperor *Augustus* and Gaulish *duron*, "door," "house," "fort."

Bayonne. *City and port, Pyrénées-Atlantiques.* The original name of the town was *Lapurdum*, from its location in **Labourd**. The present name, documented in the 12th century as *Sancta Maria Baionensis*, derives from Low Latin *baia*, "bay," and Basque *on*, "good," or according to another theory, from Basque *ibai*, "river," and *on*.

Bazas. *Town, Gironde.* The name was recorded in the 4th century as *civitas Vasates*, from Latin *civitas*, "city," "state," and the name of an Aquitanian tribe.

Bazeilles. *Village, Ardennes.* The name, recorded in the 13th century as now, derives from Latin *basilia*, a form of *basilica*, "(covered) market," "church."

Béarn. *Historic region, southwestern France.* The former province takes its name from the *Benarni*, a Gaulish tribe.

Beaucaire. *Town, Gard.* The name was recorded in the 11th century as *castrum Bellicardi*, from Latin *castrum*, "fort," and a name meaning "beautiful stone," from Latin *bellus*, "beautiful," and *quadrum*, "freestone." The town's earlier Roman name was *Ugernum*.

Beauce. *Region, north central France.* The Late Latin name of the region was *Belsia*, perhaps from Gaulish *belo-*, "strong." Some authorities link the name with the Gaulish goddess *Belisama*, sister and wife of the god Belenus, her own name also from *belo-* with the Celtic superlative suffix *-isama*.

Beauchamp. *Town, Val-d'Oise.* The name represents French *beau champ*, "beautiful field," meaning a settlement in the country.

Beauchastel. *Village, Ardèche.* The name represents Old Provençal *bel castel*, "fine castle," denoting a well-built fort.

Beaucourt. *Town, Belfort.* The name was recorded in the 12th century as *Boocor*, from a Germanic personal name *Bodo* and Latin *cortem*, accusative of *cors*, "estate."

Beaucouzé. *Village, Maine-et-Loire.* The name was recorded in the 12th century as *Vulcosiacus*, from the Germanic personal name *Willicoz* and the associative suffix *-iacum*. The present form of the name has been influenced by French *beau*, "beautiful."

Beaufort. *Resort village, Savoie.* The name represents French *beau fort*, "beautiful fort," specifically denoting a castle (which, like an ideal athlete, is both handsome and powerful).

Beaufort-en-Vallée. *Town, Maine-et-Loire.* The name has the same origin as **Beaufort**. The addition locates the town in the Loire valley (*Vallée de la Loire*).

Beaugency. *Town, Loiret.* The name was recorded in the 9th century as *Balgentium*, from the Gaulish personal name *Balgentius* and the associative suffix *-acum*.

Beaujeu. *Village, Rhône.* The name was recorded in the 14th century as *Bellojocum*, from French *beau*, "beautiful," and Latin *jugum*, "hill," influenced by *jocum*, accusative of *jocus*, "sport," "game."

Beaujolais. *Region, east central France.* The hilly region was formerly the fief of the lords of **Beaujeu**, Rhône, on the eastern edge, and takes its name from that village.

Beaulieu-en-Rouergue. *Abbey, Tarn-et-Garonne.* The name derives from Latin *bellus locus*, "beautiful place," here in the region of **Rouergue**.

Beaulieu-lès-Loches. *Village, Indre-et-*

Loire. The name derives from Latin *bellus locus*, "beautiful place," here near (*lès*) **Loches**, across the Indre River.

Beaulieu-sur-Dordogne. *Village, Corrèze*. The name derives from Latin *bellus locus*, "beautiful place," here on the **Dordogne** River.

Beaulieu-sur-Mer. *Resort town, Alpes-Maritimes*. The name was recorded in the 12th century as *Bellus Locus*, Latin for "beautiful place," here by the Mediterranean Sea.

Beaumarchés. *Village, Gers*. Beaumarchés was created as a "new town" in 1290 following an agreement between the comte de Pardiac and Eustace de *Beaumarchais*, seneschal (governor) of Toulouse. The name represents French *beau marchais*, "beautiful marsh."

Beaumes-de-Venise. *Village, Vaucluse*. The name was recorded in the 10th century as *Balmas*, from pre-Latin *balma*, "cave." The second part of the name refers to the **Comtat Venaissin** in which it is located.

Beaumont. *Village, Meurthe-et-Moselle*. The name was recorded in the 12th century as *Samboldi Mons*, from the Germanic personal name *Sinbold* ("ever bold") and Latin *mons, montis*, "mountain." The first syllable of this disappeared, and the -*bold* was taken as French *beau*, so that the name now suggests "beautiful mountain," as for **Beaumont**, Puy-de-Dôme.

Beaumont. *Town, Puy-de-Dôme*. The suburb of Clermont-Ferrand derives its name from Latin *bellus*, "beautiful," and *mons, montis*, "mountain," "hill."

Beaumont-de-Lomagne. *Town, Tarn-et-Garonne*. The name derives from Latin *bellus*, "beautiful," and *mons, montis*, "mountain," here in the *Lomagne* region.

Beaumont-en-Argonne. *Village, Ardennes*. The name derives from Latin *bellus*, "beautiful," and *mons, montis*, "mountain," here in the **Argonne** region.

Beaumont-Hague. *Village, Manche*. The name derives from Latin *bellus*, "beautiful," and *mons, montis*, "mountain," here near the *Cap de la Hague*.

Beaumont-le-Roger. *Village, Eure*. The name was recorded in the 11th century as *Belmont*, from Latin *bellus*, "beautiful," and *mons, montis*, "mountain." The addition refers to a local lord *Roger*.

Beaumont-lès-Valence. *Village, Drôme*. The name derives from Latin *bellus*, "beautiful," and *mons, montis*, "mountain," here near (*lès*) **Valence**.

Beaumont-sur-Oise. *Town, Val-d'Oise*. The name derives from Latin *bellus*, "beautiful," and *mons, montis*, "mountain," here on the **Oise** River.

Beaune. *Town, Côte-d'Or*. The town's Low Latin name was *Belna* or *Belnum*, from *Beleno Castro*, "fort of Belenos," from a Gaulish god equated with Apollo.

Beaune-la-Rolande. *Village, Loiret*. The name, recorded in the 9th century as *Belna*, has the same origin as **Beaune**. The addition is the name of a stream here.

Beaupréau. *Town, Maine-et-Loire*. The name was recorded in the 11th century as *Bello Pratello*, from French *beau*, "beautiful," and Latin *pratellum*, a diminutive of *pratum*, "meadow."

Beaurains. *Town, Pas-de-Calais*. The suburb of Arras has a name recorded in the 7th century as *Bellirino* and in the 11th century as *Belraim*, from French *beau*, "beautiful," and Latin *ramus*, "branch," meaning a wood.

Beaurecueil. *Hamlet, Bouches-du-Rhône*. The name, from French *beau*, "beautiful," and *recueil*, "shelter," is that of a château or country house dating only from 1827.

Beauregard. *Hamlet, Ain*. The name, from French *beau*, "beautiful," and *regard*, "view," originates from that of a château here by the Saône River.

Beaurepaire. *Town, Isère*. The name was recorded in the 14th century as *Bellorepayre*, from French *beau*, "beautiful," and *repaire*, "retreat," meaning a secluded place.

Beausoleil. *Resort town, Alpes-Maritimes.* The Riviera resort, bordering on Monaco, has a modern touristic name derived from French *beau*, "beautiful," and *soleil*, "sun."

Le Beausset. *Town, Var.* The name represents a diminutive of Low Latin *balteus*, from pre-Celtic *bal*, "escarpment," and the suffix *-itius*.

Beauvais. *City, Oise.* The original name of the city, recorded by Ptolemy in the 2d century AD, was *Caesaromagus*, "Caesar's market," from the name of Julius *Caesar* and Gaulish *magos*, "market." (Compare *Juliomagus* as the Roman name of **Angers**.) Its current name was recorded early as *Belloacum*, from the Gaulish tribe known as the *Bellovaci*, whose capital it was. Their own name combines *bello-*, "strong," and *uac-*, of unknown meaning.

Beauvoir-sur-Mer. *Village, Vendée.* The name was recorded in the 11th century as *Bellum Visum*, a poor Latin equivalent of *Bellum Videre*, "beautiful view." Due to the silting of the bay here, the former port is no longer actually "on sea."

Beauvois-en-Cambrésis. *Town, Nord.* The name was recorded in the 11th century as *Bellus Visus*, a latinized equivalent of French *Belvoir*, "beautiful view." The town is in **Cambrésis**.

Le Bec-Hellouin. *Hamlet, Eure.* The name was recorded in the 11th century as *Beccus*, from Old Scandinavian *bekkr*, "stream." In the 12th century it was documented as *Beccus Herlevini*, with the name of *Herluin*, first abbot of the famous abbey here, founded in 1024.

Bédarieux. *Town, Hérault.* The name was recorded in the 12th century as *Bedeiriae*, probably from Low Latin *betarivum*, from *betarium* (Latin *beta*, "beet," with the suffix *-arium*) and the suffix *-ivum*. The name seems to have been influenced by early forms of the name of **Béziers**, 20 miles to the south.

Bédarrides. *Town, Vaucluse.* The name, recorded in the 9th century as *Betoridda*, is of uncertain origin. A source in Gaulish *petor-*, "four," and *ritu-*, "ford," has been suggested, referring to the streams here, not far from the Rhône River.

Bédoin. *Village, Vaucluse.* The name was recorded in the 10th century as *Beduino*, probably from the Germanic personal name *Betwin*.

Bégard. *Town, Côtes-d'Armor.* The name probably derives from the Germanic personal name *Bighart*.

Bègles. *Town, Gironde.* The suburb of Bordeaux has a name recorded in the 8th century as *Becla*, perhaps from an Aquitanian root *beg*, as in the regional name **Bigorre**, or from Gaulish *beccos*, "bill," "headland," referring to a promontory on the Garonne River here.

Beg-Meil. *Resort village, Finistère.* The Brittany resort has a Breton name meaning "yellow cape."

Belfort. *City, Belfort.* The city was known to the Romans as *Bellofortis*, "beautiful stronghold," from Latin *bellus*, "beautiful," and *fortis*, "fort." It commands the Belfort Gap, or Burgundy Gate, the pass between the Vosges and Jura mountains, and is the capital of the *Territoire de Belfort*, the department created in 1871 from the only part of Alsace left to France after the Franco-Prussian War.

Belin-Béliet. *Village, Gironde.* The name combines two formerly separate adjacent places. *Belin* was recorded in the 11th century as *Belinum*, from the Gaulish personal name *Belinius*. *Béliet* is a diminutive of this name, representing *Belin* with the diminutive suffix *-ittum*.

Bellac. *Town, Haute-Vienne.* The name was recorded early as *Bellacum*, from the Roman personal name *Bellus* and the associative suffix *-acum*.

Belleau. *Village, Aisne.* The name was recorded in the 13th century as *Balolium*, from *Ballo*, a combining form of the Roman personal name *Ballius*, and Gaulish *ialon*, "clearing."

Belledonne. *Mountain range, southeastern France.* The range of the Dauphiné Alps has a name of uncertain origin. It can hardly be from Italian *bella donna*, "beautiful woman." The first element perhaps represents pre-Indoeuropean *bel*, "steep place."

Bellegarde. *Town, Gard.* The name was recorded in the 13th century as *Bella Garda*, as if French *belle garde*, literally "beautiful guard," denoting a fine fortress.

Bellegarde-sur-Valserine. *Town, Ain.* The first part of the name is as for **Bellegarde.** The addition denotes the town's location on the Rhône at the mouth of the small *Valserine* River.

Belle-Île. *Resort island, northwestern France.* The island, also known as *Belle-Île-en-Mer*, "beautiful island in the sea," lies off the southwest coast of Brittany. Its Breton name is quite different, as *ar Gerveur*, "the big town," from *ar*, "the," *kêr*, "town" (a feminine noun that becomes *gêr* after "the"), and *meur*, "big" (mutating after a feminine noun to *veur*).

Bellême. *Village, Orne.* The name derives from *Belisama*, that of a Gaulish goddess equated with Minerva. See **Beauce.**

Bellerive-sur-Allier. *Town, Allier.* The suburb of Vichy derives its name from Latin *bella ripa*, "beautiful bank," meaning that of the **Allier** River here.

Belleu. *Town, Aisne.* The name of the suburb of Soissons is the equivalent of *Beaulieu* (see **Beaulieu-sur-Mer**), so means "beautiful place."

Belleville. *Town, Rhône.* The name represents Low Latin *bella villa*, "beautiful estate." The town is also known as *Belleville-sur-Saône* for its location on the **Saône** River.

Belleville-sur-Loire. *Village, Cher.* The name is as for **Belleville**, the addition locating the village on the **Loire** River.

Belleville-sur-Meuse. *Village, Meuse.* The suburb of Verdun, on the **Meuse** River, shares the origin of its name with **Belleville.**

Bellevue-la-Montagne. *Village, Haute-Loire.* The original name of the village was *Saint-Just*, as for **Saint-Just-en-Chaussée.** It was renamed as now at the time of the Revolution and, unusually, retained the name, meaning "beautiful view (from) the mountain."

Belley. *Town, Ain.* The name derives from the Roman personal name *Belicius*.

Bellicourt. *Village, Aisne.* The name derives from the Germanic personal name *Beling* and Latin *cortem*, accusative of *cors*, "estate."

Belz. *Village, Morbihan.* The name, of obscure origin, was recorded in the 11th century as *Beels*.

Bénévent-l'Abbaye. *Village, Creuse.* The name may either commemorate the town of *Benevento*, Italy, known in French as *Bénévent*, or possibly represent Provençal *ben i vèn*, "it goes well," as a propitious designation. The addition refers to the historic abbey here.

Bénodet. *Resort village, Finistère.* The Brittany village probably derives its name from Breton *ben*, "head," "point," and that of the *Odet* River near the mouth of which it lies.

Bénouville. *Village, Calvados.* The name was recorded in the 11th century as *Burnolfivilla*, from the Old Norse personal name *Bjørnwulf* ("bear-wolf") and Latin *villa*, "village."

Berck. *Town, Pas-de-Calais.* The town, also known as *Berck-sur-Mer*, from its location on the English Channel coast, derives its name from Germanic *berg*, "mountain," although there is hardly much of a hill here.

Bergerac. *Town, Dordogne.* The name was recorded in the 12th century as *Brageyrack*, from the Gallo-Roman personal name *Bracarius* ("maker of breeches") and the associative suffix *-acum*. The writer

Cyrano de Bergerac did not come from here but took his name from his father's estate of *Bergerac* near Chevreuse, Yvelines, not far from Paris, where he was born.

Bergheim. *Village, Haut-Rhin*. The name was recorded in the 8th century as *Perechheim*, from Germanic *berg*, "mountain," and *heim*, "village." Bergheim lies at the foot of the Vosges mountains.

Bergues. *Town, Nord*. The name was recorded in the 10th century as *Bergan*, from Germanic *berg*, "mountain."

Berlaimont. *Village, Nord*. The name was recorded in the 12th century as *Berleinmont*, from the Germanic personal name *Berland* (or the female name *Berilind*) and Latin *mons, montis*, "mountain."

Bernay. *Town, Eure*. The name was recorded in the 12th century as *Brenaicum*, from the Gaulish personal name *Brennus* (from *branos*, "raven") and the associative suffix *-acum*.

La Bernerie-en-Retz. *Resort village, Loire-Atlantique*. The name derives from the personal name *Bernier*, of Germanic origin, and the suffix *-ie*. *Retz* is the region here, a former duchy.

Bernières-sur-Mer. *Resort village, Calvados*. The name derives from the female equivalent of the male personal name *Bernier*, of Germanic origin. The resort is on the English Channel.

Berre-l'Étang. *Town, Bouches-du-Rhône*. The name is of uncertain origin. A source in pre-Indoeuropean *ber*, "mountain," "raised plain," has been proposed. The second part of the name refers to the navigable lagoon here known as the *Étang de Berre* (from *étang*, "pond").

Berry. *Historic region, central France*. The former province takes its name from the *Bituriges*, the Gaulish tribe whose homeland it was. Their name means "kings of the world," from Gaulish *bitu-*, "world," and *rix*, "king," implying their authority over this territory.

Berry-au-Bac. *Village, Aisne*. The name, recorded in the 9th century as *Baireius*, derives from the Gaulish personal name *Barius* and the associative suffix *-acum*. The addition refers to the ferry (*bac*) over the Aisne River here.

Bersaillin. *Village, Jura*. The name derives from Old French *bersail*, "target," perhaps as a nickname for an accomplished archer or as the name of the place where a target was set up.

Berthenonville. *Village, Eure*. The name derives from Latin *Brittanorum villa*, "village of the Bretons," denoting the provenance of the original inhabitants.

Bertry. *Town, Nord*. The name was recorded in the 12th century as *Berteries*, from the Germanic personal name *Berhtari* and the associative suffix *-iacum*.

Besançon. *City, Doubs*. The name was recorded in the 1st century BC as *Vesontio*, from pre-Indoeuropean *ves*, "mountain," and the pre-Celtic suffix *-unt* followed by the suffix *-ionem*. Besançon lies at the foot of the Jura mountains.

Bessan. *Town, Hérault*. The name was recorded in the 10th century as *Betianum*, from the Roman personal name *Bessius* or *Bettius* and the suffix *-anum*.

Bessancourt. *Town, Val-d'Oise*. The name was recorded in the 12th century as *Bercencourt*, from the Germanic female personal name *Berhtsind* and Latin *cortem*, accusative of *cors*, "estate."

Besse-et-Sainte-Anastasie. *Township, Puy-de-Dôme*. As the *et* implies, the name combines two separate places. *Besse* derives from Low Latin *bettia*, "birch wood." *Sainte-Anastasie* commemorates the 4th-century martyr *St. Anastasia*.

Bessèges. *Village, Gard*. The name derives from Low Latin *bettia*, "birch wood," and a suffix *-egia* of obscure (perhaps Gaulish) origin.

Bessé-sur-Braye. *Village, Sarthe*. The name derives from the Roman personal name *Bessius* or *Bettius* and the associative suffix *-acum*. The village lies by the *Braye* River.

Bessines-sur-Gartempe. *Village, Haute-Vienne.* The name derives from the Roman personal name *Bassinius*. The second part of the name refers to the *Gartempe* River here.

Bétheny. *Town, Marne.* The suburb of Reims has a name recorded in the 9th century as *Beteneium*, from the Germanic personal name *Betto* and the double suffix *-in* and *-iacum*.

Béthisy-Saint-Pierre. *Village, Oise.* The name was recorded in the 11th century as *Bestisiacus*, from the Roman personal name *Bestitius* (from Latin *bestia*, "beast") and the associative suffix *-acum*. The second part of the name, a dedication to *St. Peter*, distinguishes the village from nearby *Béthisy-Saint-Martin.*

Béthoncourt. *Town, Doubs.* The suburb of Montbéliard derives its name from the Germanic personal name *Betto* and Latin *cortem*, accusative of *cors*, "estate."

Béthune. *Town, Pas-de-Calais.* The name was recorded in the 8th century as *Bitunia*, from the Germanic personal name *Bettun*, from *bata*, "better," implying superiority in some way, with Latin *villa*, "estate," "village," understood.

Betton. *Town, Ille-et-Vilaine.* The name derives from the Germanic personal name *Betto.*

Beuvrages. *Town, Nord.* The name of the suburb of Valenciennes, recorded in the 12th century as *Beuregia*, probably derives from a conjectural word *biberaticum*, "watering place," "drinking trough," from Latin *bibere*, "to drink," and the suffix *-aticum.*

Beuvray, Mont. *Mountain, east central France.* The mountain, in the Morvan range, takes its name from Gaulish *bebros*, "beaver," as for **Bibracte,** the historic town on its summit.

Beuvry. *Town, Pas-de-Calais.* The sub-urb of Béthune derives its name from the personal name *Biberius* (from Gaulish *bebros*, "beaver") and the associative suffix *-acum.*

Beuzeville. *Village, Eure.* The name was recorded in the 11th century as *Bosevilla*, from the Germanic personal name *Boso* and Latin *villa*, "estate."

Béville-le-Comte. *Village, Eure-et-Loir.* The name derives from the Germanic personal name *Biso* and Latin *villa*, "estate." The addition ("the count") refers to Thibaut IV, count of Blois and Champagne, who was lord here in the early 12th century.

Beylongue. *Village, Landes.* The name derives from Latin *videt longe*, "sees far," referring to the location of the village on a rise.

Beynes. *Town, Yvelines.* The name was recorded in the 12th century as *Baina*, either from Gaulish *baua*, "mud," or from Gaulish *bagos*, "beech."

Béziers. *City, Hérault.* The Roman name of the city was *Baeterrae*, from a pre-Celtic word that gave the Roman name, *Baetis*, of the Guadalquivir River in southern Spain and in turn that of the historic province of *Baetica* there.

Bezons. *Town, Val-d'Oise.* The Paris suburb derives its name from pre-Indoeuropean *bez*, "mountain," and the suffix *-onem.*

Biache-Saint-Vaast. *Town, Pas-de-Calais.* The name was recorded in the 8th century as *Bigartium*, from Germanic *bigard*, a word for an enclosed garden near a house. The second part of the name honors *St. Vedast*, 5th-century bishop of Arras.

Biarritz. *Resort town, Pyrénées-Atlantiques.* The name, recorded in the 12th century as *Bearris*, is of Basque origin, meaning either "place of two rocks," from *bi*, "two," and *harri*, "rock," or else "place of two oaks," from *bi* and *haritz*, "oak." The Basque name is *Miarritze.*

Bibracte. *Historic town, central France.* The capital and stronghold of the Gaulish

Aedui tribe, atop Mont **Beuvray**, derives its name from Gaulish *bebros*, "beaver." The beaver was the totemic animal of the Urnfield people, whose culture extended across France.

Bidache. *Village, Pyrénées-Atlantiques.* The name was recorded in the 14th century as *Vidaxen*, from Basque *bide*, "way," "path," denoting an established route.

Bidart. *Resort town, Pyrénées-Atlantiques.* The name, recorded in the 12th century as now, derives from Basque *bide*, "way," "path," and *arte*, "between," denoting a location between two established routes.

Bierry-les-Belles-Fontaines. *Village, Yonne.* The name derives from Low Latin *beria*, "plain," and the associative suffix *-acum*. The addition means "the beautiful fountains." From 1738 through 1882, and so during the Revolution, the place was known as *Anstrude*, following its erection to a barony in the former year for one M. d'*Anstrude*, a nobleman of Scottish origin with a family name that was originally *Anstruther*.

Bièvres. *Town, Essonne.* The town takes its name from that of the river here, from Gaulish *bebros*, "beaver."

Biganos. *Town, Gironde.* The name derives either from Latin *vicanus*, "villager," or from a Gaulish personal name *Vicannus*, a variant of *Vicanus*, with the Aquitanian suffix *-ossum*.

Le Bignon-Mirabeau. *Village, Loiret.* The first part of the name derives from Old French *bugnon*, "tree trunk," a word of Gaulish origin. The second part commemorates the famous orator Honoré Gabriel de Riqueti, comte de *Mirabeau* (1749-1791), who was born here.

Bigorre. *Region, southwestern France.* The former countship takes its name from the *Bigerriones* tribe, their own name based on a Mediterranean root *big* of uncertain meaning.

Bihorel. *Town, Seine-Maritime.* The suburb of Rouen derives its name from Old French *bikorel*, "night heron," perhaps as a personal nickname.

Billère. *Town, Pyrénées-Atlantiques.* The name of the suburb of Pau was recorded in the 14th century as *Vilhere*, representing a Gascon form of Latin *villella*, "little village," a diminutive of *villa*.

Billom. *Town, Puy-de-Dôme.* The name was recorded early as *Billomaco*, perhaps from the Gaulish personal name *Billios* and *magos*, "market."

Billy-Berclau. *Town, Pas-de-Calais.* The name was recorded in the 11th century as *Billiacum*, from the Gaulish personal name *Billius* and the associative suffix *-acum*. The addition of the name of nearby *Berclau* distinguishes the town from **Billy-Montigny**.

Billy-Montigny. *Town, Pas-de-Calais.* The name, recorded in the 11th century as *Billy*, has the same origin as **Billy-Berclau**, from which it is distinguished by adding the name of nearby *Montigny*.

Binic. *Resort village, Côtes-d'Armor.* The name of the Brittany village is of uncertain origin, although the second element may represent the Breton personal name *Nitos*.

Biot. *Town, Alpes-Maritimes.* The name was recorded in the 12th century as *Buzot*, perhaps from a pre-Indoeuropean root *bud*, of uncertain origin, and the suffix *-ottum*.

Biscarrosse. *Town, Landes.* The name is of uncertain origin but may derive from an Aquitanian root related to Basque *biskar*, "mound," and the suffix *-ossum*.

Bischheim. *Town, Bas-Rhin.* The suburb of Strasbourg derives its name from Germanic *bischof*, "bishop," and *heim*, "village."

Bischwiller. *Town, Bas-Rhin.* The name derives from Germanic *bischof*, "bishop," and Latin *villare*, "farmstead." The German form of the name is *Bischweiler*.

Bitche. *Town, Moselle.* The name derives from the Germanic personal name *Bito*. The town is close to the border with Germany, where it is known as *Bitsch*.

Bitschwiller-lès-Thann. *Village, Haut-Rhin.* The name derives from the Germanic personal name *Buto* and Latin *villare*, "farmstead." The addition locates the village near (*lès*) **Thann**.

Bizanet. *Village, Aude.* The name was recorded in the 10th century as *Biciano*, from the Gaulish personal name *Bitius*, a variant of *Bittius*, and the suffix *-anum*.

Bizanos. *Town, Pyrénées-Atlantiques.* The suburb of Pau takes its name from the Gaulish personal name *Bitianus*, a variant of *Bittius*, and the Aquitanian suffix *-ossum*.

Blagnac. *Town, Haute-Garonne.* The suburb of Toulouse derives its name from the Gaulish personal name *Blannius* and the associative suffix *-acum*.

Blain. *Town, Loire-Atlantique.* The name derives from the Gaulish personal name *Blanus*, a variant of *Blannius*, and the associative suffix *-acum*.

Blainville-sur-l'Eau. *Village, Meurthe-et-Moselle.* The name derives from the Germanic personal name *Bladin* and Latin *villa*, "estate." The addition ("on the water") locates the village on the Meurthe River.

Blainville-sur-Orne. *Town, Calvados.* The name, recorded in the 11th century as *Bledvilla*, shares the origin of **Blainville-sur-l'Eau**, from which it is distinguished by adding the name of the **Orne** River, near which the town is located.

Le Blanc. *Town, Indre.* The name was recorded in the 10th century as *Obliacensis*, from a pre-Celtic root *obl*, of unknown meaning, and the suffix *-incum*. The present form of the name has been influenced by an association with French *blanc*, "white."

Blanc, Mont. *Mountain, eastern France.* The name means what it says, "white mountain," referring to the Alpine peak's permanent snow cover. Its classical name, if any, is unknown. "Ninety-nine people out of a hundred appear to be under the impression that Mount Blanc is in Switzerland, whereas it is wholly within the French fron-

tier province of Haute Savoie" (C.E. Clark, *The Mistakes We Make*, 1898).

Blancheville. *Village, Haute-Marne.* The village was originally named *Villa Nova*, Latin for "new village." In 1220 it took the name of *Blanche* of Navarre, countess of Champagne.

Le Blanc-Mesnil. *Town, Seine-Saint-Denis.* The Paris suburb derives its name from French *blanc*, "white," describing the color of the ground, and nearby *Le Mesnil*, from Latin *mansionile*, "peasant dwelling."

Blanc-Nez, Cap. *Headland, northern France.* The headland, on the English Channel, has a name meaning "cape white-nose," referring to the color of the chalk cliff here, as distinct from that at *Cap Gris-Nez* (see **Gris-Nez, Cap**), 7 miles down the coast.

Blangy-sur-Bresle. *Town, Seine-Maritime.* The town has a name of the same origin as **Blanzat**, adding that of the *Bresle* River, on which it lies.

Blanquefort. *Town, Gironde.* The name was recorded in the 12th century as *Blanca Fort*, from French *blanc*, "white," and *fort*, "strong," with Latin *villa*, "estate," "village," understood, denoting a settlement with a white-stoned castle.

Blanzat. *Village, Puy-de-Dôme.* The name, recorded in the 13th century as *Blanszac*, derives from the Roman personal name *Blandius* and the associative suffix *-acum*.

Blanzy. *Town, Saône-et-Loire.* The name of the suburb of Montceau-les-Mines, recorded in the 13th century as *Blenzeius*, has the same origin as **Blanzat**.

Blayais. *Region, southwestern France.* The region is named for the town of **Blaye** here.

Blaye. *Town, Gironde.* The name was recorded in the 4th century as *Blavia*, from the Gaulish personal name *Blavus*, from *blavo*, "yellow."

Blendecques. *Town, Pas-de-Calais.* The name, recorded in the 12th century as *Blandeca*, has the same origin as **Blanzat**.

Blénod-lès-Pont-à-Mousson. *Town, Meurthe-et-Moselle.* The name was recorded early as *Beleno*, perhaps that of a local pagan god. Blénod is no longer simply "near" (*lès*) **Pont-à-Mousson** but a southern suburb of that town.

Bléré. *Town, Indre-et-Loire.* The name was recorded in the 6th century as *Briotreide*, from Gaulish *briua*, "bridge," and a second element of uncertain origin. Bléré is on the Cher River.

Blésois. *Region, west central France.* The name is an adjectival form of **Blois**, the town on which the region centers.

Bléville. *Town, Seine-Maritime.* The suburb of Le Havre has a name recorded in the 9th century as *Bladulfi villa*, from the Germanic personal name *Bladold* and Latin *villa*, "village."

Blévy. *Village, Eure-et-Loir.* The name was recorded in the 12th century as *Blesiae vicus*, from the Roman name of the *Blaise* River, in the genitive case, and Latin *vicus*, "village."

Blois. *City, Loir-et-Cher.* The name was recorded in the 7th century as *Blesis*, from *Bleso*, of pre-Celtic origin, perhaps as a river name. Blois is on the Loire River.

Blond. *Village, Haute-Vienne.* The name, recorded as *Blatomago* on early coins, is said to derive from the Gaulish personal name *Blato* and *magos*, "field," but *blato-* meant "bloom," "blossom," so a better sense is "flowery field."

Blotzheim. *Village, Haut-Rhin.* The name was recorded in the 8th century as *Flabotesheim*, from an obscure Germanic personal name (perhaps *Flobot*), subsequently replaced by *Blado*, and *heim*, "abode."

Bobigny. *Town, Seine-Saint-Denis.* The name of the Paris suburb was recorded in the 10th century as *Balbiniacum*, from the Roman personal name *Balbinius* (from Latin *balbus*, "stammerer") and the associative suffix *-acum*.

Bocage Angevin. *Region, western France.* The name of the region of bocage (wooded country interspersed with pasture) is the adjectival form of that of **Angers**, the nearby town. There are similar regions elsewhere in France, such as the *Bocage Breton* in Brittany (see **Bretagne**), *Bocage Normand* in Normandy (see **Normandie**), and *Bocage Vendéen* in Vendée. The word *bocage* is a Norman derivative of *bosc*, an early form of *bois*, "wood."

Boé. *Town, Lot-et-Garonne.* The name represents a personal name derived from Latin *bovarius*, "herdsman."

Boën. *Village, Loire.* The name derives from *Bodincus*, an early Italo-Celtic name of the *Po* River, Italy, which according to Pliny meant "deep," "bottomless." The village is also known as *Boën-sur-Lignon* for its location on the *Lignon* River.

Bohain-en-Vermandois. *Town, Aisne.* The name derives from the Germanic personal name *Bodo* or *Bolo* and *ham*, "village." The addition locates the town in **Vermandois**.

Bois-Colombes. *Town, Hauts-de-Seine.* The name of the Paris suburb derives from Low Latin *boscus*, "wood," and nearby **Colombes**.

Bois-d'Arcy. *Town, Yvelines.* The name derives from Low Latin *boscus*, "wood," and nearby *Arcy*. There is still an actual wood of the name here.

Bois de Boulogne *see* **Boulogne-Billancourt**

Bois-Guillaume. *Town, Seine-Maritime.* The suburb of Rouen derives its name from Low Latin *boscus*, "wood," and the name of its owner, *Guillaume* (William).

Bois-le-Roi. *Town, Seine-et-Marne.* The name was recorded in the 12th century as *Boscum Regis*, Latin for "king's wood," denoting its royal proprietor.

Boissy-le-Châtel. *Village, Seine-et-Marne.* The name derives from the Roman personal name *Buttius* or *Buccius* and the associative suffix *-acum*. The addition derives from Latin *castellum*, "castle."

Boissy-Saint-Léger. *Town, Val-de-Marne.* The name of the Paris suburb was recorded in the 6th century as *Bucciacus*, from Latin *buxetum*, from *buxus*, "box," "bush," and the collective suffix *-etum*. The addition honors the 7th-century martyr *St. Leger*, bishop of Autun.

Boisville-la-Saint-Père. *Village, Eure-et-Loir.* The name represents the Germanic personal name *Boda*, influenced by French *bois*, "wood," and Latin *villa*, "estate." The village was dependent on the abbey of *Saint-Père*-en-Vallée, near Chartres, its name honoring *St. Peter.*

Bolbec. *Town, Seine-Maritime.* The name is that of the small river here, itself from Scandinavian *bol*, "farmstead," and *bekkr*, "stream."

Bollène. *Town, Vaucluse.* The name was recorded in the 7th century as *Abolena*, from the Germanic personal name *Abbolenus*. The *A-* of this was taken to represent French *à*, "at," and was accordingly dropped.

Bollwiller. *Town, Haut-Rhin.* The name was recorded in the 8th century as *Ballonevillare*, from the Germanic personal name *Ballo* and Latin *villare*, "farmstead."

Bologne. *Village, Haute-Marne.* The name was recorded in the 10th century as *Bulonia*, from the Gaulish personal name *Bullonius*.

Bompas. *Town, Pyrénées-Orientales.* The name was originally *Malpas*, from Latin *malum passum*, "bad passage," denoting a difficult route, but this unfavorable name was changed to the favorable *Bompas*, as if from Latin *bonum passum*, "good passage."

Bonchamp-lès-Laval. *Village, Mayenne.* The name was recorded in the 11th century as *Malus Campus*, Latin for "bad field," then in the 13th century as *Bonus Campus*, "good field." The change of name perhaps refers to an exemption from feudal taxes or was made simply to avoid an undesirable association,

as with **Bompas**. The village is near (*lès*) **Laval**.

Bondoufle. *Town, Essonne.* The name was recorded in the 7th century as *Bonalpha*, from the Germanic personal name *Bono* and possibly *alah*, "temple."

Bondy. *Town, Seine-Saint-Denis.* The name of the Paris suburb was recorded in the 8th century as *Bonisiacus*, from a Gallo-Roman personal name *Bondius* or *Bonditius* and the associative suffix *-acum*.

Bon-Encontre. *Town, Lot-et-Garonne.* The suburb of Agen has a name meaning "good meeting" (French *bonne rencontre*), given auspiciously for a favorable future.

Bonifacio. *Village and port, Corse-du-Sud.* The village, near the southern tip of Corsica, was recorded in the 13th century as *castrum Bonifatii*, from Latin *castrum*, "fort," and the name of the Tuscan count *Boniface* (Italian *Bonifacio*), who built the fort in 838. Earlier names were *Marianon* in the 2d century and *Pallas* in the 4th century.

Bonnétable. *Town, Sarthe.* The name was recorded in the 11th century as *Malum Stabulum*, Latin for "bad stable," meaning a poor place for raising animals, but by the 13th century this had become *Bonum Stabulum*, "good stable," a change made propitiously as for **Bompas**.

Bonneuil-sur-Marne. *Town, Val-de-Marne.* Local legend derives the name of the present Paris suburb from French *bon œil*, "good eye," describing its favorable riverside site, but it in fact represents the Gaulish personal name *Bonos*, or Latin *bonus*, "good," and Gaulish *ialon*, "clearing." The addition locates the town on the **Marne** River.

Bonneval. *Town, Eure-et-Loir.* The name was recorded in the 9th century as *Bona Vallis*, Latin for "good valley." The town is on the Loir River.

Bonneval-sur-Arc. *Resort village, Savoie.* The name has the same origin as for **Bonneval**, but adding the name of the **Arc** River here for distinction.

Bonneville. *Town, Haute-Savoie.* The name was recorded in the 12th century as *Bonavilla*, from Latin *bona villa*, "good village."

Bonnières-sur-Seine. *Village, Yvelines.* The name derives from the Roman personal name *Bonus* and the suffix *-aria*. The addition locates the village on the **Seine** River.

Bonsecours. *Town, Seine-Maritime.* The suburb of Rouen has a name of religious origin meaning literally "good aid," as a title of the Virgin Mary (*Notre Dame de Bon Secours*).

Bonson. *Village, Loire.* The name is that of the stream here that flows into the Loire nearby. Its own name is of uncertain origin.

Boos. *Village, Seine-Maritime.* The name was recorded in the 11th century as *Bothus*, from Old Norse *budh*, "booth," "shelter."

Bordeaux. *City and port, Gironde.* The city's Roman name was *Burdigala*, an Aquitanian word comprising the elements *burd* and *gala*, of unknown meaning.

Bordelais. *Region, southwestern France.* The name is the adjectival form of **Bordeaux**, the region's chief town.

Bordères-sur-l'Échez. *Town, Hautes-Pyrénées.* The name derives from Old French *borde*, Provençal *borda*, "small house," "hut," here with the the suffix *-ère*, a Gascon form of the diminutive suffix *-ella*. The addition names the *Échez* River here.

Bordes. *Village, Pyrénées-Atlantiques.* The name derives from Old French *borde*, "hut," "little house," later "farm."

Bormes-les-Mimosas. *Town, Var.* The name was recorded in the 11th century as *Borma*, perhaps from pre-Indoeuropean *bar*, "height," rather than the name of *Bormo*, the Gaulish god of warm springs, as the town has no such springs. The second part of the name refers to the mimosas here. (The tree is not indigenous to this region, but was introduced from Mexico in the 1860s.)

Bornel. *Village, Oise.* The name was recorded in the 8th century as *Bordonellum*, representing Old French *borde*, "hut," as for **Bordes**, and the suffixes *-on* and *-ellum*.

Bort-les-Orgues. *Town, Corrèze.* The name was recorded early as *Boort*, perhaps representing an original form *Boduoritum*, from Gaulish *boduos*, "crow," and *ritu-*, "ford," giving a sense "ford where crows are seen." The second part of the name ("the organ") refers to nearby basalt columns that fancifully resemble organ pipes.

Bouaye. *Town, Loire-Atlantique.* The name was recorded in the 12th century as *Boia*, from the Gaulish personal name *Bovus*, a variant of *Bovius*, and the associative suffix *-acum*.

Boucau. *Town, Pyrénées-Atlantiques.* The original name of the location, recorded in the 13th century, was *Puncta*, "point," referring to a nearby headland on the Bay of Biscay. The present name probably derives from *buccale*, a derivative of Latin *bucca*, "mouth," referring to the mouth of the Adour River here, opened for navigation in 1578.

Bouc-Bel-Air. *Town, Bouches-du-Rhône.* The first part of the name probably represents pre-Latin *buk*, "mountain." Bouc lies at the foot of a huge table-shaped rock. The rest of the name is French *bel air*, "beautiful air," a name formerly popular for manor houses and farms.

Bouchain. *Town, Nord.* The name was recorded in the 12th century as *Bulcen*, probably from the Germanic female personal name *Bolsind*.

Bouchemaine. *Town, Maine-et-Loire.* The suburb of Angers has a name recorded in the 11th centuary as *Bucca Meduanae*, Latin for "mouth of the Maine," referring to the location of the town at the confluence of the **Maine** and Loire rivers.

Bouches-du-Rhône. *Department, southeastern France.* The name translates as "mouths of the Rhône," referring to the **Rhône** delta on which it is centered.

Bouffémont. *Town, Val-d'Oise.* The name was recorded in the 13th century as *Bofesmunt*, from the Germanic personal name *Boffo* and Latin *mons, montis*, "mountain."

Bougival. *Town, Yvelines.* The name of the Paris suburb was recorded in the 8th century as *Beudechisilo valle*, from the Germanic personal name *Baudegisil* and Latin *vallis*, "valley."

Bouguenais. *Town, Loire-Atlantique.* The suburb of Nantes derives its name from the (possibly Germanic) personal name *Bego* and the suffix *-ensem*.

La Bouilladisse. *Town, Bouches-du-Rhône.* The name was recorded in the 14th century as *Boythedissa*, from a Provençal derivative of French *bouillir*, "to boil," and the suffix *-adisse*, referring to a bubbling spring. Until 1910 the town was known as *La Bourine*, a name recorded in the 13th century as *Leborina*, from Latin *lepus, leporis*, "hare," and the suffix *-ina*.

Bouillargues. *Town, Gard.* The name was recorded in the 10th century as *Bulianicus*, from the Gaulish personal name *Bullius* and the suffix *-anicum*.

Boulay-Moselle. *Town, Moselle.* The first part of the name was recorded in the 12th century as *Bollei*, from Gaulish *betulla*, "birch tree." The second part names the **Moselle** River here.

Boulazac. *Town, Dordogne.* The name derives from an early form *Bullatiacum*, from the Gallo-Roman personal name *Bullatius*, from Gaulish *Bullius*, and the associative suffix *-acum*.

Boulogne-Billancourt. *Town, Hauts-de-Seine.* The Paris suburb takes the first part of its name from **Boulogne-sur-Mer**, as the church here was founded by pilgrims from that town. The second part derives from the Germanic personal name *Billa* and Latin *cortem*, accusative of *cors*, "estate." It was this Boulogne that gave the name of the *Bois de Boulogne*, the Paris park.

Boulogne-sur-Mer. *City and port, Hauts-de-Seine.* The name of the city was recorded in the 4th century as *Bolonia*, a form of *Bononia*, from Gaulish *bona*, "foundation," "fort," as perhaps also for *Bologna* in Italy. The second part of the name, denoting its location on the English Channel, distinguishes it from **Boulogne-Billancourt**. Its original Roman name was *Portus Itius*, then *Gesoriacum*.

Boulonnais. *Historic region, northern France.* The region is named adjectivally for **Boulogne-sur-Mer**, the town on which it centers.

Le Boulou. *Resort town, Pyrénées-Orientales.* The name was recorded early as *Volo*, probably representing an old name of the Tech River, on which the town stands.

Bourbon-Lancy. *Resort town, Saône-et-Loire.* The name derives from Gaulish *Borbo*, the name of the Celtic god who presided over the warm springs here. The addition, originally *l'Ancy*, names the local lord *Ancy*, distinguishing the town from **Bourbon-l'Archambault**.

Bourbon-l'Archambault. *Resort village, Allier.* The name, recorded in the 8th century as *Burbone*, shares the origin of **Bourbon-Lancy**, from which it is distinguished by the addition of *Archambault*, the name of a local lord associated with the place since 1012.

Bourbonnais. *Historic region, central France.* The name has the same origin as **Bourbon-Lancy**. It was this territory that gave the name of the French royal *Bourbon* dynasty.

Bourbonne-les-Bains. *Resort village, Haute-Marne.* The name, recorded in the 9th century as *Borbona*, has the same origin as that of **Bourbon-Lancy**. The addition ("the baths") refers to the hot saline springs here. An early Gaulish name was *Lindesina*, from *lindon*, "pool," "lake," referring to the Apance River here.

La Bourboule. *Resort village, Puy-de-*

Dôme. The name has the same origin as **Bourbon-Lancy**, relating to the hot springs here.

Bourbourg. *Town, Nord*. The name derives from Dutch *broek*, "marsh," and Germanic *burg*, "fortified place."

Bourbriac. *Village, Côtes-d'Armor*. The name derives from the Gaulish personal name *Burburius* and the associative suffix *-acum*.

Bourg. *Village, Gironde*. The name was recorded in the 12th century as *Burgus*, from Low Latin *burgus*, "fortified place," from Germanic *burg*, "castle," "fort." The village is alternately known as *Bourg-sur-Gironde*, for its location at the lower end of the **Gironde** estuary (but actually on the Dordogne River, just above its junction with the Garonne).

Bourganeuf. *Village, Creuse*. The name was recorded in the 12th century as *Borguet Nou*, from Low Latin *burgus*, "fortified place," as for **Bourg**, and *novus*, "new."

Bourg-Argental. *Village, Loire*. The name was recorded in the 11th century as *Burgus Argentavi*, from Low Latin *burgus*, "fortified place," as for **Bourg**, and the name of nearby *Argental*, from the Gaulish personal name *Argantius*, from *arganton*, "silver," and the associative suffix *-acum*.

Bourg-de-Péage. *Town, Drôme*. The name was recorded in the 15th century as *Pedagium Burgi Pisanciani*, "tollgate of the fortified place on the Isère," from Low Latin *pedaticum*, literally "right to place one's foot" (i.e. right to pass), *burgus*, "fortified place," as for **Bourg**, and a Roman name of the **Isère** River, on which the town stands.

Bourg-de-Thizy. *Village, Rhône*. The name derives from Low Latin *burgus*, "fortified place," as for **Bourg**, and the name of nearby **Thizy**.

Le Bourg-d'Oisans. *Village, Isère*. The name derives from Low Latin *burgus*, "fortified place," as for **Bourg** and the name of the *Oisans* valley here.

Le Bourg-Dun. *Village, Seine-Maritime*. The first part of the name derives from Low Latin *burgus*, "fortified place," as for **Bourg**. The second part derives from Gaulish *dunon*, "fort." The name is thus a tautological doublet.

Bourg-en-Bresse. *Town, Ain*. The name was recorded in the 13th century as *Burgus in Bressia*, from Low Latin *burgus*, "fortified place," as for **Bourg**, and the name of the **Bresse** region, of which it became the capital when Bresse passed to the house of Savoy at the end of the 13th century.

Bourges. *City, Cher*. The original name of the location, recorded by Caesar in the 1st century BC, was *Avaricum*, from *Avara*, the river now known as the *Yèvre*. In the 4th century the settlement became known as *Bituricum*, from the Gaulish tribe *Bituriges*, whose capital it was, and who themselves gave the name of **Berry**.

Le Bourget (1). *Resort village, Savoie*. The village takes its name from Low Latin *burgus*, "fortified place," as for **Bourg**. It is also known as *Le Bourget-du-Lac*, for its location near the end of the *Lac du Bourget*, named for it.

Le Bourget (2). *Town, Seine-Saint-Denis*. The Paris suburb and airport takes its name from Low Latin *burgus*, "fortified place," as for **Bourg**, and the diminutive suffix *-ittum*.

Bourg-la-Reine. *Town, Hauts-de-Seine*. The name of the Paris suburb was recorded in the 12th century as *Burgum Reginae*, "town of the queen," meaning a private royal possession.

Bourg-lès-Valence. *Town, Drôme*. The name, recorded in the 12th century as *Borc*, derives from Low Latin *burgus*, "fortified place," as for **Bourg**. The distinguishing addition locates the town near (*lès*) **Valence**, of which it is now in fact a suburb.

Bourg-Madame. *Village, Pyrénées-Orientales*. Originally called *La Guinguette*, the village was named as now in 1815 by Louis de Bourbon, duc d'Angoulême (1775-1844), the son of Charles X and the last dauphin of France (see **Dauphiné**), in honor of his wife, Marie-Thérèse de Bourbon, duchesse d'Angoulême (1778-1851), the daughter of Louis XVI, known as *Madame Royale*. *Bourg* here represents Low Latin *burgus*, "fortified place."

Bourgneuf-en-Retz. *Village, Loire-Atlantique*. The name derives from Low Latin *burgus*, "fortified place," as for **Bourg**, and *novus*, "new." This Bourgneuf is distinguished from others by its location in the former duchy of *Retz*.

Bourgogne. *Region, east central France*. The present administrative region and former province, known in English as *Burgundy*, bore the Roman name *Burgundia*, from the *Burgundians*, a Germanic tribe, who took their name either from Indoeuropean *bhrghu*, "elevated," referring to the terrain, or from Gothic *baurgjans*, "dwellers in fortified places."

Bourgoin-Jallieu. *Town, Isère*. The name was recorded in the 3d century as *Bergusia*, from a derivative of Germanic *berg*, "mountain." The second part of the name, originally that of a separate community, was recorded in the 12th century as *Jaliacum*, from the Roman personal name *Gallius* and the associative suffix *-acum*.

Bourg-Saint-Andéol. *Town, Ardèche*. The name was recorded in the 12th century as *Burgus Sancti Andeoli*, from Low Latin *burgus*, "fortified place," as for **Bourg**, and the name of the 3d-century Greek priest *St. Andeolus* (Antiochus).

Bourg-Saint-Maurice. *Resort town, Savoie*. The name was recorded in the 12th century as *Bergintrum de Sancto Mauritio*, from a pre-Latin word related to Gaulish and Germanic *berg*, "mountain," and the name of the 3d-century martyr *St. Maurice*.

Bourgtheroulde-Infreville. *Village, Eure*. The name combines two places. *Bourgtheroulde* was recorded in the 11th century as *Burgus Thoroldi*, from Low Latin

burgus, "fortified place," as for **Bourg**, and the Scandinavian personal name *Turold*, that of a local lord. *Infreville* was recorded in the 12th century as *Wifrevilla*, from the Germanic personal name *Wifred* and Latin *villa*, "estate."

Bourgueil. *Town, Indre-et-Loire*. The name was recorded in the 10th century as *Burgolium*, from Low Latin *burgus*, "fortified place," and Gaulish *ialon*, "clearing."

Bourogne. *Village, Belfort*. The name was recorded in the 13th century as *Boronia*, perhaps from the Gallo-Roman personal name *Burronius*.

Bousbecque. *Village, Nord*. The name, recorded in the 12th century as *Bosbeka*, derives from Germanic *busc*, "wood," and *bach*, "stream."

Le Bouscat. *Town, Gironde*. The suburb of Bordeaux derives its name from Old Occitan *bosc*, "wood."

Boussois. *Village, Nord*. The name was recorded in the 11th century as *Bussuth*, from Latin *buxetum*, from *buxus*, "box," "bush," and the collective suffix *-etum*.

Boussy-Saint-Antoine. *Town, Essonne*. The name was recorded in the 13th century as *Buciacum*, from the Roman personal name *Buccius* or *Buttius* and the associative suffix *-acum*. The distinguishing addition honors *St. Antony*.

Boutavent. *Village, Oise*. The name represents French *boute avant*, "push ahead," denoting a military outpost.

Bouvines. *Village, Nord*. The name was recorded in the 12th century as *Bovines* or *Bovinae villae*, from the Gallo-Roman personal name *Bovius* and the suffix *-inum*.

Bouxières-aux-Dames. *Town, Meurthe-et-Moselle*. The name was recorded in the 8th century as *Buxarias*, from Latin *buxaria*, from *buxus*, "box," and the suffix *-aria*, giving a sense "place where box trees grow." The addition ("of the ladies") refers to a nunnery here.

Bouxwiller. *Town, Bas-Rhin.* The name was recorded in the 13th century as *Buchswilre*, from the Germanic personal name *Bucco* and Latin *villare*, "farmstead."

Bouzonville. *Town, Moselle.* The name was recorded in the 12th century as *Buosonis villa*, from the Germanic personal name *Boso* and Latin *villa*, "estate."

Boves. *Village, Somme.* The name derives from Old French *bove*, "cave," "cavern."

Bozel. *Village, Savoie.* The name is of obscure origin.

Bozouls. *Village, Aveyron.* The name was recorded in the 10th century as *Pociolos*, from Latin *puteolis*, diminutive of *puteus*, "well." The present name is an altered form of this.

Braine. *Village, Aisne.* The name derives from the Gaulish personal name *Brannos*.

Bramevaque. *Village, Hautes-Pyrénées.* The name derives from Old Occitan *brama*, from the verb *bramar*, "to call," "to cry out," and *vaca*, "cow." The reference is to the poisonous plant meadow saffron, which grows locally and makes the cows low when they eat it.

Brantôme. *Village, Dordogne.* The name was recorded in the 8th century as *Branstosma*, then later as *Brantosama*, from Gaulish *brant*, of unknown meaning, and the superlative suffix *-sama*.

Brassac-les-Mines. *Village, Puy-de-Dôme.* The name was recorded in the 9th century as *Braciacus*, from the Gaulish personal name *Braccus*, a form of *Bracus*, and the associative suffix *-acum*. The addition refers to the former coal mines here.

Bray. *Region, north central France.* The small region of Normandy had the Medieval Latin name of *Brai*, from Gaulish *bracos*, "mud," "marsh."

Bray-Dunes. *Resort town, Nord.* The name probably derives from Old French *brai*, "mud," as for **Bray.** The addition refers to the sand dunes here on the North Sea coast.

Bray-sur-Seine. *Village, Seine-et-Marne.* The name relates to the region of **Bray**, while the river here is the **Seine**.

Brazey-en-Plaine. *Village, Côte-d'Or.* The name derives from the Gaulish personal name *Bracius*, from *Bracus*, and the associative suffix *-acum*. The addition ("in the plain") is found for many places along the Burgundy Canal here.

Bréal-sous-Montfort. *Village, Ille-et-Vilaine.* The name may derive from Old French *breuil*, as perhaps for **Bréhal.** The village is near (*sous*, "under") **Montfort**.

Brebières. *Town, Pas-de-Calais.* The name was recorded in the 12th century as *Berberia*, from Low Latin *berbicaria*, "sheepfold."

Brécey. *Village, Manche.* The name derives from the Gaulish personal name *Briccius* and the associative suffix *-acum*.

Brech. *Town, Morbihan.* The name, recorded in the 13th century as *Brec*, derives from Low Latin *bracium*, from Gaulish (and pre-Gaulish) *bracu*, "valley," "marsh," related to Old French *brai*, Old Provençal *brac*, "mud."

La Brède. *Village, Gironde.* The name derives from Low Latin *breda*, "thorn bush."

Bréhal. *Village, Manche.* The name may derive from Old French *breuil*, from Gaulish *brogilos*, a word for a small wood enclosed by a wall or hedge.

Breil-sur-Roya. *Village, Alpes-Maritimes.* The name was recorded in the 12th century as *Brehl*, from Old French *breuil*, as perhaps for **Bréhal.** The village is on the *Roya* River close to the border with Italy, where it is known as *Breglio*.

Bresles. *Village, Oise.* The name was recorded in the 13th century as *Braella*, probably from a derivative of Gaulish *bracu*, "mud," "marsh."

Bresse. *Region, eastern France.* The Latin name of the region, recorded in the 6th century, was *Brixia*, or *Saltus Brixiae*, "forest of

Brixia." The earlier Roman name was *Se-busia*, which may have given the later *Brixia*.

La Bresse. *Resort town, Vosges*. The name was recorded in the 15th century as *La Brasse*, translating Germanic *walle*, "rampart," "wall of a city."

Bressuire. *Town, Deux-Sèvres*. The name was recorded in the 11th century as *Berzo-rium*, apparently a blend of the Gaulish personal name *Briccius* or *Brictius* and *duron*, "fortress."

Brest. *City and port, Finistère*. The name of the Brittany city was recorded in the 9th century as *Bresta*, from Breton *bre*, "hill," related to Gaulish *briga*, as for **Brie**.

Bretagne. *Region, northwestern France*. The present administrative region and former province, better known in English as *Brittany*, takes its name from Latin *Britannia*, the Roman name of Britain, from where Celtic settlers came in the 6th century, fleeing the Anglo-Saxon invaders. Britain is now *Great Britain* (French *Grande-Bretagne*) as against this "Little Britain," formerly *Armorica* (see **Armorique**). The Breton name of Brittany is *Breizh*, abbreviated in official documentation as BZH.

Breteuil (1). *Village, Eure*. The name was recorded in the 11th century as *Britolium*, from the Gaulish personal name *Brittus* and *ialon*, "field," "clearing."

Breteuil (2). *Village, Oise*. The name was recorded early as *Brituogilum*, with the same origin as **Breteuil** (1).

Brétigny. *Hamlet, Eure-et-Loir*. The name was recorded in the 12th century as *Breteni*, from Latin *Britannus*, "Breton."

Brétigny-sur-Orge. *Town, Essonne*. The name was recorded in the 11th century as *Britiniacum*, from Latin *Britannicus*, "Breton." The addition locates the town near the **Orge** River.

Bretteville-sur-Odon. *Town, Calvados*. The name was recorded in the 11th century as *Brittavilla*, from Norman *britta villa*,

"Breton village." The addition refers to the nearby *Odon* River.

Le Breuil. *Village, Saône-et-Loire*. The name derives from Old French *breuil*, as perhaps for **Bréhal**.

Breuillet. *Town, Essonne*. The name derives from a diminutive form of Old French *breuil*, as perhaps for **Bréhal**.

Bréviandes. *Village, Aube*. The suburb of Troyes has a name as if *brève viande*, literally "brief viand," meaning a scant supply of food from land which is difficult to cultivate.

Briançon. *Town, Hautes-Alpes*. The Roman name of the town was *Brigantium*, from pre-Gaulish (here, Ligurian) *briga*, "height," with the Ligurian suffix *-ant* and the Latin suffix *-ium*. Briançon is an Alpine town and popularly claims to be the highest town in Europe.

Briançonnais. *Region, southeastern France*. The mountainous region derives its name adjectivally from that of **Briançon**, its chief town.

Briare. *Town, Loiret*. The name was recorded in the 4th century as *Brivodurum*, from Gaulish *briua*, "bridge," and *duron*, "fort." (The name reverses the elements of *Durobrivae*, the Romano-British name of Rochester, England.) A "bridge fort" is a Roman fort by a river, which in the case of Briare is the Loire.

Briatexte. *Town, Tarn*. The town was founded in 1291 by Simon Briseteste, seneschal (governor) of Carcassonne, and is named for him.

Bricquebec. *Town, Manche*. The name is of Old Norse origin, from *brekka*, "hill," and *bekkr*, "stream."

Brides-les-Bains. *Resort village, Savoie*. The name, recorded in the 17th century as *Bride*, derives from Gaulish *briua*, "bridge," and the Gaulish (and pre-Gaulish) suffix *-ate*. Brides is on the Doron River. The addition ("the baths") refers to the mineral springs here.

Brie. *Historic region, northeastern France.* The region northeast of Paris had the Medieval Latin name *Briegium*, from Gaulish *briga*, "height," "hill."

Briec. *Town, Finistère.* The name derives from the Gaulish personal name *Brigos* and the associative suffix *-acum*.

Brie-Comte-Robert. *Town, Seine-et-Marne.* The first part of the name locates the town in **Brie**. The second part honors *Robert* (died 1188), count (*comte*) of Dreux, lord (*seigneur*) of Brie, the fifth son of Louis VI.

Brienne-le-Château. *Village, Aube.* The name derives from Gaulish *briua*, "bridge," and the river suffix *-onna*. Brienne is near the Aube River. The addition refers to a castle (*château*) here.

Brienon-sur-Armançon. *Village, Yonne.* The name derives from the Gaulish personal name *Briannos* and the suffix *-onem*. The addition refers to the *Armançon* River here.

Briey. *Town, Meurthe-et-Moselle.* The name was recorded in the 11th century as *Briacensis*, from the Gaulish personal name *Brigos* (from *brigo-*, "strength") and the associative suffix *-acum*.

Brignais. *Town, Rhône.* The name was recorded in the 9th century as *Briniacas villa*, from the Gallo-Roman personal name *Brinnius*, from Gaulish *Brinnos*, and the associative suffix *-acum*, followed by Latin *villa*, "estate."

Brignoles. *Town, Var.* The name of the town was recorded in the 10th century as *Bruniola*, from pre-Latin *bron*, an altered form of *born*, "spring" (rather than the Germanic personal name *Brun*), and the suffix *-eola*.

La Brigue. *Resort village, Alpes-Maritimes.* The name was recorded in the 11th century as *Brica*, from Gaulish *briga*, "height." The village is close to the border with Italy, where it is known as *Briga* or *Briga Marittima*, for its location in the Maritime Alps.

Brionne. *Town, Eure.* The Roman name of the town was *Breviodurum*, from Gaulish *briua*, "bridge," and *duron*, "fort." The present form of the name evolved from medieval *Brionia*. Brionne is on the Risle River.

Brioude. *Town, Haute-Loire.* The name was recorded in the 5th century as *Brivas*, from Gaulish *briua*, "bridge." The bridge in question is at present *Vieille-Broude*, 2 miles to the south, over the Allier River.

Brioux-sur-Boutonne. *Village, Deux-Sèvres.* The name was recorded in the 4th century as *Brigiosum*, apparently from Gaulish *briga*, "hill," and the suffix *-osum*. But the terrain here is flat, by the *Boutonne* River, so the first element may in fact derive from the Gaulish personal name *Brigos*, although the suffix given is rarely added to personal names.

Brissac-Quincé. *Village, Maine-et-Loire.* The name was recorded in the 11th century as *Bracaseacum*, in the 12th century as *Brechesac*, and in the 15th century as *Brissesac*, as if modern French *brèche-sac* or *brise-sac*, literally "break-bag." There was a mill here, and the name appears to refer to the dishonest behavior of the miller. But the 11th-century form could also imply an origin in *Braccatiacum*, from the personal name *Braccatius*, from Gaulish *Braccius*, and the associative suffix *-acum*. *Quincé*, recorded in the 12th century as *Quinceium*, is from the Roman personal name *Quintius* and the same suffix *-acum*.

Brittany *see* **Bretagne**

Brive-la-Gaillarde. *City, Corrèze.* The city takes its name from Gaulish *briua*, "bridge," referring to a bridge over the Corrèze River here. The addition means "the vigorous," rendering *Curretia*, the Roman name of the river, with its strong current, although the term is popularly applied to the town's former ramparts, which were "so successfully defended in medieval sieges that Brive earned its sobriquet 'the gallant'" [Young, p.275]. (This account appears to confuse *gaillard*, "strong," "sprightly," with *vaillant*, "valiant," "gallant.")

Brives-Charensac. *Town, Haute-Loire.* The suburb of Le Puy-en-Velay derives the first part of its name from Gaulish *briua*, "bridge," and the second part from the Gallo-Roman personal name *Carentius*, a form of *Carantius*, and the associative suffix *-ac*. The town is on the Loire River.

Broglie. *Town, Eure.* The town was originally called *Chambrais*, a name of the same origin as **Cambrai**. It took its present name in 1742 when the land here was erected into a dukedom for the *Broglie* family, of Italian origin.

Brommat. *Village, Aveyron.* The name derives from that of the *Bromme* River here.

Bron. *City, Rhône.* The suburb of Lyon derives its name from the Germanic personal name *Bero*, here in the objective (accusative) case.

Broons. *Village, Côtes-d'Armor.* The name of the Breton village is probably that of the saint known to the Welsh as *Brychan*.

Brou (1). *Village, Ain.* The suburb of Bourg-en-Bresse derives its name from Old French *brai*, "mud."

Brou (2). *Village, Eure-et-Loir.* The name was recorded in the 11th century as *Braiolum*, from Old French *brai*, "mud," and the suffix *-eolum*.

Brouage. *Hamlet, Charente-Maritime.* The name is of uncertain origin. The first element may represent Gaulish *brog-*, "limit." The second is the suffix *-aticum*.

Bruay-la-Buissière. *Town, Pas-de-Calais.* The name was recorded in the 10th century as *Bruhaium*, from the Gaulish personal name *Brugus*, a form of *Brugos*, and the associative suffix *-acum*. The second part of the name, originally that of a nearby place, recorded in the 12th century as *Buxeria*, derives from Latin *buxaria*, from *buxus*, "box," and the suffix *-aria*, giving a sense "place where box trees grow."

Bruay-sur-l'Escaut. *Town, Nord.* The suburb of Valenciennes shares its name origin with **Bruay-la-Buissière**. The addition locates the town on the **Escaut** River.

Brumath. *Town, Bas-Rhin.* The name was recorded by Ptolemy in the 2d century AD as *Brocomagos*, from Gaulish *broccos*, "badger," or the personal name *Broccus*, and *magos*, "market."

Brunoy. *Town, Essonne.* The name was recorded in the 7th century as *Braunate*. The origin of this is uncertain. The first element may relate to the Gaulish personal name *Bratennus*. The suffix is perhaps Gaulish *-ate*, with the final *-e* giving the present *-oy*.

Brunstatt. *Town, Haut-Rhin.* The suburb of Mulhouse probably derives its name from the Germanic personal name *Brun* and *stat*, "place."

Bruyères. *Village, Vosges.* The name derives from Latin *brucaria*, from Gaulish *bruca*, "heather."

Bruyères-le-Châtel. *Town, Essonne.* The name was recorded in the 7th century as *Brocaria*, from Latin *brucaria*, a derivative of Gaulish *bruca*, "heather." The addition derives from Latin *castellum*, "castle."

Bruz. *Town, Ille-et-Vilaine.* The name perhaps derives from Gaulish *bruca*, "heather."

Bry-sur-Marne. *Town, Val-de-Marne.* The Paris suburb has a name of uncertain origin. It may derive from Gaulish *briua*, "bridge," referring to an old bridge over the **Marne** here.

Buffard. *Village, Doubs.* The name is a personal name, from French *bufe*, "cheek-piece" (the part of a helmet that covers the cheek), and the pejorative suffix *-ard*, as in English *coward, drunkard*. The personal name was thus originally a nickname meaning "chubby cheeks."

Bugey. *Region, eastern France.* The region, in the southernmost Jura, derives its name from Latin *pagus Bellicensis*, "district of Belicius," referring to its former capital, **Belley**.

La Bugue. *Village, Dordogne*. The name was recorded in the 10th century as *Albuca*, from Gaulish *albuca*, a type of white marly rock. *Albuca* became misdivided as *al Buca*, with *al* taken as French *la*, "the," giving the present name.

Buhl. *Village, Haut-Rhin*. The name represents Germanic *buhil*, "hill."

Buis-les-Baronnies. *Village, Drôme*. The name derives from Latin *buxus*, "box," here used collectively. The addition is from French *baronnie*, "barony," an old district of the Dauphiné.

Le Buisson-de-Cadouin. *Village, Dordogne* The first part of the name, recorded in the 15th century as *Buxono*, probably derives from Latin *buxus*, "box," rather than *boscus*, "wood." The second part, recorded in the 13th century as *Cadunio*, probably derives from the Gaulish personal name *Catonius*.

Bully-les-Mines. *Town, Pas-de-Calais*. The name derives from the Gaulish personal name *Bullius* and the associative suffix *-acum*. The addition refers to the former coal mines here.

Burbure. *Village, Pas-de-Calais*. The second element of this name is Germanic *bur*, "hut" (English *bower*). The first element could be Germanic *burg*, "fort," or a personal name.

Bures-sur-Yvette. *Town, Essonne*. The name represents Germanic *bur*, "hut" (English *bower*). The distinguishing addition names the **Yvette** River here.

Burgundy *see* **Bourgogne**

Busigny. *Village, Nord*. The name derives from the Germanic personal name *Boso* and the double suffix *-in* and *-iacum*.

Buxy. *Village, Saône-et-Loire*. The name derives from the Roman personal name *Bucius* and the associative suffix *-acum*.

Buzançais. *Town, Indre*. The name was recorded in the 9th century as *Bosentiacas*, either from the Roman personal name *Busentius* and the associative suffix *-acum*, or from the Germanic personal name *Boso* and a double suffix *-in* and *-iacum*.

Cabannes. *Village, Bouches-du-Rhône*. The name is a southern form of Low Latin *capanna*, "cottage" (English *cabin*).

Cabestany. *Town, Pyrénées-Orientales*. The suburb of Perpignan derives its name from Latin *caput*, "head," "end," and *stagnum*, "piece of standing water," "pond."

Cabourg. *Resort town, Calvados*. The name was recorded in the 11th century as *Cadburgus*, probably from Gaulish *catu-*, "battle," and Germanic *burg*, "fort." An origin has also been proposed in a form of Scandinavian *katr*, "happy," "cheerful," and *borg*, "fort," or in a Germanic female personal name *Hadeburg*.

Cabriès. *Town, Bouches-du-Rhône*. The name was recorded in the 11th century as *Caprarium*, from Latin *capra*, "goat," and the suffix *-arium*, giving a sense "place where goats are bred."

Cachan. *Town, Val-de-Marne*. The Paris suburb has a name recorded in the 9th century as *Caticantus*, from an obscure first element (perhaps Gaulish *catu-*, "battle," as for **Caen**) and Gaulish *cantos*, "circle," "rim."

Cadalen. *Village, Tarn*. The name is of uncertain origin. It could perhaps derive from Low Latin *catanum*, "juniper."

Cadarache. *Hamlet, Bouches-du-Rhône*. The name is usually said to derive from Low Latin *cataracta*, "cataract," "sluice," "dam," and there is in fact a modern dam on the Durance River here and a hydroelectric plant nearby. But a Gaulish origin is perhaps more likely, from *catu-*, "battle," and *rate*, "fort," giving an overall sense "(place of the) battle ramparts."

Cadenet. *Village, Vaucluse*. The name derives from Low Latin *catanum*, "juniper," and the collective suffix *-etum*.

Caderousse. *Village, Vaucluse.* The name, recorded in the 11th century as *Cadarossa*, is of uncertain origin. It may represent a pre-Indoeuropean river name *Katar*, or a Gaulish personal name *Cataros* with a pre-Celtic suffix *-ossa*.

La Cadière-d'Azur. *Village, Var.* The name, recorded in the 10th century as *Cathedra*, has the same origin as that of **Cadenet.** (The 10th-century form was influenced by Ecclesiastical Latin *cathedra*, "chair," "throne," and Provençal *cadiero* actually means "chair.") The lofty village overlooks the blue (*azur*) waters of the Mediterranean Sea. Compare **Côte d'Azur.**

Cadillac. *Town, Gironde.* The name was recorded in the 14th century as *Cadilacum*, from the Gallo-Roman personal name *Catilius* and the suffix *-anum*.

Cadouin. *Village, Dordogne.* The name, locally pronounced "Cadoon," probably derives from the Gaulish personal name *Catonius.*

Caen. *City, Calvados.* The name was recorded in the 11th century as *Cadomus*, from Gaulish *Carumago*, from *catu-*, "battle," and *magos*, "field." The site was originally that of a small inland port on the Orne River. Its evolution as a city dates from the time of William the Conqueror (11th century), who built two abbeys and a castle here, the latter as his residence.

Cagnes-sur-Mer. *Resort town, Alpes-Maritimes.* The name, recorded in the 11th century as *Caina*, could represent the Roman personal name *Canius*, but the location of the oldest part of the town on a rocky ridge suggests an alternate origin in pre-Indoeuropean *kan*, "height."

Cahors. *City, Lot.* The name was recorded in the 4th century as *Cadurcum*, from the *Cadurci*, the tribe whose capital it was. (Their name has been explained as "boars of battle," from Gaulish *catu-*, "battle," and *turcos*, "boar.") The earlier name of the city, recorded by Ptolemy in the 2d

century AD, was *Devona*, a Gaulish name meaning "holy well."

Cajarc. *Village, Lot.* The name is of uncertain origin. It could be related to Limousin *cajaroco*, "cavity."

Calacuccia. *Village, Haute-Corse.* The village, in northern Corsica, derives its name from pre-Indoeuropean *kal*, "stone," "rock," and *kuk*, "height," denoting a settlement on a hill.

Calais. *City and port, Pas-de-Calais.* The name was recorded in the 12th century as *Kalais*, representing Latin *Calesium*, from the *Caleti* tribe, whose name may come either from pre-Indoeuropean *kal*, "rock," or, less likely, from Celtic *cul*, "channel," referring to the location of Calais by the English Channel. (Pre-Indoeuropean *kal* lies behind Gaulish *caleto-*, "hard," itself related to the name of the *Caledonians* of Scotland.)

Calaisis. *Historic region, northern France.* The region centers on, and is named for, **Calais.**

Calenzana. *Village, Haute-Corse.* The village, in northern Corsica, derives its name from the Roman personal name *Calentius*, with Latin *villa*, "estate," understood, and the suffix *-ana*.

Callac. *Village, Côtes-d'Armor.* The Brittany village derives its name from the Roman personal name *Callus* and the associative suffix *-acum*. It was formerly also known as *Callac-de-Bretagne* (see **Bretagne**).

Calonne-Ricouart. *Town, Pas-de-Calais.* The name was recorded in the 11th century as *Calonna*, from Low Latin *cala*, "rock shelter," and Gaulish *unna*, "water," giving a sense "house by the water." The second part of the name represents that of a local lord.

Calvados. *Department, northwestern France.* The name comes from the *Rochers du Calvados*, a long reef of rocks off the village of Asnelles on the Normandy coast. Their own name may represent Latin *caballi dorsum*, "horse's back," referring to their appearance, or possibly *calvum dorsum,* "bald back," similarly. One unlikely theory takes the name from *Salvador,* a ship of the Spanish Armada that was wrecked here.

Calvi. *Resort town, Haute-Corse.* The name of the town, on the northwest Corscian coast, was recorded in the 13th century as *Calui,* from pre-Indoeuropean *kal,* "rock." The present form of the name has been influenced by Latin *calvus,* "bald."

Camaret-sur-Mer. *Village resort, Finistère.* The name of the Brittany resort derives from Breton *camp,* "field," and *rhed,* "current."

Camargue. *Region, southern France.* The marshy island in the delta of the Rhône River has a name of unknown origin. It is first recorded in 869 as *Camaria,* then in 923 as *Insula Camaricas,* with Latin *insula,* "island." Attempts have been made to find an origin in the personal name *Carius Marius,* or in *cara marca,* "dear frontier," or in *camp marca,* "frontier field," though none of these is likely.

Cambo-les-Bains. *Resort town, Pyrénées-Atlantiques.* The name, recorded in the 14th century as *Camboo,* could represent either Old Provençal *cambon,* "field," understood as *camp bon,* "good field," or Gaulish *cambo,* "bend," referring to a nearby height. Cambo is a spa town. Hence the addition ("the baths").

Cambrai. *City, Nord.* The name was recorded in the 4th century as *Camaracum,* from the Gallo-Roman personal name *Camarus* (from Latin *cammarus,* "prawn," "shrimp") and the associative suffix *-acum.*

Cambrésis. *Region, northern France.* The region centers on **Cambrai** and is named for it.

Camembert. *Village, Orne.* The name was recorded in the 14th century as *Campus Manberti,* from Latin *campus,* "field," and the Germanic personal name *Manberht.*

Camiers.   *Village,*   *Pas-de-Calais.*

Recorded in the 9th century as *Cafitmere,* the name is of uncertain origin.

Campan. *Village, Hautes-Pyrénées.* The name represents Gascon *campà,* from Latin *campanum,* a derivative of *campus,* "field," "estate."

Cancale. *Town and port, Ille-et-Vilaine.* The name is of uncertain origin.

Candé. *Village, Maine-et-Loire.* The name represents a western form of Gaulish *condate,* "confluence," here between the Erdre River and a tributary.

Canet-en-Roussillon. *Town, Pyrénées-Orientales.* The name probably derives from pre-Indoeuropean *kan,* "height," with the Latin suffix *-ittum* or the pre-Celtic suffix *-etum.* The second part of the name locates the town in **Roussillon**.

Canigou. *Mountain, southern France.* The Pyrenean peak bases its name on Mediterrananean *kanto,* "rock," as for **Cantal**.

Cannes. *Resort city and port, Alpes-Maritimes.* The name was recorded early as *Canna* or *Canua,* from pre-Indoeuropean *kan,* "height," and the suffix *-ua.* The old town lies at the foot of low hills.

Le Cannet. *Resort town, Alpes-Maritimes.* The name of the suburb of **Cannes** is probably a diminutive form of the city's name.

Le Cannet-des-Maures. *Village, Var.* The name may be based on pre-Indoeuropean *kan,* "height," with the Latin suffix *-ittum* or the pre-Celtic suffix *-etum* (different to the collective Latin *-etum*). The addition refers to the *Massif des Maures* here (see **Maures, Massif des**).

La Canourgue. *Village, Lozère.* The name derives from Latin *canonica,* with *villa,* "estate," or *ecclesia,* "church," understood, denoting a residence of canons or a collegiate church.

Cantal. *Department, south central France.* The department, in the Auvergne, takes its name from Mediterranean *kanto,* "rock." Cantal is a mountainous area.

Canteleu. *Town, Seine-Maritime.* The suburb of Rouen shares the origin of its name with that of **Canteloup.**

Canteloup. *Village, Calvados.* The name derives from Picard *cante*, French *chante*, "sing," and French *loup*, "wolf," denoting a place where wolves howl ("sing").

Cany-Barville. *Village, Seine-Maritime.* The first part of the name represents the Roman personal name *Canius* and the associative suffix *-acum*. The second part is the name of nearby *Barville*, from the Scandinavian personal name *Bardr* and Latin *villa*, "village."

Cap For cape names, see the main name, e.g. for *Cap Gris-Nez* see **Gris-Nez, Cap.**

Capbreton. *Town and port, Landes.* The name derives from Latin *caput*, "head," here in the sense "chief estate," and the personal name *Breton* ("Breton").

Cap-d'Ail. *Resort town, Alpes-Maritimes.* The name derives from Latin *caput*, "head," here probably in the sense "chief estate," and the Roman personal name *Alius*.

Capdenac-Gare. *Town, Aveyron.* The name derives from the Roman personal name *Capito*, *Capitonis*, with the associative suffix *-acum*. The second part of the name refers to the station (French *gare*) here, as distinct from the nearby village of *Capdenac*, which also has a station but unlike the town is not an actual railroad center.

La Capelle. *Village, Aisne.* The name was recorded in the 12th century as *Capella*, from French *chapelle*, "chapel." (For the origin of the word, see **Chapelle-aux-Saints, La.**) The village is also known as *La Capelle-en-Thiérache* for its location in the **Thiérache** region.

Capestang. *Village, Hérault.* The name was recorded in the 9th century as *Caput stanio*, from Latin *caput*, "head," "end," and *stagnum*, "piece of standing water," "pool."

Cappelle-Brouck. *Village, Nord.* The first part of the name is as for **Cappelle-la-Grande.** The second is from Old High German *bruoch*, Dutch *broek*, "marshy place."

Cappelle-la-Grande. *Town, Nord.* The suburb of Dunkerque derives its name from a Picard form of French *chapelle*, "chapel," "church," with *grande* ("great") indicating a larger or more important place than others of the same name locally, as **Cappelle-Brouck.**

Caraman. *Village, Haute-Garonne.* The name derives from pre-Indoeuropean *kar*, "rock," and Latin *magnus*, "great."

Carantec. *Resort village, Finistère.* The name is that of the saint to whom the church here is dedicated. The name itself is Breton for "kind," "pleasant."

Carbon-Blanc. *Town, Gironde.* The suburb of Bordeaux has a name meaning "white coal," that of a former inn here.

Carbonne. *Village, Haute-Garonne.* The name probably represents Latin *carbona*, a derivative of *carbo*, *carbonis*, "charcoal," meaning a place where charcoal was made.

Carcassonne. *City, Aude.* The name of the city was recorded by Caesar in the 1st century BC as *Carcassonna*, probably from pre-Indoeuropean *kar*, "rock," "stone," and *kasser*, "oak."

Carentan. *Town, Manche.* The name was recorded in the 11th century as *Karentomum*, from the Gaulish personal name *Carantus* and *magos*, "market."

Carentoir. *Village, Morbihan.* The name was recorded in the 9th century as *Carantoer*, suggesting an origin in Breton *caer an toer*, "town of the roofer."

Cargèse. *Resort village, Corse-du-Sud.* The village, on the west coast of Corsica, probably bases its name on pre-Indoeuropean *kar*, "rock." Cargèse stands on a rocky headland.

Carhaix. *Town, Finistère.* The Brittany town has the Breton name *Keraez*, from *kêr*, "town," and *Aez* or *Ahes*, which according to the philologist and historian Ferdinand Lot was the former name of the tribe known as the Osismi.

Carignan. *Village, Ardennes.* The original name of the place was *Ivoy*, recorded in the 4th century as *Epoisso*, a derivative of Gaulish *epos*, "horse." It took its present name in 1662, when the settlement was erected into a dukedom for Maurice, count of Soissons, of the *Carignano* (Piedmont) branch of the house of Savoy.

Carling. *Village, Moselle.* The village was built in 1716 on land given by Charles Louis (Karl Ludwig) (1665–1723), count of Nassau-Saarbrücken. Hence its name, from *Karl* and the Germanic suffix *-ing*. The German name of the village is *Karlingen*.

Carmaux. *Town, Tarn.* The name may derive from Low Latin *calmis*, of pre-Celtic origin, a derivative of pre-Indoeuropean *kal*, "rock," "bare height," and the Gaulish suffix *-avum*. Carmaux lies at the foot of a 60-foot rocky height.

Carnac. *Town, Morbihan.* The Brittany town probably takes its name from Breton *karn*, "tumulus," "cairn," and the associative suffix *-acum*. A more colorful origin takes the second part of the name from Celtic *hak*, "snake," giving an overall sense "tomb of the snake," supposedly denoting a former local cult of the dragon.

Carolles. *Resort village, Manche.* The name probably derives from pre-Indoeuropean *kar*, "rock," and the suffix *-olla*.

Caromb. *Village, Vaucluse.* The name was recorded in the 11th century as *Carumbum*, probably from pre-Indoeuropean *kar*, "rock," and a double Mediterranean suffix *-um* and *-p*.

Carpentras. *City, Vaucluse.* The name was recorded in the 1st century AD as *Carpentorate*, from Gaulish *carbanton*, "(two-wheeled) chariot," and *rate*, "fort," giving a meaning "fort guarding the route of the chariots," referring to a ford over the Auzon River here.

Carquefou. *Town, Loire-Atlantique.* The

name was recorded in the 12th century as *Carcafagus*, perhaps from Germanic (Saxon) *kirk*, "church," and Latin *fagus*, "beech," although one would have expected the initial *k* to palatalize to *ch*. An origin in Breton *carrec*, "rock," has also been proposed, but Breton colonization did not extend as far east as this.

Carrières-sous-Poissy. *Town, Yvelines.* The name derives from Latin *quadraria*, "quarry" (of stones). The addition locates the town near (*sous*, "under") **Poissy**.

Carrières-sur-Seine. *Town, Hauts-de-Seine.* The name of the Paris suburb has the same origin as that of **Carrières-sous-Poissy**, but here distinguished by its location on the **Seine**.

Carteret. *Resort village, Manche.* The name is of uncertain origin. It may derive from Latin *quartarius*, "rocky quarter," and the suffix *-etum*, or else pre-Indoeuropean *kar*, "rock," with an obscure suffix and *-etum*.

Carvin. *Town, Pas-de-Calais.* The name derives from the Gallo-Roman personal name *Carvinius*, from Gaulish *Carvius*.

Cassel. *Village, Nord.* The name was recorded by Ptolemy in the 2d century AD as *Castellon*, from Latin *castellum*, "castle."

Cassis. *Town and port, Bouches-du-Rhône.* The name was recorded in the 2d century as *Tutelae Charsitanae*, from Latin *tutela*, "keeper," "guardian," and a word suggesting an origin in pre-Indoeuropean *kar*, "rock," "stone," and the suffix *-ite*.

Castanet-Tolosan. *Town, Haute-Garonne.* The suburb of Toulouse derives its name from Latin *castaneum*, "chestnut," and the suffix *-etum*. The addition locates it in the environs of **Toulouse**.

Castelginet. *Town, Haute-Garonne.* The suburb of Toulouse derives its name from Latin *castellum*, "castle," and the personal name *Ginest*.

Casteljaloux. *Town, Lot-et-Garonne.* The name derives from a southern form of

Latin *castellum*, "castle," and French *jaloux*, "jealous," here in the sense "exposed," "perilous." (The name evokes the title of Sir Walter Scott's 1831 novel *Castle Dangerous*.)

Castellane. *Village, Alpes-de-Haute-Provence.* The name was recorded in the 10th century as *Petra Castellana*, from Latin *petra*, "rock," and *castellum*, a diminutive of *castrum*, "fort."

Le Castellet. *Village, Var.* The name derives from Latin *castellum*, "castle," and the diminutive suffix *-ittum*.

Castelmoron-sur-Lot. *Village, Lot-et-Garonne.* The name derives from Latin *castellum*, "castle," and the personal name *Mauron*. The addition names the **Lot** River here.

Castelnaudary. *Town, Aude.* The name was recorded in the 13th century as *Castrum novum Darri*, from Latin *castrum*, "fort," *novus*, "new," and the personal name *Ari*. Alternately, the name could represent Latin *Castellum Arianorum*, "fort of the Arians." The Visigoths, converts to Arian Christianity, settled in this part of France in the 5th century.

Castelnau-de-Médoc. *Village, Gironde.* The name represents Latin *castellum novum*, "new castle," the addition locating the village in **Médoc**.

Castelnau-le-Lez. *Town, Hérault.* The suburb of Montpellier has a name of the same origin as **Castelnau-de-Médoc**, but here distinguished by its location on the *Lez* River.

Castelsarrasin. *Town, Tarn-et-Garonne.* The name was recorded in the 9th century as *Castrum Cerrucium*, from Latin *castrum*, "fort," and the Roman personal name *Cerrucius*, from *Cerius*, and the suffix *-inum*. The present form of the name evolved by association with French *Sarrasin*, "Saracen."

Castillon-la-Bataille. *Village, Gironde.* The name derives from Latin *castellum*, "castle," and the suffix *-onem*. The addition ("the battle") refers to the French victory

over the English here in 1453, in the last great battle of the Hundred Years War.

Castillonnès. *Village, Lot-et-Garonne.* The name was recorded in the 12th century as *Castellonesium*, from Latin *castellum*, "castle," and the suffix *-ensis*.

Castres. *City, Tarn.* The name was recorded in the 11th century as *Castras*, from Latin *castra*, "camp," plural of *castrum*, "fort," referring to the former Roman encampment here.

Castries. *Town, Hérault.* The name was recorded in the 9th century as *Castra*, from Latin *castra*, "camp," the plural of *castrum*, "fort." The *i*, added later, is difficult to explain.

Le Cateau-Cambrésis. *Town, Nord.* The name was recorded in the 11th century as *Castellum*, from Latin *castellum*, "castle." (The present *Cateau* is a Picard form of French *château*.) The addition locates the town in **Cambrésis**.

Cattenom. *Village, Moselle.* The name was recorded in the 12th century as *Cathenem*, from the Germanic personal name *Catto* and (perhaps) *heim*, "abode."

Caudebec-en-Caux. *Town, Seine-Maritime.* The name, recorded in the 10th century as *Caldebec*, derives from Old Scandinavian *kald*, "cold," and *bekkr*, "stream," referring to a stream that enters the Seine River here. The town is in the Pays de **Caux**, as distinct from its namesake, **Caudebec-lès-Elbeuf**.

Caudebec-lès-Elbeuf. *Town, Seine-Maritime.* The name is identical with that of **Caudebec-en-Caux**, from which the place is distinguished by its location near (*lès*) **Elbeuf**, of which it is now actually a suburb.

Caudry. *Town, Nord.* The name was recorded in the 11th century as *Calderiacum*, from the Roman personal name *Caldarius* (from *caldus*, "hot," perhaps nicknaming a hot-bath attendant) and the associative suffix *-acum*. The town is also known as *Caudry-en-Cambrésis*, for its location in **Cambrésis**.

Caumont-sur-Durance. *Village, Vaucluse.* The name derives from Latin *calvus mons*, "bald mountain," meaning one devoid of vegetation. This addition locates the village on the **Durance** River.

Caunes-Minervois. *Village, Aude.* The name derives from Provençal *cauno*, "cave," a word of pre-Latin origin. The addition locates the village in **Minervois**.

Caussade. *Town, Tarn-et-Garonne.* The name derives from Latin *calceata*, "causeway," "road," a word often denoting a Roman or at any rate medieval road.

Causses. *Region, south central France.* The name of the limestone plateau, part of the Massif Central, and also known as the *Grands Causses*, ultimately derives from pre-Indoeuropean *kar*, "rock." See also **Larzac**.

Cauterets. *Resort village, Hautes-Pyrénées.* The name was recorded in the 10th century as *Caldarez*, from Latin *caldaria*, plural of *caldarium*, "steamroom," and the suffix *-ellum*. The village is a spa, noted for its sulfur springs and thermal establishments.

Caux, Pays de. *Region, northern France.* The chalky tableland of eastern Normandy was known by the Medieval Latin name *pagus Calcis*, from *pagus* (modern French *pays*), "country," and either the tribal name *Caleti*, as for **Calais**, or pre-Indoeuropean *kal*, "rock."

Cavaillon. *Town, Vaucluse.* The name was recorded in the 1st century as *Cabellio*, perhaps from the Roman personal name *Cabellius* or *Caballius*, or from Gaulish *cauo-*, a word of unknown meaning found in the name of the *Cavari*, the Celtic tribe whose capital this was.

Cavalaire-sur-Mer. *Resort town, Var.* The name was recorded in the 4th century as *Caccabaria*, of pre-Latin and possibly Phoenician or Mediterranean origin. Its meaning is obscure, but it was apparently recast as *Cavallaria*, probably because horses were bred here.

Cayeux-sur-Mer. *Resort village, Somme.* The name seems to represent a Latin form *Cagiacum*, from the Gaulish personal name *Cagius* and the associative suffix *-acum*.

Cazaubon. *Village, Gers.* The name derives from Latin *casale*, "smallholding," and French *bon*, "good."

Cazères. *Village, Haute-Garonne.* The name represents a Gascon form of Latin *casella*, "little house."

Cazouls-lès-Béziers. *Village, Hérault.* The name derives from Latin *casa*, "house," and the diminutive suffix *-ulum*. The addition locates the village near (*lès*) **Béziers**.

Ceillac. *Village, Hautes-Alpes.* The name was recorded in the 12th century as *Celiacum*, from the Roman personal name *Caelius* and the associative suffix *-acum*.

La Celle-Saint-Cloud. *Town, Yvelines.* The Paris suburb derives its name from Latin *cella*, "small room," "(monk's) cell," later denoting a hermitage or religious community. This one was near **Saint-Cloud**.

Celles-sur-Belle. *Village, Deux-Sèvres.* The name derives from Latin *cella*, "small room," "(monk's) cell," later denoting a hermitage or religious community. This one was on the *Belle* River.

Celles-sur-Durolle. *Village, Puy-de-Dôme.* The name derives from Latin *cella*, "small room," "(monk's) cell," later denoting a hermitage or religious community. This one was on the *Durolle* River.

Le Cendre. *Town, Puy-de-Dôme.* The name was recorded in the 11th century as *Alexandra*, short for *Alexandra villa*, "Alexander's estate." This came to be pronounced *Aussandra*, which was understood as *au Cendre*, "at Le Cendre." Hence the present form of the name

Cenis, Mont. *Mountain massif, southeastern France.* The name is said to come from Latin *cenisius*, "cinder gray," although this is hardly the prevailing local color. The origin may instead lie in pre-Indoeuropean *kend*, "mountain." The Roman name was *Cottiae Alpes*.

Cenon. *Town, Gironde.* The name of the Bordeaux suburb, recorded early as *Sanonno*, probably derives from the Gaulish personal name *Senos* or *Sannus* and the suffix *-one.*

Cenon-sur-Vienne. *Village, Vienne.* The suburb of Châtellerault has a name of the same origin as **Cenon**, but here distinguished by its location on the **Vienne** River.

Centre. *Region, central France.* The administrative region has a self-explanatory name describing its location in the center of France. Although appropriate geographically, the name is linguistically something of a paradox, as the region was established in the 1970s by the central government with the aim of decentralizing certain administrative functions.

Cépoy. *Village, Loiret.* The name derives from Latin *cippus*, "stake," "pale," and the collective suffix *-etum*, denoting a place where tree trunks were driven into the ground to form a palisade.

Cerbère. *Resort village, Pyrénées-Orientales.* The name was recorded by Pomponius Mela in the 2nd century AD as *Cervaria*, from pre-Indoeuropean *kar*, "rock," and the suffix *-aria*. The name was influenced by Latin *cervus*, "stag," as was *Mont Cervin*, the French name of the Matterhorn, the peak on the Switzerland-Italy border, and its present form has produced a folk origin: "The name of the resort is taken from Cerberus, the three-headed dog which guarded the portals of Hades" [Young, p.369].

Cercy-la-Tour. *Village, Nièvre.* The name was recorded in the 13th century as *Cerciacum*, from the Roman personal name *Cercius* and the associative suffix *-acum*. The addition means "the tower."

Cerdagne. *Region, southern France.* The high valley of the eastern Pyrenees, partly in France and partly in Spain (where it is known as *Cerdaña*), takes its name from the *Cerretani* tribe who also gave the name of **Céret**.

Cérences. *Village, Manche.* The name was recorded in the 11th century as *Cerencis*, from Old French *serence*, the word for a workshop employing a *seran*, a special cord used to separate out strands of tow (the fiber of flax or hemp) in order to spin it.

Céret. *Town, Pyrénées-Orientales.* The name was recorded by Pliny in the 1st century AD as *Cerretani*, that of an Iberian or pre-Iberian tribe who also gave the name of **Cerdagne**, in which the town lies. The name itself may relate to Basque *xerri*, "pig."

Cergy. *Town, Val-d'Oise.* The town's Medieval Latin name was *Cerviacum* or *Serviacum*, from the Roman personal name *Cervius* or *Servius* and the associative suffix *-acum*. The "new town" of *Cergy-Pontoise* (see **Pontoise**) was created in 1966.

Cérilly. *Village, Allier.* The name derives from the Roman personal name *Cerellius* and the associative suffix *-acum.*

Cerisy-la-Forêt. *Village, Manche.* The name was recorded in the 11th century as *Cerisiacus*, from the Roman personal name *Ceretius* or *Cerisius* (from *Cerius*) and the associative suffix *-acum*. The addition refers to the nearby forest named for the village.

Cerizay. *Town, Deux-Sèvres.* The name was recorded in the 12th century as *Seresiacum*, from Latin *ceresea*, "cherry tree," and the collective suffix *-etum.*

Cernay. *Town, Haut-Rhin.* The name of the town was recorded in the 14th century as *Seyreney*, suggesting an origin in *Sennheim*, its German name, from the Germanic personal name *Sanno* and *heim*, "abode." Cernay is only a few miles from the German border.

Cernay-la-Ville. *Village, Yvelines.* The name was recorded in the 8th century as *Sarnetum*, representing an original *Sarnacum*, either from the Gaulish personal name *Sarnus* and the associative suffix *-acum*, or from the base of Latin *circinum*, "circle," and the collective suffix *-etum.*

Cérons. *Village, Gironde.* The name derives from the Roman personal name *Cirus*, from *Cirius*, and the suffix *-onem*.

Cervione. *Village, Haute-Corse*. The village, in eastern Corsica, derives its name from the Roman personal name *Cervius* and the suffix *-onem*.

Cesson. *Town, Seine-et-Marne*. The name derives from the Roman personal name *Cessius* and the suffix *-onem*.

Cesson-Sévigné. *Town, Ille-et-Vilaine*. The first part of the name is as for **Cesson**. The second is nearby *Sévigné*, from the Roman personal name *Sabinius* and the associative suffix *-acum*.

Cévennes. *Region, southern France*. The mountain range takes its name from Gaulish *Cebenna* or *Cevenna*, from a pre-Celtic or Ligurian root *kem* or *kam* meaning "rounded height."

Ceyreste. *Village, Bouches-du-Rhône*. The name was recorded by Ptolemy in the 2d century AD as *Kitharistes*, a Greek-style name which is actually pre-Greek and pre-Celtic, from a conjectured original *Kitairesta*. The first part of this evokes the name of Mount *Cithaeron*, Greece, while *-esta* is a Mediterranean suffix.

Ceyzériat. *Village, Ain*. The name was recorded in the 11th century as *Saisiriacus*, from the Gallo-Roman personal name *Sacirius*, from Gaulish *Sacirus*, and the associative suffix *-acum*.

Chabanais. *Village, Charente*. The name derives from Low Latin *capanna*, "hut," "cabin," and the suffix *-ensem*.

Chabeuil. *Town, Drôme*. The name was recorded in the 12th century as *Chabiol*, from Latin *caput*, "head," "end," and Gaulish *ialon*, "field," "clearing."

Chablais. *Region, eastern France*. The name of the limestone massif, in Haute-Savoie, was recorded in the 9th century as *Caput Laci*, "head of the lake," from Latin *caput*, "head," and *lacus*, "lake," referring to the location of the region to the south of Lake Geneva.

Chablis. *Village, Yonne*. The name was recorded in the 9th century as *Capleia*, suggesting a possible origin in Medieval Latin *capuleta*, from *capulum*, "cable," and the suffix *-eta*. The import of this is uncertain, but it may relate to the floating of logs down the Serein River here.

Chabris. *Village, Indre*. The name was recorded early as *Carobrias*, from *Cares*, the Roman name of the **Cher** River, and Gaulish *briua*, "bridge," giving a sense "bridge over the Cher."

Chagny. *Town, Saône-et-Loire*. The name derives from the Gallo-Roman personal name *Catanius*, a form of *Cattanus*, or from Latin *cataneum*, "juniper grove," similar to **Cadenet**, and the associative suffix *-acum*.

Chaillé-les-Marais. *Village, Vendée*. The name derives from the Roman personal name *Callius* and the associative suffix *-acum*. The addition means "the marshes," although the marshland here has now been drained.

La Chaise-Dieu. *Resort village, Haute-Loire*. The name was recorded in the 11th century as *Casam Dei*, from Latin *casa Dei*, "house of God," denoting a church here,

Chalais. *Village, Charente*. The name derives from pre-Celtic *kal*, "rock," and the suffix *-es*.

Châlette-sur-Loing. *Town, Loiret*. The suburb of Montargis is usually said to derive its name from Low Latin *cataracta*, "cataract," "sluice," "dam," referring to such on the **Loing** River here. But as for **Cadarache** a Gaulish origin is perhaps more likely, from *catu-*, "battle," and *rate*, "fort," giving an overall sense "(place of the) battle ramparts." The name was recorded in the 11th century as *Kadelata* and in the 12th century as *Catalecta*.

Chalindrey. *Village, Haute-Marne*. The name represents an original form *Calendinacum*, from the Roman personal name *Calendinus* and the associative suffix *-acum*.

Challans. *Town, Vendée.* The name derives from pre-Celtic *kal*, "rock," and the suffix *-anc.*

Challes-les-Eaux. *Resort village, Savoie.* The original name of the settlement was *Triviers*, from the Roman personal name *Treverius*. The present name was adopted in 1579 when the village was enfeoffed to Louis of *Challes*, whose own name came from *Challes*, Ain. The addition ("the waters") refers to the sulfur springs here.

Chalonnais. *Region, east central France.* The name represents the adjectival form of the name of **Chalon-sur-Saône**, to the east of the region.

Chalonnes-sur-Loire. *Town, Maine-et-Loire.* The name was recorded in the 6th century as *Calonna*, from Low Latin *cala*, "rock shelter," "house," and Gaulish *unna*, "water," giving a sense "house by the water." The town is on the small Layon River, which flows into the **Loire** nearby.

Châlons-en-Champagne. *Town, Marne.* The town takes its name from the *Catalauni*, a Gaulish tribe, whose capital it was. Their own name comes from *catu-*, "battle," and *uellaunos*, "chief," denoting their prowess as warriors. The second part of the name refers to the town's location in **Champagne**. Until 1995 the town was known as *Châlons-sur-Marne*, from its location on the **Marne** River. The addition differentiates it from **Chalon-sur-Saône**.

Chalon-sur-Saône. *City, Saône-et-Loire.* The name of the city was recorded by Caesar in the 1st century BC as *Cabillonum*, from the same element *cab*, "height," that gave the name of **Cavaillon**. The addition, distinguishing the city from **Châlons-en-Champagne**, denotes its location on the **Saône** River.

Châlus. *Village, Haute-Vienne.* The name derives from Low Latin *castellucium*, from *castellum*, "castle," "fort," and the suffix *-ucium.*

Chamalières. *Town, Puy-de-Dôme.* The

suburb of Clermont-Ferrand derives its name from the Gaulish personal name *Camalos*, from *Camius*, and the Latin suffix *-aria.*

Chambéry. *City, Savoie.* The name was recorded in the 11th century as *Cameriacum*, from Gaulish *cambo-*, "crooked," and the associative suffix *-acum*. The reference would be to the Alpine cleft valley in which the city lies. (The name was recorded earlier that same century as *Camefriacum*, with *f* instead of *b* in error from the pen of a German scribe.)

Chambly. *Town, Oise.* The name derives from the Roman personal name *Camillius* and the associative suffix *-acum.*

Chambolle-Musigny. *Village, Côte-d'Or.* The first part of the name was recorded in the 12th century as *Cambola*, from a derivative of Gaulish *cambo-*, "curve," "bend," presumably referring to a contour of the Côte de Nuits hills here. The second part, originally the name of a separate place, recorded in the 10th century as *Musiniacus*, derives from the Roman personal name *Musinius*, a form of *Musinus*, and the associative suffix *-acum.*

Le Chambon-Feugerolles. *Town, Loire.* The name, recorded in the 11th century as *Chambo*, derives from Gaulish *cambo-*, "bend," meaning one in the Ondaine River here. The second part of the name derives from Latin *filicaria*, "fern," and the diminutive suffix *-ola.*

Le Chambon-sur-Lignon. *Resort village, Haute-Loire.* The name, recorded in the 13th century as *Cambo*, derives from Gaulish *cambo-*, "bend," here one in the *Lignon* River.

Chambord. *Village, Loir-et-Cher.* The name was recorded in the 9th century as *Cambortus*, from Gaulish *Camboritu*, from *cambo-*, "crooked" (as for **Chambéry**), and *ritu-*, "ford," a "crooked ford" being one on a river bend, here on the Cosson River.

Chambourcy. *Town, Yvelines.* The suburb of Saint-Germain-en-Laye derives its name from the Gallo-Roman personal name *Camburcius*, from Gaulish *Camburcus*, and the associative suffix *-acum*.

Chambray-lès-Tours. *Town, Indre-et-Loire.* The name was recorded in the 13th century as *Chamberium*, from the Gallo-Roman personal name *Cambarius* (from Gaulish *cambo-*, "bend") and the associative suffix *-acum*. The addition locates the town near (*lès*) **Tours**, of which it is now actually a suburb.

Chamonix. *Resort town, Haute-Savoie.* The name of the Alpine resort was recorded in the 13th century as *Chamonis*, from a pre-Celtic or possibly Ligurian root element *kam*, meaning "rounded height." The reference would be to the curving valley of the Arve River here.

Champagne. *Historic region, northeastern France.* The former province bore the Medieval Latin name *Campania*, "land of plains," from Latin *campus*, "field."

Champagné. *Village, Sarthe.* The name derives from the Roman personal name *Campanius* and the associative suffix *-acum*.

Champagne-Ardenne. *Region, northeastern France.* The administrative region takes its name from its two major geographical regions of **Champagne** and the **Ardennes**.

Champagne-sur-Seine. *Town, Seine-et-Marne.* The town, on the **Seine** River, derives its name from Latin *campania*, "plain," a derivative of *campus*, "field."

Champagney. *Village, Haute-Saône.* The name derives from the Roman personal name *Campanius* and the associative suffix *-acum*.

Champagnole. *Town, Jura.* The name was recorded in the 14th century as *Champaignole*, from a diminutive form of Latin *campania*, "plain," from *campus*, "field."

Champagny-en-Vanoise. *Resort village, Savoie.* The name derives from the Roman personal name *Campanius* and the associa-

tive suffix *-acum*. The addition locates the village in the region of the **Vanoise** massif.

Champigneulles. *Town, Meurthe-et-Moselle.* The suburb of Nancy derives its name from Latin *campineola*, a diminutive form of *campania*, "plain."

Champigny-sur-Marne. *Town, Val-de-Marne.* The Paris suburb derives its name from the Roman personal name *Campanius* and the associative suffix *-acum*. The addition names the **Marne** River here.

Champlitte. *Village, Haute-Saône.* The name was recorded early as *Cantolimete*, from Latin *campus limitis*, "field at the limit," presumably denoting the boundary of a territory.

Champniers. *Town, Charente.* The name probably represents an original *Catumarium*, from the Gaulish personal name *Catumaros*, latinized as *Catumarius*.

Champs-sur-Marne. *Town, Seine-et-Marne.* The name derives from a plural form of Latin *campus*, "field," meaning (here and elsewhere) cultivated land, as distinct from land unsuitable for cultivation. The town is distinguished by its location on the **Marne** River.

Chantilly. *Town, Oise.* The name was recorded in the 12th century as *Chantileium*, from the Gaulish personal name *Cantilius* and the associative suffix *-acum*.

Chantonnay. *Town, Vendée.* The name was recorded early as *Cantuanum*, from the Gaulish personal name *Canto, Cantonis*, and the associative suffix *-acum*.

Chaource. *Village, Aube.* The name was recorded in the 9th century as *Cadusia* and in the 12th century as *Chaorsia*, perhaps from a Gaulish personal name *Catussius* (from *catu-*, "battle"), although the alteration of *-ss-* to *-rs-* is unexplained.

La Chapelle-aux-Saints. *Hamlet, Corrèze.* The hamlet is named for its church, dedicated to *All Saints*. French *chapelle* (English *chapel*) derives from Medieval Latin *cappella*, literally "little cape," traditionally said to refer to the part of the church in Tours in which a fragment of the cloak or cape of St. Martin of Tours was preserved. The word then came to apply to a part of a church with a secondary altar (the modern chapel), then to a small church.

La Chapelle-d'Abondance. *Resort village, Haute-Savoie.* The resort, with its church, is on the Dranse d'*Abondance* River, named distinctively for nearby **Abondance.**

La Chapelle-d'Armentières. *Town, Nord.* The town, with its church, is now a suburb of **Armentières.**

La Chapelle-de-Guinchay. *Village, Saône-et-Loire.* The village, with its church, is apparently named for a place called *Guinchay.*

La Chapelle-en-Valgaudémar. *Village, Hautes-Alpes.* The village, with its church, is in the *Valgaudémar* valley, and was formed in 1963 on the merger of *Clémence-d'Ambel* and *Guillaume-Peyrouse.* The former commemorated *Clémence,* son of Raymond *d'Ambel,* lord of the far end of the Valgaudémar valley, who inherited the village at the turn of the 15th century. The latter was named for *Guillaume* (William), husband of Catherine d'Ambel, who inherited the village then. *Peyrouse* derives its name from Latin *petra,* "rock," "mountain."

La Chapelle-en-Vercors. *Village, Drôme.* The village, with its church, is in the **Vercors.**

La Chapelle-la-Reine. *Village, Seine-et-Marne.* The name means "chapel of the queen," denoting a royal possession.

La Chapelle-Saint-Luc. *Town, Aube.* The suburb of Troyes is named for its church, dedicated to *St. Luke.*

La Chapelle-Saint-Mesmin. *Town, Loiret.* The suburb of Orléans is named for its church, dedicated to *St. Maximinus,* as at **Saint-Maximin-la-Sainte-Baume.**

La Chapelle-sur-Erdre. *Town, Loire-Atlantique.* The suburb of Nantes, with its church, lies on the *Erdre* River.

La Chapelle-sur-Loire. *Village, Indre-et-Loire.* The original name of the settlement, recorded in the 9th century, was *Capella Alba,* "white church," later in French form as *La Chapelle-Blanche.* (It was in the diocese of Angers, and as such was distinct from another *La Chapelle-Blanche,* some miles to the east across the **Loire** in the diocese of Tours, Indre-et-Loire, now known as *La Chapelle-Blanche-Saint-Martin,* from its dedication to *St. Martin.*) La Chapelle-sur-Loire adopted its new name at the time of the Revolution and retained it.

Chaponost. *Town, Rhône.* The suburb of Lyon derives its name from the Gaulish personal name *Cappius* and the suffix *-oscum.*

Charbonnières-les-Bains. *Resort town, Rhône.* The name derives from Latin *carbona,* a derivative of *carbo, carbonis,* "charcoal," denoting a place where charcoal was made. The town is a spa. Hence the addition ("the baths").

Charente. *Department, western France.* The name is that of the river here, recorded by the Romans as *Carantonus,* from proto-Indoeuropean *karantono,* "sandy," from *karanto,* "sand."

Charente-Inférieure *see* **Charente-Maritime**

Charente-Maritime. *Department, western France.* The department has a name translating as "Maritime Charente," referring to the **Charente** River that flows northwest across it to enter the Atlantic. Until 1941 its name was *Charente-Inférieure* ("Lower Charente"), referring to its location, but this was changed because of its suggestion of "inferiority."

Charenton-le-Pont. *Town, Val-de-Marne.* The name derives from the Gaulish personal name *Caranto, Carantonis,* from *Carantus,* with the bridge (*pont*) over the Seine River here.

La Charité-sur-Loire. *Town, Nièvre.* The town, on the **Loire** River, gained its name from its 12th-century reputation for generosity (charity) towards the pauper pilgrims who came to worship at the famous 8th-century Benedictine abbey church here.

Charleval (1). *Village, Bouches-du-Rhône.* The villages lies on land which in 1595 was erected into a fiefdom by *Charles* of Lorraine, prince of Lambesc, and first inhabited in 1741. *Val* is "valley."

Charleval (2). *Village, Eure.* The village, in the valley (*val*) of the Andelle River, takes its name from a castle built (but never completed) here by *Charles* IX (1550–1574).

Charleville-Mézières. *City, Ardennes.* The city was created in 1966 by merging the twin towns *Charleville* and *Mézières* and three smaller communities. *Charleville* was named in 1606 for *Charles* de Gonzague, duke of Rethel, who rebuilt the town. *Mézières* was recorded in the 10th century as *Macerias*, from Latin *maceriae*, "ruins," meaning those of the Roman period.

Charlieu. *Town, Loire.* The name was recorded in the 9th century as *abbas Cariloci* (with Latin *abbas*, "abbot") and in the 10th century as both *Carilocus* and *Carus Locus*, suggesting an origin in either Latin *Caroli locus*, "Charles's place," meaning his estate, or *Carus locus*, "dear place," meaning an agreeable one.

Charly. *Village, Aisne.* The name was recorded in the 9th century as *Carliacus*, suggesting an original form *Cariliacum*, from the Gallo-Roman personal name *Carilius*, from Gaulish *Carus*, and the associative suffix *-acum*.

Charmes. *Town, Vosges.* The name derives from Low Latin *calmis*, of pre-Celtic origin, from pre-Indoeuropean *kal*, "rock," "bald height."

Charmont-sous-Barbuise. *Village, Aube.* The name of the settlement here was recorded in the 12th century as *Curtlaverzi*, from Latin *cortem*, accusative of *cors*, "estate," French *la*, "the," and the former name of the village, *Verzy*, perhaps from the

Gallo-Roman personal name *Virisius*, from *Virius*, and the associative suffix *-acum*. The present name, meaning "Charles's mountain," dates from 1669. The village is near (*sous*) the *Barbuise* River.

Charnay-lès-Mâcon. *Town, Saône-et-Loire.* The town derives its name from the Gallo-Roman personal name *Carnus* and the associative suffix *-acum*. The addition locates it near (*lès*) **Mâcon**, of which it is now actually a suburb.

Charolais. *Region, east central France.* The region is named after the town of **Charolles** here.

Charolles. *Town, Saône-et-Loire.* The name was recorded in the 11th century as *Cadrella*, from Latin *quadrum*, "square," in the sense "motte" (a mound of earth serving as the base for a fort), with the present form of the name influenced by *char*, "chariot."

Chârost. *Village, Cher.* The name was recorded in the 11th century as *Carroth*, from Latin *quadrivium*, "crossroads," with the *ch* resulting from the influence of *char*, "chariot."

Charroux. *Village, Vienne.* The name was recorded in the 8th century as *Karrofium*, from Latin *quadrivium*, "crossroads," with the *ch* resulting from the influence of *char*, "chariot," as for **Chârost**.

Chartres. *City, Eure-et-Loir.* The name was recorded in the 4th century as *Carnotum*, from the *Carnutes*, a Gaulish tribe for whom Chartres was a sacred site. Their own name is said to mean "horned ones," from Gaulish *carnon*, "horn." The Roman name of Chartres, recorded by Caesar in the 1st century BC and Ptolemy in the 2d century AD, was *Autricum*, a contracted form of *Auturicum*, from *Autura*, the present **Eure** River, on which the city stands.

Chartres-de-Bretagne. *Town, Ille-et-Vilaine.* The name of the Brittany town (see **Bretagne**) preserves the record of a region inhabited by the *Carnutes*, as at **Chartres**.

Chartrettes. *Resort village, Seine-et-Marne.* The name has an identical origin to that of **Chartres** but with a diminutive suffix for distinction from that town.

Chartreuse. *Mountains, southeastern France.* The name of the limestone mountain bloc dates from Roman times and probably derives from the *Caturiges*, the Gaulish tribe who inhabited the region. Their own name means "kings of battle," from Gaulish *catu-*, "battle," and *riges*, the plural of *rix*, "king." The monastery of *La Grande Chartreuse* was founded here *c.*1084 and was the base of the *Carthusians* until 1903, when the order was expelled.

Charvieu-Chavagneux. *Town, Isère.* The name combines those of two originally separate places. *Charvieu* takes its name from the Roman personal name *Calvius* (from *calvus*, "bald") and the associative suffix *-acum*. *Chavagneux* derives its name from *Cavannius*, a latinized form of the Gaulish personal name *Cavannus*, and the associative suffix *-acum*.

Chassagne. *Village, Puy-de-Dôme.* The name represents Latin *cassanea*, a derivative of *cassanum*, Old Provençal *cassanha*, "oak," here used in a collective sense.

Chasseneuil-du-Poitou. *Village, Vienne.* The name combines Gaulish *cassanos*, "oak," and *ialo*, "clearing." The addition locates the village in **Poitou.**

Chasse-sur-Rhône. *Town, Isère.* The name of the location was originally recorded in the 9th century as *Landatis*, representing Gaulish (or pre-Gaulish) *lindate*, from Gaulish *lindon*, "pool," and the suffix *-ate*. This name was replaced in the 15th century by *Chasse*, probably from Gaulish *cassanos*, "oak." The addition refers to the **Rhône** River here.

Chassieu. *Town, Rhône.* The suburb of Lyon derives its name from the Roman personal name *Cassius* and the associative suffix *-acum*.

La Châtaigneraie. *Village, Vendée.* The name means "the chestnut grove," from Latin *castaneum*, "chestnut tree," and the suffix *-aria.*

Château-Arnoux. *Town, Alpes-de-Haute-Provence.* The name was recorded in the 12th century as *Castrum Arnulfum*, from Latin *castrum*, "fort," and *Arnulf*, the local lord.

Châteaubourg. *Town, Ille-et-Vilaine.* The name was recorded in the 11th century as *Castelburg*, meaning "castle of the fortified town."

Châteaubriant. *Town, Loire-Atlantique.* The name was recorded in the 11th century as *Castellum Brientii*, from Latin *castellum*, "castle," and the Breton personal name *Bryan.*

Château-Chinon. *Village, Nièvre.* The name was recorded in the 12th century as *Castrum Caninum*, from Latin *castrum*, "fort," and *Caninum*, representing either a personal name or (although less likely) Latin *canis*, "dog."

Le Château-d'Oléron. *Town, Charente-Maritime.* The town arose around a citadel or castle (*château*) on the island of **Oléron.**

Château-d'Olonne. *Town, Vendée.* The town, with its castle, is a suburb of *Les Sables-d'Olonne* (see **Sables-d'Olonne, Les**).

Château-du-Loir. *Town, Sarthe.* The name was recorded in the 11th century as *Castrum Lidi*, from Latin *castrum*, "fort," and *Lidum*, a Roman name of the **Loir** River here.

Châteaudun. *Town, Eure-et-Loir.* The name was recorded in the 6th century as *Dunensem castrum*, the equivalent of *Castrodunum*, from Latin *castrum*, "fort," and Gaulish *dunon*, in the same sense. The name is thus a tautological doublet.

Châteaugiron. *Town, Ille-et-Vilaine.* The name derives from Latin *castellum*, "castle," and the Breton personal name *Giron*, presumably that of the lord here.

Château-Gontier. *Town, Mayenne.* The name was recorded in the 11th century as *Castrum Gunterii*, from Latin *castrum*, "fort," and the Germanic personal name *Gunther*, that of a local lord.

Château-Landon. *Village, Seine-et-Marne.* The name was recorded in the 9th century as *Castra Nantonense*, from Latin *castra*, "camp," and the Germanic personal name *Nanto*, a pet form of a name such as *Nanthari* or *Nantwolf*, that of a local lord.

Château-la-Vallière. *Resort village, Indre-et-Loire.* The village takes its name from Latin *castellum*, "castle," and Madame de *La Vallière*, for whom it was erected into a dukedom.

Châteaulin. *Town, Finistère.* The Brittany town has a Breton name, from *kastell*, "castle," "fort," and a second element of unknown origin.

Châteaumeillant. *Village, Cher.* The name was recorded in the 4th century as *Mediolanum*, then in the 6th century as *Mediolanensium castrum*, from Gaulish *mediolanon*, "middle (of the) plain" (as for **Meulan**), and Latin *castrum*, "fort."

Châteauneuf-du-Faou. *Village, Finistère.* The first word of the name represents Latin *castrum novum*, "new fort." The second part names the place called *le Faou*, from Latin *fagus*, "beech."

Châteauneuf-du-Pape. *Village, Vaucluse.* The name was recorded in the 12th century as *Castrum novum*, Latin for "new fort." It then became *Châteauneuf-Calcernier*, recorded in the 13th century as *Castro novo Calcenarum*, the second part deriving from Latin *calx*, "lime." The present addition, meaning "of the pope," came later, and refers to the castle built here in the 14th century as a second residence of the popes at nearby Avignon.

Châteauneuf-du-Rhône. *Village, Drôme.* The name was recorded in the 13th century as *Castrum novum*, Latin for "new fort." The addition names the **Rhône** River here.

Châteauneuf-lès-Martigues. *Town, Bouches-du-Rhône.* The main name represents Latin *novum castrum*, "new fort." The addition locates the town near (*lès*) **Martigues**.

Châteauneuf-sur-Charente. *Town, Charente.* The name was recorded in the 12th century as *Castrum novum*, Latin for "new fort." The addition locates the town on the **Charente** River.

Châteauneuf-sur-Loire. *Town, Loiret.* The name was recorded in the 11th century as *Castrum novum*, Latin for "new fort." The addition locates the town on the **Loire** River.

Châteauneuf-sur-Sarthe. *Village, Maine-et-Loire.* The name derives from Latin *castrum novum*, "new fort." The addition locates the village on the **Sarthe** River.

Châteauponsac. *Village, Haute-Vienne.* The name was recorded early as *Castrum Potentiacum*, with Latin *castrum*, "fort," prefixed to the Roman personal name *Potens* or *Potentius* and the associative suffix *-acum*.

Châteaurenard. *Village, Loiret.* The name was recorded in the 10th century as *Castellum Rainardum*, from Latin *castellum*, "castle," and the Germanic personal name *Raginhart*, that of a local lord.

Château-Renault. *Town, Indre-et-Loire.* The name was recorded in the 11th century as *Castrum Rainaldi*, from Latin *castrum*, "castle," and the Germanic personal name *Raginwald*, that of a local lord.

Châteauroux. *City, Indre.* The name was recorded in the 12th century as *Castellum Radulphi*, "Raoul's fort," from Latin *castellum*, "castle," and the name of *Raoul* le Large, who built it in the 10th century. The personal name is the equivalent of English *Ralph*. During the Revolution, the city was renamed *Indreville*, for the **Indre** River on which it lies.

Château-Salins. *Town, Moselle.* The name was recorded in the 14th century as

Chastel Sallin, from Latin *Castrum Sallum*, from *castrum*, "fort," and *sel*, "salt." There are still saltworks nearby.

Château-Thierry. *Town, Aisne.* The name was recorded in the 10th century as *Castrum Theoderici*, "Theodoric's castle," with a Germanic personal name that gave French *Thierry*. The castle was built in 718 as a royal residence for the Merovingian king *Theodoric IV* (died 737) by the Frankish ruler Charles Martel.

Châtel. *Resort village, Haute-Savoie.* The name derives from Latin *castellum*, "castle."

Châtelaillon-Plage *see* **Aunis**

Le Châtelard. *Resort village, Savoie.* The name derives from Latin *castellum*, "castle," and the suffix *-are*. (The name was recorded in the 11th century as *Castellarium*, in which *-arium* appears to have been substituted for *-are*. But it may actually represent an earlier form.)

Le Châtelet-en-Brie. *Village, Seine-et-Marne.* The name was recorded in the 12th century as *Castellarium*, from Latin *castellum*, "castle," and the suffix *-arium*, later replaced by the diminutive suffix *-ittum*. The distinguishing addition locates the village in **Brie.**

Châtelguyon. *Town, Puy-de-Dôme.* The name was recorded in the 13th century as *Castrum Guidonis*, from Latin *castrum*, "fort," and the Germanic personal name *Wido*.

Châtellerault. *Town, Vienne.* The name was recorded in the 11th century as *Castrum Araldi*, from Latin *castrum*, "fort," and the Germanic personal name *Adroaldus*.

Châtel-Montagne. *Village, Allier.* The name derives from Latin *castellum*, "castle," and French *montagne*, "mountain," referring to the location of the village in the foothills of the Massif Central.

Châtenois. *Village, Vosges.* The name derives from the Roman personal name *Castinius* and the associative suffix *-acum*.

Châtenoy-le-Royal. *Town, Saône-et-Loire.* The name derives from Latin *castaneum*, "chestnut tree," and the collective suffix *-eta*. The addition denotes a royal possession.

Châtillon. *Town, Hauts-de-Seine.* The name of the Paris suburb, now also *Châtillon-sous-Bagneux*, from its proximity to **Bagneux**, was recorded in the 12th century as *Castellionem*, from Latin *castellum*, "castle," a diminutive of *castrum*, "fort," and the suffix *-ionem*.

Châtillon-Coligny. *Village, Loiret.* The main name shares the origin of **Châtillon.** The village was earlier *Châtillon-sur-Loing*, for its location on the **Loing** River. It was then renamed as now for Admiral de *Coligny* (1519–1572), who was born here.

Châtillon-sur-Chalaronne. *Village, Ain.* The main name shares the origin of **Châtillon.** The addition locates the town on the *Chalaronne* River.

Châtillon-sur-Indre. *Village, Indre.* The main name shares the origin of **Châtillon.** The addition locates the town on the **Indre** River.

Châtillon-sur-Loire. *Village, Loiret.* The main name shares the origin of **Châtillon.** The addition locates the town on the **Loire** River.

Châtillon-sur-Marne. *Village, Marne.* The main name shares the origin of **Châtillon.** The addition locates the town near the **Marne** River.

Châtillon-sur-Seine. *Town, Côte-d'Or.* The main name shares the origin of **Châtillon.** The addition locates the town on the **Seine** River.

Chatou. *Town, Yvelines.* The name of the Paris suburb was recorded in the 13th century as *Chato*, perhaps from *Cattivum*, from the Gaulish personal name *Cattus* (from *cattos*, "cat") and the suffix *-avum*.

La Châtre. *Town, Indre.* The name has the same origin as that of **Castres.**

Chaudes-Aigues. *Resort village, Cantal.* The name derives from a plural form of Latin *calidus*, "hot," and *aqua*, Provençal *aguo*, "water," referring to the mineral springs here.

Chauffailles. *Town, Saône-et-Loire.* The name, recorded in the 14th century as *Chofalli*, is said to derive from a Germanic army contingent known as the *Taifali* or *Theofalli*, brought here by the Romans.

Chaumont. *Town, Haute-Marne.* The name was recorded in the 12th century as *Chalmunt*, from Low Latin *calmis*, a derivative of pre-Indoeuropean *kal*, "rock," and Latin *mons*, "mountain."

Chaumont-en-Vexin. *Village, Oise.* The name was recorded in the 12th century as *Castrum Calvi Montis*, Latin for "fort of the bald mountain." The present name has dropped the "fort" but added its location in **Vexin**.

Chaumont-sur-Loire. *Village, Loir-et-Cher.* The name derives from Latin *calvus mons*, "bald mountain," meaning a hill bare of vegetation. The addition locates the village on the **Loire** River.

Chauny. *Town, Aisne.* The name was recorded in the 12th century as *Chauni-acum*, from the Roman personal name *Calinius* and the associative suffix *-acum*.

Chaussin. *Village, Jura.* The name derives from the Roman personal name *Calcinus* and the associative suffix *-acum*.

Chauvigny. *Town, Vienne.* The name was recorded in the 11th century as *Calvini-aco*, from the Roman personal name *Calvinius*, a form of *Calvinus*, and the associative suffix *-acum*.

Chavanay. *Village, Loire.* The name derives from the Gaulish personal name *Cavannus* and the associative suffix *-acum*.

Chavanoz. *Village, Isère.* The name derives from the Gaulish personal name *Cavannus* and the suffix *-uscum*.

Chaville. *Town, Hauts-de-Seine.* The name was recorded in the 12th century as *Cativilla*, probably from the Gaulish personal name *Cattus* ("cat") and Latin *villa*, "estate."

Chazelles-sur-Lyon. *Town, Loire.* The name represents Latin *casa*, "house," and the diminutive suffix *-ella*. The town is on the small *Lyon* River near **Lyon**.

Chécy. *Town, Loiret.* The name was recorded in the 10th century as *Caciacus*, from the Roman personal name *Cacius* or *Cattius* and the associative suffix *-acum*.

Chef-Boutonne. *Village, Deux-Sèvres.* The name was recorded in the 11th century as *Caput Vultone*, from Latin *caput*, "head," and the name of the *Boutonne* River, at the head of which the village stands.

Chelles. *Town, Seine-et-Marne.* The name of the Paris suburb was recorded in the 11th century as *Cala*, from Low Latin *cala*, "rock shelter," from pre-Indoeuropean *kal*, "rock."

Chemillé. *Town, Maine-et-Loire.* The name was recorded in the 12th century as *Camilliacum*, from the Roman personal name *Camillius* and the associative suffix *-acum*.

Le Chemin des Dames. *Highway, Aisne.* The hilltop road between the valleys of the Aisne and the Ailette came to be known as "the ladies' road" in the 18th century, when it was used by the two daughters of Louis XV, the *Dames de France*, as a route from Paris to visit their former lady-in-waiting, the comtesse de Narbonne, at her château of La Bove near Craonne.

Chennevières-sur-Marne. *Town, Val-de-Marne.* The name derives from Latin *cannabis*, "hemp," and the suffix *-ella*, equivalent to a conjectural *cannabaria*, "field of hemp." The addition locates the town on the **Marne** River.

Chenonceaux. *Village, Indre-et-Loire.* The name probably comes from the Roman personal name *Cano, Canonis*, a variant of *Canus*, and Latin *cella*, "storeroom," "granary."

Chenôve. *Town, Côte-d'Or.* The suburb of Dijon derives its name from Latin *cannaba*, "workshop."

Cher. *Department, central France.* The name is that of the river here, known to the Romans as *Cares*, from pre-Indoeuropean *kar*, "rock," referring to its rocky bed.

Cherbourg. *City and port, Manche.* The name is probably a Germanic translation of Gallo-Roman *Coriallum* or *Coriovallum*, with Gaulish *corios*, "army," giving *hari*, and Latin *vallum*, "fort," giving *burg*. This would have produced an original form *Hariburg*, which later gave Old French *Chiersbourg* and *Cheresborc*, both recorded in the 12th century. An origin in Latin *Caesaris burgus*, "Caesar's fort," is not likely but theoretically possible.

Le Chesnay. *Town, Yvelines.* The Paris suburb derives its name from Gaulish *cassanos*, "oak," and the collective suffix *-etum*.

Cheval-Blanc. *Village, Vaucluse.* The name, meaning "white horse," is that of the former inn here around which the village arose.

Cheverny. *Village, Loir-et-Cher.* The name derives from the Roman personal name *Caprinius*, from *Caprius*, and the associative suffix *-acum*.

Chevigny-Saint-Sauveur. *Town, Côte-d'Or.* The name derives from *Cavannius*, a latinized form of the Gaulish personal name *Cavannus*, and the associative suffix *-acum*. The addition is a dedication to *St. Savior*, a title of Christ.

Chevreuse. *Town, Yvelines.* The name was recorded in the 10th century as *Cavrosa*, from Latin *capra*, "goat," presumably denoting a hill where goats lived or were kept.

Le Cheylard. *Town, Ardèche.* The name derives from Latin *castellum*, "castle," and the diminutive suffix *-are*.

Chigny-les-Roses. *Village, Marne.* The name was recorded in the 12th century as *Chigniacum*, from the Roman personal name *Canius*, and the associative suffix *-acum*. The addition is "the roses."

Chilly-Mazarin. *Town, Essonne.* The name of the Paris suburb was recorded in the 12th century as *Calliacus*, from the Roman personal name *Callius*, and the associative suffix *-acum*. The second part of the name, added in 1822, pays indirect tribute to Cardinal Jules *Mazarin* (1602–1661), whose niece Hortense Mancini married (in 1661) Armand Charles de la Porte, marquis de La Meilleraye and nephew of Antoine de Coiffier d'Effiat, former owner of the Chilly estate, making him duc de Mazarin.

Chinon. *Town, Indre-et-Loire.* The name was recorded in the 6th century as *Cainum*, from the Roman personal name *Catinus*, a form of *Catinius*, and the suffix *-onem*.

Chocques. *Village, Pas-de-Calais.* The suburb of Béthune derives its name from a Picard form of French *souche*, "tree stump," presumably referring to the stumps left after land clearance.

Choisy-le-Roi. *Town, Val-de-Marne.* The Paris suburb derives its name from the Roman personal name *Causius* and the associative suffix *-acum*. The addition ("the king") refers to Louis XV (1710–1774), who entertained his favorites at the castle here.

Cholet. *City, Maine-et-Loire.* The name was recorded in the 11th century as *Caulletum*, from Latin *caulis*, "cabbage," and either the collective suffix *-etum* or the diminutive suffix *-ittum*.

Chomérac. *Village, Ardèche.* The name represents a conjectural form *Calmiracum*, from the Gallo-Roman personal name *Calmirus* and the associative suffix *-acum*.

Chooz. *Village, Ardennes.* The name was recorded in the 9th century as *Calcum*, presumably from Latin *calx*, "lime," denoting a former limekiln here.

Chorges. *Village, Hautes-Alpes.* The name was recorded early as *Caturigomago*, a Gaulish compound, from the tribal name *Caturiges* (see **Chartreuse**) and *magos*, "market." The latter word had disappeared by the 4th century, leaving the name of the tribe alone for their capital.

Chouzé-sur-Loire. *Village, Indre-et-Loire.* The village, on the **Loire** River, derives its name from the Roman personal name *Causius* and the associative suffix *-acum*.

Ciboure. *Resort town, Pyrénées-Atlantiques.* The name of the suburb of Saint-Jean-de-Luz was recorded in the 17th century as *Subiboure*, from Basque *çubi*, "bridge," and *buru*, "head," denoting a location the other side of the Nive River from Saint-Jean-de-Luz proper.

Cinq-Mars-la-Pile. *Village, Indre-et-Loire.* The name was recorded in the 12th century as *Sanctus Medardus*, from the dedication to *St. Médard*, 6th-century bishop of Vermandois. The apparent meaning "fifth of March" arose when *Saint* was taken as *Cinq* and *Mars*, a local form of *Médard*, was taken as the name of the month. The addition represents Latin *pila*, "pillar," referring to a lofty tower here that is believed to have been a Roman beacon.

Cintegabelle. *Village, Haute-Garonne.* The name honors *St. Gabella*, the initial *Cinte-* masking the original *Sainte*.

La Ciotat. *Resort town, Bouches-du-Rhône.* The name was recorded in the 13th century as *Civitas*, from Latin *civitas*, "township," here as one dependent (until the 17th century) on nearby Ceyreste.

Cirey-sur-Blaise. *Village, Haute-Marne.* The name derives from the Roman personal name *Cirius* and the associative suffix *-acum*. The location of the village on the *Blaise* River distinguishes it from **Cirey-sur-Vezouze**.

Cirey-sur-Vezouze. *Village, Meurthe-et-Moselle.* The name derives from the Roman personal name *Cirius* and the associative suffix *-acum*. The location of the village on the *Vezouze* River distinguishes it from **Cirey-sur-Blaise.**

Cîteaux. *Abbey, Côte-d'Or.* The Medieval Latin name of the place was *Cistercium*, from Old French *cistel*, "reed," referring to the abundance of this plant here. The *Cistercian* order was established here in 1098.

Civray. *Village, Vienne.* The name derives from the Roman personal name *Severius* or *Severus* and the associative suffix *-acum*.

Clairac. *Village, Lot-et-Garonne.* The name derives from the Roman personal name *Clarius* and the associative suffix *-acum*.

Clairvaux. *Hamlet, Aube.* The name, famous as that of the (ruined) abbey here, was recorded at the time of its founding in 1115 by St. Bernard of Clairvaux as *Clara Vallis*, "bright valley," from Latin *clarus*, "clear," "bright," and *vallis*, "valley."

Claix. *Town, Isère.* The suburb of Grenoble derives its name from the Roman personal name *Clavius* and the associative suffix *-acum*.

Clamart. *Town, Hauts-de-Seine.* The name of the Paris suburb, recorded in the 12th century as *Clamardum*, is of pre-Latin but obscure origin. It may derive from the Gaulish personal name *Clamus*.

Clamecy. *Town, Nièvre.* The name was recorded in the 7th century as *Clamiciacus*, from the Gaulish personal name *Clamicius*, from *Clamus*, and the associative suffix *-acum*.

Claye-Souilly. *Town, Seine-et-Marne.* The name derives from Latin *clita*, "gate" (related to Latin *claudere*, "to shut," and so to English *close*). The second part of the name, that of a nearby place, derives from the Gaulish personal name *Sollius* or Roman personal name *Solius* and the associative suffix *-acum*.

Les Claye-sous-Bois. *Town, Yvelines.* The name derives from Latin *clita*, "gate." The distinguishing addition means "by the wood."

La Clayette. *Village, Saône-et-Loire.* The

name represents a diminutive form of Latin *clita*, "gate."

Cléguérec. *Village, Morbihan.* The Brittany village has a Breton name meaning "rocky hill," from a word related to Welsh *clegyr*, "rock," "stony place."

Clelles. *Village, Isère.* The name may represent Latin *cletellae*, a derivative of *clita*, "gate."

Cléon. *Town, Seine-Maritime.* The name is of uncertain, possibly Gaulish, origin.

Cléon-d'Andran. *Village, Drôme.* The first part of the name is probably a miscopying of *Cléou*, from Latin *clivum*, "slope." The second part may have been the original name of the village, or more likely represent the personal name *Anteran*, a variant of *Anthéron*.

Clères. *Village, Seine-Maritime.* The village takes its name from the *Claire* River on which it lies.

Clermont. *Town, Oise.* The name was recorded in the 12th century as *Clarus Mons*, Latin for "clear mountain," meaning a prominent peak that can be seen from afar.

Clermont-en-Argonne. *Village, Meuse.* The name has the same origin as **Clermont**, here distinguished by its location in **Argonne**.

Clermont-Ferrand. *City, Puy-de-Dôme.* The two communities *Clermont* and *Montferrand* combined in 1630 to form the present city. The name of *Clermont* was recorded in the 9th century as *Claromonte*, from Latin *clarus*, "clear," and *mons*, "mountain," as for **Clermont**. The town was at first known as *Nemossus*, then in the Roman era as *Augustonemetum*, from the emperor *Augustus* and Gaulish *nemeton*, "shrine." In the 3d and 4th centuries AD it was known as *Arverni*, from the tribe of this name (see **Auvergne**). *Montferrand* has a name recorded in the 11th century as *Mons Ferrandus*, from Latin *mons*, "mountain," and the personal name *Ferrandus*, meaning "iron-gray," alluding to the bearer's gray

hair. On the amalgamation, *Montferrand* was abbreviated to *Ferrand* to avoid duplication of the *mont*.

Clermont-l'Hérault. *Town, Hérault.* The name was recorded in the 12th century as *Clarus mons*, as for **Clermont**. The addition locates the town in **Hérault**.

Cléry-Saint-André. *Village, Loiret.* The name derives from the Roman personal name *Clarius* and the associative suffix *-acum*. The addition is a dedication to *St. Andrew*.

Clichy. *Town, Hauts-de-Seine.* The Paris suburb derives its name from the Roman personal name *Cleppius* and the associative suffix *-acum*.

Clichy-sous-Bois. *Town, Seine-Saint-Denis.* The Paris suburb has a name of the same origin as **Clichy**, here distinguished by its location "near the wood."

Clisson. *Town, Loire-Atlantique.* The name derives from the Roman personal name *Cliccius* and the suffix *-onem*.

Clohars-Carnoët. *Village, Finistère.* The name was recorded early as *Cluthgual*, in which *Cluth-* represents Breton *kleuz*, "ditch," probably referring to former entrenchments here. The second part of the name derives from Breton *karn*, "rock," and *hoët*, "wood."

Cloyes-sur-le-Loir. *Village, Eure-et-Loir.* The name derives from Latin *clita*, "gate." The addition locates the village on the **Loir** River.

Cluny. *Town, Saône-et-Loire.* The town's Medieval Latin name was *Cluniacum*, from the Gaulish personal name *Clunius* and the associative suffix *-acum*. The *Cluniac* order developed from the monastery founded here in 910 by the Benedictine monk St. Berno.

La Clusaz. *Resort village, Haute-Savoie.* The name derives from Latin *clusa*, "defile," "pass," here in the foothills of the Savoy Alps.

La Cluse-et-Mijoux. *Village, Doubs.* The

name derives from Latin *clusa*, "defile," "pass," here in the Jura Mountains. *Mijoux* is from Latin *medium*, "middle," and *jugum*, "mountain."

Cluses. *Town, Haute-Savoie*. The name derives from Latin *clusa*, "defile," "pass," here as a gorge through which the Arve River flows.

Cognac. *Town, Charente*. The name was recorded in the 11th century as *Comniacum*, from the Gaulish personal name *Connius* and the associative suffix *-acum*.

Cognin. *Town, Savoie*. The suburb of Chambéry derives its name from the Gaulish personal name *Cotonius* and the suffix *-anum*.

Cogolin. *Resort town, Var*. The name was recorded in the 11th century as *Cucullinus*, from a derivative of Latin *cucullus*, "hood," and the suffix *-inum*, referring to a natural hood-like feature of some kind here.

Colayrac-Saint-Cirq. *Village, Lot-et-Garonne*. The name represents a conjectural Latin *Collariacum*, from the Roman personal name *Collarius*, from *Collius*, and the associative suffix *-acum*. The addition is a dedication to the 4th-century martyr *St. Cyricus*.

La Colle-sur-Loup. *Resort town, Alpes-Maritimes*. The name derives from Latin *colla*, a form of *collis*, "hill." The town is on the *Loup* River.

Collet-d'Allevard. *Resort village, Isère*. The name represents a diminutive form of Latin *colla*, a form of *collis*, "hill," here one near **Allevard**.

Colleville-Montgomery. *Village, Calvados*. The name derives from the Scandinavian personal name *Kolli* and Latin *villa*, "village." The village, near the English Channel beaches, was originally known as *Colleville-sur-Orne*, from its location near the mouth of the **Orne** River. Following its capture by British and French forces in the Normandy invasion of World War II, however, it was renamed by way of tribute to the

English general Bernard *Montgomery* (1887–1976), whose own name, appropriately, is of Norman origin.

Colleville-sur-Mer. *Village, Calvados*. The village has a name of the same origin as **Colleville-Montgomery**, from which it is distinguished by being "on sea" (near the English Channel coast).

Collioure. *Resort village and port, Pyrénées-Orientales*. The name was recorded in the 7th century as *Caucholiberi*, from *Cauca*, presumably the original name of the settlement, and Aquitanian *ili-berri*, "new town."

Collobrières. *Village, Var*. The name was recorded in the 11th century as *Colubraira*, from Latin *colubra*, "grass snake," and the suffix *-aria*, denoting a place infested by these reptiles.

Collonges. *Village, Ain*. The name derives from Latin *colonica*, a term for land cultivated by a colonist or settler, as distinct from the earlier *colonia*, a Roman colony (as was *Cologne*).

Colmar. *City, Haut-Rhin*. The name was recorded in the 8th century as *Columbrensis*, perhaps from a Germanic personal name *Galamar*, or from Latin *columbarium*, "dovecote," from *columba*, "dove," as for **Colombes**.

Colmars. *Resort village, Alpes-de-Haute-Provence*. The name represents Latin *collis Martii*, "hill of Mars," for the Roman god of war.

Colombelles. *Town, Calvados*. The suburb of Caen has a name representing a diminutive form of Latin *columba*, "pigeon," denoting a dovecote or place where pigeons were raised.

Colombes. *Town, Hauts-de-Seine*. The Paris suburb has a name recorded in the 13th century as *Columbis*, from Latin *columba*, "dove." Doves or pigeons were kept here.

Colombey-les-Deux-Églises. *Village, Haute-Marne*. The village has a name of Latin origin recorded in the 12th century as

Columbei, ubi due ecclesie sunt ("Colombey, where there are two churches"). The name itself derives from Latin *columbarium,* "dovecote."

Colomiers. *Town, Haute-Garonne.* The suburb of Toulouse has a name recorded in the 9th century as *Colombariis,* from Latin *columbarium,* "dovecote."

Combloux. *Resort village, Haute-Savoie.* The name derives from Latin *cumulus,* "summit," and the suffix *-osum.* Combloux is high in the Alps, near Mont Blanc.

Combourg. *Town, Ille-et-Vilaine.* The name derives from the Germanic female personal name *Humburg.*

Combray *see* **Illiers-Combray**

Combres *see* **Illiers-Combray**

Combs-la-Ville. *Town, Seine-et-Marne.* The name derives from (latinized) Gaulish *cumba,* "enclosed valley," here with the distinguishing addition "the town."

Comines. *Town, Nord.* The name derives from the Gallo-Roman personal name *Comminius,* with Latin *villa,* "estate," understood. The town is on the Franco-Belgian border, divided in two by the Lys River. The French half is known in Flemish as *Komen.* The Belgian half, *Comines-Warneton,* is known as *Komen-Waasten.*

Commentry. *Town, Allier.* The name was recorded in the 11th century as *Commentriacus,* from the Gallo-Roman personal name *Commentarius,* from *Commentius,* and the associative suffix *-acum.*

Commercy. *Town, Meuse.* The name was recorded in the 9th century as *Commercium* and in the 11th century as *Commerciacum,* from the Gaulish personal name *Comartius* and the associative suffix *-acum.*

Compiègne. *City, Oise.* The name of the city was recorded in the 6th century as *Compendium,* from Latin *compendium,* "short cut." The reference is to the Roman road that crossed the Oise River here to provide a direct route between Beauvais and Soissons.

Comtat Venaissin. *Region, southeastern France.* The region, together with Avignon, was a papal possession from 1274 to 1791. Hence its name, from Latin *Comitatus Venaissini,* from *comitatus,* "court," "palace," and *Avenio,* the Roman name of **Avignon**.

Concarneau. *Town and port, Finistère.* The Brittany town derives its name from Breton *Konk-Kernev,* "bay of Cornouaille," from *konk,* "corner, "bay" (as for **Conques**), and *Kernev,* **Cornouaille**.

Conches-en-Ouche. *Town, Eure.* The original name of the town was *Châtillon,* as for **Châtillon,** recorded in the 11th century as *Castellio.* It was then renamed for **Conques,** where there was a famous abbey, adding the district name *Ouche,* perhaps from a Gaulish word meaning "enclosure."

Condé-sur-l'Escaut. *Town, Nord.* The name was recorded in the 9th century as *Condatum,* from Gaulish *condate,* "confluence," here between the **Escaut** River and what is now the Condé-Mons Canal.

Condé-sur-Noireau. *Town, Calvados.* The name derives from Gaulish *condate,* "confluence," here between the *Noireau* and Druance rivers.

Condé-sur-Vire. *Village, Manche.* The name derives from Gaulish *condate,* "confluence," here between the **Vire** River and a tributary.

Condezaygues. *Village, Lot-et-Garonne.* The name is of uncertain origin. One might propose an origin in Gaulish *condate,* "confluence," and Latin *aquas,* "waters," except that the village is some distance from the Lot River and moreover is on a mountain between two valleys.

Condom. *Town, Gers.* The name was recorded in the 7th century as *Condomum,* from the Gaulish personal name *Condus* and *magos,* "field," "market." (The town began promoting itself as a tourist attraction when it noticed English visitors joyfully posing by its roadsigns.)

Condrieu. *Village, Rhône.* The name was recorded in the 10th century as *Conriacus*, from the Gaulish personal name *Comerius*, a form of *Comarius*, and the associative suffix *-acum*.

Conflans-en-Jarnisy. *Village, Meurthe-et-Moselle.* The name derives from Latin *confluentes*, "confluence," here between the Orne and Longeau rivers. The addition names the local region.

Conflans-Sainte-Honorine. *Town, Yvelines.* The name was recorded in the 11th century as *castrum Confluencie*, then shortly after as *ecclesia Sanctae Honorinae de Confluentio*. The main name represents Latin *confluentes*, "confluence," referring to the location of the town on the Seine River just above the point where it is joined by the Oise. The second part of the name refers to the church of *St. Honorina*, an early Gaulish martyr.

Confolens. *Village, Charente.* The name was recorded in the 11th century as *Confolentis*, from Latin *confluentes*, "confluence," here between the Vienne and Goire rivers.

Conhilhac-Corbières. *Village, Aude.* The name was recorded in the 12th century as *Conneracum* and in the 13th century as *Conilhaco*. If the first of these is correct, the place seems to have changed its name. If not, it is the same as for **Conhilhac-de-la-Montagne**, although the places are too far apart (some 30 miles) for one name to have given the other. The second part of the name is as for **Lézignan-Corbières**.

Conilhac-de-la-Montagne. *Village, Aude.* The name derives from the Gallo-Roman personal name *Connilius*, from Gaulish *Connos*, and the associative suffix *-acum*. The addition ("of the mountain") refers to the lofty terrain here.

Connerré. *Village, Sarthe.* The name may represent an original *Connodurum*, from the Gaulish personal name *Connos* and *duron*, "fort," to which was later added the associative suffix *-acum*.

Conques. *Village, Aveyron.* The name, recorded in the 9th century as *Conchis*, comes from Latin *concha*, "snailshell," referring to a bowl-shaped valley here.

Conques-sur-Orbiel. *Village, Aude.* The village has a name of the same origin as **Conques**, from which it is distinguished by its location on the *Orbiel* River.

Le Conquet. *Resort village and port, Finistère.* The Brittany village has the Breton name *Konk-Leon*, "bay of Léon," referring to the region of **Léon**. The French name represents a diminutive of Breton *konk*, "corner," "angle," "bay."

Consolation-Maisonnettes. *Village, Doubs.* The village (*Maisonnettes*) grew around an oratory founded by François de la Palud in the 15th century and dedicated to Notre-Dame-de-Consolation ("Our Lady of Consolation"). In 1670 it became a Minimite monastery.

Les Contamines-Montjoie. *Resort village, Haute-Savoie.* The name derives from Medieval Latin *condominium*, meaning a portion of land near a castle that was reserved for the local lord and exempt from taxes. *Montjoie* is the nearby summit *Mont Joly*.

Contes. *Town, Alpes-Maritimes.* The name is of obscure origin. A source in pre-Indoeuropean *kun*, "hill," has been proposed. Contes is on a rocky spur overlooking a valley.

Contres. *Village, Loir-et-Cher.* The name derives from Latin *contra*, "(land) opposite."

Contrexéville. *Resort town, Vosges.* The name combines the original name of the settlement, *Gundericiacum*, from the Germanic personal name *Gunderich* and the associative suffix *-iacum*, with Latin *villa*, "village."

Coquelles. *Village, Pas-de-Calais.* The name was recorded in the 12th century as *Qualquella*, representing a diminutive form of Dutch *koek*, "cake," denoting a rounded mound of earth.

Corbas. *Town, Rhône.* The suburb of Lyon has a name recorded in the 9th century as *Petra Curba*, Latin for "rounded rock," perhaps referring to a megalith here.

Corbehem. *Village, Pas-de-Calais.* The suburb of Douai derives its name from Old French *corbel*, "crow," here presumably used as a nickname, and Germanic *heim*, "abode."

Corbeil-Essonnes. *Town, Essonne.* The first part of the name was recorded in the 4th century as *Corobilium*, from the Gaulish personal name *Corbus* and Gaulish *ialon*, "clearing," "field," "village." The second part comes from the **Essonne** River, which joins the Seine here.

Corbie. *Town, Somme.* The name, recorded in the 8th century as *Corbeia*, is of uncertain origin. It may be an old name of the Ancre River here, although a source in the Gaulish (and Latin) nickname *Corbus* ("crow") is also possible.

Corbières. *Region, southern France.* The outliers of the eastern Pyrenees, in Languedoc, derive their name from pre-Indoeuropean *kor*, a variant of *kar*, "rock," "mountain," and the Latin suffix *-arium*.

Corbigny. *Village, Nièvre.* The name was recorded in the 8th century as *Corbiniacus*, from *Corbennius*, a latinized form of the Gaulish personal name *Corbennus*, from *Corbus*, and the associative suffix *-acum*.

Cordemais. *Village, Loire-Atlantique.* The name seems to derive from the Roman personal name *Cordius* and Latin *mansus*, "farm."

Cordes. *Village, Tarn.* The village was founded in 1222 by Raymond VII, count of Toulouse, and may take its name from pre-Latin *cor-d*, "height," referring to an existing site. Some authorities, however, see an adoption of the name of the Spanish city of *Córdoba* (French *Cordoue*), and there is a similarity in the location of the two places, with Cordes high up on a steep spur (giving it the alternate name *Cordes-sur-Ciel*, "Cordes-in-the-Sky") and Córdoba lying at the foot of the Sierra Morena.

Cormeilles-en-Parisis. *Town, Val-d'Oise.* The name of the Paris suburb was recorded in the 7th century as *Cormoletum*, from *cormella*, a diminutive of Old French *corme*, "sorb apple," with the suffix *-etum*. This suffix then changed, so that the name was recorded in the 9th century as *Cormiliis*. The second part of the name, distinguishing the town from *Cormeilles-en-Vexin*, Val-d'Oise, 12 miles to the northwest, amounts to "in the Paris region."

Cormelles-le-Royal. *Town, Calvados.* The name of the suburb of Caen was recorded in the 12th century as *Cormellae*, from *cormella*, a diminutive of Old French *corme*, "sorb apple," with the collective suffix *-ia*. The addition denotes a royal possession.

Cormery. *Village, Indre-et-Loire.* The name derives from an apparent original *Cormarium*, from Old French *corme*, "sorb apple," and the associative suffix *-acum*.

Cormontreuil. *Town, Marne.* The name was recorded in the 9th century as *Curtis monasterialis*, from Latin *cortis monasterioli*, "estate of the monastery," referring to the abbey church of St. Rémi at Reims.

Cornimont. *Town, Vosges.* The name derives from Latin *cornu*, "horn," denoting a promontory, and *mons, montis*, "mountain."

Cornouaille. *Region, northwestern France.* The region of Brittany derives its name from the *Cornovii* tribe who also gave the name of *Cornwall*, England, the French name for which is *Cornouailles*. Their Celtic name means "horned ones," the "horn" in this case being the peninsula that forms the western tip of Brittany. The Breton name of Cornouaille is *Kernev-veur*, from *Kernev*, "Cornouaille," and *veur*, a mutated form of *meur*, meaning "great."

Corps. *Village, Isère.* The name represents *corbis*, a form of Latin *corbus* (Classical Latin *corvus*), "crow."

Corrèze. *Department, south central France.* The name is that of the river here, recorded in the Medieval Latin form *Curetia*, from a pre-Latin root perhaps related to Indoeuropean *ker* or *ger*, "to flow."

Corse-du-Sud. *Department, southern Corsica.* The department, created in 1976, has a name meaning "Southern Corsica," as distinct from neighboring **Haute-Corse**, to the north. (A possible matching name *Basse-Corse*, "Lower Corsica," was presumably avoided because of its suggestion of "inferiority.")

Corsica. *Island, Mediterranean Sea.* The island, an administrative region of metropolitan France (where it is known as *Corse*) since 1982 and a territorial community since 1991, had the Roman name *Corsica*, of uncertain origin. A source in Phoenician *horsi*, "wooded," has been proposed, as the Phoenicians built their boats from Corsican pine.

Corte. *Town, Haute-Corse.* The town, in north central Corsica, takes its name from Low Latin *cortis*, "court," "estate," in the sense "fortified place." Corte was the capital of Corsica from 1755 through 1769.

Cosne-Cours-sur-Loire. *Town, Nièvre.* The town was earlier known as *Cosne-sur-Loire*, from Gaulish *condate*, "confluence," and the name of the **Loire** River, which is here joined by a tributary. The name of nearby *Cours* was then added, from Latin *cortem*, accusative of *cors*, "estate."

Cosne-d'Allier. *Village, Allier.* The village was earlier known as *Cosne-sur-l'Œil*, from Gaulish *condate*, "confluence," and the name of the *Œil* River, which is here joined by a stream from the Landes lagoons. The adoption of the present name, that of the department of **Allier**, may have been suggested by its similarity to the river name.

Cossé-le-Vivien. *Village, Mayenne.* The name derives from the Roman personal name *Coccius* and the associative suffix *-acum.* The addition represents a dedication to *St. Vivian*, 5th-century bishop of Saintes.

Le Coteau. *Town, Loire.* The suburb of Roanne derives its name from a diminutive form of Latin *costa*, "slope," "hill."

Côte d'Albâtre. This name, for a stretch of the English Channel coast in northern France, means "alabaster coast," and begins a run of names based on jewels, metals, heraldic tints, and other "precious" words, designed to lure the tourist. Some of the names are genuinely descriptive, as here, where the reference is to the impressive display of white cliffs.

Côte d'Amour. The "coast of love" is a stretch of the Atlantic seaboard around La Baule.

Côte d'Argent. The "silver coast" runs along the Bay of Biscay between the Gironde and the Spanish border, its name referring to its sandy beaches and the shining waters of the Atlantic.

Côte d'Azur. The "azure coast," familiar in English as the *French Riviera*, describes the more or less blue color of the Mediterranean between Cannes and Menton.

Côte de Beauté. The "coast of beauty" extends from La Rochelle to the Gironde on the Bay of Biscay, in western France, where much of the coastline is unspoilt.

Côte d'Émeraude. The "emerald coast" runs in the region of Dinard and Saint-Malo, on the English Channel coast, where there are a number of grassy headlands.

Côte de Grâce. The "coast of grace" extends between Trouville-sur-Mer and Honfleur along the southern shore of the Seine estuary, on the English Channel coast, and takes its name from Le Havre, originally Havre-de-Grâce ("haven of grace"), on the northern shore.

Côte de Granit Rose. The "coast of pink granite" extends along the shoreline of northern Brittany, by the English Channel, with pink granite rocks prominent around Perros-Guirec.

Côte de Jade. The "jade coast" lies on

the Atlantic seaboard, around the estuary of the Loire.

Côte de Nacre. The "pearl coast" lies by the English Channel in Normandy, northwestern France.

Côte d'Opale. The "opal coast" extends along the English Channel from the estuary of the Somme to the Belgian frontier, northeastern France. The name most obviously relates to the white headlands here, but there seems to be a more subtle reference: "The coast road winds high above the sea, allowing you best to appreciate the 'opal' in the name — the sea and sky merging in an opalescent, oyster-grey continuum" [Baillie and Salmon, p.220].

Côte-d'Or. *Department, eastern France.* A name distinct from most of those above (and a few below), meaning "golden hillside," referring to the famous Burgundy vineyards here. An alternate source for the name is sometimes offered: "Although the name Côte d'Or apparently translates directly as 'golden slope', evoking its autumn aspect, it may be an abbreviation of Côte d'Orient, a reference to the fact that the escarpment on which the vines flourish faces east" [Jancis Robinson, ed., *The Oxford Companion to Wine*, 2d ed., 1999].

Côte Fleurie. The "flowery coast" extends between Honfleur and Cabourg, on the English Channel coast, taking its name from the numerous gardens and flower displays here.

Cotentin. *Peninsula, northwestern France.* The peninsula, projecting into the English Channel, takes its name from the historic capital of this Normandy region, **Coutances**.

La Côte-Saint-André. *Town, Isère.* The name was recorded in the 12th century as *Costa Sancti Andreae,* from Latin *costa,* "slope," "hill," and the dedication to *St. Andrew.* The town is in the Alpine foothills.

Côte Sauvage. The "wild coast" extends along the western, Atlantic-facing shore of the Quiberon Peninsula, western France, where the cliff path overlooks "a wild grandeur of rocky grottoes, crevices and coves, lashed by tormented seas" [Young, p.177]. There is another Côte Sauvage on the western side of the Île d'Yeu.

Côtes-d'Armor. *Department, northwestern France.* The department lies by the English Channel coast in Brittany, whose historical name is *Armorica* (see **Armorique**). Its former name, until 1990, was *Côtes-du-Nord* ("Northern Coasts"), but this bland, general name was replaced by a local, loyalist one.

Côtes de Meuse. *Hill range, northeastern France.* The hills (*côtes*) here extend along the right bank of the **Meuse** River in the department of this name.

Côtes-du-Nord *see* **Côtes-d'Armor**

Côtes du Rhône. *Hill ridge, southern France.* The low hills (*côtes*) with their vineyards here extend beside the **Rhône** River.

Côte Vermeille. The "vermilion coast" extends along the Mediterranean shore from Collioure to the Spanish border, its name describing the color of the reddish hills here.

Cotignac. *Village, Var.* The name was recorded in the 11th century as *Cotinnacus,* from the Gallo-Roman personal name *Cottinius,* from Gaulish *Cottius,* and the associative suffix *-acum.*

La Coucourde. *Village, Drôme.* The name derives from Latin *cucurbita,* "gourd," probably as an inn sign on this main route (now the N7) between Lyon and Avignon.

Coucy-le-Château-Auffrique. *Village, Aisne.* The name combines two communities. *Coucy-le-Château* was recorded in the 6th century as *Codiciacum,* from the Gallo-Roman personal name *Codicius* and the associative suffix *-acum.* (The second part of the name refers to the former medieval castle here.) *Auffrique,* recorded in the 15th century as *Auffricque,* has a name of uncertain origin, possibly from the Germanic personal name *Adalfrid.*

Coudekerque-Branche. *Town, Nord.* The suburb of Dunkerque derives its name from Flemish *koud*, "cold," and *kerk*, "church." The "branch" is that of a canal here.

Couëron. *Town, Loire-Atlantique.* The name was recorded in the 9th century as *Coiron*, perhaps from the Roman personal name *Corius* and the suffix *-onem*.

Coulaines. *Town, Sarthe.* The suburb of Le Mans has a name recorded in the 9th century as *Coloniae*, of the same origin as **Coulogne**.

Coulogne. *Town, Pas-de-Calais.* The suburb of Calais has a name recorded in the 10th century as *Colonia*, a Latin feudal term for land where a colonist has settled as a permanent, hereditary farmer, tied to the soil but free, as against the *colonia* that was a Roman colony.

Coulommiers. *Town, Seine-et-Marne.* The name was recorded in the 12th century as *Columbarium*, Latin for "dovecote," "pigeon house."

Coulonges-sur-l'Autize. *Village, Deux-Sèvres.* The name derives from Latin *colonica*, a term for land worked by a colonist or settler, as at **Collonges**. The addition refers to the *Autise* River here.

Coulounieix-Chamiers. *Town, Dordogne.* The name of the suburb of Périgueux was recorded in the 13th century as *Colemnes*, from Latin *columna*, "column," denoting a Roman column marking a boundary, and the suffix *-arium*. The second part of the name is that of a former separate place.

Courbevoie. *Town, Hauts-de-Seine.* The name of the Paris suburb was recorded in the 9th century as *Curva Via*, Latin for "curved way," referring to the bend in the road from Paris to Rouen here, or the bend in the Seine River at this point.

Courcelles-lès-Lens. *Town, Pas-de-Calais.* The name derives from Latin *corticella*, a diminutive form of *cortem*, accusative of *cors*, "estate," probably in the sense "parceling out," "division." The distinguishing addition locates the town near (*lès*) **Lens**.

La Courneuve. *Town, Seine-Saint-Denis.* The Paris suburb has a relatively modern name meaning "the new estate" (*la cour neuve*).

Cournon-d'Auvergne. *Town, Puy-de-Dôme.* The suburb of Clermont-Ferrand probably derives its name from Celtic (and pre-Celtic) *cor-n*, "escarpment," "height," and the suffix *-onem*. The addition locates it in **Auvergne**.

La Couronne. *Town, Charente.* The name was recorded in the 12th century as *Corona*, Latin for "crown," meaning a crown-shaped height.

Courpière. *Town, Puy-de-Dôme.* The name was recorded in the 11th century as *Corspetra*, apparently from Latin words that gave French *cour*, "yard," and *pierre*, "stone," implying a farm built of stone, as distinct from the more common adobe building found in the country.

Courrières. *Town, Pas-de-Calais.* The name was recorded in the 11th century as *Currierum*, from Old Picard *coure*, "hazel," and the suffix *-arium*.

Coursan. *Town, Aude.* The name was recorded in the 12th century as *Cursiacus*, then in the 13th century as *Corsant*, apparently from the Roman personal name *Curtius* and the associative suffix *-acum*, with an unexplained subsequent change of suffix.

Courseulles-sur-Mer. *Resort village, Calvados.* The name, recorded in the 11th century as *Corcella*, has the same origin as that of **Courcelles-lès-Lens**, but here with the village distinguished by its location ("on sea") on the English Channel.

Cours-la-Ville. *Town, Rhône.* The name derives from Latin *cortem*, accusative of *cors*, "estate," denoting originally the farm buildings at the center of the estate, then the whole estate, then the village that grew up around it. The distinguishing addition here emphasizes the "urban" nature of the settlement.

Courtenay. *Village, Loiret.* The name derives from the Roman personal name *Curtenus*, from *Curtus* (originally a nickname meaning "short"), and the associative suffix *-acum*.

Courthézon. *Town, Vaucluse.* The name derives from Latin *cortem*, accusative of *cors*, "estate," and the Germanic personal name *Eudo*.

Courtry. *Town, Seine-et-Marne.* The name of the Paris suburb was recorded in the 13th century as *Curtiriacum*, from the Roman personal name *Curtorius* and the associative suffix *-acum*.

Courville-sur-Eure. *Village, Eure-et-Loir.* The name derives from Latin *curva*, "curve," "bend," and *villa*, "village," denoting a place at a bend, as here by the **Eure** River.

Cousances-aux-Bois. *Village, Meuse.* The original name of the village was recorded in the 8th century as *Cusiliacum*, from the Roman personal name *Cussilius* or *Cursilius*, from *Cussius* or *Cursius*, and the associative suffix *-acum*. The present name, first recorded in the 16th century, seems to have been adopted from *Cousances-les-Forges*, a village 20 miles to the southwest, on the *Cousances* River. The respective additions refer to woods and forges.

Cousoire. *Village, Nord.* The name probably combines Latin *cortem*, accusative of *cors*, "estate," and the name of the nearby *Solre* River.

Coutances. *Town, Manche.* The Roman name of the town was *Constantia*, from the emperor *Constantius Chlorus* (died 306), who fortified the settlement around 305.

Coutras. *Town, Gironde.* The name was recorded in the 4th century as *Corterate*, with Gaulish *rate*, "fort," added to an obscure first element. A meaning "little fort" has been suggested.

La Couvertoirade. *Village, Aveyron.* The name derives from Old Provençal *cobertoira*, "cover," "lid," presumably with some kind of local topographical application.

Couzeix. *Town, Haute-Vienne.* The suburb of Limoges derives its name from Latin *cos, cotis*, "stone," and the suffix *-arium*, giving an overall meaning "stony place."

Cozes. *Village, Charente-Maritime.* The name derives from the Gaulish personal name *Cotius* or *Cottius*, with Latin *villa*, "estate," understood, or from a derivative of Latin *cos, cotis*, "stone."

Cransac. *Village, Aveyron.* The name derives from the Gallo-Roman personal name *Carentius*, a variant of *Carantius*, and the associative suffix *-acum*.

Cranves-Sales. *Village, Haute-Savoie.* The first part of the name is of obscure origin. It may be based on a Celtic word related to Old Irish *crann*, "tree." The second part derives from Germanic *seli*, "hall," "castle."

Craon. *Town, Mayenne.* The name derives from pre-Latin *cred*, perhaps from a Gaulish root word related to Latin *creta*, "chalk," and the suffix *-onem*.

Craponne. *Town, Rhône.* The suburb of Lyon derives its name from pre-Celtic *crapp*, based on *car*, "rock," "stone," and the suffix *-onem*.

Craponne-sur-Arzon. *Village, Haute-Loire.* The name has the same origin as that of **Craponne**, with the village here distinguished by its location on the *Arzon* River.

Crau. *Region, southeastern France.* The lowland region of Provence takes its name from Medieval Latin *Cravum*, a contraction of *caravus*, from Indoeuropean *kar*, "rock." The terrain here is strewn with boulders.

La Crau. *Town, Var.* The town takes its name from **Crau**, the region of its location.

Crécy-en-Ponthieu. *Village, Somme.* The name was recorded in the 7th century as *Cressiacum* or *Crisciacum*, from the Gaulish personal name *Crixsius* and the associative suffix *-acum*. *Ponthieu* comes from Latin *Pontivus pagus*, from *pontus*, "bridge," and *pagus*, "country." The village name is often shortened to *Crécy*, especially for the battle of 1346, the first in the Hundred Years War, a victory for the English over the French.

Crécy-la-Chapelle. *Village, Seine-et-Marne*. The name shares the origin of **Crécy-en-Ponthieu**, from which, among other places, the village is distinguished by its chapel.

Créhange. *Village, Moselle*. The name was recorded in the 12th century as *Krichinga*, from the Germanic personal name *Hricho* and the suffix *-ing*.

Creil. *Town, Oise*. The name was recorded in the 7th century as *Crioilum*, from the Gaulish personal name *Critos* and *ialon*, "clearing."

Crémieu. *Village, Isère*. The name was recorded in the 12th century as *Cremiacum*, from the Gaulish personal name *Cremius* and the associative suffix *-acum*.

Créon. *Village, Gironde*. The name is of uncertain origin. It may derive from *crevonem*, an altered form of *cravonem*, from the *caravus* that gave the name of **Crau**.

Crépy. *Village, Aisne*. The name derives from the Roman personal name *Crispius* and the associative suffix *-acum*.

Crépy-en-Valois. *Town, Oise*. The origin of the name is as for **Crépy**, from which the town is distinguished by its location in **Valois**.

Le Crès. *Town, Hérault*. The suburb of Montpellier derives its name from Languedocian *cres*, Provençal *gres*, "stony," "rocky," from pre-Indoeuropean *kar*, "rock."

Crespin. *Town, Nord*. The name derives from the Roman personal name *Crispinus*, a form of *Crispius*.

Crest. *Town, Drôme*. The name represents a dialect form of French *crête*, "crest."

Crest-Voland. *Resort village, Savoie*. The first part of the name is as for **Crest**. The

distinguishing addition names nearby *Voland*.

Crêt de la Neige. *Mountain, eastern France*. The highest summit of the Jura Alps has a name meaning "crest of snow."

Créteil. *City, Val-de-Marne*. The Paris suburb has a name recorded in the 10th century as *Cristoilum*, from the Gaulish personal name *Cristos* and *ialon*, "clearing," "field."

Creuse. *Department, west central France*. The name is that of the river here, recorded in the Medieval Latin form *Crosa*, from Gaulish *croso*, "hollow," "deep," referring to its gorge.

Le Creusot. *Town, Saône-et-Loire*. The name comes from Gaulish *croso*, "hollow," and the Latin suffix *-ottum*, referring to the local topography.

Creutzwald. *Town, Moselle*. The Benedictine abbey of *Sainte-Croix* ("Holy Cross") was founded here in the 11th century and the settlement that evolved adopted a Germanic dialect form of its name, adding *wald*, "forest," for its location. The town is on the border with Germany, where it is known as *Kreuzwald*, and a fuller form of its French name is the somewhat tautological *Creutzwald-la-Croix*.

Crèvecœur-le-Grand. *Village, Oise*. The name denotes infertile land, which "breaks the heart" (*crève le cœur*) of the peasant farmer. There is a corresponding *Crèvecœur-le-Petit*.

Criel-sur-Mer. *Resort village, Seine-Maritime*. The name is of uncertain origin. It may derive from the Gaulish personal name *Critos* and the suffix *-ellum*.

Crillon. *Village, Oise*. The original name of the village was *Caigny*, from the Roman personal name *Canius* and the associative suffix *-acum*. The present name is that of the famous *Crillon* family of French soldiers, notably Louis des Balbes de Berton de *Crillon* (1541–1615), which itself came from *Crillon*, Vaucluse, a placename of uncertain origin.

Criquetot-l'Esneval. *Village, Seine-Maritime.* The name derives from the Germanic personal name *Criach* and Norse *topt,* "farmstead." The addition of the local placename *Esneval* distinguishes the village from several other places of the name here.

Le Croisic. *Town and port, Loire-Atlantique.* The town has a Breton name recorded in the 15th century as *Croaizic,* meaning "little cross."

Croissy-sur-Seine. *Town, Yvelines.* The Paris suburb, by the **Seine** River, derives its name from the Gaulish personal name *Crossius* and the associative suffix *-acum.*

Le Croisty. *Village, Morbihan.* The Brittany village derives its name from Breton *kroaz,* "cross," and *ti,* "house," as a 12th-century foundation of the Knights Templars.

Croix. *Town, Nord.* The suburb of Roubaix has a name meaning "cross" (French *croix*), referring either to a cross erected as a Christian symbol or to a crossroads (or to both).

Crolles. *Town, Isère.* The name derives from the Gaulish personal name *Crollus,* with Latin *villa,* "estate," understood.

Cro-Magnon. *Archaeological site, Dordogne.* The cave near Les Eyzies in which distinctive human skulls were found in 1868 takes its name from the local word *cro,* "cave," and the Roman personal name *Magnio, Magnionis.*

Crosne. *Town, Essonne.* The name derives from Old French *crosne,* "waterhole," a word of Gaulish origin. Crosne is at the confluence of the Seine and Yerres rivers.

Le Crotoy. *Village and port, Somme.* The name, recorded in the 12th century as now, derives from a form of Latin *crypta,* "underground cave," and the collective suffix *-etum.*

Crouy. *Village, Aisne.* The suburb of Soissons has a name recorded early as *Croviacus,* from the Gaulish personal name *Crodius* and the associative suffix *-acum.*

Crozon. *Resort town, Finistère.* The Brittany town has a name recorded in the 11th century as *Crauthon,* perhaps from pre-Breton *crav,* as for **Crau,** and the Gaulish suffix *-enna.*

Cruas. *Village, Ardèche.* The name probably derives from a form of pre-Indoeuropean *kar,* "stone," "rock," and the Gaulish suffix *-ate.* Cruas lies at the foot of a limestone cliff.

Cruseilles. *Village, Haute-Savoie.* The name derives from a diminutive form of Latin *crux, crucis,* "cross," denoting a religious memorial or a crossroads.

Cubzac-les-Ponts. *Village, Gironde.* The name derives from the Roman personal name *Cupitius* and the associative suffix *-acum.* The addition refers to the bridges (*ponts*) here over the Dordogne River.

Cucq. *Town, Pas-de-Calais.* The name probably derives from pre-Indoeuropean *cucc,* "rounded height," referring to the dunes here, near the English Channel.

Cuers. *Town, Var.* The name was recorded in the 11th century as *Corius,* from *corium,* a latinized form of *kor,* a variant of pre-Indoeuropean *kar,* "stone," "rock."

Cugnaux. *Town, Haute-Garonne.* The suburb of Toulouse derives its name from Gascon *cugn,* "corner."

Cuincy. *Town, Nord.* The name derives from the Roman personal name *Quintius* and the associative suffix *-acum.*

Cuiseaux. *Village, Saône-et-Loire.* The name may derive either from the Roman personal name *Cusillus,* from *Cusius,* or from *Cusius* and the suffix *-ellum.*

Cuise-la-Motte. *Village, Oise.* The name could derive from the Roman personal name *Cusius,* with Latin *villa,* "estate," understood, but the village lies on the edge of the Forest of Compiègne, recorded in the 6th century as *Cotia silva,* and this seems a more likely origin. The addition is "the mound."

Cuisery. *Village, Saône-et-Loire.* The name derives from the Roman personal name *Cusirius*, from *Cusius*, and the associative suffix *-acum.*

Culoz. *Village, Ain.* The name derives from a dialect form of French *culée*, a derivative of *cul*, "bottom," "end," from Latin *culus.*

Cultures. *Village, Lozère.* The name derives from Latin *cultura*, "cultivating," referring to the growing of wheat here on south-facing slopes overlooking the Lot River.

Curebourse, Col de. *Mountain road, Cantal.* The pass (*col*), above the Cère River, is one where the traveler risks being robbed, from *curer*, "to clean out," and *bourse*, "purse."

Cusset. *Town, Allier.* The name derives from the Roman personal name *Cucius* and the associative suffix *-acum.*

Cussy-la-Colonne. *Village, Côte-d'Or.* The name derives from the Roman personal name *Cucius* or *Cussius* and the associative suffix *-acum.* The addition relates to a Roman column (*colonne*) here.

Cuzac-d'Aude. *Town, Aude.* The name derives from the Gallo-Roman personal name *Cucucius*, a variant of Gaulish *Cococios*, and the associative suffix *-acum.* The distinguishing addition locates the town on the **Aude** River.

Cys-la-Commune. *Village, Aisne.* The name derives from the Gaulish personal name *Cisius.* The village was created a commune by Thibaut of Champagne in 1191.

Cysoing. *Village, Nord.* The name derives from the Gaulish personal name *Cisonius*, a derivative of *Cisius.*

Dainville. *Town, Pas-de-Calais.* The suburb of Arras derives its name from the Germanic personal name *Daginus* and Latin *villa*, "estate."

Dambach-la-Ville. *Town, Bas-Rhin.* The name derives from Germanic *dam*, "deer," and *bach*, "stream," meaning a stream where deer come to drink. The rest of the name ("the town") denotes the status of the place.

Damery. *Village, Marne.* The name derives from Latin *domnus*, "saint," and *Regius*, a saint's name not recorded anywhere else.

Damiatte. *Village, Tarn.* The name was adopted from that of *Damietta*, Egypt, commemorating the victory of St. Louis (Louis IX) there in 1250 in the Seventh Crusade.

Dammarie-les-Lys. *Town, Seine-et-Marne.* The suburb of Melun derives its name from Latin *domina*, "female saint," and *Maria*, "Mary," denoting a dedication to the Virgin Mary. The distinguishing addition is "the lilies."

Dammartin-en-Goële. *Town, Seine-et-Marne.* The name derives from Latin *domnus*, "saint," and *Martin*, meaning St. Martin of Tours, the apostle of the Gauls. The district name *Goële* serves to distinguish this Dammartin from others.

Damparis. *Village, Jura.* The suburb of Dole derives its name from Latin *domnus*, "saint," and *Patricius*, referring not to St. Patrick but to a local monk called *Paris*, who founded a monastery here around 1150.

Dampierre-en-Burly. *Village, Loiret.* The name derives from Latin *domnus*, "saint," and French *Pierre*, "Peter," here distinguished by the district name *Burly.*

Dampierre-en-Yvelines. *Village, Yvelines.* The name shares its origin with **Dampierre-en-Burly**, but here the distinctive addition names the department of **Yvelines.**

Damville. *Village, Eure.* The name apparently represents Latin *domini villa*, "estate of the lord."

Dangé-Saint-Romain. *Village, Vienne.* The name derives from an original form *Damiacum*, from the Roman or Gaulish personal name *Damius* and the associative suffix *-acum.* The dedication is to *St. Romanus*, a 4th-century martyr (or a 7th-century bishop of Rouen).

Danjoutin. *Village, Belfort*. The suburb of Belfort derives its name from Latin *domnus*, "saint," and *Justin*, 5th-century bishop of Tarbes.

Dannemarie. *Village, Haut-Rhin*. The name derives from Latin *domina*, "female saint," and *Maria*, "Mary," honoring the Virgin Mary.

Dardilly. *Town, Rhône*. The name may represent an original *Dardiliacum*, from the Roman personal name *Dardilius*, a variant of *Dardenus*, and the associative suffix *-acum*.

Darney. *Village, Vosges*. The name probably represents an original *Darniacum*, from the Gallo-Roman personal name *Darnos* and the associative suffix *-iacum*.

Dauphiné. *Historic region, southeastern France*. The nucleus of the former province was the countship of Viennois, which was originally part of the kingdom of Arles and a fief of the Holy Roman Empire. The southern part of the countship was enfiefed in the 11th century to Guigues I, count of Albon, who extended his domain to include other parts of the kingdom of Arles. His grandson, Guigues IV, count from 1133 to 1142, bore the additional name *Dauphin*, "dolphin," from the heraldic symbol on his coat of arms. This became a hereditary title of later counts of Albon, and passed from them to the province in the 13th century. In 1349 the future Charles V of France was made Dauphin of Viennois and Dauphiné was ceded to him. He became king in 1364, and in 1368 granted Dauphiné to his son, the future Charles VI, so establishing the precedent whereby the eldest son of the king of France, the heir apparent, bore the title Dauphin. Louis de France (1661–1711), the son of Louis XIV, was known as *le Grand Dauphin*. The tradition continued until 1830.

Dax. *Town, Landes*. The name is really *d'ax*, from *de* "of," and *ax*, from Latin *aquis*, the ablative (locative) plural of *aqua*, "water," referring to the hot mineral springs here. The name was recorded in the 4th century as *Aquae Tarbellicae*, from the *Tarbelli* tribe, then later as *Aquae Augustae*, "famous waters." In medieval times Dax became a viscountship under the name *Acqs*, then *Dacqs*.

Deauville. *Resort town, Calvados*. The name was recorded in the 11th century as *Auevilla*, from Germanic *auwa* or *auwja*, "damp plain," and Latin *villa*, "estate." The initial *D-* represents French *de*, "of."

Débats-Rivière-d'Orpra. *Village, Loire*. The village consists of two parishes, *Débats* and *Les Rivières-d'Orpra*, the former deriving its name from *débat*, apparently a term for the action of churning the water upstream in order to drive fish into hoop nets cast downstream, so denoting a place where this was done.

Decazeville. *Town, Aveyron*. The name is that of the French politician, duc Élie *Decazes* et de Glücksberg (1780–1860), who exploited the coal deposits here from 1826.

Dechy. *Town, Nord*. The suburb of Douai derives its name from the Gaulish personal name *Deppius* and the associative suffix *-acum*.

Décines-Charpieu. *Town, Isère*. The suburb of Lyon derives the first part of its name from the Roman personal name *Dissinius*, with Latin *villa*, "estate," understood. The second part is of uncertain origin.

Decize. *Town, Nièvre*. The name derives from the Gaulish personal name *Decetos*, latinized as *Decetius*.

La Délivrande *see* **Douvres-la-Délivrande**

Demoiselles, Grotte des. *Cavern, Hérault*. The huge limestone cavern, lined with stalactites and stalagmites, "was thus called by the peasants, who thought it the abode of the fairies or *demoiselles*" [Young, p. 371].

Denain. *Town, Nord.* The name was recorded in the 9th century as *Dononium*, from the Gaulish personal name *Donnos* and the suffix *-onem*, replaced by the Germanic suffix *-ing*.

Déols. *Town, Indre.* The suburb of Châteauroux has a name of uncertain origin. It may derive from a form of pre-Latin *tull*, "height."

Derval. *Village, Loire-Atlantique.* The name derives from Gaulish *deruos*, "oak," and the suffix *-alis*.

Descartes. *Town, Indre-et-Loire.* The town was originally known as *La Haye-en-Touraine*, "the hedged enclosure in Touraine" (see **Touraine**). In 1802 it was renamed *La Haye-Descartes*, for the philosopher René *Descartes* (1596–1650), who was born here. The present name was adopted in 1967 when the town merged with the nearby village of Balesmes.

Désertines. *Town, Allier.* The name of the suburb of Montluçon is a derivative of Latin *desertum*, "abandoned place," denoting barren ground.

Desvres. *Town, Pas-de-Calais.* The name, recorded in the 13th century as *Davre*, is of uncertain origin. A derivation in Gaulish *dubron*, "water," "river," is possible.

Dettwiller. *Village, Bas-Rhin.* The name derive from the Germanic personal name *Detto* and Latin *villare*, "farmstead." The German form of the name is *Dettweiler*.

Deuil. *Town, Val-d'Oise.* The name derives from Gaulish *deuos*, "god," and *ialon*, "clearing," "field."

Les Deux-Alpes. *Resort village, Isère.* The "two Alps" of the Alpine winter resort are the twin villages *L'Alpe-de-Mont-de-Lans* and *L'Alpe-de-Venosc*, named for two summits in the **Alps** that are themselves named for the respective villages of **Mont-de-Lans** and **Venosc**.

Deux-Chaises. *Village, Allier.* The name does not mean "two chairs" but derives from Latin *duae casae*, "two houses."

Deux-Évailles. *Village, Mayenne.* The name derives from French *deux*, "two," and Latin *aqualis*, "water pipe."

Les Deux-Fays. *Village, Jura.* The name derives from French *deux*, "two," and Latin *fageus*, "beech," an adjective here used as a noun.

Deux-Jumeaux. *Village, Calvados.* The name was recorded in the 11th century as *Duo Gemelli*, Latin for "two twins," either denoting two trees or deriving from an inn sign.

Deux-Sèvres. *Department, western France.* The name means "two Sèvres," from the local rivers *Sèvre Nantaise* and *Sèvre Niortaise* (see **Sèvre**).

Deux-Verges. *Hamlet, Cantal.* The name was recorded in the 14th century as *Duae Virgiae*, from Latin *duo*, "two," and either Old Provençal *verga*, "branch," or *verge*, "virgin." The reading is too late to determine which. The origin is probably in an inn sign in any case.

Deuxville. *Village, Meurthe-et-Moselle.* The name represents Latin *duae villae*, "two villages." The present village consists of two parishes divided by a stream.

Les Deux-Villes. *Village, Ardennes.* The two former villages of Chamouilly and Giversy combined here in the late 16th century to form the present community.

Déville-lès-Rouen. *Town, Seine-Maritime.* The suburb of Rouen apparently derives its name from Latin *Dei villa*, "village of God." The addition locates the town near (*lès*) **Rouen**.

Diane-Capelle. *Village, Moselle.* The original chapel (*Capelle*) here was rebuilt in the 17th century by *Diane* de Dommartin.

Die. *Town, Drôme.* The name was recorded in the 4th century as *Dea Augusta Vocontiorum*, from Latin *dea*, "goddess," *augustus*, "great," and the name of the *Vocontii*, a Gaulish tribe, whose capital it was. Their own name is said to mean "the twenty," from *uo-*, a form of *duo-*, "two," and *conto-*, "hundred." The present name has retained only the "goddess" element.

Dieppe. *Resort town and port, Seine-Maritime.* The name was recorded in the 11th century as *Dieppa*, from Old English *dēop*, "deep," referring to the deep water of the Arques estuary here.

Dieulefit. *Village, Drôme.* The name represents French *Dieu le fit*, "God made it," originally applied to a castle here whose site was so strong and solid that it seemed God had created it.

Dieulouard. *Town, Meurthe-et-Moselle.* The name was recorded in the 10th century as *Deilauvart*, equating to modern French *Dieu le garde*, "May God guard it."

Dieuze. *Town, Moselle.* The name probably represents an original form *Dousa*, from the Gaulish personal name *Dous*, with Latin *villa*, "estate," understood.

Digne. *Resort town, Alpes-de-Haute-Provence.* The name was recorded in the 1st century as *Dinia*, standing for *Dinia villa*, from the Roman (or possibly Gaulish) personal name *Dinius* and Latin *villa*, "village." The spa town is also known as *Digne-les-Bains* ("the baths").

La Digne-d'Amont. *Village, Aude.* The name represents *Latiniana*, from the Roman personal name *Latinius* and the suffix *-ana*, with Latin *villa*, "estate," understood. The initial *La-* of this was later taken to be French *la*, "the." The village is upstream (*amont*) on the Cougain River from *La Digne-d'Aval*, which is thus downstream (*aval*).

Digoin. *Town, Saône-et-Loire.* The name was recorded early as *Degontium*, a form of *Divicontium*, from the Gaulish personal name *Divicos* and the suffix *-ont*.

Dijon. *City, Côte-d'Or.* The name was recorded in the 6th century as *Divio, Divionis*, from the Roman personal name *Divius* (from Latin *divus*, "divine") and the suffix *-onem*.

Dinan. *Town and port, Côtes-d'Armor.*

The name represents a conjectured Gaulish original *Divonantos*, from *divos*, "holy," and *nanto*, "valley," referring to the Rance River here.

Dinard. *Resort town, Ille-et-Vilaine.* The Brittany town has the Breton name *Dinarz*, from *din*, "hill," and *arzh*, "bear," presumably referring to the outline of the hill in question.

Dives-sur-Mer. *Town and port, Calvados.* The name was recorded in the 11th century as *Portus Divae*, from the *Dives* River nearby. The river name comes from Latin (and Gaulish) *Diva*, "divine," naming the goddess believed to dwell in its waters.

Divonne-les-Bains. *Resort town, Ain.* The name was recorded in the 12th century as *Divonna*, Gaulish *Diuona*, "divine," implying "holy well," "sacred spring," and referring to the cold mineral springs here. The town is a spa with a thermal establishment ("the baths").

Dol-de-Bretagne. *Town, Ille-et-Vilaine.* The name was recorded early as *Dolum*, perhaps from the same source as **Dole**. The town is in *Brittany* (**Bretagne**).

Dole. *Town, Jura.* The Roman name of the town was *Dola Sequanorum*, from the Celtic tribe known as the *Sequani*, whose name may relate to the *Sequana*, the Roman name of the **Seine**. The main name, later *Dolum*, is perhaps from the Roman personal name *Dullus*, or else from *tul*, a variant of pre-Indoeuropean *tar* or *ter*, "hill," "height." Dole stands on a hill slope.

Dombasle-sur-Meurthe. *Town, Meurthe-et-Moselle.* The name derives from Latin *domnus*, "saint," and the personal name *Basolus*, that of a 7th-century hermit. The addition locates the town on the **Meurthe** River.

Dombrot-sur-Vair. *Village, Vosges.* The village, on the *Vair* River, was originally called *Bouzet*, from the Germanic personal name *Boso* and the associative suffix *-iacum*. It took its present name in 1715, when its lord also held *Dombrot-le-Sec* ("the dry"), some 8 miles to the south. *Dombrot* itself derives from Latin *domnus*, "saint," and the personal name *Brice*.

Domène. *Town, Isère*. The name derives from that of a wood, from Latin *dumus*, "bush," and the Gaulish suffix *-ennum*.

Domérat. *Town, Allier*. The name was recorded in the 11th century as *Domairac*, from the Roman personal name *Armalius* or *Armarius* and the associative suffix *-acum*. The initial *D-* represents *de*, "of."

Domfront. *Town, Orne*. The name was recorded in the 11th century as *Domnus Frons*, from Latin *domnus*, "saint," and the personal name *Fronto*.

Domont. *Town, Val-d'Oise*. The Paris suburb derives its name from the Germanic personal name *Dodo* and Latin *mons, montis*, "mountain."

Dompierre-sur-Besbre. *Village, Allier*. The name derives from Latin *domnus*, "saint," and French *Pierre*, "Peter." The addition names the *Besbre* River here.

Dompierre-sur-Mer. *Village, Charente-Maritime*. The name has the same origin as that of **Dompierre-sur-Besbre**, the addition locating it "on sea" (but in fact some distance from it).

Domrémy-la-Pucelle. *Hamlet, Vosges*. The name was recorded in the 16th century as *Dompremy la Pucelle*, but in the 15th century as *Dompnum Remigium*, from Latin *domnus*, "saint," and the name of *Remigius* (modern *Rémi*), 6th-century archbishop of Reims. *La Pucelle*, "the maid," refers to Joan of Arc, who was born here. See also **Arc-en-Barrois**.

Donnemarie-Dontilly. *Village, Seine-et-Marne*. The name combines two formerly separate communities. *Donnemarie* has the same origin as **Dannemarie**. *Dontilly* derives its name from the Roman personal name *Dontilius*, from *Dontio*, or *Domitilius*, from *Domitilla*, a derivative of *Domitius*, and the associative suffix *-acum*.

Donville-les-Bains. *Resort village, Manche*. The name derives from the Germanic personal name *Dono* or *Dodo* and Latin *villa*, "estate." There is bathing ("the baths") here on the English Channel coast.

Donzenac. *Village, Corrèze*. The original form of the name was probably *Domitianacum*, from the Roman personal name *Domitianus* and the associative suffix *-acum*.

Donzère. *Town, Drôme*. The name derives from pre-Gaulish *dus*, "height," and the pre-Gaulish suffix *-era*.

Donzy. *Village, Nièvre*. The name derives from the Roman personal name *Domitius* and the associative suffix *-acum*.

Le Dorat. *Village, Haute-Vienne*. The name may derive from *Dore*, as the former name of the stream here on which the town stands. It is popularly said to derive from *dorée*, "gilded," referring to the 13th-century copper angel atop the spire of St. Peter's church here, "from which (when it was gilded) the town probably took its name" [Young, p.283].

Dordogne. *Department, southwestern France*. The name is that of the river here, known to the Romans as *Duranius*, from Indoeuropean *dur* or *dor*, "current," and *anun*, "deep." The upper reaches of the Dordogne cut through a narrow gorge for almost 100 miles.

Dormans. *Village, Marne*. The name was recorded in the 11th century as *Duromannensis*, from Gaulish *duron*, "fort," and an element *man* of unknown origin.

Dortan. *Village, Ain*. The name was recorded in the 9th century as *Dortincum*, from the Germanic personal name *Dorta* and the suffix *-ing*.

Douai. *Town, Nord*. The name was recorded in the 10th century as *Doacense castellum*, from the Gaulish personal name *Dous* and the associative suffix *-acum*. Latin *castellum* is "castle."

Douarnenez. *Town, Finistère*. The Brittany town takes its name from *Doarn*, from

St. *Tutuarn*, who founded a monastery on a nearby island, and Breton *enez*, "island."

Douaumont. *Hamlet, Meuse.* The name of the former village, destroyed in World War I, was recorded in the 14th century as *Dewamont*, from *Deva*, the Gaulish goddess of a stream here (as at **Dives-sur-Mer**), and Latin *mons, montis*, "mountain," "hill."

Doubs. *Department, eastern France.* The name is that of the river here, from Gaulish *dubus*, "dark," "black," referring to the color of the water.

Douchy-les-Mines. *Town, Nord.* The name represents the Roman personal name *Dulcius* and the associative suffix *-acum*. The second part of the name refers to the former coal mines here.

Doudeville. *Village, Seine-Maritime.* The name derives from the Germanic personal name *Dodo* and Latin *villa*, "village."

Doué-la-Fontaine. *Town, Maine-et-Loire.* The name, recorded in the 9th century as *Theodadus*, is popularly taken as French *doué*, "gifted," referring to the abundance of spring water here ("the fountain"), but it really represents the Germanic personal name *Theudoad*.

Doullens. *Town, Somme.* The name was recorded in the 10th century as *Donincum*, apparently from the Gaulish personal name *Donnos* and the suffix *-incum*.

Dourdan. *Town, Essonne.* The name was recorded in the 10th century as *Dordincum*, apparently from an original *Durotincum*, itself a variant of *Tincodurum*, with Gaulish *duron*, "fort," following a first element of uncertain meaning.

Doussard. *Village, Haute-Savoie.* The name derives from the Germanic personal name *Tozohart*.

Douvaine. *Village, Haute-Savoie.* The name is Gaulish in origin but of unknown meaning.

Douvres-la-Délivrande. *Town, Calvados.* The name was recorded in the 9th cen-

tury as *Dopra*, from Gaulish *dubron*, "(current of) water." (The origin is identical to that of *Dover*, England, which the French know as *Douvres*.) Nearby *La Délivrande* is a village long visited by pilgrims to honor a statue of the Virgin Mary. Its name is thus popularly understood to mean something like "deliverer," but it is actually of Celtic origin, from the same source as **Ingrandes**.

Douvrin. *Town, Pas-de-Calais.* The name is of uncertain origin, but may represent a Germanic personal name *Dubrin* or *Dubhari* and the suffix *-ing*.

Dozulé. *Village, Calvados.* The name was recorded in the 12th century as both *Cul Uslé* and *Dorsum Uslatum*, which seems to suggest an origin in Latin *culum ustulatum*, "scorched bottom," meaning the end of a wood cleared by burning, with *culum* replaced by *dorsum*, "back," to give the present name. Dozulé is on a slight ridge ("back").

Drac. *River, southeastern France.* The Alpine river had the Medieval Latin name of *Drachum* or *Dracus*, perhaps from Occitan *drac*, "dragon," referring to the god in its waters.

Draguignan. *Town, Var.* The name was recorded in the 10th century as *Dragontano*, from the Roman personal name *Draconius* (from Latin *draco*, "dragon") and the suffix *-anum*.

Drancy. *Town, Seine-Saint-Denis.* The name was recorded in the 11th century as *Derenciacum*, from the Gallo-Roman personal name *Darentius*, from Gaulish *Darios*, and the associative suffix *-acum*.

Drap. *Town, Alpes-Maritimes.* The name may derive from a pre-Roman personal name *Drappus*.

Dravell. *Town, Essonne.* The name was recorded in the 7th century as *Dravernum*, from a Gaulish element of uncertain origin (perhaps a plant name, given *drauoca*, "rye grass"), and a subsequently altered suffix *-ernum*.

Dreux. *Town, Eure-et-Loir.* The name was recorded in the 4th century as *Durocassis*, from the Gaulish tribe *Durocasses.* (Their name is problematic, since *duro-* is "fort," and *-casses* "bronze" or "hair," words that do not readily combine to give a valid meaning.)

Drôme. *Department, southeastern France.* The name is that of the river here, from Latin *Druma* or *Droma*, from proto-Indoeuropean *drawa* or *druna*, "current," as for the *Drava* River of south central Europe.

Drulingen. *Village, Bas-Rhin.* The name derives from the Germanic personal name *Trullo* and the suffix *-ing.*

Drusenheim. *Town, Bas-Rhin.* The name derives from the Germanic personal name *Drusun* and *heim*, "abode."

Ducey. *Village, Manche.* The name derives from the Roman personal name *Dussius* or *Duccius* and the associative suffix *-acum.*

Duclair. *Village, Seine-Maritime.* The name was recorded in the 10th century as *Durclarum*, a variant of *Clarodunum*, from Latin *clarum*, "clear," and Gaulish *duron*, "fort," representing a sort of Gallo-Roman equivalent to **Clermont.**

Duesme. *Village, Côte-d'Or.* The name derives from Gaulish *dubisama*, from *dubis*, "black," "dark," and the superlative suffix *-sama*, presumably referring to a river. Duesme is at the confluence of a stream with the Seine.

Dugny. *Town, Seine-Saint-Denis.* The name derives from the Gallo-Roman personal name *Dunius*, from Gaulish *Dunos*, and the associative suffix *-acum.*

Duingt. *Resort village, Haute-Savoie.* The name may derive from the Germanic personal name *Dugo* and the suffix *-ing.*

Dunkerque. *City and port, Nord.* The city, more familiar to English speakers as *Dunkirk*, derives its name from Middle Dutch *dunen*, "dune," and *kerke*, "church," referring to the church built by the sand

dunes here on the Strait of Dover some time before the 9th century.

Dunkirk *see* **Dunkerque**

Dun-sur-Auron. *Town, Cher.* The town derives its name from Gaulish *dunon*, "hill," "fort," here distinguished by its location near the *Auron* River.

Durance. *River, southeastern France.* The river's Roman name was *Dorentia*, from Indoeuropean *dur* or *dor*, "current."

Durtal. *Town, Maine-et-Loire.* The first element of the name is of obscure origin. The second is Germanic *stall*, "stable," "inn."

Eaubonne. *Town, Val-d'Oise.* The name was recorded in the 7th century as *Aqua Putta*, from Latin *aqua*, "water," and *putus*, "pure," then in the 12th century as *Aquabona*, as if from *aqua* and *bonus*, "good."

Les Eaux-Bonnes. *Resort village, Pyrénées-Atlantiques.* The name means "good waters," referring to the sulfurous hot springs here.

Les Eaux-Chaudes. *Resort village, Pyrénées-Atlantiques.* The name means "hot waters," referring to the hot sulfur springs here.

Eauze. *Town, Gers.* The name, recorded in the 4th century as *Elusa*, is perhaps of Aquitanian origin, giving the tribal name *Elusates*, recorded by Caesar in the 1st century BC and Pliny in the 1st century AD. Their name may derive from Gaulish *elu-*, "numerous." Elusa was the capital of the *Auscii*, who gave the name of **Auch.**

Les Échelles. *Village, Savoie.* The name derives from Latin *scalae*, "ladder," "steps," referring to the steep slope here.

Échirolles. *Town, Isère.* The suburb of Grenoble has a name recorded in the 11th century as *Eschirolis*, from Low Latin *scuriolus*, "squirrel," meaning a place noted for this animal.

Eckbolsheim. *Town, Bas-Rhin.* The

name was recorded in the 9th century as *Eggiboldesheim*, from the Germanic personal name *Agebald* or *Acbold* and *heim*, "abode."

Écommoy. *Town, Sarthe.* The name was recorded in the 7th century as *Iscomodiacus*, from an obscure Gallo-Roman personal name (perhaps *Scomodius* or *Excommodius*) and the associative suffix *-acum*.

Écouen. *Town, Val-d'Oise.* The name was recorded in the 12th century as *Escuem*, from Latin *Scotomagus*, from the Gaulish personal name *Scotus* and Gaulish *magos*, "market."

Écrouves. *Town, Meurthe-et-Moselle.* The name, recorded in the 9th century as *Scribulum*, is of obscure origin.

Écully. *Town, Rhône.* The suburb of Lyon derives its name from the Gaulish personal name *Scopilius* and the associative suffix *-acum*.

Égletons. *Town, Corrèze.* The Limousin name of the town is *aus Gletous*, "on a knoll."

Éguilles. *Town, Bouches-du-Rhône.* The name was recorded in the 11th century as *Aculia*, from the Roman personal name *Aculius*, with Latin *villa*, "estate," understood, and the associative suffix *-acum*.

Eguisheim. *Village, Haut-Rhin.* The name was recorded in the 8th century as *Aginesheim*, from the Germanic personal name *Agino* and *heim*, "abode."

Éguzon-Chantôme. *Village, Indre.* The first part of the name derives from the Roman personal name *Acutius* and the suffix *-onem*. The second part, the name of a nearby place, derives from pre-Celtic *cant*, "height," and the superlative suffix *-sama*. Chantôme stands on a hillcrest.

Eincheville. *Village, Moselle.* The name derives from the Germanic personal name *Anso* and Latin *villare*, "farmstead." Until 1870 the village was known as *Einchwiller*, and the present name represents the local pronunciation, with the stress on the *i* of *-willer*.

Élancourt. *Town, Yvelines.* The name derives from the Germanic personal name *Ella* and Latin *cortem*, accusative of *cors*, "estate."

Elbeuf. *Town, Seine-Maritime.* The name was recorded in the 10th century as *Wellebou*, and in the 12th century as *Wellebued*, from the Germanic personal name *Ellebod*.

Elne. *Town, Pyrénées-Orientales.* The town was founded in the early 4th century by the Roman emperor Constantine the Great with the name *Castrum Helenae*, "fort of Helen," after his mother, St. *Helen*.

Elven. *Village, Morbihan.* The name may be that of St. *Elwin*, a 7th-century English bishop.

Embrun. *Town, Hautes-Alpes.* The Roman name of the town was *Eburodunum*, from either the Gaulish personal name *Eburo*, meaning "yew," or the *Eburones*, a Gaulish tribe whose totemic tree was the yew, and Gaulish *dunon*, "height," "fort."

Émerainville. *Town, Seine-et-Marne.* The name was recorded in the 12th century as *Hemeri*, representing the Germanic personal name *Haimrich*. French *ville*, "town," was added later to this. The middle *-ain-* is unexplained.

Enchastrayes. *Village, Alpes-de-Haute-Provence.* The name represents Latin *incastrata*, from *in*, "in," and *castrum*, "castle," meaning a place protected by a semicircle of mountains.

Enghien-les-Bains. *Resort town, Val-d'Oise.* The name of the present Paris suburb was originally given to **Montmorency** when in 1689 it passed from the duke of that name to the Condé family, dukes of *Enghien* in Belgium. It remained there until the Revolution, when the old name of Montmorency was restored and the Enghien name was adopted for this resort.

Enguinegatte. *Village, Pas-de-Calais.* The name derives from the Germanic personal name *Inguin* and *gata*, "way," "road." The name is familiar in the form *Guinegatte* for the Battle of the Spurs in 1513, when the English under Henry VIII and the Flemish under Maximilian defeated the French under Louis XII.

Ennezat. *Village, Puy-de-Dôme.* The name was recorded in the 10th century as *Enisiacus*, from the Gallo-Roman personal name *Enicius*, from Gaulish *Enos*, and the associative suffix *-acum*.

Ensisheim. *Town, Haut-Rhin.* The name derives from the Germanic personal name *Ansigis*, a variant of *Anschis*, and *heim*, "abode."

Entraigues-sur-la-Sorgue. *Town, Vaucluse.* The town has a name recorded in the 11th century as *Interaquis*, from Latin *inter aquas*, "between the waters," referring to its location between the Sorgue River (see **Sorgues**), which flows just east of the town, and the Ouvrèze.

Entraygues. *Village, Aveyron.* Also known as *Entraygues-sur-Truyère*, the village has a name recorded in the 12th century as *Antraiguas*, from Latin *inter aquas*, "between the waters," as for **Entraigues-sur-la-Sorgue**, referring to its location in the angle of the Lot and Truyère rivers.

Entre-deux-Mers. *Region, southwestern France.* The name of the wine-growing region means "between two seas," referring to its situation between the tidal waters of the Garonne and Dordogne rivers.

Entrevaux. *Village, Alpes-de-Haute-Provence.* The name derives from Latin *inter*, "between," and *vallis*, "valley," denoting a site at a confluence of two rivers, as here, where the Chalvagne flows into the Var.

Entzheim. *Village, Bas-Rhin.* The name was recorded in the 10th century as *Anisheim*, from the Germanic personal name *Anno* and *heim*, "abode."

Envermeu. *Village, Seine-Maritime.* The name is of uncertain origin, although the suffix may have been *-avum*.

Les Éparres. *Village, Isère.* The name derives from Old French *esparre*, related to English *spar*, the word for a wooden crossbar joining the two sides of a cart, or an iron bar supporting doors and windows. This literal sense is here applied to a rocky ledge on a mountainside.

Épernay. *Town, Marne.* The name was recorded in the 6th century as *Sparnacus*, from Gaulish *sparno-*, "thorn," and the associative suffix *-acum*.

Épernon. *Town, Eure-et-Loir.* The name was recorded in the 11th century as *Sparro*, an error for *Sparno*, from Gaulish *sparno-*, "thorn," and the suffix *-onem*.

Épinac. *Village, Saône-et-Loire.* The original form of the name was *Spinacum*, from the Roman personal name *Spinus* and the associative suffix *-acum*. The village is also known as *Épinay-les-Mines*, for the former coal mines here.

Épinal. *Town, Vosges.* The name was recorded in the 10th century as *Spinal*, from Latin *spina*, "thorn," "thorn bush," and the suffix *-ale*.

Épinay-sous-Sénart. *Town, Essonne.* The name of the Paris suburb derives from Latin *spina*, "thorn," "thorn bush," and Gaulish *ialon*, "clearing." The addition, referring to the Forest of *Sénart* here, distinguishes the town from **Épinay-sur-Orge** and **Épinay-sur-Seine**.

Épinay-sur-Orge. *Town, Essonne.* The town has a name of the same origin as that of **Épinay-sous-Sénart**, from which, as well as **Épinay-sur-Seine**, it is distinguished by its location on the **Orge** River.

Épinay-sur-Seine. *Town, Seine-Saint-Denis.* The Paris suburb has a name of the same origin as that of **Épinay-sous-Sénart**, from which, as well as **Épinay-sur-Orge**, it is distinguished by its location on the **Seine** River.

L'Épine. *Village, Marne.* The name, formerly spelled *Lépine*, derives from Latin *spina*, "thorn," referring to the dedication of the village, a place of pilgrimage since medieval times, to *Notre Dame de l'Épine* (Our Lady of the Crown of Thorns).

Épône. *Town, Yvelines.* The name, of obscure origin, was recorded in the 10th century as *Spedona.*

Eppeville. *Village, Somme.* The name derives from the Germanic personal name *Eppo* and Latin *villa,* "estate."

Équeurdreville-Hainneville. *Town, Manche.* The suburb of Cherbourg combines the name of two separate places. *Équeurdreville* derives from the Germanic personal name *Scildhar* and Latin *villa,* "estate." *Hainneville* represents the Germanic personal name *Hagino* and French *ville,* "town."

Éragny. *Town, Val-d'Oise.* The suburb of Pointoise, also known as *Éragny-sur-Oise,* for its location by the **Oise** River, derives its name from the Roman personal name *Herinnius* and the associative suffix *-acum.*

Ergué-Gabéric. *Town, Finistère.* The suburb of Quimper has the Breton name *Erge-Vras,* "Great Erge," by contrast with *Ergué-Armel,* with Breton name *Erge-Vihan,* "Little Erge." The meaning of the main name is uncertain.

Ermenonville. *Village, Oise.* The name was recorded in the 12th century as *Herminoltvillare,* from the Germanic personal name *Irminold* and Latin *villa,* "estate."

Ermont. *Town, Val-d'Oise.* The Paris suburb has a name of obscure origin, recorded in the 9th century as *Ermedonis viculus* (the latter word a diminutive of Latin *vicus,* "village").

Ernée. *Town, Mayenne.* The town presumably takes its name from the *Ernée* River here.

Erquinghem-Lys. *Town, Nord.* The name derives from the Germanic personal name *Ercho* and the double suffix *-ing* and *-hem.* The addition, from the *Lys* River here, distinguishes the town from nearby *Erquinghem-le-Sec* ("the dry"), not on a river.

Erquy. *Resort town and port, Côtes-d'Ar-* mor. The name of the Brittany resort, recorded in the 12th century as *Erque,* is of uncertain origin. It may represent Breton *ar c'herregi,* "the rocks."

Erstein. *Town, Bas-Rhin.* The name derives from the Germanic personal name *Ero* and *stein,* "stone."

Esbly. *Town, Seine-et-Marne.* The name derives from the Gaulish personal name *Ebelius* and the associative suffix *-acum.*

Escalquens. *Town, Haute-Garonne.* The original form of the name was probably *Scalkingos,* from the Germanic (Visigothic) personal name *Scalco* and the suffix *-ing.*

Escaudain. *Town, Nord.* The suburb of Denain derives its name from the **Escaut** River here and the suffix *-inum.*

Escaudœuvres. *Town, Nord.* The suburb of Cambrai derives its name from the **Escaut** River here and Gaulish *briga,* "height," here in the sense "fort."

Escaut. *River, northeastern France.* The river, better known as the *Scheldt,* rises in northern France, then flows north and northeast through Belgium to enter the North Sea in the Netherlands. Its Roman name was *Scaldis,* from a pre-Latin root perhaps meaning "shallow."

Escautpont. *Town, Nord.* The town derives its name from the **Escaut** River, on which it stands, and Latin *pons, pontis,* "bridge."

Eschau. *Village, Bas-Rhin.* The name derives from Germanic *ask,* "ash tree," and *au,* "wetland," "marsh."

Escornebœuf. *Village, Gers.* A lighthearted name for a place where the wind is strong enough to blow the horns off an ox (*écorner,* "to dehorn," and *bœuf,* "ox").

Espalion. *Town, Aveyron.* The name represents an early form *Spalione,* from a Gallo-Roman personal name *Spalia* and the suffix *-onem.* The first element could also derive from pre-Celtic *spal,* "cliff."

Espaly-Saint-Marcel. *Village, Haute-*

Loire. The suburb of Le-Puy-en-Velay derives its name from pre-Celtic *spal,* "cliff," and the Gaulish (and pre-Gaulish) suffix *-ate.* The addition is a dedication to the 4th-century pope (or 5th-century bishop of Paris) *St. Marcellus.*

Espira-de-l'Agly. *Village, Pyrénées-Orientales.* The name derives from the Roman personal name *Asperius* and the suffix *-anum.* The addition locates the village on the *Agly* River.

Les Essarts. *Town, Vendée.* The town takes its name from Latin *exsartum,* "preparation of land for cultivation," from *ex,* "out," and *sartum,* the supine (verbal noun) of *sarcire,* "to mend," "to repair."

Les Essarts-le-Roi. *Town, Yvelines.* The name has the same origin as for *Les Essarts* (see **Essarts, Les**), with the addition ("the king") denoting a royal connection.

Essey-lès-Nancy. *Town, Meurthe-et-Moselle.* The suburb of Nancy has a name recorded in the 10th century as *Aciacum,* from the Roman personal name *Ascius* or *Assius* and the associative suffix *-acum.* The addition denotes a location near (*lès*) **Nancy.**

Essonne. *Department, north central France.* The department, created in 1964, is named for the river here, from Medieval Latin *Exona,* of the same origin as the **Aisne** (but stressed on the second syllable).

Estagel. *Village, Pyrénées-Orientales.* The name represents a diminutive form of Old Occitan *estatge,* "residence."

Estaires. *Town, Nord.* The name was recorded in the 8th century as *Stegras,* from Germanic *steger,* "mooring place." The town is on the Lys River.

Esterel. *Mountain range, southeastern France.* The name was recorded in the 14th century as *Estelell,* perhaps from Greek *stēlē,* "pillar," or more likely from pre-Indoeuropean *est,* "rock," and the Ligurian suffix *-elu.*

Estrées-Saint-Denis. *Village, Oise.* The name represents Latin *strata,* "street," here

as usually elsewhere denoting a Roman road. The addition is a dedication to *St. Denis,* 3d-century bishop of Paris.

Esvres. *Town, Indre-et-Loire.* The town has a pre-Latin name of uncertain origin.

Étables-sur-Mer. *Resort village, Côtes-d'Armor.* The Brittany village derives its name from Latin *stabulum,* "stable," "inn." It is "on sea" by the English Channel.

Étain. *Village, Meuse.* The name was recorded in the 9th century as *Stagnum,* Latin for "piece of standing water," "pool."

Étampes. *Town, Essonne.* The name represents Low Latin *Stampae,* of unknown origin.

L'Étang-la-Ville. *Town, Yvelines.* The name was recorded in the 12th century as *Stagnum,* Latin for "piece of standing water," "pond." The addition ("the town") denotes the town's proximity to Paris (formally designated *la ville de Paris*).

Étaples. *Town and port, Pas-de-Calais.* The settlement here was recorded in the 8th century as *Wic,* from Latin *vicus,* "village." In the 9th century the town is documented as *Stapulae,* from Old French *estaple,* "entrepôt."

Étel. *Village, Morbihan.* The Breton village has a name of uncertain origin.

Étival-Clairefontaine. *Village, Vosges.* The name was recorded in the 9th century as *Stivagium,* from Latin *aestaticum,* "place of pasturing cattle in summer," with the form of the name influenced by Latin *vallis,* "valley." The second part of the name means "clear spring."

Étrechy. *Town, Essonne.* The name derives from Latin *stirps,* "tree stump," and the associative suffix *-iacum,* although the Roman personal name *Stirpius* could also offer an origin.

Étreham *see* **Ouistreham**

Étrépagny. *Village, Eure.* The name was recorded in the 7th century as *Sterpinacium,* from Low Latin *sterpinium,* "land full of tree stumps," and the associative suffix -acum. The Roman personal name *Sterpinius* could also be considered as an origin.

Étretat. *Village and port, Seine-Maritime.* Early forms of the name are *Strutat*, recorded in the 11th century, and later *Estrudard*, *Estrefal*, *Estretal*, and *Estretat*. The origin is uncertain, but the following have been tentatively (and in some cases fancifully) proposed: (1) Old Scandinavian *stadr*, "place," preceded by *stur*, "great," or the personal name *Thor*; (2) Old Scandinavian *strutr*, "cone-shaped ornament on headdress"; (3) Old Scandinavian *strud*, "point"; (4) Old Norman *West Tot*, "western hamlet"; (5) Medieval Latin *stratae talus*, "end of the road"; (6) Latin *ex structa ardua*, from *structus*, "layered," "heaped up," and *arduus*, "high," "steep." A source in Germanic *thur*, "door," has also been suggested, while a map of 1534 is said to have shown the name as *Esttretat*, supposedly a misreading of *ici est tr etat*, "here is state treasure," with *tr* an abbreviated form of *tresor*, "treasure."

Eu. *Town, Seine-Maritime.* The name was recorded in the 10th century as *Auga* or *Alga*, from Germanic *auwa*, "island," "wet plain." Eu is an inland port on the Bresle River, near its mouth on the English Channel.

Eugénie-les-Bains. *Resort village, Landes.* The village, with its springs ("the baths"), has a modern name commemorating the empress *Eugénie* (1826-1920), wife of Napoleon III.

Eure. *Department, northwestern France.* The name is that of the river here, known to the Romans as *Audura*, from Gaulish *Autura*, probably a shortened form of *Avitura*, from the root element *av*, "water," and *ur*, "water." Hence *Autricum*, the Roman name of **Chartres**.

Eure-et-Loir. *Department, northwestern France.* The name is that of the department's two main rivers, the **Eure** in the north and the **Loir** in the south.

Évaux. *Resort village, Creuse.* The name derives from a pre-Latin root of uncertain

origin and the Gaulish suffix -aulo. The village is also known as *Évaux-les-Bains* ("the baths") for its hot springs.

Évian-les-Bains. *Resort town, Haute-Savoie.* The name of the spa town was recorded in the 8th century as *Laquatico*, from Latin *aquianum*, a derivative of *aqua*, "water." The addition ("the baths") refers to the mineral springs here.

Évin-Malmaison. *Town, Pas-de-Calais.* The name derives from the Germanic personal name *Agiwin*. The second part of the name means "bad house," implying one built on unsuitable ground.

Évrecy. *Village, Calvados.* The name derives from the Germanic personal name *Eboric* and the associative suffix -iacum.

Évreux. *City, Eure.* The name was recorded in the 4th century as *Civitas Ebroicorum*, from Latin *civitas*, "city," and *Eburovices*, the Gaulish tribe whose capital it was and who also gave the name of **Embrun**. Their own name means "conquering with the yew," from Gaulish *eburos*, "yew," and *-uices*, "who conquer" (the source of Latin *vincere*, "to conquer"). They presumably made their spears or bows from yew wood. The earlier Roman name for what is now *Le Vieil-Évreux* was *Mediolanum*, "middle of the plain," as for **Meulan**.

Évron. *Town, Mayenne.* The name derives from the Gaulish personal name *Eburos* and (probably) *magos*, "market."

Évry. *City, Essonne.* The name was recorded in the 11th century as *Avriacum*, from the Gallo-Roman personal name *Eburo*, "yew," as for **Embrun**, and the associative suffix -acum.

Excideuil. *Village, Dordogne.* The name was recorded in the 6th century as *Exidolium*, from Gaulish *ialon*, "clearing," and a first element of obscure origin.

Exincourt. *Village, Doubs.* The suburb of Montbéliard derives its name from a Germanic personal name (perhaps *Answin*) and Latin *cortem*, accusative of *cors*, "estate."

Eybens. *Town, Isère.* The suburb of Grenoble has a name with a first element of uncertain origin. The second element may be either Gaulish *-inco* or Germanic *-ing.*

Eyguières. *Town, Bouches-du-Rhône.* The name was recorded in the 11th century as *Aqueria,* of obscure origin. A connection with French *aiguière,* "ewer," in a transferred sense, is not appropriate for the topology.

Eymet. *Village, Dordogne.* The name was recorded in the 14th century as *Aymetum,* perhaps from the Gaulish personal name *Aimos* and the suffix *-eto.*

Eymoutiers. *Village, Haute-Vienne.* The name, recorded in the 9th century as *Agentum,* is a contraction of a form such as *Aenmoutier,* from the Gaulish placename *Agentum* and Latin *monasterium,* "monastery."

Ézanville, *Town, Val-d'Oise.* The Paris suburb derives its name from the accusative form of the Germanic personal name *Heiza* and Latin *villa,* "estate."

Èze. *Village, Alpes-Maritimes.* The name was recorded in the 4th century as *Avisio,* from a pre-Celtic root *av* of uncertain meaning. The village, overlooking the Mediterranean, is not far from the border with Italy, where it is known as *Eza.*

Ézy-sur-Eure. *Village, Eure.* The name was recorded early as *Asiacum,* from the Roman personal name *Asius* and the associative suffix *-acum.* The village is on the **Eure** River.

Fabrègues. *Town, Hérault.* The name represents a southern form of Latin *fabrica,* "workshop."

Faches-Thumesnil. *Town, Nord.* The suburb of Lille derives the first part of its name from Germanic *fak,* "enclosure." The second part, the name of a nearby hamlet, is of uncertain origin, but may represent Germanic *thu,* "farm," and Latin *mansionile,* "peasant dwelling," "house with a plot of land." The two names combined in 1914. The spelling of *Faches* long varied between *Fâches* and *Faches,* but in 1951 the form without the circumflex was officially adopted.

Fagnières. *Town, Marne.* The name was recorded in the 6th century as *Fascinariae,* from Latin *fascina,* "faggot," and the suffix *-aria,* denoting a wood.

Falaise. *Town, Calvados.* The town's name, recorded in the 11th century as *Falesia,* is the French word for "cliff," referring to the escarpment on which the medieval castle stands here.

Fanjeaux. *Village, Aude.* The name derives from Latin *fanum Jovis,* "temple of Jupiter."

Le Faouët. *Village, Morbihan.* The name derives from Latin *fagus,* "beech," and the collective suffix *-etum.*

Farébersviller. *Town, Moselle.* The name derives from the Germanic personal name *Farabert* and Latin *villare,* "farmstead."

La Fare-les-Oliviers. *Town, Bouches-du-Rhône.* The name derives from Germanic *fara,* properly "family," here probably denoting a family estate. The addition means "the olive trees."

Faremoutiers. *Village, Seine-et-Marne.* The original name of the settlement here was recorded in the early 7th century as *Eboriacum,* with the same origin as **Évry.** The present name derives from the female personal name *Fare,* that of the woman who founded a nunnery here around 615, and Latin *monasterium,* "monastery."

La Farlède. *Town, Var.* The name derives from Latin *ferula,* "fennel," and the collective suffix *-eta.*

Faucigny. *Valley, Haute-Savoie.* The valley of the Arve River is named for a castle here, itself so called from the Roman personal name *Fulcinius* and the associative suffix *-acum.*

Le Fauga. *Village, Haute-Garonne.* The name derives from Latin *filex,* "fern," and the suffix *-arium.*

Faulquemont. *Town, Moselle.* The name derives from the Germanic personal name *Falco* and Latin *mons, montis,* "mountain." The town is not far from the border with Germany, where it is known as *Falkenberg.*

Faverges. *Town, Haute-Savoie.* The name shares the exact origin of **Fabrègues**.

Fayence. *Village, Var.* The name was recorded in the 10th century as *Fagentia,* from Latin *fagus,* "beech," and the suffix *-entia.*

Fécamp. *Resort town, Seine-Maritime.* The name was recorded early as as *Fiscannum,* from Germanic *fisk,* "fish," and *hafn,* "port." Fécamp was an active fishing port down to the 17th century, when it was superseded by Le Havre.

Fegersheim. *Village, Bas-Rhin.* The name derives from the Germanic personal name *Fagher* and *heim,* "abode."

Feignies. *Town, Nord.* The name derives from the Roman personal name *Fenius* and the associative suffix *-acum.*

Felletin. *Town, Creuse.* The name derives from the Germanic personal name *Feletheus* and the suffix *-inum.*

Fenain. *Town, Nord.* The name may have evolved from an original form *Fidenanum,* from the Roman personal name *Fidenus* and the suffix *-anum.*

Fénétrange. *Village, Moselle.* The name derives from the Germanic personal name *Filista* and the suffix *-ing.*

La Fère. *Town, Aisne.* The name derives from Germanic *fara,* "family," here denoting a family estate.

Fère-Champenoise. *Village, Marne.* The name derives from Germanic *fara,* "family," meaning a family estate, and *Champenoise,* the (feminine) adjectival form of **Champagne.**

Fère-en-Tardenois. *Town, Aisne.* The name derives from Germanic *fara,* "family," meaning a family estate, and the local regional name *Tardenois.*

Ferney-Voltaire. *Town, Ain.* The Old French name of the town was *Fernay,* from the Roman personal name *Ferennus,* a variant of *Ferentus,* and the associative suffix *-acum.* The writer *Voltaire* lived here from 1759 to his death in 1778, and his name was added at the time of the Revolution, then again in 1881.

Ferrette. *Village, Haut-Rhin.* The village was originally a fortified settlement, and its name may thus be an altered form of Latin *firmitas,* "firmness," "strength."

La Ferrière. *Village, Vendée.* The name derives from Latin *ferraria,* from *ferrum,* "iron," and the suffix *-aria,* denoting a forge.

Ferrière-la-Grande. *Town, Nord.* The suburb of Mauberg derives its name from Latin *ferraria,* from *ferrum,* "iron," and *-aria,* denoting an iron mine. The addition ("the great") distinguishes the town from nearby *Ferrière-la-Petite.*

Ferrières. *Village, Loiret.* The name derives from Latin *ferraria,* from *ferrum,* "iron," and the suffix *-aria,* denoting here, as elsewhere, either forges or iron mines.

La Ferté-Alais. *Village, Essonne.* The first part of the name is Old French *ferté,* "fortress," from Latin *firmitas, firmitatis,* "firmness," from *firmus,* "firm." The second part represents the Germanic female name *Adelhaidis.*

La Ferté-Bernard. *Town, Sarthe.* The first part of the name is as for *La Ferté-Alais* (see **Ferté-Alais, La**). The second part represents the Germanic personal name *Bernhard.*

La Ferté-Gaucher. *Village, Seine-et-Marne.* The first part of the name is as for *La Ferté-Alais* (see **Ferté-Alais, La**). The second part represents the Germanic personal name *Walhahari.*

La Ferté-Macé. *Town, Orne.* The first part of the name is as for *La Ferté-Alais* (see **Ferté-Alais, La**). The second part represents the personal name *Mathieu.*

La Ferté-Milon. *Village, Aisne.* The first part of the name is as for *La Ferté-Alais* (see **Ferté-Alais, La**). The second part represents the Germanic personal name *Milo*.

La Fertés-Saint-Aubin. *Town, Loiret.* The first part of the name is as for *La Ferté-Alais* (see **Ferté-Alais, La**). The second part represents a dedication to *St. Albinus*, 6th-century bishop of Angers (or 4th-century bishop of Lyon).

La Ferté-sous-Jouarre. *Town, Seine-et-Marne.* The first part of the name is as for *La Ferté-Alais* (see **Ferté-Alais, La**). The second part denotes that the town is near (*sous*) **Jouarre**.

Fesches-le-Châtel. *Village, Doubs.* The name derives from Latin *fisca*, the feminine form of *fiscus*, "treasury," here in the sense of a house belonging to the church. The second part of the name represents Latin *castellum*, "castle."

Fessenheim. *Village, Haut-Rhin.* The name derives from the Germanic personal name *Fezzo* and *heim*, "abode."

Feuquières-en-Vimeu. *Village, Somme.* The name derives from Latin *filicaria*, "fern." The second part of the name is that of the local region *Vimeu*, itself named for the *Vimeuse* River.

Feurs *see* **Forez**

Feytiat. *Town, Haute-Vienne.* The name derives from the Roman personal name *Festius* and the associative suffix *-acum*.

Feyzin. *Town, Rhône.* The suburb of Lyon has a name that was perhaps originally *Fasianum*, from the Roman personal name *Fasius*, a variant of *Fassius*, and the suffix *-anum*.

Figeac. *Town, Lot.* The name was recorded in the 8th century as *Figiacus*, from the Roman personal name *Fidius* or *Fibius*, a variant of *Fabius*, and the associative suffix *-acum*.

Finistère. *Department, northwestern France.* The department, at the western end of the Brittany peninsula, takes its name from Latin *finis terrae*, "end of the land," a rendering of the Breton name *Penn-ar-Bed*, "head of the world," from *penn*, "head," *ar*, "the," and *bed*, "world." The Latin name has its counterpart in *Cape Finisterre*, a promontory in northwestern Spain, in *Land's End*, the westernmost peninsula in Cornwall, England, and in *Pembroke*, a town near the coast in southwestern Wales, UK, where the name represents Welsh *Pen-fro*, from *pen*, "head," and *bro*, "land." All these "land's ends" are on western coasts, suggesting a common drive to the west.

Firminy. *Town, Loire.* The name was recorded in the 10th century as *Firminiaco*, from the Roman personal name *Firminius* and the associative suffix *-acum*.

Fismes. *Town, Marne.* The name probably represents Latin *finibus*, the ablative (locative) plural form of *finis*, "end," "limit," denoting a place located at the limit of two Gaulish cities. However, the *m* in the name is hard to explain.

Fitz-James. *Village, Oise.* The village was originally called *Warty*, from the Germanic personal name *Warto* and the associative suffix *-iacum*. In 1710 it was erected into a dukedom and peerdom for James *Fitzjames*, duke of Berwick (1670-1734), illegitimate son of James II of England. (Anglo-Norman *fitz* corresponds to French *fils*, "son," and can indicate an illegitimate son when followed by the name of a royal parent, as here.)

Fixin. *Village, Côte-d'Or.* The name is a diminutive form of *Fixey*, a nearby hamlet, itself from the Roman personal name *Fiscius* and the associative suffix *-acum*.

Flamanville. *Village, Manche.* The name was recorded in the 10th century as *Flamenovilla*, from the personal name *Flamand* ("Fleming," i.e. a person from Flanders) and Latin *villa*, "estate," "village."

Flanders. *Region, northern France.* The region, known in French as *Flandre* or *Flandres*, extends along the North Sea and to the west of the Scheldt River. Its French part, known also in English as *French Flanders*, is bounded to the east by the border with Belgium, where its Flemish name is *Vlaanderen*. The name probably comes from Flemish *vlakte*, "plain," or *vlak*, "flat," and *wanderen* or *wandelen*, "to wander," implying an extensive level region.

La Flèche. *Town, Sarthe.* The name was recorded in the 11th century as *Feza, Fecia* and *Fissa*, among others. The origin may lie in the Roman personal name *Fiscius*, or in Latin *fiscus*, "treasury." The present form of the name has been influenced by *flèche*, "arrow."

Flers. *Town, Orne.* The name may come from Germanic *hlara*, "common pasture land." The town is also known as *Flers-de-l'Orne*, although not actually on the **Orne** River.

Flers-en-Escrebieux. *Town, Nord.* The suburb of Douai shares the origin of its name with **Flers**, here distinguished by its location in the district of *Escrebieux*.

Flesselles. *Village, Somme.* The name derives from Old French *flais*, "faggot," as applied to a bundle of thin branches used for fishing, and the suffix *-aria*, later replaced by *-elles*.

Fleurance. *Town, Gers.* The name, recorded in 1289 as *Florencie*, was originally that of a medieval stronghold here, itself named after the Italian town of *Florence*.

Fleury. *Village, Aude.* The original name of the settlement, as recorded in the 11th century, was *Perignanum*, from the Roman personal name *Perennius* and the suffix *-anum*. In 1736 the village was raised to a dukedom and peerdom for Jean-Hercule de Rosset de *Fleury*, and renamed for him.

Fleury-les-Aubrais. *Town, Loiret.* The suburb of Orléans derives its name from the Roman personal name *Florus* and the associative suffix *-acum*. The distinguishing addition is a local placename.

Fleury-Mérogis. *Town, Essonne.* The first part of the name is as for **Fleury-les-Aubrais.** The second part is a local placename.

Fleury-sur-Andelle. *Village, Eure.* The first part of the name is as for **Fleury-les-Aubrais.** The second part locates the village on the *Andelle* River here.

Fleury-sur-Orne. *Village, Calvados.* The suburb of Caen, on the **Orne** River, shares the origin of its name with that of **Fleury-les-Aubrais.**

Flines-lez-Raches. *Town, Nord.* The name derives from Latin *figlina*, a form of *figulina*, "potter's workshop." The addition locates the town near (*lez*) *Raches*, itself named for the river here.

Flins-sur-Seine. *Village, Yvelines.* The Paris suburb derives its name from Latin *figulinum*, "potter's work." The distinguishing addition locates it on the **Seine**.

Floirac. *Town, Gironde.* The suburb of Bordeaux derives its name from the Roman personal name *Florus* and the associative suffix *-acum*.

Florac. *Village, Lozère.* The name has the same origin as that of **Floirac**.

Florange. *Town, Moselle.* The name derives from a Germano-Roman personal name *Flor* and the Germanic suffix *-ing*.

Florensac. *Village, Hérault.* The name was recorded in the 10th century as *Florencagium*, from the Roman personal name *Florentius* and the associative suffix *-acum*.

Foëcy. *Village, Cher.* The name was recorded in the 14th century as *Fossiacum*, from the Roman personal name *Fuscius* and the associative suffix *-acum*.

Foix. *Town, Ariège.* The name was recorded in the 9th century as *Fuxum*, of pre-Celtic origin but unknown meaning.

Folembray. *Village, Aisne.* The name probably derives from a Germanic personal name such as *Folabraht*.

Le Folgoët. *Village, Finistère.* The second part of the name is Breton *goet*, "wood." The first part is of obscure origin.

Folschviller. *Town, Moselle.* The name derives from the Germanic personal name *Fulco* and Latin *villare,* "farmstead." The town is close to the border with Germany, where it is known as *Folschweiler.*

Fondettes. *Town, Indre-et-Loire.* The suburb of Tours has a name of uncertain origin. The place is on a plateau, so any connection with French *fond,* "bottom," seems unlikely.

Fonsorbes. *Town, Haute-Garonne.* The name derives from Latin *fons,* "spring," and Old Provençal *orba,* "blind," presumably denoting a hidden spring or well.

Fontaine. *Town, Isère.* The suburb of Grenoble takes its name from Latin *fontana,* "fountain."

Fontainebleau. *Town, Seine-et-Marne.* The name was recorded in the 12th century as *Fontem Blahaud,* from Latin *fontana,* "fountain," and the Germanic personal name *Blahaud* (from *Blitwald*).

Fontaine-de-Vaucluse *see* **Vaucluse**

Fontaine-Henry. *Village, Calvados.* The name was recorded in the 13th century as *Fontes Henrici,* from Latin *fontana,* "fountain," and the personal name *Henricus,* that of the local lord.

Fontaine-le-Dun. *Village, Seine-Maritime.* The name derives from Latin *fontana,* "fountain," and the *Dun* River, which at one time rose near here.

Fontaine-lès-Dijon. *Town, Côte-d'Or.* The suburb of Dijon derives its name from Latin *fontana,* "fountain," and its location near (*lès*) **Dijon.**

Fontaine-sur-Saône. *Town, Rhône.* The suburb of Lyon derives its name from Latin *fontana,* "fountain," and its location on the **Saône** River.

Fontenay-aux-Roses. *Town, Hauts-de-Seine.* The name of the Paris suburb was recorded in the 10th century as *Fontanetum,* from Latin *fontana,* "fountain," and the collective suffix *-etum.* The addition means "by the roses."

Fontenay-le-Comte. *Town, Vendée.* The name was recorded in the 11th century as *Fontanetum,* from Latin *fontana,* "fountain," and the collective suffix *-etum.* The distinguishing addition, meaning "the count," dates from the 13th century, when Louis IX appointed a count to oversee this new capital of Bas-Poitou.

Fontenay-le-Fleury. *Town, Yvelines.* The name was recorded in the 12th century as *Fontanetum,* from Latin *fontana,* "fountain," and the collective suffix *-etum.* The distinguishing addition has a name of the same origin as that of **Fleury-les-Aubrais.**

Fontenay-sous-Bois. *Town, Val-de-Marne.* The name of the Paris suburb was recorded in the 9th century as *Fontanetum,* from Latin *fontana,* "fountain," and the collective suffix *-etum.* The distinguishing addition ("by the wood") refers to the Bois de Vincennes nearby.

Fontenay-Trésigny. *Town, Seine-et-Marne.* The first part of the name derives from Latin *fontana,* "fountain," and the collective suffix *-etum.* The second part names a nearby place.

Fontevrault-l'Abbaye. *Village, Maine-et-Loire.* The name was recorded in the 12th century as *Fons Evraldi,* from Latin *fons,* "spring," and *Evraldus,* the Latin form of the Germanic personal name *Ebrald.* The Benedictine abbey that gave the second part of the name was founded in 1101.

Fontoy. *Town, Moselle.* The name derives from Latin *fons, fontis,* "spring," and the collective suffix *-etum.*

Font-Romeu. *Resort village, Pyrénées-Orientales.* The winter-sports center has a chapel with a statue of the Virgin Mary and a "miraculous" fountain that attracts pilgrims. Hence the name, meaning "pilgrim's fountain." The full name of the village is *Font-Romeu-Odeillo-Via,* the additions being the names of two nearby places. (The latter, recorded in the 9th century as *Avizano,* derives from the Roman personal name *Avitius* and the suffix *-anum.*)

Fontvieille. *Village, Bouches-du-Rhône.* The name was recorded in the 12th century as *Fonoietl* (a scribal error for *Fonvietl*), from Latin *fons*, "spring," and *vetula*, "old."

Forbach. *Town, Moselle.* The name was recorded in the 10th century as *Furpac*, from Germanic *fohra*, "spruce," and *bach*, "stream."

Forcalquier *Village, Alpes-de-Haute-Provence.* The name was recorded in the 11th century as *Forcalcherio*, from Latin *Forcalquerium* or *Forum Calcarium*, from *furnus*, "oven," and *calcarius*, the adjectival form of *calx, calcis*, "lime."

La Force. *Village, Dordogne.* The name was recorded in the 14th century as *Forcia*, from Low Latin *fortia*, "fortress."

Forez. *Region, east central France.* The historic region, a medieval countship, takes its name from Latin *Forensis pagus*, "land of Feurs," from the town of *Feurs*, Loire, its former capital. Its own name, from Latin *forum*, "public square," "market," was recorded in the 4th century as *Forum Segusiavorum*, from the *Segusiavi* tribe, whose capital it was. Their own name is based on Gaulish *sego-*, "victory," "strength."

Forges-les-Eaux. *Resort village, Seine-Maritime.* The name derives from French *forge*, "forge," "smithy," itself from Latin *fabrica*, "workshop." The second part of the name ("the waters") refers to the cold mineral springs here.

Formerie. *Village, Oise.* The name was recorded in the 9th century as *Framerie*, from the Germanic personal name *Framerich* and the suffix *-iaca*.

Formigny. *Village, Calvados.* The name was recorded in the 12th century as *Formigneium*, from the Roman personal name *Forminius*, from *Formius*, and the associative suffix *-acum*.

Fort-Mardyck. *Town, Nord.* The first part of the name denotes a modern military fort here. The second part names its site, from Middle Dutch *mare*, "piece of standing water," "pool," and *dijc*, "dyke."

Fos, Golfe de. *Sea inlet, southeastern France.* The inlet of the Golfe du Lion takes its name from the nearby town of *Fos-sur-Mer*, recorded in Roman times as *Fossa Mariana*, from the ditch or trench (Latin *fossa*) dug here in 106 BC by the Roman general Marius. *Fos-sur-Mer*, now understood as "Fos-on-Sea," thus really evolved from *Fossa Mariana*.

Fosses. *Town, Val-d'Oise.* The name derives from Latin *fossa*, "ditch," "little valley."

Fos-sur-Mer *see* **Fos, Golfe du**

Fougères. *Town, Ille-et-Vilaine.* The name was recorded in the 12th century as *Fulgerii*, from Latin *filicaria*, "fern" (French *fougère*).

Fougerolles. *Town, Haute-Saône.* The name shares the origin of **Fougères**.

La Fouillouse. *Town, Loire.* The name derives from Latin *folia*, "leaf," "wood," and the suffix *-osa*.

Foulayronnes. *Town, Lot-et-Garonne.* The name is traditionally derived from Latin *fons latrorum*, "spring of thieves," but a more likely origin is Old Provençal *folaire*, "presser," meaning a vineyard worker who presses grapes at the time of the wine harvest.

Fouquières-lès-Lens. *Town, Pas-de-Calais.* The name derives from Latin *filicaria*, "fern" (French *fougère*). The addition locates the town near (*lès*) **Lens**.

Fourchambault. *Town, Nièvre.* The name derives from Latin *furnus*, "oven" (for a manufacturing process), and the personal name *Archambaud*.

Fourmies. *Town, Nord.* The name derives from the Roman personal name *Formius* and the associative suffix *-acum*.

Fourques. *Village, Gard.* The name represents Old French *fourc*, Old Provençal *forc*, "fork," meaning a fork in the road, from Latin *furca* in the same sense.

Fourqueux. *Village, Gard.* The Paris

suburb derives its name from Latin *filex*, "fern," and the suffix *-osum*.

Fraisses. *Village, Loire*. The name derives from Latin *fraxinum*, "ash tree."

Fraize. *Town, Vosges*. The name derives from Low Latin *fractia*, from *fracta*, "breach," "cleft."

Framecourt. *Village, Pas-de-Calais*. The name was recorded in the 11th century as *Wulfrancourt*, from the Germanic personal name *Wulfran* and Latin *cortem*, accusative of *cors*, "estate." By the 14th century the name was appearing as *Auframacourt*. The initial *Au-* of this was taken as French *au*, "at the," and so was dropped as if not part of the name.

France. *Country, western Europe*. The Latin name of France was *Francia*, from *Francus*, "Frank," referring to the *Franks*, the Germanic people who invaded and settled in what was then Gaul from the 3d century AD. The name of the Franks themselves is of uncertain origin. It is popularly related to *frank*, meaning a people who were free, not enslaved, but a more likely source is in the Germanic word *wrang*, from *wringen*, "to twist" (English *wring*), denoting those who have been "wrung" or wrenched from their native land.

France, Île de *see* **Île de France**

Franche-Comté. *Region, east central France*. The name of the present administrative region means "free countship" (French *comté*, now masculine, was originally feminine), referring to the countship of Burgundy, as distinct from the duchy of Burgundy, further to the west. In 1032 the former kingdom of Burgundy passed to the Holy Roman emperor Conrad II, and in 1127 one of its counts, Raynald III, refused to do homage to king (later Holy Roman emperor) Lothair III. He thus became a "free count" (German *Freigraf*), and his territory became *Franche-Comté*.

Francheville. *Town, Rhône*. The suburb of Lyon derives its name from French *franc*, "free," "enfranchized," and Latin *villa*, "estate."

Franconville. *Town, Val-d'Oise*. The Paris suburb derives its name from the Germanic personal name *Franco* and Latin *villa*, "estate."

Franqueville-Saint-Pierre. *Town, Seine-Maritime*. The name shares the origin of **Francheville**, while the addition is a dedication to *St. Peter*.

Fréjus. *Town, Var*. The name evolved from the town's Roman name, *Forum Julii*, referring to the market (Latin *forum*) founded here in 49 BC by *Julius* Caesar.

French Riviera *see* **Côte d'Azur**

Freneuse. *Village, Yvelines*. The name derives from Latin *fraxinum*, "ash tree," and the suffix *-osa*.

Le Freney-d'Oisans. *Resort village, Isère*. The name shares the origin of **Fresnay-sur-Sarthe**, with the addition from the *Oisans* valley here.

Fresnay-sur-Sarthe. *Village, Sarthe*. The name derives from a shortened form of Latin *fraxinum*, "ash tree," and the collective suffix *-etum*. The addition locates the village on the **Sarthe** River.

Fresnes. *Town, Val-de-Marne*. The Paris suburb derives its name from Latin *fraxinum*, "ash tree."

Fresnes-sur-Escaut. *Town, Nord*. The name is identical in origin to that of **Fresnes**, with the addition locating the town on the **Escaut** River.

Fresnoy-le-Grand. *Village, Aisne*. The name derives from a shortened form of Latin *fraxinum*, "ash tree," and the collective suffix *-etum*. The addition is "the great."

Fresse-sur-Moselle. *Village, Moselle*. The name shares the origin of **Fraize**, but with an addition locating the village on the **Moselle** River.

Fréteval. *Village, Loir-et-Cher*. The name derives from Latin *fractus*, "broken," and *vallis*, "valley," denoting a valley eroded by a current of water. Fréteval is on the Loir River.

Fretin. *Village, Nord.* The name derives from the Germanic personal name *Fridin.*

La Frette-sur-Seine. *Town, Val-d'Oise.* The name derives from Latin *fracta*, "broken," here referring to ground that has been dug out to form an entrenchment or fortification. The addition locates the town on the **Seine.**

Frévent. *Town, Pas-de-Calais.* The name, of uncertain origin, was recorded in the 12th century as *Fevrent.* A personal name may be involved.

Freyming-Merlebach. *Town, Moselle.* The town, on the German border, combines two names. *Freyming* derives from the Germanic personal name *Fretmod* and the suffix *-ing. Merlebach* derives from the Germanic personal name *Merila* and *bach*, "stream."

Friville-Escarbotin. *Town, Somme.* The first part of the name may derive from the Germanic personal name *Frido* and Latin *villa*, "estate." The second part is of uncertain origin.

Froges. *Village, Isère.* The name derives from the Germanic personal name *Frotgius.*

Fronsac. *Village, Gironde.* The name derives from the Roman personal name *Frontius* and the associative suffix *-acum.*

Frontenay-Rohan-Rohan. *Village, Deux-Sèvres.* The first part of the name derives from the Roman personal name *Frontenas*, from *Fronto*, and the associative suffix *-acum.* The duplicated second part refers to the combined dukedom and peerdom raised here in 1714 for Hercule Mériadec de *Rohan* (1669-1749).

Frontignan. *Town, Hérault.* The name was recorded in the 12th century as *Frontinianum*, from the Roman personal name *Frontinius* and the suffix *-anum.*

Fronton. *Village, Haute-Garonne.* The name derives from the Roman personal

name *Fronto, Frontonis*, or from the personal name *Frontus* and the suffix *-onem.*

Frouard. *Town, Meurthe-et-Moselle.* The name derives from the Germanic personal name *Frothard.*

Fruges. *Village, Pas-de-Calais.* The name may derive from Latin *fraucia*, a variant of *frauces*, "fallow land."

Fumay. *Town, Ardennes.* The name is of uncertain origin. It may derive from the Germanic personal name *Fumo* and the associative suffix *-acum.*

Fumel. *Town, Lot-et-Garonne.* The name is of obscure origin. A personal name *Fumel* is found in documents dated 1348.

Fuveau. *Town, Bouches-du-Rhône.* The name, recorded in the 11th century as *Affluel*, is of uncertain origin.

Gabas. *Resort village, Pyrénées-Atlantiques.* The name derives from French *gave*, "mountain stream." The village stands at the junction of two tributaries of such a stream.

Gacé. *Village, Orne.* The name derives from the Gallo-Roman personal name *Vassius* and the associative suffix *-acum.* (The *V-* of the personal name became *G-* as for **Gap.**)

Gagny. *Town, Seine-Saint-Denis.* The Paris suburb derives its name from the Gallo-Roman personal name *Gannius* and the associative suffix *-acum.*

Gaillac. *Town, Tarn.* The name derives from the Roman personal name *Gallius* and the associative suffix *-acum.*

Gaillard. *Town, Haute-Savoie.* The name represents the identical personal name.

Gaillon. *Town, Eure.* The name derives from the Germanic personal name *Wadal* and the suffix *-ionem.*

Gamaches. *Village, Somme.* The name was recorded in the 8th century as *Gammapium*, from pre-Latin *gamapia*, from *gam*, of unknown origin, and *apia*, "water." Gamaches is on the Bresle River.

Gambsheim. *Town, Bas-Rhin*. The name derives from the Germanic personal name *Wamb* and *heim*, "abode."

Ganges. *Village, Hérault*. The name was recorded in the 12th century as *Agange*, perhaps from a word *acanthicum*, from Latin *acanthus*, denoting a place where this plant grew.

Gannat. *Town, Allier*. The name derives from the Germanic personal name *Waddin* and the associative suffix *-acum*.

Gap. *Town, Hautes-Alpes*. The Romans knew the town as *Vapincum*, a name of unknown origin. Under French influence, the initial *V-* was regarded as a Germanic *W-*, so became *G-*. According to the poet Frédéric Mistral, *Gap* came from Provençal *gavot*, "goitrous," the name given to local Alpine inhabitants, so called from the goitres from which they suffered.

Garches. *Town, Hauts-de-Seine*. The name of the Paris suburb may be a variant form of *Guerche*, as in *La Guerche-de-Bretagne* (see **Guerche-de-Bretagne, La**).

Garchizy. *Town, Nièvre*. The name probably derives from the Germanic personal name *Waricho* and the associative suffix *-iacum*.

Gard. *Department, southern France*. The name is that of the river here, from Latin *Wardo*, from Indoeuropean *var*, "water." The Gard is formed by the confluence of the *Gardon d'Anduze* and *Gardon d'Alès*, with names of the same basic origin.

Gardanne. *Town, Bouches-du-Rhône*. The name derives from Germanic *gart*, "garden," and the suffix *-ana*, with Latin *villa*, "estate," understood.

La Garde. *Town, Var*. The suburb of Toulon derives its name from Germanic *wart*, "fort," a word related to English *guard* and *ward*.

La Garde-Freinet. *Village, Var*. The first part of the name is as for *La Garde* (see **Garde, La**). The second part means "ash wood," from a word related to modern French *frêne*, "ash."

La Garenne-Colombes. *Town, Hauts-de-Seine*. The Paris suburb derives the first part of its name from Low Latin *warenna*, "warren," "game reserve," a word that blends pre-Latin *varenna*, as for **Varennes-en-Argonne**, and Germanic *wardon*, "to guard," meaning a place where one keeps watch, or *waron*, "to keep safe," referring to the game. The second part of the name refers to nearby **Colombes**.

Gargas. *Village, Vaucluse*. The name probably derives from a pre-Latin root *garg*, meaning "rock" or "gorge," with the suffix *-aceus*.

Gargenville. *Town, Yvelines*. The name probably derives from the Gaulish personal name *Garganus* and Latin *villa*, "estate."

Garges-lès-Gonesse. *Town, Val-d'Oise*. The Paris suburb may take its name from Germanic *wardja*, "lookout place." The second part of the name locates it near (*lès*) **Gonesse**.

Gargilesse-Dampierre. *Hamlet, Indre*. The name is of uncertain origin. A derivation in Germanic *warginissa*, "prisoners' base," has been suggested. (The *Gargilesse* River here took its name from the place.) The second part of the name is as for **Dampierre-en-Burly**.

Garonne. *River, southwestern France*. The river rises in the Pyrenees just inside Spain, where it is known as the *Garona*, then flows northeast and northwest to join the Dordogne. Its name derives from pre-Indoeuropean *kar*, or *gar*, "rock," referring to its rocky source. (Some authorities object to this interpretation on the grounds that the river would be originally named from its broad lower reaches in flat country, rather than from its source.)

Gascogne. *Historic region, southwestern France*. The former duchy, more familiar to English speakers as *Gascony*, was known to the Roman as *Vasconia*, from Latin *Vasco*, *Vasconis*, "Basque," this being the *Basque Region* (see **Basque, Pays**).

Gascony *see* **Gascogne**

Gâtinais. *Region, north central France.* The region had the Latin name *pagus Vastiniensis*, from *pagus*, "land," "country," and a word related to French *gâtine*, "wasteland." Although later an agricultural region, it was originally a sandy, barren waste.

Gauchy. *Town, Aisne.* The suburb of Saint-Quentin derives its name from the Roman personal name *Gallicius* and the associative suffix *-acum*.

La Gaude. *Town, Alpes-Maritimes.* The name derives from Latin *gabata*, "bowl," denoting a gully or hollowed place here.

Gaul. *Historic country, western Europe.* Although originally covering a region corresponding to modern France and Belgium, with parts of Germany and the Netherlands, and formerly part of northern Italy, the name is now mainly associated with France, where its French form is *Gaule*. The Romans knew Gaul as *Gallia*, from its inhabitants, a Celtic people whose name may derive from Gaulish *gala*, "brave," or from a Celtic word meaning "white." It could equally have come from Germanic *walho*, "stranger," making it akin to the name of *Wales* (in French *Pays de Galles*). The cockerel that is France's symbolic bird arose from a supposed linguistic identity between Latin *Gallus*, "Gallic," and *gallus*, "cockerel."

Gavarnie. *Village, Hautes-Pyrénées.* The name comprises French *gave*, "mountain stream," and possibly the double suffix *-arn*, of pre-Latin origin, and *-ia*.

Geispolsheim. *Town, Bas-Rhin.* The name derives from the Germanic personal name *Gaispod* and *heim*, "abode."

Gelos. *Village, Pyrénées-Atlantiques.* The suburb of Pau derives its name from the Gaulish personal name *Gelos* and the Aquitanian suffix *-ossum*.

Gémenos. *Town, Bouches-du-Rhône.* The name may derive from Latin *geminus*, "twin," referring to the Roque Fourcade, a nearby mountain with two summits.

Gémozac. *Village, Charente-Maritime.* The name derives from the Gallo-Roman personal name *Gemutius* and the associative suffix *-acum*.

Genas. *Town, Rhône.* The name derives from the Roman personal name *Junius* and the suffix *-aceum*.

Gençay. *Village, Vienne.* The name derives from the Roman personal name *Gentius* and the associative suffix *-acum*.

Geneva, Lake. *Lake, eastern France.* The lake, on the Swiss-French border between the Alps and the Jura mountains, takes its name from the Swiss city of *Geneva*, at its western end. Its own name derives either from proto-Indoeuropean *gan*, "mouth," referring to the emergence of the Rhône River from the lake at this point, or from Indoeuropean *gen*, "bend," describing the curve in the shore of the lake here. The French name of Lake Geneva is *Lac Léman*, perhaps from Gaulish *lemo-*, "elm," or a Celtic word that gave Latin *limus*, "mud."

Genlis. *Town, Côte-d'Or.* The name derives from the Gallo-Roman personal name *Genilius* and the associative suffix *-acum*.

Gennes. *Village, Maine-et-Loire.* The name, recorded in the 6th century as *Gegina*, is of uncertain origin. Early forms of the name do not square with Gaulish *genaua*, "river mouth," even though the village lies at the point where a tributary joins the Loire River.

Gennevilliers. *Town, Hauts-de-Seine.* The Paris suburb derives its name from the Germanic personal name *Gin* and Latin *villare*, "farmstead."

Gentilly. *Town, Val-de-Marne.* The name was recorded in the 7th century as *Gentiliacus*, from the Roman personal name *Gentillus*, a variant of *Gentilius*, and the associative suffix *-acum*.

Gérardmer. *Town, Vosges.* The name derives from the Germanic personal name *Gerwald*, subsequently altered to *Gérard*, and Latin *mare*, "sea," "lake." The town lies at the eastern end of the lake of the same name.

Gerbier des Joncs. *Mountain, southern France*. The extinct volcano, in the Massif Central, has a rounded top, suggesting the appearance of a *gerbier*, or stack of sheaves of corn. The second part of the name, meaning "of rushes," is unexplained, as no rushes grow here.

Germigny-des-Prés. *Hamlet, Loiret*. The name was recorded in the 9th century as *Germiniacus*, from the Roman personal name *Germinius* and the associative suffix *-acum*. The addition ("of the meadows") distinguishes this place from others of the name.

Gers. *Department, southwestern France*. The name is that of the river here, known to the Romans as *Aegirxius*, perhaps from pre-Indoeuoprean *kar* or *gar*, "rock," or else from Indoeuropean *gir*, "height." The Gers rises at the foot of the Pyrenees.

Gerstheim. *Village, Bas-Rhin*. The name derives from the Germanic personal name *Garst* and *heim*, "abode."

Gerzat. *Town, Puy-de-Dôme*. The name derives from the Gallo-Roman personal name *Geritius*, from Gaulish *Gerus*, and the associative suffix *-acum*.

Gétigné. *Village, Loire-Atlantique*. The name derives from the Roman personal name *Gestinius* and the associative suffix *-acum*.

Les Gets. *Village, Haute-Savoie*. The name derives from French *jet* in the local and topographical sense of a chute for sending down timber. Les Gets is high up in a valley.

Gévaudan. *Historic region, southern France*. The former countship was known to the Romans as *Gabaldanum*, from the tribal name *Gaballi*, recorded in the 1st century AD by Pliny, itself from a pre-Celtic root *gab* or *gav*, "mountain stream." See also **Javols**.

Gevrey-Chambertin. *Village, Côte-d'Or*.

The name was recorded in the 7th century as *Gibriacus*, from the Gallo-Roman personal name *Gabrius* (from Gaulish *gabros*, "goat") and the associative suffix *-acum*. The second part of the name derives from Latin *campus*, "field," and the Germanic personal name *Bertin*.

Gex. *Resort town, Ain*. The name was recorded in the 12th century as Latin *Gaesium* and French *Gaix*, probably from the Roman personal name *Gaius*.

Ghisonaccia. *Town, Haute-Corse*. The town, in eastern Corsica, has a diminutive form (with suffix *-acea*) of the name of the village of *Ghisoni*, some 12 miles to the northwest, recorded in the 16th century as *Chisone*, from the Germanic personal name *Wiso*.

Giberville. *Town, Calvados*. The suburb of Caen derives its name from the Germanic personal name *Gisbert* and Latin *villa*, "estate."

Gien. *Town, Loiret*. The name was recorded in the 6th century as *Giomum*, from Gaulish *Givomago*, from a first element of uncertain origin (perhaps a personal name) and *magos*, "market."

Gières. *Town, Isère*. The suburb of Grenoble derives its name from pre-Latin *gar*, "rock," and the suffix *-ia*. Gières is at the foot of the Belledonne massif.

Gif-sur-Yvette. *Town, Yvelines*. The Paris suburb has a name of obscure but probably pre-Latin origin. The river here is the *Yvette*.

Gignac. *Village, Hérault*. The name was recorded in the 10th century as *Gignachum*, from the Gaulish personal name *Gennius* and the associative suffix *-acum*.

Gignac-la-Nerthe. *Town, Bouches-du-Rhône*. The name shares the origin of **Gignac**, with the addition naming the local region.

Gigondas. *Village, Vaucluse*. The name was recorded in the 10th century as *Jocundatis*, from the Latin nickname *Jucundus*, "pleasant," and the suffix *-atis*.

Gimont. *Village, Gers.* The name probably derives from the Germanic personal name *Gimmund*. The *Gimone* River here is named for the village.

Giocatojo. *Village, Haute-Corse.* The village, in northeastern Corsica, seems to derive its name from an original *Jocatorium*, from Latin *jocum*, "game," denoting a place where contests were held (wrestling, racing, or the like).

Giromagny. *Village, Belfort.* The name derives from the Germanic personal name *Girard* and Latin *mansionile*, "farmstead."

Gironde. *Department, southwestern France.* The name is that of the estuary of the Garonne and Dordogne rivers, forming a deep inlet of the Bay of Biscay. The Roman name was *Garunda*, a variant of *Garunna*, the Latin name of the **Garonne.**

Gisors. *Town, Eure.* The name of the town was recorded in the 10th century as *Gisortis* or *Gisortium*, perhaps from the Gaulish personal name *Gisus* and *ritu-*, "ford." Gisors is on the Epte River.

Givenchy-en-Gohelle. *Village, Pas-de-Calais.* The name derives from the Roman personal name *Juventius* and the associative suffix *-acum*. The addition names the local region.

Giverny. *Village, Eure.* The name of the settlement here was recorded in the 7th century as *Warnacus*, perhaps from a Germanic personal name *Warin* and the associative suffix *-iacum*. The present name, recorded in the 11th century as *Givernacus*, was apparently influenced by that of nearby *Giverville*, itself from the Germanic personal name *Gibert* and Latin *villa*, "estate."

Givet. *Town, Ardennes.* The name derives from the Germanic personal name *Gabilo*.

Givors. *Town, Rhône.* The name derives either from pre-Latin *gaba*, "stream," and Gaulish *ritu-*, "ford," or possibly from a Gaulish personal name *Givo* and a pre-Latin suffix *-oricum*. Givors lies at the junction of the Gier and Rhône rivers.

Givry. *Village, Saône-et-Loire.* The name derives from the Gallo-Roman personal name *Gabrius* (from Gaulish *gabros*, "goat") and the associative suffix *-acum*.

La Glacerie. *Town, Manche.* The suburb of Cherbourg presumably derives its name from the glass (*glace*) made here.

Gleizé. *Town, Rhône.* The suburb of Villefranche-sur-Saône derives its name from French *glaise*, "clay," and the suffix *-é*, denoting the clayey soil here near the Saône River.

Goderville. *Village, Seine-Maritime.* The name derives from the Germanic personal name *Godehard* and Latin *villa*, "estate."

Goetzenbruck. *Village, Moselle.* The name derives from the Germanic personal name *Godizo* and *bruck*, "bridge."

Golbey. *Town, Vosges.* The suburb of Épinal has a name recorded in the 12th century as *Golobes*, probably from Germanic *bach*, "stream," and a first element of uncertain origin

Golfe For names beginning thus, see the main name, e.g. for *Golfe de Fos* see **Fos, Golfe de.**

Golfe-Juan *see* **Juan-les-Pins**

Gondecourt. *Village, Nord.* The name derives from the Germanic personal name *Godo* and Latin *cortem*, accusative of *cors*, "estate."

Le Gond-Pontouvre. *Town, Charente.* The suburb of Angoulême derives the first part of its name from the Germanic female personal name *Algundis*, the *Al-* of which was dropped when it was taken to represent French *au*, "at the." The second part of the name represents French *pont*, "bridge," and the name of the *Touvre* River here.

Gonesse. *Town, Val-d'Oise.* The name of the Paris suburb, recorded in the 9th century as *Gaunissa*, is of uncertain origin.

Gonfreville-l'Orcher. *Town, Seine-Maritime.* The suburb of Le Havre derives its name from the Germanic personal name

Gundfrid and Latin *villa*, "estate." The addition refers to the nearby *Château d'Orcher*.

Gordes. *Village, Vaucluse*. The name was recorded in the 11th century as *castro Gordone*, from Latin *castrum*, "fort," and apparently a pre-Latin root element *gor-d*, "mountain."

La Gorgue. *Town, Nord*. The name represents a Picard form of French *gorge*, "throat," used here for the place where water flows down after turning a mill wheel.

Gorron. *Village, Mayenne*. The name derives from Le Mans dialect *gor*, "river dam," meaning a deep place where the water is still. Gorron is on the Colmont River.

Gouesnou. *Town, Finistère*. The suburb of Brest derives its name from Breton *gwezenn*, "trees."

La Goulafrière. *Village, Eure*. The name derives from Old French (also Norman) *goulafrer*, "to devour," here used ironically for an estate that "swallowed up" the owner's profits.

Gourdon. *Town, Lot*. The town had the Medieval Latin name of *Gordo, Gordonis*, from pre-Latin *gor* or *gord*, "mountain." Gourdon stands on a hill.

Gournay-en-Bray. *Town, Seine-Maritime*. The name derives from the Gallo-Roman personal name *Gordinus*, from Gaulish *Gordus*, and the associative suffix *-acum*. The addition locates the town in **Bray**.

Gournay-sur-Marne. *Town, Seine-Saint-Denis*. The name has the same origin as **Gournay-en-Bray**, but this Gournay is on the **Marne** River.

Goussainville. *Town, Val-d'Oise*. The Paris suburb derives its name from the Germanic female personal name *Gunza* and Latin *villa*, "estate."

Gradignan. *Town, Gironde*. The suburb of Bordeaux derives its name from the Roman personal name *Gratinius* and the suffix *-anum*.

Gramat. *Village, Lot*. The name probably derives from the Gaulish personal name *Gramus* and the associative suffix *-acum*, although a source in Provençal *grame*, "couch grass," is also possible, or in a Roman personal name *Garmus*, a form of *Garmanus*.

Le Grand-Bornand. *Resort village, Haute-Savoie*. The name is that of the *Borne* River here. The prefixed word ("great") distinguishes the village from a smaller place of identical name, as it does for many of the names below.

Grandcamp-Maisy. *Village and port, Calvados*. The first part of the name derives from Latin *grandis campus*, "big field." The second part derives from the Roman personal name *Masius* and the associative suffix *-acum*.

Grand-Champ. *Village, Morbihan*. The name derives from Latin *grandis campus*, "big field."

Grand-Charmont. *Town, Doubs*. The suburb of Montbéliard has a name apparently meaning "mountain of Charles," referring to a possessor or lord. It is "great" (*grand*) by comparison with some neighboring place, although there is no *Petit-Charmont*.

La Grand-Combe. *Town, Gard*. The name represents (latinized) Gaulish *cumba*, "enclosed valley" (Welsh *cwm*, English *coomb*), a term usually implying a dry valley with no stream, although La Grand-Combe lies by the Gardon d'Alès River.

Grand-Couronne. *Town, Seine-Maritime*. The name derives from Scandinavian *holmr*, "hill," with the modern form of the name influenced by French *couronne* (as for **Couronne**). The town is "great" (*grand*) by contrast with nearby *Petit-Couronne*.

La Grand-Croix. *Town, Loire*. The name means "the big cross," referring either to a cross erected here or to a crossroads, and perhaps "great" (*grand*) by comparison with nearby *Sainte-Croix-en-Jarez*.

La Grande-Brière. *Wetland, western*

France. The peat bog, in Loire-Maritime, has a name meaning "the great heath," from Latin *brucaria,* French *bruyère.*

La Grande-Motte. *Resort town, Hérault.* The name means "the great mound," from Low Latin *motta,* "height."

Grand-Fort-Philippe. *Resort town and port, Nord.* The locality here is first mentioned in 1657 as *Fort-Saint-Philippe,* after *Philip* IV (1605-1665), king of Spain, who had enlarged the entrance to the nearby port of Gravelines, which Grand-Fort-Philippe and *Petit-Fort-Philippe,* opposite each other at the mouth of the Aa River, had been built to defend.

Grand-Fougeray. *Village, Ille-et-Vilaine.* The name derives from Latin *filicaria,* "bracken." The village is "great" (*grand*) by comparison with *Le Petit-Fougeray* some 15 miles to the northeast.

Le Grand-Lemps. *Village, Isère.* The name, recorded in the 12th century as *Leems* or *Leemps,* is of uncertain, probably pre-Latin origin.

Le Grand-Lucé. *Village, Sarthe.* The name derives from the Roman personal name *Lucius* and the associative suffix *-acum.*

Le Grand-Pressigny. *Village, Indre-et-Loire.* The name was recorded in the 6th century as *Prisciniacus,* from the Roman personal name *Priscinius,* from *Priscius,* and the associative suffix *-acum.*

Grandpuits. *Village, Seine-et-Marne.* The name means "big well" (*grand puits*).

Le Grand-Quevilly. *Town, Seine-Maritime.* The name of the suburb of Rouen was recorded in the 9th century as *Civiliacum,* from the Gaulish personal name *Cabilius* and the associative suffix *-acum.* The town is "great" (*grand*) by contrast with nearby *Le Petit-Quevilly.*

Grandvillars. *Village, Belfort.* The name derives from Latin *grandis,* "big," and *villare,* "farmstead."

Grandvilliers. *Village, Oise.* The name has the same origin as that of **Grandvillars.**

Granges-sur-Vologne. *Village, Vosges.* The village, on the *Vologne* River, derives its name from Latin *granica,* "granary," "farm."

Granville. *Resort town and port, Manche.* The name was recorded in the 11th century as *Grandevilla,* from Latin *grandis,* "big," and *villa,* "estate," "village."

Grasse. *Resort town, Alpes-Maritimes.* The name was recorded in the 11th century as *Grassis* or *Grassa,* from the Roman personal name *Crassus* (from Latin *crassus,* "fat").

Le Grau-du-Roi. *Town and port, Gard.* The name represents the local word *grau* (from Latin *gradus,* "step," "stage") used for a channel connecting a lagoon with the sea, as here, on the Gulf of Aigues-Mortes, where a maritime canal was dug in 1725. The addition means "of the king."

Graulhet. *Town, Tarn.* The name was recorded in the 10th century as *Granolhetum,* from Latin *ranuncula,* "frog," and the collective suffix *-etum.*

La Grave. *Resort village, Hautes-Alpes.* The name derives from pre-Latin *grava,* "rock," "stone," meaning a stony or gravelly place, as here.

Gravelines. *Town, Nord.* The name was recorded in the 11th century as *Graveninga,* from the Germanic personal name *Grawin* and the suffix *-ing.*

Gravelotte. *Village, Moselle.* The name derives from pre-Latin *grava,* "stone," "pebble," denoting a stony or gravelly place, and the double diminutive suffix *-ell* and *-otta.*

Graves. *Vineyard region, Gironde.* The name derives from pre-Latin *grava,* "stone," "pebble," denoting a gravelly soil, offering good drainage for the vines here.

Gravigny. *Village, Eure.* The suburb of Évreux derives its name from the Gallo-Roman personal name *Gravinius* (from Gaulish *graua,* "gravel") and the associative suffix *-acum.*

Gray. *Town, Haute-Saône*. The name derives from an original *Gradiacus*, from the Roman personal name *Gratus*, a variant of *Gratius*, and the associative suffix *-acum*.

Grenade. *Town, Haute-Garonne*. The town adopted the name of the Spanish city of *Granada* (French *Grenade*).

Grenade-sur-l'Adour. *Village, Landes*. The name is as for **Grenade**, with the addition locating the village on the **Adour** River.

Grenay. *Town, Pas-de-Calais*. The name derives from the Roman personal name *Granus*, a nickname from Latin *granum*, "grain," "seed," and the associative suffix *-acum*.

Grenoble. *City, Isère*. The name was recorded in the Roman era as *Cularo, Cularonis*, apparently from Gaulish *cularo-*, "cucumber." This name was replaced in the 4th century by *Gratianopolis*, from the Roman emperor *Gratianus* (Gratian) and Greek *polis*, "town." (The city asked to take this name because Gratian had founded a bishopric here.) The aristocratic name was changed during the Revolution to *Grelibre*, so that apparent *noble*, "noble," was replaced by *libre*, "free."

Gréoux-les-Bains. *Resort village, Alpes-de-Haute-Provence*. The name represents a derivative (or precursor) of Provençal *greso*, "fallow land," and the Ligurian suffix *-elum*. The addition ("the baths") refers to the sulfurous springs here.

Grésy-sur-Aix. *Resort village, Savoie*. The name derives from the Roman personal name *Gratius* and the associative suffix *-acum*. The village is just outside **Aix-les-Bains**.

Gretz-Armainvilliers. *Town, Seine-et-Marne*. The first part of the name derives from Gallo-Roman *gresum*, "rocky terrain." The name of the nearby *Château d'Armainvilliers* was added to the original in 1950.

Grigny (1). *Town, Essonne*. The name derives from the Roman personal name *Grinius*, a variant of *Granius*, and the associative suffix *-acum*.

Grigny (2). *Town, Rhône*. The origin of the name is as for **Grigny** (1).

Grimaud. *Resort town, Var*. The name was recorded in the 9th century as *Grimaldo*, from the Germanic personal name *Grimald*.

Gris-Nez, Cap. *Headland, northern France*. The headland, on the narrowest part of the Strait of Dover, has a name meaning "cape gray-nose," referring to the color of the cliff here, by contrast with the white chalk at *Cap Blanc-Nez* (see **Blanc-Nez, Cap**) further up the coast.

Groix. *Island, northwestern France*. The island, off the Brittany coast, has the Breton name *Groe*, perhaps from *gro*, "shore."

Grosbliederstroff. *Village, Moselle*. The name derives from Germanic *gross*, "great," the personal name *Blithar*, and *dorf*, "village." Across the Saar River, which here forms the frontier between France and Germany, is its German counterpart, *Kleinblittersdorf*.

Gruissan. *Village, Aude*. The name was recorded in the 11th century as *Gruxan*, from the Gaulish personal name *Grussius* and the suffix *-anum*.

Guebwiller. *Town, Haut-Rhin*. The name was recorded in the 8th century as *Gebunwillare*, from the Germanic personal name *Gebo* and Latin *villare*, "farmstead." The town is not far from the border with Germany, where it is known as *Gebweiler*.

Guéméné-Penfao. *Town, Loire-Atlantique*. The name was recorded in the 11th century in the Breton and Latin form *Wenmened, id est Candidus Mons*, meaning "white mountain" (Breton *gwen*, "white," and *méné*, "mountain"). The second part of the name, that of a former priory nearby, is also Breton, meaning "end of the ash wood" (*pen*, "head," and *faou*, "ash tree").

Guénange. *Town, Moselle*. The name derives from the Germanic personal name *Wino* and the suffix *-ing*.

Guer. *Town, Morbihan.* The Brittany town derives its name from Breton *gwern*, "alder."

Guérande. *Town, Loire-Atlantique.* The name was recorded in the 9th century as *Guerran*, from Breton *gwen*, "white," and *ran*, "region," referring to the color of the local salt pans.

La Guerche-de-Bretagne. *Village, Ille-et-Vilaine.* The name derives from Frankish *werki*, "fortification" (English *work*), meaning a defensive post set up by the Franks in western France against attacks by the Bretons and the Visigoths. This one is in *Brittany* (**Bretagne**).

La Guerche-sur-l'Aubois. *Village, Cher.* The name is as for *La Guerche-de-Bretagne* (see **Guerche-de-Bretagne, La**), but here with the distinguishing location on the *Aubois* River.

Guéret. *Town, Creuse.* The town arose around a monastery founded in 669 on a wide expanse of fallow land (French *guéret*).

Guérigny. *Village, Nièvre.* The name derives from the Germanic personal name *Warin* and the associative suffix *-iacum*.

Guerville. *Village, Yvelines.* The name derives from the Scandinavian personal name *Gerri* and Latin *villa*, "estate."

Guesnain. *Town, Nord.* The name derives from the Germanic female personal name *Gisina*.

Guichen. *Town, Ille-et-Vilaine.* The Brittany town derives its name from Breton *gwik*, "village" (Latin *vicus*), and *hen*, "old."

Guidel. *Resort town, Morbihan.* The Brittany town derives its name from the Breton saint *Vitalo*.

Guienne *see* **Guyenne**

Guilers. *Town, Finistère.* The Brittany town may derive its name from Breton *gwiler*, "public square."

Guilherand. *Town, Ardèche.* The suburb of Valence derives its name from the Germanic personal name *Williramn*.

Guillestre. *Resort village, Hautes-Alpes.* The name, recorded in the 12th century as *Guillestra*, presumably refers to the *Guil* River here, unless the river took its name from the place. A reading of the name as *Wilistra* has also been proposed, from the Germanic personal name *Wil* and a suffix. Another reading is *Guillu-extra*, "beyond the Guil."

Guimiliau. *Village, Finistère.* The Brittany village derives its name from Breton *gwik*, "village" (from Latin *vicus*), and *Miliau*, the name of its patron saint.

Guinegatte *see* **Enguinegatte**

Guînes. *Town, Pas-de-Calais.* The name derives from the Germanic personal name *Wiso* and the suffix *-ina*, with Latin *villa*, "estate," understood.

Guingamp. *Town, Côtes-d'Armor.* The Brittany town has a Breton name, *Gwengamp*, from *gwen*, "white," and *kamp*, "camp."

Guipavas. *Town, Finistère.* The suburb of Brest derives its name from Breton *gwik*, "village" (from Latin *vicus*) and *Pavas*, the name of its patron saint.

Guiry-en-Vexin. *Hamlet, Val-d'Oise.* The name derives from the Roman personal name *Gurrius* and the associative suffix *-acum*. The hamlet is located in **Vexin**.

Guiscriff. *Village, Morbihan.* The Brittany village may derive its name from Breton *gwik*, "village," and the name of its patron saint.

Guise. *Town, Aisne.* The name was recorded in the 12th century as *Gusia*, from the personal name *Cutius*. The territory became a countship in the 13th century, then in 1528 a duchy, giving the name of the dukes of Guise, among them François de Lorraine, 2d duke of Guise, who took Calais from the English in 1558.

Gujan-Mestras. *Town, Gironde.* The first part of the name derives from the Gaulish personal name *Gudius* and the suffix *-anum*. The second part is of uncertain origin.

Guyancourt. *Town, Yvelines*. The Paris suburb derives its name from the Germanic personal name *Wido* and Latin *cortem*, accusative of *cors*, "estate."

Guyenne. *Historic region, southwestern France*. The name of the former province, also spelled *Guienne*, evolved as a corrupt form of Latin *Aquitania* (*see* **Aquitaine**) via the intermediate forms *Aguienne* and *Aguiaine*.

Habsheim. *Village, Haut-Rhin*. The name derives from the Germanic personal name *Habuini* and *heim*, "abode."

Haegen. *Village, Bas-Rhin*. The name was recorded in the 9th century as *Hegenheim*, from the Germanic personal name *Hago* and *heim*, "abode." The latter element then disappeared, leaving the personal name alone.

Hagetmau. *Town, Landes*. The name derives from Latin *fagus*, "ash tree," and the collective suffix *-etum*, with French *mauvais*, "bad," added subsequently to describe poor ground.

Hagondange. *Town, Moselle*. The name derives from the Germanic personal name *Ingold* and the suffix *-ing*. The town is near the border with Germany, where it is known as *Hagendingen*.

Haguenau. *Town, Bas-Rhin*. The name was recorded in the 12th century as *Hagenowa*, from the Germanic personal name *Hagino* (from *hago*, "forest") and *auwa*, "water." The German form of the name is *Hagenau*.

Le Haillan. *Town, Gironde*. The name may represent an original *Fadilianum*, from the Roman personal name *Fadilius* and the suffix *-anum*, but the definite article (*le*, "the") militates against a proper name in favor of a common noun.

Haillicourt. *Town, Pas-de-Calais*. The name was recorded in the 11th century as *Dahellicut*, from the Germanic personal name *Dahilo* and Latin *cortem*, accusative of *cors*, "estate." The initial *D-* of the original name was dropped when it was taken to represent French *de*, "of."

Haisnes. *Town, Pas-de-Calais*. The name derives from the Germanic personal name *Hagino* or the female personal name *Hagana*.

Hallennes-lez-Haubourdin. *Village, Nord*. The name may be related to Old High German *hali*, "slippery," applied to dry soil. The village is near (*lez*) **Haubourdin**.

Halluin. *Town, Nord*. The name derives from the Germanic personal name *Halewin*.

Ham. *Town, Somme*. The name derives from Germanic *haim*, "village," a word of Frankish origin found in northern France and related to German *Heim* and English *home* and *hamlet*.

Hambach. *Village, Moselle*. The name derives from the Germanic personal name *Hagino* and *bach*, "stream."

Hambye. *Village, Manche*. The name is Germanic in origin but of uncertain meaning.

Hangenbieten. *Village, Bas-Rhin*. The name derives from German *hangend*, "hanging," denoting a high location, and the Germanic personal name *Buto* followed by *heim*, "abode."

Harfleur. *Town, Seine-Maritime*. The town had the Medieval Latin name *Harflevium* or *Arefluctus*, recorded in the 11th century as *Harofloth*, from Scandinavian *har*, "high," and Old English *flēot*, "inlet." Harfleur lies at the mouth of the Seine on the English Channel.

Harnes. *Town, Pas-de-Calais*. The name derives from the Germanic personal name *Harina*.

Hartmannswiller. *Village, Haut-Rhin*. The name derives from the Germanic personal name *Hartmann* and Latin *villare*, "farmstead."

Hasparren. *Town, Pyrénées-Atlantiques*. The name derives from Basque *aspe*, "behind," and *barnea*, "house."

Hastingues. *Village, Landes.* The name is that of *Hastings*, England, adopted in commemoration of the famous battle (October 14, 1066), in which William the Conqueror defeated the Anglo-Saxon king Harold II, so delivering England to the Normans.

Haubourdin. *Town, Nord.* The suburb of Lille derives its name from the Germanic personal name *Haribod* and *heim*, "abode."

Haute-Corse. *Department, northern Corsica.* The department, created in 1976, has a name meaning "Upper Corsica," as distinct from neighboring **Corse-du-Sud.**

Haute-Garonne. *Department, southwestern France.* The name translates as "Upper Garonne," as the department includes the upper reaches of the **Garonne** River.

Haute-Goulaine *see* **Basse-Goulaine**

Haute-Loire. *Department, south central France.* The name translates as "Upper Loire," as the department includes the upper reaches of the **Loire** River.

Haute-Marne. *Department, northeastern France.* The name translates as "Upper Marne," as the department includes the upper reaches of the **Marne** River.

Haute-Normandie. *Region, northern France.* The name of the region, meaning "Upper Normandy," refers to its inclusion of Rouen as the capital of *Normandy* (see **Normandie**) as a whole, making it "superior" to neighboring **Basse-Normandie.**

Hauterives. *Village, Drôme.* The name was recorded in the 13th century as *Altarippa*, meaning "high bank" (French *haute rive*), referring to its location by the Galaure River.

Hautes-Alpes. *Department, southeastern France.* The name translates as "Upper Alps," denoting the department's location in a more elevated part of the **Alps** than the former *Basses-Alpes*, now **Alpes-de-Haute-Provence.**

Haute-Saône. *Department, eastern France.* The name translates as "Upper Saône," as the department includes the upper reaches of the **Saône** River.

Haute-Savoie. *Department, southeastern France.* The name translates as "Upper Savoy," as the department is situated in a more elevated region than neighboring **Savoie.**

Hautes-Pyrénées. *Department, southwestern France.* The name translates as "Upper Pyrenees," as the department includes the highest ranges of the **Pyrenees.**

Les Hautes-Rivières. *Village, Ardennes.* The name does not mean "high rivers" (as if *hautes rivières*) but "high banks" (*hautes rives*), meaning those of the Semoy River here.

Haute-Vienne. *Department, west central France.* The name translates as "Upper Vienne," as the department includes the upper reaches of the **Vienne** River.

Hauteville-Lompnes. *Town, Ain.* The name combines those of two separate places. *Hauteville* derives from Latin *alta villa*, "high village." *Lompnes* probably derives from the Roman personal name *Lumnus* with Latin *villa*, "estate," understood.

Hautmont. *Town, Nord.* The name derives from Latin *altus*, "high," and *mons, montis*, "mountain."

Haut-Rhin. *Department, northeastern France.* The name translates as "Upper Rhine." The department borders an upper stretch of the **Rhine** by contrast with neighboring **Bas-Rhin**, which borders a lower stretch.

Hauts-de-Seine. *Department, north central France.* The department, created in 1964, has a name translating as "Upper Reaches of the Seine," describing its location relative to others lower down the **Seine**, such as **Seine-Maritime.**

Haverskerque. *Village, Nord.* The name derives from a Germanic personal name (perhaps *Hawirih*) and *kirikka*, "church."

Le Havre. *City and port, Seine-Maritime.*

The port, founded by Francis I in 1517, was originally named *Havre-de-Grâce*, from the former chapel here dedicated to *Notre-Dame-de-Grâce*, "Our Lady of Grace." (Our Lady of Grace is the Virgin Mary, whose name, through association with Latin *mare*, "sea," came to be connected with ships and sailors.) *Havre* is "haven."

Hayange. *Town, Moselle.* The name derives from the Germanic personal name *Hago* and the suffix *-ing*.

Haybes. *Village, Ardennes.* The name derives from a Germanic personal name, perhaps *Hasbo*.

La Haye-Bellefond. *Village, Manche.* The name was recorded in the 14th century as *Haia Hugonis*, from Old French *haie*, "wood enclosed by a hedge," and the name of the lord *Hugon*, later replaced by *Bellefond*, "beautiful spring."

La Haye-du-Puits. *Village, Manche.* The main word of the name represents Old French *haie*, "hedge," "wood enclosed by a hedge." The addition means "of the well" (*puits*).

L'Haÿ-les-Roses. *Town, Val-de-Marne.* The name was recorded in the 8th century as *Laiacum*, from the Roman personal name *Laius* and the associative suffix *-acum*. The expected current form of the name would be *Lay*, but the initial *L-* was taken as *L'*, "the." The addition names the town's glory: "These are probably the best rose gardens in the world, and in the grounds is a Rose Museum of absorbing interest and delight" [Young, p.115].

Hazebrouck. *Town, Nord.* The name derives from Germanic *hase*, "hare," and *bruoch*, "marsh."

Hédé. *Village, Ille-et-Vilaine.* The name is of uncertain origin. It may derive from a Germanic personal name such as *Haido* and the associative suffix *-acum*.

Hegenhaim. *Village, Haut-Rhin.* The name derives from the Germanic personal name *Hagino* and *heim*, "abode."

Heillecourt. *Town, Meurthe-et-Moselle.* The suburb of Nancy derives its name from the Germanic personal name *Hadulf* or *Haidulf* and the associative suffix *-acum*, with Latin *cortem*, accusative of *cors*, "estate."

Hem. *Town, Nord.* The suburb of Lille and Roubaix has a name of the same origin as **Ham.**

Hénaménil. *Village, Meurthe-et-Moselle.* The name was originally recorded in the 7th century as *Iminivilla*, from the Germanic personal name *Imino* and Latin *villa*, "estate." *Imino* was then replaced by *Huni* and *villa* by *mansionile*, "farmstead."

Hendaye. *Town, Pyrénées-Atlantiques.* The name of the town, on the Spanish border, was recorded in the 16th century as *Handaye*, from Basque *handi*, "great," "famous," and a second element of unknown origin. The Spanish form of the name is *Hendaya*.

Hengwiller. *Village, Bas-Rhin.* The name was recorded in the 9th century as *Hemmingesbura*, from the Germanic personal name *Hemming* and *bur*, "habitation." The village was then destroyed in the 18th century and rebuilt under its present name, with the same personal name followed by Latin *villare*, "farmstead" (here, "village").

Hénin-Beaumont. *Town, Pas-de-Calais.* The first part of the name derives from the Germanic personal name *Henno* and the suffix *-inum*. The second part is as for **Beaumont.**

Hennebont. *Town, Morbihan.* The Brittany town derives its name from Breton *hen*, "old," and Latin *pons, pontis*, "bridge." Hennebont is on the Blavet River.

Henrichemont. *Village, Cher.* The village was planned and founded in 1608 by Henry IV's finance minister Sully. The name combines *Henri* in its latinized form *Henricus* and Latin *mons, montis*, "mountain," while also happening to suggest *Richemont*, "rich mountain."

Hérault. *Department, southern France.* The name is that of the river here, recorded by Pliny in the 1st century AD as *Arauris*, from *ar-av-aris*, from the European river root *ar*.

Les Herbiers. *Town, Vendée.* The name was recorded in the 12th century as *de villis de Herbertis*, showing an origin in the Germanic personal name *Herbert*. The present form of the name has been influenced by French *herbier*, "herbarium."

Herbignac. *Town, Loire-Atlantique.* The name derives from the Roman personal name *Arbenius* and the associative suffix *-acum*.

Herblay. *Town, Val-d'Oise.* The name was recorded in the 8th century as *Acebrelidum*, from Low Latin *acerabulus*, "maple," and the collective suffix *-etum*.

Hergnies. *Village, Nord.* The name derives from the Roman personal name *Herennius* and the associative suffix *-acum*.

Héricourt. *Town, Haute-Saône.* The name was recorded in the 12th century as *Oricourt*, from the Germanic personal name *Audericus*, and Latin *cortem*, accusative of *cors*, "estate." The present spelling has been influenced by names beginning *Héri-*, such as **Hérimoncourt**.

Hérimoncourt. *Village, Doubs.* The name was recorded in the 12th century as *Arymoncort*, from the Germanic personal name *Harimund* and Latin *cortem*, accusative of *cors*, "estate."

Hérin. *Town, Nord.* The name derives from the Germanic personal name *Herin*.

Hermanville-sur-Mer. *Resort village, Calvados.* The name derives from the Germanic personal name *Hermann* and Latin *villa*, "estate." The resort is "on sea" by the English Channel.

Hérouville-Saint-Clair. *Town, Calvados.* The name of the suburb of Caen was recorded in the 11th century as *Herufi villa*, from the Germanic personal name *Herulf* and Latin *villa*, "estate," "village." The sec-

ond part of the name honors *St. Clarus*, 3d-century bishop of Nantes.

Herrlisheim. *Town, Bas-Rhin.* The name derives from the Germanic personal name *Herileich* and *heim*, "abode." The German form of the name is *Herlisheim*.

Herserange. *Town, Meurthe-et-Moselle.* The suburb of Longwy derives its name from the Germanic personal name *Hirzula* and the suffix *-ing*.

Hersin-Coupigny. *Town, Pas-de-Calais.* The first part of the name derives from the Germanic personal name *Herisind*. The second part derives from the Roman personal name *Cuppenius*, a derivative of *Cuppius*, and the associative suffix *-acum*.

Hesdin. *Village, Pas-de-Calais.* The original name of the place, recorded in the 12th century, was *Maisnils*, from Latin *mansionile*, "farm." In 1554 the settlement was replaced by the present village, its name perhaps representing Germanic *husi-duna*, from *husi*, "house," and *duna*, "hill," "down," denoting a shelter for people or animals on open land.

Hettange-Grande. *Town, Moselle.* The name derives from the Germanic personal name *Hatto* and the suffix *-ing*. The town is not far from the border with Germany, where it is known as *Groß-Hettingen*.

Heudicourt-sous-les-Côtes. *Village, Meuse.* The original name of the settlement was recorded in the 8th century as *Tronione*, from the Roman personal name *Trunnius* and the suffix *-onem*. In 1737 the village adopted its present name, from the marquis of *Heudicourt*, his title from *Heudicourt*, Eure, or *Heudicourt*, Somme. The addition means "below the slopes."

Heyrieux. *Village, Isère.* The name was recorded in the 9th century as *Ariacum*, from the Roman personal name *Arius* and the associative suffix *-acum*.

Hillion. *Village, Côtes-d'Armor.* The name probably derives from a personal name.

Hirsingue. *Village, Haut-Rhin.* The name derives from the Germanic personal name *Hiruz* and the suffix *-ing.* The German name form of the name is *Hirsingen.*

Hirson. *Town, Aisne.* The name probably equates to modern French *hérisson,* "hedgehog."

Hochfelden. *Village, Bas-Rhin.* The name derives from Germanic *hoch,* "high," and *feld,* "field."

Hoëdic *see* **Houat**

Hœnheim. *Town, Bas-Rhin.* The suburb of Strasbourg derives its name from Germanic *hoh,* "high," and *heim,* "village."

Hœrdt. *Village, Bas-Rhin.* The name derives from Germanic *herd,* "hearth," "home."

Le Hohwald. *Resort village, Bas-Rhin.* The name derives from Germanic *hoh,* "high," and *wald,* "forest." The village lies in the Vosges Mountains in a densely wooded area.

Hombourg-Haut. *Town, Moselle.* The name derives from the Germanic personal name *Huni* and *burg,* "fortified village," with French *haut,* "high." The German name is *Oberhomburg.*

Homécourt. *Town, Meurthe-et-Moselle.* The name derives from the Germanic personal name *Hamo* and the associative suffix *-iacum,* followed by Latin *cortem,* accusative of *cors,* "estate."

Hondschoote. *Town, Nord.* The name of the frontier town, at the Belgian border, derives from the Germanic personal name *Hundo* and Dutch *schoot,* "enclosure."

Honfleur. *Town and port, Calvados.* The name was recorded in the 12th century as *Honneflo,* from Old Scandinavian *Hunnfloth,* from the Germanic personal name *Hun* or *Hunn* and Old English *flēot,* "estuary," "inlet." Honfleur, like its (literally) opposite number **Harfleur,** is at the mouth of the Seine River on the English Channel.

L'Hôpital. *Town, Moselle.* The name derives from Latin *hospitale,* "guesthouse," denoting a house and shelter for the needy. The German name of the town is *Spittel,* of the same origin.

Horbourg. *Town, Haut-Rhin.* The suburb of Colmar derives its name from a Germanic personal name (perhaps *Hor*) and *burg,* "fortified village."

L'Horme. *Town, Loire.* The name derives from Latin *ulmus,* "elm."

L'Hospitalet-près-l'Andorre. *Village, Ariège.* The name derives from a diminutive form of Latin *hospitale,* "guesthouse," here referring to a religious house set up by the Knights of the Hospital of St. John at Jerusalem (the Knights Hospitalers). The addition denotes the location of the village near **Andorra.**

Houat. *Island, northwestern France.* The island, off the Brittany coast, has the Breton name *Houad,* from *houad,* "duck," referring to its shape. The nearby smaller island of *Hoëdic,* with Breton name *Heudig,* has a diminutive form of this name.

Les Houches. *Resort village, Haute-Savoie.* The name derives from Gaulish *olca,* "plowable land."

Houdain. *Town, Pas-de-Calais.* The name was recorded in the 11th century as *Husdinium,* from the Germanic personal name *Hosed* and the suffix *-ing.*

Houdan. *Village, Yvelines.* The name, recorded early as *Hosdingus,* has the same origin as that of **Houdain.**

Houilles. *Town, Yvelines.* The Paris suburb has a name of uncertain origin. A derivation in Old French *holle,* "height," is possible (but hardly in modern French *houille,* "coal").

Houlgate. *Resort village, Calvados.* The name derives from Scandinavian *hol,* "hole," and *gate,* "way," "road."

Le Houlme. *Town, Seine-Maritime.* The name derives from Latin *ulmus,* "elm."

Houplines. *Town, Nord.* The suburb of Armentières derives its name from the Germanic personal name *Oppila*, from *Oppo*, and the suffix *-ina.*

Hourtin. *Village, Gironde.* The name may represent a local form of French *fortin*, "(small) fort."

Huelgoat. *Resort town, Finistère.* The name of the Brittany town represents its Breton name *An Uhelgoad*, from *an*, "the," *uhel*, "high," and *goad*, the mutated form of *koad*, "wood."

Huningue. *Town, Haut-Rhin.* The name derives from the Germanic personal name *Huno* and the suffix *-ing.* The German form of the name is *Hüningen.*

Huriel. *Village, Allier.* The name was recorded in the 11th century as *Huriacum*, from a Gaulish personal name *Uria* or a Germanic name *Uro* and the associative suffix *-iacum.*

Hussigny-Godbrange. *Village, Meurthe-et-Moselle.* The first part of the name derives from the Germanic personal name *Huso* or *Husso* and the double suffix *-in* and *-iacum.* The second part is a placename from over the nearby Luxembourg border.

Huttenheim. *Village, Bas-Rhin.* The name derives from the Germanic personal name *Hutto* and *heim*, "abode." The German form of the name is *Hüttenheim.*

Hyères. *Resort city, Var.* The name of the Mediterranean resort was recorded in the 10th century as *Eyras*, from Latin *area*, "piece of level ground." It in turn gave the name of the three *Îles d'Hyères* off the coast here. The island are also known as *Îles d'Or*, "Golden Isles," "probably from the golden tone the cliffs take from the sunlight" [Young, p.412].

Idron. *Village, Pyrénées-Atlantiques.* The name was recorded in the 11th century as *Idronium*, perhaps from a Roman personal name *Ituraeus* and the suffix *-onem.*

Igny. *Town, Essonne.* The name derives from the Roman personal name *Ignius* and the associative suffix *-acum.*

Île. For unhyphenated names beginning thus, see the main name, e.g. *Île de Ré* as **Ré, Île de.**

Île-aux-Moines. *Resort island, Morbihan.* The largest island in the Gulf of Morbihan has a name meaning "island of monks," referring to its early ownership by the abbey of Redon.

L'Île-Bouchard. *Village, Indre-et-Loire.* The name, recorded in the 10th century as *Insula* and in the 12th century as *Insula Buchardi*, derives from Latin *insula*, "island," and the name of the local lord, *Bouchard* I, known to be here in 887. The "island" is raised land by the Vienne River here.

Île-de-France. *Region, north central France.* The name of the present administrative region and former province means "island of France," either because it is bounded by rivers, or (less likely) because it was at the center of the crown lands of the Capetian kings.

L'Île-Rousse. *Village and port, Haute-Corse.* The village, on the northwest coast of Corsica, was founded in 1758 by the Corsican patriot Pascal Paoli (1725-1807) as a rival to the Genoese stronghold of Calvi, further down the coast. It takes its name from the red rocks of the *Île de la Pietra* here, itself recorded in the 13th century as *Izula Lero* and in the 17th century as *Isola Rossa*, "red island." The Corsican name of the port is the plural form *Isole Rosse*, "red islands," and it seems likely the French name is a mistranslation of this.

L'Île-Saint-Denis. *Town, Seine-Saint-Denis.* The Paris suburb, on a narrow island (*île*) in the Seine River, takes its name from nearby **Saint-Denis.**

Ille. *River, northwestern France.* The Brittany river takes its name from a pre-Celtic root element meaning simply "river."

Ille-et-Vilaine. *Department, northwestern France.* The Brittany department takes its name from two of its main rivers, the

Ille flowing south to joint the **Vilaine** at Rennes.

Ille-sur-Têt. *Town, Pyrénées-Orientales.* The name derives from Aquitanian *ili,* "town." The second part of the name locates the town on the *Têt* River.

Illiers-Combray. *Town, Eure-et-Loir.* The first part of the name was recorded in the 12th century as *Illetum,* perhaps from a Germanic personal name *Illhari.* The second part is the name given to Illiers in the writings of Marcel Proust (1871-1922), who spent many of his childhood holidays here. It was officially added to the original name on June 29, 1970. The real *Combray* is in Calvados, and Proust probably based the name on that of *Combres,* a village near Illiers. Both *Combray* and *Combres* take their names from Old French *combre,* "weir," "dam," from Gaulish *comberos.*

Illkirch-Graffenstaden. *Town, Bas-Rhin.* The suburb of Strasbourg derives the first part of its name from the *Ill* River and Germanic *kirche,* "church." The second part of the name, from words related to German *Graf,* "count," and *Stadt,* "town," dates from the late 13th century, when Holy Roman emperor Rudolf I raised several citizens of Strasbourg to the rank of knight following their armed aid in 1272 against Otakar II, king of Bohemia.

Imphy. *Town, Nièvre.* The name derives from the Roman personal name *Amphius* and the associative suffix *-acum.*

Indre (1). *Department, central France.* The name is that of the river here, perhaps from Frankish *anger,* "meadow," or from Celtic *ik,* "to go out."

Indre (2). *Village, Loire-Atlantique.* The suburb of Nantes has a name of uncertain but probably pre-Latin origin.

Indre-et-Loire. *Department, west central France.* The department takes its name from two of its main rivers, the **Indre** flowing northwest to join the **Loire** below Tours.

Ingersheim. *Town, Haut-Rhin.* The name derives from the Germanic personal name *Ongis,* a form of *Aungis,* and *heim,* "abode."

Ingrandes. *Village, Vienne.* The name may derive from Gaulish *equoranda,* "territorial limit." An alternate possible meaning is "level limit," with a first element from Latin and Italic *aequus,* "level," "even." Ingrandes is on the Vienne River.

Ingré. *Town, Loire.* The name may derive from the Germanic personal name *Ingrad.*

Ingwiller. *Village, Bas-Rhin.* The name derives from the Germanic personal name *Ingo* and Latin *villare,* "farmstead."

Inzinzac-Lochrist. *Town, Morbihan.* The first part of the name of the Brittany town derives from the Roman personal name *Disentius,* from *Disius,* and the associative suffix *-acum.* The initial *D-* of the personal name was taken as *de,* "of," so was subsequently dropped. The second part of the name means "Christ's church," from Breton *loc,* "church site," "parish" (see **Locminé**) and the name of *Christ.*

Irigny. *Town, Rhône.* The name derives from the Roman personal name *Ireneus* or *Irinius* and the associative suffix *-acum.*

Isbergues. *Town, Pas-de-Calais.* The name derives from the Germanic female personal name *Iduberga.*

Isère. *Department, southeastern France.* The name is that of the river here, from a pre-Celtic root of uncertain origin (*is,* "holy," has been suggested) and the river root *ar.*

Isigny-le-Buat. *Village, Manche.* The name derives from the personal name *Isinius,* a latinized form of the Gaulish name *Isina,* and the associative suffix *-acum.* The addition distinguishes this Isigny from **Isigny-sur-Mer.**

Isigny-sur-Mer. *Town and port, Calvados.* The name shares the origin of **Isigny-le-Buat,** although this Isigny is "on sea" near the English Channel coast.

Isle. *Town, Haute-Vienne.* The name derives from Latin *insula*, "island," here meaning raised ground by the Vienne River.

L'Isle-Adam. *Resort town, Val-d'Oise.* The name was recorded in the 12th century as *Insula* and in the 13th century as *Insula Ade*, from Latin *insula*, "island," and the name of a local lord. "Island" refers to the raised ground on which the town stands by the Oise River, rather than to the two islands in the river itself at this point.

Isle-Aumont. *Village, Aube.* The name derives from Latin *insula*, "island," denoting the location of the village on raised ground near the Seine. In 1665 Isle was erected into a dukedom and peerdom for Antoine d'*Aumont*, lord of an estate in Picardy.

L'Isle-d'Abeau. *Town, Isère.* There are two towns of this name, *L'Isle-d'Abeau* proper and, 3 miles to the west, the New Town of *L'Isle-d'Abeau (Ville Nouvelle)*. The name derives from Latin *insula*, "island," referring to the raised land by the Bourbre River on which the original town stands, and the name of a local lord.

L'Isle-d'Espagnac. *Town, Charente.* The suburb of Angoulême derives the first part of its name from Latin *insula*, "island," referring to raised ground by the Charente River, and the second part, a former name of the village here, from the Gallo-Roman personal name *Spanius* and the associative suffix *-acum*.

L'Isle-en-Dodon. *Village, Haute-Garonne.* The first part of the name derives from Latin *insula*, "island," referring to raised ground by the Save River here. The second part is a local district name.

L'Isle-Jourdain. *Town, Gers.* The first part of the name derives from Latin *insula*, "island," referring to raised ground by the Save River here. The second part is the name of a local lord.

L'Isle-sur-la-Sorgue. *Town, Vaucluse.* The name derives from Latin *insula*, "island," meaning raised ground by the *Sorgue* River (see **Sorgues**) on which the town stands.

L'Isle-sur-le-Doubs. *Village, Doubs.* The name derives from Latin *insula*, "island," meaning raised ground by the **Doubs** River on which the town stands.

Isola 2000. *Resort village, Alpes-Maritimes.* Although close to the Italian border, the winter sports resort does not take its name from Italian *isola*, "island," but from a pre-Latin word based on Ligurian *lev*, "slope," and a double suffix *-it* and *-ola*. (The name was recorded in the 11th century as *Leudola*, in the 14th century as *Liausola*, and in the 17th century as *Lisola*, then *Isola*.) The figure *2000* denotes the approximate altitude of the place in meters.

Isolaccio-di-Fiumorbo. *Village, Haute-Corse.* The village, in eastern Corsica, derives its name from a diminutive form of Latin *isola*, "island," denoting the raised location here. The addition is as for **Prunelli-di-Fiumorbo.**

Issarlès. *Village, Ardèche.* The name derives from Latin *exsartum*, "preparation of land for cultivation" and a double suffix *-ell* and *-ensem*.

Issoire. *Town, Puy-de-Dôme.* The name was recorded in the 6th century as *Iciodorensium vicum*, from the Gaulish personal name *Iccius* and *duron*, "fort," with Latin *vicus*, "village."

Issoudun. *Town, Indre.* The name was recorded in the 10th century as *Uxelodurum*, from Gaulish *uxellos*, "high," "elevated," and *dunon*, "fort."

Is-sur-Tille. *Town, Côte-d'Or.* The name derives from the Gaulish personal name *Icius* or *Itius*. The *Tille* River is nearby.

Issy-les-Moulineaux. *Town, Hauts-de-Seine.* The name of the Paris suburb was recorded in the 11th century as *Issiacum*, from the Gaulish personal name *Iccius* and the associative suffix *-acum*. *Moulineaux* is a diminutive of *moulin*, "mill," with the suffix *-ellum*.

Istres. *Town, Bouches-du-Rhône.* The name was recorded in the 10th century as *Ystro*, a pre-Latin form perhaps based on *is*, "height."

Itteville. *Town, Essonne.* The name derives from the Germanic personal name *Itto* and Latin *villa*, "estate."

Ivry-la-Bataille. *Village, Eure.* The first part of the name derives from Gaulish *iuos*, "yew," and the associative suffix *-acum*. The addition refers to the battle of 1590 in which the future king Henry IV defeated the Catholic League led by the duke of Mayenne.

Ivry-sur-Seine. *City, Val-de-Marne.* The name of the Paris suburb has the same basic origin as that of **Ivry-la-Bataille.** The addition locates the town on the **Seine** River.

Jabrun. *Village, Cantal.* The name implies an original *Gabrodunum*, from the Gaulish personal name *Gabros* ("Goat") and *dunon*, "fort."

Jacou. *Village, Hérault.* The name derives from the Germanic personal name *Jacco* rather than French *Jacques*.

Janzé. *Town, Ille-et-Vilaine.* The name derives from the Gallo-Roman personal name *Gennitius*, from Gaulish *Gennius*, and the associative suffix *-acum*.

Jargeau. *Village, Loiret.* The name was recorded in the 10th century as *monasterium Gargogilensis*, from the Gaulish personal name *Gargo* and *ialon*, "clearing."

Jarnac. *Town, Charente.* The name was recorded in the 8th century as *Agannagum*, from the (latinized) Germanic personal name *Agarnus* and the associative suffix *-acum*.

Jarny. *Town, Meurthe-et-Moselle.* The name was recorded in the 10th century as *Garniacum*, from the Roman personal name *Garinius* and the associative suffix *-acum*.

Jarrie. *Town, Isère.* The suburb of Grenoble derives its name from Languedocian *garric*, "kermes oak" (*Quercus coccifera*), denoting the type of rocky terrain where this shrub grows.

La Jarrie. *Village, Charente-Maritime.* The name is identical in origin to that of **Jarrie**.

Jarville-la-Malgrange. *Town, Meurthe-et-Moselle.* The suburb of Nancy derives its name from the Germanic personal name *Garo* and Latin *villa*, "estate." The addition names a château here.

Jassans-Riottier. *Town, Ain.* The first part of the name, recorded in the 14th century as now, derives from the Germanic personal name *Jazo* and the suffix *-ing*. The second part, recorded in the 10th century as *Redorterio*, comes from Old Provençal *redorta*, Latin *retorta*, "bent thing" (English *retort*, "flask with bent-back neck"), here a pliable branch used for plashing, and the suffix *-arium*.

Jaunay-Clan. *Town, Vienne.* The name was recorded in the 7th century as *vicus Gallinacus*, with Latin *vicus*, "village," followed by the Roman personal name *Gallinus* and the associative suffix *-acum*. The addition names the nearby *Clain* River.

Javols. *Village, Lozère.* The name of the original settlement was recorded by Ptolemy in the 2d century AD as *Anderedon*, and by the Romans in the 4th century as *Anderitum*, from Gaulish *ande*, an intensive prefix meaning "great," and *ritu*, "ford." (The same Roman name is recorded for Pevensey, Sussex, England.) In the 4th century the settlement took the name of the *Gaballi*, the tribe whose capital it was, and they in turn gave the name of **Gévaudan**.

Jeumont. *Town, Nord.* The name, recorded as now in the 12th century, probably derives from Latin *Jovis*, the genitive form of the god name *Jupiter*, and *mons, montis*, "mountain."

Jœuf. *Town, Meurthe-et-Moselle.* The name derives from the personal name *Juif* ("Jew").

Joigny. *Town, Yonne.* The name,

recorded in the 9th century as *Jauniacus* and in the 12th century as *Joviniacum*, comes from the Roman personal name *Jovinus* and the associative suffix *-iacum*.

Joinville. *Town, Haute-Marne*. The name derives from the Germanic personal name *Juni* and Latin *villa*, "estate."

Joinville-le-Pont. *Town, Val-de-Marne*. The Paris suburb was so named in 1831 for François d'Orléans (1818-1900), prince of **Joinville**, third son of king Louis-Philippe. The bridge (*pont*) is over the Marne River here. The original name of the place, recorded in the 12th century, was *Pons Olini*, from Latin *pons*, "bridge," and the Roman personal name *Olinus*.

Jonage. *Town, Rhône*. The name derives from the Christian name *Johannes* (John) and the Latin suffix *-aticum*.

Jonquières. *Village, Vaucluse*. The name derives from Latin *juncus*, "(bul)rush," and the suffix *-aria*.

Jonzac. *Town, Charente-Maritime*. The name was recorded in the 10th century as *Joenzacus*, from the Roman personal name *Juentius*, a variant of *Juventius* (from *juventus*, "youth"), and the associative suffix *-acum*.

Josselin. *Village, Morbihan*. The name of the Brittany village was recorded in the early 11th century as *Thro*, probably from Breton *tro*, "tower," "castle." Later that century it appears as *Goscelinus castellum*, with Latin *castellum*, "castle," added to the Germanic personal name *Gauzelin*, that of the son of Guethenoc, who built the original castle here in 1008.

Jouarre. *Town, Seine-et-Marne*. The name was recorded in the 7th century as *Jotrum*, an alteration of Latin *Diodurum*, a popular form of *Divodurum*, from Gaulish *deuo-*, "divine," and *duron*, "fort," "stronghold."

Jouars-Pontchartrain. *Town, Yvelines*. The first part of the name is as for **Jouarre**. The second part names a château here.

Joué-lès-Tours. *Town, Indre-et-Loire*. The name was recorded in the 6th century as *Gaudiacus*, from the Roman personal name *Gaudius* and the associative suffix *-acum*. The addition is French *lès*, "near," and **Tours**, of which the town is now a suburb.

Jougne. *Village, Doubs*. The name probably derives from the Roman personal name *Jovinius*, with Latin *villa*, "estate," understood.

Jouques. *Town, Bouches-du-Rhône*. The name is probably based on pre-Latin *jokk*, "top."

Jouy-en-Josas. *Town, Yvelines*. The name derives from the Roman personal name *Gaudius* and the associative suffix *-acum*. The addition is a local district name.

Jouy-le-Moutier. *Town, Val-d'Oise*. The origin of the main name is as for **Jouy-en-Josas**. The addition derives from Latin *monasterium*, "monastery," "church."

Juan-les-Pins. *Resort town, Alpes-Maritimes*. The name was given in the late 19th century, from the *Golfe Juan* (Gulf of Juan) here on the Mediterranean. The earlier name of the gulf was *Gourjan* or *Gourjean*, which became *Gour Jouan*, then *Golfe Jouan*, then finally *Golfe Juan*. The origin of this is unknown, although *gour* could mean "river." The second part of the name refers to the pine trees by the sea here, while *Golfe-Juan* is a nearby resort.

Jublains. *Village, Mayenne*. The original name of the site, recorded in the 2d century, was *Noviodunum*, from Gaulish *nouio-*, "new," and *dunon*, "fort," referring to the Roman encampment here. This name was replaced in the 4th century by *civitas Diablintum*, from Latin *civitas*, "city," and the name of the Gaulish city of the *Diablintes*, a tribe who had disappeared by the end of the Roman era but whose capital this was. The present form of the name thus evolved from the tribal name.

Juillan. *Village, Hautes-Pyrénées*. The

name derives from the Roman personal name *Julius* and the suffix *-anum*.

Jumelles see **Longué**

Jumièges. *Village, Seine-Maritime.* The Low Latin name of the village was *Gemedicum* or *Gemmeticum*, probably from a personal name (from the root *gem* meaning "twin," Latin *gemellus*) and the suffix *-eticum*.

Jura. *Department, eastern France.* The name is that of the mountain range here, from Gaulish *iuris*, "wooded mountain." The Jura are noted for the forests on their rounded crests.

Jurançon. *Town, Pyrénées-Atlantiques.* The suburb of Pau derives its name from the Gallo-Roman personal name *Jurantius*, from Gaulish *Jurius*, and the suffix *-onem*.

Juvisy-sur-Orge. *Town, Essonne.* The name was recorded in the 12th century as *Gevisiacum*, from the Roman personal name *Gavitius*, from *Gavius*, and the associative suffix *-acum*. The town is on the **Orge** River near the point where it joins the Seine.

Kaysersberg. *Village, Haut-Rhin.* The name was recorded in the 13th century as *Kesyrsperch*, from Germanic *Kaiser*, "emperor," and *berg*, "mountain," referring to the castle built here in the 13th century by the Holy Roman emperor Frederick II.

Kembs. *Village, Haut-Rhin.* The name was recorded in the 3d century as *Cambeten*, from Gaulish *cambo-*, "curve," "bend," for the location of the village at a bend in the Rhine River.

Kervignac. *Village, Morbihan.* The Brittany village derives its name from Breton *kêr*, "village," and the Roman personal name *Veneius* with the associative suffix *-acum*.

Kingersheim. *Town, Haut-Rhin.* The suburb of Mulhouse derives its name from the Germanic personal name *Chuneger* and *heim*, "abode."

Kleinfrankenheim. *Village, Bas-Rhin.* The name derives from Germanic *klein*,

"little," *Franken*, "Franks," and *heim*, "village," denoting a small settlement of the named people.

Knutange. *Village, Moselle.* The name derives from the Germanic personal name *Knut* and the suffix *-ing*.

Kœur-la-Grande. *Village, Meuse.* The name was recorded in the 8th century as both *Ulmus* and *Coria*, and the place is described in a Latin text of 1571 as a *villa quae dicitur Ulmus et in popolo vocatur Coria*, "village which is called Ulmus and by the people named Coria." Latin *ulmus*, "elm," has thus been replaced by *corylus*, "hazel," to give the present name. The village is "great" (*grande*) by comparison with nearby *Kœur-la-Petite*.

Le Kremlin-Bicêtre. *Town, Val-de-Marne.* The first part of the name of the Paris suburb represents a former inn sign here, *Au sergent du Kremlin*, "The Kremlin Sergeant," a reminder of Napoleon's retreat from Moscow in 1812. The second part was formerly thought to be a corruption of the name of the English city of *Winchester*, whose bishop represented the king in Paris in the 15th century. According to an article in the 1972 *Revue internationale onomastique*, however, the word represents Old French *bissexte*, "bissextile day," meaning the extra day the Julian calendar inserted in a leap year (now February 29), which was regarded as unlucky. Hence modern French *bissêtre* or *bicêtre*, "misfortune," "accident," later "haunted ruins."

L' For names beginning thus, see the next word, e.g. for *L'Île-Rousse* see **Île-Rousse, L'.**

La For names beginning thus, see the next word, e.g. for *La Rochelle* see **Rochelle, La.**

Labaroche. *Village, Haut-Rhin.* The village was recorded in the 15th century as *Zell*, from Latin *cella*, "hermitage." By the 17th century it had become *Bas-Roche*, suggesting "lower (place of the) rock" but actually representing a form of Latin *basilica*, "market," "church," influenced by *parrochia*, "parish." Former *La Baroche* is now thus *Labaroche*.

Labarthe-sur-Lèze. *Village, Haute-Garonne.* The name derives from Gascon and Languedocian *barto*, "thicket." The addition locates the village on the *Lèze* River.

Labastide-Rouairoux. *Village, Tarn.* The village arose around a medieval *bastide* or stronghold. The second part of the name derives from Latin *robur, roboris*, "oak," and the double suffix *-ari* and *-osum*.

Labouheyre. *Village, Landes.* The name was recorded in the 13th century as *le Boere*, with French *la*, "the," prefixed to Latin *bovaria*, from *bos, bovis*, "ox," and the suffix *-aria*, meaning a place where oxen are kept.

Labourd. *Historic region, southwestern France.* The region, now part of the Basque Country, has the Basque name *Lapurdi*, from *Lapurdum*, the Roman name of **Bayonne**, of Ligurian origin.

Labruguière. *Town, Tarn.* The name originates in Latin *brucaria*, a derivative of Gaulish *bruca*, "heather."

Lacanau. *Resort village, Gironde.* The name derives from Old Provençal *canal*, "channel." Lacanau lies on the eastern side of the lake of the same name, while *Lacanau-Océan*, to the west, is a seaside bathing resort.

Lacapelle-Marival. *Village, Lot.* The first part of the name represents a form of French *chapelle*, "chapel," "church." The second part is the name of a nearby place.

Lacaune. *Resort village, Tarn.* The name derives from French *la*, "the," and Provençal *cauno*, "cave," a word of pre-Latin origin.

Lacq. *Village, Pyrénées-Atlantiques.* The name, recorded in the 12th century as *Lag*, probably represents Latin *Laccum fundum*, referring to a place founded by a man with the Gaulish name *Laccos*.

Lacroix-Saint-Ouen. *Village, Oise.* The name was recorded in the 10th century as *Crux Sancti Audoeni*, from Latin *crux*, "cross," and the name of *St. Ouen*, 7th-century bishop of Rouen.

Laferté-sur-Aube. *Village, Aube.* The name derives from Latin *firmitas*, "fortified place," with an addition locating the village on the **Aube** River.

Lafrançaise. *Village, Tarn-et-Garonne.* The name implies "the (fortress of the) French."

Lagnieu. *Town, Ain.* The name was recorded in the 9th century as *Latiniacus*, from the Roman personal name *Latinius* and the associative suffix *-acum*.

Lagny-sur-Marne. *Town, Seine-et-Marne.* The name shares the origin of **Lagnieu**, with the distinguishing addition locating the town on the **Marne** River.

Lagord. *Town, Charente-Maritime.* The suburb of La Rochelle has a name of obscure origin.

Laguiole. *Village, Aveyron.* The name was recorded in the 13th century as *La Glazole* or *La Gliole*, from French *la*, "the," and Latin *ecclesiola*, a diminutive of *ecclesia*, "church."

Laissac. *Village, Aveyron.* The name derives from the Gaulish personal name *Lascius* or *Lacceius* and the associative suffix *-acum*.

Laissaud. *Village, Savoie.* The name represents Old French *les soz*, "the lower regions," referring to the location of the village below an old road.

Lalacelle. *Village, Orne.* The name derives from Christian Latin *cella*, "hermitage." French *la*, "the," was added to this to give *Lacelle*, then another *La* to give the present name.

Lalinde. *Village, Dordogne.* The name was recorded in the 13th century as *La Lynda*, from the English seneschal John de la Linde, who founded a *bastide* (stronghold) here in 1267.

Lallaing. *Town, Nord.* The name is of uncertain origin. It may represent the Germanic personal name *Lalling.*

Lalouvesc. *Village, Ardèche.* The name derives from Germanic *lupus,* "wolf," and the suffix *-iscum.*

Lamalou-les-Bains. *Resort village, Hérault.* The name appears to come from a Gaulish personal name *Amalo.* The village is a spa. Hence the addition ("the baths").

Lamastre. *Town, Ardèche.* The name is of uncertain origin. A derivation in Provençal *mastro,* "kneading trough," seems unlikely.

Lamballe. *Town, Côtes-d'Armor.* The name is of obscure origin.

Lambersart. *Town, Nord.* The suburb of Lille derives its name from the Germanic personal name *Lambert* and Latin *exsartum,* "preparation of land for cultivation."

Lambesc. *Town, Bouches-du-Rhône.* The name seems to derive from pre-Latin *lamb,* "mountain" (rather than a personal name) and the Ligurian suffix *-iscum.*

Lambres-lez-Douai. *Town, Nord.* The town derives its name from the Gaulish personal name *Lambrus,* with Latin *villa,* "estate," understood. The addition locates it near (*lez*) **Douai,** of which it is now in fact a suburb.

Lamorlaye. *Town, Oise.* The name derives from Germanic *morlaka,* "marsh."

Lamotte-Beuvron. *Town, Loir-et-Cher.* The town, on the *Beuvron* River, derives its name from Latin *motta,* "height," "mound," meaning a mound on which a castle is built, and by extension the castle itself.

Lançon-Provence. *Town, Bouches-du-Rhône.* As for **Alençon,** the name derives from the Gaulish personal name *Alantius* and the suffix *-onem.* The town is located in **Provence.**

Landerneau. *Town, Finistère.* The Brittany town derives its name from Breton *lann,* "territory," and the saint's name *Ternok.* See also **Landes.**

Landes. *Department, southwestern France.* The name is that of the extensive tract of sand and former marshland here, from Gaulish *landa,* "enclosure," "moorland," or *lano-,* "plain."

Landivisiau. *Town, Finistère.* The Brittany town derives its name from Breton *lann,* "territory," and the saint's name *Thivisiau.*

Landrecies. *Town, Nord.* The name derives from the Germanic personal name *Landerich* and the associative suffix *-iacum.*

Landser. *Village, Haut-Rhin.* The name derives from Germanic *land,* "country," and an element of uncertain origin.

Lanester. *Town, Morbihan.* The Brittany town, now a suburb of Lorient, derives its name from Breton *lann,* "territory," and a second element of uncertain origin.

Laneuveville-devant-Nancy. *Town, Meurthe-et-Moselle.* The name means essentially "the new town before Nancy," referring to a new estate (Latin *nova villa*) built in front of (*devant*) the city of **Nancy,** of which it is now an outer suburb.

Langeac. *Town, Haute-Loire.* The name derives from the Gallo-Roman personal name *Langius,* from Gaulish *Langos,* and the associative suffix *-acum.*

Langeais. *Town, Indre-et-Loire.* The name was recorded in the 6th century as *Alingavias,* from *Aling,* probably from the tribal name *Lingones* (see **Langres**) and the suffix *-avus.*

Langogne. *Town, Lozère.* The name was recorded in the 10th century as *Lingonia,* from the Gaulish personal name *Lingo* and the suffix *-ia.*

Langon. *Town, Gironde.* The name was recorded in the 5th century as *Alingonis,* with the same origin as for **Langeais.** The initial *A-* of the later form *Alangon* appears to have been understood as French *à,* "to," giving the present form *Langon.*

Langres. *Town, Haute-Marne.* The

town's Gallo-Roman name, recorded in the 4th century, was *Andemattunnum.* Its present name, first recorded in the 5th century, derives from the *Lingones,* the Gaulish tribe whose capital it was. Their name probably derives from Gaulish *ling-,* "to jump," perhaps referring to a war dance.

Langrune-sur-Mer. *Village, Calvados.* The name is of uncertain origin and meaning.

Languedoc. *Historic region, southern France.* The Medieval Latin name of the former province was *Languedocia,* from Occitan *Lengadòc,* the land whose people spoke the *lenga d'òc,* "language of oc," meaning Occitan, as distinct from the *langue d'oil,* "language of oil," spoken in the north. Both *oc* and *oil* mean "yes," the latter giving modern French *oui.*

Languedoc-Roussillon. *Region, southern France.* The administrative region takes its name from the former provinces of **Languedoc** and **Roussillon.**

Langueux. *Town, Côtes-d'Armor.* The Brittany town derives its name from Breton *lann,* "territory," and a saint's name that may be *Kenan.*

Languidic. *Town, Morbihan.* The Brittany town derives its name from Breton *lann,* "territory," and a saint's name that may be *Kintic.*

Lanmeur. *Village, Finistère.* The Brittany village derives its name from Breton *lann,* "territory," and *meur,* "great," but with the latter element possibly a personal name.

Lannemezan. *Town, Hautes-Pyrénées.* The name derives from French *lande,* "moorland," from Gaulish *landa,* as for **Landes,** and Latin *medianum,* "middle." The town lies in the southern part of the plateau of the same name.

Lannilis. *Town, Finistère.* The Brittany town derives its name from Breton *lann,* "territory," and *ilis,* "church."

Lannion. *Town, Côtes-d'Armor.* The Brittany town derives its name from Breton *lann,* "territory," and the saint's name *Yon.*

Lannoy. *Village, Nord.* The suburb of Roubaix derives its name from Latin *alnus,* "alder," and the collective suffix *-etum.* The initial *L-* represents prefixed French *le,* "the."

Lans-en-Vercors. *Village, Isère.* The name derives from the Roman personal name *Lancius* or *Lantius.* The second part of the name locates this Lans in the **Vercors** mountain range. The main name gave the distinguishing addition to the name of **Villard-de-Lans.**

Lanslebourg-Mont-Cenis. *Village, Savoie.* The name derives from the Roman personal name *Lancius* or *Lantius* and Low Latin *burgus,* "fortified place." The second part of the name refers to nearby *Mont Cenis* (see **Cenis, Mont**).

Lanslevillard. *Village, Savoie.* The name derives from the Roman personal name *Lancius* or *Lantius* and Latin *villare,* "farmstead," as for **Villard-de-Lans.**

Lanton. *Resort village, Gironde.* The name derives from the Gaulish personal name *Lantos* and the suffix *-onem.*

Lanvéoc. *Village, Finistère.* The Brittany village derives its name from Breton *lann,* "territory," and the saint's name *Méoc.*

Laon. *Town, Aisne.* The name was recorded in the 7th century as *Laodunum, Laudunum* and *Leudunum,* from an earlier *Lugdunum,* as for **Lyon.**

Lapalisse. *Village, Allier.* The name derives from Old French *palisse,* in the local sense "hedge."

Lapoutroie. *Village, Haut-Rhin.* The original name of the locality, near the crest of the Vosges Mountains, was recorded in the 12th century as *Sconerloch,* from Germanic *schön,* "beautiful," and *loch,* "lake." The present name, recorded in the 17th century as *La Poutroye,* may derive from Old French *poutre,* "mare," and the collective suffix *-eta,* perhaps denoting a place where mares were bred.

Lapugnoy. *Village, Pas-de-Calais.* The

name derives from Latin *pugnus*, "fist," "fistful," denoting a measure of land, and the collective suffix *-eta*.

Laragne-Montéglin. *Village, Hautes-Alpes.* The name was recorded in the 15th century as *Aranea*, from an old inn sign showing a spider (French *araignée*). *Montéglin* presumably derives its name from Latin *mons, montis*, "mountain," and a personal name.

Lardy. *Village, Essonne.* The name was recorded in the 10th century as *Larziacum*, from the Roman personal name *Laritius* and the associative suffix *-acum*.

Largentière. *Town, Ardèche.* The name was recorded in the 9th century as *Argenteria*, from Latin *argentum*, "silver," and the suffix *-aria*. Silver was mined here from the 10th through 15th centuries by the counts of Toulouse.

Laroquebrou. *Village, Cantal.* The name derives from pre-Latin *rocca*, "rock," and an element of uncertain origin.

Laroque-d'Olmes. *Village, Ariège.* The name derives from pre-Latin *rocca*, "rock," and the placename *Olmes*, from Latin *ulmus*, "elm."

Laruns. *Village, Pyrénées-Atlantiques.* The name was recorded in the 11th century as now, from Basque *lar*, "moorland," and the pre-Latin suffix *-untium*.

Larzac. *Region, southwestern France.* The region, one of the *Grands Causses* (see **Causses**), was recorded in an early Occitan text as the *montanha vulgarmen apelada Larsac*, "mountain commonly called Larsac," from a Gallo-Roman name that itself comes from the personal name *Larcius* or *Lartius* and the associative suffix *-acum*. The name of the mountain then spread to the whole region.

Lascaux. *Historic site, southwestern France.* The cave near Montignac, Dordogne, in which paintings of prehistoric animals were discovered in 1940, takes its name from obsolete French *las*, "the," and

Low Latin *calmis*, from pre-Indoeuropean *kal*, "rock," "bald height."

Lassay-les-Châteaux. *Village, Mayenne.* The name derives from the Gaulish personal name *Lascius* or *Lacceius* and the associative suffix *-acum*. The addition to the name refers to the castles or châteaux here, including Lassay's own 15th-century one.

Latour-de-Carol. *Village, Pyrénées-Orientales.* The name derives from Latin *turris*, "tower," and the *Carol* River here by the Spanish border.

Lattes. *Town, Hérault.* The name, recorded in the 1st century as *Latara* and *Latera*, is of pre-Celtic origin and uncertain meaning.

Laudun. *Town, Gard.* The name was recorded in the 11th century as *Laudunum*, from the Gaulish personal name *Laucus* and *dunon*, "fortress."

Launaguet. *Village, Haute-Garonne.* The name is a diminutive form of *Launac*, a village to the west across the Garonne River. Its own name derives from the Roman personal name *Lavenus* and the associative suffix *-acum*.

Lauragais. *Region, southern France.* The small region, a former district of Languedoc, takes its name from the onetime military settlement of *Laurac*, itself from the Gaulish personal name *Larus* and the associative suffix *-acum*. The name was formerly spelled *Lauraguais*.

Lautaret, Col du. *Mountain road, Hautes-Alpes.* The pass (*col*) derives its name from a diminutive form of Latin *altare*, "altar," prefixed by French *le*, "the." Another *le* was then added to give the present name *Le Lautaret*.

Lautenbach. *Village, Haut-Rhin.* The name derives from the Germanic personal name *Luto* and *bach*, "stream."

Lauterbourg. *Village, Bas-Rhin.* The name derives from the *Lauter* River here and Germanic *burg*, "fort," "town."

Lautrec. *Village, Tarn.* The name was recorded in the 10th century as *Lautricum*, either from Latin *altura*, "height," with the suffix *-iccum*, or (more likely) from Occitan *autreg*, "granted (fief)," from *autrejar*, modern French *octroyer*, "to grant," prefixed by *l'*, "the." (The Occitan and French verbs are in turn related to English *authorize*.)

Le Lauzet-Ubaye. *Village, Alpes-de-Haute-Provence.* The the name derives from a diminutive form of Provençal *laus*, "lake," meaning the small one near the *Ubaye* River here.

Laval. *City, Mayenne.* The name was recorded in the 11th century as *Vallis Guidonis*, and later as *la Valle Guidonis*. A fortified castle here was built by one *Guion*. The name *Laval* means simply "the valley." Laval stands on a hill overlooking the Mayenne River.

Le Lavandou. *Resort town, Var.* The name represents an altered form of *lavadou*, from Latin *lavatorium*, "washing place."

Lavardac. *Village, Lot-et-Garonne.* The name derives from the Gaulish personal name *Lavaratus* and the associative suffix *-acum*.

Lavardin (1). *Village, Loir-et-Cher.* The name derives from the Roman personal name *Laberitius*, from *Laberius*, and the suffix *-inum*.

Lavardin (2). *Village, Sarthe.* The original settlement of *Tucé* here was incorporated in 1561 into the barony of *Lavardin*, comprising a castle and hamlet belonging to nearby *Mézières* (see **Mézières**), now known as *Mézières-sous-Lavardin*, and eventually adopted its name, itself from the Gaulish personal name *Lavaratus* or *Lavaritus* and the suffix *-inum*.

Lavaur. *Town, Tarn.* The name was recorded in the 11th century as *Vaurum*, from Gaulish *uobera*, "hidden stream," "forest," subsequently prefixed by French *la*, "the."

Lavelanet. *Town, Ariège.* The name,

recorded in the 13th century as *Avellaneto*, means "place of hazels," from French *l'*, "the," Latin *avellana*, "hazel," and the collective suffix *-etum*.

Laventie. *Town, Pas-de-Calais.* The name, recorded in the 11th century as *Le Venties*, is of uncertain origin and meaning.

Laxou. *Town, Meurthe-et-Moselle.* The suburb of Nancy has a name of obscure origin.

Layrac. *Village, Lot-et-Garonne.* The name derives from the Roman personal name *Larius* and the associative suffix *-acum*.

Le For names beginning thus, see the next word, e.g. for *Le Mans* see **Mans, Le.**

Lectoure. *Town, Gers.* The name was recorded in the 4th century as *Lactora*, either from Occitan *leca*, "flat rock," a word of pre-Celtic origin, or from the Gallo-Roman personal name *Liccus*.

Leers. *Town, Nord.* The name derives from Germanic *ler*, "clearing," "uncultivated land."

Leffrinckoucke. *Town, Nord.* The name derives from the Germanic personal name *Laitfried* and the suffix *-ing*, then Flemish *houcke*, "corner of land."

Leforest. *Town, Pas-de-Calais.* The name means "the forest," from Old French *forest*, itself from Latin *forestis silva*, "outside wood," meaning a royal forest reserved for hunting.

Légé. *Village, Loire-Atlantique.* The name derives from the Roman personal name *Laevius* and the associative suffix *-acum*.

Lège-Cap-Ferret. *Resort town, Gironde.* The first part of the name is as for **Légé**. The second part names nearby *Cap Ferret*, as which the resort is itself more usually known.

Léguevin. *Town, Haute-Garonne.* The original form of the name may have been *Licovinum*, from a Gaulish personal name

Licovius, from *Licos*, a variant of *Liccus*, and the suffix *-inum*.

Léman, Lac *see* **Geneva, Lake**

Lembach. *Village, Bas-Rhin.* The name derives from Germanic *laim*, "clay," and *bach*, "stream."

Lempdes. *Town, Puy-de-Dôme.* The suburb of Clermont-Ferrand derives its name from Gaulish *lemo-*, "elm," and the pre-Latin suffix *-ate*.

Lencloître. *Village, Vienne.* The name derives from Old French *encloître*, "convent" (literally "in a cloister"). The village is in a well wooded region.

Lens. *Town, Pas-de-Calais.* The name was recorded in the 9th century as *Lennis*, from the Roman female personal name *Lenna*.

Lentilly. *Village, Rhône.* The name was recorded in the 10th century as *Lentiliacus*, from the Gallo-Roman personal name *Lentilius* and the associative suffix *-acum*.

Léognan. *Town, Gironde.* The name derives from the Roman personal name *Leonius* and the suffix *-anum*.

Léon (1). *Region, northwestern France.* The region of northwestern Brittany has a name of uncertain origin. It may ultimately come from the name of the Celtic god *Lug*, as for **Lyon**.

Léon (2). *Village, Landes.* The name derives from the Roman personal name *Leo, Leonis*.

Les For names beginning thus, see the next word, e.g. for *Les Andelys* see **Andelys, Les.**

Lescar. *Town, Pyrénées-Atlantiques.* The suburb of Pau originally bore the Iberian name *Beneharnum*, recorded in the 4th century. The town was destroyed by the Normans in 841 and a new settlement was built, with a name recorded in the 9th century as *Lascurris*, probably of pre-Celtic origin but related to Spanish *lasca*, "flat rock," with the pre-Latin suffix *ur* or Basque *uri*, "water."

Lescure-d'Albigeois. *Village, Tarn.* The first part of the name derives from Germanic *skur*, "granary." The second part locates the village in the region of **Albi**, of which it is now a suburb.

Lésigny. *Town, Seine-et-Marne.* The Paris suburb derives its name from the Roman personal name *Licinius* and the associative suffix *-acum*.

Lesneven. *Town, Finistère.* The Brittany town derives its name from Breton *lis*, "court," and *neven*, "new."

Lesparre-Médoc. *Town, Gironde.* The town was recorded in the 12th century as *Sparra*, from Occitan *esparra*, "beam," "post" (related English *spar*). The second part of the name locates the town in **Médoc**.

Lespugue. *Hamlet, Haute-Garonne.* The name may represent a form of *l'espigno*, "the thorn bush."

Lesquin. *Town, Nord.* The suburb of Lille has a name of obscure origin.

Lessay. *Village, Manche.* The name derives from the Gaulish personal name *Lascius* or *Lacceius* and the associative suffix *-acum*.

Lestrem. *Village, Pas-de-Calais.* The name was recorded in the 12th century as *Strumum*, from Germanic *stroom*, "stream," "current," prefixed with French *le*, "the."

Leucate. *Village, Aude.* The name was recorded in the 1st century as *Leucata*, from Greek *leukas*, "white," a word used by ancient Greek seamen to describe the Mediterranean coast here. The village is also known as *Port-Leucate*.

Levainville. *Village, Eure-et-Loir.* The name was recorded in the 9th century as *Lavana Fontana*, from the Germanic female personal name *Liuba* or *Lupa*, in its objective (accusative) form, and Latin *fontana*, "fountain," later replaced by *villa*, "estate."

Levallois-Perret. *Town, Hauts-de-Seine.* The former town, now a Paris suburb, was founded in 1867 on the amalgamation of four hamlets: *Levallois* and *Courcelles*, in the township of Clichy, and *Champerret* and *Villiers*, in the township of Neuilly. *Levallois* takes its name from Nicolas-Eugène *Levallois* (1816–1879), who founded it in 1846. *Perret* is a shortened form of the name of *Champerret*, from Latin *campus petrosus*, "stony field." (By coincidence the land here was apportioned by Jean-Jacques *Perret*.) The hamlet names are preserved in the Paris street names *Porte de Champerret*, *Rue de Courcelles*, and *Avenue de Villiers*.

Levie. *Village, Corse-du-Sud.* The village, in south central Corsica, derives its name from the Roman personal name *Laevius*, with Latin *villa*, "estate," understood, rather than from local French *le vie*, "the ways," from Latin *via*, "way," "road."

Levier. *Village, Doubs.* An origin in Latin *aquarium*, proposed by some scholars, seems unlikely.

Levroux. *Village, Indre.* The name was recorded in the 6th century as *vicus Leprosus*, apparently implying a leprosarium, but an origin in Latin *lepus, leporis*, "hare," and the suffix *-osum*, seems more likely.

Lezay. *Village, Deux-Sèvres.* The name was recorded in the 11th century as *Leziacus*, from the Roman personal name *Lisius* and the associative suffix *-acum*.

Lézignan-Corbières. *Town, Aude.* The name was recorded in the 9th century as *Lisinianus*, from the Roman personal name *Lisinianus* and the suffix *-anum*. The formerly separate *Corbières* derives its name from a Gascon form of Latin *corbaria*, a variant of *corvaria*, from *corvus*, "raven," "crow," and the suffix *-aria*, denoting a place frequented by these birds.

Lezoux. *Town, Puy-de-Dôme.* The name derives from Latin *lutosus*, "muddy." Lezoux is in a low-lying area amid streams.

Liancourt. *Town, Oise.* The name was recorded in the 9th century as *Landulficurtis*, from the Germanic personal name *Landulf* and Latin *cortem*, accusative of *cors*, "estate."

Libourne. *Town, Gironde.* The name was recorded in the 13th century as *Leybourne*, from the English seneschal *Roger de Leybourne*, governor of Gascony, then part of the fief of the Plantagenet kings of England. (Roger, from *Leybourne*, Kent, is himself said to have built the town around 1270 on the orders of Edward I of England as a *bastide* or fortified village against the French.) The earlier name of the town was *Condate*, from Gaulish *condate*, "confluence." Libourne lies on the Dordogne at the mouth of the Isle River.

Liesse-Notre-Dame. *Village, Aisne.* The name was recorded in the 9th century as *Lientia*, perhaps from the Roman personal name *Licentius*. The second part of the name relates to the 12th-century image of Our Lady (*Notre Dame*), the Virgin Mary, long visited by pilgrims.

Lieusaint. *Town, Seine-et-Marne.* The name was recorded in the 10th century as *Locus sanctus*, Latin for "holy place," denoting a shrine or a cemetery, but the real origin of the name could be in the Germanic personal name *Liutsind*, corrupted to give the present sense.

Liévin. *Town, Pas-de-Calais.* The name was recorded in the 12th century as *Laivin*, from the Germanic personal name *Laidwin*.

Liffol-le-Grand. *Village, Vosges.* The name derives from Latin *lucus*, "wood," and *fagus*, "beech." The addition ("the great") contrasts the village with nearby *Liffol-le-Petit*.

Liffré. *Town, Ille-et-Vilaine.* The name may derive from the Germanic personal name *Liutfred*.

Ligné. *Village, Loire-Atlantique.* The name was recorded in the 12th century as *Lingiacum*, from the Gallo-Roman personal name *Lemnius*, from Gaulish *Lemnos*, and the associative suffix *-acum*.

Ligny-en-Barrois. *Town, Meuse.* The name was recorded in the 10th century as *Lineium*, from the Roman personal name

Linius, from *Linus*, and the associative suffix *-acum*. The addition locates the town in **Barrois**.

Ligueil. *Village, Indre-et-Loire*. The name was recorded in the 8th century as *Luggogalus*, from the Gaulish personal name *Luggo* and *ialon*, "field."

Ligugé. *Town, Vienne*. The name was recorded in the 6th century as *Locogeiacum*, from the Gaulish personal name *Lucotius* and the associative suffix *-acum*.

Lille. *City, Nord*. The name probably derives from the Germanic personal name *Rizili*, altered to *Rizle* or *Lizle*. This gave a form popularly understood as *l'isle*, "the island," recorded in the 11th century as Latin *Insula*, since the town arose around the foot of a castle amidst marshland. The personal name origin is backed by the city's Flemish name of *Rijssel*.

Lillebonne. *Town, Seine-Maritime*. The name was recorded in the 11th century as *Lillebonensis*, an altered form of *Juillebonne*, from the Roman name *Juliobona*, from the name of *Julius* Caesar and Gaulish *bona*, "village."

Lillers. *Town, Pas-de-Calais*. The name was recorded in the 12th century as *Lilirs*, from Germanic *lar*, "clearing," and a first element of uncertain origin.

Limagne. *Region, central France*. The fertile lowland, with its alluvial soil, has a name that ultimately derives from the Celtic source of Latin *limus*, "mud," "sludge."

Limas. *Village, Rhône*. The name derives from the Gaulish personal name *Lima* or *Limus* and the associative suffix *-acum*.

Limay. *Town, Yvelines*. The origin of the name is as for **Limas**.

Limeil-Brévannes. *Town, Val-de-Marne*. The first part of the name derives from Gaulish *limo-*, "elm," and *ialon*, "clearing." The origin of the second part is uncertain.

Limoges. *City, Haute-Vienne*. The original name of the settlement here, recorded in the 2d century, was *Augustoritum*, from the Roman emperor *Augustus* and Gaulish *ritu-*, "ford." The present name derives from the *Lemovices*, the Gaulish tribe whose capital it was. Their own name means "conquering with the elm," from Gaulish *lemo*, "elm," and *-uices*, "who conquer" (the source of Latin *vincere*, "to conquer"). They presumably made their spears or bows from elm wood. See also **Limousin**.

Limonest. *Village, Rhône*. The name apparently derives from the Gallo-Roman personal name *Limonius* and the associative suffix *-acum*.

Limours. *Town, Essonne*. The name derives from Gaulish *limo-*, "elm," and the suffix *-ausus*.

Limousin. *Region, central France*. The present administrative region and former province takes its name from Latin *Lemovicinus*, from the Gaulish *Lemovices* people who gave the name of **Limoges**, its capital.

Limoux. *Town, Aude*. The name was recorded in the 9th century as *Limosum*, from Latin *limosus*, "muddy," from *limus*, "mud," "sludge." Limoux lies on the Aude River.

Linas. *Town, Essonne*. The name was recorded in the 10th century as *Linaias*, perhaps from an old, pre-Latin name of the Selmouille River here.

Linselles. *Town, Nord*. The name derives from Latin *linteolus*, Old French *lincel*, "sheet," probably denoting the manufacture of linen fabrics here. (Nearby Lille is a major textile center, long noted for its lisle.)

Lion, Golfe du. *Sea inlet, southern France*. The great gulf of the Mediterranean is popularly said to take its name from former statues of *lions* near the coast here, but a more likely origin is in the roaring of the sea when the mistral blows, fancifully compared to that of lions.

Le Lion-d'Angers. *Village, Maine-et-Loire*. The name was recorded in the 11th century as *Legio*, either from the Roman personal name *Legius* and the suffix *-onem*, or from Latin *legio, legionis*, "legion," denoting a Roman legionary camp (like *León* in Spain). The addition locates the town near **Angers**.

Lion-sur-Mer. *Resort village, Calvados*. The name is said to derive from Latin *leo, leonis*, "lion," referring to lion-shaped rocks off the coast here, but an origin identical to that of **Lyon** is also theoretically possible.

Liré. *Village, Maine-et-Loire*. The name derives from the Gaulish personal name *Lirus* and the associative suffix *-acum*.

Lisieux. *Town, Calvados*. The name was recorded in the 4th century as *civitas Lexoviorum*, from Latin *civitas*, "city," and the Gaulish tribe known as the *Lexovii*. Their own name derives from Gaulish *lexsouio-*, "leaning," perhaps referring to men who limp (through battle injuries.) An earlier name, recorded in the 2d century, was *Noviomagos*, "new market," as for **Noyon**.

Lisle-sur-Tarn. *Village, Tarn*. The name derives from Latin *insula*, "island," prefixed by French *la*, "the," referring to the raised ground on which the town stands by the **Tarn** River.

Lisses. *Town, Essonne*. The name derives from the Gaulish personal name *Liccius*, with Latin *villa*, "estate," understood.

Little Saint Bernard *see* **Petit-Saint-Bernard**

Livarot. *Village, Calvados*. The name was recorded in the 12th century as *Livaron*, possibly as a derivative of Gaulish *iuos*, "yew."

Liverdun. *Town, Meurthe-et-Moselle*. The name was recorded in the 10th century as *Liberdunum*, from the Roman personal name *Liber* and Gaulish *dunon*, "fort."

Livron-sur-Drôme. *Town, Drôme*. The name derives from the Roman personal name *Liber* and the suffix *-onem*. The town is on the **Drôme** River.

Livry-Gargan. *Town, Seine-Saint-Denis*. The name of the Paris suburb was recorded in the 12th century as *Livriacum*, from the Roman personal name *Liberius*, from *Liber*, and the associative suffix *-acum*. The second part of the name presumably derives from the Gaulish personal name *Garganus*.

Lizy-sur-Ourcq. *Village, Seine-et-Marne*. The name derives from the Roman personal name *Lisius* and the associative suffix *-acum*. The village is on the *Ourcq* River.

Loches. *Town, Indre-et-Loire*. The name was recorded in the 6th century as *Lucca* or *Locca*, from Gaulish *Locca*, of uncertain origin.

Locmaria-Plouzané. *Village, Finistère*. The first part of the Breton name derives from *loch*, "church site" (see **Locminé**), and *Maria*, "Mary." The second part derives from *plou*, "parish," and the Irish saint's name *Sané*.

Locmariaquer. *Village, Morbihan*. The Breton name amounts to "St. Mary's," from *loch*, "church site" (see **Locminé**), *Maria*, "Mary," and *kêr*, "house," "town."

Locminé. *Town, Morbihan*. As elsewhere in Brittany, the *Loc-* of the name represents Breton *loch*, "church site," "parish," from Latin *locus*, "place." The meaning is thus "parish of the monks," from *loch* and Breton *menec'h*, plural of *manac'h*, "monk," from Latin *monachus*.

Locronan. *Hamlet, Finistère*. The Breton name means "St. Ronan's church," from *loch*, "church site" (see **Locminé**), and the saint's name *Ronan*.

Loctudy. *Village, Finistère*. The Breton name means "St. Tudy's church," from *loch*, "church site" (see **Locminé**), and the saint's name *Tudy*.

Lodève. *Town, Hérault*. The name was recorded in the 4th century as *Luteva*, from Gaulish *luto-*, "marsh," as probably for *Lutetia*, the Roman name of **Paris**, and the suffix *-eva*.

Lognes. *Town, Seine-et-Marne.* The name probably derives from the Gaulish personal name *Lauconius*, from *Laucus.*

Logrian-Florian. *Village, Gard.* The first part of the name derives from the Roman personal name *Lucrio* and the suffix *-anum.* The second part names the French fabulist Jean-Pierre Claris de *Florian* (1755–1794), who was born here.

Loing. *River, north central France.* The river, a tributary of the Seine, was recorded in the 9th century as Latin *Luva* or *Lupa,* from the pre-Celtic river root *low.*

Loir. *River, north central France.* The river, a tributary of the Sarthe, derives its name from Gaulish *ledo,* "current." Despite appearances, the name bears no relation to that of the **Loire.**

Loire. *Department, east central France.* The name, recorded earlier in the Latin form *Liger,* is that of the river here, the longest in France, from the Indoeuropean root *leg* or *lig,* perhaps related to Basque *liga,* "mud," "silt," if not preserving the name of the god *Lug,* as for **Lyon.** The end of the word probably represents the river root *ar.*

Loire-Atlantique. *Department, western France.* The department is named for its chief river, the **Loire,** which crosses it from east to west, and the *Atlantic* Ocean into which it flows. Until 1957 the department was known as *Loire-Inférieure* ("Lower Loire") but the name was changed because of its suggestion of "inferiority."

Loire-Inférieure *see* **Loire-Atlantique**

Loire-sur-Rhône. *Village, Rhône.* The name derives from the Roman personal name *Laurius* or *Lorius,* with Latin *villa,* "estate," understood. The village is on the **Rhône** River.

Loiret. *Department, north central France.* The name is that of a river, recorded earlier in the Latin form *Ligeritus,* a diminutive of *Liger,* now the **Loire,** as the department's main river.

Loir-et-Cher. *Department, north central France.* The department takes its name from two of its main rivers, the **Loir** in its northern part and the **Cher** in its southern.

Loison-sous-Lens. *Town, Pas-de-Calais.* The name derives from the Roman personal name *Lausius* or *Lautius* and the suffix *-onem.* The town was originally near (*sous,* "below") **Lens** but is now a suburb.

Lomme. *Town, Nord.* The suburb of Lille derives its name from Latin *ulmus,* "elm," prefixed by French *le,* "the."

La Londe-les-Maures. *Town, Var.* In 1673, Antoine Lemonnier, sire of *La Londe,* Seine-Maritime, bought land here and built a house called *Château de La Londe.* (The name itself is probably a blend of *lande,* "moor," as for **Landes,** and Old Norse *lundr,* "wood.") In 1901, the second part of the name was added, for the town's location at the foot of the *Massif des Maures* (see **Maures, Massif des**).

Longeville-lès-Metz. *Town, Moselle.* The town takes its name from French *long,* "long," and Latin *villa,* "village." The addition denotes its location near (*lès*) **Metz,** of which it is now in fact a suburb.

Longeville-lès-Saint-Avold. *Town, Moselle.* The name is as for **Longeville-lès-Metz.** The addition locates the town near (*lès*) **Saint-Avold,** of which it is today actually a suburb.

Longjumeau. *Town, Essonne.* The name was recorded in the 13th century as *Longjumel,* a corrupt form of the 11th-century name *Nongemellum,* a diminutive of *Nogeom,* itself from *Noviomo* or *Noviomagus,* from Gaulish *nouio-* "new," and *magos,* "market." The same name gave that of **Noyon.** The present form of the name appears to have been influenced by French *long,* "long," and *jumeau,* "twin."

Longlaville. *Village, Meurthe-et-Moselle.* The suburb of Longwy has a name recorded in the 17th century as *Langlaville-la-Grande,* suggesting an origin in French *la,* "the," the personal name *Anglard*, and *ville*, "town."

Longpont-sur-Orge. *Town, Essonne.* The name derives from French *long*, "long," and *pont*, "bridge," relating to a bridge over the **Orge** River here.

Longué. *Town, Maine-et-Loire.* The name derives from French *long*, "long," and Latin *vadum*, "ford," denoting one over a stream here. The town is also known as *Longué-Jumelles*, for the nearby village of *Jumelles*, from Latin *gemellus*, "twin," either as a personal name or denoting two similar natural objects, such as rocks or hilltops.

Longueau. *Town, Somme.* The suburb of Amiens derives its name from French *long*, "long," and *eau*, "water." Longueau is on the Avre River near the point where it enters the Somme.

Longuyon. *Town, Meurthe-et-Moselle.* The name was recorded in the 7th century as *Longagio*, probably from Latin *longa*, "long," and Germanic *awja*, "damp meadow," with the suffix *-onem*.

Longvic. *Town, Côte-d'Or.* The suburb of Dijon derives its name from French *long*, "long," and Latin *vicus*, "village."

Longwy. *Town, Meurthe-et-Moselle.* The name was recorded in the 7th century as *Longwich*, from Latin *longus*, "long," and *vicus*, "village."

Lons. *Town, Pyrénées-Atlantiques.* The name, recorded in the 11th century as *Lod*, is of obscure origin.

Lons-le-Saunier. *Resort town, Jura.* The name was recorded in the 14th century as *Ledo Salnerius*, the first word probably from Gaulish *ledone*, "neap tide," here in the sense "stagnant water," the second from *saunier*, "worker in a saltworks." The town has been a saltwater spa since Roman times.

Loon-Plage. *Resort town, Nord.* The name derives from Germanic *lōh* (Dutch *loo*), "wood." The addition denotes that the town has a beach (*plage*).

Loos. *Town, Nord.* The suburb of Lille derives its name from Germanic *lōh*, "wood."

Loos-en-Gohelle. *Town, Pas-de-Calais.* The main name is as for **Loos**. The addition names the local region.

Lorette. *Town, Loire.* The original name of the settlement was *Le Reclus*, "the secluded place." The present name dates from the 19th century, when a railroad station opened here. It was probably adopted from *Loreto*, Italy, a place of pilgrimage, known in French as *Lorette*.

Lorgues. *Town, Var.* The name was recorded in the 10th century as *Lonicus*, from the Gaulish personal name *Lonus* and the Latin suffix *-icum*.

Lorient. *City and port, Morbihan.* The port was founded in 1664 with the name *L'Orient*, "the east," to serve the French East India Company (*Compagnie des Indes Orientales*). This apparently "eastern" town is actually in northwestern France, in southern Brittany.

Loriol-sur-Drôme. *Town, Drôme.* The name derives from Latin *auriolus*, "oriole," with the initial *L-* representing French *le*, "the." The town is near (rather than on) the **Drôme** River.

Lormont. *Town, Gironde.* The suburb of Bordeaux derives its name, originally that of a castle here, from the Gaulish personal name *Laurus* and Latin *mons, montis*, "mountain."

Le Loroux-Bottereau. *Town, Loire-Atlantique.* The name derives from Latin *oratorium*, "oratory" (place of prayer), with the initial *L-* representing French *le*, "the." The second part of the name is that of *Botterelus*, a 12th-century lord.

Lorraine. *Region, northeastern France.* The present administrative region and former province had the Medieval Latin name of *Lotharingia*, from *Lotharii regnum*, "kingdom of Lothair," from *Lothair* II (835–869), second son of Lothair I, the grandson of Charlemagne.

Lorris. *Village, Loiret.* The name is of obscure origin. The double *r*, present in the name from the 12th century, rules out a derivation in the Roman personal name *Lorius* or *Laurius.*

Lot. *Department, south central France.* The name is that of the river here, from Latin *Oltis*, from pre-Celtic *ol*, "to flow." The direct source is in Occitan *L'Òlt*, with the river name preceded by *l'*, "the."

Lot-et-Garonne. *Department, southwestern France.* The department is named for its two main rivers, the **Lot** joining the **Garonne** below Agen.

Loudéac. *Town, Côtes-d'Armor.* The name derives from the Roman personal name *Laudius* and the associative suffix *-acum.*

Loudun. *Town, Vienne.* The name was recorded in the 9th century as *Laucidunensis*, from *Laucidunum*, from the Gaulish personal name *Laucus* and *dunon*, "fort."

Louhans. *Town, Saône-et-Loire.* The name was recorded in the 9th century as *Lovingum*, from the Germanic personal name *Lauba* and the suffix *-ing.*

La Loupe. *Village, Eure-et-Loir.* The name was recorded in the 13th century as *Lopa*, perhaps from some common noun of uncertain meaning.

Lourches. *Village, Nord.* The name derives from the Roman personal name *Orcius* or *Ursius*, prefixed with French *le*, "the," and with Latin *villa*, "estate," understood.

Lourdes. *Town, Hautes-Pyrénées.* The name was recorded in the 15th century as *Lorda*, from the Roman personal name *Luridus* or *Lordus*. It is said that the local lord here, when besieged by Charlemagne in the 9th century, agreed to be baptized under the name *Lordus.*

Le Louroux. *Village, Indre-et-Loire.* The name was recorded in the 12th century as *Loratorium*, from French *le*, "the," and Latin *oratorium*, "oratory." Another *le* was then added later.

Louveciennes. *Town, Yvelines.* The Paris suburb derives its name from the Roman personal name *Lupicius* and the suffix *-anum.*

Louviers. *Town, Eure.* The name derives from Latin *lupus*, "wolf," and the suffix *-arium.*

Louvigné-du-Désert. *Town, Ille-et-Vilaine.* The name derives from the Roman personal name *Lupinius*, or a derivative of Latin *lupus*, "wolf," and the associative suffix *-acum*. The distinguishing addition refers to an uncultivated (*désert*) piece of land.

Louvres. *Town, Val-d'Oise.* The name probably derives from Latin *lupus*, "wolf," and the suffix *-ara*, denoting a place frequented by wolves.

Louvroil. *Town, Nord.* The suburb of Maubeuge derives its name from the Roman personal name *Luparius* and Gaulish *ialon*, "clearing," "field."

Lozère. *Department, southern France.* The name is that of a mountain here, in the Cévennes, recorded by Pliny in the 1st century AD as *Lesura*, from a pre-Latin root of unknown origin.

Lubersac. *Village, Corrèze.* The name derives from the Roman personal name *Lupercius* and the associative suffix *-acum.*

Luc. *Town, Aveyron.* The name derives from Latin *lucus*, "sacred wood."

Le Luc. *Town, Var.* The origin of the name is as for **Luc.**

Luçay-le-Libre. *Village, Indre.* The name derives from the Roman personal name *Lucius* and the associative suffix *-acum*. In the 17th century the village was known alternately as *Luçay-le-Captif*, "Luçay the Captive," and *Luçay-le-Chétif*, "Luçay the Poor," then in 1793, during the Revolution, as *Luçay-le-Libre*, "Luçay the Free," a name it has since retained.

Lucé. *Town, Eure-et-Loir.* The suburb of Chartres derives its name from the Roman personal name *Lucius* and the associative suffix *-acum.*

Luçon. *Town, Vendée.* The name was recorded in the 11th century as *Lucionnum,* from the Roman personal name *Luccius* or *Lussius* and the suffix *-onem.*

Luc-sur-Mer. *Resort village, Calvados.* The origin of the name is as for **Luc.** The resort is "on sea" by the English Channel.

Le Lude. *Town, Sarthe.* The name derives from Latin *lucidus,* "clear," denoting a clearing.

Ludres. *Town, Meurthe-et-Moselle.* The suburb of Nancy derives its name from Latin *lucidus,* "clear," denoting a clearing.

Luisant. *Town, Eure-et-Loir.* The suburb of Chartres probably derives its name from the Roman personal name *Lucentius.*

Lumbres. *Town, Pas-de-Calais.* The original name of the place, recorded in the 11th century, was *Laurentia,* from the Roman personal name *Laurentius.* By the 16th century this had been replaced by a Germanic personal name of uncertain form or origin.

Lunel. *Town, Hérault.* The name probably derives from the Gaulish personal name *Lunus* and the suffix *-ellum.*

Lunéville. *Town, Meurthe-et-Moselle.* The name was recorded in the 11th century as *Lienatis villa.* The first word is of uncertain origin, while the second is Latin *villa,* "village."

Lurcy-Lévis. *Village, Allier.* The name derives from the Roman personal name *Lupercius* and the associative suffix *-acum.* The second part of the name derives from the Roman personal name *Laevius* and the same suffix.

Lure. *Town, Haute-Saône.* The name was recorded in the 10th century as *Lutra,* probably from Gaulish *lautron,* "bath."

Lusignan. *Town, Vienne.* The name was recorded in the 11th century as *Lezinan,* from the Roman personal name *Licinius* and the associative suffix *-acum.*

Lusigny-sur-Barse. *Village, Aube.* The name derives from the Roman personal name *Lucinius* and the associative suffix *-acum.* The addition names the *Barse* River here.

Lussac. *Village, Gironde.* The name derives from the Roman personal name *Lucius* and the associative suffix *-acum.*

Lussac-les-Châteaux. *Village, Vienne.* The name shares the origin of **Lussac.** The addition refers to the châteaux in the region.

Lutetia *see* **Paris**

Lutterbach. *Town, Haut-Rhin.* The suburb of Mulhouse has a name meaning "pure stream," from Germanic *hluttar,* "pure," and *bach,* "stream."

Luxeuil-les-Bains. *Resort town, Haute-Saône.* The name was recorded in the 2d century as *Luxovium,* from *Luxsa,* either the name of a Gaulish god or a Gaulish personal name, and the suffix *-ovius,* later replaced by *ialon,* "clearing." Luxeuil is a thermal spa, and the second part of the name ("the baths") refers to the mineral springs here.

Luynes. *Town, Indre-et-Loire.* The original name of the place, recorded in the 5th century as *Malleium,* was *Maillé,* as for **Mailly-le-Camp.** In 1619 the settlement here was erected into a dukedom for Charles d'Albert, lord of *Luynes,* Bouches-du-Rhône, itself a stream name.

Luzarches. *Village, Val-d'Oise.* The name was recorded in the 7th century as *Lusareca,* from a pre-Latin root of uncertain origin and the double suffix *-ar* and *-ica.*

Luzech. *Village, Lot.* The name was recorded in the 13th century as *Luzeteg,* probably from Gaulish *Lucetio,* from the personal name *Luto* and the suffix *-etio.*

Luz-Saint-Sauveur. *Resort village, Hautes-Pyrénées.* The name probably comes from the Roman personal name *Lucius.* The second part of the name is a dedication to *St. Savior,* a title of Christ.

Luzy. *Town, Nièvre.* The name was

recorded in the 4th century as *Lausea*, from the Roman personal name *Lausius*, to which in medieval times was added the associative suffix *-acum*.

Lyon. *City, Rhône.* The city was founded in 43 BC by Lucius Munatius Plancus and named *Lugdunum*, from Gaulish *Lug*, the name of a god equated with Mercury, and *dunon*, "fort." (Lug's own name means "light," as does related Welsh *golau*.) The usual English form of the name is *Lyons*. The Gaulish settlement at the junction of the Rhône and Saône rivers here was *Condate*, "confluence." During the Revolution, Lyon was renamed *Ville-Affranchie*, "enfranchized town," as it was "freed" in 1793 by Revolutionary troops after an uprising by the citizenry.

Lyonnais. *Historic region, east central France.* The former province takes its name from its capital, **Lyon**.

Lyons *see* **Lyon**

Lyons-la-Forêt. *Village, Eure.* The name was originally that of an 11th-century castle here, itself apparently adopted from that of the nearby forest. The origin of the name is unknown.

Lys. *River, northern France.* The river rises in northern France, then flows northeast to form the Franco-Belgian border between Armentières and Menin before continuing into Belgium, where it is known as the *Leie*, to join the Scheldt at Ghent. Its name derives from Gaulish *liga*, "mud," "sediment" (related to English *lees*).

Lys-lez-Lannoy. *Town, Nord.* The suburb of Roubaix derives its name from the **Lys** River, although not actually on it or near it. The addition locates the suburb near (*lez*) **Lannoy**.

Mably. *Town, Loire.* The name is of uncertain origin. It may derive from the Gallo-Roman personal name *Mapilius* and the associative suffix *-acum*.

Macau. *Village, Gironde.* The Roman name of the settlement here was *Noviomagus*, meaning "new market" (as for **Noyon**). The present name, recorded in the 13th century as now, may represent Latin *malum cavum*, literally "bad hollow," meaning a place with infertile soil or one difficult to cultivate.

Machecoul. *Town, Loire-Atlantique.* The name was recorded in the 11th century as *Machicol*, purportedly from French *mâche*, imperative of *mâcher*, "to crush," and *col*, "neck." (This is said to be the origin of French *mâchicoulis*, English *machicolation*, the term for an opening between the corbels of a projecting parapet in a castle, supposedly so called because projectiles launched from it would crush the neck of an assailant.) But this explanation is just as unlikely as the one deriving the name from Lithuanian *Maisiogala*, "castle on a rock."

La Machine. *Town, Nièvre.* The name of the former coal-mining center means what it says, "the machine," referring to the novel mining machinery installed here in 1670.

Mâcon. *Town, Saône-et-Loire.* The Roman name of the town, recorded by Caesar in the 1st century BC, was *Matisco, Matisconis*, from the Ligurian root *mat*, "mountain," and the suffix *-asco*, changed by the Romans to *-isco*.

Mâconnais. *Region, east central France.* The hill district takes its name from its historic capital, **Mâcon**.

La Madeleine. *Town, Nord.* The suburb of Lille takes its name from a chapel here dedicated to *St. Mary Magdalene*, whose cult spread throughout France from the 12th century.

Magescq. *Village, Landes.* The name represents the masculine form of Old Provençal *magesca*, Gascon *majesque*, a term for the special tax payable by a wine seller. The village would thus have been a place where such a tax applied.

Magnac-Laval. *Village, Haute-Vienne.* The name was recorded in the 9th century as *Magniacus*, from the Roman personal name *Magnius*, and the associative suffix *-acum*. The distinguishing addition means "the valley."

Magnac-sur-Touvre. *Village, Charente*. The suburb of Angoulême has a name of the same origin as **Magnac-Laval**, but here distinguished by its location on the *Touvre* River.

Magny-Cours. *Village, Nièvre*. The name shares the origin of **Magnac-Laval**, but here distinguished by Latin *cortem*, accusative of *cors*, "estate."

Magny-en-Vexin. *Town, Val-d'Oise*. The town has a name of the same origin as **Magnac-Laval**, but here distinguished by its location in **Vexin**.

Magny-les-Hameaux. *Town, Yvelines*. The town shares its name with **Magnac-Laval**, but is here distinguished by its location among "the hamlets."

Maîche. *Town, Doubs*. The name is said to derive from Old French *mache*, "haystack," but this seems unlikely.

Maignelay-Montigny. *Village, Oise*. The first part of the name derives from the Roman personal name *Magnilla* and the associative suffix *-acum*, rather than the Germanic personal name *Magin* and *lar*, "clearing," as has also been proposed. The second part, recorded in the 8th century as *Muntigniagum*, derives from the Roman personal name *Montinius*, a variant of *Montinus*, and the associative suffix *-acum*.

Maillane. *Village, Bouches-du-Rhône*. The name was recorded in the 11th century as *Maliana*, from the Roman personal name *Magilius* or *Mailius* and the suffix *-anum*.

Maillezais. *Village, Vendée*. The name may represent *Malliacensis*, an adjectival form of *Malliacum*, from the Roman personal name *Magilius* and the associative suffix *-acum*. An alternate origin could be in the Roman personal name *Mallitius*, from *Mallius*, with *-acum*.

Mailly-le-Camp. *Village, Aube*. The name was recorded in the 9th century as

Malliacus, from the Roman personal name *Magilius* and the associative suffix *-acum*. The second part of the name refers to the large military camp nearby.

Maine. *Historic region, northwestern France*. The former province takes its name from the river here, either from Gaulish *magio-*, "great," or from the tribal name *Cenomanni*, who gave the name of *Le Mans* (see **Mans, Le**). It is possible the US state of *Maine* was named by French colonists from this province.

Maine-et-Loire. *Department, western France*. The name is that of two rivers here, the short **Maine**, formed by the confluence of the Mayenne and the Sarthe, and the much larger **Loire**, which crosses the department from east to west.

Maing. *Town, Nord*. The name derives from the Germanic personal name *Mato* and the suffix *-ing*.

Maintenon. *Town, Eure-et-Loir*. The name, recorded in the 12th century as *Mextenum*, is of uncertain origin. An unlikely derivation has been proposed in a Roman personal name *Mestinus*, a form of *Mestrius*, and the suffix *-onem*.

Mainvilliers. *Town, Eure-et-Loir*. The suburb of Chartres has a name meaning "middle farm," from Latin *medianus*, "middle," and *villare*, "farmstead."

Maisons-Alfort. *Town, Val-de-Marne*. The Paris suburb derives its name from a plural form of Latin *mansio, mansionis*, "stopping place," meaning one on a Roman road. The second part of the name relates to nearby *Alfortville*, so called from a former château here, recorded in the 14th century as *Herefort*, then as *Hallefort*, and finally as *Alfort*, from the Germanic personal name *Hari* and Latin *fortis*, "strong," or (perhaps better) Germanic *furt*, "ford."

Maisons-Laffitte. *Town, Yvelines*. The name of the Paris suburb, formerly *Maisons-sur-Seine*, was recorded in the 9th century as *Mansionibus*, the ablative (locative) plural form of Latin *mansio*, "stopping place," as for **Maisons-Alfort**. The second part of the name, added in the 19th century, is that of the French banker Jacques *Laffitte* (1767–1844).

Maizières-lès-Metz. *Town, Moselle*. The name derives from Latin *maceriae*, "ruins," meaning those of a Roman settlement. The addition locates the town near (*lès*) **Metz**.

Malakoff. *Town, Hauts-de-Seine*. The original hamlet was raised to a village in 1883 and adopted the name of *Malakhov* in the Crimea, captured by the French on September 8, 1855, during the Crimean War, a victory that led to the fall of Sebastopol. The name was originally that of an inn here, *À la tour de Malakoff*, "The Malakoff Tower," so called because situated below the tower of this name. The tower was destroyed in 1870 during the Siege of Paris.

Malaucène. *Village, Vaucluse*. The name derives from Provençal *malausseno*, "molasse" (in the geological sense of a type of sandstone or sandy marl).

Malaunay. *Town, Seine-Maritime*. The name derives from Latin *malus*, "bad," and *alnetum*, "place of alders."

Malemort-sur-Corrèze. *Town, Corrèze*. The name derives from French *mal*, "bad," and *mort*, "death," meaning a dangerous route or passage, here by the **Corrèze** River.

Malesherbes. *Town, Loiret*. The name derives from French *mal*, "bad," and *herbe*, "grass," denoting a poor pasture.

Malestroit. *Village, Morbihan*. The name was recorded in the 12th century as *Malestrictum*, from Old French *mal*, "bad," and *estroit* (from Latin *strictus*), "narrow passage."

Malicorne-sur-Sarthe. *Village, Sarthe*. The name derives from French *mal y corne*, literally "trumpet your woe," referring to a grouchy miller, here one by the **Sarthe** River.

Mallemort. *Village, Bouches-du-Rhône*. The name means "bad death," as for **Male-**mort-sur-Corrèze, here referring to a passage by the Durance River.

Malo-les-Bains. *Resort town, Nord*. The town, now a part of Dunkerque, takes its name from *Maclovius*, the saint who also gave the name of **Saint-Malo**. The addition ("the baths") relates to the bathing facilities at this seaside resort.

Malzéville. *Town, Meurthe-et-Moselle*. The suburb of Nancy derives its name from the Roman personal name *Maritius* and the associative suffix *-acum*, followed by Latin *villa*, "estate," "village."

Mamers. *Town, Sarthe*. The name was recorded in the 8th century as *Mamertum*, from a Roman personal name *Mamertus*.

Manche. *Department, northwestern France*. The name refers to the region's location by the English Channel, the French name for which is *La Manche*, "the sleeve," so called from its shape, with the Strait of Dover (*Pas de Calais*) at the eastern end forming the "cuff."

Mandelieu-la-Napoule. *Resort town, Alpes-Maritimes*. The suburb of Cannes is said to derive its name from pre-Celtic *manda*, "height," "limit," and Latin *locus*, "place." The addition names nearby *La Napoule*.

Mandeure. *Town, Doubs*. The name was recorded in the 4th century as *Epomanduodurum*, from Gaulish *epos*, "horse," *mandus*, "pony," and *duron*, "fort." The *Epo-* was subsequently dropped from the lengthy name.

Manduel. *Town, Gard*. The suburb of Nîmes derives its name from the Gaulish personal name *Manduos* (from *mandus*, "pony") and *ialon*, "clearing," "field."

Manosque. *Town, Alpes-de-Haute-Provence*. The name was recorded in the 10th century as *Manoasca*, from pre-Indoeuropean *man*, "rock," "height," and the Ligurian suffix *-asca*.

Le Mans. *City, Sarthe*. The historic form of the name is *Celmans*, a contracted form of *Cenomannis*, the ablative of *Cenomanni*, the Gaulish tribe whose capital this was. Their own name may come from Gaulish *ceno-*, "far," and a root meaning "to go." The *Cel-* of *Celmans* was later taken to represent *cel*, "which," and as this made poor sense it was replaced by *le*, "the." The original name of the town, recorded in the 2d century BC, was *Vindinon*, from Gaulish *uindos*, "white."

Mantes-la-Jolie. *City, Yvelines.* The name was recorded in the 13th century as *Medanta* or *Medantum*, from the river name *Medante fluminia*, itself from the river root *med*. (Mantes is actually on the Seine.) The city was earlier known as *Mantes-Gassicourt* or *Mantes-sur-Seine*, the addition (now *la jolie*, "the pretty") distinguishing it from nearby **Mantes-la-Ville**.

Mantes-la-Ville. *Town, Yvelines.* The town (*la ville*) shares the name of nearby **Mantes-la-Jolie**, of which it is now a suburb.

Le Marais *see* Appendix 4.

Marange-Silvange. *Town, Moselle.* The name derives from the Germanic personal name *Maro* and the suffix *-ing*. Nearby *Silvange* was officially united with Marange in 1809.

Marans. *Town, Charente-Maritime.* The name derives from the Roman personal name *Marentius*, from *Marius*.

Marche. *Region, central France.* The former province was a northern border fief (French *marche*, English *march*) of the duchy of Aquitaine. The name is used of other borderlands, such as the *Marches* in central Italy or the *Welsh Marches* between England and Wales.

Marchiennes. *Town, Nord.* The name derives from the Roman personal name *Marcius* or *Martius* and the suffix *-anum.*

Marcigny. *Town, Saône-et-Loire.* The name derives from the Roman personal name *Marcinius* and the associative suffix *-acum.*

Marck. *Town, Pas-de-Calais.* The suburb of Calais derives its name from Germanic *marca*, "border," "frontier."

Marckolsheim. *Village, Bas-Rhin.* The name derives from the Germanic personal name *Marcold* and *heim*, "abode."

Marcoing. *Village, Nord.* The name derives from the Roman personal name *Marconius*, from *Marco.*

Marcoussis. *Town, Essonne.* The name derives from Low Latin *marcocia*, "pasture," and the suffix *-icium.*

Marcq-en-Barœul. *Town, Nord.* The name is that of a river here, in the district of *Barœul.*

Mardyck. *Village, Nord.* The suburb of Dunkerque derives its name from Middle Dutch *mare*, "pool," "stretch of water," and *dijc*, "dyke."

Marennes. *Town, Charente-Maritime.* The name was recorded in the 12th century as *Marennia*, from Latin *maritima villa*, "village by the sea." Marennes lies near the mouth of the Seudre River, on the Bay of Biscay.

Mareuil-sur-Lay. *Village, Vendée.* The name derives from Gaulish *maros*, "great," and *ialon*, "field," "clearing." The village is on the *Lay* River.

Margaux. *Village, Gironde.* The name is of obscure origin. It could represent Gaulish *marga*, "marl," and a suffix *-alem*, or else a personal name based on *Marguerite.*

Margny-lès-Compiègne. *Town, Oise.* The name derives from the Roman personal name *Matrinius* and the associative suffix *-acum*. The addition locates the town near (*lès*) **Compiègne**, of which it is now actually a suburb.

Marguerittes. *Town, Gard.* The suburb of Nîmes derives its name from the female personal name *Marguerite*, perhaps originally with *Sainte* to honor *St. Margaret.*

Marignane. *Town, Bouches-du-Rhône.* The name was recorded in the 10th century as *Marignana*, from the Roman personal name *Marinius* and the suffix *-ana*.

Marignier. *Town, Haute-Savoie.* The name probably derives from the Roman personal name *Marinius* and the associative suffix *-acum*.

Marigny. *Village, Manche.* The name derives from the Roman personal name *Marinius* and the associative suffix *-acum*.

Marimont-lès-Bénestroff. *Village, Moselle.* The name was recorded in the 13th century as *Morsperc*, from the Germanic personal name *Moro* and *berg*, "mountain," replaced in the present name by *mons, montis*, its Latin equivalent. The addition locates the village near (*lès*) *Bénestroff*, a name deriving from the Germanic personal name *Benno* and *dorf*, "village."

Marines. *Village, Val-d'Oise.* The name derives either from the Roman personal name *Marinus* or from *Marius* and the suffix *-ina*, with Latin *villa*, "estate," understood.

Maringues. *Village, Puy-de-Dôme.* The name derives from the Germanic personal name *Maro* and the suffix *-ing*.

Marle. *Village, Aisne.* The name derives from Gaulish *marga*, Old French *marle*, "marl."

Marlenheim. *Village, Bas-Rhin.* The name derives from the Germanic personal name *Marila* and *heim*, "abode."

Marles-les-Mines. *Town, Pas-de-Calais.* The name has the same origin as **Marle**, with the addition referring to the former coal mines here.

Marly (1). *Town, Moselle.* The suburb of Metz derives its name from the Roman personal name *Marillius* or *Merulius* and the associative suffix *-acum*.

Marly (2). *Town, Nord.* The suburb of Valenciennes has a name of identical origin to **Marly** (1).

Marly-la-Ville. *Town, Val-d'Oise.* The name has the same origin as that of **Marly** (1), with the addition identifying this Marly as "the town."

Marly-le-Roi. *Town, Yvelines.* The town has a name of the same origin as that of **Marly** (1). The addition ("the king") denotes a royal possession, as the country estate of Louis XIV.

Marmande. *Town, Lot-et-Garonne.* The name was recorded in the 13th century as *Myremande*, from Old French *mirmande* or *mirande*, "fortified house."

Marmoutier. *Town, Bas-Rhin.* The name was recorded in the 8th century as *Moresmunister*, from the Germanic personal name *Moro* and Latin *monasterium*, "monastery."

Marnaz. *Town, Haute-Savoie.* The name is akin to that of the Roman mother goddess *Matrona*, from Gaulish *matir*, "mother," denoting a stream here as for the **Marne**.

Marne. *Department, northern France.* The name is that of the river here, known to the Romans as *Matrona*, from Gaulish *matir*, "mother," probably referring to the mother goddess believed to inhabit its waters.

Marne-la-Vallée. *Town, Seine-et-Marne.* The new town, one of five planned in the 1960s to relieve congestion in the suburbs of Paris, takes its name from its location in the valley of the **Marne** to the east of Paris.

Marolles-en-Brie. *Town, Val-de-Marne.* The name derives from Latin *materiola*, a diminutive form of *materia*, "timber." The addition locates the town in **Brie**.

Marolles-en-Hurepoix. *Town, Essonne.* The origin of the name is as for **Marolles-en-Brie**, but with the addition locating the town in the local region of *Hurepoix*.

Marolles-les-Braults. *Village, Sarthe.* The name is as for **Marolles-en-Brie**, with the addition a local placename.

Marpent. *Village, Nord.* The name is of uncertain origin. It may represent a Germanic female name *Merabind*.

Marquette-lez-Lille. *Town, Nord.* The name represents a diminutive form of the river name as for **Marcq-en-Barœul**. The addition locates the town near (*lez*) **Lille**, of which it is now in fact a suburb.

Marquion. *Village, Pas-de-Calais*. The name was recorded in the 11th century as *Marchium*, representing an earlier *Marke-dunum*, apparently from a Celtic word meaning "border" related to Old Irish *mruig*, "boundary," and Gaulish *dunon*, "fort." The settlement here would thus have been on the edge of tribal territory.

Marquise. *Town, Pas-de-Calais*. The name derives from Germanic *marka*, "border," "limit," and a suffix (added later) *-itia*.

Marsal. *Village, Moselle*. The name derives from Gaulish *maros*, "great," and Latin *sal*, "salt," referring to the mining of salt here in Gallo-Roman times.

Marsannay-la-Côte. *Town, Côte-d'Or*. The name was recorded in the 7th century as *Marcenniacus*, from the Roman personal name *Marcenus* and the associative suffix *-acum*. The town is on a slope (*côte*) of the Côte-d'Or hills.

Marseillan. *Town, Hérault*. The name derives from the Roman personal name *Marcellius* or *Marcilius* and the suffix *-anum*.

Marseille. *City and port, Bouches-du-Rhône*. The city's name, often spelled *Marseilles* by English speakers, derives from the Roman form *Massilia*, recorded in the 1st century BC, itself an alteration of *Massalia*, recorded in the 6th century BC, from a pre-Latin (possibly Ligurian) root *mas*, "spring," and the pre-Latin suffix *-alia*, probably denoting a tribal name. During the Revolution, as a punishment for its royalist views, the city was renamed *Ville-sans-Nom*, "town without a name," which is nevertheless a name.

Marsillargues. *Town, Hérault*. The name was recorded in the 11th century as *Marcianicus*, from the Roman personal name *Marcilius* and the suffix *-anicum*.

Martel. *Village, Lot*. The village is named

for Charles *Martel* ("The Hammer") (*c.*688–741), leader of the Franks and grandfather of Charlemagne, who repulsed the Muslims in the battle of Poitiers (732), pursued them southward, and finally destroyed them near here.

Martignas-sur-Jalle. *Town, Gironde*. The suburb of Bordeaux derives its name from the Roman personal name *Martinus* and the associative suffix *-iacum*. The town lies on the *Jalle* River.

Martigné-Ferchaud. *Village, Ille-et-Vilaine*. The first part of the name shares its origin with **Martignas-sur-Jalle**. The second part is French *fer chaud*, "hot iron," denoting a forge here.

Martigues. *City and port, Bouches-du-Rhône*. The name was recorded in the 10th century as *Martigum*, from pre-Indoeuropean *mart*, "rock," and the suffix *-icum*, originally applied to the navigable lagoon here known as the *Étang de Berre* (see **Berre-l'Étang**).

Martres-Tolosane. *Village, Haute-Garonne*. The name derives from Latin *martyres*, "martyrs," then "cemetery," as here, where the parish church is built over an ancient burial site. The second part of the name locates the village on the plain of **Toulouse**.

Marvejols. *Town, Lozère*. The name was recorded in the 12th century as *Maroiol*, from Gaulish *maros*, "great," and *ialon*, "clearing."

Le Mas-d'Agenais. *Village, Lot-et-Garonne*. The name derives from Latin *mansus*, a feudal term for a small farm held by a single tenant. This one is in the region centering on **Agen**.

Le Mas-d'Azil. *Village, Ariège*. The name derives from Latin *mansus*, a feudal term for a small farm held by a single tenant. This one is identified by a local placename.

Masevaux. *Town, Haut-Rhin*. The name derives from the Germanic personal name *Maso* and Latin *vallis*, "valley."

Masnières. *Town, Nord.* The name represents a feminine form of the Latin infinitive *manere*, "to dwell," denoting a residence, such as a castle or château.

Masny. *Town, Nord.* The name derives from Latin *mansionile*, a term for a peasant dwelling with a plot of land.

Masseube. *Village, Gers.* The *Mas-* of the name represents Latin *mansus*, a feudal term for a small farm held by a single tenant. The *-seube* represents Latin *silva*, "forest."

Massiac. *Resort village, Cantal.* The name derives from the personal name *Matthaeus* (Matthew) and the associative suffix *-acum*.

Massif. For names beginning thus, apart from the next below, see the main name, e.g. for *Massif du Mont-Dore* see **Mont-Dore, Massif du**.

Massif Central. *Plateau region, central and southern France.* The name denotes the location of the massif, or large mountainmass, in the (approximate) center of France. Its Occitan name is *Massís septentrional*, "northern massif," denoting its situation relative to Occitania (see **Occitanie**).

Massy. *Town, Essonne.* The Paris suburb derives its name from the Roman personal name *Macius* or *Maccius* and the associative suffix *-acum*.

Matha. *Village, Charente-Maritime.* The name derives from a diminutive form of pre-Indoeuropean *matta*, "bush," "forest," and a suffix of uncertain origin.

Mathay. *Village, Doubs.* The name derives from the Roman personal name *Mattus*, a variant of *Mattius*, and the associative suffix *-acum*.

Maubeuge. *Town, Nord.* The Medieval Latin name of the town was *Malbodium*, from the Germanic personal name *Malbold*.

Maubourguet. *Village, Hautes-Pyrénées.* The name derives from Latin *malum*, "bad," and *burgus*, "stronghold," with the diminutive suffix *-ittum*. The implication is of a castle built on unsuitable terrain or from faulty materials.

Maule. *Town, Yvelines.* The name was recorded in the 13th century as *Manlia*, of uncertain meaning.

Mauléon. *Town, Deux-Sèvres.* The name is said to derive from Latin *malus*, "bad," and *leo, leonis*, "lion," referring to a group of rocks here resembling a lion in outline.

Mauléon-Licharre. *Village, Pyrénées-Atlantiques.* The first part of the name is as for **Mauléon**. The second part names a nearby village that formally joined Mauléon in 1841.

Maure-de-Bretagne. *Village, Ille-et-Vilaine.* The name derives from the Roman personal name *Maurus*, with Latin *villa*, "estate," understood. The addition locates the village in *Brittany* (**Bretagne**).

Maurepas. *Town, Yvelines.* The name apparently derives from French *mal*, "bad," and *repas*, "meal," implying land difficult to cultivate.

Maures, Massif des. *Mountains, southeastern France.* The name derives from Latin *maurus*, "dark," either from the color of the rocks, or from the dark green pine woods by the coast. The full French name, *Monts des Maures*, is popularly explained as meaning "mountains of the Moors," as if for the Moors (Saracens) who occupied the region for over a century.

Mauriac. *Town, Cantal.* The name was recorded in the 9th century as *Mauriacus*, from the Roman personal name *Maurius* and the associative suffix *-acum*.

Mauron. *Village, Morbihan.* The name derives from the Roman personal name *Maurus* and the suffix *-anum*.

Maurs. *Village, Cantal.* The village arose on the site of a Roman settlement occupied by Moorish mercenaries. Hence the name (French *Maure*, "Moor").

Mauzé-sur-le-Mignon. *Village, Deux-Sèvres.* The name was recorded in the 11th century as *Malsiacus*, from the Roman personal name *Maletius* or Gaulish name *Mausos* and the associative suffix *-acum*. The village is on the *Mignon* River.

Maxéville. *Town, Meurthe-et-Moselle.* The suburb of Nancy has a name recorded in the 13th century as *Marchevilla*, probably from the Germanic female personal name *Marica* and Latin *villa*, "estate."

Mayenne. *Department, western France.* The name is that of the river here, from Latin *Meduana*, from the pre-Indoeuropean river root *med*, or possibly from Gaulish *medios*, "middle," referring to the location of the river between the Sarthe and the Vilaine. The town of *Mayenne* here, on the river itself, has a name of the same origin.

Mayet. *Village, Sarthe.* The name may derive from Gaulish *magos*, "field," "market," and the diminutive suffix *-ittum*.

Le Mayet-de-Montagne. *Village, Allier.* The name was recorded in the 13th century as *Masetus*, perhaps from a diminutive form of *mas*, from Latin *mansus*, as for **Masseube**. An origin in Old French *maiet*, a diminutive of *mai*, "May," has also been proposed, denoting a tree planted in May. The addition refers to the proximity of the village to **Châtel-Montagne**.

Le May-sur-Èvre. *Village, Maine-et-Loire.* The name was recorded in the 11th century as *Ulmetum*, from Latin *ulmus*, "elm," and the collective suffix *-etum*. The present *May* thus represents the stressed second syllable of *Ulmetum*. The village is on the *Èvre* River.

Mazamet. *Town, Tarn.* The name may represent a blend of *mas*, from Latin *mansus*, as for **Masseube**, and the personal name *Azamet*, a diminutive of *Azam*.

Mazé. *Village, Maine-et-Loire.* The name derives from the Roman personal name *Masius* and the associative suffix *-acum*.

Mazères. *Village, Ariège.* The name derives from Latin *maceriae*, "ruins," referring to a former Roman settlement here.

Mazingarbe. *Town, Pas-de-Calais.* The name derives from the Germanic personal name *Mazo* and *garba*, "sheaf," "place where corn grows."

Meaux. *City, Seine-et-Marne.* The name was recorded by Strabo in the 1st century BC in the Greek form *Meldole*, probably from root elements *mel*, "gentleness," "softness," and *dol*, "valley," "winding river." This gave the name of the Celtic tribe known as the *Meldi*. Meaux lies in a loop of the Marne River in an intensively cultivated region.

Médoc. *Region, southwestern France.* The Roman name of the region was *Medulicus*, from the tribal name *Meduli*.

Les Mées. *Village, Alpes-de-Haute-Provence.* The name was recorded in the 11th century as *Metas*, from Latin *meta*, "boundary stone," referring to nearby pillar-like rocks (known locally as "The Penitents").

Le Mée-sur-Seine. *Town, Seine-et-Marne.* The suburb of Melun, on the **Seine** River, derives its name from Latin *mansus*, a feudal term for a small farm held by a single tenant.

Megève. *Resort town, Haute-Savoie.* The name probably comes from a pre-Latin root *meg* or *mag*, "height," and the regional suffix *-eva*. Megève is in the French Alps.

Mehun-sur-Yèvre. *Resort town, Cher.* The name was recorded in the 9th century as *Maidunus*, implying an original *Magdunum*, from the Gaulish personal name *Maglo* ("Noble One") and *dunon*, "fort." The town is on the *Yèvre* River.

Meilly-sur-Rouvres. *Village, Côte-d'Or.* The name derives from an original *Meletum*, perhaps from Gaulish *melatia*, "larch." The *Rouvres* is a stream here.

Meisenthal. *Village, Moselle.* The name derives from German *Meise*, "(blue)tit," and *Thal*, "valley."

Melesse. *Town, Ille-et-Vilaine.* The name may derive from the Gallo-Roman personal name *Melicius*, with Latin *villa*, "estate," understood.

Mélicocq. *Village, Oise.* The name was recorded in the 8th century as *Molinus-*

cottus, from Latin *molinus*, "mill," and Germanic *kot*, "cottage."

Melle. *Town, Deux-Sèvres.* The name was recorded in the 8th century as *Medolus*, probably of Gaulish origin, but popularly derived from Latin *metallum*, "metal," "mine," referring to a Roman mint here and to the local silver-bearing mines.

Melun. *Town, Seine-et-Marne.* The Roman name of the town, recorded in the 1st century BC, was *Melodunum*, from Gaulish *metelo-*, "harvester," and *dunon*, "fort."

Mende. *Town, Lozère.* The name was recorded in the 6th century as *Memmate*, from a root *mem*, of uncertain meaning, and the Gaulish suffix *-ate*.

Ménerbes. *Village, Vaucluse.* The name derives from *Minerva*, the Roman goddess of handicrafts.

Mennecy. *Town, Essonne.* The name was recorded in the 13th century as *Mannasi-acum*, from the Roman personal name *Man-acius*, a form of *Menacius*, and the associative suffix *-acum*.

Menou. *Village, Nièvre.* The original name of the settlement was recorded in the 9th century as *Nantivinea*, from Gaulish *nanto-*, "valley," and Latin *vinea*, "vine." In 1697 the village was erected into a marquisate for François-Charles de *Menou* de Charnizay, and took his name.

Mens. *Village, Isère.* The name derives from the Gaulish personal name *Mincius*, with Latin *fundum*, "farm," understood.

Menthon-Saint-Bernard. *Resort village, Haute-Savoie.* The name may come from the Roman personal name *Mento, Mentonis*, but a more likely origin is in pre-Celtic *men-t*, "rock," and the suffix *-onem*. The second part of the name honors *St. Bernard* of Menthon, founder of the hospices on the Great and Little St. Bernard passes (see **Petit-Saint-Bernard**), who was born near here.

Menton. *Resort town, Alpes-Maritimes.*

The name was recorded in the 13th century as *Mentonum*, either from pre-Celtic *men*, "rock," and the suffix *-onem*, or (less likely) from the Roman personal name *Mento, Mentonis*. Menton lies below a ring of mountains.

Mer. *Town, Loir-et-Cher.* The name derives from Latin *mare*, "sea," here used in the sense "pool," "pond." Mer is near the Loire River.

Mercurey. *Village, Saône-et-Loire.* The name derives from the Roman personal name *Mercurius* and the associative suffix *-acum*.

Merdrignac. *Village, Côtes-d'Armor.* The name derives from the Roman personal name *Matrinius* and the associative suffix *-acum*.

Méréville. *Village, Essonne.* The name was recorded in the 11th century as *Merelisvilla*, from the Germanic personal name *Merila* and Latin *villa*, "estate."

Méricourt. *Town, Pas-de-Calais.* The suburb of Lens derives its name from the Germanic personal name *Ermenrich* and Latin *cortem*, accusative of *cors*, "estate."

Mérignac. *City, Gironde.* The suburb of Bordeaux derives its name from the Roman personal name *Matrinius* and the associative suffix *-acum*.

Merkwiller-Pechelbronn. *Village, Bas-Rhin.* The first part of the name derives from the Germanic personal name *Marc* and Latin *villare*, "farmstead." The second part means "source of pitch," from Germanic *pech*, "pitch," and *brunn*, "spring," "well," referring to the historic oil wells here.

Mers-les-Bains. *Resort village, Somme.* The name of the swimming resort ("the baths") derives from Latin *mare*, "sea," referring to its location on the English Channel.

Mertzwiller. *Village, Bas-Rhin.* The first part of the name probably derives from a Germanic form of the Roman personal name *Martinus*. The second part is Latin *villare*, "farmstead."

Méru. *Town, Oise.* The name is of uncertain origin. It may derive from the Roman personal name *Matrius* and the suffix *-ivum.*

Merville. *Town, Nord.* The name derives from Latin *minor,* "lesser," "smaller," and *villa,* "estate," "village."

Merville-Franceville-Plage. *Resort village, Calvados.* The name was recorded in the 11th century as *Matervilla,* from the Germanic personal name *Mather* and Latin *villa,* "estate." *Franceville* arose in the 19th century as a bathing beach (*plage*) designed for Parisians.

Méry-sur-Oise. *Town, Val-d'Oise.* The town, on the **Oise** River, has a name recorded in the 12th century as *Mederiacum,* from the Roman personal name *Materius* and the associative suffix *-acum.*

Meslay-du-Maine. *Village, Mayenne.* The name derives from Latin *mespilum,* "medlar," and the collective suffix *-etum.* The addition locates the village in **Maine.**

Meslay-le-Grenet. *Village, Eure-et-Loir.* The name derives from the Roman personal name *Merula* (or the Germanic name *Merila*) and the associative suffix *-acum.* Jean *Grenet* is recorded as the lord here in 1560.

Le Mesnil-Esnard. *Town, Seine-Maritime.* The suburb of Rouen takes its name from Latin *mansionile,* as for **Masny.** The second part of the name represents that of a local lord.

Mesnil-Follemprise. *Village, Seine-Maritime.* The first part of the name is as for **Masny.** The village was originally known as *Le Mesnil-aux-Moines,* the addition meaning "of the monks." During the Revolution this name was changed to *Mesnil-Follemprise,* implying a "foolish undertaking" (*folle emprise*) of some kind.

Le Mesnil-le-Roi. *Town, Yvelines.* The first part of the name is as for **Masny.** The second denotes possession by the king (*le roi*).

Le Mesnil-sur-Oger. *Village, Marne.*

The first part of the name is as for **Masny.** The second locates the village on the *Oger* River.

Messac. *Village, Ille-et-Vilaine.* The name derives from the Gaulish personal name *Mettius* and the associative suffix *-acum.*

Messei. *Village, Orne.* The name shares the origin of **Messac.**

Les Métairies. *Village, Charente.* French *métairie* is a term for a smallholding or farm held on a *métayage* agreement, under which the farmer pays rent in kind. (The word derives from an early form of French *moitié,* "half.")

Metz. *City, Moselle.* The name was recorded in the 4th century as *Mediomatricum,* then in the early 5th century as *Mettis,* apparently a shortened form of *Mediomatrici,* the name of the Gaulish tribe whose capital this was. Their own name is usually said to mean "those living between the rivers," from Gaulish *medios,* "middle," and *matir,* "mother," the latter referring to the mother goddess who personified a Gaulish river, but a more likely sense is "those of the median mothers," as if *Mediomateres,* referring to the mothers of the "world in the middle," i.e. between heaven and hell. The Roman name, recorded in the 1st century, was *Divodurum,* from Gaulish *diuo-,* "divine," and *duron,* "fort."

Metz-en-Couture. *Village, Pas-de-Calais.* The name derives from the Germanic female personal name *Magiswinda* and Latin *cultura,* "cultivated land." The first part of the name has been influenced by Old French *mes* or *metz,* from Latin *mansus,* as for **Masseube.**

Meudon. *City, Hauts-de-Seine.* The name was recorded in the 1st century BC as *Meclodunum,* from Gaulish *metelo-,* "harvester," and *dunon,* "fort."

Meulan. *Town, Yvelines.* The name was recorded in the 11th century as *Mellentum,* from Gaulish *mediolanon,* "middle (of the) plain." Meulan lies by the Seine on level land that was presumably regarded as midway between two similar areas or that was itself in the middle of a plain, perhaps as a sacred site. The Roman name of the Italian city of *Milan* was *Mediolanum*, of identical origin.

Meung-sur-Loire. *Town, Loiret.* The name represents an original *Magdunum*, from the Gaulish personal name *Maglo* ("prince") and *dunon*, "fort." The second part of the name locates the town on the **Loire**.

Meurchin. *Village, Pas-de-Calais.* The name derives from the Germanic personal name *Marchuni*.

Meursault. *Village, Côte-d'Or.* The name derives from Latin *murus*, "wall," with the Germanic suffix *-iscum*, and Latin *saltus*, "wood," denoting a wood enclosed by a wall.

Meurthe. *River, northeastern France.* The name was recorded in the 7th century as *Murta*, from a pre-Latin source of unknown meaning. Germanic *muor*, "marsh," has been suggested.

Meurthe-et-Moselle. *Department, northeastern France.* The name is that of the two main rivers here, the **Meurthe** joining the **Moselle** just below Nancy.

Meuse. *Department, northeastern France.* The name is that of the river here, from Latin and Gaulish *Mosa*, perhaps from Germanic *mos*, "marsh." The Meuse flows from France across Belgium into the Netherlands, where it is known as the *Maas*.

Meximieux. *Town, Ain.* The name was recorded in the 12th century as *Maximiacus*, from the Roman personal name *Maximius* and the associative suffix *-acum*.

Meylan. *Town, Isère.* The suburb of Grenoble derives its name from Gaulish *mediolanon*, "middle (of the) plain," as for **Meulan**.

Meymac. *Village, Corrèze.* The name derives from the Roman personal name *Maximus* and the associative suffix *-acum*.

Meyrueis. *Resort village, Lozère.* The name derives from the Roman personal name *Matrius* and Gaulish *ialon*, "field," "clearing."

Meyzieu. *Town, Rhône.* The name derives from the Roman personal name *Masius* and the associative suffix *-acum*.

Mèze. *Town, Hérault.* The name was recorded in the 10th century as *Mesoa*, from the pre-Celtic root *mis*, probably meaning "marsh," and the pre-Latin suffix *-ua*. Mèze lies on the shore of the Étang de Thau, a lagoon near the Mediterranean coast.

Mézidon-Canon. *Town, Calvados.* The name was recorded in the 11th century as *Mesodon*, from Latin *mansus*, as for **Masseube**, and a personal name. The second part of the name, originally that of a separate place, derives either from the Roman personal name *Canus* and the suffix *-onem* or from a form of the Gaulish personal name *Cano*.

Mézières. *Village, Indre.* The name derives from Latin *maceriae*, "ruins," meaning those of a Roman settlement. There are other places of the name, and this one is usually distinguished as *Mézières-en-Brenne*, from the region of its location. See also **Lavardin** (2).

Mézin. *Village, Lot-et-Garonne.* The name derives from the Roman personal name *Metius* and the Latin suffix *-inus*.

Midi. *Region, southern France.* The name is used generally for the south of France, where the sun is at its zenith at midday (French *midi*). An inhabitant of the Midi is known as a *Méridional* (from Latin *meridianus*, from *meridies*, "midday").

Midi, Aiguille du. *Mountain, southeastern France.* The name of the peak, in the Mont Blanc Massif, means "midday needle," since the sun is high over it at midday when seen from the north, as typically in Chamonix. Other peaks have similar names, so that the *Pic du Midi* in the Pyrenees lies in the same relation south of Pau, and the Swiss mountain *Dent du Midi* (French *dent*, "tooth") lies south of Vevey and other towns at the upper end of Lake Geneva.

Midi-Pyrénées. *Region, southwestern France.* The administrative region encompasses an extensive area that includes part of the **Midi**, or south of France, and much of the territory bounded to the south by the **Pyrenees.**

Miélan. *Village, Gers.* The name derives from Gaulish *mediolanon*, "middle (of the) plain," as for **Meulan.**

Migennes. *Town, Yonne.* The name was recorded in the 7th century as *Mitiganna*, perhaps from the Germanic personal name *Mitiwan* and a suffix -*a*.

Migné-Auxances. *Town, Vienne.* The suburb of Poitiers derives its name from the Roman personal name *Magnius* and the associative suffix -*acum*. The second part of the name is that of the *Auxances* River here.

Mijoux. *Resort hamlet, Ain.* The ski resort derives its name from Latin *medium*, "middle," and *jugum*, "mountain," describing its location in the Jura Mountains.

Milhaud. *Town, Gard.* The suburb of Nîmes derives its name from the Roman personal name *Aemilius* and the suffix -*avum*.

Millas. *Village, Pyrénées-Orientales.* The name derives from Latin *milliarium*, "milliary stone," otherwise a Roman milestone.

Millau. *Town, Aveyron.* The Old Occitan name of the town, recorded in the 11th century, was *Amigliauvo*, from the Roman personal name *Aemilius* and the suffix -*avum*.

Millevaches, Plateau de. *Upland region, central France.* The name does not mean "thousand cows," despite the extensive use of the tableland for bovine pasturage, but comes from Gaulish *metelo-*, "harvester" (as for **Melle** and **Melun**), and Low Latin *vacius*, from Classical Latin *vacuus*, "empty." The plateau rises to over 3,000 feet (914 m).

Milly-la-Forêt. *Town, Essonne.* The name derives from the Gaulish personal name *Milius* and the associative suffix -*acum*. The addition refers to the Forest of Fontainebleau nearby.

Mimizan. *Town, Landes.* The name derives from the Roman personal name *Mimisius*, from *Mimus*, and the suffix -*anum*.

Minervois. *Region, southern France.* The name comes from the old capital of the region, *Minerve*, Hérault, so called from a temple of *Minerva* there, later replaced by a church.

Mions. *Town, Rhône.* The suburb of Lyon perhaps derives its name from Gaulish *metelo-*, "harvester," and *dunon*, "hill," "fort."

Mios. *Village, Gironde.* The name derives from the Gaulish personal name *Minus* and the Aquitanian suffix -*ossum*.

Miramas. *Town, Bouches-du-Rhône.* The name derives from Occitan *mirar*, "to watch," "to survey," and Latin *mare*, "sea." The town overlooks the lagoon known as the Étang de Berre.

Miramont-de-Guyenne. *Town, Lot-et-Garonne.* The name derives from French *mirer*, Old Provençal *mirar*, "to look at," and Latin *mons, montis*, "mountain." The addition locates the town in **Guyenne.**

Mirande. *Town, Gers.* The town has an Occitan name meaning "watchtower," from *mirar*, "to watch," "to survey."

Mirebeau. *Village, Vienne.* The name was recorded in the 10th century as *Mirebellum*, from words corresponding to French *mirer*, "to look at," and *beau, bel*, "beautiful," referring to a height from which a good view can be had.

Mirecourt. *Town, Vosges.* The name derives from the Germanic personal name *Moderich* and Latin *cortem*, accusative of *cors*, "estate."

Mirepoix. *Town, Ariège.* The Occitan name of the town is *Mirapeis*, "watching the fish," from *mirar*, "to look at," and *peis*, "fish." Mirepoix lies on the Hers River.

Miribel. *Town, Ain.* The name derives from Occitan *mirar*, "to watch," "to survey," and Old French *bel*, "beautiful," denoting a site with a good view.

Modane. *Town, Savoie.* The name was recorded in the 11th century as *Amaldana*, from the Germanic female personal name *Amaldana*. The initial *A-* was then dropped, to give *Modane* by the 17th century.

Moëlan-sur-Mer. *Resort town, Finistère.* The Brittany town may derive its name from the Breton personal name *Moal* and *lan*, "church." It is "on sea" by the Bay of Biscay.

Moirans. *Town, Isère.* The name derives from the Germanic personal name *Maurus* or *Moro* and the suffix *-ing*.

Moirans-en-Montagne. *Village, Jura.* The name was recorded in the 10th century as *Moringum*, from the same source as **Moirans**. The village lies near the Jura Mountains.

Moissac. *Town, Tarn-et-Garonne.* The name derives from the Roman personal name *Mustius* or *Muscius* and the associative suffix *-acum*.

Moissy-Cramayel. *Town, Seine-et-Marne.* The Paris suburb has a name of the same origin as **Moissac**. The second part of the name is of disputed origin.

Le Molay-Littry. *Village, Calvados.* The first part of the name derives from Latin *mola*, "stack," and the collective suffix *-etum*. The second part is from the Gaulish personal name *Lister* and the associative suffix *-acum*.

Molines-en-Queyras. *Village, Hautes-Alpes.* The name comes from Latin *molina*, plural of *molinum*, "mill." The second part of the name, distinguishing this Molines from others, locates it in the *Queyras* region of the French Alps.

Molitg-les-Bains. *Resort village, Pyrénées-Orientales.* The name probably derives from

pre-Latin *mol*, "height," and the suffix *-idium*. There is a thermal establishment ("the baths") here.

Molsheim. *Town, Bas-Rhin.* The name comes from *Mols*, probably a personal name, and Germanic *heim*, "abode."

Monaco. *Principality, southeastern France.* The enclave of France, long an independent principality (but annexed by France during the period 1793–1814), is said to derive its name from Greek *Monoikos*, "solitary," an epithet of Hercules, to whom there was a temple here in the 7th century BC. But this is probably a popular etymology, and the name is more likely to derive from Ligurian *monegu*, "rock," a word preserved in the adjectival *Monégasque*. The present form of the name has been influenced by Latin *monachus*, "monk."

Le Monastier-sur-Gazeille. *Village, Haute-Loire.* The name derives from Latin *monasterium*, "monastery." The addition locates the village on the *Gazeille* River.

Monbazillac. *Village, Dordogne.* The name was recorded in the 15th century as *Mons Bazalanus*, from Latin *mons*, "mountain," and *Bazalanus*, the adjectival form of the personal name *Basilius*, and the associative suffix *-acum*.

Moncontour. *Village, Côtes-d'Armor.* The name derives from Latin *mons*, "mountain," and either Old Provençal *comtor*, "comptor," the title of a functionary responsible to a count, or Old French *conteor*, "treasurer."

Moncoutant. *Village, Deux-Sèvres.* The name derives from Latin *mons*, "mountain," and the Roman personal name *Constantius*.

Mondeville. *Town, Calvados.* The suburb of Caen derives its name from the Scandinavian personal name *Amundi* and Latin *villa*, "estate."

Mondoubleau. *Village, Loir-et-Cher.* The name derives from Latin *mons*, "mountain," and a diminutive form of French *double*, "double."

Monein. *Town, Pyrénées-Atlantiques.* The name derives from the Germanic personal name *Munda* and the suffix *-ing*.

Monestier-de-Clermont. *Resort village, Isère.* The name was recorded in the 13th century as *Monasterium Claromontis*, from Latin *monasterium*, "monastery," "church," and a placename of the same origin as **Clermont**.

Monéteau. *Town, Yonne.* The name was recorded in the 9th century as *Monasteriolum*, as for **Montreuil**.

Le Monêtier-les-Bains. *Resort town, Hautes-Alpes.* The name comes from Latin *monasterium*, "monastery," here distinguished by "the baths," the town's mineral springs.

Monflanquin. *Village, Lot-et-Garonne.* The first part of the name is Latin *mons*, "mountain." The rest is obscure, but possibly from a Germanic personal name *Frankin*.

Monistrol-sur-Loire. *Town, Haute-Loire.* The name derives from Latin *monasteriolum*, as for **Montreuil**. The town is near (but not actually on) the **Loire** River.

Monnaie. *Village, Indre-et-Loire.* The name derives from the Roman personal name *Modinnus* and the associative suffix *-acum*.

La Monnerie-le-Montel. *Village, Puy-de-Dôme.* The first part of the name derives from the personal name *Monier* and the suffix *-ie*. The second part is from Latin *mons, montis*, "mountain," and the suffix *-ilium*.

Monnetier-Mornex. *Village, Haute-Savoie.* The first part of the name derives from Latin *monasterium*, "monastery," "church." The second part, naming a nearby village, apparently derives from the Roman personal name *Maurinus* and the associative suffix *-acum*.

Monpazier. *Village, Dordogne.* The name was recorded in the 13th century as *castrum montis Pazerii*, from Latin *castrum*, "fort,"

mons, montis, "mountain," and Old Provençal *pazier*, "peacekeeper," a term for a guardian of the peace (or a personal name of this origin).

Mons-en-Barœul. *Town, Nord.* The suburb of Lille derives its name from Latin *mons*, "mountain," and the district name *Barœul*.

Mont For mountain names, see the main name, e.g. for *Mont Blanc* see **Blanc, Mont**.

Montagnac. *Village, Hérault.* The name was recorded in the 10th century as *Montanacum*, from the Roman personal name *Montanius* and the associative suffix *-acum*.

La Montagne. *Town, Loire-Atlantique.* The name derives from Latin *montanea*, a derivative of *mons*, "mountain."

Montaigu. *Town, Vendée.* The name derives from Latin *mons, montis*, "mountain," and *acutus*, "pointed."

Montalieu-Vercieu. *Village, Isère.* The first part of the name derives either from the Roman personal name *Montilius* and the associative suffix *-acum*, or from Latin *montilius*, a derivative of *mons*, "mountain," and *-acum*. The second part is from the Roman personal name *Vercius* and *-acum*.

Montargis. *Town, Loiret.* The name was recorded in the 12th century as *Monte Argis*, from Latin *mons*, "hill," and the Gaulish personal name *Argio*, with the associative suffix *-acum*.

Montastruc-la-Conseillère. *Village, Haute-Garonne.* The name derives from Latin *mons, montis*, "mountain," and the local personal name *Astruc*. The addition is literally "the councillor."

Montataire. *Town, Oise.* The name derives from Latin *mons, montis*, "mountain," and the *Thérain* River on which the town lies.

Montauban. *City, Tarn-et-Garonne.* The name was recorded in the 12th century as *Montalba*, from Latin *mons, montis*, "mountain," and *albanus*, "white."

Montbard. *Town, Côte-d'Or.* The name was recorded in the 11th century as *Barris Mons*, from pre-Celtic Gaulish *barr*, "summit," and Latin *mons*, "mountain," giving a virtual tautology. The present form of the name has reversed the two elements.

Montbazon. *Village, Indre-et-Loire.* The name derives from Latin *mons, montis*, "mountain," and the Germanic personal name *Baso*.

Montbéliard. *Town, Doubs.* The name was recorded in the 11th century as *Mons Biligardis*, from Latin *mons*, "mountain," and a personal name of Germanic origin.

Montbrison. *Town, Loire.* The name was recorded in the 11th century as *Castellum Montibrisonis*, from Latin *castellum*, "castle," *mons, montis*, "mountain," and the Germanic personal name *Briso, Brisonis*.

Montbron. *Village, Charente.* The name derives from Latin *mons, montis*, "mountain," and the Germanic personal name *Berulf.*

Montceau-les-Mines. *Town, Saône-et-Loire.* The name was recorded in the 10th century as *Villa Moncellis*, from Latin *villa*, "village," and Low Latin *monticellum*, a diminutive of *mons, montis*, "mountain," Old French *moncel*, "hill." The second part of the name refers to the coal mines here.

Montcenis. *Village, Saône-et-Loire.* The suburb of Le Creusot derives its name from Latin *mons, montis*, "mountain," and *cenisius*, "ash-gray."

Montchanin. *Town, Saône-et-Loire.* The suburb of Le Creusot derives its name from Latin *mons, montis*, "mountain," and possibly the Roman personal name *Caninius.*

Mont-Dauphin. *Village, Hautes-Alpes.* The village arose around a fort built by the military engineer Vauban in 1693 and is named for its location in the region of **Dauphiné.**

Mont-de-Lans. *Village, Isère.* The name derives from Latin *mons, montis*, "mountain," and the Roman personal name *Lentus* or *Lentius.*

Mont-de-Marsan. *Town, Landes.* The name was recorded in the 13th century as *Montis Marcianus*, from Latin *mons, montis*, "mountain," and the Roman personal name *Marcianus.*

Montdidier. *Town, Somme.* The name was recorded in the 11th century as *Castrum Montis Desiderii*, from Latin *castrum*, "fort," *mons, montis*, "mountain," and the Roman personal name *Desiderius* (French *Didier*).

Le Mont-Dore *see* **Mont-Dore, Massif du**

Mont-Dore, Massif du. *Massif, central France.* The mass of volcanic cones and peaks, in the Auvergne, takes its name from the *Dore* River here, its own name coming from Indoeuropean *dur* or *dor*, "stream," as for the **Dordogne.** The Roman name of the massif was *Duranius mons*. The resort town of *Le Mont-Dore*, Puy-de-Dôme, lies amidst the mountains.

Montebourg. *Village, Manche.* The name derives from Latin *mons, montis*, "mountain," and Germanic *burg*, "township." A source in the Germanic female name *Mundeberg* has also been proposed.

Monte Carlo. *Resort town, Monaco.* The Monegasque capital derives its name from Italian *monte*, "mountain," and *Carlos*, "Charles," for Prince *Charles* III of Monaco (1818–1889), who founded the town in 1866.

Montech. *Village, Tarn-et-Garonne.* The name is of obscure origin. It may derive from a Roman personal name *Montidius*, a derivative of Latin *mons, montis*, "mountain."

Montélimar. *Town, Drôme.* The name was recorded in the 13th century as *Montellum Aymardi*, from Latin *montellum*, a diminutive of *mons, montis*, "mountain," and the Germanic personal name *Aymard.*

Montendre. *Village, Charente-Maritime.* The name derives from Latin *mons, montis*, "mountain," and the Germanic personal name *Andar.*

Montereau-Fault-Yonne. *Town, Seine-et-Marne.* The name derives from Latin *monasteriolum*, as for **Montreuil.** The town is located at the point where the **Yonne** River falls (*fault*) into the Seine.

Montesquieu-Volvestre. *Village, Haute-Garonne.* The first part of the name derives from Latin *mons, montis,* "mountain," and Old Provençal *esquiu*, "wild," "fierce," in a warlike sense. The second part names the region of *Volvestre* in which the village lies.

Montesson. *Town, Yvelines.* The Paris suburb derives its name from Latin *mons, montis,* "mountain," and a nickname adopted from Latin *taxo, taxonis,* "badger."

Monteux. *Town, Vaucluse.* The name derives from Latin *mons, montis,* "mountain," and the suffix *-ilium.*

Montfaucon-d'Argonne. *Village, Meuse.* The name derives from Latin *mons, montis,* "mountain," and *falco, falconis,* "falcon," or possibly the Germanic personal name *Falco.* The second part of the name locates the village in **Argonne.**

Montfaucon-en-Velay. *Village, Haute-Loire.* The name is as for **Montfaucon-d'Argonne,** but here the addition locates the village in **Velay.**

Montfermeil. *Town, Seine-Saint-Denis.* The Paris suburb derives its name from Latin *mons, montis,* "mountain," and Old French *fermeil,* a variant of *fermail,* "clasp," here meaning a castle marking the boundary of an estate.

Montfort. *Town, Ille-et-Vilaine.* The name derives from Latin *mons, montis,* "mountain," and *fortis,* "strong," "fortified."

Montfort-l'Amaury. *Village, Yvelines.* The name is as for **Montfort,** with the addition named a local lord.

Montfort-le-Gesnois. *Village, Sarthe.* The name resulted from the union in 1985 of the two communities of *Montfort-le-Rotrou,* as for **Montfort,** the addition naming a local lord, and *Pont-de-Gennes,* from French *pont,* "bridge," and Gaulish *genaua,*

"river mouth" (or perhaps the Germanic female personal name *Geneda*), with *Gesnois* the adjectival form of *Gennes.*

Montfrin. *Village, Gard.* The name derives from Latin *mons, montis,* "mountain," and an element of uncertain origin, but possibly from the Roman personal name *Frennius.*

Montgenèvre. *Resort village, Hautes-Alpes.* The name was recorded in the 11th century as *Mons Genevus,* from Latin *mons,* "mountain," and a combination of pre-Gaulish *gen,* "angle," "bend," and the pre-Celtic suffix *-evus.* The name was then recorded in the 15th century as *Mont Genevre,* under the influence of French *genièvre,* "juniper."

Montgeron. *Town, Essonne.* The name derives from Latin *mons, montis,* "mountain," and the Germanic personal name *Giso.*

Montgiscard. *Village, Haute-Garonne.* The name derives from Latin *mons, montis,* "mountain," and the Germanic personal name *Wisichart.*

Montguyon. *Village, Charente-Maritime.* The name derives from Latin *mons, montis,* "mountain," and the Germanic personal name *Wido.*

Monthermé. *Village, Ardennes.* The name derives from Latin *mons, montis,* "mountain," and the Germanic personal name *Herimer.*

Montier-en-Der. *Village, Haute-Marne.* The name derives from Latin *monasterium.* "monastery," "church," and its location in *Der,* a forest name, from Gaulish *deruos,* "oak."

Montignac. *Village, Dordogne.* The name was recorded in the 11th century as *Montignacum,* from the Roman personal name *Montinius,* from *Montinus,* and the associative suffix *-acum.*

Montigny-en-Gohelle. *Town, Pas-de-Calais.* The name was recorded in the 14th century as *Montigniacum,* from the Roman personal name *Montinius*, a form of *Montinus*, and the associative suffix *-acum*. The addition names the local region.

Montigny-en-Ostrevent. *Town, Nord.* The suburb of Douai derives its name from Latin *montinus*, from *mons*, "mountain," "hill," and the name of the local region.

Montigny-le-Bretonneux. *Town, Yvelines.* The suburb of the new town of Saint-Quentin-en-Yvelines has a name recorded in the 14th century as *Montiniacum le Brestonneux*, from the Roman personal name *Montinius*, a form of *Montinus*, and the associative suffix *-acum*. The addition may have evolved from pre-Gaulish *bracu*, "marsh."

Montigny-lès-Cormeilles. *Town, Val-d'Oise.* The name of the Paris suburb was recorded in the 13th century as *Montiniacum*, from the Roman personal name *Montinius*, a form of *Montinus*, and the associative suffix *-acum*. The addition locates the town near (*lès*) **Cormeilles-en-Parisis.**

Montigny-lès-Metz. *Town, Moselle.* The name was recorded in the 14th century as *Montigni*, from Latin *montinus*, from *mons*, "mountain," "hill." The addition locates the town near (*lès*) **Metz**, of which it is now actually a suburb.

Montivilliers. *Town, Seine-Maritime.* The suburb of Le Havre has a name recorded in the 13th century as *Monasterium villare*," from Latin *monasterium*, "monastery," "church," and *villare*, "farmstead."

Montjean-sur-Loire. *Village, Maine-et-Loire.* The name derives from Latin *mons, montis*, "mountain," and the personal name *Jean* (John), perhaps that of the saint. The village is on the **Loire** River.

Montlhéry. *Town, Essonne.* The name derives from Latin *mons, montis*, "mountain," and the Germanic personal name *Liuderich*.

Montlouis. *Village, Pyrénées-Orientales.* The name derives from Latin *mons, montis*,

"mountain," and the Germanic personal name *Hlodwig*.

Montlouis-sur-Loire. *Town, Indre-et-Loire.* The name was recorded in the 6th century as *Mons Laudiacus*, from Latin *mons*, "mountain," followed by the Roman personal name *Laudius* and the associative suffix *-acum*. The town is on the **Loire** River.

Montluçon. *City, Allier.* The name derives from Latin *mons*, "mountain," followed by the Roman personal name *Luccius* or *Lussius* and the suffix *-onem*.

Montluel. *Town, Ain.* The name derives from Latin *mons, montis*, "mountain," and probably *locellum*, a diminutive of *locus*, "place."

Montmagny. *Town, Val-d'Oise.* The Paris suburb derives its name from Latin *mons, montis*, "mountain," followed by the Roman personal name *Manius* and the associative suffix *-acum*.

Montmartre see Appendix 4.

Montmaurin. *Village, Haute-Garonne.* The name derives from Latin *mons, montis*, "mountain," and the Roman personal name *Maurinus*.

Montmédy. *Village, Meuse.* The name derives from Latin *mons, montis*, "mountain," followed by the Gaulish personal name *Madia* and the associative suffix *-acum*.

Montmélian. *Town, Savoie.* The name derives from Latin *mons, montis*, "mountain," and Gaulish *mediolanon*, "middle (of the) plain," as for **Meulan.**

Montmerle-sur-Saône. *Village, Ain.* The name derives from Latin *mons, montis*, "mountain," and French *merle*, "blackbird." The village is on the **Saône** River.

Montmirail. *Village, Marne.* The name derives from Latin *mons, montis*, "mountain," and Old French *mirail*, Old Provençal *miralh*, "mirror," meaning a military lookout post.

Montmoreau-Saint-Cybard. *Village, Charente.* The name derives from Latin *mons, montis,* "mountain," and the Roman personal name *Maurellus.* The second part of the name is a dedication to *St. Eparchius,* a 6th-century hermit honored at Angoulême.

Montmorency. *Town, Val-d'Oise.* The name of the Paris suburb was recorded in the 10th century as *Mons Maurenciacus,* from Latin *mons,* "hill," and the Roman personal name *Maurentius,* with the associative suffix *-acum.* Montmorency was the seat of the dukes of this title until 1689, when the town passed to the Condé family, dukes of Enghien in Belgium, who renamed it *Enghien.* When this happened, the Montmorency name was transferred to *Beaufort,* Aube, now **Montmorency-Beaufort.** The Enghien name remained here until the Revolution, when it passed to the new resort of **Engien-les-Bains** nearer Paris.

Montmorency-Beaufort. *Village, Aube.* The village was originally *Beaufort,* French for "beautiful fort." In 1689 the name of **Montmorency** was transferred here by order of the duke of Montmorency, lord (seigneur) of Beaufort.

Montmorillon. *Town, Vienne.* The name was recorded in the 11th century as *Mons Maurilionis,* from Latin *mons,* "mountain," and the Roman personal name *Maurilio,* a diminutive of *Maurus.*

Montmorot. *Village, Jura.* The suburb of Lons-le-Saunier derives its name from Latin *mons, montis,* "mountain," and the Roman personal name *Maurittus,* a diminutive form of *Maurus.*

Montoir-de-Bretagne. *Town, Loire-Maritime.* The name derives from Latin *monasterium,* "monastery," "church." The distinguishing addition locates the town in *Brittany* (**Bretagne**).

Montoire-sur-le-Loir. *Town, Loir-et-Cher.* The name derives from Latin *mons, montis,* "mountain," and *aureus,* "golden." The town is located on the **Loir** River.

Montparnasse *see* Appendix 4.

Montpellier. *City, Hérault.* The name was recorded in the 10th century as *Mons pislerius,* a variant of *Mons pestellarius,* from Latin *mons,* "mountain," and *pestellum,* from *pastellum,* "pastel," "dye," probably with reference to the dyes produced hereabouts. The Occitan name of Montpellier is *Lo Clapàs,* diminutive *Clapasson,* "the rock," "the heap of stones," from the root element *klapp,* an extended form of *kal,* "rock."

Montpezat-de-Quercy. *Village, Tarn-et-Garonne.* The village, in the region of **Quercy,** derives its name from Latin *mons, montis,* "mountain," and Provençal *pesat,* a form of the verb *pedare,* "to pole up vines," implying a height whose enclosure had firm foundations.

Montpon-Ménestérol. *Town, Dordogne.* The first part of the name, recorded in the 12th century as *Montpao,* derives from Latin *mons, montis,* "mountain," and possibly Latin *pavo, pavonis,* "peacock." The second part is Latin *monasteriolum,* a diminutive of *monasterium,* "monastery," "church."

Montréal. *Village, Aude.* The name derives from Latin *mons, montis,* "mountain," and *regalis,* "royal," denoting a possession of the king.

Montredon-Labessonnié. *Village, Tarn.* The first part of the name is as for **Montrond-les-Bains.** The second part is presumably based on Gaulish *betua,* "birch."

Montréjeau. *Village, Haute-Garonne.* The name has the same origin as **Montréal.**

Montreuil. *Town, Seine-Saint-Denis.* The name of the Paris suburb was recorded in the 10th century as *Monsteroll,* from Latin *monasteriolum,* a diminutive of *monasterium,* "monastery," "church." The town is also known as *Montreuil-sous-Bois* ("by the wood"), for its location near the Bois de Vincennes.

Montreuil *see* **Montreuil-sur-Mer**

Montreuil-Bellay. *Town, Maine-et-Loire.* The first part of the name is identical to that of **Montreuil**. The second part derives from Latin *betulla*, "birch."

Montreuil-Juigné. *Town, Maine-et-Loire.* The suburb of Angers derives the first part of its name from the same source as **Montreuil**. The second part represents the Roman personal name *Juvenius* and the associative suffix *-acum*.

Montreuil-sur-Mer. *Town, Pas-de-Calais.* The name, recorded in the 11th century as *Monasteriolum*, has an identical origin to that of **Montreuil**, from which it is distinguished by its addition, although it is no longer actually "on sea" and the suffix is often omitted.

Montrevel-en-Bresse. *Village, Ain.* The name derives from Latin *mons, montis*, "mountain," and *rebellis*, "rebellious," "impregnable," implying military resistance. The village is in the region of **Bresse**.

Montrichard. *Village, Loir-et-Cher.* The name derives from Latin *mons, montis*, "mountain," and either the Germanic personal name *Trecchard* or French *tricheur*, "trickster," denoting a hazard. The latter part of the name was later assimilated to *Richard*.

Montrond-les-Bains. *Resort village, Loire.* The name derives from Latin *mons, montis*, "mountain," and *rotundus*, "round." The village has thermal springs ("the baths").

Montrouge. *Town, Hauts-de-Seine.* The Paris suburb derives its name from Latin *mons, montis*, "mountain," and *rubeus*, "red," describing the color of the soil.

Monts. *Town, Indre-et-Loire.* The name derives from a plural form of Latin *mons, montis*, "mountain."

Monts For mountain names, see the main name, e.g. for *Monts d'Arrée* see **Arrée, Monts d'**.

Mont-Saint-Aignan. *Town, Seine-Maritime.* The suburb of Rouen derives its name from Latin *mons, montis*, "mountain," and a dedication to *St. Anianus*, 5th-century bishop of Orléans.

Mont-Saint-Éloi. *Village, Pas-de-Calais* The name derives from Latin *mons, montis*, "mountain," and a dedication to *St. Eligius*, 7th-century bishop of Noyon.

Mont-Saint-Martin. *Town, Meurthe-et-Moselle.* The suburb of Longwy derives its name from Latin *mons, montis*, "mountain," and a dedication to *St. Martin* of Tours, 4th-century evangelizer of Gaul.

Le Mont-Saint-Michel. *Islet, northwestern France.* The name of the fortified rock off the coast of northwestern France was recorded in the 10th century as *Mons Sancti Michaelis*, "St. Michael's mount." It was given this Latin name in 709, when the abbey here was founded and dedicated to the Archangel Michael. It has an almost exact counterpart in *St. Michael's Mount*, off the coast of Cornwall, England, where St. Michael was said to have appeared in 710. This St. Michael's Mount was later given to its French namesake, either by Edward the Confessor in *c.*1030 or by Robert, count of Mortain, in *c.*1070. The reason for the donation was presumably the similarity of the two sites and their dates of origin.

Montsalvy. *Village, Cantal.* The name derives from Latin *mons, montis*, "mountain," and the Roman personal name *Salvius*.

Montsec. *Village, Meuse.* The name was recorded in the 9th century as *Motissovilla*, from the Roman personal name *Moticius*, from *Motius*, and the suffix *-onem*, apparently later changed to the associative suffix *-acum*. The present form of the name is popularly taken to mean "dry mountain," as if from Latin *mons siccus*.

Montségur. *Hamlet, Ariège.* The name was recorded in the 13th century as *castrum Montissecuri*, from Latin *castrum*, "fort," and a conjectural *mons securus*, "safe mountain." But this etymology probably masks a Basque origin in *muno*, "mountain," "hill," and *eguzki* or *iguzki*, "sun," or *egun*, "day," denoting an ancient site of sun worship.

Montville. *Town, Seine-Maritime.* The name may derive from the Germanic personal name *Modo* and Latin *villa,* "estate."

Morangis. *Town, Essonne.* The Paris suburb stands on the site of place originally called *Louans,* from the Germanic personal name *Lauba* and the suffix *-ing.* In 1689 the settlement was raised to a countship for the seigneur (lord) of *Morangis,* Marne, and took his name, itself apparently from Latin *mons,* "mountain," and the Germanic personal name *Rango,* a variant of *Renco,* with the associative suffix *-iacum.*

Morbecque. *Village, Nord.* The name derives from Dutch *moer,* "moor," "marsh," and *beek* (Germanic *bach*), "stream."

Morbihan. *Department, northwestern France.* The name comes from the *Golfe du Morbihan* (Gulf of Morbihan) on the southern coast of Brittany, with Breton name *Mor-Bihan,* from *mor bihan,* "little sea," from *mor,* "sea," and *bihan,* "little."

Morcenx. *Town, Landes.* The name may derive from the Germanic personal name *Mauricho* and the suffix *-ing.*

Morestel. *Village, Isère.* The name is of uncertain origin. It may have evolved from a derivative of pre-Celtic *mor,* "rocky hill," and a double suffix *-est* and *-ellum,* rather than from the Germanic personal name *Maurisier* or a derivative of Latin *maurus,* "black."

Moret-sur-Loing. *Town, Seine-et-Marne.* The name derives from Latin *murus,* "wall," and the diminutive suffix *-ittum.* The town is on the **Loing** River.

Moreuil. *Town, Somme.* The name derives from Latin *morus,* "blackberry," and Gaulish *ialon,* "clearing."

Morey-Saint-Denis. *Village, Côte-d'Or.* The name, recorded in the 12th century as *Mirriaca,* is of uncertain origin. It may derive from the Germanic personal name *Maur* and the associative suffix *-iacum.* The second part of the name is a dedication to *St. Denis* (see **Saint-Denis**).

Morhange. *Town, Moselle.* The name derives from the Germanic personal name *Mauricho* and the suffix *-ing.*

Morienval. *Village, Oise.* The name was recorded in the 6th century as *Mauriniane vallis,* from the Roman personal name *Maurinius* and the suffix *-anum* with Latin *vallis,* "valley."

Morières-lès-Avignon. *Town, Vaucluse.* The name derives from Latin *morus,* "blackberry bush" and the suffix *-aria.* The town is near (*lès*) **Avignon,** of which it is now a suburb.

Morizécourt. *Village, Vosges.* The name derives from the Roman personal name *Maletius* and the associative suffix *-acum,* followed by Latin *cortem,* accusative of *cors,* "estate." The present form is due to an association with St. *Maurice,* the patron saint of the parish.

Morlaàs. *Village, Pyrénées-Atlantiques.* The name derives from the Roman personal name *Maurilus* or *Maurellus* and the suffix *-anum.*

Morlaix. *Town, Finistère.* The name derives from the Roman personal name *Maurilus* or *Maurellus* and the associative suffix *-acum.*

Mornant. *Village, Rhône.* The name probably derives from Latin *maurus,* "black," "dark," and Gaulish *nanto-,* "valley."

Morosaglia. *Village, Haute-Corse.* The village, in north central Corsica, has a name of uncertain origin. It may have evolved from a derivative of the Roman personal name *Maurusius.*

Morsang-sur-Orge. *Town, Essonne.* The name of the Paris suburb was recorded in the 10th century as *Murcinctus,* from Latin *murocinctus,* "surrounded by walls," denoting a fortified place. The town is by the **Orge** River.

Morsbronn-les-Bains. *Resort village, Bas-Rhin.* The name derives from the Germanic personal name *Maur* or *Moro* and *brunn,* "spring." The village is a spa ("the baths").

Morschwiller-le-Bas. *Village, Haut-Rhin.* The suburb of Mulhouse derives its name from the Germanic personal name *Maurus* or *Moro* and Latin *villare,* "farmstead." The village is *bas* ("below") by contrast with *Obermorschwiller* (Germanic *ober,* "above"), a few miles to the south.

Mortagne-au-Perche. *Town, Orne.* The name derives from the *Mauritani,* "Mauritanians," meaning the North African people who had immigrated elsewhere in the Roman Empire. The town is in the region of **Perche.**

Mortagne-sur-Sèvre. *Town, Vendée.* The name has the same origin as for **Mortagne-au-Perche,** but here the distinguishing addition locates the town on the **Sèvre** Nantaise River.

Mortain. *Village, Manche.* The name was recorded in the 11th century as *Moretoin,* from Latin *Mauritanum fundum,* "(village) founded by *Mauritanus.*"

Morteau. *Town, Doubs.* The name was recorded in the 12th century as *Mortua Aqua,* Latin for "dead water," as for **Aigues-Mortes,** but here on the Doubs River.

Morvan. *Region, east central France.* The mountainous region, in the Massif Central, takes its name from the Roman personal name *Morvennum.*

Morzine. *Village, Haute-Savoie.* The origin of the name is uncertain. It may derive from pre-Celtic *mor,* "rocky hill."

Moselle. *Department, northeastern France.* The name is that of the river here, known to the Romans as *Mosella,* a diminutive form of *Mosa,* the **Meuse.** The Moselle rises in France but then flows north and northeast to enter Germany, where it is known as the *Mosel.*

La Mothe-Achard. *Village, Vendée.* The first part of the name derives from Latin *motta,* "height," "motte," meaning a mound on which a castle is built, and by extension

the castle itself. The second part is the Germanic name of a local lord.

La Mothe-Saint-Héray. *Village, Deux-Sèvres.* The first part of the name derives from Latin *motta,* "height," "motte," meaning a mound on which a castle is built, and by extension the castle itself. The second is a dedication to *St. Aradius.*

La Motte-Servolex. *Town, Savoie.* The suburb of Chambéry derives the first part of its name from Latin *motta,* "height," "motte," meaning a mound on which a castle is built, and by extension the castle itself. The community was originally *La Motte-Montfort,* as for **Montfort,** but took its present name name in 1802 after uniting with the nearby parish of *Servolex,* a name popularly derived from Latin *silvula,* "little wood," but more likely from a personal name with the associative suffix *-acum.*

Mougins. *Resort town, Alpes-Maritimes.* The name derives from pre-Celtic *mug,* "rock," "mound," and the Latin suffix *-inum.*

Mouguerre. *Village, Pyrénées-Atlantiques.* The suburb of Bayonne derives its name from Basque *muger,* "steep," referring to the hill above Bayonne on which the village lies.

Mouilleron-en-Pareds. *Village, Vendée.* The name derives from Latin *mollaria* (from *mollis,* "soft," and the suffix *-aria*) and the suffix *-onem,* denoting a damp place in the *Pareds* region.

Moulins. *Town, Allier.* The name was recorded in the 10th century as *villa Molinis,* from Latin *villa,* "village," and *molinum,* "mill."

Moulins-lès-Metz. *Town, Moselle.* The town, with a name as for **Moulins,** is near (*lès*) **Metz,** of which it is now actually a suburb.

Moulis-en-Médoc. *Village, Gironde.* The village, in the region of **Médoc,** derives its name from Latin *molinum,* "mill."

Mourenx. *Town, Pyrénées-Atlantiques.*

The name derives from the Germanic personal name *Maurus* or *Moro* and the suffix *-ing*.

Mouriès. *Village, Bouches-du-Rhône.* The name derives from Latin *morus*, "blackberry bush," and the suffix *-arium*.

Mourmelon-le-Grand. *Town, Marne.* The name derives from Latin *murmur*, "murmur," and the suffix *-onem*, referring to a mill that "murmurs." The town is "great" (*grand*) by comparison with nearby *Mourmelon-le-Petit*.

Mouroux. *Village, Seine-et-Marne.* The name probably derives from Latin *morus*, "blackberry," and the suffix *-osum*.

Le Moustier. *Archaeological site, southwestern France.* The cave near Les Eyzies, Dordogne, noted for its important archaeological finds, takes its name from Latin *monasterium*, "monastery."

Moustiers-Sainte-Marie. *Resort village, Alpes-de-Haute-Provence.* The name was recorded in the 11th century as *ecclesia Sancte Marie in Monasterio*, Latin for "St. Mary's church in the monastery." The chapel of Notre-Dame-de-Beauvoir here is a place of pilgrimage.

Mouthe. *Village, Doubs.* The name may represent a local form of French *motte*, from Latin *motta*, "mound," meaning one on which a castle is built, and by extension the castle itself.

Mouthiers-sur-Boëme. *Village, Charente.* The name derives from Latin *monasterium*, "monastery," "church." The addition locates the village on the *Boëme* River.

Moûtiers. *Town, Savoie.* The name derives from Latin *monasterium*, "monastery," "church."

Mouvaux. *Town, Nord.* The suburb of Roubaix has a name of obscure origin. It may derive from the Germanic personal name *Modo* and Latin *vallis*, "valley."

Mouy. *Town, Oise.* The name derives from the Roman personal name *Modius* and the associative suffix *-acum*.

Mouzon. *Village, Ardennes.* The name was recorded in the 5th century as *Musmagenses*, from the **Meuse** River on which the village lies and Gaulish *magos*, "market."

Moyenmoutier. *Village, Vosges.* The name was recorded in the 9th century as *Meieni monasterium*, from the Germanic personal name *Megino* and Latin *monasterium*, "monastery," "church." The first part of the name was subsequently influenced by Latin *medianum*, "middle."

Moyeuvre-Grande. *Town, Moselle.* The name was recorded in the 9th century as *Modover superior*, apparently from *Modo*, the name of a stream here, and Gaulish *briga*, "fortified place." The town is "great" (*grande*) by contrast with nearby *Moyeuvre-Petite*.

Mozac. *Village, Puy-de-Dôme.* The name comes from the Roman personal name *Maletius* or Gaulish personal name *Mausos* and the associative suffix *-acum*.

La Mulatière. *Town, Rhône.* The name derives from Latin *mulatus*, a derivative of *mulus*, "mule," and the suffix *-aria*, denoting a relay post for mules (rather than a place where they were bred).

Mulhouse. *City, Haut-Rhin.* The name was recorded in the 9th century as *Mullenhausen*, from Germanic *mühle*, "mill," and *haus*, "house." The city is close to the border with Germany, where it is known as *Mülhausen*. (Along with the rest of Alsace, Mulhouse was actually annexed by Germany from 1870 through 1918 and again in World War II.)

Mulsanne. *Town, Sarthe.* The name, recorded in the 11th century as *Murcenae*, is of uncertain origin. The suffix is probably Celtic *-enna*.

Munster. *Town, Haut-Rhin.* The name was recorded in the 8th century as *Monasteriolo*, from an Alsatian form of Latin *monasterium*, "monastery."

Mur-de-Bretagne. *Village, Côtes-d'Armor.* The name means literally "wall of

Brittany," from Latin *murus*, "wall," denoting a fortification of some kind, and French **Bretagne**.

Murat. *Village, Cantal.* The name was recorded in the 11th century as *Muratum*, from Latin *murus*, "wall," denoting a fortified place, and the suffix *-atum*.

La Mure. *Town, Isère.* The name derives from Latin *murus*, "wall," here denoting the walls of a ruined building.

Les Mureaux. *Town, Yvelines.* The name derives from Latin *murus*, "wall," and the diminutive suffix *-ellum*.

Muret. *Town, Haute-Garonne.* The name was recorded in the 10th century as *Murellum*, a diminutive of Latin *murus*, "wall," denoting an early fortification here.

Murol. *Resort village, Puy-de-Dôme.* The name was recorded in the 14th century as now, from Latin *murus*, "wall," meaning a fortified place, and the diminutive suffix *-olum*.

Murviel-lès-Béziers. *Village, Hérault.* The name derives from Latin *murus*, "wall," and *vetulus*, "old," denoting a former fortified site. The village is near (*lès*) **Béziers**.

Mutzig. *Town, Bas-Rhin.* The name was recorded in the 10th century as *Muzzeca*, from the Roman personal name *Mustius* or *Muscius* and the associative suffix *-acum*.

Le Muy. *Village, Var.* The name was recorded in the 12th century as *Modius*, perhaps from Latin *modius*, "birch."

Muzillac. *Village, Morbihan.* The name was recorded in the 12th century as *Musuliacum*, from the Gallo-Roman personal name *Musullius*, from Gaulish *Musius*, and the associative suffix *-acum*.

Naintré. *Town, Vienne.* The name, recorded in the 9th century as *Nintriacum*, is of uncertain origin. It may derive from the Gaulish personal name *Nemeturius*, from the *Nemeturi*, an Alpine tribe, and the associative suffix *-acum*.

Najac. *Village, Aveyron.* The name derives from the Roman personal name *Navius* and the associative suffix *-acum*.

Nançay. *Village, Cher.* The name was recorded in the 13th century as *Nanciacum*, from the same origin as **Nancy**.

Nancy. *City, Meurthe-et-Moselle.* The name was recorded in the 9th century as *Nanceiacum* or *Nantiacum*, from the Gaulish personal name *Nantio* and the associative suffix *-acum*.

Nandy. *Town, Seine-et-Marne.* The name probably derives from the Germanic personal name *Nandius* and the associative suffix *-acum*.

Nangis. *Town, Seine-et-Marne.* The name derives from the Germanic personal name *Nantgis* and the associative suffix *-iacum*.

Nanterre. *City, Hauts-de-Seine.* The name was recorded in the 6th century as *Nemptum Dorum*, from Gaulish *Nemeto Duru*, from *nemeton*, "sanctuary," "holy wood," and *duron*, "house," "village."

Nantes. *City, Loire-Atlantique.* The name was recorded in the 6th century as *Namnetas*, from the *Namnetes*, the Gaulish tribe whose capital was here, their own name perhaps deriving from Gaulish *nanto-*, "valley." The Breton name of Nantes is *Naoned*, and its earlier Roman name was *Condevincum*.

Nanteuil-le-Haudouin. *Village, Oise.* The name derives from Gaulish *nanto-*, "valley," "stream," and *ialo*, "clearing." The addition derives from the Germanic personal name *Hildiwin*, that of a local lord.

Nanteuil-lès-Meaux. *Town, Seine-et-Marne.* The name has the same origin as that of **Nanteuil-le-Haudouin**, but the addition here locates the town near (*lès*) **Meaux**.

Nantiat. *Village, Haute-Vienne.* The name probably derives from the Gaulish personal name *Nantuus*, from *Nantius*, and the associative suffix *-iacum*.

Nantua. *Town, Ain.* The name was

recorded in the 9th century as *Nantoadis*, from Gaulish *nanto-*, "valley," "stream," and the Gaulish suffix *-ate*.

Narbonne. *City, Aude.* The name was recorded in the 6th century BC as *Narba*, perhaps of Iberian or Aquitanian origin, from a source related to the root *nar*, found in river names. (Ptolemy, in the 2d century AD, named the Aude River as *Narbon*.) Other possibilities are an origin in *Narbo*, the name of an Iberian god, or in Basque *nare*, "calm," "peaceful," and *baia*, "bay," referring to the former lagoon to the south of the city, in Roman times a thriving port.

Naucelle. *Village, Aveyron.* The name derives from Latin *nova*, "new," and *cella*, "cell," "holy place."

Navarre. *Region, southwestern France.* The former kingdom of northern Spain and southwestern France, on both sides of the Pyrenees, had the Medieval Latin name of *Navarra*, from pre-Latin *nava*, "plain," and *arra*, of unknown origin. The name is now that of a province of northern Spain, the Spanish form of the name being *Navarra*.

Naves. *Village, Corrèze.* The name derives from pre-Latin *nava*, "plain," "plateau."

Nay-Bourdettes. *Village, Pyrénées-Atlantiques.* The first part of the name is perhaps from the Gaulish personal name *Nadius*, with Latin *fundum*, "farm," understood. The second part derives from Old French *borde*, Provençal *borda*, "cottage," "small farm," and the diminutive suffix *-ittum*.

Neauphle-le-Château. *Village, Yvelines.* The name derives from Germanic *nivi*, "new," and *alah*, "temple." The castle (*château*) is that of Pontchartrain nearby.

Nemours. *Town, Seine-et-Marne.* The name, popularly said to represent French *ne mourra* ("shall not die"), was recorded in the 9th century as *Nemausus*, as for **Nîmes**, but here stressed on the second syllable, in the Latin manner.

Nérac. *Town, Lot-et-Garonne.* The name was recorded in the 12th century as *Neriacum*, from the Gaulish personal name *Nerius* and the associative suffix *-acum*.

Néris-les-Bains. *Resort village, Allier.* The name was recorded in the 4th century as *Aquis Neris*, from Latin *aquae*, "waters," and the god *Nerius*. There were Roman baths here.

Nérondes. *Village, Cher.* The name derives from a root *nirum* or *nirom*, of uncertain origin, and the Gaulish (and pre-Gaulish) suffix *-ate*.

Nersac. *Village, Charente.* The name derives from the Gaulish personal name *Nartius* or *Narissius* and the associative suffix *-acum*.

Nesle. *Village, Somme.* The name seems to derive from Germanic *nige*, "new," and Latin *villa*, "estate," corresponding to Latin *nova villa*, as for **Neuville-sur-Saône**.

Le Neubourg. *Village, Eure.* The name was recorded in the 11th century as *Novus Burgus*, Latin for "new stronghold."

Neuf-Brisach. *Village, Haut-Rhin.* The name means "new Brisach," referring to the fortress built near the Rhine in 1698 opposite Germany's *Breisach-am-Rhein* (French *Vieux-Brisach*). The name derives from the Gaulish personal name *Brisios* and the associative suffix *-acum*.

Neufchâteau. *Town, Vosges.* The name was recorded in the 11th century as *Novum Castrum*, Latin for "new fort."

Neufchâtel-en-Bray. *Town, Seine-Maritime.* The name shares the origin of **Neufchâteau**. The addition locates the town in **Bray**.

Neuilly-en-Thelle. *Village, Oise.* The name is as for **Neuilly-sur-Seine**, but with an addition locating the village in the local region of *Thelle*.

Neuilly-Plaisance. *Town, Seine-Saint-Denis.* The main name of the Paris suburb is as for **Neuilly-sur-Seine**. The addition is the formerly separate *Plaisance*, apparently named for the Italian city of *Piacenza*, known in French as *Plaisance*, literally "pleasure."

Neuilly-Saint-Front. *Village, Aisne.* The name is as for **Neuilly-sur-Seine**, with the addition a dedication to *St. Fronto*, 4th-century bishop of Périgueux.

Neuilly-sur-Marne. *Town, Seine-Saint-Denis.* The Paris suburb, on the **Marne** River, shares the origin of its name with **Neuilly-sur-Seine**.

Neuilly-sur-Seine. *Town, Hauts-de-Seine.* The Paris suburb, near the **Seine** River, derives its name from Latin *novellus*, a diminutive of *novus*, "new," referring to newly cleared land.

Neuves-Maisons. *Town, Meurthe-et-Moselle.* The name, recorded in the 15th century as *Les Nueves Manson*, means "new houses."

Neuvic (1). *Resort village, Corrèze.* The name derives from Latin *novus*, "new," and *vicus*, "village."

Neuvic (2). *Village, Dordogne.* The name has the same origin as **Neuvic** (1).

Neuville-aux-Bois. *Village, Loiret.* The name is as for **Neuville-sur-Saône**, the addition ("by the woods") referring to the Forest of Orléans here.

Neuville-de-Poitou. *Village, Vienne.* The name is as for **Neuville-sur-Saône**, the addition locating the village in **Poitou**.

Neuville-en-Ferrain. *Town, Nord.* The name is as for **Neuville-sur-Saône**, the addition being a local region.

Neuville-Saint-Rémy. *Village, Nord.* The name is as for **Neuville-sur-Saône**, the addition being a dedication to *St. Remigius* (see **Reims**).

Neuville-Saint-Vaast. *Village, Pas-de-Calais.* The name is as for **Neuville-sur-Saône**, the addition being a dedication to *St. Vedas*, 5th-century bishop of Arras.

Neuville-sur-l'Escaut. *Village, Nord.*

The name is as for **Neuville-sur-Saône**, the addition locating the village on the **Escaut** River.

Neuville-sur-Saône. *Town, Rhône.* The name derives from Latin *nova villa*, "new estate." The addition locates the town on the **Saône** River.

Neuvy-Deux-Clochers. *Village, Cher.* The name derives from Latin *novus vicus*, "new village." The addition refers to two bell towers (*deux clochers*) here.

Neuvy-Saint-Sépulchre. *Village, Indre.* The name was recorded in the 11th century as *Novus Vicus ante altare Sancti Sepulchri*, "new village before the altar of the Holy Sepulcher." The round church here is patterned on the Holy Sepulcher in Jerusalem.

Nevers. *City, Nièvre.* The name was recorded in the 4th century as *Nevirnum*, from *Nevera*, the Latin name of the **Nièvre** River, on which the town stands. The Roman name of Nevers, recorded by Caesar in the 1st century BC, was *Noviodunum*, from Gaulish *nouio-*, "new," and *dunon*, "fort."

Nexon. *Village, Haute-Vienne.* The name, recorded early as *Aneisso*, derives from the Gaulish personal name *Anectius* and the suffix *-onem*.

Niaux. *Hamlet, Ariège.* The name may derive from Latin *nidale*, "hollow," as if describing a place in a nest (Latin *nidus*).

Nice. *Resort city, Alpes-Maritimes.* The name was recorded in the 1st century BC as *Nicaea*, from Greek *Nikaia*, "giving victory," from *Nike*, the goddess of victory, to whom the place was dedicated following a victory by the Massaliotes over the Ligurians or the Etruscans. The city is not far from the border with Italy, where it is known as *Nizza*.

Nicole. *Village, Lot-et-Garonne.* The name apparently represents a form of *Lincoln*, the English city.

Niederbronn-les-Bains. *Resort town, Vosges.* The name derives from Germanic *nieder*, "lower," and *brunn*, "spring," by contrast with nearby *Oberbronn* (Germanic *ober*, "higher"). The town has a thermal establishment with mineral springs ("the baths").

Nieul-sur-Mer. *Town, Charente-Maritime.* The suburb of La Rochelle derives its name from Gaulish *nouio-*, "new," and *ialon*, "clearing," "field." It is not on the sea (*sur mer*) but near it.

Nièvre. *Department, central France.* The name is that of the river here, known to the Romans as *Nevera*, from a root element *nev* of uncertain origin. See also **Nevers**, **Nivernais**.

Nilvange. *Town, Moselle.* The first part of the name is of uncertain origin. It may represent a Germanic personal name derived from *Nilo*. The suffix is Germanic *-ing*.

Nîmes. *City, Gard.* The name was recorded in the 2d century as *Nemausus*, from Gaulish *nemeton*, "sanctuary" and the Latin suffix *-ausus*. The Latin name is identical to that of **Nemours**, but in this case was stressed on the first syllable, in the Gaulish manner.

Niort. *City, Deux-Sèvres.* The early Latin name of the city was *Noiordo*, from Gaulish *Novioritu*, from *nouio-*, "new," and *ritu*, "ford." Niort stands on the Sèvre Niortaise River.

Nissan-lez-Ensérune. *Village, Hérault.* The name derives from the Roman personal name *Anicius* and the suffix *-anum*. The village is near (*lez*) the ancient fort of *Ensérune*.

Nivernais. *Region, central France.* The former province, with historic capital **Nevers**, was known to the Romans as *pagus Nivernensis*, from Latin *pagus*, "land," "country," and *Niver* or *Nevera*, the **Nièvre** River.

Noailles. *Village, Corrèze.* The name was recorded in the 14th century as *Novalium*, from Latin *novalia*, "newly prepared lands," from *novus*, "new." The name gave that of the noble house of *Noailles*, one noted member being Louis-Marie, vicomte de

Noailles (1756–1804), who served under Lafayette in the US War of Independence.

Nœux-les-Mines. *Town, Pas-de-Calais.* The name derives from Latin *nauda*, "marshy place." The addition refers to the former coal mines here.

Nogent-le-Roi. *Village, Eure-et-Loir.* The name was recorded in the 11th century as *Novigentum*, from Gaulish *nouio-*, "new," and the suffix *-entum*, which in Gaulish times denoted a new settlement, on the lines of the later *Neuville* (as for **Neuville-sur-Saône**) and *Villeneuve* (as for **Villeneuve-d'Ascq**). The addition ("the king") denotes a royal possession.

Nogent-le-Rotrou. *Town, Eure-et-Loir.* The name was recorded in the 11th century as *Nogiomum*, from Gaulish *nouio-*, "new," and *magos*, "market." The addition names *Rotrou* (*Hrodtrud*), the first count of Perche.

Nogent-sur-Marne. *Town, Val-de-Marne.* The name is as for **Nogent-le-Roi**. The addition locates the town on the **Marne** River.

Nogent-sur-Oise. *Town, Oise.* The name is as for **Nogent-le-Roi**. The addition locates the town near the **Oise** River.

Nogent-sur-Seine. *Town, Aube.* The name is as for **Nogent-le-Roi**. The addition locates the town on the **Seine** River.

Nogent-sur-Vernisson. *Village, Loiret.* The name is as for **Nogent-le-Rotrou**. The addition locates the village on the *Vernisson* River.

Noguères. *Village, Pyrénées-Atlantiques.* The name derives from Latin *nucaria*, a feminine form of *nucarium*, "nut tree."

Nohant-Vic. *Rural district, Indre.* The name combines two villages. *Nohant* is as for **Nogent-le-Roi**. *Vic* is as for **Vic-en-Bigorre**.

Noirétable. *Resort village, Loire.* The name derives from Latin *nigrum*, "black," and *stabulum*, "stable."

Noirmoutier. *Island, western France.* The

island, in the Bay of Biscay, bore the Medieval Latin name of *Nigrum Monasterium*, a corruption of *Nerium Monasterium*, from the phrase *in Herio monasterio*, "in the monastery of Herus," from *Herus*, the original name of the island, of unknown origin. The main town on the island is *Noirmoutier-en-l'Île*.

Noisiel. *Town, Seine-et-Marne*. The name derives from Latin *nux, nucis*, "nut," and the diminutive suffix *-ellum*, meaning a small area of nut trees.

Noisy-le-Grand. *City, Seine-Saint-Denis*. The name of the Paris suburb was recorded in the 11th century as *Nociacum*, from Latin *nux, nucis*, "nut," and the suffix *-etum*, referring to nut trees here. The addition ("the great") distinguishes this Noisy from nearby **Noisy-le-Sec**.

Noisy-le-Roi. *Town, Yvelines*. The name is as for **Noisy-le-Grand**, but here with an addition denoting a royal possession ("the king").

Noisy-le-Sec. *Town, Seine-Saint-Denis*. The Paris suburb has a name recorded in the 11th century as *Nusiacum Siccum*, as for **Noisy-le-Grand**, but here with Latin *siccus*, "dry."

Nolay. *Village, Côte-d'Or*. The name derives from the Roman personal name *Novellus* and the associative suffix *-acum*.

Nomexy. *Village, Vosges*. The name derives from the Germanic personal name *Nunnberht* and the associative suffix *-iacum*.

Nonancourt. *Village, Eure*. The name derives either from Old French *nonnain*, "nun," or the Germanic female personal name *Nonna*, from *Nonno*, and Latin *cortem*, accusative of *cors*, "estate."

Nontron. *Town, Dordogne*. The name was recorded in the 8th century as *Nantronum*, perhaps from the Gallo-Roman personal name *Nantirius*, from Gaulish *Nantius*, and the suffix *-onem*.

Nonza. *Coastal village, Haute-Corse*. The village, in northern Corsica, derives its name from the Roman personal name *Nuntius*, with Latin *villa*, "estate," understood.

Nord. *Department, northern France*. The name means "north," describing the location of the department in the extreme north of France.

Nord-Pas-de-Calais. *Region, northern France*. The administrative region comprises the departments of **Nord** and **Pas-de-Calais**.

Normandie. *Historic region, northwestern France*. The former province, known to English speakers as *Normandy*, takes its name from its inhabitants, the *Normans* (French *Normands*), descendants of the Vikings or *Norsemen* who settled here from the 8th century. Their own name comes from Old Norse *nordmann*, "northman," from *nord*, "north," and *mann*, "man."

Normandy *see* **Normandie**

Nort-sur-Erdre. *Town, Loire-Atlantique*. The name was recorded in the 11th century as *Honort*, apparently from Latin *honor*, Old French *onor*, "fief," with the initial syllable taken to represent French *à*, "at," or *en*, "in." The town is on the *Erdre* River.

La Norville. *Town, Essonne*. The name was recorded in the 13th century as *Lanorvilla*, from a Germanic personal name of uncertain form (perhaps *Lanort*) and Latin *villa*, "estate."

Notre-Dame-de-Bellecombe. *Resort village, Savoie*. The first part of the name ("Our Lady") denotes a church dedicated to the Virgin Mary. The addition, the name of a nearby village, derives from French *belle*, "beautiful," and Low Latin *comba*, "valley."

Notre-Dame-de-Bondeville. *Town, Seine-Maritime*. The first part of the name is as for **Notre-Dame-de-Bellecombe**. The addition derives from the Germanic personal name *Bonido* and Latin *villa*, "estate."

Nouâtre. *Village, Indre-et-Loire*. The name was recorded in the 10th century as *Nogastrum*, from Latin *nux, nucis*, "nut," and the pejorative suffix *-aster* (as in English *poetaster*). The reference may be to a type of wild nut growing here.

Le Nouvion-en-Thiérache. *Village, Aisne.* The name derives from Gaulish *nouio-*, "new," and *magos*, "market." The addition locates the village in **Thiérache.**

Nouvion-sur-Meuse. *Village, Ardennes.* The name is as for **Nouvion-en-Thiérache,** with the village here distinguished by its location on the **Meuse** River.

Nouzonville. *Town, Ardennes.* The name derives from the Germanic personal name *Nozo* and Latin *villa*, "estate."

Noves. *Town, Bouches-du-Rhône.* The name derives from Latin *novas*, accusative plural of *novus*, "new," with *terras*, "lands," or *villas*, "estates," understood.

Noyal-sur-Vilaine. *Town, Ille-et-Vilaine.* The name probably derives from Latin *novialum*, a variant of *novalis*, "newly prepared land." The town is on the **Vilaine** River.

Noyelles-Godault. *Town, Pas-de-Calais.* The first part of the name is as for **Noyelles-sous-Lens.** The second part names a local lord.

Noyelles-sous-Lens. *Town, Pas-de-Calais.* The name was recorded in the 12th century as *Noyella*, apparently from Germanic *nige*, "new," and Latin *villa*, "estate," "village," the equivalent of Latin *nova villa*, as for **Neuville-sur-Saône.** The second part of the name locates the town near (*sous*, "under") **Lens,** of which it is now actually a suburb.

Noyen-sur-Sarthe. *Village, Sarthe.* The name derives from Gaulish *nouio-*, "new," and *magos*, "market." The addition locates the village on the **Sarthe** River.

Noyon. *Town, Oise.* The Roman name of the town was *Noviomagus*, from Gaulish *nouio-*, "new," and *magos*, "market."

Nozay. *Village, Loire-Maritime.* The name derives from the Roman personal name *Nautius* and the associative suffix *-acum*.

Nuits-Saint-Georges. *Town, Côte-d'Or.* The town takes its name from the *Côte de Nuits*, or hillside of *Nuits*, whose own name may derive from Latin *nauda*, "marshy place." The second part of the name honors *St. George*, a saint perhaps favored for this fertile region because his name, of Greek origin, means "farmer" (literally "earth worker").

Nyons. *Town, Drôme.* The name was recorded in the 2d century as *Noimagos*, from Gaulish *nouio-*, "new," and *magos*, "market." The market here was "new" by contrast with the one at nearby *Saint-Pierre-de-Senos*, originally *Senomagus*, from Gaulish *senos*, "old," and *magos*.

Obernai. *Town, Bas-Rhin.* The common name of both this town and the nearby village of *Niedernai* was recorded in the 11th century as *Ehenheim*, from the Germanic personal name *Echo* and *heim*, "abode." The two places were then differentiated as *Obernai*, from a reduced form of this name prefixed by Germanic *ober*, "above," "higher," and *Niedernai*, formed identically but with Germanic *nieder*, "beneath," "lower." Both places are at the foot of the Vosges mountains, but Obernai is closer to the summits and more elevated.

Oberschaeffolsheim. *Village, Bas-Rhin.* The name derives from Germanic *ober*, "higher," prefixed to a Germanic personal name and *heim*, "abode." The name contrasts with *Niederschaeffolsheim*, prefixed with Germanic *nieder*, "lower," a few miles to the north.

Objat. *Village, Corrèze.* The name may derive from the Gaulish personal name *Obius* and the associative suffix *-acum*.

Occitanie. *Region, southern France.* The name is used for those parts of southern France where the *langue d'oc* (see **Languedoc**) is spoken. The Medieval Latin name for the region was *Occitania*, based on that of *Aquitania* (see **Aquitaine**), with *oc* for *Aqu-*.

Offemont. *Town, Belfort.* The suburb of

Belfort derives its name from the Germanic personal name *Offo* and Latin *mons, montis,* "mountain."

Offranville. *Village, Seine-Maritime.* The name derives from the Germanic personal name *Wulfran* and Latin *villa,* "estate."

Ogenne-Camptort. *Village, Pyrénées-Atlantiques.* The first part of the name represents Basque *oihen,* a Navarrese variant of *oihu,* "twisted." The second part is a translation of this, from Latin *campus,* "field," and *tortus,* "twisted." A "twisted" field has an irregular shape.

Oignies. *Town, Pas-de-Calais.* The name derives from the Roman personal name *Osinius* and the associative suffix *-acum.*

Oiron. *Village, Deux-Sèvres.* The name derives from the Roman personal name *Aurius* or *Orius* and the suffix *-onem.*

Oise. *Department, northern France.* The name is that of the river here, known to the Romans as *Isara,* of the same origin as the name of the **Isère.**

Oissel. *Town, Seine-Maritime.* The name derives from Gaulish *osca,* "enclosure," and the diminutive suffix *-ellum.*

Oléron. *Island, western France.* The island, in the Bay of Biscay, was known by the Roman name of *Ularius,* of Venetian origin.

Olivet. *Town, Loiret.* The suburb of Orléans apparently derives its name from the biblical *Olivet,* or *Mount of Olives,* a hill near Jerusalem that was a frequent resort of Jesus and the scene of his Ascension.

Ollioules. *Town, Var.* The name derives from Latin *olivus,* "olive tree," and the diminutive suffix *-ula,* serving here as a collective.

Olonne-sur-Mer *see* **Sables-d'Olonne, Les**

Oloron-Sainte-Marie. *Town, Pyrénées-Atlantiques.* The name, recorded in the 4th century as *Iluro,* derives from Iberian *ili,* "town." The second part of the name is the

dedication of the former cathedral here to St. Mary.

Onzain. *Village, Loir-et-Cher.* The name derives from the Gallo-Roman personal name *Unitius,* from *Unius,* and the suffix *-anum.*

Oradour-sur-Glane. *Village, Haute-Vienne.* The name is from Occitan *orador,* "oratory," from Latin *oratorium.* The village is on the *Glane* River, from Gaulish *glanna,* "bank."

Oraison. *Village, Alpes-de-Haute-Provence.* The name derives from the pre-Indoeuropean root *ar,* "height," and the pre-Latin suffix *-aus,* to which has been added the suffix *-ionem.*

Orange. *Town, Vaucluse.* The name was recorded in the 2d century as *Arausio,* from pre-Indoeuropean *ar,* "height," and the suffix *-aus,* as for **Oraison.** In 1544 the town passed to William the Silent of the house of Nassau, among whose descendants were William III of England, "William of *Orange*" (1650–1702) and the ruling family of the Netherlands. Hence the former *Orange Free State* in South Africa and the *Orange Order* of Irish Protestants, who originally supported William. The name has nothing to do with oranges, and the theory that the town is so called because it lay on the route by which oranges were brought into France from Mediterranean ports is a complete fiction.

Orbec. *Village, Calvados.* The name, recorded as now in the 12th century, represents Old High German *uro,* "aurochs," and Scandinavian *bekkr,* "stream."

Orbey. *Village, Haut-Rhin.* The name derives from Old High German *uro,* "aurochs," and *bah,* "stream."

Orcières. *Resort village, Hautes-Alpes.* The name was recorded in the 12th century as *Urseria,* from Latin *ursus,* "bear," and the suffix *-aria.*

Orcival. *Village, Puy-de-Dôme.* The name probably derives from the Roman (or

Germanic) personal name *Ursus* and Latin *vallis*, "valley."

Orge. *River, north central France.* The name of the river, a tributary of the Seine, was recorded in the 6th century as *Urbia*, from the river root *or* or *ar*.

Orgeval. *Town, Yvelines.* The name derives from the Germanic personal name *Orgis* and Latin *vallis*, "valley."

Orgon. *Village, Bouches-du-Rhône.* The name could represent the Gaulish personal name *Orgus* and the suffix *-onem* but is more likely to derive from a Mediterranean root *or-g* meaning "height."

Orléanais. *Region, north central France.* The former province takes its name from its historic capital, **Orléans.**

Orléans. *City, Loiret.* When the city was rebuilt in the 3d century AD, it was given the name *Aurelianum* in honor of the Roman emperor *Aurelius.* Its earlier name was *Genabum*, from proto-Indoeuropean *gen*, "river bend," and pre-Indoeuropean *apa*, "water." Orléans lies on a broad bend of the Loire River.

Orly. *Town, Val-de-Marne.* The name of the Paris suburb was recorded in the 8th century as *Aureliacum*, from the Roman personal name *Aurelius* and the associative suffix *-acum*.

Ormesson-sur-Marne. *Town, Val-de-Marne.* The name derives from Latin *ulmus*, "elm," and the double suffix *-ici* and *-onem.* The town is on the **Marne** River.

Ornans. *Town, Doubs.* The name was recorded in the 12th century as *Ornens*, from the Germanic personal name *Aurwin* and the suffix *-ing*.

Orne. *Department, northwestern France.* The name is that of the river here, recorded early as *Olina*, perhaps from Celtic *olno*, "ash tree."

Les Orres. *Resort village, Hautes-Alpes.* The name derives from Latin *horreum*, "granary."

Orsay. *Town, Essonne.* The name was recorded in the 13th century as *Orceiacum*, from the personal name *Orcius* and the associative suffix *-acum*.

Orthez. *Town, Pyrénées-Atlantiques.* The name was recorded in the 12th century as *Ortez*, from Latin *horta*, a form of *hortus*, Old Provençal *orta*, "garden," and the suffix *-ensem*.

Orvault. *Town, Loire-Atlantique.* The suburb of Nantes derives its name from Latin *aurea*, "golden," and *vallis*, "valley," denoting rich soil or good pasture. See also **Vallauris.** (The name *Golden Valley* is found in a similar sense in the English-speaking world, as for counties in Montana and North Dakota, and in England for the valley of the Dore River in Herefordshire, the latter giving a folk origin for the river name in French *d'or*, "golden.")

Osny. *Town, Val-d'Oise.* The name may derive from the Roman personal name *Osinius* and the associative suffix *-acum*.

Ostricourt. *Town, Nord.* The name derives from the Germanic personal name *Austoric* and Latin *cortem*, accusative of *cors*, "estate."

Ostwald. *Town, Bas-Rhin.* The suburb of Strasbourg derives its name from Germanic *ost*, "east," and *wald*, "wood."

Ottmarsheim. *Village, Haut-Rhin.* The name derives from the Germanic personal name *Audomar* and *heim*, "abode."

Ouessant. *Island, northwestern France.* The Roman name of the rockbound island, off the west coast of Brittany, was *Axanthos* or *Uxantis*, from Gaulish *ux-*, "high," and the superlative ending *-isamo*, related to Latin *-issimus.* The English form of the name is *Ushant*.

Ouistreham. *Resort town and port, Calvados.* The name was recorded in the 11th century as *Oistreham*, from Germanic *ooster*, "eastern," and *ham*, "homestead." The town is "eastern" with regard to *Étreham*, Calvados, some 25 miles to the west, where the name is from *wester*, "western," and *ham*.

Outreau. *Town, Pas-de-Calais*. The original name of what is now a suburb of Boulogne-sur-Mer was recorded in the 9th century as *Walbodeghem*, from the Germanic personal name *Walbodo* and *heim*, "abode." The present name was recorded in the 12th century as *Ultra aquam*, from Latin *ultra*, "beyond," and *aqua*, "water."

Ouzouer-sur-Loire. *Village, Loiret*. The name was recorded in the 12th century as *Oroium super Ligerim*, from Latin *oratorium*, "oratory," *super*, "on," and *Liger*, the Latin name of the **Loire** River.

Oye-Plage. *Resort town, Pas-de-Calais*. The name was recorded in the 8th century as *Ogia*, from Germanic *auwja*, "damp meadow." The town has a beach (*plage*) on the North Sea.

Oyonnax. *Town, Ain*. The name was recorded in the 12th century as *Oiaonacus*, from the Roman personal name *Audienus* and the associative suffix *-acum*.

Ozoir-la-Ferrière. *Town, Seine-et-Marne*. The first part of the name derives from Latin *oratorium*, "oratory." The second part derives from Latin *ferraria*, from *ferrum*, "iron," and the suffix *-aria*, denoting an iron mine or a forge.

Pacé. *Town, Ille-et-Vilaine*. The suburb of Rennes derives its name from the Roman personal name *Paccius* and the associative suffix *-acum*.

Pacy-sur-Eure. *Town, Eure*. The name, recorded in the 12th century as *Paceium*, derives from the Roman personal name *Paccius* and the associative suffix *-acum*. The addition locates the town on the **Eure** River.

Padirac. *Village, Lot*. The name derives from the Roman personal name *Paterius* and the associative suffix *-acum*.

Pagny-sur-Moselle. *Town, Meurthe-et-Moselle*. The name derives from the Roman personal name *Paternius* and the associative suffix *-acum*. The town is on the **Moselle** River.

Paimbœuf. *Village, Loire-Maritime*. The Brittany village derives its name from Breton *pen*, "head," "end," and possibly a Germanic word related to English *booth*. The Breton form of the name, *Pembro*, has been influenced by Breton *bro*, "country."

Paimpol. *Resort town and port, Côtes-d'Armor*. The Brittany town has the Breton name *Pempoull*, from *pen*, "head," and *poull*, "hole," "ditch," "marsh."

Paimpont. *Village, Ille-et-Vilaine*. The Brittany village derives its name from Breton *pen*, "head," and Latin *pons, pontis*, "bridge." The name gave that of the *Forêt de Paimpont* here, the last relic of the primeval forest of Armorica.

Paladru. *Resort village, Isère*. The name, recorded as *Peladru* in the 12th century, is of obscure origin. It may derive from a Germanic female personal name *Bilidruth*, but this does not account for the *a*. A popular origin in Provençal *pela-dru*, "stealing much," is hardly likely. The *-dru* element may represent Gaulish *druco-*, "bad," or *drutos*, "strong."

Le Palais. *Village and port, Morbihan*. The name derives from Latin *palatium*, "palace."

Palaiseau. *Town, Essonne*. The name was recorded in the 6th century as *Palatidus* and in the 9th century as *Palatiolum*, from Latin *palatius*, "palace," and the diminutive suffix *-eolum*.

Palais-sur-Vienne, Le. *Town, Haute-Vienne*. The suburb of Limoges, on the **Vienne** River, derives its name from Latin *palatium*, "palace."

Palasca. *Village, Haute-Corse*. The village, in northern Corsica, derives its name from pre-Indoeuropean *pal*, "mountain," and the pre-Latin suffix *-asca*.

Palavas-les-Flots. *Resort town and port, Hérault*. The name was recorded in the 10th century as *Pavallanum*, from the Roman personal name *Papilus* and the suffix *-anum*. The ending of the name then changed, partly under the influence of Latin *palus*, "marsh." The second part of the name ("the waves") refers to the town's seaside location.

La Palud-sur-Verdon. *Village, Alpes-de-Haute-Provence.* The name derives from Latin *palus, paludis,* "marsh," and the name of the **Verdon** River here.

Pamiers. *Town, Ariège.* The name was recorded in the 12th century as *Appamia,* a borrowing of the name of the Syrian town *Apamea,* built by the Selucid king Seleucus Nicator, who called it after his wife, *Apama.* The name of the French town was originally that of its castle, itself probably so called by Roger II de Foix in memory of the First Crusade of 1096.

Pampelonne. *Village, Tarn.* The name of the original *bastide* (stronghold) here was adopted from the Spanish city of *Pamplona,* known in French as *Pampelune.*

Panazol. *Town, Haute-Vienne.* According to Marcel Villoutreix, *Les Noms de Lieux en Haute-Vienne* ("Placenames in Haute-Vienne") (1981), the name probably derives from *pan,* a variant form of pre-Indoeuropean *pal,* "rock," "cliff," and the double suffix *-ate* and *-otum.*

Pancheraccia. *Village, Haute-Corse.* The village, in northern Corsica, has a name probably deriving from Italian *panca,* "bench," with a double suffix *-aria* and *-acea.* The reference would be to a hilly region where the land is cultivated in terraces.

Panissières. *Village, Loire.* The name probably derives from Latin *panicum,* "panic grass," and the suffix *-aria.*

Pantin. *City, Seine-Saint-Denis.* The name of the Paris suburb was recorded in the 11th century as *Pentinum,* either from a pre-Latin word meaning "marsh" or from the Gaulish personal name *Pentino,* "fifth," a name given to the fifth child in a family.

Paray-le-Monial. *Town, Saône-et-Loire.* The name was recorded in the 11th century as *Paredus,* from Latin *paries, parietis,* "wall," "enclosure." The second part of the name represents Old French *monial,* "(re-

lating to a) monk," referring both to the Basilica of the Sacré Cœur here, initiated in 1109 by the Abbot of Cluny, and more recently to the cult of the Sacred Heart of Jesus founded here in the 17th century by Sister Margaret Mary Alacoque. (French *moniale* means "nun belonging to an enclosed order.")

Paray-Vieille-Poste. *Town, Essonne.* The name, recorded in the 13th century as *Paretum,* has the same origin as **Paray-le-Monial.** The distinguishing addition means "old post," referring to a former staging post for horses here on the road into Paris.

Pardies. *Village, Pyrénées-Atlantiques.* The name was recorded in the 10th century as *Pardines,* from Latin *prata,* the plural of *pratum,* "meadow," and the suffix *-ina.*

Parentis-en-Born. *Town, Landes.* The name derives from the Roman personal name *Parentius.* The addition locates the town in the district of *Born.*

Pargny-sur-Saulx. *Village, Marne.* The name derives from the Roman personal name *Paternius* and the associative suffix *-acum.* The village is on the *Saulx* River.

Paris. *City, Paris.* The French capital, on the Seine River, takes its name from the Gaulish tribe *Parisii,* whose capital was *Lutetia* (in full Latin form, *Lutetia Parisiorum*). Their own name is of uncertain origin, but the following sources have been (tentatively) proposed: (1) Celtic *par,* "boat," and *gwys,* "men"; (2) Celtic *par* and *bêr,* "lance"; (3) Greek *baris,* "boat," a word of Egyptian origin. This last is said to explain the coat of arms of Paris, depicting a wave-tossed galley below a chief semé of fleurs de lis, with the Latin motto "Fluctuat nec mergitur" ("It is tossed about but does not sink"). More likely, the name was that of a Celtic god, meaning "shaper," "maker," from a source that also gave Welsh *peri,* "to cause."

The Gaulish capital *Lutetia* (French *Lutèce*), recorded in the 1st century BC, probably derives its name from Gaulish *luto-*, "marsh" (Welsh *llaid*, "mire"), with the double suffix *-et* and *-la*, although there have been various fanciful interpretations, such as that of Rabelais: "Paris, whose name formerly was Leucotia, as Strabo testifieth, lib. quarto, from the Greek word leukothēs, whiteness — because of the white thighs of the ladies of that place" (François Rabelais, *Gargantua*, 1534, translated by Thomas Urquhart, 1653). A link with the Ligurian god *Lug* has also been proposed, as for **Lyon**.

Paris-l'Hôpital. *Village, Saône-et-Loire.* The name may be a transfer of that of **Paris** or else derive from the Roman personal name *Patricius*. The addition, from Latin *hospitale*, "guesthouse," refers to a religious house founded here in the 13th century by the Knights of the Hospital of St. John at Jerusalem (the Knights Hospitalers).

Parmain. *Town, Val-d'Oise.* The name may derive from Old French *parmain*, "pearmain" (a type of pear).

Parthenay. *Town, Deux-Sèvres.* The name was recorded in the 11th century as *Parteniacum*, from the Roman personal name *Partenus* and the associative suffix *-acum*.

Partinello. *Village, Corse-du-Sud.* The name of the village, in western Corsica, is a diminutive form of *partino*, "ruined walls."

Pas-de-Calais. *Department, northern France.* The department extends inland from the Strait of Dover (French *Pas de Calais*, "strait of **Calais**") and the English Channel. Hence its name.

Le Passage. *Town, Lot-et-Garonne.* The suburb of Agen derives its name from Latin *passus*, "pass," "defile," denoting a route through the valley of the Garonne River here.

Passy (1). *Town, Haute-Savoie.* The name derives from the Roman personal name *Paccius* and the associative suffix *-acum*.

Passy (2) see Appendix 4.

Pau. *Resort city, Pyrénées-Atlantiques.* The Medieval Latin name of the city was *Palum*, from Old Occitan *Pal*, itself either from pre-Indoeuropean *pal*, "mountain," possibly of Ligurian origin, or perhaps from Latin *palus*, "stake," referring to the custom whereby a stake was driven in the ground to mark the site of a future settlement.

Patrimonio. *Village, Haute-Corse.* The village, in northern Corsica, derives its name from Latin *patrimonium*, "patrimony," denoting an estate inherited from the owner's ancestors.

Pauillac. *Town, Gironde.* The name was recorded in the 4th century as *Pauliacus*, from the Roman name *Paulius* and the associative suffix *-acum*.

Paulhaguet. *Village, Haute-Loire.* The name is a diminutive form of the original of **Pauillac**.

Paulhan. *Village, Hérault.* The name was recorded in the 9th century as *Paulianum*, from the Roman personal name *Paulius* and the suffix *-anum*.

Pavant. *Village, Aisne.* The name was recorded in the 9th century as *Penvennum*, apparently from an original *Pennovindos*, from Gaulish *penno-*, "head," "end," and *uindos*, "white."

Les Pavillons-sous-Bois. *Town, Seine-Saint-Denis.* The Paris suburb derives its name from Old French *pavillon*, "tent," "small building." The addition is "by the woods."

Pavilly. *Town, Seine-Maritime.* The name was recorded in the 9th century as *Pauliacum*, from the Roman personal name *Pavilius* and the associative suffix *-acum*.

Pays For names beginning thus, aside from the one below, see the main name, e.g. for *Pays Basque* see **Basque, Pays**, for *Pays de Caux* see **Caux, Pays de**.

Pays de la Loire. *Region, western France.* The administrative region has a name meaning "Loire Country," referring to its chief river, the **Loire**, which flows through it to the Atlantic coast through the departments of **Maine-et-Loire** and **Loire-At-lantique**.

Le Péage-de-Roussillon. *Town, Isère.* The name represents French *péage*, "right of way," as for **Bourg-de-Péage**. The distinguishing addition relates to **Roussillon** (2).

Le Pecq. *Town, Yvelines.* The name was recorded in the 7th century as *Alpicum*, from pre-Celtic *alp*, "height" (see **Alps**). Le Pecq lies at the foot of the height of Saint-Germain-en-Laye.

Pecquencourt. *Town, Nord.* The name derives from the Germanic female personal name *Picca* and Latin *cortem*, accusative of *cors*, "estate."

Pégomas. *Town, Alpes-Maritimes.* The name derives from Old Provençal *pegomas*, "pitch plaster," meaning a place where it was made or used as a nickname for a person who made it.

Peisey-Nancroix. *Village, Savoie.* The first part of the name derives from Latin *picea*, "spruce," and the collective suffix *-etum*. The second part derives from Gaulish *nanto-*, "valley," "stream," and an element perhaps based on pre-Celtic *car*, "stone," "rock."

Pélissanne. *Town, Bouches-du-Rhône.* The suburb of Salon-de-Provence derives its name from the Roman personal name *Pellicius* and the suffix *-ana*.

Le Pellerin. *Village, Loire-Atlantique.* The name derives from Latin *peregrinus*, "pilgrim," either adopted as a personal name or marking a staging point for pilgrims.

Pélussin. *Village, Loire.* The name probably derives from the Roman god *Pollux*, *Pollucis*, and the suffix *-inum*.

Pelvoux. *Mountain, southeastern France.* The peak in the Dauphiné Alps derives its name from pre-Indoeuropean *pala* or *pela*, "rocky height."

Penmarch. *Town, Finistère.* The Brittany town derives its name from Breton *penn*, "head," and *march*, "horse," denoting a nearby headland where horses were kept.

Penne-d'Agenais. *Village, Lot-et-Garonne.* The name was recorded in the 12th century as *Pena*, from pre-Latin (probably Ligurian) *penna*, "rocky height." The former fortress town is on a steep hill in the historic region of *Agenais*, named for its capital, **Agen**.

Les Pennes-Mirabeau. *Town, Bouches-du-Rhône.* The first part of the name is as for **Penne-d'Agenais**. The second part is as for **Mirebeau**.

La Penne-sur-Huveaune. *Town, Bouches-du-Rhône.* The suburb of Aubagne has a name of the same origin as **Penne-d'Agenais**, but here the addition locates the town on the *Huveaune* River.

Perche. *Region, northwestern France.* The agricultural region had the Medieval Latin name *saltus Perticus*, from *saltus*, "wooded pasture," and *pertica*, "pole" (English *perch*), referring to the abundant woodland here.

Percy. *Village, Manche.* The name derives from the Roman personal name *Persius* and the associative suffix *-acum*.

Pérenchies. *Town, Nord.* The name may derive from the Germanic female personal name *Perinza* and the associative suffix *-iacum*.

Périers. *Village, Manche.* The name probably derives from Latin *pirarius*, "pear tree."

Périgny. *Town, Charente-Maritime.* The suburb of La Rochelle derives its name from the Roman personal name *Patrinius* and the associative suffix *-acum*.

Périgord. *Region, southwestern France.* The Roman name of the region was *Petrucorii*, from the Gaulish tribe who gave the name of **Périgueux**, one of its chief towns.

Périgueux. *Town, Dordogne.* The name was recorded in the 4th century as *civitas Petrucoriorum*, from Latin *civitas*, "city," and the *Petrucorii*, the Gaulish tribe whose capital it was. Their own name derives from Gaulish *petru-*, "four" (related to Latin *quattuor*), and *corios*, "army," referring to the military resources of four administrative regions here. (But some authorities interpret the second part of their name a little differently: "The Petrucorii are a tribe whose name in Gaulish denotes 'the Four Kinship-Groups' (*coriae*—we can find the word in Irish as *cuire* for a population-group)" [C.E. Stevens, "Roman Gaul," in Wallace-Hadrill and McManners, p.22].) The Gallo-Roman name of the town, recorded in the 2d century AD by Ptolemy (as *Ouesuna*), was *Vesunna*, the name of a Gaulish goddess, from *uesu-*, "good," "worthy."

Pernes-les-Fontaines. *Town, Vaucluse.* The name derives from the Roman personal name *Paternus* with Latin *villa*, "estate," understood. The addition refers to the fountains here.

Pérols. *Town, Hérault.* The name derives from Latin *petra*, "rock," and the suffix *-olum*.

Péronnas. *Town, Ain.* The suburb of Bourg-en-Bresse derives its name from the Roman personal name *Petro, Petronis* and the associative suffix *-acum*.

Péronne. *Town, Somme.* The name was recorded in the 6th century as *Perruna* or *Perona*, from the Gaulish personal name *Perro* and the river suffix *-onna*.

Perpignan. *City, Pyrénées-Orientales.* The name was recorded in the 10th century as *Perpiniano* or *Perpeniacum*, from the Gaulish personal name *Perpennio* and the associative suffix *-acum*.

Le Perray-en-Yvelines. *Town, Yvelines.* The name derives from Latin *petra*, "stone," "rock," and the collective suffix *-etum*. The addition locates the town in **Yvelines**.

Le Perreux-sur-Marne. *Town, Val-de-Marne.* The Paris suburb, on the **Marne** River, derives its name from Latin *petra*, "stone," "rock," and the suffix *-osum*.

Perros-Guirec. *Resort town, Côtes-d'Armor.* The first part of the name of the Brittany town represents Breton *penn*, "head,"

and *roz*, "mound," "hill." The second part names the local saint *Guirec* (Kirech), who built a church here in the 6th century.

Persan. *Town, Val-d'Oise.* The name may derive from the Germanic female personal name *Berahtsind*.

Le Perthus. *Village, Pyrénées-Orientales.* The name derives from Low Latin *pertusium*, "hole," "pass," referring to a pass in the Pyrenees on the border between France and Spain.

Pertuis. *Town, Vaucluse.* The name derives from Low Latin *pertusium*, "hole," "pass."

Pessac. *Town, Gironde.* The suburb of Bordeaux derives its name from the Roman personal name *Peccius* and the associative suffix *-acum*.

Petit-Couronne *see* **Grand-Couronne**

Petit-Croix. *Village, Belfort.* The name was recorded in the 13th century as *Petit Creux*, implying an origin in French *petit*, "little," and Latin *crosum*, "hollow." The latter word (French *creux*) gave the German name of the place, *Klein Kreuz*, and *Kreuz*, "cross," was then translated by French *Croix*.

Petite-Forêt. *Town, Nord.* The suburb of Valenciennes has a name meaning "little forest."

La Petite-Pierre. *Village, Bas-Rhin.* The name means "little rock."

Petite-Rosselle. *Town, Moselle.* The name, prefixed by *petit*, "little," is that of the *Rosselle* River on which the town lies. Its own name derives from Old French *rossel*, "reed."

Le Petit-Quevilly *see* **Grand-Quevilly, Le**

Petit-Saint-Bernard. *Mountain pass, southeastern France.* The Alpine pass, known in English as the *Little Saint Bernard*, leads from Bourg-Saint-Maurice, Savoie, to La Thuile, Piedmont, Italy, and takes its name from a hospice founded nearby around 960 by *St. Bernard* of Menthon (923–1008). He also founded a hospice near the *Grand-Saint-Bernard* (*Great Saint Bernard*) pass, some 25 miles to the northeast, between Valais, Switzerland, and the Valle d'Aosta, Italy.

Peypin. *Town, Bouches-du-Rhône.* The name derives from Latin *podium*, "height," "hill," and *pinus*, "pine," here in a collective sense.

Peyrat-le-Château. *Village, Haute-Vienne.* The name derives from the Roman personal name *Parius* and the associative suffix *-acum*. The addition denotes the *château* (castle) here.

Peyrehorade. *Village, Landes.* The name derives from Latin *petra*, "stone," "rock," and *forata*, "pierced," referring to an ancient stone here.

Peyrolles-en-Provence. *Village, Bouches-du-Rhône.* The name was recorded in the 12th century as *Peyrolas*, from Latin *petra*, "stone," "rock," and the feminine suffix *-ola*. This Peyrolles is distinguished from others by its location in **Provence**.

Peyruis. *Village, Alpes-de-Haute-Provence.* The name was recorded in the 11th century as *Petroxium*, from Latin *petra*, "stone," "rock," and the suffix *-ucium*.

Pézenas. *Town, Hérault.* The name was recorded in the 10th century as *Pedinatis*, from the name of the *Peyne* River here, itself from a pre-Latin root of unknown meaning.

Pfaffenhoffen. *Village, Bas-Rhin.* The name derives from the Germanic personal name *Papo* and *hof*, "farm."

Pfastatt. *Town, Haut-Rhin.* The suburb of Mulhouse derives its name from the Germanic personal name *Papo* and *stat*, "place."

Phalsbourg. *Town, Moselle.* The garrison here was founded in 1570 by the prince palatine Georg-Johann, and thus derives its name from German *Pfalz*, "palatinate," and Germanic *burg*, "stronghold."

Philippsbourg. *Village, Moselle.* The name derives from *Philippe*, count of Hanau, who built a castle (Germanic *burg*) here in 1590.

Le Pian-Médoc. *Town, Gironde.* The name derives from Old Provençal *pea*, "portion of land," meaning one suitable for building. The addition locates the town in **Médoc**.

Piazzali. *Village, Haute-Corse.* The village, in northeastern Corsica, derives its name from Latin *platea*, "flat area," and the suffix *-alem*.

Pibrac. *Town, Haute-Garonne.* The suburb of Toulouse probably derives its name from the Roman personal name *Piper* and the associative suffix *-acum*.

Picardie. *Region, northern France.* The administrative region and former province, known in English as *Picardy*, had the Medieval Latin name of *Picardia*, from Old French *pic* or *pique*, "pike," the preferred weapon of its indigenous inhabitants.

Picquigny. *Village, Somme.* The name derives from the Germanic personal name *Pinco* and the double suffix *-in* and *-iacum*.

Piedicroce. *Village, Haute-Corse.* The village, in northeastern Corsica, derives its name from Latin *plebs, plebis*, "canton" (an administrative and religious term, related to the *ple* and *plou* of Breton names, as for **Plabennec**), Italian *di*, "of," and Latin *crux*, "cross."

Pierre-Bénite. *Town, Rhône.* The suburb of Lyon derives its name from Latin *petra*, "rock," and French *bénite*, "blessed," "holy."

Pierre-Buffière. *Village, Haute-Vienne.* The name derives from Latin *petra*, "rock," and *bufaria*, "windy place."

Pierrefeu-du-Var. *Town, Var.* The name derives from Latin *petra*, "stone," "rock," and *focus*, "fire," referring to local flint or quartz. The addition locates the town in **Var**.

Pierrefitte-sur-Seine. *Town, Seine-Saint-Denis.* The Paris suburb derives its name from Latin *petra*, "stone," and *ficta*, "fixed," referring to an ancient stone fixed in the ground here. The addition locates the town near the **Seine** River.

Pierrefonds. *Resort village, Oise.* The name was recorded in the 11th century as *Pietrafonte*, from Latin *petra*, "rock," and *fons, fontis*, "fountain," referring to the mineral springs here.

Pierrefontaine-les-Varans. *Village, Doubs.* The name derives from Latin *petra*, "stone," "rock," and *fontana*, "fountain." The addition locates the village near (*les*) *Varans*.

Pierrelatte. *Town, Drôme.* The name derives from Latin *petra*, "stone," "rock," and *lata*, "broad," "wide," presumably referring to an ancient stone here.

Pierrelaye. *Town, Val-d'Oise.* The name has the same origin as that of **Pierrelatte.**

Pierry. *Village, Marne.* The suburb of Épernay derives its name from the Roman personal name *Petreius* and the associative suffix *-acum*.

Les Pieux. *Village, Manche.* The name apparently derives from Latin *palus*, "stake," "pale."

Pignan. *Town, Hérault.* The suburb of Montpellier derives its name from the Roman personal name *Pinius* and the suffix *-anum*.

Pignans. *Village, Var.* The name has the same origin as that of **Pignan.**

Le Pin-au-Haras. *Village, Orne.* The first part of the name derives from Latin *pinus*, "pine." The latter half is French *haras*, "stud farm," describing the former royal stud farm here, now a noted equestrian center known as the *Haras National du Pin*. (French *haras* may derive from Old Scandinavian *hárr*, "gray," related to English *hoary*, referring to gray horses.)

Piolenc. *Village, Vaucluse.* The name derives from Latin *podium*, "mound," "hill," and the Germanic personal name *Ottolin*.

Piriac-sur-Mer. *Resort village, Loire-At-lantique.* The name derives from Breton *penn*, "head," "end," and either the Gaulish personal name *Carius* or pre-Latin *kar*, "rock," and the associative suffix *-acum*. The resort is "on sea" by the Bay of Biscay.

Pissotte. *Village, Vendée.* The name derives from *pisser*, "to piss," and the suffix *-otte*, denoting a trickling spring.

Pithiviers. *Town, Loiret.* The name was recorded in the 11th century as *Pitveris castrum*, from the Gaulish personal name *Petuario*, "fourth," given to the fourth child in a family, and Latin *castrum*, "fort."

Plabennec. *Town, Finistère.* The Brittany town derives its name from Breton *ple*, "parish" (from Latin *plebs*, "the common people"), and the personal name *Abennoc*.

La Plagne. *Resort village, Savoie.* The name derives from Latin *planea*, a collective form of *planum*, "plain," meaning specifically "plateau," "level area," here in the French Alps.

Plaisance-du-Touch. *Town, Haute-Garonne.* The suburb of Toulouse has apparently adopted the name of the Italian city of *Piacenza*, known to the French as *Plaisance*. Both names means literally "pleasure." The town is on the *Touch* River.

Plaisir. *Town, Yvelines.* The name is an alteration of *plessis*, denoting a fortified place, from Old French *plaissié*, "enclosure of plashed branches."

Plancoët. *Village, Côtes-d'Armor.* The Brittany village may derive its name from Breton *plaen*, "flat," and *coat*, "wood."

Plan-de-Cuques. *Town, Bouches-du-Rhône.* The suburb of Marseille derives its name from Latin *planum*, "flat region," "plain," and the small *Cuques* River here.

Pleaux. *Village, Cantal.* The name is said to derive from Old Provençal *pleu*, "guarantee," "security," presumably denoting a safe place.

Plédran. *Town, Côtes-d'Armor.* The name of the Brittany town derives from Breton *ple*, "parish," and an element of uncertain origin.

Plélan-le-Grand. *Village, Ille-et-Vilaine.* The Brittany village has a Breton name, from *ple*, "parish," and the personal name *Alan*. It is "great" (*le grand*) for distinction from "little" *Plélan-le-Petit*, Côtes-d'Armor, although there the second part of the main name is from Breton *lan*, "monastery."

Plémet. *Village, Côtes-d'Armor.* The name of the Brittany village derives from Breton *ple*, "parish," and an element of uncertain origin.

Pléneuf-Val-André. *Town, Côtes-d'Armor.* The name of the Brittany town derives from Breton *ple*, "parish," and an element of uncertain origin. The second part of the name is that of the nearby resort *Val-André*, presumably from Latin *vallis*, "valley," and a personal name.

Plérin. *Town, Côtes-d'Armor.* The name of the Brittany town derives from Breton *ple*, "parish," and the personal name *Rin*, perhaps that of a local saint.

Le Plessis-Bouchard. *Town, Val-d'Oise.* The Paris suburb derives the first part of its name from *plessis*, denoting a fortified place, from Old French *plaissié*, "enclosure of plashed branches." The second part is a local distinguishing name.

Le Plessis-Robinson. *Town, Hauts-de-Seine.* The Paris suburb derives the first part of its name from *plessis*, denoting a fortified place, from Old French *plaissié*, "enclosure of plashed branches." The original name was *Le Plessis-Picquet*, after its owner, financier Jean de la Haye, known as *Picquet*. In 1848 a *guinguette*, a type of outdoor wine parlor and dance hall, was opened here and named after the *Swiss Family Robinson* of Johann Wyss's novel (not *Robinson Crusoe*, as popularly believed), and this name was adopted in 1909. (The *guinguette* itself was presumably so named as it was laid out in "tunnels" under the trees, evoking the desert island tree house built by the fictional shipwrecked Swiss family.)

Le Plessis-Trévise. *Town, Val-de-Marne.* The Paris suburb derives the first part of its name from *plessis*, denoting a fortified place, from Old French *plaissié*, "enclosure of plashed branches." The second part is a local distinguishing name.

Plestin-les-Grèves. *Resort village, Côtes-d'Armor.* The name of the Brittany resort derives from Breton *ple*, "parish," and the saint's name *Justin*. The second part of the name means "the coasts," referring to those nearby on the English Channel.

Pleubian. *Village, Côtes-d'Armor.* The Breton name of the Brittany village represents *pleu*, "parish," and *bihan*, "little."

Pleumeur-Bodou. *Town, Côtes-d'Armor.* The Breton name of the Brittany town means "big parish in the bushes," from *pleu*, "parish," *veur*, the mutated form of *meur*, "big," and *bodoù*, the plural of *bod*, "bush."

Pleyben. *Village, Finistère.* The Brittany village has a Breton name, from *ple*, "parish," and *penn*, "head."

Ploëmeur. *Town, Morbihan.* The suburb of Lorient derives its name from Breton *plou*, "parish," and the personal name *Mur*.

Ploërmel. *Town, Morbihan.* The Brittany town has a Breton name, from *plou*, "parish," and *Armel*, formerly *Arthmael*, a saint's name.

Plœuc-sur-Lié. *Village, Côtes-d'Armor.* The name derives from Breton *plou*, "parish," and an element of uncertain origin. The village is on the *Lié* River.

Plombières-les-Bains. *Resort town, Vosges.* The name was recorded in the 13th century as *Ploumieres*, from Latin *plumbus*, "lead" (the metal), and the suffix *-aria*. The second part of the name ("the baths") refers to the radioactive springs here, used since Roman times.

Plomelin. *Town, Finistère.* The Brittany town derives its name from Breton *plou*, "parish," and the saint's name *Merin*.

Plonéour-Lanvern. *Town, Finistère.* The

Brittany town derives the first part of its name from Breton *plou*, "parish," and the saint's name *Eneour*. The second part is a local placename, presumably from Breton *lann*, "territory," and a saint's name.

Plouagat. *Village, Côtes-d'Armor.* The name of the Brittany village derives from Breton *plou*, "parish," and the saint's name *Egat*.

Plouaret. *Village, Côtes-d'Armor.* The name of the Brittany village derives from Breton *plou*, "parish," and the saint's name *Barvet* or *Barvoet*.

Plouay. *Town, Morbihan.* The name of the Brittany town derives from Breton *plou*, "parish," and an element of uncertain origin.

Ploubalay. *Village, Côtes-d'Armor.* The name of the Brittany village derives from Breton *plou*, "parish," and the saint's name *Palay*.

Ploubazlanec. *Village, Côtes-d'Armor.* The name of the Brittany village derives from Breton *plou*, "parish," and the original village name *Bazlanec*, from Breton *banad-loc*, "place where broom grows."

Ploudalmézeau. *Town, Finistère.* The name of the Brittany town derives from Breton *plou*, "parish," and an element (or elements) of obscure origin.

Plouescat. *Village, Finistère.* The name of the Brittany village was recorded in the 14th century as *Ploe Rescat* (in error for *Plou Jescat*), from Breton *plou*, "parish," and the saint's name *Judcat*.

Ploufragan. *Town, Côtes-d'Armor.* The suburb of Saint-Brieuc derives its name from Breton *plou*, "parish," and the personal name *Fracan*.

Plougasnou. *Village, Finistère.* The name of the Brittany village derives from Breton *plou*, "parish," and perhaps a form of the saint's name *Catoc*.

Plougastel-Daoulas. *Town, Finistère.* The Breton form of the Brittany town's name is *Plougastell-Daoulaz*, from *plou*, "parish," *kastell*, mutated as *gastell*, "castle," and the Breton form of the personal name *Douglas*.

Plouguerneau. *Town, Finistère.* The Brittany town derives the first part of its name from Breton *plou*, "parish." The rest of the name may be based on *kern*, "point."

Plouha. *Village, Côtes-d'Armor.* The name of the Brittany village derives from Breton *plou*, "parish," and an element of uncertain origin.

Plouhinec. *Town, Finistère.* The name of the Brittany town derives from Breton *plou*, "parish," and either a conjectural word *eithinoc*, "place growing with gorse," or the personal name *Eithin*.

Plouigneau. *Town, Finistère.* The name of the Brittany town derives from Breton *plou*, "parish," and the saint's name *Igno* (sometimes confused with St. Ignatius).

Ploumagoar. *Town, Côtes-d'Armor.* The name of the Brittany town derives from Breton *plou*, "parish," and Latin *maceria*, "ruins," meaning Roman remains.

Plourin-lès-Morlaix. *Town, Finistère.* The name of the Brittany town derives from Breton *plou*, "parish," and either *rin*, "secret," or the saint's name *Rin*. The town is near (*lès*) **Morlaix**.

Plouzanè. *Town, Finistère.* The name of the Brittany town derives from Breton *plou*, "parish," and the Irish saint's name *Saneus*.

Pluvigner. *Town, Morbihan.* The name of the Brittany town derives from Breton *plou*, "parish," and the saint's name *Guinner*.

Podensac. *Village, Gironde.* The name derives from the Roman personal name *Potentius* and the associative suffix *-acum*.

Le Poiré-sur-Vie. *Town, Vendée.* The name probably derives from Latin *pirarius*, "pear tree." The town lies on the *Vie* River.

Poissy. *Town, Yvelines.* The name was recorded in the 9th century as *Pinciacum*, from the Roman personal name *Pincius* and the associative suffix *-acum*. The present form of the name evolved through *Pissiacum* (11th century), *Penci* (13th), and *Poissiaci* (15th).

Poitiers. *City, Vienne.* The name was recorded in the 4th century as *Pictavis* or *Pictavium*, from *Pictavi* or *Pictones*, a Gaulish tribal name, itself from that of the *Picts.* Earlier, in the 1st century BC, the name was recorded by Caesar as *Limonum*, from Gaulish *lemo-*, "elm."

Poitou. *Historic region, western France.* The former province was known to the Romans as *Pictavum*, from the *Pictones* or *Picts* who gave the name of **Poitiers**, its capital.

Poitou-Charentes. *Region, western France.* The administrative region was formed in the early 1980s to include part of the former province of **Poitou** in the north and territory in the departments of **Charente** and **Charente-Maritime** (hence plural *Charentes*) in the south.

Poix-de-Picardie. *Village, Somme.* The main name is that of the river here, itself probably from Latin *piscis*, "fish." The addition locates the village in *Picardy* (**Picardie**).

Polignac. *Village, Haute-Loire.* The name, recorded in the 10th century as *Podaniacum*, is of uncertain origin. It appears to represent a personal name with the associative suffix *-acum.*

Poligny. *Town, Jura.* The name was recorded in the 9th century as *Pollemniacum*, from the Roman personal name *Poleminius* and the associative suffix *-acum.*

Pomerol. *Village, Gironde.* The name derives from Latin *pomarium*, "apple tree," and the suffix *-olum.*

Pommard. *Village, Côte-d'Or.* The name was recorded in the 9th century as *Polmarcum*, from Germanic *pol*, "marsh," and *marka*, "land," "territory."

La Pommeraye. *Village, Maine-et-Loire.*

The name derives from Latin *pomarium*, "apple tree" and the collective suffix *-eta.*

Pompey. *Town, Meurthe-et-Moselle.* The name probably derives from the Roman personal name *Pompennius.*

Pons. *Town, Charente-Maritime.* The name derives from Latin *pons*, "bridge," here one over the Seugne River.

Ponson-Debat-Pouts. *Village, Pyrénées-Atlantiques.* The first part of the name derives from the Roman personal name *Pontius* and the suffix *-onem.* The second part means "below" (French *de bas*). The third part names nearby *Pouts*, from Latin *podium*, "height," "hill." The village thus lies below Pouts, while to the south is *Ponson-Dessus*, above it (*dessus*).

Pontacq. *Village, Pyrénées-Atlantiques.* The name derives from the Roman personal name *Pontus*, a variant of *Pontius*, and the associative suffix *-acum.*

Pont-à-Marcq. *Village, Nord.* The name derives from Latin *pons, pontis*, "bridge," and the *Marcq* River that it crosses here.

Pont-à-Mousson. *Town, Meurthe-et-Moselle.* The name was recorded in the 9th century as *Pontus sub castro Montionis*, Latin for "bridge by the fort of Mousson," denoting a bridge over the Moselle River here between the town proper and what is now the virtual suburb of *Mousson.* Its own name, recorded in the 10th century as *castrum Montionis*, derives from the Roman personal name *Montius* and the suffix *-onem.*

Pontarlier. *Town, Doubs.* The name derives from Latin *pons, pontis*, "bridge," and *Ariola*, the original name of the place, recorded in the 4th century. The town is on the Doubs River.

Pont-Audemer. *Town, Eure.* The name derives from Latin *pons, pontis*, "bridge," and the Germanic personal name *Haldemar.* The town is on the Risle River.

Pontault-Combault. *Town, Seine-et-Marne.* The Paris suburb derives the first part of its name from Latin *pons, pontis,* "bridge," and the diminutive suffix *-ellum.* The second part derives from (latinized) Gaulish *cumba,* "enclosed valley," and the same suffix.

Pont-Aven. *Village, Finistère.* The Brittany village derives its name from Latin *pons, pontis,* "bridge," and the *Aven* River, on which it lies.

Pontcharra. *Town, Isère.* The name derives from Latin *pons, pontis,* "bridge," and *carralis,* "for the chariots," enabling them to cross the Isère River nearby.

Pontchâteau. *Town, Loire-Atlantique.* The name derives from Latin *pons, pontis,* "bridge," and *castellum,* "castle." The town is on the Brive River. The castle is nearby La Bretesche.

Pont-Croix. *Village, Finistère.* The name derives from Latin *pons, pontis,* "bridge," and *crux,* "cross." The village is on the Goyen River.

Pont-d'Ain. *Village, Ain.* The name derives from Latin *pons, pontis,* "bridge," and the **Ain** River that it crosses here.

Le Pont-de-Beauvoisin. *Village, Isère and Savoie.* The name derives from Latin *pons, pontis,* "bridge," and *bellum vicinium,* "beautiful village," the latter word denoting a jointly owned *vicus.* The bridge spans the Guiers River to join the the two halves of the village.

Pont-de-Buis-lès-Quimerch. *Village, Finistère.* The name derives from Latin *pons, pontis,* "bridge," and *buxus,* "box," "group of box trees," the latter being near (*lès*) Quimerch.

Pont-de-Chéruy. *Town, Isère.* The name derives from Latin *pons, pontis,* "bridge," and the small *Chéruy* River that flows into the Bourbre River here.

Pont-de-Claix. *Town, Isère.* The suburb of Grenoble derives its name from Latin *pons, pontis,* "bridge," and nearby **Claix.** The river here is the Drac.

Pont-de-l'Arche. *Village, Eure.* The name derives from Latin *pons, pontis,* "bridge," and *arca,* "arch." The bridge here was one of the first to be built over the lower Seine.

Pont-de-Roide. *Town, Doubs.* The name derives from Latin *pons, pontis,* "bridge," and the smalle *Roide* River that flows into the Doubs River here.

Pont-de-Vaux. *Village, Ain.* The name derives from Latin *pons, pontis,* "bridge," and a plural form of *vallis,* "valley." The village is near the point where several rivers join to enter the Saône.

Pont-du-Château. *Town, Puy-de-Dôme.* The name derives from Latin *pons, pontis,* "bridge," and *castellum,* "castle." The town is on the Allier River.

Le Pontet. *Town, Vaucluse.* The suburb of Avignon derives its name from Latin *pons, pontis,* "bridge," and the diminutive suffix *-ittum.*

Pont-Évêque. *Town, Isère.* The suburb of Vienne derives its name from Latin *pons, pontis,* "bridge," and *episcopus,* "bishop," denoting its possessor.

Pontigny. *Village, Yonne.* The name was recorded in the 12th century as *Pontiniacum,* from the Roman personal name *Potentinius,* a form of *Potentinus,* and the associative suffix *-acum.*

Pontivy. *Town, Morbihan.* The Brittany town, on the Blavet River, derives its name from Latin *pons, pontis,* "bridge," and *Ivy,* a saint who founded a monastery here in the 7th century. A new town was built here by Napoleon in 1805 as the military headquarters for Brittany, and was known as *Napoléonville* under Napoleons I and III (1805–14, 1848–71).

Pont-l'Abbé. *Town, Finistère.* The name derives from Latin *pons, pontis,* "bridge," and *abbas,* "abbot," denoting the possessor. The bridge itself was built by monks.

Pont-l'Évêque. *Town, Calvados.* The name was recorded in the 12th century as

Pons Episcopi, Latin for "bridge of the bishop," referring to the longstanding right of the bishop of Liseux to claim tolls charged for crossing a bridge over the Touques River here.

Pontoise. *Town, Val-d'Oise.* The name is first recorded in the 4th century as *Briva Isarae*, from Gaulish *briua*, "bridge," and the **Oise** River. It then appears in the 9th century as *Pons Hiserae*, with Latin *pons* translating Gaulish *briua*, and in the 11th century as *Pons Isara*.

Pontorson. *Town, Manche.* The name was recorded in the 12th century as *Pons Urso*, from Latin *pons, pontis*, "bridge," and the Germanic personal name *Urso*.

Pont-Sainte-Marie. *Town, Aube.* The suburb of Troyes derives its name from Latin *pons, pontis*, "bridge," and a dedication to *St. Mary*. The river here is the Seine.

Pont-Sainte-Maxence. *Town, Oise.* The name derives from Latin *pons, pontis*, "bridge," and a dedication to *St. Maxentia*. The river here is the Oise.

Pont-Saint-Esprit. *Town, Gard.* The name derives from Latin *pons, pontis*, "bridge," and a dedication to the Holy Spirit (*Saint-Esprit*) but originally to St. Saturninus (St. Sernin). The river here is the Rhône.

Pont-Saint-Martin. *Village, Loire-Atlantique.* The name derives from Latin *pons, pontis*, "bridge," and a dedication to *St. Martin*. The village is on the Ognon River.

Pont-Saint-Vincent. *Village, Meurthe-et-Moselle.* The name derives from Latin *pons, pontis*, "bridge," and a dedication to *St. Vincent*. The village is on the Moselle River.

Pont-Scorff. *Village, Morbihan.* The name derives from Latin *pons, pontis*, "bridge," and the *Scorff* River that it crosses.

Les Ponts-de-Cé. *Town, Maine-et-Loire.* The name derives from Latin *pons, pontis*, "bridge," and a place nearby with a name recorded in the 9th century as *Seium*. The town lies on several islands in the Loire River, crossed here by successive bridges.

Pont-sur-Yonne. *Village, Yonne.* The name derives from Latin *pons, pontis*, "bridge," and the **Yonne** River that it crosses here.

Porcelette. *Village, Moselle.* The village was founded in 1621 by Jean des *Porcelets* de Maillane, abbot of Saint-Avold and bishop of Toul.

Pordic. *Town, Côtes-d'Armor.* The Brittany town derives its name from Breton *porzh*, "port," and the diminutive suffix *-ic*.

Pornic. *Resort town, Loire-Atlantique.* The Brittany town probably derives its name from Latin *portus*, Breton *porzh*, "port," and the Breton personal name *Nicos*.

Pornichet. *Resort town, Loire-Atlantique.* The name of the Brittany town appears to be a diminutive form of that of **Pornic**, some 15 miles to the southeast across the Loire estuary.

Porquerolles. *Village and port, Var.* The port, on the island of the same name, the westernmost of the three *Îles d'Hyères* (see **Hyères**), has a name meaning "pigpens" (French *porcheries*).

Port-Camargue. *Resort complex, Gard.* The entire complex, on the Mediterranean Sea, arose in the 1970s with a name from French *port*, "port," and the **Camargue** region here.

Port-de-Bouc. *Town, Bouches-du-Rhône.* The name derives from Latin *portus*, "port," and pre-Latin *buk*, "mountain," referring to the raised site where the railroad station now stands.

Le Portel. *Town and port, Pas-de-Calais.* The suburb of Boulogne-sur-Mer derives its name from Latin *portus*, "port," and the diminutive suffix *-ellum*.

Port-en-Bessin. *Village and port, Calvados.* The name derives from Latin *portus*, "port," and the regional name *Bessin*.

Portes-lès-Valence. *Town, Drôme.* The

name derives from Latin *porta*, "pass," "defile," here denoting a through route by the Rhône River near (*lès*) **Valence**.

Portet-sur-Garonne. *Town, Haute-Garonne.* The suburb of Toulouse derives its name from Latin *portus*, "pass," "defile," and the diminutive suffix *-ellum*, referring to a through route by the **Garonne** River here.

Port-la-Nouvelle. *Village and port, Aude.* The name has French *port*, "port," suffixed to *La Nouvelle*, "the new," a name recorded in 1528 for a newly created port on the Gulf of Lion.

Port-Louis. *Village and port, Morbihan.* The suburb of Morbihan arose around a fort built to command the entrance to Lorient harbor and named by Richelieu in 1598 in honor of *Louis* XIII. The earlier name of the place was recorded in the 15th century as *Locpezran*, from Breton *loch*, "church site," "parish," and a saint's name.

Le Port-Marly. *Town, Yvelines.* The Paris suburb derives its name from Latin *portus*, "port," and what is now **Marly-le-Roi**. The town is on the Seine River.

Porto-Vecchio. *Resort town and port, Corse-du-Sud.* The town, on Corsica's southwest coast, has an Italian name meaning "old port" that dates from the 13th century.

Port-Sainte-Marie. *Village, Lot-et-Garonne.* The name derives from Latin *portus*, "port," and a dedication to *St. Mary*. The village is on the Garonne River.

Port-Saint-Louis-du-Rhône. *Town, Bouches-du-Rhône.* The town, at the mouth of the **Rhône** River, derives its name from Latin *portus*, "port," and a dedication to *St. Louis*.

Port-sur-Saône. *Village, Haute-Saône.* The village derives its name from Latin *portus*, "port," and the **Saône** River on which it lies.

Port-Vendres. *Town and port, Pyrénées-Orientales.* The name was recorded in the 1st century AD as *Portus Veneris*, from Latin *portus*, "port," and the genitive form of the name of *Venus*, the Roman goddess of beauty and love.

Pouancé. *Village, Maine-et-Loire.* The name was recorded in the 11th century as *Poenciacum*, from the Roman personal name *Potentius* and the associative suffix *-acum*.

Pougnadoresse. *Village, Gard.* The name derives from Latin *pugnator*, "fighter," "combatant," and the suffix *-icia*, describing a fortified position.

Pouillon. *Village, Landes.* The name derives from the Roman personal name *Pullius* and the suffix *-onem*.

Pouilly-sous-Charlieu. *Village, Loire.* The name derives from the Roman personal name *Paullius* and the associative suffix *-acum*. The addition locates the village near (*sous*, "under") **Charlieu**.

Pouilly-sur-Loire. *Village, Nièvre.* The village has a name of the same origin as **Pouilly-sous-Charlieu**, from which it is distinguished by its location on the **Loire** River.

Le Pouliguen. *Resort town and port, Loire-Atlantique.* The Brittany town derives its name from Breton *poull*, "pool," "swamp," and *gwen*, "white."

Poussan. *Village, Hérault.* The name derives from the Roman personal name *Porcius* and the suffix *-anum*.

Pouzauges. *Town, Vendée.* The name derives from Latin *puteus*, "well," and the suffix *-alia*, referring to a full-flowing spring at the top of the town.

Le Pouzin. *Village, Ardèche.* The name may either derive from Old Provençal *polzin*, "chicken," or represent a derivative of Latin *podium*, "height," "hill."

Prades. *Town, Pyrénées-Orientales.* The name was recorded in the 9th century as *Prata*, from Latin *prata*, the plural of *pratum*, "meadow."

Le Pradet. *Town, Var.* The suburb of

Toulon derives its name from Latin *prata*, the plural of *pratum*, "meadow," and the diminutive suffix *-ittum*.

Pralognan-la-Vanoise. *Resort village, Savoie.* The name derives from Latin *prata*, the plural of *pratum*, "meadow," and *longianum*, "long." The village is high in the **Vanoise** Massif.

Pré-en-Pail. *Village, Mayenne.* The name derives from Latin *prata*, the plural of *pratum*, "meadow." The addition locates the village in (now near) the *Forêt de Pail*.

Preignac. *Village, Gironde.* The name was recorded in the 6th century as *Praemiacum*, from the Roman personal name *Primius* and the associative suffix *-acum*.

Prémery. *Village, Nièvre.* The name derives from the Roman personal name *Primarius* and the associative suffix *-acum*.

Prémontré. *Village, Aisne.* The name was recorded in 1120 as *Premonstratum*, said to derive from Latin *pratum*, "meadow," and a second element of uncertain origin, but perhaps a derivative of *monasterium*, "monastery." The *Premonstratensian* order of canons was founded here in 1120 by St. Norbert, who is said to have prophetically pointed the place out for the purpose (Latin *praemonstratus locus*, "place foreshown").

Le Pré-Saint-Gervais. *Town, Seine-Saint-Denis.* The Paris suburb derives its name from Latin *prata*, the plural of *pratum*, "meadow," and a dedication to *St. Gervase*.

Presles. *Village, Val-d'Oise.* The name was recorded in the 9th century as *Pretarium*, from Latin *prata*, the plural of *pratum*, "meadow," and the suffix *-arium*.

Preuilly-sur-Claise. *Village, Indre-et-Loire.* The name was recorded in the 10th century as *Pruliacus*, from the Roman personal name *Probilius* and the associative suffix *-acum*. The village is on the *Claise* River.

Prévessin-Moëns. *Village, Ain.* The first part of the name derives from the Roman personal name *Privicius*, from *Privus*, and the suffix *-anum*. The second part comes either from the Germanic personal name *Mod* and the suffix *-ing* or from the Germanic personal name *Modings*.

Prigonrieux. *Village, Dordogne.* The name derives from Latin *profundus*, "deep," and *rivus*, "stream."

Printzheim. *Village, Bas-Rhin.* The name derives from German *Prinz*, "prince," and Germanic *heim*, "village," denoting a royal possession.

Privas. *Town, Ardèche.* The name is that of *St. Privatus*, 3d-century bishop of Mende and martyr.

Propriano. *Resort village, Corse-du-Sud.* The name of the village, in southwestern Corsica, was recorded in the 13th century as *Proprianum*, from Latin *proprius*, "special," "peculiar," or the Roman personal name *Properius*.

Provence. *Historic region, southeastern France.* The former province takes its name from Latin *Provincia*, "province," from *provincia romana*, "Roman province." Provence was the first Transalpine province in the Roman Empire, founded around 130 BC as part of Roman *Gallia Narbonensis* (see **Gallia, Narbonne**).

Provence-Alpes-Côte d'Azur. *Region, southeastern France.* The extensive administrative region, created in the 1980s, has the historic province of **Provence** at its core and includes all of the southern **Alps** in its northern part and the **Côte d'Azur** (French Riviera) in the south.

Proville. *Village, Nord.* The suburb of Cambrai derives its name from a Germanic personal name such as *Perolt* and Latin *villa*, "estate."

Provin. *Village, Nord.* The name probably has the same origin as that of **Provins**.

Provins. *Town, Seine-et-Marne.* The name derives from the Roman personal name *Probus* and the suffix *-inum*.

Prunelli-di-Fiumorbo. *Village, Haute-Corse.* The village, in eastern Corsica, has an Italian name, from Latin *prunellum*, "sloe," and the *Fium'Orbo* River here (Italian *fiume*, "river").

Publier. *Town, Haute-Savoie.* The name appears to derive from the Roman personal name *Publius* and the suffix *-arium*.

Puellemontier. *Village, Haute-Marne.* The name derives from Latin *puella*, "girl," and the suffix *-arium*, followed by *monasterium*, "monastery," "convent." A nunnery was founded here in the 7th century.

Puget-sur-Argens. *Town, Var.* The name derives from Latin *podium*, "height," "hill," and the diminutive suffix *-ittum*. The town is on the *Argens* River.

Puilboreau. *Town, Charente-Maritime.* The name derives from Latin *podium*, "height," "hill," and probably French *le*, "the," and the personal name *Boreau*.

Puiseaux. *Village, Loiret.* The name derives from Latin *puteus*, "well," and the suffix *-eolum*.

Puisserguier. *Village, Hérault.* The name derives from Latin *podium*, "height," "hill," and *sericarius*, "maker of serge."

Pujols. *Village, Lot-et-Garonne.* The name derives from Latin *podium*, "height," "hill," and the diminutive suffix *-eolum*.

Puligny-Montrachet. *Village, Côte-d'Or.* The first part of the name derives from the Germanic personal name *Puolo* and the double suffix *-in* and *-iacum*. The second part derives from Latin *mons, montis*, "mountain," and an element of uncertain origin.

Pulnoy. *Town, Meurthe-et-Moselle.* The name derives from Latin *prunus*, "plum tree," and apparently the double suffix *-ar* and *-etum*.

Pulversheim. *Village, Haut-Rhin.* The name, recorded in the 8th century as *Wolfrigeshaim*, derives from the Germanic personal name *Vulferich* and *heim*, "abode."

Puteaux. *Town, Hauts-de-Seine.* The Paris suburb derives its name from Latin *putidellum*, Old French *putel*, "mire," "marsh." Puteaux lies by the Seine.

Le Puy. *Town, Haute-Loire.* The name was recorded in the 10th century as *Podium*, from Latin *podium*, "height," referring to the mountainous volcanic region in which the town lies. The full name is *Le Puy-en-Velay*, from its location in **Velay**.

Puy-de-Dôme. *Department, central France.* The name is that of a volcanic mountain in Auvergne, with *Puy* from Latin *podium*, as for *Le Puy* (see **Puy, Le**), and *Dôme*, from Gaulish *Duma*, the actual mountain name.

Puy-Guillaume. *Village, Puy-de-Dôme.* The name derives from Latin *podium*, "height," "hill," and the Germanic personal name *Wilihelm*.

Puylaurens. *Village, Tarn.* The name derives from Latin *podium*, "height," "hill," and the Roman personal name *Laurentius*.

Puy-l'Évêque. *Village, Lot.* The name, recorded in the 13th century as simply *Podium*, derives from Latin *podium*, "height," and French *l'évêque*, "the bishop," the feudal lord.

Le Puy-Sainte-Réparade. *Town, Bouches-du-Rhône.* The name derives from Latin *podium*, "height," and a dedication to *St. Reparata*, beheaded in Caesarea, Palestine, in the 3d century.

Puy-Saint-Vincent. *Resort village, Hautes-Alpes.* The name derives from Latin *podium*, "height," and a dedication to *St. Vincent*.

Pyrenees. *Mountain range, southwestern France.* The range, forming the border between France (where they are called *Pyrénées*) and Spain (where they called *Pirineos*), has a name adopted as recently as the 17th century from that used by ancient geographers. The Romans knew the mountains as *Pyreneus mons*, from Greek *Purenaia*, from *Pyrene*, the mythical daughter of

Bebryx, king of Narbonne, who was raped by Hercules, killed by wild beasts, and buried in the Pyrenees. In medieval times there was no overall name for the range, and the inhabitants of this region knew only the names of local mountains and valleys.

Pyrénées-Atlantiques. *Department, southwestern France.* The department borders the **Pyrenees** to the south and the *Atlantic* to the west. Hence its name. Until 1969 it was known as *Basses-Pyrénées* ("Lower Pyrenees"), by contrast with neighboring **Hautes-Pyrénées**, but the name was changed because of its suggestion of "inferiority."

Pyrénées-Orientales. *Department, southern France.* The name means "Eastern Pyrenees," describing the department's location at the eastern end of the **Pyrenees**, bordering the Mediterranean.

Quarouble. *Village, Nord.* The name was recorded in the 7th century as *Karubium*, apparently from Latin *quadruvium*, "crossroads."

Quarré-les-Tombes. *Village, Yonne.* The name derives from Latin *quadrata*, "square," with *villa*, "village," understood, meaning a settlement built on a rectangular plan. The addition ("the tombs") refers to a Roman burial ground here.

Quercitello. *Village, Haute-Corse.* The village, in northern Corsica, derives its name from Latin *quercus*, "oak," and the collective suffix *-etum*, with the diminutive suffix *-ellum*. The name implies a small settlement by an oak grove.

Quercy. *Region, southwestern France.* The region of the Aquitaine Basin had the Latin name *Cadurcinum*, from the *Cadurci*, the Celtic tribe who gave the name of **Cahors**.

Querqueville. *Town, Manche.* The suburb of Cherbourg derives its name from Dutch *kerke*, "church," and Latin *villa*, "estate," "village." The 10th-century chapel here is one of the oldest religious buildings in western France.

Le Quesnoy. *Town, Nord.* The name was recorded in the 12th century as *Quercetum* and in the 13th century as *Chaisnoyt*. The first form derives from Latin *quercus*, "oak," and the collective suffix *-etum*; the second from Gaulish *cassanos*, "oak," and the same suffix.

Quesnoy-sur-Deûle. *Town, Nord.* The name is identical in origin to that of *Le Quesnoy* (see **Quesnoy, Le**). The addition locates the town on the *Deûle* River,

Quetigny. *Town, Côte-d'Or.* The suburb of Dijon derives its name from the Roman personal name *Quintinius* and the associative suffix *-acum*.

La Queue-en-Brie. *Town, Val-de-Marne.* The Paris suburb derives its name from Latin *cauda*, "tail," denoting an elongated stretch of land. The addition locates the town in **Brie**.

Queuille. *Village, Puy-de-Dôme.* The name derives from Low Latin *collia*, a collective form of Latin *collis*, "hill."

Quéven. *Town, Morbihan.* The Brittany town derives its name from Breton *gwen*, "white," and a first element of uncertain origin.

Quiberon. *Town, Morbihan.* The Brittany town takes its name from that of the peninsula on which it lies, recorded in the 11th century as *Keberpen* or *Kemberoen*. This name is of uncertain origin, but possible Breton sources are: (1) *Kêr Broenn*, "town of reeds," from the marshes here; (2) *Gwez brein*, "rotten trees"; (3) *Kebrienn*, "chevron," from the V-shape of the peninsula; (4) *Kêr brec'hagn*, "barren town." A source has also been proposed in Old Welsh *co*, "high," "great," and *peroen*, "owner," "possessor," referring to the 5th-century immigration from Britain here.

Quiévrechain. *Town, Nord.* The name may derive from Latin *capra*, "goat," and the double suffix *-ic* and *-inum*.

Quillan. *Village, Aude.* The name was recorded in the 12th century as *Quillianum*, from the Roman personal name *Quelius* and the suffix *-anum*.

Quimper. *City, Finistère.* The Breton name of the Brittany city is *Kemper*, from *kember*, "confluence," referring to the junction of the Steir and Odet rivers here. In Roman times the city was called *Civitas Corisopitum*, and in the Revolution it was named *Montagne-sur-Odet*.

Quimperlé. *Town, Finistère.* The Breton name of the Brittany town is *Kemperle*, recorded in the 11th century as *Kemperelegium*, from *kember*, "confluence," as for **Quimper**, here referring to the junction of the Ellé and Isole rivers, and the Roman name of the *Ellé* itself.

Quincampoix. *Village, Seine-Maritime.* The name represents Old French *cui qu'en poïst*, "(belonging) to whoever does the weighing," an ironic reference to a mean miller.

Quincy-sous-Sénart. *Town, Essonne.* The Paris suburb derives its name from the Roman personal name *Quintius* and the associative suffix *-acum*. The addition locates the town near (*sous*, "under") the Forest of *Sénart*.

Quincy-Voisins. *Town, Seine-et-Marne.* The first part of the name is as for **Quincy-sous-Sénart**. The second part derives from a plural form of Latin *vicinium*, "hamlet," "village."

La Quinte. *Village, Sarthe.* The name derives from Latin *quinta*, Old French *quinte*, "fifth," denoting a community of five villages.

Quintin. *Village, Côtes-d'Armor.* The name derives either from the Roman personal name *Quintinus* or from a modern form of this.

Quissac. *Village, Gard.* The name was recorded in the 12th century as *Quintiacum*, from the Roman personal name *Quintius* and the associative suffix *-acum*.

Rabastens. *Village, Tarn.* The name derives from a blend of the Germanic personal name *Hratgast* or *Ratgast* and the suffix *-ing* with Old Provençal *rabasta*, "quarrel," referring to disputed territory.

Rabodanges. *Village, Orne.* The original name of the settlement was recorded in the 11th century as *Cuelleit*, from the Roman personal name *Cullius* and the associative suffix *-acum*. Around 1650 the village was erected into a marquisate for Louis de *Rabodanges*, and adopted his name (from the Germanic personal name *Radbodo* and the suffix *-ing*).

Raillimont. *Village, Aisne.* The name derives from Latin *mons, montis*, "mountain," added to the former name of the village, from the Germanic female personal name *Rocula* and the associative suffix *-iacum*.

Le Raincy. *Town, Seine-Saint-Denis.* The name of the Paris suburb was recorded in the 11th century as *Reinse* or *Reinsiacum*, from the Gallo-Roman personal name *Remicius* and the associative suffix *-acum*.

Raismes. *Town, Nord.* The suburb of Valenciennes may derive its name from Latin *rama*, a feminine form of *ramus*, Old French *raime*, "branch," used collectively to mean "wood." A large forest lies to the north of the town.

Rambervillers. *Town, Vosges.* The name, recorded in the 12th century as *Rambertivillaris*, derives from the Germanic personal name *Raginberht* and Latin *villare*, "farmstead."

Rambouillet. *Town, Yvelines.* The name was recorded in the 12th century as *Rambullet*, a diminutive form of *Rambeuil*, from the Germanic personal name *Rambo* or *Rampo* and Gaulish *ialon*, "clearing," "village."

Ramonville-Saint-Agne. *Town, Haute-Garonne.* The suburb of Toulouse derives its name from the Germanic personal name *Raginmund* and Latin *villa*, "estate." The second part of the name is a dedication to St. *Anianus*, 5th-century bishop of Orléans.

Rancogne. *Village, Charente.* The name

was recorded in the 13th century as *Ranconia*, apparently from the Graeco-Latin verb *rhonchare*, "to snore," Gaulish *onno*, "river," and the suffix *-ia*. The reference would be to the deep gurgling sound of streams flowing through the large caves here.

Rang-du-Fliers. *Village, Pas-de-Calais.* The name was recorded in the 15th century as *Le Rencq de Faez*, perhaps from Old French *renc* or *ranc*, "opening," "gap." The second part of the name is a river name.

Rantigny. *Village, Oise.* The name derives from the Roman personal name *Rantinius*, from *Rantius*, and the associative suffix *-acum*.

Raon-l'Étape. *Town, Vosges.* The name derives from a local form of Old French *regon*, "mixed crop of wheat and rye," Germanic *rogon*, "rye." The addition is French *étape*, "staging post," distinguishing the town from *Raon-lès-Leau* ("near Leau") and *Raon-sur-Plaine* ("on the Plaine River"), a few miles to the northeast.

Rapaggio. *Village, Haute-Corse.* The village, in northern Corsica, derives its name from Latin *rapa*, "rape" (the crop plant), and the suffix *-arium*.

Rasteau. *Village, Vaucluse.* The name derives from Latin *rastellum*, "rake," referring to a local relief feature.

Ravel. *Village, Drôme.* The name derives from Old Provençal *revel*, "rebellion," used metaphorically for a castle or fort.

La Ravoire. *Town, Savoie.* The suburb of Chambéry derives its name from Latin *roboria*, "oak wood."

Razimet. *Village, Lot-et-Garonne.* The name derives from Latin *racemus*, "bunch of grapes," and the collective suffix *-etum*, referring to a local vineyard.

Ré, Île de. *Island, western France.* The island, in the Bay of Biscay, was known to the Romans as *Ratis*, later changed to *Rhea*, the name of a goddess. The original name probably derived from Gaulish *rate*, "fort."

Réalmont. *Village, Tarn.* The name was recorded in the 14th century as *Regalis montis*, from Latin *regalis*, "royal," implying an estate belonging to the king, and *mons, montis*, "mountain."

Recouvrance. *Village, Belfort.* The name is that of the dedication of a chapel here, to *Notre-Dame de Recouvrance*, "Our Lady of Succour."

Le Reculey. *Village, Calvados.* The name derives from French *reculé*, "remote," denoting an isolated place.

Redon. *Town, Ille-et-Vilaine.* The name was recorded in the 6th century as *Redone*, from the *Redones*, a Gaulish tribe who also gave the name of **Rennes**. An alternate origin in Latin *rotundus*, "round," has also been proposed.

Réhon. *Village, Meurthe-et-Moselle.* The suburb of Longwy has a name of obscure origin. It may derive from the Germanic personal name *Rehan* or *Reon*.

Reichshoffen. *Town, Bas-Rhin.* The name derives from the Germanic personal name *Richini* and *hof*, "farm." The German form of the name is *Reichshofen*.

Reichstett. *Town, Bas-Rhin.* The suburb of Strasbourg derives its name from the Germanic personal name *Rico* and *stat*, "place."

Reignier. *Town, Haute-Savoie.* The name derives from the Germanic personal name *Raginhari*.

Reims. *City, Marne.* The city, still sometimes known to English speakers as *Rheims*, takes its name from the *Remi*, a Gaulish tribe whose own Celtic name means "dominant ones." The earlier Roman name, recorded in the 1st century BC, was *Durocortorum*, from Gaulish *duron*, "fort." The name has been associated with that of St Remigius, 6th-century bishop of Reims, although his own name is generally held to be of Latin origin.

Le Relecq-Kerhuon. *Town, Finistère.* The suburb of Brest derives the first part of its name from Breton *releg*, "relic," meaning a chapel or cemetery. The second part derives from Breton *kêr*, "town," and the personal name *Huon*.

Remiremont. *Town, Vosges.* The name was recorded in the 7th century for this part of the Vosges as *montiis Romarici*, from Latin *mons, montis*, "mountain," and the name of *St. Romaric*, who founded a monastery here in 620.

Renage. *Village, Isère.* The name may derive from the Gaulish personal name *Renos* and the associative suffix *-acum*.

Renazé. *Village, Mayenne.* The name may derive from the Germanic personal name *Rinhath* and the associative suffix *-iacum*.

Rencurel. *Village, Isère.* The name derives from Old Provençal *rancura*, "rancor," either as a nickname for a spiteful person or describing a castle difficult to capture.

Rennes. *City, Ille-et-Vilaine.* The name of the Brittany city was recorded in the 4th century as *Redonas*, from the *Redones*, the Gaulish tribe whose capital it was. Their own name comes from Gaulish *redo-*, "to ride," "to journey." The Breton name of Rennes is *Roazhon*. Its earlier Gaulish name, recorded in the 2d century BC, was *Condate*, "confluence," from the junction of the Ille and Vilaine rivers here.

La Réole. *Town, Gironde.* The name was recorded in the 11th century as *Regulatensis ecclesia*, from Latin *regula*, "straight edge," "rule," here in the sense of "slatted enclosure" or "monastery."

Restinclières. *Village, Hérault.* The name derives from Languedocian *restincle*, "lentisk" (the mastic tree).

Rethel. *Town, Ardennes.* The name probably derives from Germanic *roden*, "to clear land."

Rethondes. *Village, Oise.* The name was recorded in the 7th century as *Rotundae*, apparently from Latin *rotundus*, "round," as possibly for **Redon**.

Retournac. *Village, Haute-Loire.* The name derives from the Gaulish personal name *Rittius* and the associative suffix *-acum*, with the spelling of the personal name influenced by Old Provençal *retornar*, "to return."

Reutenbourg. *Village, Bas-Rhin.* The name derives from German *reuten*, a dialect form of *roden*, "to clear land," and *Burg*, "castle."

Revel. *Town, Haute-Garonne.* The name represents Old Provençal *revel*, "rebellion," used metaphorically for a castle or fort.

Revigny-sur-Ornain. *Village, Meuse.* The name derives from the Germanic personal name *Rubo* and the double suffix *-in* and *-iacum*. The village is on the *Ornain* River.

Réville. *Village, Manche.* The name may derive from Latin *regis villa*, "king's estate."

Revin. *Town, Ardennes.* The name, recorded in the 8th century as *Ruivinium*, is of uncertain origin. It may derive from a Germanic personal name *Rugwin*.

Reyrevignes. *Village, Lot.* The name derives from Old Provençal *reire*, "behind," and *vinha*, "vine," denoting the location of the village in relation to a vineyard.

Reyrieux. *Town, Ain.* The name derives from the Roman personal name *Rarus* and the associative suffix *-iacum*.

Rezé. *Town, Loire-Atlantique.* The suburb of Nantes has a name recorded in the 2d century AD as *Ratiaton*, from the Roman personal name *Rasius* or *Ratius*, or Gaulish *ratis*, "fern," and the suffix *-ate*.

Rezza. *Village, Corse-du-Sud.* The village, in west central Corsica, derives its name from the Roman personal name *Raetius*, with Latin *villa*, "estate," understood.

Rheims *see* **Reims**

Rhinau. *Village, Bas-Rhin.* The village derives its name from that of the *Rhin* River (see **Rhine**), on which it lies, and Germanic *au*, "damp meadow."

Rhine. *River, northeastern France.* The Upper Rhine, which rises in Switzerland, flows north along the eastern border of **Bas-Rhin** and **Haut-Rhin** as the western frontier of Germany. Its name (French *Rhin*, German *Rhein*) was recorded by the Romans as *Rhenus*, probably from Gaulish *renos*, "river," or less likely from Germanic *hrinan*, "to low" (of cattle), describing its roaring sound.

Rhône. *Department, east central France.* The name is that of the main river here, known to the Romans as *Rhodanus*, perhaps from pre-Indoeuropean *rod* or *rot*, "to run," or Celtic *rho*, "river," and *dan*, "rapid," or Celtic *rhuit-an*, "rapid water," related to Welsh *rhedeg*, "to run."

Rhône-Alpes. *Region, southeastern France.* The administrative region includes the middle **Rhône** valley in its western part and most of the French **Alps** in the east. Hence its name.

Riaillé. *Village, Loire-Maritime.* The name derives from the Gallo-Roman personal name *Rialius* and the associative suffix *-acum*.

Rians. *Village, Var.* The name derives from the Roman personal name *Reius* and the suffix *-anum*.

Ribeauvillé. *Town, Haut-Rhin.* The name was recorded in the 8th century as *Ratbaldo villare*, from the Germanic personal name *Ratbald* and Latin *villare*, "farmstead." Ribeauvillé is not far from the border with Germany, where it is known as *Rappoltsweiler*.

Ribécourt. *Village, Oise.* The name derives from the Germanic personal name *Ricberht* and Latin *cortem*, accusative of *cors*, "estate."

Ribemont. *Village, Aisne.* The name derives from the Germanic personal name *Ricbodo* and Latin *mons, montis*, "mountain."

Ribérac. *Town, Dordogne.* The name, recorded in the 10th century as *Ribairac*, is from Latin *riparia*, "riverside land," with the associative suffix *-acum*. Ribérac is near the Dronne River.

La Ricamarie. *Town, Loire.* The name derives from the French family name *Recamier*.

La Riche. *Town, Indre-et-Loire.* The suburb of Tours probably derives its name from French *riche*, "rich," referring to rich soil or pasture here.

Richelieu. *Village, Indre-et-Loire.* The name was recorded in the 13th century as *Richeloc*, from French *riche*, "rich," and Latin *locus*, "place." The first part of the name could also represent the Germanic female personal name *Ricburgis*. The present town was planned and built in 1631 for Cardinal *Richelieu*, who was born here.

Richemont. *Village, Moselle.* The name, recorded in the 13th century as now, derives from the Germanic personal name *Richer* and Latin *mons, montis*, "hill." The village is not far from the border with Germany, where it is known as *Reichersberg*.

Richwiller. *Village, Haut-Rhin.* The name probably derives from a Germanic personal name *Rich*, short for a name such as *Richmund*, and Latin *villare*, "farmstead." The German form of the name is *Reichweiler*.

Riec-sur-Bélon. *Town, Finistère.* The name derives from the Breton saint's name *Rioc*. The town is on the *Bélon* River.

Riedisheim. *Town, Haut-Rhin.* The suburb of Mulhouse derives its name from the Germanic personal name *Ruodin* and *heim*, "abode."

Riervescemont. *Village, Belfort.* The name derives from Old French *rière*, "behind," and nearby **Vescemont**, which the village overlooks.

Rieupeyroux. *Village, Aveyron.* The name derives from Latin *rivus*, "stream," and *petrosus*, "stony," "rocky."

Riez. *Village, Alpes-de-Haute-Provence.* The Roman settlement here was recorded in the 1st century as *Alebaece Reiorum Apol-linarium*, from the Ligurian people known as the *Reii*.

Rimbach-près-Guebwiller. *Village, Haut-Rhin*. The name derives from *Rindr*, the Germanic goddess who was the consort of Odin, and Germanic *bach*, "stream." The addition locates the village near (*près*) **Guebwiller**, as distinct from *Rimbach-près-Masevaux*, some 10 miles to the southwest, not far from **Masevaux**.

Rimplas. *Village, Alpes-Maritimes*. The name derives from the Germanic personal name *Ragin* and Latin *placitum*, "that which is pleasing," referring to a local court of justice. (It is known historically as a *plaid*, and was an assembly of counts and bishops in Frankish times.)

Riom. *Town, Puy-de-Dôme*. The name was recorded in the 6th century as *Ricomagensis vicus*, from Gaulish *Ricomago* (from *rix*, "king," and *magos*, "market") and Latin *vicus*, "village."

Riom-ès-Montagne. *Town, Cantal*. The name has the same origin as **Riom**. The addition ("in the mountains") locates the town in the regional park of the Auvergne Volcanoes.

Riquewihr. *Village, Haut-Rhin*. The name derives from the Germanic personal name *Ricco* and Latin *villare*, "farmstead." The village is not far from the border with Germany, where it is known as *Reichenweier*.

Ris-Orangis. *Town, Essonne*. The first part of the name may represent Gaulish *rica*, "line," "furrow." The second part, recorded in the 12th century as *Orengiacum*, derives from the Germanic personal name *Uring* and the associative suffix *-iacum*.

Rive-de-Gier. *Town, Loire*. The town derives its name from Latin *ripa*, "bank," and the *Gier* River on which it lies.

Rives. *Town, Isère*. The town derives its name from Latin *ripa*, "bank," referring to its location on the Fure River.

Rivesaltes. *Town, Pyrénées-Orientales*. The town derives its name from a plural form of Latin *ripa*, "bank," and *alta*, "high," referring to its location on the Agly River.

Riviera *see* **Côte d'Azur**

Rixheim. *Town, Haut-Rhin*. The suburb of Mulhouse derives its name from the Germanic personal name *Richeni* and *heim*, "abode."

Roanne. *City, Loire*. The name was recorded in the 2nd century as *Rodumna*, from the pre-Indoeuropean or Celtic river root *rod* (as for **Rhône**) and the Gaulish suffix *-umna*.

Rocamadour. *Village, Lot*. The name is Occitan, from *roc*, "rock," and the saint's name *Amator*. The Latin name *Rupis Amatoris*, recorded in the 12th century, has the same sense. The village is built along and up the side of a sheer cliff and there is a chapel here dedicated to St. Amator. (According to local legend this Amator is not the saint who gave the name of **Saint-Amadou** but the name taken by the biblical Zaccheus when he came here as a hermit and built a shrine to the Virgin Mary which attracts pilgrims to this day.)

Rochechouart. *Town, Haute-Vienne*. The name was recorded in the 12th century as *Rochehardouin*, from pre-Latin *rocca*, French *roche*, "rock," and the Germanic personal name *Hardwin*. "Rock" in a name such as this (and those below) often means "rocky mount," hence "fort built on a rocky mount," hence "fortress," "stronghold."

Rochecorbon. *Village, Indre-et-Loire*. The suburb of Tours derives its name from pre-Latin *rocca*, French *roche*, "rock," and the personal name *Hardouin*, latinized as *Corbo, Corbonis*.

Rochefort. *City and port, Charente-Maritime*. The name derives from pre-Latin *rocca*, "rock," and Latin *fortis*, "strong." The city is also known as *Rochefort-sur-Mer* ("on sea").

La Rochefoucauld. *Town, Charente*. The

name was recorded in the 11th century as *Rupes Fulcaudi*, from Latin *rupes*, "cave," and the personal name *Fulcaudus*. Pre-Latin *rocca*, French *roche*, "rock," was then prefixed.

Roche-la-Molière. *Town, Loire.* The name derives from pre-Latin *rocca*, French *roche*, "rock," and *Molière*, from Latin *mollis*, "soft," and the suffix *-aria*, denoting an area of soft or damp land.

La Rochelle. *City and port, Charente-Maritime.* The name was recorded in the 10th century as *Rupella*, from Latin *rupes*, "cave," and the suffix *-ella*, but in the 12th century as *Rochella*, from French *roche*, "rock."

Rochemaure. *Village, Ardèche.* The name derives from pre-Latin *rocca*, French *roche*, "rock," and Latin *maura*, "black." Medieval castle ruins here lie atop a black basalt rock-spur.

La Roche-Posay. *Resort village, Vienne.* The name derives from pre-Latin *rocca*, French *roche*, "rock," and that of the nearby village of *Posay*.

Rocheservière. *Village, Vendée.* The name was recorded in the 11th century as *Rocha Cerveria*, from pre-Latin *rocca*, French *roche*, "rock," and Latin *cervus*, "stag," "hart."

La Roche-sur-Foron. *Town, Haute-Savoie.* The town derives its name from pre-Latin *rocca*, French *roche*, "rock," and the *Foron* River on which it lies.

La Roche-sur-Yon. *City, Vendée.* The name was recorded in the 13th century as *Roca super Eon*, from Latin *roca*, "rock," and the name of the *Yon* river. An earlier name, recorded in the 11th century, was *Oinis* or *Oionis*, from a pre-Latin river name.

La Rochette. *Village, Savoie.* The name derives from pre-Latin *rocca*, French *roche*, "rock," and the diminutive suffix *-itta*.

Rocquencourt. *Village, Yvelines.* The name derives from the Germanic personal name *Rocco* and Latin *cortem*, accusative of *cors*, "estate."

Rodez. *Town, Aveyron.* The name was recorded in the 6th century as *Rutenis*, from the *Ruteni*, the Gaulish tribe who had their capital here. Their name may mean "swift ones," from a Gaulish word derived from Indoeuropean *reu*, "to move rapidly." An earlier name, recorded in the 2d century, was *Segodunum* or *Segedunum*, from Gaulish *sego-*, "victory," "strength," and *dunon*, "fort."

Rognac. *Town, Bouches-du-Rhône.* The name derives from the Gallo-Roman personal name *Rutenius*, from *Rutenus* (from the *Ruteni* who gave the name of **Rodez**), and the associative suffix *-acum*.

Rohan. *Town, Morbihan.* The Brittany town takes its name from Breton *roc'h*, "rock."

Rohrbach-lès-Bitche. *Village, Moselle.* The name derives from Germanic *ror*, "reed," and *aha*, "water" (subsequently lost), with *bach*, "stream." The village is near (*lès*) **Bitche**.

Roissy-en-Brie. *Town, Seine-et-Marne.* The town, on the edge of the **Brie** region, derives its name from the Roman personal name *Rossius* or *Roscius* and the associative suffix *-acum*.

Roissy-en-France. *Town, Val-d'Oise.* The Paris suburb has a name identical to that of **Roissy-en-Brie**, from which it is distinguished by its location in *France*, a name applied to this region before it came to be used for the country as a whole.

Romagnat. *Town, Puy-de-Dôme.* The suburb of Clermont-Ferrand has a name recorded in the 6th century as *Romaniacum*, from the Roman personal name *Romanius* and the associative suffix *-acum*.

Romagne-sous-Montfaucon. *Village, Meuse.* The name derives from the Roman personal name *Romanus*, with Latin *villa*, "estate," understood. The village is near (*sous*, "under") **Montfaucon-d'Argonne**.

Romainville. *Town, Seine-Saint-Denis.* The Paris suburb derives its name from the

Roman personal name *Romanus* and Latin *villa*, "estate."

Romanèche-Thorins. *Village, Saône-et-Loire*. The first part of the name derives from the Roman personal name *Romanus* and the Germanic suffix *-isca*. The second part names nearby *Les Thorins*.

Romans-sur-Isère. *Town, Drôme*. The name was recorded in the 10th century as *villa Romanis*, from *villa*, "estate," "village," and the Roman personal name *Romanus*, from *Roma*, "Rome." The town is on the **Isère** River.

Rombas. *Town, Isère*. The name derives from the Germanic personal name *Rumo* and *bach*, "stream." The German name of the village is thus *Rombach*.

Romette. *Village, Hautes-Alpes*. The name is said to represent a diminutive form of *Rome*, the Italian city.

Romilly-sur-Andelle. *Village, Eure*. The name derives from the Roman personal name *Romilius* and the associative suffix *-acum*. The addition locates the village on the *Andelle* River.

Romilly-sur-Seine. *Town, Aube*. The town has a name of the same origin as **Romilly-sur-Andelle**, from which, among others, it is distinguished by its location on the **Seine** River.

Romorantin-Lanthenay. *Town, Loir-et-Cher*. Two communities merged to give this name. *Romorantin* was recorded in the 12th century as *rivus Morentinus*, from Latin *rivus*, "stream," and *Morentinus*, the name of the *Morantin* River, from the Roman personal name *Maurentius*. *Lanthenay* was recorded in the 14th century as *Lanthenayum*, probably from the Gaulish personal name *Lenteno*.

Ronchamp. *Village, Haute-Saône*. The name probably derives from Latin *rotundus*, "round," and French *champ*, "field."

Ronchin. *Town, Nord*. The suburb of Lille has a name recorded in the 9th century

as *Runcinium*, from the Roman personal name *Ronsinus*.

Roncq. *Town, Nord*. The name may derive from the Germanic personal name *Hrodo* or *Hrogo*.

Roquebrune-Cap-Martin. *Resort town, Alpes-Maritimes*. The name was recorded in the 12th century as *Rocam brunam*, Latin for "brown rock," describing the headland here. The town is distinguished from **Roquebrune-sur-Argens** by its addition of nearby *Cap-Martin*, "St. Martin's cape." The latter, recorded in the 12th century as *caput Sancti Martini*, was earlier *Cap-Saint-Martin* but by the 17th century was appearing on maps in its present form.

Roquebrune-sur-Argens. *Town, Var*. The name has the same origin as that of **Roquebrune-Cap-Martin**, from which it is distinguished by its location on the *Argens* River.

Roquecourbe. *Village, Tarn*. The name derives from pre-Latin *rocca*, French *roche*, "rock," and Latin *curva*, "bent," "curved."

Roquefort. *Village, Landes*. The name derives from pre-Latin *rocca*, French *roche*, "rock," and Latin *fortis*, "strong," denoting a stronghold.

Roquefort-la-Bédoule. *Town, Bouches-du-Rhône*. The name is as for **Roquefort**, with an addition of uncertain origin.

Rocquefort-les-Pins. *Town, Alpes-Maritimes*. The name is as for **Roquefort**, but with an addition meaning "the pines."

Roquefort-sur-Soulzon. *Village, Aveyron*. The name is as for **Roquefort**, but with an addition locating the village on the *Soulzon* River.

Roquemaure. *Village, Gard*. The name derives from pre-Latin *rocca*, French *roche*, "rock," and Latin *maura*, "black."

La Roquette-sur-Siagne. *Village, Alpes-Maritimes*. The village, on the *Siagne* River, derives its name from pre-Latin *rocca*, French *roche*, "rock," and the diminutive suffix *-itta*.

Roquevaire. *Town, Bouches-du-Rhône.* The name derives from pre-Latin *rocca*, French *roche*, "rock," and Latin *varius*, "varied," "mottled," describing the appearance of the rock.

Roscoff. *Resort town and port, Finistère.* The Brittany town has the Breton name *Rosgo*, from *roz*, "mound," "hill," and *gov*, "smithy."

Rosenwiller. *Village, Bas-Rhin.* The name, recorded in the 19th century as *Rosenweiler*, derives from that of General *Rosen* and Latin *villare*, "farmstead."

Rosières-aux-Salines. *Village, Meurthe-et-Moselle.* The name derives from Germanic *raus*, "reed," and the suffix *-aria*. The addition represents Latin *salina*, "salt-works."

Rosières-en-Santerre. *Village, Somme.* The name is as for **Rosières-aux-Salines**, with the addition here from the regional name *Santerre*.

Les Rosiers. *Village, Maine-et-Loire.* The name derives from Latin *rosa*, "rose," meaning the dog rose, and the suffix *-arium*.

Rosny-sous-Bois. *Town, Seine-Saint-Denis.* The name of the Paris suburb was recorded in the 12th century as *Rodoniacum*, from the Gallo-Roman personal name *Rutenius*, from *Rutenus* (from the *Ruteni* who gave the name of **Rodez**), and the associative suffix *-acum*. The addition means "near the wood."

Rosny-sur-Seine. *Town, Yvelines.* The town has a name of the same origin as **Rosny-sous-Bois**, but here with an addition locating it on the **Seine** River.

Rosporden. *Town, Finistère.* The Brittany town derives its name from Breton *roz*, "mound," and an element of uncertain origin.

Rosselange. *Village, Moselle.* The name derives from the Germanic personal name *Roacheri* and the suffix *-ing*. The German form of the name is *Rosslingen*.

Rostrenen. *Town, Côtes-d'Armor.* The Brittany town derives its name from Breton *roz*, "mound," and an element of uncertain origin.

Roubaix. *City, Nord.* The name was recorded in the 9th century as *Rusbacus*, from Germanic *hros*, "horse," and *baki*, "stream." A "horse stream" is one where where horses regularly crossed or came to drink.

Rouen. *City, Seine-Maritime.* The name was recorded in the 4th century as *Rotomagus*, from Gaulish *roto-*, "wheel," and *magos*, "field," probably referring to the Celtish love of chariot racing.

Rouergue. *Region, southern France.* The Roman name of the region was *Rutenicum*, from the *Ruteni*, the Gaulish people who gave the name of **Rodez**, the region's historic capital.

Rouffach. *Town, Haut-Rhin.* The name was recorded in the 7th century as *Rubiaco*, from the Gallo-Roman personal name *Rubius* and the associative suffix *-acum*. The German form of the name is *Rufach*.

Rougé. *Village, Loire-Atlantique.* The name derives from the Gallo-Roman personal name *Rubius* and the associative suffix *-acum*.

Rougegoutte. *Village, Belfort.* The name derives from Latin *rubeus*, "red," and *gutta*, "drop" (of water), "small stream." The color would be that of the earth or stream bed here.

Rougemont-le-Château. *Village, Belfort.* The name derives from Latin *rubeus*, "red," and *mons, montis*, "mountain," referring to the color of the soil. The addition is "the castle."

Rouillac. *Village, Charente.* The name was recorded in the 9th century as *Roliacum*, from the Roman personal name *Rullius* and the associative suffix *-acum*.

Roumazières-Loubert. *Village, Charente.* The first part of the name derives from Latin *rubeus*, "red," and *maceriae*, "ruins," referring to the color of the Roman remains here. The second part probably derives from the Germanic personal name *Liudberht*.

Rousies. *Town, Nord*. The suburb of Maubeuge may derive its name from the Germanic personal name *Rozzo* and the suffix *-aca*.

Les Rousses. *Resort village, Jura*. The origin of the name is uncertain. It may derive from Latin *russus*, "russet," "red," describing the color of the soil here

Roussillon (1) *Region, southern France*. The former province had the Latin name *Ruscino*, that of the region's former capital before Perpignan, perhaps from Semitic *rosh*, "head," "cape."

Roussillon (2). *Town, Isère*. The name derives from the Roman personal name *Russilius* or *Roscilius*, from *Russus* or *Roscus*, and the suffix *-onem*. An alternate origin has been proposed in Old French *rossel*, a variant of *roseau*, "reed."

Roussillon (3). *Village, Vaucluse*. The name has the same origin as that of **Roussillon** (2).

Route des Alpes. *Highway, eastern France*. The "highway of the Alps," in the French Alps, links Lake Geneva at Thonon-les-Bains with the Mediterranean at Menton.

Route des Crêtes. *Highway, northeastern France*. The "highway of the crests" is a north-south road along the crest of the Vosges Mountains, between Alsace and Lorraine, extending from the Col du Bonhomme pass in the north to Thann in the south.

Route Napoléon. *Highway, southeastern France*. The "Napoleon highway" is a road segment in the French Alps that was followed by Napoleon in 1815 on his return from his first exile to the island of Elba. After landing at Golfe-Juan on the Riviera, he and his men marched north past Grasse to Digne-les-Bains, Sisteron, Gap, and finally to Grenoble, where he was hailed as the returning emperor. The route is identified by commemorative markers.

Rouvroy. *Town, Pas-de-Calais*. The suburb of Lens derives its name from Latin *robur, roboris*, "oak," and the collective suffix *-etum*.

Royan. *Town, Charente-Maritime*. The name derives from the Roman personal name *Roius* and the Latin suffix *-anum*.

Royat. *Resort town, Puy-de-Dôme*. The name was recorded in the 12th century as *Rubiacum*, from the Gallo-Roman personal name *Rubius* and the associative suffix *-acum*.

Roye. *Town, Somme*. The name was recorded early as *Rauga*, from the Gaulish personal name *Rodios*.

Rozay-en-Brie. *Village, Seine-et-Marne*. The name was recorded in the 11th century as *Rosetum*, from Germanic *raus*, "reed," and the collective suffix *-etum*. The addition locates the village in **Brie**.

Rue. *Village, Somme*. The name derives from Latin *ruga*, "road," "street."

Rueil-Malmaison. *Town, Hauts-de-Seine*. The name of the Paris suburb was recorded in the 6th century as *Rotoialinsem villam*, from Gaulish *roto-*, "wheel," "race," and *ialon*, "field." denoting a site of chariot racing. The second part of the name, on record from the 13th century, means "bad house," denoting a house built on unsuitable ground, such as marshland or soft soil.

Ruelle-sur-Touvre. *Town, Charente*. The name derives from Gaulish *roto-*, "wheel," perhaps denoting a ford, and the suffix *-ela*, the ford itself being over the *Touvre* River.

Ruffec. *Town, Charente*. The name derives from the Roman personal name *Ruffius* and the associative suffix *-acum*.

Rumilly. *Town, Haute-Savoie*. The name derives from the Roman personal name *Romilius* and the associative suffix *-acum*.

Ruynes-en-Margeride. *Village, Cantal*. The name derives from Latin *ruina*, "ruin." The village lies in the *Margeride* Mountains.

Saales. *Village, Bas-Rhin.* The name probably derives from Germanic *seli*, "hall," "castle."

Saar. *River, northeastern France.* The river, known in French as *Sarre*, rises in northeastern France but then flows north into Germany as a tributary of the Moselle. Its Medieval Latin name was *Sara*, from Indoeuropean *ser*, "to flow."

Les Sables-d'Olonne. *Town and port, Vendée.* The first word derives from Latin *sabulum*, "sand," referring to the sandy beach here. The rest of the name refers to the nearby town of *Olonne-sur-Mer*, its own name perhaps from a Celtic original *Olona*, from an Indoeuropean root *olb*, "height," meaning land raised above water level. Olonne is not actually "on sea."

Les Sables-d'Or-les-Pins. *Resort village, Côtes-d'Armor.* The main name of the seaside resort translates as "the golden sands." The addition refers to the pines (*les pins*) that extend to the beach here.

Sablé-sur-Sarthe. *Town, Sarthe.* The name of the town was recorded in the 9th century as *Sabolium*, from Latin *sabulum*, "sand," and Gaulish *ialon*, "clearing." The second part of the name refers to the **Sarthe** River here.

Saclay. *Village, Essonne.* The Paris suburb has a name of uncertain origin. The second element may represent Gaulish *clita*, "pillar."

Sahune. *Village, Drôme.* The name was recorded in the 13th century as *Anseduna*, perhaps from the Roman personal name *Ansius* and Gaulish *dunon*, "fort," although the final *-a* is a problem. The initial *An-* of this was taken as French *en*, "in," and was dropped.

Saincaize-Meauce. *Village, Nièvre.* The first part of the name derives from *Sinquatis*, the name of a Gaulish god. The second part names nearby *Meauce*.

Sains-du-Nord. *Village, Nord.* The name derives from Latin *sanctus*, "holy," denoting a sacred place or a shrine with holy relics. The addition locates the village in **Nord**.

Sains-en-Gohelle. *Town, Pas-de-Calais.* The town has a name of the same origin as **Sains-du-Nord**, but with an addition locating it in the region of *Gohelle*.

St-, Ste-, etc. Names beginning thus have the first element spelled out as *Saint-*, *Sainte-*, etc.

Saint-Acheul. *Village, Somme.* The name of the suburb of Amiens honors *St. Aciolus*, martyred at Amiens in 290.

Saint-Adjutory. *Village, Charente.* The name honors *Adjutorius*, the original name of St. Maxentius (who gave the name of **Saint-Maixent-l'École**).

Saint-Affrique. *Town, Aveyron.* The name was recorded in the 13th century in the Occitan form *Sang Affrican*, after *St. Africanus*, 6th-century bishop of Comminges.

Saint-Agnan. *Village, Charente-Maritime.* The name honors *St. Anianus*, 5th-century bishop of Orléans.

Saint-Agrève. *Village, Ardèche.* The name honors Spanish-born *St. Agrippanus*, 7th-century bishop in Languedoc.

Saint-Aignan. *Village, Loir-et-Cher.* The name is identical in origin to that of **Saint-Agnan**.

Saint-Alban. *Town, Haute-Garonne.* The name honors *St. Alban*, 3d-century English martyr.

Saint-Alban-Leysse. *Town, Savoie.* The first part of the name is as for **Saint-Alban**. The second part names nearby *Leysse*.

Saint-Alban-sur-Limagnole. *Village, Lozère.* The name is as for **Saint-Alban**, with a distinguishing addition locating the village on the *Limagnole* River.

Saint-Amadou. *Village, Ariège.* The name honors *St. Amator*, 5th-century bishop of Auxerre.

Saint-Amancet. *Village, Tarn.* The name is a diminutive form of *Saint-Amans*, meaning that the village, although dedicated to the same saint, is smaller by comparison to **Saint-Amans-Soult**, 20 miles to the east.

Saint-Amand-les-Eaux. *Town, Nord.* The name honors *St. Amand*. The addition ("the waters") refers to a nearby thermal establishment.

Saint-Amand-Montrond. *Town, Cher.* The name is as for **Saint-Amand-les Eaux**, with the addition referring to the nearby hillock *Mont-Rond*, "round mount," a favorite place of public recreation and relaxation.

Saint-Amans-Soult. *Village, Tarn.* The village was originally named *Saint-Amans-la-Bastide*, as for **Saint-Amand-les-Eaux**, but with Latin *bastita*, "fortified place." The present name honors Marshal *Soult* (1769–1851), who was born here.

Saint-Amarin. *Village, Haut-Rhin.* The name honors *St. Amarin*, 7th-century abbot.

Saint-Ambroix. *Village, Gard.* The name honors *St. Ambrose*, 4th-century archbishop of Milan.

Saint-Amé. *Village, Vosges.* The name honors *St. Amatus*, 7th-century abbot. (He converted Romaric, the founder of Remiremont, and was the first abbot at the monastery there.)

Saint-Amour. *Village, Jura.* The name honors *St. Amor*, bishop of Besançon and martyr.

Saint-André (1). *Town, Alpes-Maritimes.* The suburb of Nice has a name that honors *St. Andrew*.

Saint-André (2). *Town, Nord.* The suburb of Lille has a name that honors *St. Andrew*.

Saint-André-de-Cubzac. *Town, Gironde.* The town has a name honoring *St. Andrew*, and an addition locating it near **Cubzac-les-Ponts**.

Saint-André-de-l'Eure. *Village, Eure.* The village has a name honoring *St. Andrew*, and an addition locating it in **Eure**.

Saint-André-de-Sangonis. *Village, Hérault.* The village has a name honoring *St. Andrew*. The second part of the name is the original, recorded in the 10th century as *Sangonias*.

Saint-André-les-Vergers. *Town, Aube.* The suburb of Troyes has a name honoring *St. Andrew*, and an addition referring to its orchards (*vergers*).

Saint-Antonin-Noble-Val. *Village, Tarn-et-Garonne.* The village has a name honoring *St. Antoninus*, while the addition refers to the "noble valley," that of the Aveyron River here.

Saint-Apollinaire. *Town, Côte-d'Or.* The name honors *St. Apollinaris*, 6th-century bishop of Valence.

Saint-Arnoult-en-Yvelines. *Town, Yvelines.* The town has a name honoring *St. Arnulf*, and an addition locating it in **Yvelines**.

Saint-Astier. *Town, Dordogne.* The name honors *St. Asterius*, 5th-century bishop of Amasea.

Saint-Aubain-de-Médoc. *Town, Gironde.* The town has a name honoring *St. Alban*, 3d-century English martyr, and an addition locating it in **Médoc**.

Saint-Aubin-du-Cormier. *Village, Ille-et-Vilaine.* The village has a name honoring *St. Alban*, 3d-century English martyr, while the addition refers to nearby *Le Cormier*, its name from Old French *corme*, "sorb apple," meaning a group of service trees.

Saint-Aubin-lès-Elbeuf. *Town, Seine-Maritime.* The town has a name honoring *St. Alban*, 3d-century English martyr, and an addition locating it near (*lès*) **Elbeuf**, of which it is now actually a suburb.

Saint-Aubin-sur-Mer. *Resort village, Calvados.* The name honors *St. Alban*, 3d-century English martyr. The resort is "on sea" by the English Channel.

Saint-Avaugourd-des-Landes. *Village, Vendée.* The saint's name is an altered form, influenced by the Breton barony of *Avau-*

gour, of *Vaubourg*, as for the village of *Sainte-Vaubourg*, Ardennes, honoring *St. Walburga*, 8th-century abbess of Heidenheim. The addition names the region (now also department) of **Landes**.

Saint-Avertin. *Town, Indre-et-Loire*. The suburb of Tours has a name honoring *St. Avertinus*, a local 12th-century hermit.

Saint-Avold. *Town, Moselle*. The name honors *St. Nabor*, 4th-century Roman martyr. (The initial *N-* of his name was dropped when it was represented in speech by the *n* of *saint*.)

Saint-Barbant. *Village, Haute-Vienne*. The name was originally *Sainte-Barbe-en-Poitou*, honoring *St. Barbara*, a 3d-century virgin martyr, and locating the village in **Poitou**. The present form of the name evolved from the spoken form of this, *Saint'-Barb'-en* (omitting *Poitou*), creating a bogus *St. Barbant*.

Saint-Barthélemy-d'Anjou.   *Town, Maine-et-Loire*. The suburb of Angers has a name honoring *St. Bartholomew*, and an addition locating it in **Anjou**.

Saint-Benoît. *Town, Vienne*. The name honors *St. Benedictus*, 6th-century founder of the Benedictine order.

Saint-Benoît-sur-Loire. *Village, Loiret*. The name honors *St. Benedict*, as at **Saint-Benoît**, and his remains are preserved here. The addition locates the village on the **Loire** River.

Saint-Bernard (1). *Village, Ain*. The name honors *St. Bernard* of Menthon, founder of the hospices at the Great St. Bernard and Little St. Bernard passes (see **Petit-Saint-Bernard**).

Saint-Bernard (2). *Village, Côte-d'Or*. The settlement here was founded in 1613 by Cistercian monks, whose monastery at Clairvaux was founded by *St. Bernard* in 1115.

Saint-Berthevin. *Town, Mayenne*. The suburb of Laval has a name honoring *St. Bertwin*, 9th-century deacon and martyr.

Saint-Bertrand-de-Comminges. *Hamlet, Haute-Garonne*. The name honors *St. Bertrand*, 12th-century bishop of *Comminges*, now the name of the region here, but earlier the Gallo-Roman city of *Civitas Convenarum* or *Lugdunum Convenarum*, for the *Convenae* tribe.

Saint-Bonnet-de-Mure. *Town, Rhône*. The town has a name honoring *St. Bonitus*, 7th-century bishop of Clermont, and an addition locating it near *Mure*.

Saint-Brévin-les-Pins. *Resort town, Loire-Atlantique*. The town has a name honoring *St. Bregwin*, 8th-century archbishop of Canterbury. The addition refers to its pines.

Saint-Briac-sur-Mer. *Village, Ille-et-Vilaine*. The name honors *St. Briac*, a Breton saint of Irish origin. The village is "on sea" by the English Channel.

Saint-Brice-en-Coglès. *Village, Ille-et-Vilaine*. The village has a name honoring *St. Brice*, 5th-century bishop of Tours, successor to St. Martin. The addition locates it in the local region of *Coglès*.

Saint-Brice-sous-Forêt. *Town, Val-d'Oise*. The Paris suburb has a name honoring *St. Brice*, 5th-century bishop of Tours, and an addition locating it near (*sous*, "under") the Forest of Montmorency.

Saint-Brieuc. *City, Côtes-d'Armor*. The name of the Brittany city honors the 6th-century Breton *St. Brieuc*. During the Revolution the town was renamed *Port-Brieuc*.

Saint-Calais. *Town, Sarthe*. The name honors *St. Carilefus*, a 6th-century hermit.

Saint-Cannat. *Village, Bouches-du-Rhône*. The name honors *St. Cannatus*, 6th-century bishop of Marseille.

Saint-Cast-le-Guildo. *Resort town, Côtes-d'Armor*. The resort has a name honoring the Breton *St. Cast*. The addition names nearby *Le Guildo*.

Saint-Céré. *Village, Lot*. The name honors *St. Serenus*, a 3d-century martyr.

Saint-Chamas. *Town, Bouches-du-Rhône.* The name honors *St. Amantius*, a 6th-century hermit in the diocese of Angoulême, or the first bishop of Rodez. (The local pronunciation of Latin *sanctus* as *sanch* caused the name to be misdivided, so that *Sanctus Amantius* became *Sanch Amas*, then *San Chamas*.)

Saint-Chamond. *Town, Loire.* The name honors *St. Aunemund*, 7th-century bishop of Lyon. (Latin *Sanctus Annemundus* became *Sanch Amond*, then *San Chamond*.)

Saint-Chaptes. *Village, Gard.* The name was recorded in the 12th century as *villa Sancta Agatha*, showing that the saint honored is actually the 3d-century virgin martyr *St. Agatha*. (The name has been misdivided, as with **Saint-Chamas**.)

Saint-Chély-d'Apcher. *Town, Lozère.* The name honors *St. Hilarus*, 6th-century bishop of Gévaudan. (Latin *Sanctus Hilarus*, with the saint's name stressed on the first syllable, became *Sanch Eler*, then *San Chély*.) The addition names nearby *Apcher*, from the Roman personal name *Appius* and the suffix *-arium*.

Saint-Chéron. *Town, Essonne.* The name honors *St. Caraunus*, a 5th-century martyr.

Saint-Chinian. *Village, Hérault.* The name honors *St. Anianus*, 5th-century bishop of Orléans. (As with **Saint-Chamas**, the name has been misdivided.)

Saint-Christol. *Village, Vaucluse.* The name honors *St. Christopher*, 3d-century martyr.

Saint-Christol-lès-Alès. *Town, Gard.* The town has a name honoring *St. Christopher*, and an addition locating it near (*lès*) **Alès**.

Saint-Ciers-sur-Gironde. *Village, Gironde.* The village has a name honoring *St. Cyricus*, a 4th-century martyr, and an addition locating it on the **Gironde** River.

Saint-Cirq-Lapopie. *Village, Lot.* The village has a name honoring *St. Cyricus*, as at **Saint-Ciers-sur-Gironde**, and an addi-tion naming a local lord who built a castle here.

Saint-Clair-de-la-Tour. *Village, Isère.* The village has a name honoring *St. Clarus*, 3d-century bishop of Nantes, and an addition naming *La Tour-du-Pin* (see **Tour-du-Pin, La**), of which it is now a suburb.

Saint-Clair-sur-Epte. *Village, Val-d'Oise.* The village has a name honoring *St. Clarus*, 3d-century bishop of Nantes, and an addition locating it on the *Epte* River.

Saint-Claude. *Town, Jura.* The name honors *St. Claudius*, 7th-century bishop of Besançon. The Gaulish name of the town was *Condate*, "confluence."

Saint-Clément-de-Rivière. *Town, Hérault.* The town has a name honoring *St. Clement*, and an addition locating it on the small river here.

Saint-Cloud. *Town, Hauts-de-Seine.* The name honors *St. Clodoald*, 6th-century grandson of Clovis I, king of the Franks, who founded a monastery here.

Saint-Cyprien. *Town, Pyrénées-Orientales.* The name honors *St. Cyprian*, 3d-century bishop of Carthage and martyr.

Saint-Cyr-au-Mont-d'Or. *Town, Rhône.* The suburb of Lyon has a name honoring the 4th-century martyr *St. Cyricus*, and an addition locating it near the "Golden Hill" mentioned.

Saint-Cyr-l'École. *Town, Yvelines.* The name honors the 4th-century martyr *St. Cyricus*. A school (*école*) for the daughters of impoverished noblemen was founded here in 1685 and the building later housed the famous military academy founded by Napoleon in 1808.

Saint-Cyr-les-Vignes. *Village, Loire.* A document of 1218 refers to the location as a *vinea sita ad Sanctum Cereum*, "vineyard situated by [the church of] St. Cyricus," and this gave the present name.

Saint-Cyr-sur-Loire. *Town, Indre-et-Loire.* The suburb of Tours, on the **Loire**

River, has a name honoring *St. Cyricus*, 4th-century martyr.

Saint-Cyr-sur-Mer. *Town, Var*. The town has a name honoring *St. Cyricus*, 4th-century martyr, and the addition locates it on (actually near) the Mediterranean Sea.

Saint-Dalmas-de-Tende. *Resort village, Alpes-Maritimes*. The resort has a name honoring the 4th-century *St. Dalmatius*, and an addition locating it near **Tende**. The village was part of Italy until 1947, when it was known as *San Dalmazzo di Tenda*.

Saint-Dalmas-le-Selvage. *Village, Alpes-Maritimes*. The village has a name honoring the 4th-century *St. Dalmatius*, while the addition represents Latin *selvaticus*, "wooded."

Saint-Denis. *City, Seine-Saint-Denis*. The name of the Paris suburb was recorded in the 8th century as *Sanctus Dionysius*, in honor of *St. Denis*, bishop of Paris, who was beheaded at **Montmartre** in 258 together with two companions, Rusticus and Eleutherius, a priest and a deacon. They were buried here and over their tomb was built the abbey of Saint Denis, later the burial place of French kings.

Saint-Denis-en-Val. *Town, Loiret*. The suburb of Orléans has a name honoring *St. Denis*, as at **Saint-Denis**, and an addition locating it in the valley (*en val*) of the Loire River.

Saint-Didier-au-Mont-d'Or. *Town, Rhône*. The suburb of Lyon has a name honoring *St. Desiderius*, as for **Saint-Dizier**. The addition locates it near the same "Golden Hill" as **Saint-Cyr-au-Mont-d'Or**.

Saint-Didier-en-Velay. *Village, Haute-Loire*. The village has a name honoring *St. Desiderius*, as at **Saint-Dizier**, and an addition locating it in **Velay**.

Saint-Dié. *Town, Vosges*. The name honors *St. Deodatus*, 7th-century bishop of Nevers, and later a hermit in the Vosges mountains.

Saint-Dizier. *Town, Haute-Marne*. The name honors *St. Desiderius*, 3d-century bishop of Langres (or 6th-century bishop of Vienne).

Saint-Donat-sur-l'Herbasse. *Village, Drôme*. The village has a name honoring *St. Donatus*, 6th-century hermit of Sisteron (or 7th-century bishop of Besançon), and an addition locating it on the *Herbasse* River.

Saint-Dos. *Village, Pyrénées-Atlantiques*. The name was recorded in the 12th century as *Sendos*, from the Roman personal name *Sintus* and the Aquitanian suffix *-ossum*. There is thus no actual saint behind the name.

Saint-Doulchard. *Town, Cher*. The suburb of Bourges has a name honoring *St. Dulcardus*, a 6th-century hermit.

Sainte-Adresse. *Town, Seine-Maritime*. The suburb of Le Havre has a name apparently honoring *St. Andrew*.

Sainte-Alvère. *Village, Dordogne*. The name honors *St. Alvera*, a local saint martyred in the 3d century.

Sainte-Anne-d'Auray. *Village, Morbihan*. The village has a name honoring *St. Anne*, mother of the Virgin Mary, and an addition locating it near **Auray**.

Sainte-Catherine-de-Fierbois. *Village, Indre-et-Loire*. The village has a name honoring *St. Catherine*, 2d-century virgin and martyr of Alexandria. The addition is a local placename.

Sainte-Croix-de-Verdon. *Village, Alpes-de-Haute-Provence*. The village has a name honoring *St. Cross*, a devotional term for the Holy Cross on which Christ was crucified. The addition locates the village on the **Verdon** River (now dammed to form a reservoir).

Sainte-Croix-du-Mont. *Village, Gironde*. The village has a name honoring *St. Cross*, as for **Sainte-Croix-de-Verdon**, and an addition locating it on a hill (*mont*).

Sainte-Eulalie. *Village, Gironde*. The name honors 12-year-old *St. Eulalia* of Merida, martyred at Barcelona in 304.

Sainte-Eusoye. *Village, Oise.* The name honors the 4th-century pope *St. Eusebius.* The spoken form of his name has caused him to change gender in the placename.

Sainte-Florine. *Village, Haute-Loire.* The name honors *St. Florina,* martyred in Auvergne.

Sainte-Foy-la-Grande. *Village, Gironde.* The name honors the 3d-century virgin *St. Faith,* martyred at Agen. The village is "great" (*grande*) by comparison with others of the name.

Sainte-Foy-lès-Lyon. *Town, Rhône.* The town has a name honoring the 3d-century virgin *St. Faith.* The addition locates it near (*lès*) **Lyon,** of which it it is now actually a suburb.

Sainte-Geneviève-des-Bois. *Town, Essonne.* The town has a name honoring *St. Genevieve,* 5th-century patron of Paris, and an addition locating it near woods (*bois*).

Saint-Egrève. *Town, Isère.* The suburb of Grenoble has a name honoring Spanish-born *St. Agrippanus,* 7th-century bishop in Languedoc.

Sainte-Hermine. *Village, Vendée.* The name honors *St. Irmina,* 8th-century abbess, daughter of Dagobert II, king of Austrasia.

Sainte-Livrade-sur-Lot. *Town, Lot-et-Garonne.* The town has a name honoring *St. Liberata,* 4th-century virgin and martyr, and an addition locating it on the **Lot** River.

Saint-Éloi. *Village, Ain.* This name usually honors St. Eligius, but early records show that the saint commemorated here is in fact *St. Eulalia* (see **Sainte-Eulalie**). In the Latin form of her name, *Sancta Eulalia,* the final -*a* of *Sancta* has been lost before the initial *E-* of *Eulalia.*

Saint-Éloy-les-Mines. *Town, Puy-de-Dome.* The town has a name honoring *St. Eligius,* 7th-century bishop of Noyon. The addition refers to the former coal mines here.

Sainte-Luce-sur-Loire. *Town, Loire-Atlantique.* The suburb of Nantes has a name honoring *St. Lucy,* 3d-century virgin and martyr of Syracuse, and an addition locating it on the **Loire.**

Sainte-Marie. *Village, Cantal.* Most places of this name honor the Virgin Mary. This one, however, was recorded in the 14th century as *ecclesia Sancti Mari,* showing a dedication to *St. Marius,* abbot of the monastery of Bevons, near Sisteron, in the 6th century. The name subsequently became associated with St. Mary, and was recorded as *Saincte Marye* in 1613.

Sainte-Marie-aux-Mines. *Town, Haut-Rhin.* The name honors *St. Mary,* with the addition referring to the former silver and lead mines here. The town is not far from the border with Germany, where it is known as *Markirch* ("St. Mary's church").

Sainte-Maure-de-Touraine. *Town, Indre-et-Loire.* The original name of the town, recorded in the 6th century, was *Arciacum,* from the Gaulish personal name *Artius* and the associative suffix -*acum.* The present name honors *St. Maura,* 6th-century saint of **Touraine.**

Sainte-Maxime. *Town, Var.* The name honors *St. Maxima,* a local saint of obscure origin.

Sainte-Menehould. *Town, Marne.* The name honors *St. Manehildis,* 5th-century virgin of Le Perthois.

Sainte-Mère-Église. *Village, Manche.* The first part of the name, apparently meaning "holy mother," is said to be a variant of *Sainte-Marie,* for *St. Mary,* but according to one account is really a corruption of the Germanic personal name *Sintmer.* The second part is "church."

Saint-Émilion. *Town, Gironde.* The name honors *St. Aemilianus,* 8th-century bishop of Nantes.

Sainte-Odile. *Abbey, Bas-Rhin.* The abbey takes its from the Alsatian nun and patron saint of Alsace, *St. Odile* (*c.*660-

c.720), who founded it on the hill now known as *Mont Sainte-Odile*.

Saintes. *Town, Charente-Maritime.* The name was recorded in the 4th century as *Mediolanum Santonum*, from *Mediolanum* (as for **Meulan**) and the Gaulish tribe *Santones*.

Sainte-Savine. *Town, Aube.* The suburb of Troyes has a name honoring the 3d-century martyr *St. Sabina*.

Sainte-Scolasse-sur-Sarthe. *Village, Orne.* The name honors *St. Scholastica* (*c.*480–*c.*543), sister of St. Benedict and herself the first Benedictine nun. The addition locates the village on the **Sarthe** River.

Sainte-Sigolène. *Town, Haute-Loire.* The name honors *St. Sigolena*, 8th-century abbess in Albigeois.

Saintes-Maries-de-la-Mer. *Resort village, Bouches-du-Rhône.* The name has been successively recorded as *ecclesia Sanctae Mariae de Ratis* (5th century), *ecclesia Sanctae Mariae de Mare* (12th century), *Nostre Dame de la Mer* (15th century), and *la ville des Trois Maries* (17th century). The present form of the name means "Holy Marys of the Sea," referring to the dedication of the church here to the three Marys of the Gospel: *Mary Magdalene*, *Mary* the wife of Cleophas, the Virgin Mary's sister, known in French as *Marie-Jacobé*, and *Mary* the mother of James and John, known as *Marie-Salomé*. According to a confused mixture of legend and history, these three Marys, together with their black servant, Sara, and certain other saints, among them St. Martha, St. Lazarus, and St. Maximinus (see **Saint-Maximin-la-Sainte-Baume**), left Palestine in a boat without sail or oars and landed here on the Mediterranean coast at a point to the west of the town known as *Le Grand Radeau*, "the great raft," from Latin *Ratis*. They then began to evangelize southern Gaul.

Saint-Estèphe. *Village, Gironde.* The name honors *St. Stephen*, the first martyr (or some other saint of the name, as for the identical dedications below).

Saint-Estève. *Town, Pyrénées-Orientales.* The suburb of Perpignan has a name honoring *St. Stephen*, the first martyr.

Saint-Étienne. *City, Loire.* The name honors *St. Stephen*, the first martyr.

Saint-Étienne-de-Montluc. *Town, Loire-Atlantique.* The town has a name honoring *St. Stephen*, the first martyr, and an addition locating it near *Montluc*.

Saint-Étienne-de-Saint-Geoirs. *Village, Isère.* The village has a name honoring *St. Stephen*, the first martyr, and an addition locating it near *Saint-Geoirs*, so named for *St. George*.

Saint-Étienne-de-Tinée. *Resort village, Alpes-Maritimes.* The village has a name honoring *St. Stephen*, the first martyr, and an addition locating it on the *Tinée* River here.

Saint-Étienne-du-Rouvray. *Town, Seine-Maritime.* The suburb of Rouen has a name honoring *St. Stephen*, the first martyr. The addition locates it by the Forest of *Rouvray*, itself named from Latin *robur, roboris*, "oak."

Sainte-Tulle. *Village, Alpes-de-Haute-Provence.* The name honors *St. Tullia*, sister of St. Consortia, probably the daughter of Eucherius, 6th-century bishop in Provence.

Sainte-Verge. *Village, Deux-Sèvres.* The name honors *St. Virgana*, a shepherdess from the Thouars region.

Sainte-Vertu. *Village, Yonne.* The name means "holy virtue," regarding this abstract quality as an object of religious devotion.

Sainte-Victoire, Mont. *Mountain ridge, southern France.* The ridge is said to take its name from the priory of *Notre-Dame-de-Sainte-Victoire*, "Our Lady of Holy Victory," on its summit, and itself perhaps so called from the site near Pourrières where the Roman general Marius won a victory over the invading Germanic tribes in the 2d century BC.

Saint-Fargeau-Ponthierry. *Town, Seine-et-Marne.* The first part of the name honors *St. Ferreolus,* 6th-century bishop of Limoges (or 3d-century martyr at Besançon, or 4th-century martyr at Vienne). The second part names nearby *Ponthierry.*

Saint-Florentin. *Town, Yonne.* The name honors *St. Florentinus,* 6th-century abbot of Arles (or 5th-century hermit near Autun).

Saint-Florent-le-Vieil. *Village, Maine-et-Loire.* The name honors *St. Florentius,* who founded an abbey here in the 4th century. Hence "old" (*vieil*) by contrast with newer places.

Saint-Florent-sur-Cher. *Town, Cher.* The name honors *St. Florentius,* and an addition locating the town on the **Cher** River.

Saint-Flour. *Town, Cantal.* The name honors *St. Florus,* 5th-century apostle of the Auvergne.

Saint-Fulgent. *Village, Vendre.* The name honors *St. Fulgentius,* 6th-century African bishop.

Saint-Galmier. *Town, Loire.* The name honors *St. Waldomar,* here confused with the 7th-century monk *St. Baldomar.*

Saint-Gaudens. *Town, Haute-Garonne.* The name honors *St. Gaudentius,* martyred in 475 near Toulouse.

Saint-Gaultier. *Village, Indre.* The name honors *St. Walter,* 11th-century abbot of L'Esterp, near Confolens, Charente.

Saint-Genest-Lerpt. *Town, Loire.* The town has a name honoring *St. Genesius.* The addition represents a local form of *l'ermite,* "the hermit."

Saint-Geniez-d'Olt. *Village, Aveyron.* The village has a name honoring *St. Genesius,* and an addition locating it on the **Lot** River.

Saint-Genis-Laval. *Town, Rhône.* The suburb of Lyon has a name honoring *St. Genesius,* and an addition meaning "in the valley" (of a tributary of the nearby Rhône River).

Saint-Georges-de-Didonne. *Resort town, Charente-Maritime.* The town has a name honoring *St. George,* and an addition locating it near *Didonne.*

Saint-Georges-de-Reneins. *Village, Rhône.* The village has a name honoring *St. George,* and an addition locating it near *Reneins.*

Saint-Georges-des-Groseillers. *Village, Orne.* The village has a name honoring *St. George,* and an addition referring to its currant bushes (*groseilliers*).

Saint-Georges-sur-Loire. *Village, Maine-et-Loire.* The village, near the **Loire** River, has a name honoring *St. George.*

Saint-Germain-des-Fossés. *Village, Allier.* The village has a name honoring *St. Germanus,* 5th-century bishop of Auxerre, and an addition referring to its ditches (*fossés*).

Saint-Germain-du-Puy. *Town, Cher.* The town has a name honoring *St. Germanus,* 5th-century bishop of Auxerre, and an addition from Latin *podium,* "height."

Saint-Germain-en-Laye. *City, Yvelines.* The Paris suburb has a name honoring *St. Germanus,* 5th-century bishop of Auxerre, and an addition locating it in *Laya,* the old name of the Forest of Saint-Germain, *Forêt de Laye,* from *l'aye,* "the hedge," in the sense "forest."

Saint-Germain-lès-Arpajon. *Town, Essonne.* The town has a name honoring *St. Germanus,* 5th-century bishop of Auxerre, and an addition locating it near (*lès*) **Arpajon.**

Saint-Germain-lès-Corbeil. *Town, Essonne.* The town has a name honoring *St. Germanus,* 5th-century bishop of Auxerre, and an addition locating it near (*lès*) **Corbeil-Essonnes.**

Saint-Gervais-les-Bains. *Resort town, Haute-Savoie.* The name honors *St. Gervase* of Milan, 1st-century martyr with his twin brother Protase. The addition ("the baths") refers to the thermal baths here.

Saint-Gildas-des-Bois. *Village, Loire-Atlantique*. The village has a name honoring *St. Gildas*, a 6th-century Scottish saint, and an addition locating it near woods (*bois*).

Saint-Gilles. *Town, Gard*. The name honors the 7th-century hermit *St. Giles*, who founded a monastery here and who is buried here. (A 9th-century Latin document mentions the *monasterium Sancti Petri, in quo quiescit corpus Beati Ægidii*, "monastery of St. Peter, in which reposes the body of St. Ægidius").

Saint-Gilles-Croix-de-Vie. *Resort town, Vendée*. The name combines those of two towns, either side of the *Vie* River estuary: *Saint-Gilles-de-Vie*, with a name honoring *St. Giles*, as at **Saint-Gilles**, and *Croix-de-Vie*, with a name from Latin *crux*, "cross," as at **Croix**.

Saint-Gingolph. *Resort village, Haute-Savoie*. The name honors *St. Gangulf*, an 8th-century Burgundy saint.

Saint-Girons. *Town, Ariège*. The name honors *St. Gerontius*, 5th-century bishop of Milan.

Saint-Gobain. *Village, Aisne*. The name honors *St. Gobbanus*, a 7th-century Irish saint.

Saint-Gourson. *Village, Charente*. The name was recorded early as *Sergonson*, from the Celtic personal name *Serguntius* and the suffix *-onem*. The *Ser-* of this was taken as *Saint-*, creating a bogus St. Gourson.

Saint-Gratien. *Town, Val-d'Oise*. The Paris suburb has a name honoring the 3d-century martyr *St. Gratian*.

Saint-Gregoire. *Town, Ille-et-Vilaine*. The name honors *St. Gregory*.

Saint-Guilhem-le-Désert. *Village, Hérault*. The village has a name honoring *St. William* the Great (*c.*755–812), count of Toulouse and duke of Aquitaine, grandson of the Frankish ruler Charles Martel, who conquered the Saracens in Languedoc and in 804 founded a monastery here at a site

then called Gellone, where he became a Benedictine monk and where he died. (He later became the hero of a cycle of medieval *chansons de geste*.) The addition refers to the hillsides round about the village, which are bare except for scrub bushes.

Saint-Héand. *Village, Loire*. The name honors *St. Eugendus*, 6th-century abbot of Condate (now Saint-Claude, Jura).

Saint-Herblain. *Town, Loire-Atlantique*. The suburb of Nantes has a name honoring *St. Hermelandus*, 8th-century abbot on the island of Indre in the Loire River, near Nantes.

Saint-Hilaire. *Village, Isère*. The name honors *St. Hilary*, 4th-century bishop of Poitiers (or 5th-century bishop of Arles).

Saint-Hilaire-de-Riez. *Town, Vendée*. The town has a name honoring *St. Hilary*, as at **Saint-Hilaire**, and an addition locating it near *Riez*.

Saint-Hilaire-Saint-Florent. *Town, Maine-et-Loire* The suburb of Saumur has a name honoring both *St. Hilary*, as at **Saint-Hilaire**, and *St. Florentius*, as at **Saint-Florent-le-Vieil**.

Saint-Hippolyte. *Village, Haut-Rhin*. The name honors the 3d-century martyr *St. Hippolytus*.

Saint-Hippolyte-du-Fort. *Village, Gard*. The name was recorded in the 13th century as *prioria Sancti Ypoliti de Rupe Furcata*, "priory of St. Hippolytus of the Forked Rock," honoring *St. Hippolytus*, as at **Saint-Hippolyte**. The fort (*fort*) of the name was built in 1687. The village lies at the foot of the Cévennes mountains.

Saint-Honoré-les-Bains. *Resort village, Nièvre*. The name honors *St. Honoratus*, 5th-century bishop of Arles (or 6th-century bishop of Amiens). The second part of the name ("the baths") refers to the hot springs here.

Saint-Igny-de-Vers. *Village, Rhône*. The name of the village, near *Vers*, was recorded in the 11th century as *Semtiniacus*, from the

Gallo-Roman personal name *Sentinius* and the associative suffix *-acum*. This name was later taken to be that of a (nonexistent) *St. Igny*.

Saint-Inglevert. *Village, Pas-de-Calais.* The name was recorded in the 13th century as *Santingheveld*, from the Germanic personal name *Sando* and the suffix *-ing* followed by *feld*, "field." The *Sant-* was subsequently taken as *Saint-*, giving a fictional St. Inglevert.

Saint-Ismier. *Town, Isère.* The name honors *St. Hymerius*, apostle of the Swiss Jura.

Saint-Jacques-de-la-Lande. *Town, Ille-et-Vilaine.* The suburb of Rennes has a name honoring *St. James*, and an addition referring to the former moorland (*lande*) here.

Saint-James. *Village, Manche.* The name honors *St. James*.

Saint-Jean-Bonnefonds. *Town, Loire.* The town has a name honoring *St. John*, and an addition from Latin *bona fons*, "good spring."

Saint-Jean-Cap-Ferrat. *Village, Alpes-Maritimes.* The village, known as *Saint-Jean-sur-Mer* until 1904, has a name honoring *St. John*, and an addition locating it on *Cap Ferrat*.

Saint-Jean-d'Angély. *Town, Charente-Maritime.* The name of the town was recorded in the 11th century as Latin *Angeliacense Monasterium*, from the personal name *Angelus* or *Angel* and the associative suffix *-acum*. According to legend, the original name was replaced by *Saint Jouan* in 817 when the duke of Aquitaine received from a monk in Alexandria the supposed head of *St. John* the Baptist, and the Benedictine abbey here was built to house it.

Saint-Jean-de-Losne. *Village, Côte-d'Or.* The village has a name honoring *St. John*, and an addition locating it near *Losne*, where there was a shrine to the Roman goddess *Latona*.

Saint-Jean-de-Luz. *Resort town and port, Pyrénées-Atlantiques.* The name was recorded in the 12th century as *Sanctus Johannes de Luis*, perhaps from the personal name *Lucius*, or according to some from the god *Lug* who gave the name of **Lyon**. The Basque name of the town is *Donibane-Lohizon*, from *done*, "saint," *Iban*, "John," and *lohizun*, "muddy." This suggests that *Luz* may in fact come from Gaulish *luto-*, "marsh," rather than a personal name.

Saint-Jean-de-Maurienne. *Town, Savoie.* The name of the town was recorded in the 8th century as *Sanctus Johannes Baptiste Maurigenna*, honoring *St. John the Baptist*. *Maurienne* may represent the personal name *Maurus* with the Celtic suffix *-genna*, "son," "daughter." A less likely theory takes the name from *mau rieu*, representing Latin *malus rivus*, "bad stream," referring to the capricious current of the Arc River here.

Saint-Jean-de-Monts. *Town, Vendée.* The town has a name honoring *St. John*, and an addition locating it in the *Pays de Monts*, "land of hills."

Saint-Jean-du-Gard. *Village, Gard.* The village has a name honoring *St. John*, and an addition locating it on the *Gardon d'Anduze* River here (see **Gard**).

Saint-Jean-en-Royans. *Village, Drôme.* The village has a name honoring *St. John*, and an addition locating it in the region of *Royans*.

Saint-Jean-Pied-de-Port. *Village, Pyrénées-Atlantiques.* The name was recorded in the 14th century as *Sanctus Johannes sub pede Portus*, "St. John at the foot of the pass" (Latin *portus*, "pass"), referring to the nearby Roncesvalles pass over the Pyrenees to Spain.

Saint-Jeoire. *Village, Haute-Savoie.* The name honors *St. George*.

Saint-Joachim. *Town, Loire-Atlantique.* The name honors *St. Joachim*, father of the Virgin Mary.

Saint-Jorioz. *Resort town, Haute-Savoie.* The name honors *St. George*.

Saint-Juéry. *Town, Tarn.* The name honors *St. George.*

Saint-Julien-Beychevelle. *Village, Gironde.* The village has a name honoring *St. Julian*, and an addition locating it near the château of *Beychevelle.*

Saint-Julien-de Concelles. *Town, Loire-Atlantique.* The suburb of Nantes has a name honoring *St. Julian*, and an addition locating it on the *Concelles* River near the Loire.

Saint-Julien-du-Sault. *Village, Yonne.* The village has a name honoring *St. Julian*, and an addition from Latin *salix*, "willow."

Saint-Julien-en-Genevois. *Town, Haute-Savoie.* The town has a name honoring *St. Julian*, and an addition locating it in the region around *Geneva*, Switzerland, of which it is now a suburb.

Saint-Junien. *Town, Vienne.* The name honors *St. Junianus*, a 5th-century Limousin hermit.

Saint-Juste-Malmont. *Village, Haute-Loire.* The village has a name honoring *St. Justus*, 4th-century bishop of Lyon, and an addition locating it near *Malmont.*

Saint-Just-en-Chaussée. *Town, Oise.* The town has a name honoring *St. Justus*, 4th-century bishop of Lyon, and an addition locating it on an old Roman road (*chaussée*).

Saint-Just-Saint-Rambert. *Twin towns, Loire.* The name respectively honors *St. Justus*, 4th-century bishop of Lyon, and *St. Rambert* (Raginberht), 7th-century martyr in Jura.

Saint-Lary-Soulant. *Resort village, Hautes-Pyrénées.* The village has a name honoring *St. Hilary*, as at **Saint-Hilaire**, and an addition locating it near *Soulan*, its own name either from the Roman personal name *Solus* and the suffix *-anum* or from Latin *solana*, "sunny slope."

Saint-Laurent-Blangy. *Town, Pas-de-Calais.* The suburb of Arras has a name honoring the 3d-century martyr *St. Laurence*, and an addition locating it near *Blangy*, from the Roman personal name *Blandius* and the associative suffix *-acum.*

Saint-Laurent-de-la-Salanque. *Town, Pyrénées-Orientales.* The town has a name honoring the 3d-century martyr *St. Laurence*, and an addition locating it in the region of *Salanque.*

Saint-Laurent-des-Arbres. *Village, Gard.* The village has a name honoring the 3d-century martyr *St. Laurence*, and an addition referring to the trees (*arbres*) here. The locality is still well wooded.

Saint-Laurent-du-Pont. *Town, Isère.* The town has a name honoring the 3d-century martyr *St. Laurence*, and an addition locating it by a bridge (*pont*).

Saint-Laurent-du-Var. *Town, Alpes-Maritimes.* The town has a name honoring the 3d-century martyr *St. Laurence*, and an addition locating it near the (mouth of the) **Var** River.

Saint-Laurent-le-Minier. *Village, Gard.* The village has a name honoring the 3d-century martyr *St. Laurence*, and an addition referring to the gold and silver mines here.

Saint-Laurent-Médoc. *Village, Gironde.* The village has a name honoring the 3d-century martyr *St. Laurence*, and an addition locating it in the region of **Médoc.**

Saint-Laurent-Nouan. *Village, Loir-et-Cher.* The village has a name honoring the 3d-century martyr *St. Laurence*, and an addition locating it near *Nouan-sur-Loire*, probably from Gaulish *nouio-*, "new," and the suffix *-entum.*

Saint-Laurent-sur-Mer. *Village, Calvados.* The name was recorded in the 13th century as *Sanctus Laurencius super mare*, "St. Laurence on sea," honoring the 3d-century martyr *St. Laurence.* The village is near the English Channel coast.

Saint-Laurent-sur-Sèvre. *Town, Vendée.* The town has a name honoring the 3d-century martyr *St. Laurence*, and an addition locating it on the *Sèvre-Nantaise* River (see **Deux-Sèvres**).

Saint-Léger-des-Vignes. *Village, Nièvre*. The suburb of Decize has a name honoring *St. Leger*, 7th-century bishop of Saintes, and an addition referring to its vines (*vignes*).

Saint-Léger-sous-Beuvray. *Village, Saône-et-Loire*. The village has a name honoring *St. Leger*, 7th-century bishop of Saintes, and an addition locating it near *Mont Beuvray* (see **Beuvray, Mont**).

Saint-Léonard. *Town, Pas-de-Calais*. The suburb of Boulogne-sur-Mer has a name honoring *St. Leonard*.

Saint-Léonard-de-Noblat. *Town, Haute-Vienne*. The town has a name honoring *St. Leonard*. The "addition" is in fact its original name, recorded in the 9th century as *Nobiliacus*, from the Roman personal name *Nobilis* and the associative suffix *-iacum*.

Saint-Leu-d'Esserent. *Town, Oise*. The suburb of Creil has a name honoring *St. Lupus*, 5th-century bishop of Troyes (or 7th-century bishop of Sens), and an addition locating it near *Esserent*.

Saint-Leu-la-Forêt. *Town, Val-d'Oise*. The town has a name honoring *St. Lupus*, as at **Saint-Leu-d'Esserent**, and an addition locating it by the Forest of Montmorency.

Saint-Lizier. *Village, Ariège*. The suburb of Saint-Girons has a name honoring *St. Glycerius*, 7th-century bishop of Couserans. The earlier name of the former village, recorded in the 6th century as *Consorannis*, derives from the *Consoranni*, an Aquitanian tribe.

Saint-Lô. *Town, Manche*. The name honors *St. Laudus*, 6th-century bishop of Coutances. An earlier name was *Briovera*, "bridge over the (River) Vire."

Saint-Loubès. *Village, Gironde*. The name probably honors *St. Lupercius*, a 3d-century martyr at Eauze.

Saint-Louis. *Town, Haut-Rhin*. The town arose near a fortress built here in 1680 by Louis XIV, who in 1684 named it *Saint-Louis*, partly for himself, and partly for his predecessor, Louis IX (*St. Louis*). During the Revolution, the name was changed to *Bourg-Libre*, as if "Freetown."

Saint-Loup-sur-Semouse. *Town, Haute-Saône*. The town has a name honoring *St. Lupus*, as at **Saint-Leu-d'Esserent**, and an addition locating it on the *Semouse* River.

Saint-Lubin-des-Joncherets. *Town, Eure-et-Loir*. The town has a name honoring *St. Lupinus*, 6th-century bishop of Chartres. The addition refers to the reed beds (*joncheraies*) here by the Avre River.

Saint-Lunaire. *Village, Ille-et-Vilaine*. The name honors *St. Leonorius*, a 6th-century Breton bishop.

Saint-Lys. *Town, Haute-Garonne*. The name is said to refer to the fleurs-de-lys in the French royal coat of arms.

Saint-Macaire. *Village, Gironde*. The name honors *St. Macarius*, a 4th-century saint of Egypt.

Saint-Macaire-en-Mauges. *Town, Maine-et-Loire*. The town has a name honoring *St. Macarius*, as at **Saint-Macaire**, and an addition locating it in the region of *Mauges*.

Saint-Maixent-l'École. *Town, Deux-Sèvres*. The town has a name honoring *St. Maxentius*, an obscure saint of the 5th or 6th century. The addition refers to the infantry school (*école*) established here in 1874, now a training school for noncommissioned army officers.

Saint-Malo. *Resort town and port, Ille-et-Vilaine*. The name honors *St. Maclovius*, 6th-century bishop of Aleth (now Saint-Servan-sur-Mer).

Saint-Mammès. *Village, Seine-et-Marne*. The name honors *St. Mammes*, 3d-century martyr of Cappadocia.

Saint-Mandé. *Town, Val-de-Marne*. The Paris suburb has a name honoring *St. Maudetus*, a 6th-century Breton recluse.

Saint-Mandrier-sur-Mer. *Town, Var.* The town has a name honoring *St. Mandreas*, 6th-century saint of Toulouse, and an addition locating it on the Mediterranean Sea.

Saint-Marcel. *Town, Saône-et-Loire.* The suburb of Chalon-sur-Saône has a name honoring the 4th-century pope *St. Marcellus* (or the 5th-century bishop of Paris of the same name).

Saint-Marcel-lès-Valence. *Village, Drôme.* The village has a name honoring *St. Marcel*, as at **Saint-Marcel**, and an addition locating it near (*lès*) **Valence**.

Saint-Marcellin. *Town, Isère.* The name honors *St. Marcellinus*, 3d-century pope and martyr.

Saint-Mars-la-Jaille. *Village, Loire-Atlantique.* The village has a name honoring *St. Médard*, 6th-century bishop of Noyon, and an addition from the château of *La Jaille* here.

Saint-Martin-Boulogne. *Town, Pas-de-Calais.* The suburb of **Boulogne-sur-Mer** has a name honoring *St. Martin* of Tours, the 4th-century evangelizer of Gaul.

Saint-Martin-de-Belleville. *Resort village, Savoie.* The village has a name honoring *St. Martin*, as at **Saint-Martin-Boulogne**, and an addition from nearby *Belleville*, as for **Belleville**.

Saint-Martin-de-Crau. *Town, Bouches-du-Rhône.* The town has a name honoring *St. Martin*, as at **Saint-Martin-Boulogne**, and an addition locating it in the **Crau** region.

Saint-Martin-de-Londres. *Village, Hérault.* The name was recorded in the 11th century as *ecclesia Sancti Martini de Londres*, from *St. Martin*, as at **Saint-Martin-Boulogne**, and an addition apparently adopted from *London*, England (French *Londres*).

Saint-Martin-d'Entraigues. *Village, Deux-Sèvres.* The village has a name honoring *St. Martin*, as at **Saint-Martin-Boulogne**. The addition derives from Latin *inter aquas*, "between the waters," denoting a location by the Boutonne River and its streams.

Saint-Martin-de-Queyrières. *Village, Hautes-Alpes.* The name was recorded in the 12th century as *Sanctus Martinus de Caireria*, honoring *St. Martin*, as at **Saint-Martin-Boulogne**, and referring to the stone quarries (*carrières*) here.

Saint-Martin-des-Champs. *Town, Finistère.* The suburb of Morlais has a name honoring *St. Martin*, as at **Saint-Martin-Boulogne**, and an addition locating it in the fields (*champs*).

Saint-Martin-de-Seignanx. *Village, Landes.* The village has a name honoring *St. Martin*, as at **Saint-Martin-Boulogne**, and an addition locating it in the region of *Seignanx*.

Saint-Martin-de-Valgalgues. *Town, Gard.* The suburb of Alès has a name honoring *St. Martin*, as at **Saint-Martin-Boulogne**, and an addition locating it in the valley (*val*) of the *Gardon d'Alès* River (see **Gard**).

Saint-Martin-d'Uriage. *Resort village, Isère.* The village has a name honoring *St. Martin*, as at **Saint-Martin-Boulogne**, and an addition probably from Latin *aureus*, "golden," and the suffix *-aticum*, perhaps referring to the color of the soil.

Saint-Martin-la-Plaine. *Village, Loire.* The village has a name honoring *St. Martin*, as at **Saint-Martin-Boulogne**, and an addition locating it in the Jarez Plain.

Saint-Martin-le-Vinoux. *Town, Isère.* The suburb of Grenoble has a name honoring *St. Martin*, as at **Saint-Martin-Boulogne**, and an addition from Latin *vinosus*, "planted with vines."

Saint-Martin-Vésubie. *Resort village, Alpes-Maritimes.* The village has a name honoring *St. Martin*, as at **Saint-Martin-Boulogne**, and an addition locating it on the *Vésubie* River.

Saint-Maur. *Village, Indre.* The suburb of Châteauroux has a name honoring *St. Maurus*, 6th-century monk of Anjou.

Saint-Maur-des-Fossés. *Town, Val-de-Marne.* The name of the Paris suburb was recorded in the 7th century as *castello Fossatus*, referring to the entrenched fortification here (Latin *fossa*, "trench"), in a bend of the Marne River. The dedication to *St. Maur*, as at **Saint-Maur**, was then added.

Saint-Maurice. *Town, Val-de-Marne.* The Paris suburb has a name honoring *St. Maurice*, 3d-century soldier saint and commander of the Theban Legion, martyred at Agaunum (now *Saint-Maurice*, Switzerland).

Saint-Maurice-de-Beynost. *Village, Ain.* The suburb of Lyon has a name honoring *St. Maurice*, as at **Saint-Maurice**, and an addition locating it near *Beynost*, from the Gaulish personal name *Baginus* (from *bagos*, "beech") and the Ligurian suffix *-oscum*.

Saint-Max. *Town, Meurthe-et-Moselle* The suburb of Nancy has a name honoring *St. Mark*.

Saint-Maximin-la-Sainte-Baume. *Town, Var.* The town has a name honoring *St. Maximinus*, either the 5th-century companion of the four saints Mary Magdalen (supposedly buried here), Martha, Lazarus, and Mary the wife of Cleophas, who together are said to have evangelized Provence (see **Saintes-Maries-de-la-Mer**), or the 4th-century bishop of Trier. The second part of the name refers to the *Sainte-Baume* range here.

Saint-Médard-en-Jalles. *Town, Gironde.* The town has a name honoring *St. Médard*, 6th-century bishop of Noyon, and an addition locating it in the district of *Jalles*.

Saint-Méen-le-Grand. *Village, Ille-et-Vilaine.* The village has a name honoring *St. Mevennus*, a 6th-century Breton abbot, and an addition describing it as "great" by comparison with its namesake in Finistère.

Saint-Memmie. *Town, Marne.* The suburb of Châlons-en-Champagne has a name honoring *St. Memmius*, 3d-century (and first) bishop of Châlons.

Saint-Michel. *Village, Aisne.* The name honors the *St. Michael* the Archangel.

Saint-Michel-Chef-Chef. *Village, Loire-Atlantique.* The village has a name honoring *St. Michael* the Archangel, and an addition perhaps from Old French *chevecher*, "scoundrel."

Saint-Michel-de-Maurienne. *Village, Savoie.* The village has a name honoring *St. Michael* the Archangel, and an addition locating it in the *Maurienne* valley (see **Saint-Jean-de-Maurienne**).

Saint-Michel-en-l'Herm. *Resort village, Vendée.* The village has a name honoring *St. Michael* the Archangel, and an addition from Old French *erm*, "desert," denoting its location in coastal wetland.

Saint-Michel-l'Observatoire. *Village, Alpes-de-Haute-Provence.* The village, also known as *Saint-Michel-de-Provence*, has a name honoring *St. Michael* the Archangel, The addition refers to the astrophysical observatory nearby.

Saint-Michel-sur-Orge. *Town, Essonne.* The town has a name honoring the archangel *St. Michael*, and an addition locating it on the **Orge** River.

Saint-Mihiel. *Town, Meuse.* The town has a name honoring *St. Michael* the Archangel, to whom its 8th-century Benedictine abbey was dedicated.

Saint-Mitre-les-Remparts. *Town, Bouches-du-Rhône.* The town has a name honoring *St. Mitrias*, a 4th-century saint of Aix-en-Provence (rather than St. Demetrius, as sometimes proposed), and an addition referring to the medieval ramparts still here.

Saint-Nabord. *Village, Vosges.* The name honors *St. Nabor*, a 4th-century Roman martyr.

Saint-Nazaire. *City and port, Loire-At-*

lantique. The name honors *St. Nazarius*, 5th-century abbot of Lerins.

Saint-Nectaire. *Village, Puy-de-Dôme*. The name honors *St. Nectarius*, 1st-century companion of St. Austremonius.

Saint-Nicolas. *Town, Pas-de-Calais*. The name honors *St. Nicholas*, 4th-century bishop of Myra.

Saint-Nicolas-d'Aliermont. *Village, Seine-Maritime*. The village has a name honoring *St. Nicholas*, as at **Saint-Nicolas**, and an addition locating it near *Aliermont*, from the Germanic personal name *Adalhari* and Latin *mons, montis*, "mountain."

Saint-Nicolas-de-Port. *Town, Meurthe-et-Moselle*. The name was recorded in the 10th century as *Port*, referring to the port on the Meurthe River here. The dedication to *St. Nicholas*, as at **Saint-Nicolas**, was then added.

Saint-Nicolas-de-Redon. *Village, Loire-Atlantique*. The village has a name honoring *St. Nicholas*, as at **Saint-Nicolas**, and an addition locating it near **Redon**.

Saint-Nizier-du-Moucherotte. *Resort village, Isère*. The village has a name honoring *St. Nicetius*, 6th-century bishop of Lyon (or 7th-century bishop of Besançon), and an addition locating it near the summit of *Le Moucherotte*.

Saint-Nom-la-Bretèche. *Town, Yvelines*. The town has a name honoring *St. Nummius*, and an addition referring to its brattice (*bretèche*) or battlements.

Saint-Omer. *Town, Pas-de-Calais*. The name honors *St. Audemar*, 7th-century bishop of Thérouanne, who founded the abbey of Saint-Bertin here.

Saintonge. *Region, western France*. The former province took its name from its historic capital, **Saintes**.

Saint-Orens-de-Gameville. *Town, Haute-Garonne*. The town has a name honoring *St. Orientius*, 5th-century bishop of Auch, and an addition from the local placename *Gameville*.

Saint-Ouen. *Town, Seine-Saint-Denis*. The Paris suburb was earlier known as *Clichy-la-Garenne*, with a name identical to **Clichy** and an addition from Low Latin *warenna*, "warren" (a game reserve). It was then renamed in honor of *St. Ouen*, 7th-century bishop of Rouen, who died here.

Saint-Ouen-l'Aumône. *Town, Val-d'Oise*. The town has a name honoring *St. Ouen*, as at **Saint-Ouen**, and an addition meaning "alms," "charity."

Saint-Pair-sur-Mer. *Resort village, Manche*. The village has a name honoring *St. Paternus*, 4th-century bishop of Avranches, and an addition locating it "on sea" by the English Channel.

Saint-Palais. *Village, Pyrénées-Atlantiques*. The name honors *St. Palladius*, 6th-century bishop of Saintes (or a 5th-century Greek saint).

Saint-Palais-sur-Mer. *Resort village, Charente-Maritime*. The village has a name honoring *St. Palladius*, as at **Saint-Palais**, and an addition locating it "on sea" by the Bay of Biscay.

Saint-Pathus. *Town, Seine-et-Marne*. The name honors *St. Patuscius*, a 6th-century canon of Meaux.

Saint-Paul-de-Fenouillet. *Village, Pyrénées-Orientales*. The village has a name honoring *St. Paul*, and an addition locating it near *Fenouillet*, from Latin *feniculum*, "fennel," and the collective suffix *-etum*. (The whole of the region here is known as *Fenouillèdes*.)

Saint-Paul-de-Vence. *Village, Alpes-Maritimes*. The village has a name honoring *St. Paul*, and an addition locating it near **Vence**.

Saint-Paulien. *Village, Haute-Loire*. The name honors *St. Paulianus*, 6th-century bishop of Le Puy.

Saint-Paul-lès-Dax. *Town, Landes*. The town has a name honoring *St. Paul*, and an addition locating it near (*lès*) **Dax**, of which it is now actually a suburb.

Saint-Paul-sur-Isère. *Village, Savoie.* The name was recorded in the 12th century as *ecclesia Sancti Hippolyti*, showing that the original dedication was to *St. Hippolytus*, as at **Saint-Hippolyte**. The saint's name gradually changed to *Paul* (first *Hippolyte*, then *Polyte*, then *Pol*, then *Paul*).

Saint-Paul-Trois-Châteaux. *Town, Drôme.* The name was recorded in the 6th century as *Civitas Trecastininsis*, from the *Tricastini*, a Gaulish tribe mentioned by Livy. Their own name has the same origin as that of the *Tricasses* (see **Troyes**). This gave the second part of the name, now altered as if to mean "three castles." The reference is not to the biblical St. Paul but to *St. Paul*, 4th-century bishop of Tricastin (as the town was then known). The earlier Roman name was *Noviomagus*, as for **Noyon**.

Saint-Pé-de-Bigorre. *Village, Hautes-Pyrénées.* The village has a name honoring *St. Peter* (in the Gascon form of his name), and an addition locating it in **Bigorre**.

Saint-Péravy-Épreux. *Village, Loiret.* The name represents *Saint-Père à vi*, from the name of *St. Peter* (as for **Saint-Père**) and Latin *ad vicum*, "to the village." The addition derives from Latin *speratorium*, "lookout post." A 12th-century record of the parish name was *parrochia Sancti Petri Vici Hesperi*.

Saint-Père. *Hamlet, Yonne.* The name honors *St. Peter*.

Saint-Philbert-de-Grand-Lieu. *Town, Loire-Atlantique.* The town has a name honoring *St. Philbert*, 7th-century abbot of Jumièges, whose tomb is here, and an addition meaning "great place," the name of the large lake nearby.

Saint-Pierre-d'Albigny. *Village, Savoie.* The village has a name honoring *St. Peter*, and an "addition" that is the original name of the place, recorded in the 11th century as *Albiniacum*, from the Roman personal name *Albinius* and the associative suffix *-acum*.

Saint-Pierre-d'Oléron. *Resort town,* *Charente-Maritime.* The town, on the island of **Oléron**, has a name honoring *St. Peter*.

Saint-Pierre-du-Mont. *Town, Landes.* The suburb of **Mont-de-Marsan** has a name honoring *St. Peter*.

Saint-Pierre-lès-Elbeuf. *Town, Seine-Maritime.* Ther town has a name honoring *St. Peter*, and an addition locating it near (*lès*) **Elbeuf**, of which it is now actually a suburb.

Saint-Pierre-sur-Dives. *Town, Calvados.* The town has a name honoring *St. Peter*, and an addition locating it on the *Dives* River (see **Dives-sur-Mer**).

Saint-Point. *Village, Saône-et-Loire.* The name honors *St. Pontius*.

Saint-Pol-de-Léon. *Town, Finistère.* The Brittany town has the Breton name *Kastell-Paol*, "Paul's castle," honoring *St. Paul Aurelian*, who came from Wales in the 6th century and worked here as bishop. The town's Roman name was *Castellum Leonense*, "Leo's castle."

Saint-Pol-sur-Mer. *Town, Nord.* The suburb of Dunkerque takes its name from the inn sign *Au Grand Saint Pol*, commemorating the Chevalier de *Saint-Pol*, a companion of the French privateer and naval officer Jean Bart (1650–1702), himself a Dunkerque man.

Saint-Pol-sur-Ternoise. *Town, Pas-de-Calais.* The town, on the *Ternoise* River, is named for *St. Paul*.

Saint-Pons-de-Thomières. *Village, Hérault.* The village is named for *St. Pontius*, the added placename distinguishing it from *Saint-Pons-de-Mauchiens*, some 38 miles to the east.

Saint-Pourçain-sur-Sioule. *Town, Allier.* The town, on the *Sioule* River, is named for *St. Portianus*, a 6th-century abbot of Auvergne.

Saint-Priest. *Town, Rhône.* The suburb of Lyon has a name honoring *St. Praejectus*, 7th-century bishop in Auvergne.

Saint-Privat-la-Montagne. *Village, Moselle.* The village has a name honoring *St. Privatus*, 3d-century bishop of Mende, and an addition meaning "the mountain."

Saint-Prix. *Town, Val-d'Oise.* The Paris suburb has a name honoring *St. Praejectus*, as for **Saint-Priest**.

Saint-Pryvé-Saint-Mesmin. *Town, Loiret.* The suburb of Orléans has a name honoring both *St. Privatus*, as at **Saint-Privat-la-Montagne**, and *St. Maximinus*, as at **Saint-Maximin-la-Sainte-Baume**.

Saint-Puy. *Village, Gers.* The name was recorded in the 13th century as *castrum Summi Podii*, from Latin *castrum*, "castle," *summum*, "top," and *podium*, "height," "hill," giving an overall sense "castle on the top of a hill." The name was gradually "smoothed" to *Sempuy*, in which *Sem-* was taken as *Saint-*, so creating a nonexistent St. Puy.

Saint-Quay-Portrieux. *Resort village, Côtes-d'Armor.* The village has a name honoring an Irish bishop, and an addition locating it near *Portrieux*.

Saint-Quentin. *City, Aisne.* The name honors *St. Quentin*, martyred here in the 3d century. The city's Roman name was *Augusta Veromanduorum*, as capital of the *Veromandui* (see **Vermandois**).

Saint-Rambert-d'Albon. *Town, Drôme.* The town has a name honoring *St. Rambert*, as at **Saint-Just-Saint-Rambert**, and an addition locating it near **Albon**.

Saint-Rambert-en-Bugey. *Village, Ain.* The village has a name honoring *St. Rambert*, as at **Saint-Just-Saint-Rambert**, and an addition locating it in the region of **Bugey**.

Saint-Raphaël. *Resort town, Var.* The name honors *St. Raphael* the Archangel.

Saint-Rémy. *Town, Saône-et-Loire.* The suburb of Chalon-sur-Saône has a name honoring *St. Remigius*, 4th-century bishop of Reims.

Saint-Rémy-de-Provence. *Town,* *Bouches-du-Rhône.* The town has a name honoring *St. Remigius*, as at **Saint-Rémy**, and an addition locating it in **Provence**.

Saint-Rémy-lès-Chevreuse. *Town, Yvelines.* The town has a name honoring *St. Remigius*, as at **Saint-Rémy**, and an addition locating it near (*lès*) **Chevreuse**.

Saint-Rémy-sur-Avre. *Village, Eure-et-Loir.* The village has a name honoring *St. Remigius*, as at **Saint-Rémy**, and an addition locating it on the *Avre* River.

Saint-Renan. *Town, Finistère.* The name honors *St. Renan*, a 6th-century Breton hermit.

Saint-Riquier. *Village, Somme.* The name honors *St. Riquier*, 7th-century founder of an abbey at nearby Celles, now **Abbeville**, named after it.

Saint-Roch. *Village, Indre-et-Loire.* The name honors the famous Montpellier hermit *St. Roch* (*c.*1350–1380), reputed to have miraculously cured sufferers from the plague.

Saint-Romain. *Village, Charente.* The name was recorded in the 11th century as *Romanorevilla*, and this gave the present name, as if honoring *St. Romanus*, as at **Saint-Romain-le-Puy**.

Saint-Romain-le-Puy. *Village, Loire.* The village has a name honoring *St Romanus*, a 4th-century martyr (or a 7th-century bishop of Rouen), and an addition from Latin *podium*, "height," referring to the elevated site on which it lies.

Saintry-sur-Seine. *Town, Essonne.* The suburb of Corbeil-Essonnes, on the **Seine** River, probably derives its name from the Roman personal name *Sanctitius*, from *Sanctius*, and the associative suffix *-acum*.

Saint-Saëns. *Village, Seine-Maritime.* The name honors *St. Sidonius*, a 7th-century abbot.

Saint-Saulve. *Town, Nord.* The suburb of Valenciennes has a name honoring *St. Salvius*, 6th-century hermit of the Bray region (or 6th-century bishop of Albi).

Saint-Sauveur-le-Vicomte. *Village, Manche.* The village has a name honoring *St. Savior*, a title of Christ, and an addition referring to the viscounts who held the town. (The earliest known was Roger, who founded the Benedictine abbey of St. Savior here in the 10th century.)

Saint-Sauveur-sur-Tinée. *Hamlet, Alpes-Maritimes.* The hamlet has a name honoring *St. Savior*, a title of Christ, and an addition locating it on the *Tinée* River.

Saint-Savin. *Village, Vienne.* The name honors *St. Sabinus*, the name of various saints of Poitou and Bigorre.

Saint-Savinien. *Village, Charente-Maritime.* The name honors *St. Sabinianus*, 3d-century (and first) bishop of Sens and martyr.

Saint-Sébastien-sur-Loire. *Town, Loire-Atlantique.* The suburb of Nantes, on the **Loire** River, has a name honoring *St. Sebastian*, born at Narbonne and martyred in Rome in 288.

Saint-Servan-sur-Mer. *Resort area and port, Ille-et-Vilaine.* The resort, "on sea" by the English Channel, has a name honoring *St. Servanus*, 6th-century Scottish bishop and apostle of the Orkney Islands.

Saint-Sever. *Town, Landes.* The name honors *St. Severus*, one of several in the 5th and 6th centuries.

Saints-Geosmes. *Village, Haute-Marne.* The name was recorded in the 9th century as *monasterium Sanctorum Geminorum*, from Latin *Gemini*, "Twins," referring to the so-called *Saints Jumeaux*, "Twin Saints" (in fact triplets) Speusippe, Eleosippe, and Melasippe, three young Christian brothers said to have been martyred here. (The tympanum over the church door at Saint-Broingt-les-Fosses, a few miles to the south, shows the brothers being baptized by St. Benignus, the 2nd-century apostle of Burgundy who gave the name of this village.)

Saint-Sulpice. *Town, Tarn.* The name honors *St. Sulpicius*, 7th-century bishop of Bourges.

Saint-Sylvain-d'Anjou. *Town, Maine-et-Loire.* The town has a name honoring *St. Silvinus*, 8th-century bishop of Thérouanne, and an addition locating it near **Anjou.**

Saint-Symphorien-d'Ozon. *Town, Rhône.* The town has a name honoring *St. Symphorian*, 2d-century martyr at **Autun**, and an addition locating it on the *Ozon* River.

Saint-Trojan-les-Bains. *Resort village, Charente-Maritime.* The village has a name honoring *St. Troianus*, 6th-century bishop of Saintes, and an addition ("the baths") referring to the bathing facilities here on the Île d'Oléron.

Saint-Tropez. *Resort town, Var.* The name honors *St. Torpes*, 1st-century martyr from Pisa.

Saint-Vaast-la-Hougue. *Resort town and port, Manche.* The town has a name honoring *St. Vedast*, 6th-century bishop of Arras, and an addition locating it on the former island of *La Hougue.*

Saint-Valéry-en-Caux. *Resort town and port, Seine-Maritime.* The town has a name honoring *St. Walaric*, a 7th-century abbot in Picardy, and an addition locating it in the Pays de **Caux.**

Saint-Valéry-sur-Somme. *Village, Somme.* The village has a name honoring *St. Walaric*, as at **Saint-Valéry-en-Caux**, and an addition locating it on (the estuary of) the **Somme** River.

Saint-Vallier. *Town, Drôme.* The name honors *St. Valerius*, 3d-century martyr (or 5th-century bishop of Couserans, or 5th-century bishop of Antibes).

Saint-Varent. *Village, Deux-Sèvres.* The name honors *St. Veranus*, 5th-century bishop of Vence (or 6th-century bishop of Cavaillon, or 5th-century recluse in Champagne).

Saint-Victoret. *Town, Bouches-du-Rhône.* The fortified settlement that is now a suburb of Marignane formerly depended on the abbey of *St. Victor* at Marseille. Hence its name.

Saint-Vincent-de-Tyrosse. *Town, Landes*. The name honors *St. Vincent de Paul* (1581–1660), priest and philanthropist, born at Pouy (now Saint-Vincent-de-Paul), near Dax. The second part of the name probably derives from the Roman personal name *Tiro* and the Aquitanian suffix *-osa*.

Saint-Vit. *Village, Doubs*. The name honors *St. Vitus*, 1st-century martyr.

Saint-Vrain. *Village, Essonne*. The Paris suburb has a name honoring *St. Veranus*, as at **Saint-Varent**.

Saint-Wandrille-Rançon.   *Hamlet, Seine-Maritime*. The hamlet has a name honoring *St. Wandrille*, 7th-century abbot of Fontanelle, near Rouen, and an addition locating it near *Rançon*.

Saint-Yorre. *Town, Allier*. The name probably honors *St. George*.

Saint-Yrieix-la-Perche. *Town, Haute-Vienne*. The town has a name honoring *St. Aredius*, 7th-century abbot in Limousin, and an addition from nearby *La Perche*, from Latin *pertica*, "pole" (English *perch*), denoting the abundant woodland here.

Saint-Yrieix-sur-Charente. *Town, Charente*. The suburb of Angoulême has a name honoring *St. Aredius*, as at **Saint-Yrieix-la-Perche**, and an addition locating it on the **Charente** River.

Saint-Zacharie. *Village, Var*. The name was recorded in the 10th century as *Segalarias*, from Latin *secale*, "rye," and the suffix *-aria*. This gave the present name, as if honoring *St. Zacharias*.

Saivres. *Village, Deux-Sèvres*. The name was recorded in the 11th century as *Severa*, perhaps from the Roman personal name *Severus*, with Latin *villa*, "estate," understood. It is probably not from the Sèvre Niortaise River, to the south, as the village is actually on the Chambon.

Salaise-sur-Sanne. *Village, Isère*. The name derives from Latin *salix*, "willow," and the suffix *-ia*. The second part of the name locates the village on the *Sanne* River.

Salbris. *Town, Loir-et-Cher*. The name derives from *Salera*, the historical name of the *Sauldre* River here, and Gaulish *briua*, "bridge."

Salernes. *Village, Var*. The name probably derives from pre-Celtic *sal*, "mountain," and the pre-Latin suffix *-erna*. Salernes is in the Provence Alps.

Salers. *Hamlet, Cantal*. The name, recorded in the 12th century as *Salernum*, has the same origin as **Salernes**. Salers was built atop a volcanic rock in the Massif du Cantal.

Sales. *Village, Haute-Savoie*. The Medieval Latin name of the village, the birthplace of St. Francis of Sales (1567–1622), was *Salesius*, from Germanic *seli*, "hall," "castle."

Salies-de-Béarn. *Resort town, Pyrénées-Atlantiques*. The town is noted for its salt springs. Hence the name, from Latin *salina*, "salt works," distinguished by their location in **Béarn**.

Salies-du-Salat. *Village, Haute-Garonne*. The name is as for **Salies-de-Béarn**, referring to the salt mines here, with an addition locating the village on the *Salat* River.

Salindres. *Village, Gard*. The name probably derives from a former name of the Avène River here.

Salins-les-Bains. *Resort village, Jura*. The village is a spa with brine baths and rock-salt mines. Hence the name, from Latin *salina*, "salt works," and French *les bains*, "the baths."

Sallanches. *Resort town, Haute-Savoie*. The name may be an altered form of *Chalanche*, a dialectal variant of Provençal *calanque*, as for **Challans**.

Salles. *Village, Gironde*. The name probably derives from Germanic *seli*, "hall," "house."

Salles-Curan. *Village, Aveyron.* The first part of the name is as for **Salles**. The second part relates to nearby *Curan*.

Salmbach. *Village, Bas-Rhin.* The name derives from Germanic *salm*, "salmon," and *bach*, "stream."

Salon-de-Provence. *Town, Bouches-du-Rhône.* The name was recorded in the 9th century as *Villa Salone*, from Germanic *seli*, "hall," "castle," and the suffix *-onis*. The second part of the name locates the town in **Provence**.

Salonnes. *Village, Moselle.* The name is that of the river here, from Latin *sal*, "salt."

Salses-le-Château. *Village, Pyrénées-Orientales.* The name derives from Latin *salsus*, "salty," referring to the *Étang de Salses* here, a lagoon on the Mediterranean. The *château* is the nearby fort (*Fort de Salses*) built in the 15th century.

La Salvetat-Saint-Gilles. *Town, Haute-Garonne.* The name comes from Latin *salvitas*, Old Provençal *salvetat*, "place of refuge," "hospice," here one dedicated to *St. Giles*.

Sambre. *River, northeastern France.* The river rises in northern France, then flows northeast into Belgium to join the Meuse at Namur. Its Gaulish name was *Samara*, perhaps from a root meaning "peaceful," "calm," referring to its slow current.

Samer. *Village, Pas-de-Calais.* The earlier name of the village, recorded in the 11th century, was *Silviacus*, from the Roman personal name *Silvus* and the associative suffix *-acum*. The present name, recorded in the 12th century as *Sanctus Ulmarus*, derives from Latin *sanctus*, "holy," and the Germanic personal name *Wulmar*, that of an obscure saint.

Samoëns. *Village, Haute-Savoie.* The first part of the name is of obscure origin. It may represents a Germanic personal name *Samo*. The second part is the Germanic suffix *-ing*.

Sanary-sur-Mer. *Resort town, Var.* Until the end of the 19th century the name was identical with that of **Saint-Nazaire** and was pronounced locally *San Nàri*. The townsfolk demanded their name be spelled "properly," although the spoken form was really a southern translation of the original. The town is "on sea" by the Mediterranean.

Sancergues. *Village, Cher.* As a Latin text of 1124 implies, the village here arose around the *ecclesia de Sancirgio que in honore beati Cirici consecrata est*, "church of Sancirgius which was consecrated in honor of Blessed Cyricus." But *Sancirgius*, which gave the present name, is simply a form of *Sanctus Cyricus*, otherwise the 4th-century martyr *St. Cyricus*, known in French as *Saint Cyr* (as at **Saint-Cyr-l'École** and elsewhere).

Sancerre. *Village, Cher.* The name honors *St. Satyrus*, said to be the brother of St. Ambrose, 4th-century bishop of Milan.

Sangatte. *Resort village, Pas-de-Calais.* The name derives from Dutch *zand*, "sand," and *gat*, "gate," denoting a way to the sandy shore here on the Strait of Dover. (Sangatte has its exact counterpart across the water in *Sandgate*, a district of Folkestone, Kent, England, and each place happens to adjoin a terminal of the Channel Tunnel.)

San-Gavino-di-Fiumorbo. *Village, Haute-Corse.* The village, in eastern Corsica, has a name honoring *St. Gavino*, 4th-century martyr in Sardinia. The addition is as for **Prunelli-di-Fiumorbo**.

Sannerville. *Village, Calvados.* The name derives from Latin *salinarius*, "salt merchant," probably given as a personal name, and *villa*, "estate."

Sannois. *Town, Val-d'Oise.* The name of the Paris suburb was recorded in the 12th century as *Centinodium*, perhaps from Latin *centinodium*, "knotgrass."

Santa-Maria-Poggio. *Village, Haute-Corse.* The village, in eastern Corsica, has a name honoring *St. Mary*. The addition is the Corsican equivalent of French *Puy*, as for *Le Puy* (see **Puy, Le**).

Sanvignes-les-Mines. *Town, Saône-et-Loire.* The name derives from Latin *sine*, "without," and *vinea*, "vine," implying a poor site for a vineyard. The second part of the name refers to the former coal mines here.

Saône. *River, east central France.* The Roman name of the river, recorded in the 1st century AD, was *Souconna*, later *Sauconna*, from *Sauc*, perhaps the name of a god, and the Gaulish suffix *-onna* meaning "river." Its earlier name was *Arar* or *Araris*, from the river-name root *ar*.

Saône-et-Loire. *Department, east central France.* The department takes its name from its two main rivers. The **Saône** crosses it from north to south and forms part of its eastern border, and the **Loire** flows south to north and forms most of its western border.

Saorge. *Village, Alpes-Maritimes.* The name probably derives from pre-Indoeuropean *sab*, "river," and the pre-Latin suffix *-urgium*, rather than a pre-Latin personal name *Savurgius*.

Sarcelles. *City, Val-d'Oise.* The name of the Paris suburb was recorded in the 9th century as *Cercilla*, later *Sercellae*, perhaps from Latin *circellum*, "little circle," "curve."

Sare. *Resort village, Pyrénées-Atlantiques.* The name derives from Basque *sara*, "wood."

Sarlat-la-Canéda. *Town, Dordogne.* The name was recorded in the 9th century as *Sarlatum*, from pre-Latin *serra*, "long mountain." The second part of the name is that of nearby *La Canéda*, said to have been adopted from the Cretan city of *Canea* (Khaniá), known to the French as *La Canée*, and so called because because facing a *canneta*, "place of reeds."

Sarrebourg. *Town, Moselle.* The name was recorded in the 8th century as *Saraburgum*, from the **Saar** River, on which the town lies, and Germanic *burg*, "fort." Sarrebourg is not far from the border with Germany, where it is known as *Saarburg*.

Sarreguemines. *Town, Moselle.* The name was recorded in the 16th century as *Sargemünt*, from the **Saar** River, on which the town lies, and Germanic *gamundi*, "mouth." It is not far from the border with Germany, where it is known as *Saargemünd*.

Sarre-Union. *Town, Bas-Rhin.* The town comprises two formerly separate villages: the medieval village of *Bouquenom* (German *Bockenheim*), on the right bank of the Saar River, and the modern planned village of *Ville-Neuve* (German *Neusarrewerden*), built in the 18th century by the princes of Nassau on the left bank. On June 16, 1794, the two villages amalgamated under the present name, from **Saar** and French *union*, "union."

Sarrians. *Town, Vaucluse.* The name derives from the Roman personal name *Sarius* or *Sarrius* and the suffix *-anum*.

Sarthe. *Department, western France.* The name is that of the river here, recorded in the 9th century as *Sarta*, from Indoeuropean *ser* or *sar*, "to flow."

Sartrouville. *City, Yvelines.* The name of the present Paris suburb was recorded in the 11th century as *Satorvilla*, from the Germanic personal name *Saduru* and Latin *villa*, "estate."

Sassenage. *Town, Isère.* The suburb of Grenoble derives its name from pre-Latin *cassano*, "oak," and the suffix *-aticum*.

Sathonay-Camp. *Town, Rhône.* The name derives from the Roman personal name *Satto*, *Sattonis*, a variant of *Sato*, and the associative suffix *-acum*. The addition refers to the military base here.

Sauclières. *Village, Aveyron.* The name derives from Latin *circulus*, "circle," "hoop," and the suffix *-aria*, the source of Old Provençal *celclaria* and Languedocian *céuclieiro*, the word for a copse of chestnut trees whose stump sprouts were used to make hoops.

Saugues. *Resort village, Haute-Loire.* The name derives from Gaulish *salico-*, "willow."

Saujon. *Resort town, Charente-Maritime.* The name derives from the Roman personal name *Salvius* and the suffix *-onem*.

Saulnes. *Village, Meurthe-et-Moselle.* The name derives from the Gaulish personal name *Salinus*, with Latin *villa*, "estate," understood.

Saulx-les-Chartreux. *Town, Essonne.* The name derives from Latin *salix*, "willow." The second part of the name refers to a Carthusian (*Chartreux*) monastery here.

Saulxures-sur-Moselotte. *Village, Vosges.* The name derives from Latin *salsus*, "salty," denoting a salt-water spring, and the suffix *-ura*. The village is on the *Moselotte* River.

Saumur. *Town, Maine-et-Loire.* The name of the town was recorded in the 10th century as Latin *Salmurus*, from pre-Celtic *sala*, "marshland," and an element of unknown meaning

Sausset-les-Pins. *Town and port, Bouches-du-Rhône.* The name derives from Latin *salix*, "willow," and the suffix *-etum*. The addition to the name refers to the pines here.

Sauternes. *Village, Gironde.* The name may derive from Latin *saltu terra*, "wooded terrain," or *salva terra*, "land of refuge," or Celtic *sau*, "mound," "hillock," and *ternevan*, "bank."

Sautron. *Town, Loire-Atlantique.* The name probably derives from the Roman personal name *Saltarius* and the suffix *-onem*.

Sauveterre-de-Béarn. *Village, Pyrénées-Atlantiques.* The name represents Latin *salva terra*, "safe land," meaning land where refuge could be obtained. The addition to the name locates the village in **Béarn**.

Sauveterre-de-Guyenne. *Village, Gironde.* The name shares the origin of **Sauveterre-de-Béarn**, but with the addition locating the village in **Guyenne**.

Le Sauze. *Resort village, Alpes-de-Haute-Provence.* The name derives from Latin *salix*, "willow."

Savasse. *Village, Drôme.* The name perhaps derives from the Roman personal name *Sapaudus*.

Savenay. *Town, Loire-Atlantique.* The name derives from the Roman personal name *Sabinus* and the associative suffix *-acum*.

Saverne. *Town, Bas-Rhin.* The name was recorded in the 4th century as *Tabernis*, from Latin *taberna*, "tavern." Saverne was a staging post on an important Roman route.

Savigné-l'Évêque. *Village, Sarthe.* The village derives its name from the Roman personal name *Sabinius* and the associative suffix *-acum*. It was a fief of the bishop (*évêque*).

Savigny-lès-Beaune. *Village, Côte-d'Or.* The name is as for **Savigné-l'Évêque**. The village is near (*lès*) **Beaune**.

Savigny-le-Temple. *Town, Seine-et-Marne.* The town has a name as for **Savigné-l'Évêque**. In 1149 Louis VII, returned from the Second Crusade, gave the village of Savigny and its lands to the Knights Templars, an event preserved in the second part of the name.

Savigny-sur-Braye. *Village, Loir-et-Cher.* The name is as for **Savigné-l'Évêque**. The second part of the name locates the village on the *Braye* River.

Savigny-sur-Orge. *Town, Essonne.* The town, on the **Orge** River, has a name of the same origin as **Savigné-l'Évêque**.

Savoie. *Historic region, southeastern France.* Known to English speakers as *Savoy*, the region derives its name, now that of a department, from Latin *Sapaudia*, of uncertain origin.

Savoy *see* **Savoie**

Saxon-Sion. *Village, Meurthe-et-Moselle.* The name combines that of two distinct communities. *Sion* was earlier *pagus Segetensis*, "district of the Saintois," perhaps from *seges*, *segetis*, "field," or *seion*, "path." The name has been popularly linked with the biblical *Mount Sion*, the Jerusalem height, which may have influenced the present form of the name but which is hardly likely to be the origin. According to the scholarly Benedictine Dom Augustin Calmet (1672–1757), author of the great *Dictionnaire historique, critique, chronologique, géographique et littéral de la Bible* (1720–1), the historic name of Sion was *Semita*, but any association with the *Semites* is doubtful. *Saxon*, recorded in the 12th century as *Saisons*, may take its name either from the *Saxons* or from Latin *saxum*, "sacred stone." The nearby hill *Sion-Vaudémont*, a pilgrimage center since the 10th century, has a name explained by the writer Maurice Barrès (1862–1923) to mean "Wotan's hill," after the Norse god *Wotan* (Odin), but Dom Calmet prefers an origin in *Wood* and *Got*, a name of Mercury, which amounts to much the same. A source in the Germanic personal name *Wado* seems more likely, however.

Sceaux. *Town, Hauts-de-Seine*. The name of the Paris suburb was recorded in the 12th century as *Celsiacus*, from the Roman personal name *Celsius*.

Schaeffersheim. *Village, Bas-Rhin*. The name derives from the Germanic personal name *Schaeffer* ("shepherd") and *heim*, "abode."

Scheldt *see* **Escaut**

Schiltigheim. *Town, Bas-Rhin*. The suburb of Strasbourg derives its name from the Germanic personal name *Schiltung* and *heim*, "abode."

Schneckenbusch. *Village, Moselle*. The name derives from German *Schnecke*, "snail," "slug," and *Busch*, "bush," "copse."

Schœnau. *Village, Bas-Rhin*. The name represents German *schön*, "beautiful," and *Au*, "damp meadow."

Schweighouse-sur-Moder. *Town, Bas-Rhin*. The name probably derives from the Germanic personal name *Swaidico* and *haus*, "house." The town is on the *Moder* River. The German form of the name is *Schweighausen*.

Scolca. *Village, Haute-Corse*. The village, in northern Corsica, is said to derive its name from Low Latin *exculcae*, "garrison," "military post."

Scy-Chazelles. *Village, Moselle*. The suburb of Metz derives the first part of its name from the Germanic personal name *Sigo* and the associative suffix *-iacum*. The second part represents Latin *casella*, from *casa*, "house," and the diminutive suffix *-ella*.

Seclin. *Town, Nord*. The name derives from the Germanic personal name *Sigolenus*.

Secondigny. *Village, Deux-Sèvres*. The name derives from the Roman personal name *Secundinius* and the associative suffix *-acum*.

Sedan. *Town, Ardennes*. The name was recorded in the 10th century as *Villa Sedensi*, from Latin *villa*, "estate," "village," and perhaps Gaulish *setu*, "long," with the suffix *-ennu*.

Sées. *Town, Orne*. The name was recorded in the 10th century as *Sagium*, from the *Sagii*, a Gaulish tribe.

Ségala. *Region, southern France*. The plateau, in the Massif Central, has the Occitan name *Segalar*, "land of rye," from *segal*, "rye."

Segonzac. *Village, Charente*. The name was recorded in the 11th century as *Secundiacum*, apparently from the Roman personal name *Secundius* and the associative suffix *-acum*, but more likely from a Gaulish personal name *Segontios* ("strong one") and this suffix.

Segré. *Town, Maine-et-Loire*. The name was recorded in the 11th century as *castellum Secretum*, from Latin *castellum*, "castle," and possibly either *secretum*, "secret," "isolated," or the Roman personal name *Securus*, with the associative suffix *-acum*.

Seichamps. *Town, Meurthe-et-Moselle*. The name derives from Latin *siccus*, "dry," and *campus*, "field."

Seiches-sur-le-Loir. *Village, Maine-et-Loire*. The name derives from the Roman personal name *Ceppius*, with Latin *villa*, "estate," understood. The village is on the **Loir** River.

Seillans. *Village, Var.* The name derives from the Roman personal name *Caelius* and the suffix *-anum.*

Sein. *Island, northwestern France.* The Medieval Latin name of the island, off the west coast of Brittany, was *Sena*, from Breton *Enez-Sun*, from *enez*, "island," and the proper name *Sun.*

Seine. *River, northern France.* The major waterway was known to the Romans as *Sequana*, a name perhaps from Celtic *soghan*, "calm," referring to its slow current and gentle profile, making it France's most navigable river.

Seine-et-Marne. *Department, north central France.* The department is named for its two main rivers, the **Seine** in its southern part and the **Marne** in its northern region.

Seine-Inférieure *see* **Seine-Maritime**

Seine-Maritime. *Department, northern France.* The name means "Maritime Seine," referring to the **Seine** that meanders across the south of the department and the English Channel coast that forms its northern border. Until 1955 the department was known as *Seine-Inférieure* ("Lower Seine"), but the name was changed because it implied "inferiority."

Seine-Saint-Denis. *Department, north central France.* The department was created in 1964 and takes its name from the **Seine** that forms its western boundary and the long-established city (now Paris suburb) of **Saint-Denis** that lies on the river's right bank.

Sélestat. *Town, Bas-Rhin.* The name was recorded in the 8th century as *Scalistatus*, from Old High German *sclade*, "marshland," and *stat*, "place." The town is near the border with Germany, where it is known as *Schlettstadt.*

Selles-sur-Cher. *Town, Loir-et-Cher.* The name derives from Latin *cella*, "hermitage." The town is on the **Cher** River.

Seloncourt. *Town, Doubs.* The name derives from the Germanic personal name *Selo* and Latin *cortem*, accusative of *cors*, "estate."

Selongey. *Village, Côte-d'Or.* The name probably derives from the Roman personal name *Solemnius* and the associative suffix *-acum.*

Séméac. *Town, Hautes-Pyrénées.* The suburb of Tarbes probably derives its name from the Roman personal name *Semius* and the associative suffix *-acum.*

Semur-en-Auxois. *Town, Côte-d'Or.* The name, recorded in the 6th century as *Sinemuro*, derives from pre-Indoeuropean *sin*, "mountain," and Latin *murus*, "wall," describing the site of the town atop a rocky bluff. The second part of the name distinguishes this Semur from others by locating it in the region of *Auxois.*

Sénas. *Town, Bouches-du-Rhône.* The name was recorded in the 9th century as *Sinaca*, from the Gallo-Roman personal name *Senius*, from Gaulish *Senos*, and the associative suffix *-acum.*

Séné. *Town, Morbihan.* The suburb of Vannes derives its name from the Gaulish personal name *Senos* and the associative suffix *-acum.*

Senez. *Hamlet, Alpes-de-Haute-Provence.* The name was recorded in the 2nd century as *Sanition*, from pre-Indoeuropean *san*, "height," and the pre-Latin suffix *-etium.*

Senlis. *Town, Oise.* The name was recorded in the 4th century as *civitas Silvanectum*, from Latin *civitas*, "city," and the Gaulish tribe known as the *Silvanectes.* Their own name, properly *Selvanectes*, but influenced by Latin *silva*, "wood," derives from Gaulish *selua*, "possession," "property." The earlier Roman name of the settlement was *Ratomagus*, from Gaulish *rate*, "fort," and *magos*, "market."

Sennecey-le-Grand. *Village, Saône-et-Loire.* The name derives from the Gallo-Roman personal name *Senicius* and the associative suffix *-acum.* The village is "great" (*grand*) by comparison with others of the name.

Senonches. *Village, Eure-et-Loir.* The

name derives from the Gaulish personal name *Seno, Senonis*, from the *Senones* who gave the name of **Sens**, and the suffix *-ica*, with Latin *villa*, "estate," understood.

Senones. *Village, Vosges*. The name has the same origin as that of **Senonches**, but with the suffix *-a*.

Sens. *Town, Yonne*. The name was recorded in the 4th century as *Senones*, the Latin name of the Gaulish tribe whose capital it was. Their own name may come from Gaulish *senos*, "old."

Septèmes-les-Vallons. *Town, Bouches-du-Rhône*. The first part of the name derives from Latin *septimus*, "seventh," denoting a Roman milestone 7 miles from Marseille. The second part means "little valleys," from a plural form of Latin *vallis*, "valley," and the suffix *-one*.

Septimanie. *Historic region, southern France*. The coastal region, between the Pyrenees and the Rhône River, was known to the Romans as *Septimania*, from Latin *septimanus*, "relating to seven," from *septem*, "seven," from a colony of veterans of the 7th Roman Legion set up here in the reign of the emperor Augustus.

Sept-Laux. *Resort area, Isère*. The name derives from Latin *septem*, "seven," and *lacus*, "lake," referring to the 7 lakes dotted around the area.

Sérifontaine. *Village, Oise*. The name probably derives from the Germanic personal name *Sigric* and Latin *fontana*, "spring."

Sérignan. *Town, Hérault*. The name derives from the Roman personal name *Serenius* (or possibly *Surinus*) and the suffix *-anum*.

Serres. *Village, Hautes-Alpes*. The name derives from pre-Latin *serra*, "long mountain."

Serrières. *Village, Ardèche*. The name probably derives from Latin *ceresia*, "cherry," and the suffix *-aria*, although the loss of the *s* is hard to explain.

Servian. *Village, Hérault*. The name derives from the Roman personal name *Cervius* or *Servius* and the suffix *-anum*.

Sète. *Town and port, Hérault*. The name goes back to Greek *Setion*, recorded in the 2d century AD, from pre-Indoeuropean *set*, "mountain," referring to Mont Saint-Clair that overlooks the town. The name was spelled *Cette* from the time of Louis XIV (17th century) to 1936, and the town's coat of arms shows a whale (Latin *cetus*) by way of a visual pun.

Seurre. *Village, Côte-d'Or*. The name perhaps derives from Latin *saburra*, "sand," referring to the sandy soil here by the Saône River.

Sévérac-le-Château. *Village, Aveyron*. The name derives from the Roman personal name *Severus* and the associative suffix *-acum*. The second part of the name refers to the (now ruined) medieval castle here.

Sevran. *Town, Seine-et-Oise*. The Paris suburb derives its name from Medieval Latin *Severanum*, from the Gallo-Roman personal name *Severus* and the suffix *-anum*.

Sèvre. *River, western France*. The name is that of two rivers, *Sèvre Nantaise* and *Sèvre Niortaise*, which together gave the name of the department of **Deux-Sèvres**. The *Sèvre Nantaise* enters the Loire near **Nantes**, while the *Sèvre Niortaise* flows through **Niort**, its head of navigation. The basic name was recorded in the 10th century as *Severa* or *Savara*, perhaps from pre-Indoeuropean *sav*, "hollow," and the river root *ar*.

Sèvres. *Town, Hauts-de-Seine*. The name of the present Paris suburb was recorded in the 6th century as *Savara*, a river name of the same origin as **Sèvre**.

Seyne. *Resort village, Alpes-de-Haute-Provence*. The name derives from pre-Indoeuropean *set*, "height," and the pre-Latin suffix *-ena*. The village is also called *Seyne-les-Alpes*.

La Seyne-sur-Mer. *Town and port, Var*. The suburb of Toulon derives its name from

Low Latin *sania*, "muddy marsh," implying an unhealthy place. The town is "on sea" in a bay of the Mediterranean.

Seyssel. *Village, Ain*. The name derives from Latin *saxum*, "rock," and the diminutive suffix *-ellum*.

Seysses. *Town, Haute-Garonne*. The name derives from Latin *saxa*, the plural of *saxum*, "rock."

Seyssins. *Town, Isère*. The suburb of Grenoble derives its name from the Roman personal name *Saxius* and the suffix *-inum*.

Sézanne. *Town, Marne*. The name probably derives from the Roman personal name *Setius* and the suffix *-ana*.

Sierck-les-Bains. *Village, Moselle*. The name derives from Latin *circus*, "circle," "round building." The addition to the name ("the baths") refers to the mineral springs in the village.

Sigean. *Village, Aude*. The name derives from the Roman personal name *Seius* and the suffix *-anum*.

Sillé-le-Guillaume. *Village, Sarthe*. The name derives from the Roman personal name *Silius* or *Cilius* and the associative suffix *-acum*. The second part of the name is that of the first known lord, *Guillaume*, in the 11th century, added to distinguish the village from *Sillé-le-Philippe*, some 22 miles to the east.

Sillery. *Village, Marne*. The name was recorded in the 12th century as *Seleriacum*, from the Roman personal name *Sellarius* and the associative suffix *-acum*.

Simiane-Collongue. *Town, Bouches-du-Rhône*. The original village of *Collongue*, with a name origin as for **Collonges**, was held by a family from Clapiers, Hérault. In 1684 it passed to a family from *Simiane*, now *Simiane-la-Rotonde*, Alpes-de-Haute-Provence, and prefixed that name (from the Roman personal name *Simius* and the suffix *-ana*) to the original.

Sion-Vaudémont *see* **Saxon-Sion**

Sissonne. *Village, Aisne*. The name derives from Latin *Saxo, Saxonis*, "Saxon," and the suffix *-ia*.

Sisteron. *Town, Alpes-de-Haute-Provence*. The name was recorded in the 4th century as *Segustero*, from Gaulish *sego-*, "victory," "strength," and the suffix *-ster*, related to the name of the **Esterel**.

Six-Fours-les-Plages. *Resort town, Var*. The name was recorded in the 11th century as *Sex Furnos*, presumably meaning "six ovens." The addition (*les plages*) relates to the beaches below.

Sixt-Fer-à-Cheval. *Resort village, Haute-Savoie*. The village derives its basic name from Latin *sextum*, "sixth (milliary column)," referring to its location, 6 miles from the Tenneverge pass. The rest of the name refers to the *Cirque du Fer-à-Cheval* ("Horseshoe Cirque"), the spectacular horseshoe-shaped natural amphitheater 4 miles from the village.

Soissons. *Town, Aisne*. The name was recorded in the 6th century as *Suession*, after the Gaulish tribe known as the *Suessiones*, whose capital it was. Their own name perhaps derives from Gaulish *suexs*, "six." (For other Gaulish "number names," see **Die**, **Périgueux**.)

Soisy-sous-Montmorency. *Town, Val-d'Oise*. The Paris suburb derives its name from the Roman personal name *Sosius* and the associative suffix *-acum*. The addition locates it near (*sous*, "under") **Montmorency**.

Soisy-sur-Seine. *Town, Essonne*. The name shares the origin of **Soisy-sous-Montmorency**, but the addition here locates the town on the **Seine** River.

Le Soler. *Town, Pyrénées-Orientales*. The name derives from Latin *solarium*, "sunny place."

Solesmes (1). *Town, Nord*. The name derives from the Roman personal name *Solemnius*.

Solesmes (2). *Village, Sarthe*. The name

has an identical origin to that of **Solesmes** (1).

Solignac. *Village, Haute-Vienne.* The name was recorded in the 9th century as *Solempniacensis*, probably from the Roman personal name *Solemnius* and the associative suffix *-acum*.

Soligny-la-Trappe. *Village, Orne.* The name was recorded in the 12th century as *Soligneium*, from the Roman personal name *Solemnius*. The second part of the name refers to the 12th-century monastery *Notre Dame de La Trappe*, parent house of the Trappist order, its own name from Low Latin *trappa*, "trap," "snare," a word of Germanic origin.

Solliès-Pont. *Town, Var.* The name derives from Latin *solarium*, "sunny place," referring not to the town, with its bridge (*pont*), but to the nearby old quarter of *Solliès-Ville*, on a hillside.

Sologne. *Region, north central France.* The name comes from pre-Celtic *sek-alonia*, from the river-name root *sek* as in *Sequana*, the Roman name of the **Seine**, and two elements of unknown meaning. The region is situated inside a great bend of the Loire.

Solutré-Pouilly. *Village, Saône-et-Loire.* The name was recorded in the 9th century as *Sulistriacus*, from an obscure Gallo-Roman personal name, perhaps from Gaulish *Sollius*, and the Latin suffixes *-ister* and *-acum*. The second part of the name derives from the Roman personal name *Pollius* and the associative suffix *-acum*.

Somain. *Town, Nord.* The name may derive from the Germanic personal name *Suluman* or from Germanic *solmanium*, a term for dark, marshy soil.

Somme. *Department, northern France.* The name is that of the river here, recorded by Caesar in the 1st century BC as *Samara*, from Gaulish *su-*, "good," and a root perhaps meaning "gentle."

Sommières. *Village, Gard.* The name derives from Latin *summum*, "summit," and the suffix *-aria*.

Sorbiers. *Town, Loire.* The suburb of Saint-Étienne probably derives its name from Latin *sorbus*, "service tree," and the diminutive suffix *-ellum*.

Sorède. *Village, Pyrénées-Orientales.* The name is that of the river here, recorded in the 10th century as *Sunereda*.

Sorèze. *Village, Tarn.* The name is that of the river here, recorded in the 9th century as *Soricinius*.

Sorgues. *Town, Vaucluse.* The name was recorded in the 11th century as *villam Sorgam*, from the *Sorgue* River, which rises near *Fontaine-de-Vaucluse* (see **Vaucluse**), east of Avignon, and enters the Ouvèze River, on which Sorgues stands, at Bédarrides, to the north of the town. The river's own name is pre-Gaulish in origin.

Sospel. *Village, Alpes-Maritimes.* The name was recorded in the 11th century as *Cespedelli*, from Latin *caespes, caespitis*, "turf," "hut covered with turf," and the suffix *-ellum*.

Sotteville-lès-Rouen. *Town, Seine-Maritime.* The town derives its name from the Scandinavian personal name *Soti* and Latin *villa*, "estate." The addition locates it near (*lès*) **Rouen**, of which it is now actually a suburb.

Soubise. *Town, Charente-Maritime.* The name was recorded early as *Sopitia villa*, from the Roman personal name *Sopitius*, a variant of *Sopitus* ("sleeper"), and Latin *villa*, "estate."

Souillac. *Town, Lot.* The name derives from the Gaulish personal name *Sollius*, or Roman personal name *Solius*, and the associative suffix *-acum*.

Souilly. *Hamlet, Meuse.* The name may derive from the Gaulish personal name *Sollius* or Roman name *Solius* and the associative suffix *-acum*.

Soulac-sur-Mer. *Resort village, Gironde.* The name derives from the Roman personal name *Solus* and the associative suffix *-acum*. The village is "on sea" by the Bay of Biscay.

Soule. *Historic region, southwestern France*. The name represents Basque *Zubero* or *Zibero*.

Soultz-Haut-Rhin. *Town, Haut-Rhin*. The name derives from Old High German *sulza*, "salt water." The addition locates the town in **Haut-Rhin.**

Soultzmatt. *Village, Haut-Rhin*. The name derives from Old High German *sulza*, "salt water," and *mato*, "meadow."

Soultz-sous-Forêts. *Village, Bas-Rhin*. The name is as for **Soultz-Haut-Rhin** but with an addition locating the village "near the forests," respectively the *Hochwald* to the north and *Forêt de Haguenau* to the south.

Souppes-sur-Loing. *Town, Seine-et-Marne*. The name derives fron Germanic *suppa*, "waterlogged place," here by the **Loing** River.

Sourdeval. *Village, Manche*. The name derives from Latin *surdus*, "hidden," and *vallis*, "valley."

La Souterraine. *Town, Creuse*. The name means what it says, "subterranean," referring to the town's famous pre-Roman crypt.

Souvigny. *Village, Allier*. The name derives from the Roman personal name *Silvinius* and the associative suffix *-acum*.

Soyaux. *Town, Charente*. The suburb of Angoulême derives its name from Low Latin *sutis*, "pigpen," and the diminutive suffix *-ellum*.

Spada. *Village, Meuse*. The original name of the settlement was recorded in the 10th century as *Girbodi villa*, from the Germanic personal name *Garbod* and Latin *villa*, "estate. In 1516 the village was erected into a marquisate for the marquis of *Spada*, an Italian nobleman.

Spay. *Village, Sarthe*. The name derives from Latin *cippus*, "stake," "pale," and the collective suffix *-etum*, referring to a palisade here.

Staffelden. *Village, Haut-Rhin*. The name represents German *Staffel*, "echelon," and *Feld*, "field," describing a series of stepped pastures.

Stains. *Town, Seine-Saint-Denis*. The Paris suburb derives its name from the Germanic personal name *Sittin*.

Stazzona. *Village, Haute-Corse*. The village, in northern Corsica, derives its name from Latin *statio*, "station," "post," here in the Corsican sense of "forge."

Steenvoorde. *Town, Nord*. The name derives from Dutch *steen*, "stone," and *voord*, "ford," meaning a stony ford or one laid with stones for ease of crossing.

Stenay. *Town, Meuse*. The name was recorded in the 8th century as *Sathanagium*, perhaps from a temple of *Saturn* here, on the site of which the present church of St. Dagobert was built, or else from the Gallo-Roman personal name *Satto* or *Setinus*.

Stiring-Wendel. *Town, Moselle*. The first part of the name derives from a Germanic personal name based on *Sir* or *Stir* and the suffix *-ing*. The second part represents the name of the French industrial family of *Wendel*, who founded the coal-mining town in 1857.

Strasbourg. *City, Bas-Rhin*. The name was recorded in the 6th century as *Strateburgum*, from Germanic *straza*, "street" (German *Straße*, English *street*), and *burg*, "castle," "fort." The "fort on a street" is on an important route leading westward from the Rhine over the Vosges mountains. The earlier name of the town, recorded in the 2d century, was *Argentoraton*, from Gaulish *arganton*, "silver," and *rate*, "fort," perhaps given symbolically. The Rhine here forms the border with Germany, where the city is known as *Straßburg*.

Sucy-en-Brie. *Town, Val-de-Marne*. The Paris suburb has a name recorded in the 9th century as *Sulciacum*, from the Roman personal name *Sulcius* and the associative suffix *-acum*. The second part of the name locates it in **Brie.**

Suippes. *Town, Marne.* The name is that of the river here, recorded in the 12th century as *Sopia*.

Suisse Normande. *Region, northwestern France.* The region of Normandy, with its cliffs and crags, is somewhat suggestive of Switzerland. Hence its name, "Norman Switzerland."

Sully-sur-Loire. *Town, Loiret.* The name was recorded in the 7th century as *Soliaco*, from the Gaulish personal name *Sollius* or *Solius*.

Superbagnères. *Resort village, Haute-Garonne.* The winter sports resort is located above (Latin *super*) **Bagnères-de-Luchon.**

Suresnes. *Town, Hauts-de-Seine.* The Medieval Latin name of the Paris suburb was *Soresnae*, *Surisnae*, or *Syrenae*, of unknown origin. The final *-na*, together with the fact that these names are plural, suggests a possible river name. Suresnes is actually on the Seine.

Surgères. *Town, Charente-Maritime.* The name may derive from the Roman personal name *Surbius* and the suffix *-aria*.

Sury-le-Comtal. *Town, Loire.* The name derives from the Roman personal name *Surius* and the associative suffix *-acum*. *Comtal* means "belonging to a count," and refers to the counts of Forez who made Sury their residence from the 11th century.

La Suze-sur-Sarthe. *Village, Sarthe.* The name was recorded in the 11th century as *Secusa*, from Gaulish *sego-*, "victory," "strength," and the Gaulish suffix *-usa*. The village is on the **Sarthe** River.

Le Syndicat. *Village, Vosges.* The village is referred to in a document of 1790 as the *communauté du Syndicat de Saint Amé*, from French *syndicat* in the sense "commune," from *syndic*, "head of a community." **Saint-Amé** is the adjacent village.

Le Taillan-Médoc. *Town, Gironde.* The suburb of Bordeaux derives its name from the Roman personal name *Autellius*, from *Autius*, and the suffix *-anum*. The initial *Au-* of the name was dropped when it was taken as French *au*, "at the." The second part of the name locates the town in the region of **Médoc.**

Tain-l'Hermitage. *Town, Drôme.* The name was recorded in the 4th century as *Tegna*, from the Roman personal name *Tennius*. The second part of the name, which gave that of a noted Rhône wine, refers to the nearby hill *Hermitage*, itself said to be so called from a ruin on its summit that was originally a hermit's cell. "The origin of the name Hermitage is not so much shrouded in mystery as obscured by many conflicting legends, most of them concerning a hermit, *ermite* in French" [Jancis Robinson, ed., *The Oxford Companion to Wine*, 1999].

Taizé. *Village, Saône-et-Loire.* The name derives from the Roman personal name *Tatius* and the associative suffix *-acum*.

Talange. *Town, Moselle.* The name derives from the Germanic personal name *Tatili* and the suffix *-ing*.

La Talaudière. *Town, Loire.* The suburb of Saint-Étienne probably derives its name from the personal name *Talaud*, from Germanic *tal*, "valley," and *wald*, "wood."

Talence. *Town, Gironde.* The suburb of Bordeaux has a name recorded in the 12th century as *Talencia*, from the Roman personal name *Tallentius*.

Talmont-Saint-Hilaire. *Town, Vendée.* The name was recorded in the 11th century as *Talamun*, from pre-Indoeuropean *tala*, "earth," "clay," and a double suffix *-am* and *-one*. The second part of the name, from nearby *Saint-Hilaire-de-Talmont*, dedicated to *St. Hilary*, 4th-century bishop of Poitiers, distinguishes this Talmont from *Talmont-sur-Gironde*, Charente-Maritime, on the **Gironde** estuary.

Tancarville. *Village, Seine-Maritime.* The name derives from the Germanic personal name *Thancwar* and Latin *villa*, "estate."

Taninges. *Village, Haute-Savoie*. The name derives from the Roman personal name *Tannius* and the suffix *-anicum*.

Tarare. *Town, Rhône*. The name was recorded in the 11th century as *Taradrum*, from the Gaulish personal name *Taros* and *duron*, "fort."

Tarascon. *Town, Bouches-du-Rhône*. The name was recorded in the 4th century as *Tarasco, Tarasconis*, perhaps from pre-Indoeuropean *tar*, "rock," "stone," and the double suffix *-asc* and *-on*, or more likely from the *Taruscans*, the tribe who founded the place, as well as *Tarascon-sur-Ariège*, Ariège, and *Tarragona* in Spain. The tribal name is probably related to that of the *Etruscans*.

Tarascon-sur-Ariège *see* **Tarascon**

Tarbes. *City, Hautes-Pyrénées*. The city was recorded in the 4th century as *Turba*, a Latin form of an Aquitanian name related to that of the tribe known as the *Tarbelles*.

Tarn. *Department, southern France*. The name is that of the river here, known to the Romans as *Tarnis*, perhaps from Indoeuropean *tar*, "rapid water," or else from Gaulish *taranus*, "storm," referring to the same noisy stream. The Tarn flows through many gorges.

Tarn-et-Garonne. *Department, southwestern France*. The department takes its name from two of its main rivers, the **Tarn** joining the **Garonne** below Moissac.

Tarquimpol. *Village, Moselle*. The name was recorded in the 4th century as *Decem pagi*, from Latin *decem*, "ten," and *pagus*, "village."

Tartas. *Village, Landes*. The name, recorded as now in the 11th century, derives from the Gaulish personal name *Tartos* and the associative suffix *-acum*.

Tassin-la-Demi-Lune. *Town, Rhône*. The suburb of Lyon derives its name from the Roman personal name *Tattius* or *Tas-*

cius and the suffix *-anum*. The addition refers to a historic fort here built as a *demi-lune* or ravelin (defined by *Webster* as "a detached work … consisting of two embankments forming a salient angle in front of the curtain of the fortified position").

Tavaux. *Town, Jura*. The name probably derives from Gaulish *tauo-*, "quiet," a river name, and the suffix *-ellum*.

Taverny. *Town, Val-d'Oise*. The name derives from Latin *taberna*, "shop," "peasant dwelling," and the associative suffix *-acum*.

Le Teich. *Village, Gironde*. The name probably represents Latin *tectum*, Old Provençal *tech*, "roof," "house," rather than Latin *taxus*, Gascon *tech*, "yew."

Le Teil. *Town, Ardèche*. The name derives from Latin *tilium*, a form of *tilia*, Old French *til*, "lime," "linden."

Templemars. *Village, Nord*. The suburb of Lille is generally held to have a name meaning "temple of Mars," from Latin *templum*, "temple," and the Roman war god *Mars*. But it may actually be based on a derivative of pre-Indoeuropean *tapp*, "mound of earth."

Templeuve. *Town, Nord*. The name is usually said to derive from Latin *templum*, "temple," denoting a former shrine, and the pre-Latin suffix *-ova*. But, like **Templemars**, it may really represent a derivative of pre-Indoeuropean *tapp*, "mound of earth," and this suffix.

Tence. *Village, Haute-Loire*. The name derives from the Gaulish personal name *Tincius*.

Tende. *Village, Alpes-Maritimes*. The name was recorded in the 11th century as *Tenda*, from Latin *tenda*, "tent," "dwelling place," "village."

Tergnier. *Town, Aisne*. The name was recorded in the 13th century as *Terniacum*, probably from the Gaulish personal name *Tarinus* and the associative suffix *-iacum*, with a subsequent alteration of the final element.

Terrasson-Lavilledieu. *Town, Dordogne.* The first part of the name derives from French *terrasse*, "terrace," "overhanging ground," and the suffix *-onem*. The second half derives from Latin *villa Dei*, "village of God."

Territoire de Belfort *see* **Belfort**

Terville. *Town, Moselle.* The suburb of Thionville derives its name from the Germanic personal name *Darb* and French *ville*, "town."

Tessy-sur-Vire. *Village, Manche.* The village, on the **Vire** River, has a name recorded in the 6th century as *Teudeciaco villa*, from the Roman personal name *Teudicius* and the associative suffix *-acum*.

La Teste-de-Buch. *Resort town, Gironde.* The suburb of Arcachon derives its name from Latin *testa*, "head," "forward part," describing the town's location on the southern shore of the Arcachon Basin. The town added the name of the celebrated lordship of *Buch* in 1994.

Téteghem. *Town, Nord.* The suburb of Dunkerque derives its name from the Germanic personal name *Tatto* and an element corresponding to the *-ingham* of many English names, such as *Birmingham*, meaning "homestead of the family or followers of [the named person]."

Thann. *Town, Haut-Rhin.* The name was recorded in the 10th century as *Danne*, from the Germanic personal name *Tanna*, "fir."

Thaon-les-Vosges. *Town, Vosges.* The name may derive from the Germanic personal name *Tato*. The second part of the name locates the town in the (lee of the) **Vosges** Mountains.

Theix. *Town, Morbihan.* The Brittany town may derive its name from that of a Breton saint, *Taicus*.

Thenailles. *Village, Aisne.* The name derives from Low Latin *telonia*, from Greek *telonion*, "tollhouse," "custom house," here meaning a place where a feudal tax had to be paid. The present form of the name has been influenced by French *tenailles*, "tongs," "pincers."

Thérouanne. *Village, Pas-de-Calais.* The name was recorded in the 2d century as *Tarouanoi*, from the Gaulish personal name or god name *Tarvo* ("bull") and the suffix *-enna*.

Thiais. *Town, Val-de-Marne.* The Paris suburb derives its name from the Germanic personal name *Theodasius*, a masculine form of *Theodasia*.

Thiant. *Village, Nord.* The name derives from the Germanic personal name *Theudo*, which also gave the name of **Thionville**.

Thiaucourt-Regniéville. *Village, Meurthe-et-Moselle.* The name combines two formerly distinct places. *Thiaucourt* derives its name from the Germanic personal name *Theald* and Latin *cortem*, accusative of *cors*, "estate." *Regniéville* has French *ville*, "village," added to the original name, from the Germanic personal name *Ragino* (rather than Gallo-Germanic *Renius*) and the associative suffix *-acum*.

Thiérache. *Region, northern France.* The name was recorded in the 9th century as *Terascia*, from Ligurian *Teorasca*, of unknown meaning, with the Ligurian suffix *-asca*.

Thiers. *Town, Puy-de-Dôme.* The name was recorded in the 6th century as *Tigernum*, probably from the Gaulish personal name *Tigernos*.

Thierville-sur-Meuse. *Town, Meuse.* The suburb of Verdun, on the **Meuse** River, derives its name from the Germanic personal name *Theudhari* and Latin *villa*, "estate."

Le Thillot. *Town, Vosges.* The name derives from Latin *tilium*, a form of *tilia*, Old

French *til*, "lime," "linden," and the diminutive suffix *-ottum*.

Thionville. *City, Moselle.* The name derives from the Germanic personal name *Theudo* (from *theud*, "people") and Latin *villa*, "estate." The town was in German hands from 1871 through 1919 with the name *Diedenhofen*, from the same personal name but with Germanic *hof*, "farm," "estate."

Thiverval-Grignon. *Village, Yvelines.* The first part of the name derives from the Germanic personal name *Thiotwar* and Latin *vallis*, "valley." The second part derives from the Roman personal name *Grinius*, a variant of *Granius*, and the suffix *-onem*.

Thiviers. *Village, Dordogne.* The name derives from the Roman personal name *Tiberius*.

Thizy. *Village, Rhône.* The name derives from the Roman personal name *Titius* and the associative suffix *-acum*.

Thoiry. *Village, Yvelines.* The name derives from the Roman personal name *Taurius* or *Torius* and the associative suffix *-acum*.

Thoissey. *Village, Ain.* The name derives from the Roman personal name *Tuscius* or *Tossius* and the associative suffix *-acum*.

Thomery. *Village, Seine-et-Marne.* The name probably derives from the Gaulish personal name *Talomaros* and the associative suffix *-acum*.

Thonon-les-Bains. *Resort town, Haute-Savoie.* The name was recorded in the 12th century as *Thonuns*, and although a charter dated 929 mentions a *Villa Donona*, located in Chablais, it is not certain that this was the ancestor of Thonon. The name could be of Celtic origin, from a word meaning "town built on water," or derive from a Germanic word related to Old English *tūn*, modern *town*. The addition ("the baths") refers to the alkaline springs here.

Le Thor. *Town, Vaucluse.* The name derives from Latin *torus*, "height."

Thorens-Glières. *Village, Haute-Savoie.* The first part of the name may derive from Latin *torus*, "height," and the pre-Latin suffix *-incum*. The second part is a local mountain name.

Thorigny-sur-Marne. *Town, Marne.* The name derives from the Roman personal name *Taurinius* or *Torinius* and the associative suffix *-acum*. The town is on the **Marne** River.

Le Thoronet. *Village, Var.* The name derives from Old Provençal *toron*, "gushing spring," and the diminutive suffix *-ettum*.

Thouarcé. *Village, Maine-et-Loire.* The name derives from a personal name of uncertain origin, perhaps Germanic *Toawart*, and the associative suffix *-iacum*.

Thouaré-sur-Loire. *Town, Loire-Atlantique.* The name derives from the Roman personal name *Taurius* or *Torius* and the associative suffix *-acum*. The town is on the **Loire** River.

Thouars. *Town, Deux-Sèvres.* The name was recorded in the 8th century as *Toarcis*, from the *Thouet* River here, its own name deriving from Gaulish *tauo-*, "quiet," "peaceful."

Thourotte. *Town, Oise.* The name derives from Latin *turris*, "tower," "castle," and the suffix *-otta*.

Thuir. *Town, Pyrénées-Orientales.* The name may derive from the Roman personal name *Turius*.

Thury-Harcourt. *Resort village, Calvados.* Local legend derives the first part of this name from French *Thor, Aïc!* , "Help us, Thor!", an appeal to the Scandinavian thunder god, but in fact it represents the Roman personal name *Taurius* or *Torius*. The second part is the name of the local lord Henri de *Harcourt*, raised to the rank of duke by Louis XIV in 1700.

Tiercé. *Village, Maine-et-Loire.* The

name derives from the Roman personal name *Tessius* and the associative suffix *-acum*.

Tignes. *Village, Savoie.* The name comes from the Roman personal name *Tinius* or from a pre-Latin river root that also gave the name of the *Tinée* River, Alpes-Maritimes.

Tignieu-Jameyzieu. *Town, Isère.* The first part of the name derives from the Roman personal name *Tennius* or *Tineius* and the associative suffix *-acum*. The second part derives from the Gaulish personal name *Gematius* and the same suffix.

Tinchebray. *Village, Orne.* The name derives from Old French *tenerge*, "dark," and *brai*, Gaulish *bracos*, "mud," "marsh," describing the terrain here.

Tinténiac. *Village, Ille-et-Vilaine.* The name derives from the Roman personal name *Tintinius* and the associative suffix *-acum*.

Tirepied. *Village, Manche.* The name derives from French *tirer*, "to pull," and *pied*, "foot," meaning a place with a steep ascent. Tirepied is on a hilly road between Avranches and Brécey.

Tombebœuf. *Village, Lot-et-Garonne.* The name derives from French *tomber*, "to fell," and *bœuf*, "ox," denoting an abattoir.

Tomblaine. *Town, Meurthe-et-Moselle.* The suburb of Nancy derives its name from the root of Latin *tumulus*, "tumulus," "burial mound," and the diminutive suffix *-eline*.

Tonnay-Charente. *Town, Charente-Maritime.* The name derives from the Gaulish personal name *Talenus* and the associative suffix *-acum*. The town lies on the **Charente** River.

Tonneins. *Town, Lot-et-Garonne.* The name derives from the Germanic personal name *Tunno* and the suffix *-ing*.

Tonnerre. *Town, Yonne.* The name was recorded in the 4th century as *Ternodurum*, from the Gaulish personal name *Torno* and *duron*, "fort."

Torcy. *Town, Seine-et-Marne.* The Paris suburb derives its name from the Roman personal name *Torcius*, a variant of *Turcius*, and the associative suffix *-acum*.

Torigny-sur-Vire. *Village, Manche.* The village, near the **Vire** River, derives its name from the Roman personal name *Taurinius* or *Torinius* and the associative suffix *-acum*.

Le Torp-Mesnil. *Village, Seine-Maritime.* The name was recorded in the early 13th century as *Torp*, from Old Norse *thorp*, "farmstead." The second part of the name, from Latin *mansionile*, "peasant dwelling with a plot of land," was then added to this as a "translation."

Toucy. *Village, Yonne.* The name derives from the Roman personal name *Toccius* and the associative suffix *-acum*.

Toufflers. *Village, Nord.* The name derives from Germanic *lar*, "clearing," and a first element of uncertain origin. It probably represents a Germanic personal name.

Toul. *Town, Meurthe-et-Moselle.* The name was recorded in the 1st century BC as *Tullum*, from Celtic *tol*, "mountain," "height." It was also known as *Civitas Leucorum*, from the Celtic tribal name *Leuces*, from Gaulish *leucos*, "bright," "shining."

Toulon. *City and port, Var.* The name was recorded in the 4th century as *Telo Martius*, from Celtic *tol*, "mountain," "height," or Ligurian *tol* or *tel*, "spring." Toulon is surrounded by fortified heights, and during the Revolution was known for a time as *Port-de-la-Montagne.*

Toulon-sur-Arroux. *Village, Saône-et-Loire.* The name shares the origin of **Toulon**, from which the village is distinguished by its location on the *Arroux* River.

Toulouse. *City, Haute-Garonne.* The name of the city was recorded by Caesar in the 1st century BC as *Tolosa*, perhaps from Celtic *tol*, "height," or of Iberian or Ligurian origin. Toulouse was the capital of the *Tectosages*, suggesting a possible connection between Celtic *tol* and Latin *tectum*, "roof."

Le Touquet. *Resort town, Pas-de-Calais.* The name is of pre-Latin origin from a word for a wood standing between areas of cleared land. The full name of the town and its airport is *Le Touquet-Paris-Plage*, implying a desirably fashionable beach (*plage*) for visitors from **Paris**.

Touraine. *Historic region, west central France.* The former province takes its name from its capital, **Tours**.

Tourch. *Village, Finistère.* The name may derive from Breton *tourc'h*, "boar."

Tourcoing. *City, Nord.* The name was recorded in the 11th century as *Torcoin*, from the Germanic personal name *Thorkun*.

La Tour-d'Aigues. *Village, Vaucluse.* The name was recorded in the 11th century as *Turris de Aquis*, from Latin *turris*, "tower," "castle," and the name of **Aix-en-Provence**.

La Tour-du-Pin. *Town, Isère.* The name was recorded in the 7th century as *Turris de Pinu*, Latin for "tower of the pine."

Tourlaville. *Town, Manche.* The suburb of Cherbourg derives its name from the Scandinavian personal name *Thorlakr* and Latin *villa*, "estate."

Tournan-en-Brie. *Town, Seine-et-Marne.* The name derives from the Gaulish personal name *Turnus*, or pre-Latin *turno*, "height," and Gaulish *magos*, "market." The town lies in the region of **Brie**.

Tournefeuille. *Town, Haute-Garonne.* The suburb of Toulouse derives its name from French *tourne feuille*, "turn (a) leaf," perhaps denoting an occupation of some kind.

Tournon-sur-Rhône. *Town, Ardèche.* The name was recorded in the 12th century as *Tornonis*, perhaps from the Gaulish personal name *Turnus*, or from pre-Latin *turno*, "height." The town is on the **Rhône** River.

Tournus. *Town, Saône-et-Loire.* The name was recorded in the 4th century as *Tinurtium*, of unknown origin.

Tourouvre. *Village, Orne.* The name derives from Latin *tortus*, "twisted," and *robur*, "oak."

Tours. *City, Indre-et-Loire.* The name was recorded in the 4th century as *Turones*, from the Gaulish tribe who had their capital here. Their own name may come from a Celtic word meaning "powerful." The earlier name, recorded in the 2d century, was *Caesarodunum*, from Julius *Caesar* and Gaulish *dunon*, "fort."

Tourves. *Village, Var.* The name derives from Latin *turribus*, the ablative (locative) plural form of *turris*, "tower," "castle."

Toury. *Village, Eure-et-Loir.* The name was recorded in the 11th century as *Thauriacus*, from the Roman personal name *Taurius* and the associative suffix *-acum*.

Toussaint. *Village, Seine-Maritime.* The name was recorded in the 14th century as *Omnes Sancti*, Latin for "All Saints," denoting the dedication of a church or chapel here.

Le Touvet. *Village, Isère.* The name derives from pre-Latin *tob*, "sloping ground," and the diminutive suffix *-ittum*.

Trainel. *Village, Aube.* The name was recorded in the 12th century as *Triangulum*, Latin for "triangle," to which the suffix *-ellum* was added. The reference is presumably to the location of the original settlement on a triangular piece of land.

Tramezaïgues. *Village, Hautes-Pyrénées.* The name derives from Latin *inter*, "between," *ambas*, "both," and *aquas*, "waters," referring to the location of the village between the Neste d'Aure and Rioumajou rivers.

La Tranche-sur-Mer. *Resort village, Vendée.* The name seems to represent French *tranche*, "slice," perhaps referring to the outline of the coast here.

Trans-en-Provence. *Town, Var.* The town, in **Provence**, has a name deriving from pre-Celtic *tr*, "height," and the double suffix *-ant* and *-ium*.

Trappes. *Town, Yvelines.* The name derives from French *trappe*, "trap," meaning one for birds or animals.

Trébeurden. *Resort village, Côtes-d'Armor.* The name of the Brittany village derives from *trev*, "parish," and a second element of unknown origin.

Treffort. *Village, Isère.* The name derives from Latin *trans*, "across," "beyond," and *fortis*, "fort."

Tréfols. *Village, Marne.* The name derives from Latin *tres*, "three," and *fagus*, "beech."

Trégastel. *Resort village, Côtes-d'Armor.* The Brittany resort derives its name from Breton *trev*, "parish," and Latin *castellum*, "castle."

Trégueux. *Town, Côtes-d'Armor.* The suburb of Saint-Brieuc derives its name from Breton *trev*, "parish," and an element of uncertain origin.

Tréguier. *Town, Côtes-d'Armor.* The Brittany town has the Breton name *Tregêr*, from *trev*, "parish," and *kêr*, mutated as *gêr*, "house."

Trégunc. *Resort town, Finistère.* The Brittany town derives its name from Breton *trev*, "parish," and *konk*, "angle," "corner."

Treignac. *Village, Corrèze.* The name derives from the Roman personal name *Trinius* and the associative suffix *-acum*.

Treillières. *Town, Loire-Atlantique.* The name derives from Latin *trichila*, "bower," "arbor," and the suffix *-aria*.

Treize-Septiers. *Village, Vendée.* The name probably derives from French *treize*, "thirteen," and *setiers*, from Latin *sextarius*, "sixth part (of a given measure)," here applied to an area of sowing.

Treize-Vents. *Village, Vendée.* The name is French for "thirteen winds," denoting an exposed location.

Trélázé. *Town, Maine-et-Loire.* The name probably derives from the Roman personal name *Trelasius*, from *Trellius*, and the associative suffix *-acum*.

La Tremblade. *Town, Charente-Maritime.* The name derives from Latin *tremulus*, "aspen," and the suffix *-ata*.

Tremblay-en-France. *Town, Seine-Saint-Denis.* The Paris suburb derives its name from Latin *tremulus*, "aspen," and the collective suffix *-etum*. The addition to the name refers to the local region of *France*, so called before the name was applied to the country as a whole.

Le Tréport. *Resort town, Seine-Maritime.* The name of the once thriving port derives from Latin *trans*, "across," and *portus*, "port," meaning a port opposite Mers-les-Bains at the mouth of the Bresle River.

Trets. *Town, Bouches-du-Rhône.* The name probably derives from pre-Indoeuropean *tr*, "height," and the double suffix *-itt* and *-ium* rather than a Roman personal name *Trittius*, from *Tritus*.

Le Triadou. *Village, Hérault.* The name was recorded in the 12th century as *Triatorium*, a term for a rectangular enclosure where ewes are sorted (French *trier*) and counted.

Tricastin. *Region, southern France.* The region, beside the Rhône River, is known by the adjectival form of the name of its historic capital, **St-Paul-Trois-Châteaux.**

Triel-sur-Seine. *Town, Yvelines.* The name originates from a derivative of Frankish *thresk*, "fallow land." The town is on the **Seine** River.

Trignac. *Town, Loire-Atlantique.* The name derives from the Roman personal name *Trinius* and the associative suffix *-acum*.

Trilport. *Village, Seine-et-Marne.* The name was recorded in the 13th century as *Tria portus*, from Frankish *thresk*, "fallow land," and Latin *portus*, "port," "shelter." Trilport is on the Marne River opposite Meaux.

La Trinité. *Town, Alpes-Maritimes.* The suburb of Nice derives its name from a dedication to the Holy Trinity.

La Trinité-sur-Mer. *Resort village and port, Morbihan*. The name derives from a dedication to the Holy Trinity. The Brittany resort is "on sea" by the Bay of Biscay.

La Trinité-Victor. *Village, Alpes-Maritimes*. The village, with a church dedicated to the Holy Trinity, was erected into a commune in 1818 by *Victor*-Emmanuel I (1759–1824), king of Sardinia. The settlement is now usually known as simply *La Trinité*.

Trith-Saint-Léger. *Town, Nord*. The first part of the name derives from Latin *trajectus*, "crossing," meaning a terrain crossed by a stream or river, here the Escaut (Scheldt). The second part of the name is a dedication to *St. Leger*, 7th-century bishop of Saintes.

Troarn. *Village, Calvados*. The name blends the Germanic personal names *Truhthard* and *Droctarn*, a father and son mentioned in the *Polyptique* of the abbé Irminon, a 9th-century survey of the estates held by the abbey at Saint-Germain-des-Prés.

Les Trois-Évêchés. *Historic region, eastern France*. The name means "the three bishoprics," referring to the self-governing towns of Metz, Toul, and Verdun in the historic duchy of Lorraine. Their independent government was not abolished until the Revolution.

Les Trois-Vallées. *Region, southeastern France*. The region, an upland area in the Alps of Savoy, has a name meaning "the three valleys," meaning the side valleys of the main valley of the Isère River.

La Tronche. *Town, Isère*. The suburb of Grenoble derives its name from Latin *truncus*, "(tree) trunk," meaning a wood.

Tronville-en-Barrois. *Village, Meuse*. The name derives from the Germanic personal name *Trudo* and Latin *villa*, "estate." The village lies in the region of **Barrois**.

Trouville-sur-Mer. *Resort town, Calvados*. The name was recorded in the 13th century as *Torouvilla*, from the Scandinavian personal name *Thorulf* and Latin *villa*, "estate."

Troyes. *City, Aube*. The name was recorded in the 4th century as *civitas Tricassium*, from Latin *civitas*, "city," and the Gaulish tribe *Tricasses*, whose own name means "those with three tresses," from Gaulish *tri-*, "three," and *-casses*, "hair." (The name evokes Cúchulainn, the great hero of Irish legend, whose hair was of three colors: brown at the roots, blood-red in the middle, and blond at the crown.) The city's earlier name, recorded in the 2d century, was *Augustobona*, from the name of the emperor *Augustus* and Gaulish *bona*, "foundation." The present form of the name may have been influenced by that of the ancient city of *Troy*, known in French as *Troie*.

Tulle. *Town, Corrèze*. The name was recorded in the 10th century as *Tutelae*, from the Roman god name *Tutela*.

Tullins. *Town, Isère*. The name derives from the Roman personal name *Tullius* and the suffix *-anum*.

La Turbie. *Village, Alpes-Maritimes*. Ptolemy recorded the name in the 2d century in the Greek form *tropaia Sebastou*, from *tropaion*, "trophy," and *Sebastos*, the Greek name of the Roman emperor Augustus, who built a monument here in 6 BC to commemorate his subjugation of the local hill tribes.

Turckheim. *Village, Haut-Rhin*. The name derives from the Germanic personal name *Thuring* and *heim*, "abode." The German form of the name is *Türkheim*.

Ucciani. *Village, Corse-du-Sud*. The village, in central Corsica, derives its name from the Roman personal name *Uccius* and the suffix *-anum*.

Uckange. *Town, Moselle*. The name derives from the Germanic personal name *Ucho*, a variant of *Hugo*, and the suffix *-ingen*. The German form of the name is *Uckingen*.

Ueberstrass. *Village, Haut-Rhin*. The

name derives from Germanic *über*, "over," and *strass*, "road," denoting the location of the village the other side of a Roman road.

Ugine. *Town, Savoie.* The name represents a diminutive form of Savoyard *ougia*, a derivative of Latin *alveus*, "cavity," "watercourse."

Unias. *Village, Loire.* The name derives from Latin *unitas*, "unity," denoting a village formed by a union of hamlets, as at *L'Union* (see **Union, L'**).

Unieux. *Town, Loire.* The name derives from the Germanic personal name *Huno* and the associative suffix *-iacum*.

L'Union. *Town, Haute-Garonne.* The two communities of Le Cornaudric and Belbèze, forming a single parish, originally occupied the present territory of Saint-Jean and L'Union. In 1790 the Directoire ordered them to unite, which they initially did under the dedication name *Saint-Jean-de-Kyrie-Eleison*, the second part of this representing the Greek invocation in the Mass meaning "Lord, have mercy." This was soon altered to a simpler and more logical *L'Union*. Two other communities later united to form the present nearby Saint-Jean.

Urdos. *Village, Pyrénées-Atlantiques.* The name has its origin in the Gallo-Roman personal name *Urdo* and the Aquitanian suffix *-ossu*.

Ushant *see* **Ouessant**

Ussel. *Town, Corrèze.* The name derives from Gaulish *uxellos*, "high," "elevated." The town lies in the Massif Central on the slopes of the Millevaches Plateau.

Ustaritz. *Town, Pyrénées-Atlantiques.* The name derives from Basque *uste*, "empty space," "plain," and *haritz* "oak."

Utelle. *Village, Alpes-Maritimes.* The name is from pre-Celtic *ut*, of uncertain meaning (probably "height"), and the Ligurian suffix *-elu*. Utelle is on a hillside.

Uzerche. *Town, Corrèze.* The name was recorded in the 9th century as *Usercensium*, probably from pre-Celtic *uc*, "height," and an element *erica*. The town stands on a height above the gorge of the Vézère River.

Uzès. *Town, Gard.* The name was recorded in the 6th century as *Ucetia*, probably from pre-Celtic *uc*, "height," and a suffix *-etium*.

Vagney. *Village, Vosges.* The name derives from the Germanic personal name *Walo* (from *valah*, "foreigner") and the double suffix *-in* and *-iacum*.

Vailly-sur-Aisne. *Village, Aisne.* The name derives from the Germanic personal name *Wazili* and the associative suffix *-iacum*. The village lies on the (canalized) **Aisne** River.

Vaires-sur-Marne. *Town, Seine-et-Marne.* The name derives from Gaulish *uerna*, "alder." The town is on the (canalized) **Marne** River.

Vaison-la-Romaine. *Town, Vaucluse.* The name, recorded in the 2d century as *Vasio*, represents pre-Celtic *vas*, "spring," and the suffix *-io*. The town arose on the site of a Roman resort. Hence the second part of the name.

Valbonne. *Town, Alpes-Maritimes.* The name derives from Latin *vallis*, "valley," and *bona*, "good," meaning one with good pasture or the like.

Valdahon. *Town, Doubs.* The name derives from Germanic *wald*, "forest," and the personal name *Hago*.

Le Val-d'Ajol. *Town, Vosges.* The name derives from Latin *vallis*, "valley," and the region of *L'Ajol* here.

Val-de-Marne. *Department, north central France.* The department, created in 1964, has a name meaning "valley of the Marne," describing its inclusion of the lower **Marne** River.

Val-d'Isère. *Resort village, Savoie.* The name means "valley of the Isère," describing the location of the village near the headwaters of the **Isère** River.

Valdoie. *Town, Belfort.* The name derives from Latin *vadum*, "ford," and Germanic *ahwjo*, "watery," the latter giving the name of the *Oie* River here.

Val-d'Oise. *Department, north central France.* The department, created in 1964, has a name meaning "valley of the Oise," describing its inclusion of the lower **Oise** River.

Valençay. *Town, Indre.* The name was recorded in the 12th century as *Valentiacum*, from the Roman personal name *Valentius* and the associative suffix *-acum*.

Valence. *City, Drôme.* The name was recorded in the 1st century as *Valentia*, from the Roman personal name *Valentius*.

Valenciennes. *Town, Nord.* The name was recorded in the 8th century as *Valentianas*, from *Valentinianae*, from the name of the Roman emperor *Valentinian* (321–375).

Valensole. *Village, Alpes-de-Haute-Provence.* The name was recorded in the 10th century as *Valentiola*, representing a diminutive form of the name of **Valence**.

Valentigney. *Town, Doubs.* The name derives from the Roman personal name *Valentinius* and the associative suffix *-acum*.

Valentine. *Village, Haute-Garonne.* The name probably derives from the Roman personal name *Valens*, *Valentis* and the suffix *-inum*, although according to August Longnan, in *Les Noms de lieu de la France* (1929), the name could represent one of the forms under which **Valenciennes** was mentioned in *Garin de Loherain*, a medieval *chanson de geste*.

Valenton. *Town, Val-de-Marne.* The name derives from the Roman personal name *Valens*, *Valentis* and the suffix *-one*.

La Valette-du-Var. *Town, Var.* The suburb of Toulon derives its name from Latin *vallis*, "valley," and the diminutive suffix *-ittum*. The addition relates to the **Var** department.

Vallauris. *Town, Alpes-Maritimes.* The name was recorded in the 11th century as *Vallauria* or *Vallis Aurea*, Latin for "golden valley," referring to the fertile land here. See also **Orvault**.

Valleroy. *Village, Meurthe-et-Moselle.* The name derives from Latin *vallis*, "valley," and the double suffix *-ar* and *-etum*.

Vallet. *Town, Loire-Atlantique.* The name derives from Latin *vallis*, "valley," and the diminutive suffix *-ittum*.

Valloire. *Resort village, Savoie.* The name was recorded in the 11th century as *Valle Aurea*, from Latin *vallis*, "valley," and *aurea*, "golden," as for **Vallauris**.

Vallon-Pont-d'Arc. *Village, Ardèche.* The first part of the name derives from Latin *vallis*, "valley," and the suffix *-one*. The second part refers to the *Pont d'Arc*, "arched bridge," a huge natural archway just below the village over the Ardèche River.

Vallorcine. *Resort hamlet, Haute-Savoie.* The name derives from Latin *vallis*, "valley," and Latin *ursina*, "of the bears."

Vallouise. *Village, Hautes-Alpes.* The name was originally *Vallis*, Latin for "valley." In 1480 the name of *Louis* XI (1423–1483) was added.

Valmy. *Village, Marne.* The name was recorded in the 12th century as *Walesmeium*, from the Germanic personal name *Walismus* and the associative suffix *-iacum*.

Valognes. *Town, Manche.* The name was recorded in the 11th century as *Valaugias*, possibly from Latin *vallis*, "valley," the Gaulish tribal name *Alauni*, and the suffix *-ia*. The tribal name derives from Gaulish *alaunos*, "wanderer," describing a nomadic people.

Valois. *Historic region, northern France.* The region was known in the 8th century as *pagus Vadensis*, from Latin *pagus*, "land," "country," and possibly *vadum*, "ford." The royal house of *Valois*, reigning from 1328 through 1589, took their name from the region.

Valras-Plage. *Resort town and port, Hérault*. The name derives from the Roman personal name *Valerus* and the suffix *-anum* (with a silent *n*). Valras has a long sandy beach (*plage*).

Valréas. *Town, Vaucluse*. The name was recorded in the 12th century as *Valleriaz*, from the Roman personal name *Valerius* and the associative suffix *-iacum*.

Vals-les-Bains. *Resort town, Ardèche*. The name derives from a plural form of Latin *vallis*, "valley." The town is a spa with a thermal establishment. Hence the addition ("the baths").

Vals-près-le-Puy. *Village, Haute-Loire*. The village was originally simply *Vallis*, Latin for "valley." Its addition locates it near (*près*) Le Puy (see **Puy, Le**), of which it is now a suburb.

Vanault-les-Dames. *Village, Marne*. The name derives from the Germanic personal name *Wazo*, *Wazone* and the Gaulish suffix *-avum*. The addition ("the ladies") refers to the nuns of St. Paul de Verdun.

Vandœuvre-lès-Nancy. *Town, Meurthe-et-Moselle*. The name was recorded in the 10th century as *Vindopera*, from Gaulish *uindos*, "white," or a personal name, and *briga*, "height." The addition locates the town near (*lès*) **Nancy**, of which it is now actually a suburb.

Vannes. *Town, Morbihan*. The Brittany town has the Breton name *Gwened*, recorded in the 4th century as *Benetis* and in the 7th century as *Venetis*, from Gaulish *Veneto*, the name of a Celtic tribe, the *Veneti*, who had their capital here. Their own name comes from Gaulish *uenet-*, "related," "friendly." The town took their name in the 4th century, before which it was known as *Darioritum*, from the Gaulish personal name *Dario* and *ritu-*, "ford."

Vanoise. *Mountain massif, southeastern France*. The group of the Savoy Alps takes its name from the pre-Celtic root word *van*, "scatttered rocks."

Vanves. *Town, Hauts-de-Seine*. The name was recorded in the 10th century as *Venva*, of obscure origin.

Var. *Department, southeastern France*. The name is that of the river formerly here, recorded in the Latin form *Varus*. (The river was in the Grasse district, which in 1860 passed to Alpes-Maritimes. The department is thus named after a river that no long runs through it.) The origin of the river name is uncertain, although Indoeuropean *vara*, "current of water," or the river root *ar* have been suggested.

Varangéville. *Town, Meurthe-et-Moselle*. The name derives from the Germanic personal name *Warengar* and Latin *villa*, "village."

Varengeville-sur-Mer. *Resort village, Seine-Maritime*. The name has the same origin as that of **Varangéville**. The resort is (almost) "on sea" by the English Channel coast.

Varennes-en-Argonne. *Village, Meuse*. The name derives from pre-Latin *varenna*, "riverside wasteland," from Indoeuropean *vara*, "water," referring here to the Aire River. The village is in the region of **Argonne**.

Varennes-sur-Allier. *Town, Allier*. The name has the same origin as that of **Varennes-en-Argonne**, but here the river is the **Allier**.

Varennes-Vauzelles. *Town, Nièvre*. The town was formerly *Varennes-lès-Nevers*, with an origin as for **Varennes-en-Argonne** and an addition locating it near (*lès*) **Nevers**, of which it is now a suburb. The second part of the present name is that of another suburb.

Varilhes. *Village, Ariège*. The name derives from Latin *vallis*, "valley," and the suffix *-ilis*.

Vaucluse. *Department, southeastern France*. The name relates to the village of *Fontaine- de-Vaucluse*, east of Avignon, near which the Sorgue River (see **Sorgues**) emerges from a grotto in a "fountain." The village name was recorded in the 11th century as *Vallis Clusa*, Latin for "enclosed valley."

Vaucouleurs. *Village, Meuse.* The name derives from Latin *vallis*, "valley," and an element of uncertain origin and meaning.

Vaucresson. *Town, Hauts-de-Seine.* The name was recorded in the 11th century as *Vallis Crisonis*, from Latin *vallis*, "valley," and the Germanic personal name *Crisso*.

Vaugneray. *Village, Rhône.* The name was recorded in the 10th century as *Vallis Neriacensis*, from Latin *vallis*, "valley," followed by the Roman personal name *Nerius* and the associative suffix *-acum*.

Vaujours. *Town, Seine-Saint-Denis.* The Paris suburb derives its name from Latin *vallis*, "valley," and perhaps the Germanic personal name *Joco*.

Vaulx-en-Velin. *City, Rhône.* The suburb of Lyon, in the local district of *Velin*, derives its name from Latin *vallis*, "valley."

Vauréal. *Town, Val-d'Oise.* The suburb of Pontoise derives its name from Latin *vallis*, "valley," and *regalis*, "royal."

Vausseroux. *Village, Deux-Sèvres.* The name was recorded in the 12th century as *Vallis Sororum*, as if Latin for "valley of the sisters," referring to a nunnery. But the second part of the name is more likely to represent the personal name *Seroux*.

Vauvenargues. *Village, Bouches-du-Rhône.* The name derives from Latin *vallis*, "valley," followed by the Roman personal name *Veranus* and the suffix *-icum*.

Vauvert. *Town, Gard.* The name derives from Latin *vallis*, "valley," and *viridis*, "green."

Vaux-le-Pénil. *Town, Seine-et-Marne.* The suburb of Melun derives its name from Latin *vallis*, "valley," and an addition assimilated to French *pénil*, "mons pubis," referring to a mound here.

Vaux-sur-Seine. *Village, Yvelines.* The name derives from Latin *vallis*, "valley." The village lies by the **Seine** River.

Veauche. *Town, Loire.* The name is of uncertain origin.

Vedène. *Town, Vaucluse.* The name derives from pre-Celtic *ved*, of uncertain meaning (perhaps "height"), and the suffix *-ena*.

Velaux. *Town, Bouches-du-Rhône.* The name is of uncertain origin. It may derive from pre-Celtic *vel*, "height," and the Mediterranean suffix *-aur*, rather than from the Gaulish personal name *Vellavus*.

Velay. *Region, south central France.* The Medieval Latin name of the region was *Vellavum*, from the Gaulish tribe known as the *Vellavii*.

Vélizy-Villacoublay. *Town, Yvelines.* The Paris suburb derives the first part of its name from the Roman personal name *Velitius* and the associative suffix *-acum*. The second part derives from Latin *villa*, "village," and probably a personal name.

Venarey-les-Laumes. *Village, Côte-d'Or.* The first part of the name derives from the Roman personal name *Venerius* and the associative suffix *-acum*. The second part probably derives from pre-Latin *lamma*, "muddy place."

Vence. *Resort town, Alpes-Maritimes.* The name was recorded in the 2d century as *Ouintion*, perhaps from pre-Celtic *vin* or *vint*, "height." Vence lies on a rocky height between two ravines.

Vendée. *Department, western France.* The name is that of the river here, perhaps from Gaulish *uindos*, "white."

Vendeuvre-sur-Barse. *Village, Aube.* The name, recorded early as *Vindovera*, derives from Gaulish *uindos*, "white," or a personal name, and *ialon*, "field," "clearing." The village is on the *Barse* River.

Vendin-le-Vieil. *Town, Pas-de-Calais.* The name derives from the Germanic personal name *Windo* and the suffix *-oinium*.

The addition to the name ("the old") distinguishes the town from nearby *Vendin-lès-Béthune* (Vendin near **Béthune**).

Vendôme. *Town, Loir-et-Cher.* The name was recorded early as *Vindocino*, from Gaulish *uindos*, "white," and an element of unknown meaning.

Venelles. *Town, Bouches-du-Rhône.* The name derives from pre-Celtic *ven*, "mountain," or the Gaulish personal name *Venna*, and the Latin suffix *-ella*.

Vénissieux. *City, Rhône.* The name of the suburb of Lyon derives from the Roman personal name *Venicius* or *Venissius* and the associative suffix *-acum*.

Venosc. *Village, Isère.* The name derives from the Roman personal name *Vennus* and the suffix *-oscum*.

Ventoux, Mont. *Mountain, southeastern France.* The mountain, in the Maritime Alps, takes its name from pre-Celtic *vint*, as perhaps for **Vence**, and the suffix *-ur*.

Verberie. *Village, Oise.* The name probably derives from Gaulish *uerna*, "alder," and *briua*, "bridge." The village is on the Oise River.

Vercors. *Region, southeast France.* The limestone massif derives its name from the Gaulish personal name *Vertamacorius*, itself of tribal origin and meaning "armies of the peak" or "excellent armies," from Gaulish *uertamos*, "peak," "excellent," and *corios*, "army."

Verdon. *River, southeastern France.* The name was recorded in the 11th century as *Virdones*, from the root elements *var-d-one*, as for the **Gard**, with the Latin name influenced by *viridis*, "green."

Le Verdon-sur-Mer. *Village, Gironde.* The name derives from Latin *viridis*, "green," and the suffix *-onem*. The village is "on sea" at the mouth of the Gironde estuary.

Verdun. *Town, Meuse.* The name was recorded in the 4th century as *Virodunum*

or *Verodunum*, perhaps from the Gaulish personal name *Vero* and *dunon*, "fort."

Verdun-sur-Garonne. *Village, Tarn-et-Garonne.* The name has the same origin as **Verdun**. The addition locates the village on the **Garonne** River.

Verfeil. *Village, Haute-Garonne.* The name derives from Latin *viridis*, "green," and *folium*, "leaf," "wood."

Vergèze. *Village, Gard.* The name derives from the Gaulish personal name *Vergetius*, with Latin *villa*, "estate," understood.

Vermandois. *Region, northern France.* The region takes its name from the village of *Vermand*, Aisne, recorded in the 12th century as *Virmandus*, from the Gaulish tribe *Veromandui*, whose capital it was. (It was replaced in the Roman era by Saint-Quentin.) Their own name means "horse-like men" (perhaps in the sense "centaurs"), from Gaulish *uiros*, "man," related to Latin *vir*, "man," and *mandus*, "pony."

Vermelles. *Town, Pas-de-Calais.* The name is of uncertain origin. It may derive from Germanic *walm*, "boiling," referring to turbulent water, and the diminutive suffix *-ella*.

Vernet-les-Bains. *Resort village, Pyrénées-Orientales.* The name was recorded in the 9th century as *Verneto*, from Gaulish *uerna*, "alder," and the collective suffix *-etum*. The second part of the name ("the baths") refers to the hot sulfur springs here.

Verneuil-en-Halatte. *Village, Oise.* The name derives from Gaulish *uerna*, "alder," and *ialon*, "clearing." The addition locates the village in the Forest of *Halatte*.

Verneuil-sur-Avre. *Town, Eure.* The name has the same origin as that of **Verneuil-en-Halatte**. The addition locates the town on the *Avre* River.

Verneuil-sur-Seine. *Town, Yvelines.* The name has the same origin as that of **Verneuil-en-Halatte**. The addition locates the town on the **Seine** River.

Vernon. *Town, Eure.* The name was recorded in the 12th century as *Vernum*, perhaps from Gaulish *uerna*, "alder."

Vernouillet (1). *Town, Eure-et-Loir.* The original name of the settlement here, on the site of the present suburb of Dreux, was recorded in the 13th century as *Sanctus Sulpicius*, as for **Saint-Sulpice**. The present name is a diminutive form of the name of **Verneuil-sur-Avre**, some 20 miles to the west.

Vernouillet (2). *Town, Yvelines.* The town is adjacent to **Verneuil-sur-Seine** and its name is a diminutive form of that name.

Vernoux-en-Vivarais. *Village, Ardèche.* The name derives from Gaulish *uerna*, "alder," and the suffix *-osum*. The second part of the name locates the village in *Vivarais* (see **Viviers**).

La Verpillière. *Town, Isère.* The name derives from Latin *vulpicula*, "fox," the source of Old French *goupil* (replaced by modern French *renard*), and the suffix *-aria*.

Verquin. *Town, Pas-de-Calais.* The suburb of Béthune probably derives its name from the Germanic personal name *Werika* and the suffix *-ing*.

La Verrie. *Village, Vendée.* The name derives from Latin *vitraria*, from *vitrum*, "glass," and the suffix *-aria*.

La Verrière. *Town, Yvelines.* The name derives from Latin *vitraria*, from *vitrum*, "glass," and the suffi *-aria*.

Verrières-le-Buisson. *Town, Essonne.* The Paris suburb derives its name from Latin *vitraria*, from *vitrum*, "glass," and the suffix *-aria*. The addition represents *boscione*, a derivative of Low Latin *boscus*, "wood," here meaning a small group of trees (English *bosk*).

Versailles. *City, Yvelines.* The name was recorded in the 11th century as *Versaliae*. Various origins have been proposed for this, some more plausible than others, including: (1) Latin *versus*, "side," "slope," and the suffix *-alia*; (2) Latin *versum*, from *vertere*,

"to turn," and *alae*, "wings," from a former windmill here; (3) Medieval Latin *Versagium*, the name of a forest tax; (4) Old French *Val de Gallie*, "valley of Gaul," a name found on early documents. The place was gradually built up by French kings around a hunting lodge of Louis XIII.

Versailleux. *Village, Ain.* The name derives from Gaulish personal name *Vassalus* and the associative suffix *-iacum*, with the form of the name influenced by **Versailles**.

Ver-sur-Mer. *Resort village, Calvados.* The name derives from Gaulish *uerna*, "alder." The village is (almost) "on sea" by the English Channel.

Vertaizon. *Village, Puy-de-Dôme.* The name derives from pre-Celtic *vert*, of unknown meaning, and the double prefix *-asi* and *-onem*.

Vertou. *Town, Loire-Atlantique.* The suburb of Nantes has a name recorded in the 9th century as *Vertavus*, from pre-Celtic *vert*, of unknown meaning, and the Gaulish suffix *-avum*.

Vert-Saint-Denis. *Town, Seine-et-Marne.* The first part of the name derives from Gaulish *uerna*, "alder." The second part is as for **Saint-Denis**.

Vertus. *Village, Marne.* The name is said to derive from the Gaulish god *Virotutes*, later identified with Apollo. His own name means either "man of the people" or "true tribe," from Gaulish *uiros*, "man," "true," and *touta*, "tribe," "people."

Vervins. *Village, Aisne.* The name was recorded in the 3d century as *Verbinum*, of uncertain origin.

Verzy. *Village, Marne.* The name may derive from the Gallo-Roman personal name *Virisius*, from *Virius*, and the associative suffix *-acum*.

Vescemont. *Village, Belfort.* The name derives from the Germanic personal name *Wiso* and Latin *mons, montis*, "mountain" (or possibly from the Germanic personal name *Wizmund*).

Vescovato. *Village, Haute-Corse.* The village, in northeastern Corsica, takes its name from Latin *episcopatum*, "bishopric." Mgr. Pernice built a castle here in 1269 and the community remained a bishopric until 1569.

Vésines. *Village, Ain.* The village was originally known as *Aisne*, from the Germanic personal name *Anno* and the suffix *-iscum*. In 1790 it adopted the present name, from a feminine form of Latin *vicinium*, "hamlet," "village."

Le Vésinet. *Town, Yvelines.* The Paris suburb derives its name from a diminutive form of Latin *vicinium*, "hamlet," "village."

Vesoul. *Town, Haute-Saône.* The name was recorded in the 9th century as *Vesulium*, from pre-Celtic *ves*, "mountain," and the suffix *-ulum*. The town is built around the hill of La Motte, and that is the "mountain."

La Vespière. *Village, Calvados.* The name derives from Latin *vespa*, "wasp," and the suffix *-aria*. Presumably these insects were troublesome here.

Veules-les-Roses. *Resort village, Seine-Maritime.* The name derives from Old English *wella*, "spring." The village was originally known as *Veules-en-Caux*, from its location in the Pays de **Caux**, but in 1897 adopted its present name, for its rose garden.

Vexin. *Historic region, northern France.* The name was recorded in the 9th century as *pagus Valcassinus*, from Latin *pagus*, "land," "country," and the Gaulish tribe *Veliocasses* (see **Arcachon**).

Veynes. *Town, Hautes-Alpes.* The name shares the origin of **Vedène**.

Veyre-Monton. *Village, Puy-de-Dôme.* The first part of the name derives from that of the river here. The second is from Latin *mons*, "mountain," and the suffix *-onem*, referring to the height that overlooks the river.

Vézelay. *Village, Yonne.* The name was recorded in the 9th century as *Vidiliacus*, from the Roman personal name *Vitellius* and the associative suffix *-acum*.

Vézère. *River, south central France.* The name was recorded in the 9th century as *Visera*, from the river root *vis* or *ves* and the pre-Latin suffix *-ara*.

Vibraye. *Village, Sarthe.* The name derives from Latin *vicus*, "village," and the *Braye* River here.

Vic-en-Bigorre. *Town, Hautes-Pyrénées.* The town derives its name from Latin *vicus*, "village," with the addition locating it in *Bigorre* (see **Bagnères-de-Bigorre**).

Vichy. *Town, Allier.* The name is of uncertain origin. It may represent the Roman personal name *Vippius*, with the place name suffix *-acum*, or else derive from Latin *vicus calidus*, "warm village," referring to the hot springs here.

La Vicomté-sur-Rance. *Village, Côtes-d'Armor.* The name denotes land belonging to a viscount by the *Rance* River.

Vic-sur-Cère. *Village, Cantal.* The name derives from Latin *vicus*, "village." The addition locates the village on the *Cère* River.

Vidauban. *Town, Var.* The name derives from Latin *vitis alba*, Provençal *vidaubo*, "old man's beard," "traveler's joy" (the climbing plant *Clematis vitalba*).

Viefvillers. *Village, Oise.* The name derives from Latin *vetulus*, "old," and *villare*, "farmstead."

Le Vieil-Armand. *Mountain, eastern France.* The summit, in the Vosges Mountains, derives its name from French *vieil*, "old," and the French equivalent of *Hartmann* in the name of the nearby village of **Hartmannswiller**. The German name of the peak is thus *Hartmannswillerkopf*, with *Kopf*, "head."

Vienne (1). *Department, west central France.* The name is that of the river here, recorded in the 6th century as *Vingenna* by the Frankish prelate Gregory of Tours and as *Vigenna* by the Roman poet Fortunatus, perhaps from Indoeuropean *veg*, "damp," and the Gaulish suffix *-enna*.

Vienne (2). *Town, Isère.* The name was recorded by Caesar in the 1st century BC as *Vienna*, from a Gaulish name of unknown meaning. An origin in Indoeuropean *vindo*, "white," has been proposed.

Vierville-sur-Mer. *Resort village, Calvados.* The name derives from the Germanic personal name *Wighari* and Latin *villa*, "village." The resort is "on sea" by the English Channel.

Vierzon. *Town, Cher.* The name was recorded in the 9th century as *Virsio*, from the Roman personal name *Virisius*, from *Virius*, and the suffix *-one*.

Vieux. *Village, Calvados.* The name of the location was recorded in the 2d century as *Arigenus*. The present name, recorded in the 12th century as *Veiocae*, derives from the *Viducasses*, the Gaulish tribe whose capital it was. Their own name means "those with tree-like (i.e. unkempt) hair," from Gaulish *uidu-*, "tree," "wood," and *-casses*, "hair."

Vieux-Condé. *Town, Nord.* The town is "old" (*vieux*) and adjacent to **Condé-sur-l'Escaut.**

Vieux-Thann. *Village, Haut-Rhin.* The village is "old" (*vieux*) as a suburb of **Thann.**

Vif. *Town, Isère.* The name derives from Latin *vicus*, "village."

Le Vigan. *Town, Gard.* The name was recorded in the 11th century as *Vicanum*, from a pre-Latin name of unknown origin. The present form of the name was influenced by Latin *vicus*, "village."

Viggianello. *Village, Corse-du-Sud.* The village, in southwestern Corsica, derives its name from the region of *Viggiano* (from the Roman personal name *Vidius* and the suffix *-anum*) and the diminutive suffix *-ellum*.

Vignemale. *Mountain, southwestern France.* The highest peak in the French Pyrenees derives its name from the root

elements *vin* and *mala*, the latter meaning "mountain."

Vigneulles-lès-Hattonchâtel. *Village, Meuse.* The name derives from Latin *vinea*, "vineyard," and the suffix *-eola*. The village is near (*lès*) *Hattonchâtel*, from the Germanic personal name *Hatto* and Latin *castellum*, "castle."

Vigneux-de-Bretagne. *Town, Loire-Atlantique.* The name derives from Latin *vinea*, "vineyard" and (possibly) the suffix *-oc*. The village is in *Brittany* (**Bretagne**).

Vigneux-sur-Seine. *Town, Essonne.* The Paris suburb, on the **Seine** River, has a name recorded in the 6th century as *Vicus Novus*, Latin for "new village."

Vihiers. *Town, Maine-et-Loire.* The name derives from Latin *vivarium*, "vivarium," "piece of water where fish are kept."

Vijon. *Village, Indre.* The name derives from Latin *videre*, "to see," and the suffix *-onem*. Vijon lies at the foot of the highest summit in the department.

Vilaine. *River, northwestern France.* The name of the Brittany river was recorded in the 6th century by Gregory of Tours as *Vicinonia*, from a pre-Latin toot element of uncertain origin. The modern form of the name arose by the process known as dissimilation (the first *n* became *l* for distinction from the second one) and the influence of French *vilain*, "bad."

Village-Neuf. *Village, Haut-Rhin.* The village is on the left bank of the Rhine, here marking the border with Germany, and its name thus translates its German name of *Neudorf.*

Villaines-les-Rochers. *Village, Indre-et-Loire.* The name derives from Latin *villana*, from *villa*, "farmstead," "estate." The distinguishing addition means "the rocks."

Villandraut. *Village, Gironde.* The name derives from Latin *villa*, "estate," "village," and the Germanic personal name *Andrald*.

Villandry. *Village, Indre-et-Loire.* The

name derives from Latin *villa*, "estate," "village," and the Germanic personal name *Andric*.

Villard-Bonnot. *Town, Isère.* The name derives from Latin *villare*, "farmstead," "estate," and the Germanic personal name *Bonald*, that of the local lord.

Villard-de-Lans. *Resort town, Isère.* The first part of the name is as for **Villard-Bonnot.** The second locates the town near **Lans-en-Vercors.**

Villard-les-Dombes. *Village, Ain.* The first part of the name is as for **Villard-Bonnot.** The second locates the village in the local *Dombes* district.

Villarodin-Bourget. *Village, Savoie.* The first part of the name derives from Latin *villare*, "farmstead," "estate," and the Germanic personal name *Aldin*, that of the local lord. The second part is from Low Latin *burgus*, "fortified place," and the diminutive suffix *-ittum*.

Villars. *Town, Loire.* The name was recorded in the 12th century as *Vilarium*, from Latin *villare*, "farmstead," "estate."

Villebois-Lavalette. *Town, Charente.* The first part of the name derives from Latin *villa*, "estate," "village," and the Germanic personal name *Baudast*. The second part was added in 1622 in honor of the French admiral Jean-Louis de Nogaret de *La Valette*, duc d'Épernon (1554–1642), favorite of Henri III.

Villebon-sur-Yvette. *Town, Essonne.* The Paris suburb derives its name from Latin *villa*, "estate," "village," and the Germanic personal name *Abbo*, that of the lord here. The town is on the **Yvette** River.

Villecresnes. *Town, Val-de-Marne.* The name of the Paris suburb was recorded in the 12th century as *Villa Cranea*, from Latin *villa*, "estate," "village," and probably Old French *escrenne*, "hovel," "small cottage."

Ville-d'Avray. *Town, Hauts-de-Seine.* The name was recorded in the 12th century as *villa Davren*, from Latin *villa*, "estate,"

"village," and (probably) a Germanic personal name (perhaps *Davhring*).

Villedieu-les-Poêles. *Town, Manche.* The name represents Latin *villa Dei*, "village of God," denoting a religious community. The addition to the name, meaning "the frying pans," refers to the local manufacture of copper and aluminum kitchen utensils.

Villedieu-sur-Indre. *Village, Indre.* The name is as for **Villedieu-les-Poêles,** but here with an addition locating the village on the **Indre** River.

La Ville-du-Bois. *Town, Essonne.* The Paris suburb derives its name from Latin *villa*, "estate," "village," and an addition locating it by or in a wood (*bois*).

Villefontaine. *Town, Isère.* The name derives from Latin *villa*, "estate," "village," and *fontana*, "fountain," "spring."

Villefranche-de-Conflent. *Village, Pyrénées-Orientales.* The name was recorded in the 13th century as *Villafranca Confluentis*, from Latin *villa franca*, "free town," and the *Conflent* River here, its own name meaning "confluence." A "free town" is a settlement founded by a local lord, lay or religious, who grants exemption from feudal taxes to attract new residents.

Villefranche-de-Lauragais. *Village, Haute-Garonne.* The name is as for **Villefranche-de-Conflent,** but here with an addition locating the village in **Lauragais.**

Villefranche-de-Rouergue. *Town, Aveyron.* The name is as for **Villefranche-de-Conflent,** but here with an addition locating the town in **Rouergue.**

Villefranche-sur-Mer. *Resort town, Alpes-Maritimes.* The name is as for **Villefranche-de-Conflent,** but here with an addition locating the town "on sea" in the French Riviera.

Villefranche-sur-Saône. *Town, Rhône.* The name is as for **Villefranche-de-Conflent,** but here with an addition locating the town on the **Saône** River.

Villejuif. *City, Val-de-Marne.* The Paris suburb derives its name from Latin *villa*, "village," and *Judaeus*, "Jew," denoting a Jewish community.

Villemandeur. *Town, Loiret.* The name derives from Latin *villa*, "estate," "village," and an element of uncertain origin.

Villemaréchal. *Village, Seine-et-Marne.* The name derives from Latin *villa*, "estate," "village," and Old French *marchais*, "marsh." (The present form has been influenced by *maréchal*, "marshal.") The village lies at the source of a stream.

Villemoisson-sur-Orge. *Town, Essonne.* The name derives from Latin *villa*, "estate," "village," and a stream named after a place called *Moisson*, perhaps from the Roman personal name *Mustius* or *Muscius* and the suffix *-onem*. The town is on the **Orge** River.

Villemomble. *Town, Seine.* The Paris suburb derives its name from Latin *villa*, "estate," "village," and the Germanic personal name *Mummulus*, presumably that of a local lord.

Villemur-sur-Tarn. *Town, Haute-Garonne.* The name derives from Latin *villa*, "estate," "village," and *murus*, "wall." The town is on the **Tarn** River.

Villenauxe-la-Grande. *Village, Aube.* The name derives from the Gaulish personal name *Villoneos* or *Vellaunos* and the suffix *-issa*. The addition ("the great") contrasts the village with *Villenauxe-la-Petite*, Seine-et-Marne.

Villeneuve-d'Ascq. *City, Nord.* The suburb of Lille was created as a new town in 1970 by combining the existing suburbs of Annappes, Flers, and *Ascq*, the latter name deriving from Germanic *ask*, "ash tree." The "new town of Ascq" thus has a name patterned on the older *Villeneuve* names below.

Villeneuve-de-Berg. *Village, Ardèche.* The name derives from Latin *villa nova*, "new town," denoting a medieval settlement founded by a lord or religious community but without the tax concessions accorded to a *villa franca* (see **Villefranche-de-Conflent**). The addition derives from Germanic *berg*, "mountain."

Villeneuve-de-Marsan. *Village, Landes.* The name has an origin as for **Villeneuve-de-Berg**, but here with an addition from nearby **Mont-de-Marsan**.

Villeneuve-la-Garenne. *Town, Hauts-de-Seine.* The name of the Paris suburb has an origin as for **Villeneuve-de-Berg**, but here with an addition from Low Latin *warenna*, "warren," "game reserve."

Villeneuve-l'Archevêque. *Village, Yonne.* The has an origin as for **Villeneuve-de-Berg**, but here with an addition denoting a new town created by the archbishop (*archevêque*).

Villeneuve-le-Roi. *Town, Val-de-Marne.* The name has an origin as for **Villeneuve-de-Berg**, but here with an addition denoting a new town created by the king (*le roi*).

Villeneuve-lès-Avignon. *Town, Gard.* The name has an origin as for **Villeneuve-de-Berg**, but here with an addition locating the town near (*lès*) **Avignon**.

Villeneuve-lès-Béziers. *Village, Hérault.* The name has an origin as for **Villeneuve-de-Berg**, but here with an addition locating the village near (*lès*) **Béziers**, of which it is now a suburb.

Villeneuve-Loubet. *Resort town, Alpes-Maritimes.* The name has an origin as for **Villeneuve-de-Berg**, but here with an addition from nearby *Loubet*.

Villeneuve-Saint-Georges. *Town, Val-de-Marne.* The name has an origin as for **Villeneuve-de-Berg**, but here with an addition honoring *St. George*. (The 8th-century record of this name as *Villa Nova* is the earliest "new town" known.)

Villeneuve-sur-Lot. *Town, Lot-et-Garonne.* The name has an origin as for **Villeneuve-de-Berg**, but here with an addition locating the town on the **Lot** River.

Villeneuve-sur-Yonne. *Town, Yonne.* The name has an origin as for **Villeneuve-de-Berg**, but here with an addition locating the town on the **Yonne** River.

Villeneuve-Tolosane. *Town, Haute-Garonne.* The name has an origin as for **Villeneuve-de-Berg**, but here with an addition locating the town near **Toulouse**.

Villennes-sur-Seine. *Town, Yvelines.* The name derives from Latin *villana*, from *villa*, "farm," "estate." The addition locates the town on the **Seine** River.

Villenoy. *Village, Seine-et-Marne.* The suburb of Meaux derives its name from the Roman personal name *Villanius* and Gaulish *ialon*, "field," "clearing."

Villeparisis. *Town, Seine-et-Marne.* The Paris suburb derives its name from Latin *villa*, "farm," "estate," and *Parisis*, the name of the historic region centering on **Paris**.

Villepinte. *Town, Seine-Saint-Denis.* The Paris suburb derives its name from Latin *villa*, "farm," "estate," and *pincta*, "painted," referring to the variegated color of the soil or stones.

Villepreux. *Town, Yvelines.* The name derives from Latin *villa*, "farm," "estate," and *pira*, "pear," denoting a pear-tree orchard.

Villequier. *Village, Seine-Maritime.* The name derives from Latin *villa*, "farm," "estate," and *quadrum*, "corner." (This name was transferred in 1666 to *Villequiers*, Cher, formerly Montfaucon, through Louis d'Aumont, marquis of Villequier, and in 1774 to *Villequier-Aumont*, Aisne, formerly Genlis, when that place was raised to a dukedom.)

Villers-Bocage. *Village, Calvados.* The name derives from Low Latin *villare*, "farmstead," and the *Bocage Normand* (see **Bocage Angevin**) in which the village lies. The final *-s* of *Villers* and also **Villars** is hard to explain. It may have been added on an analogy with the ablative (locative) plural *-is* endings of Latin first and second declension nouns.

Villers-Bretonneux. *Village, Somme.* The name derives from Low Latin *villare*, "farmstead," and the *Breton* people who formerly inhabited this place (not itself in Brittany).

Villers-Cotterêts. *Resort town, Aisne.* The name derives from Low Latin *villare*, "farmstead," and an obscure element. It may represent a Germanic personal name *Godrest.*

Villers-en-Cauchie. *Village, Nord.* The name derives from Low Latin *villare*, "farmstead." The district name derives from Latin *calceata*, "causeway," referring to a Roman road from Cambrai to Bavay.

Villersexel. *Village, Haute-Saône.* The name derives from Low Latin *villare*, "farmstead," followed by the Germanic personal name *Saxo* and the suffix *-el.*

Villers-Guislain *see* **Villers-Outréaux**

Villers-le-Lac. *Resort town, Doubs.* The name derives from Low Latin *villare*, "farmstead," and *lacus*, "lake," referring to the Chaillexon Lake, a widening of the Doubs River nearby.

Villers-lès-Nancy. *Town, Meurthe-et-Moselle.* The name derives from Low Latin *villare*, "farmstead." The addition locates the town near (*lès*) **Nancy**, of which it is now actually a suburb.

Villers-le-Tilleul. *Village, Ardennes.* The name derives from Low Latin *villare*, "farmstead," and French *tilleul*, "lime tree." The name has been retained since the Revolution, when it replaced *Villers-le-Teigneux*, from *teigneux*, "rough," referring to the rugged terrain.

Villers-Outréaux. *Village, Nord.* The name derives from Low Latin *villare*, "farmstead." and Latin *ultra aquam*, "beyond the water." The village lies east of the Escaut (Scheldt) River, opposite *Villers-Guislain* (from the Germanic personal name *Gisila*), to the west of it.

Villers-Pol. *Village, Nord.* The name derives from Low Latin *villare*, "farmstead," and *Pol*, the name of the mayor, representing the bishop of Cambrai.

Villers-Saint-Paul. *Town, Oise*. The name derives from Low Latin *villare*, "farmstead," and a dedication to *St. Paul*.

Villers-Semeuse. *Village, Ardennes*. The suburb of Charleville-Mézières has a name recorded in the 13th century as *Villare ante Macerias*, from Low Latin *villare*, "farmstead," and Latin *ante*, "before," and *maceriae*, "ruins," meaning those of a Roman settlement. The village is on the Meuse River, leading to the present form of the name (as if *sur-Meuse*).

Villers-sur-Mer. *Resort village, Calvados*. The name derives from Low Latin *villare*, "farmstead." The village is "on sea" by the English Channel.

Villerupt. *Town, Meurthe-et-Moselle*. The name derives from Latin *villa*, "farm," "estate," and an element of uncertain origin. It may represent Latin *rivus*, "stream."

Ville-sous-la-Ferté. *Village, Aube*. The name derives from Latin *villa*, "farm," "estate," with an addition locating the village near (*sous*, "under") **Laferté-sur-Aube**.

Villetaneuse. *Town, Seine-Saint-Denis*. The Paris suburb derives its name from Latin *villa*, "farm," "estate," and French *teigneuse*, "rough," referring to the rugged terrain here.

La Villette see Appendix 4.

Villeurbanne. *City, Rhône*. The suburb of Lyon has a name recorded in the 9th century as *villa Orbana*, from Latin *villa*, "village," and either *urbana*, "urban," giving something of a tautology, or a feminine form of the Roman personal name *Urbanus*.

Villeveyrac. *Village, Hérault*. The name derives from Latin *villa*, "farm," "estate," and the placename *Veyrac*, from the Roman personal name *Varius* and the associative suffix *-acum*.

Villiers-Charlemagne. *Village, Mayenne*. The name derives from Low Latin *villare*, "farmstead," and the Germanic personal name *Karl*. The present form has been influenced by the name of the emperor *Charlemagne*.

Villiers-le-Bel. *Town, Val-d'Oise*. The Paris suburb derives its name from Low Latin *villare*, "farmstead," and the name of the tenant, as recorded in a text of 1094: *Villare ... unde solvuntur Rodulfo Bello XV denarios*, "A farm ... whence they are paid 15 denarii by Hrodwulf the Fair."

Villiers-le-Morhier. *Village, Eure-et-Loir*. The name derives from Low Latin *villare*, "farmstead," and the name of Philippe *Morhier*, who founded a chapel here in 1330.

Villiers-le-Roux. *Village, Charente*. The name was recorded in the 11th century as *villa Latronorum*, from Latin *villa*, "village," and *latro*, "robber." The present addition is not thus French *le roux*, "the red," but the equivalent of *larron*, "thief."

Villiers-sur-Marne. *Town, Val-de-Marne*. The name derives from Low Latin *villare*, "farmstead" and an addition locating the town on the **Marne** River.

Vimoutiers. *Town, Orne*. The name was recorded in the 11th century as *Vimonasterium*, from the *Vie* River here and Latin *monasterium*, "monastery."

Vimy. *Town, Pas-de-Calais*. The name probably derives from the Germanic personal name *Wimo* and the associative suffix *-iacum*. Nearby *Vimy Ridge* saw fierce trench warfare in World War I.

Vinay. *Village, Isère*. The name derives from Latin *vinetum*, "vineyard."

Vincennes. *City, Val-de-Marne*. The Paris suburb has a name recorded in the 9th century as *Vilcena*, perhaps from the Gaulish personal name *Vilicus*, a derivative of *Villo*, and the suffix *-enna*.

Vineuil. *Town, Loir-et-Cher*. The name derives from Latin *vinea*, "vineyard," and Gaulish *ialon*, "field."

Violaines. *Village, Pas-de-Calais*. The name derives from Latin *villana*, from *villa*, "farm," "estate."

Vire. *Town, Calvados*. The name was recorded in the 11th century as *Vira*, from the *Vire* River here, recorded in the 6th century as *Viria*, a name of the same origin as the **Var**.

Viriat. *Town, Ain*. The suburb of Bourg-en-Bresse derives its name from the Gallo-Roman personal name *Virius* and the associative suffix *-acum*.

Virieu-le-Grand. *Village, Ain*. The name has the same origin as that of **Viriat**. The village is "great" (*grand*) by comparison with *Viriat-le-Petit*, a few miles to the north.

Viroflay. *Town, Yvelines*. The suburb of Versailles has a name recorded in the 12th century as *villa Offleni*, from Latin *villa*, "estate," "village," and the Germanic personal name *Offlin*.

Viry-Châtillon. *Town, Essonne*. The first part of the name is as for **Viriat**. The second part derives from Latin *castellum*, "castle," and the suffix *-ionem*.

Viterbe. *Village, Tarn*. The name was adopted from the Italian town of *Viterbo* (French *Viterbe*).

Vitré. *Town, Ille-et-Vilaine*. The name derives from the Roman personal name *Victorius* and the associative suffix *-acum*.

Vitrolles. *Town, Bouches-du-Rhône*. The name derives from Latin *vitrum*, "glass," and the suffix *-eola*.

Vitry-en-Artois. *Town, Pas-de-Calais*. The name has the same origin as **Vitré**, with an addition locating the town in **Artois**.

Vitry-le-François. *Town, Marne*. The town, with a name of identical origin to that of **Vitré**, was founded in 1545 by Francis (*François*) I to replace the nearby settlement Vitry-en-Perthois, burned down by Charles V the previous year.

Vitry-sur-Seine. *Town, Val-de-Marne*. The name of the Paris suburb shares the origin of **Vitré**. The distinguishing addition located the town on the **Seine** River.

Vittel. *Resort town, Vosges*. The name derives from the Gaulish personal name *Vittus* or *Vitus* and the suffix *-ellum*.

Vivarais *see* **Viviers**

Viviers. *Town, Ardèche*. The name was recorded in the 5th century as *Vivarium*, from Latin *vivarium*, "vivarium," meaning a place where animals or fish are kept for food. Viviers is on the Rhône River. The town was the historic capital of *Vivarais*, a mountainous region on the edge of the Massif Central.

Vivonne. *Village, Vienne*. The name derives from Latin *vicus*, "village," and the *Vonne* River here.

Vizille. *Town, Isère*. The name, recorded in the 10th century as *Visilia*, derives from the Roman personal name *Visilius*, a derivative of *Visius*.

Vœgtlinshofen. *Village, Haut-Rhin*. The name was recorded in the 13th century as *Fockelinishoven*, from the Germanic personal name *Fukelin* and *hof*, "farm."

Void. *Village, Meuse*. The name is that of the river here. The village is also known as *Void-Vacon*, for nearby *Vacon*, probably from the Germanic personal name *Wacco*. The settlement was referred to in a 7th-century document as *Novientum super fluviolum Vidum*, "Novientum on the little river Void," with *Novientum* as for **Nogent-le-Rotrou**.

Voie Sacrée. *Highway, northeastern France*. The "Sacred Way" is the name given to the section of the present N35 road between Verdun and Bar-le-Duc as the only route by which supplies and reinforcements could be brought to beleaguered Verdun in World War I. Until relatively recently the road had no number but was simply known as "N (Voie Sacrée)." The name itself was adopted from the *Via Sacra*, the triumphal way in Rome that led through the Forum to the Capitol, so called from the sacred buildings that it passed.

Voiron. *Town, Isère.* The name is of uncertain origin. It may derive from pre-Celtic *vor*, a variant of *kar*, "rock," and the suffix *-ionem*.

Voisins-le-Bretonneux. *Town, Yvelines.* The name derives from Latin *vicinium*, "hamlet," "village." The addition refers to the local Breton inhabitants.

Volgelsheim. *Village, Haut-Rhin.* The name derives from the Germanic personal name *Folcoald* and *heim*, "abode."

Volnay. *Village, Côte-d'Or.* The name derives from the Roman personal name *Volumnus*, a variant of *Volumnius*, and the associative suffix *-acum*.

Volvic. *Town, Puy-de-Dôme.* The name may come from the pre-Latin root *vol*, "mountain," and Latin *vicus*, "village," if not from the Roman personal name *Volovicus*.

Voreppe. *Town, Isère.* The name probably derives from pre-Celtic *vor*, a variant of *kar*, "rock," and the pre-Latin suffix *-appa*.

Vosges. *Mountain massif, northeastern France.* The Latin form of the name was *Vogesus* or *Vosegus*, from Gaulish *Vosego* or *Vosago*, either from Celtic *vos*, "peak," or from the name of a Celtic god, from *vo*, "under," and *sego*, "strength," "height." The name gave that of a department here. (The first Latin form above, with *-ges-* rather than *-seg-*, gave *Vogesen* as the German name of the mountains.)

Vougeot. *Village, Côte-d'Or.* The name is that of one of the streams that form the *Vouge* River here.

Vouillé. *Village, Vienne.* The name was recorded in the 11th century as *Volliaco*, from the Roman personal name *Vollius* and the associative suffix *-acum*.

Voujeaucourt. *Village, Doubs.* The suburb of Montbéliard derives its name from a Germanic personal name (perhaps *Wiliawass*) and Latin *cortem*, accusative of *cors*, "estate."

La Voulte-sur-Rhône. *Town, Ardèche.* The name derives from Old Provençal *volta*, "turn," "river bend," meaning one in the **Rhône** River here.

Vouvray. *Village, Indre-et-Loire.* The name was recorded in the 8th century as *Vobridus*, from Gaulish *uobera*, "stream hidden in a wood," as for **Woëvre**.

Vouziers. *Town, Ardennes.* The name was recorded in the 12th century as *Vosiers*, from the Germanic personal name *Wulshari*.

Voves. *Village, Eure-et-Loir.* The name derives from Gaulish *uidua*, "forest."

Vrigne-aux-Bois. *Village, Ardennes.* The name is that of the river here, a tributary of the Meuse. The addition locates the village in the woods (*aux bois*) at the foot of the Ardennes.

Wallers. *Town, Nord.* The name derives from the Germanic personal name *Walo* or *Wallo* and *lar*, "clearing."

Wambrechies. *Town, Nord.* The suburb of Lille derives its name from the Germanic personal name *Winebert* and the associative suffix *-iacum*.

Wangenbourg. *Village, Bas-Rhin.* The name derives from Germanic *wanc*, "field," "plain," or the personal name *Wanniko*, and *burg*, "fortified settlement."

La Wantzenau. *Town, Bas-Rhin.* The suburb of Strasbourg derives its name from the Germanic personal name *Wanzo* and *au*, "damp meadow."

Wasquehal. *Town, Nord.* The suburb of Roubaix derives its name from the Germanic personal name *Wasco* and Frankish *halle*, "market."

Wasselonne. *Town, Bas-Rhin.* The name derives from the Germanic personal name *Wezil* and *heim*, "abode."

Wassy. *Village, Haute-Marne.* The name derives from the Germanic personal name *Waso* and the associative suffix *-iacum*.

Watten. *Village, Nord.* The name may derive from the Germanic personal name *Watto* and *heim*, "abode."

Wattignies. *Town, Nord.* The suburb of Lille derives its name from the Germanic personal name *Watto* and the double suffix *-in* and *-iacum.*

Wattignies-la-Victoire. *Town, Nord.* The name is as for **Wattignies.** The addition ("the victory") refers to the defeat of the Austrians here by the French under Marshal Jourdan in 1793.

Wattrelos. *Town, Nord.* The suburb of Roubaix derives its name from Flemish *water,* "water," and Germanic *lōh,* "wood."

Waville. *Village, Meurthe-et-Moselle.* The name was recorded in the 9th century as *Imvaldi villa,* from the Germanic personal name *Inguald* and Latin *village.* The *In-* of the personal name was later taken as Latin *in,* "in," so was dropped, giving the present form of the name.

Wavrin. *Town, Nord.* The name derives from the Germanic personal name *Waifar* and the suffix *-inum.*

Wemaers-Cappel. *Village, Nord.* The name derives from the Germanic personal name *Winimar,* that of the founder of the settlement, and Latin *cappella,* "chapel."

Wervicq-Sud. *Town, Nord.* The name derives from the Gaulish personal name *Virovios* and the associative suffix *-acum.* The town is south (*sud*) in relation to *Wervik,* to the north across the Belgian border.

West-Cappel. *Village, Nord.* The original name was recorded in the 12th century as *Arnuldi Capella,* from the Germanic personal name *Arnulf,* that of the founder of the settlement, and Latin *cappella,* "chapel." The personal name was later replaced by *west,* "west."

Wignehies. *Village, Nord.* The name is of uncertain origin. It may derive from the Germanic female personal name *Winigis* and the associative suffix *-iacum.*

Willerwald. *Village, Moselle.* The name derives from Low Latin *villare,* "farmstead," and Germanic *wald,* "forest." The village was founded in 1601 on the site of a razed settlement with a name recorded in the 15th century as *Alberzwiller.*

Wimereux. *Resort town, Pas-de-Calais.* The town takes its name from the *Wimereux* River, at the mouth of which it lies.

Wingles. *Town, Pas-de-Calais.* The name was recorded in the 11th century as *Wistrewingles,* from Germanic *wester,* "westerly," and *winchil,* "corner." The first part of this was then lost.

Wintersbourg. *Village, Moselle.* The name derives from the personal name *Winther* and Germanic *berg,* "mountain," later replaced by *bourg,* as if from *burg,* "fortified place."

Wintzenheim. *Town, Haut-Rhin.* The name derives from the Germanic personal name *Winzo* and *heim,* "abode."

Wissant. *Resort village, Pas-de-Calais.* The name derives from Dutch *wit,* "white," and *sant,* "sand." The resort is noted for its large beach.

Wissembourg. *Town, Bas-Rhin.* The name was recorded in the 8th century as *Uuizunburg* and *Wizenburg,* perhaps from German *weiß,* "white," or more likely from the Germanic personal name *Wizo,* and *burg,* "castle, "fort." The town is almost on the border with Germany, where it is known as *Weißenburg.*

Wissous. *Town, Essonne.* The name of the Paris suburb was recorded in the 12th century as *Vizeorium,* probably from Latin *vicus,* "village," and *Suevorum,* the genitive plural form of the name of the Germanic people known as the *Suevi,* from what is now Swabia (Schwaben).

Witry-lès-Reims. *Town, Marne.* The name derives from the Roman personal name *Victorius* and the associative suffix *-acum.* The addition locates the town near (*lès*) **Reims.**

Wittelsheim. *Town, Haut-Rhin.* The name derives from the Germanic personal name *Witolt* and *heim,* "abode."

Wittenheim. *Town, Haut-Rhin.* The suburb of Mulhouse derives its name from the Germanic personal name *Witto* or (better) *Witin* or *Wieding* and *heim*, "abode."

Wizernes. *Village, Pas-de-Calais.* The name is of uncertain origin. It could represent *Viserina*, from the Gaulish personal name *Viserinus*, with Latin *villa*, "estate," understood.

Wœrth. *Village, Bas-Rhin.* The name derives from Germanic *warid*, "island," describing the location of the village on raised ground by the Sauer River.

Woëvre. *Region, northeastern France.* The tableland in Lorraine was formerly known as *Voivre*, from Gaulish *uobera*, "stream hidden in a wood."

Woippy. *Town, Moselle.* The suburb of Metz derives its name from the Germanic personal name *Wappo* and the associative suffix *-iacum*.

Wormhout. *Town, Nord.* The name derives from Germanic *holz*, "wood," and a first element of uncertain origin. It may represent a Germanic personal name based on *Worm*.

Xaintrailles. *Village, Lot-et-Garonne.* The name masks that of *St. Eulalia* (see **Sainte-Eulalie**).

Xammes. *Village, Meurthe-et-Moselle.* The name derives from Latin *scamnum*, "stool," "bank of earth."

Xertigny. *Village, Vosges.* The name derives from the Germanic personal name *Scatto* and the double suffix *-in* and *-iacum*.

Yenne. *Village, Savoie.* The name is of uncertain origin. It may derive from the Gaulish personal name *Hedius* and the Latin suffix *-ana* (or perhaps Gaulish *-enna*).

Yerres. *Town, Essonne.* The name is that of the river here, itself of pre-Celtic origin.

Yeu, Île d'. *Island, western France.* The name of the island, in the Bay of Biscay, was recorded in the 6th century as *Oia*, from Germanic *au*, "water."

Yonne. *Department, north central France.* The name is that of the river here, recorded in the 2d century as *Icauna*, from the pre-Celtic river root *ic* and the Gaulish suffix *-auna*.

Ys. *Legendary city, northwestern France.* The legendary Breton city is said to have been drowned in the Bay of Douarnenez in the 4th or 5th century. Its Breton name is *Kêr-Iz*, "low town," from *kêr*, "town," and *iz*, "low," but the French name preserves only the second part of this. The city is the subject of Lalo's opera *Le Roi d'Ys* (1888) and inspired Debussy's piano piece *La Cathédrale engloutie* ("The Submerged Cathedral") (1910).

Yser. *River, northern France.* The Romans knew the river as *Isarus*, from the pre-Celtic river root *is* and the suffix *-ara*.

Yssingeaux. *Town, Haute-Loire.* The name was recorded in the 10th century as *Issinguaudum*, from the Germanic personal name *Isingaud*, from *isin* or *isan*, an extended form of *is*, "ice," symbolizing durability, and *waldan*, "ruler."

Yvelines. *Department, north central France.* The name comes from the Forest of *Yvelines*, part of the Forest of Rambouillet, recorded variously in early texts as *Aequaline silva*, *Equalina*, *Aqualina*, *Eulina*, and *Egilina*. The form *Yvelina* appeared only in the 13th century. The early names all seem to stem from a Celtic root meaning "water." There are many streams in the region.

Yvetot. *Town, Seine-Maritime.* The name was recorded in the 11th century as *Ivetot*, from the Germanic personal name *Ivo* and Old Scandinavian *toft*, "farm."

Yvette. *River, north central France.* The river, a tributary of the Orge in the Paris region, had the Medieval Latin name *Aquata*, probably from *aqua*, "water." A meaning "river of yews," from Gaulish *eburos*, "yew," is less likely.

Yvoire. *Resort village, Haute-Savoie.* The name probably derives from Gaulish *eburos*, "yew," and the suffix *-ea*.

Yvré-l'Évêque. *Village, Sarthe.* The name derives from the Gallo-Roman personal name *Eburius* and the associative suffix *-acum.* The addition means "the bishop," denoting the feudal possessor.

Yzeure. *Town, Allier.* The suburb of Moulins derives its name from a Gaulish original *Itiodurum,* from the personal name *Itius* and *duron,* "fort."

Zoteux. *Village, Pas-de-Calais.* The name was recorded in the 12th century as *Altaria,* from Latin *altare,* "altar," denoting a place of worship. A record of 1559 has the name as *Desauteulx,* showing a form of the plural original prefixed by French *des,* "of the," and this was later misdivided so that the *-s* of *des* became the initial *Z-* of the present name.

Appendix 1: French Habitative Names

Most French places, from towns and cities to quite small villages, have a distinctive habitative name for a person who was born or who has long lived in the place in question, the equivalent of the New Yorker of New York or Angeleno of Los Angeles. Such forms are mostly found in media reports, especially at a local level, but also occur in a wide range of written or printed contexts or in everyday speech.

The form of the habitative name sometimes preserves a historic form of the placename. Thus a native of *Aubervilliers* is an *Albertivilliarien*, echoing the 11th-century form *Albertivillare*, while an inhabitant of *Épernay* is a *Sparnacien*, mirroring the 9th-century form *Spernaco*. Sometimes the habitative name is quite unlike the modern placename, either because the original form has significantly smoothed or altered over the years, so that a person born in *Elne* is an *Illibérien*, from the 1st-century form *Illiberi*, or because the place in question has changed its name. Thus a resident of *Bourg-Madame* is a *Guingettois*, from the pre–1815 name *La Guingette*.

Compound placenames may derive their habitative from either or any part, so that a native of *Ax-les-Thermes* is an *Axéen*, but a resident of *Azay-le-Rideau* is a *Ridelois*. Similarly, a person from *Bagnères-de-Bigorre* is a *Bagnérais*, but one from *Bagnères-de-Luchon* is a *Luchonnais*. Sometimes in such cases there are alternate names, so that an inhabitant of *Amélie-les-Bains-Palalda* can be either an *Amélien* or a *Paladéen*. In a placename based on a saint's name, the "saint" element may be included or omitted, giving a person from *Saint-Girons* as a *Saint-Gironais*, but a native of *Saint-Gobain* as a *Gobanais*. (In a few names of this type, the "saint" element is represented by *San-*, as a *Sanclaudien* from *Saint-Claude*.)

The endings of such names, which are the adjectival forms adopted for noun use, are often *-ais* or *-ois*, as *Agenais* from *Agen* or *Agathois* from *Agde*, but *-ien* is also widely found, as *Arlésien* from *Arles* and *Parisien* from *Paris*. Occasionally *-iot* is found, as for *Condriot* from *Condrieu* or (unexpectedly) *Malakoffiot* from *Malakoff*. These forms are all masculine, and the corresponding feminine form (adding *-e* and doubling the *-n* of *-ien*) will apply to a female native or resident (*Agenaise, Agathoise, Arlésienne, Parisienne, Condriote*). All of the forms listed below are masculine plural, with added plural *-s* where appropriate. (The plurals of *-ais* or *-ois* forms, which already have *-s*, are identical.)

Abbeville : Abbevillois
Achères : Achérois
Agde : Agathois
Agen : Agenais
Aigle, L' : Aiglons
Aigueperse : Aiguepersois
Aigues-Mortes : Aigues-Mortais
Aire-sur-l'Adour : Alturins
Aire-sur-la-Lys : Airois
Airvault : Airvaudais
Aix-en-Othe : Aixois
Aix-en-Provence : Aixois
Aixe-sur-Vienne : Aixois
Aix-les-Bains : Aixois
Aizenay : Agésinates
Albens : Albanais
Albertville : Albertvillois
Albi : Albigeois
Alençon : Alençonnais
Alès : Alésiens
Alfortville : Alfortvillais
Allauch : Allaudiens
Allevard : Allevardais
Allonnes : Allonnais
Altkirch : Altkirchois
Ambérieu-en-Bugey : Ambarrois
Ambert : Ambertois
Amboise : Amboisiens
Amélie-les-Bains-Palalda: Améliens or
   Paladéens
Amiens : Amiénois
Amnéville : Amnévillois
Ancenis : Anceniens
Andelys, Les : Andelysiens
Andrésy : Andrésiens
Andrézieux-Bouthéon : Andréziens-
   Bouthéonais
Anet : Anétais
Angers : Angevins
Anglet : Angloys
Angoulême : Angoumoisins
Aniane : Anianais
Aniche : Anichois
Annecy : Anneciens
Annemasse : Annemassiens
Annonay : Annonéens
Antibes : Antibois
Antony : Antoniens
Anzin : Anzinois
Apt : Aptésiens or Aptois
Aramon : Aramonais
Arbois : Arboisiens
Arbresle, L' : Arbreslois
Arcachon : Arcachonnais

Arcis-sur-Aube : Arcisiens
Arcueil : Arcueillais
Ardentes : Ardentais
Ardres : Ardrésiens
Argelès-Gazost : Argelésiens
Argelès-sur-Mer : Argelésiens
Argentan : Argentanais
Argentat : Argentacois
Argenteuil : Argenteuillais
Argentière-la-Bessée : Argentiérois
Argenton-sur-Creuse : Argentonnais
Argentré : Argentréens
Argent-sur-Sauldre : Argentais
Arlanc : Arlancois
Arles : Arlésiens
Armentières : Armentiérois
Arpajon : Arpajonnais
Arras : Arrageois
Asnières-sur-Seine : Asniérois
Athis-Mons : Athégiens
Aubagne : Aubagnais
Aubenas : Albenassiens
Aubervilliers : Albertivilliariens
Aubusson : Aubussonnais
Auch : Auscitains
Auchel : Auchellois
Audenge : Audengeois
Audierne : Audiernais
Audincourt : Audincourtois
Audruicq : Audruicquois
Audun-le-Roman : Audunois
Aulnat : Aulnatois
Aulnay-sous-Bois : Aulnaisiens
Ault : Aultois
Aumale : Aumalois
Aunay-sur-Odon : Aunais
Auray : Alréens
Aurignac : Aurignaciens
Aurillac : Aurillacois
Auterive : Auterivains
Autun : Autunois
Auvers-sur-Oise : Auversois
Auxerre : Auxerrois
Auxi-le-Château : Auxilois
Auxonne : Auxonnois
Avallon : Avallonnais
Avesnes-le-Comte : Avesnois
Avesnes-sur-Helpe : Avesnois
Avignon : Avignonnais
Avon : Avonnais
Avranches : Avranchinais
Ax-les-Thermes : Axéens
Ay : Agéens
Azay-le-Rideau : Ridelois

Baccarat : Bachamois
Bagnères-de-Bigorre : Bagnérais
Bagnères-de-Luchon : Luchonnais
Bagneux : Balnéolais
Bagnolet : Bagnoletais
Bagnols-les-Bains : Bagnolais
Bagnols-sur-Cèze : Bagnolais
Bailleul : Bailleulois
Bain-de-Bretagne : Bainais
Bains-les-Bains : Balnéens
Bandol : Bandolais
Bannalec : Bannalécois
Banyuls-sur-Mer : Banyulencs
Bapaume : Bapalmois
Barbezieux-Saint-Hilaire : Barbeziliens
Barentin : Barentinois
Barjols : Barjolais
Bar-le-Duc : Barisiens
Barlin : Barlinois
Barsac : Barsacais
Bar-sur-Aube : Baralbins or Barsuraubois
Bar-sur-Loup : Aubarnois
Bar-sur-Seine : Barrois
Bas-en-Basset : Bassois
Bassée, La : Basséens
Bassens : Bassenais
Batz-sur-Mer : Batziens
Baugé : Baugeois
Baule-Escoublac, La : Baulois
Baume-les-Dames : Baumois
Bavay : Bavaisiens
Bayeux : Bayeusins or Bajocasses
Bayonne : Bayonnais
Bazas : Bazadais
Bazeilles : Bazeillais
Beaucaire : Beaucairois
Beauchamp : Beauchampois
Beaucourt : Beaucourtois
Beaufort : Beaufortains
Beaufort-en-Vallée : Beaufortais
Beaugency : Balgenciens
Beaujeu : Beaujolais
Beaulieu-sur-Mer : Berlugans
Beaumes-de-Venise : Balméens
Beaumont : Beaumontois
Beaumont-de-Lomagne : Beaumontois
Beaune : Beaunois
Beaupréau : Bellopratains
Beaurepaire : Beaurepairois
Beausoleil : Beausoleillois
Beausset, Le : Beaussetans
Beauvais : Beauvaisiens
Bec-Hellouin, Le : Bexiens
Bédarieux : Bédariciens

Bédarrides : Bédarridais
Bégard : Bégarrois
Bègles : Béglais
Belfort : Belfortains
Bellac : Bellachons
Bellegarde-sur-Valserine : Bellegardiens
Bellême : Bellémois
Belleville : Bellevillois
Belleville-sur-Loire : Bellevillois
Belley : Belleysans
Benfeld : Benfeldois
Bénodet : Bénodetois
Berck : Berckois
Bergerac : Bergeracois
Bergues : Berguois
Berlaimont : Berlaimontois
Bernay : Bernayens
Berre-l'Étang : Berratins
Berzé-la-Ville : Berzélavilliens
Besançon : Bisontins
Besse-et-Saint-Anastaise : Bessois
Bessèges : Bességeois
Béthune : Béthunois
Betton : Bettonais
Beuzeville : Beuzevillais
Beynes : Beynois
Béziers : Biterrois
Biache-Saint-Vaast : Biachois
Biarritz : Biarrots
Bidart : Bidartars
Billom : Billomois
Binic : Binicais
Biot : Biotois
Bischheim : Bischheimois
Bischwiller : Bischwillerois
Bitche : Bitchois
Blagnac : Blagnacais
Blain : Blinois
Blainville-sur-l'Eau : Blainvillois
Blainville-sur-Orne : Blainvillais
Blanc, Le : Blancois
Blanc-Mesnil : Blanc-Mesnilois
Blangy-sur-Bresle : Blangeois
Blanzy : Blanzynois
Blaye : Blayais
Bléré : Blérois
Blois : Blésois
Bobigny : Balbyniens
Bois-d'Arcy : Arcisiens
Bolbec : Bolbécais
Bollène : Bollénois
Boncourt : Boncourtois
Bondoufle : Bondouflois
Bondues : Bonduois

Bonnétable : Bonnétabliens
Bonneuil-sur-Marne : Bonneuillois
Bonneval : Bonnevalais
Bonneville : Bonnevillois
Bonnières-sur-Seine : Bonniérois
Bordeaux : Bordelais
Bordes : Bordais
Bouaye : Boscéens
Bouc-Bel-Air : Boucains
Bougival : Bougivalais
Bouguenais : Bougenaisiens
Boulay-Moselle : Boulageois
Boulogne-Billancourt : Boulonnais
Boulogne-sur-Mer : Boulonnais
Boulou, Le : Boulounencqs
Bourbon-Lancy : Bourbonnais
Bourbon-l'Archambault : Bourbonnais
Bourbonne-les-Bains : Bourbonnais
Bourboule, La : Bourbouliens
Bourbourg : Bourbourgeois
Bourganeuf : Bourganiauds
Bourg-Argental : Bourguisans
Bourg-de-Péage : Péageois
Bourg-d'Oisans, Le : Bourcats
Bourg-en-Bresse : Burgiens or Bressans
Bourges : Berruyers
Bourg-la-Reine : Réginaborgiens
Bourg-lès-Valence : Bourcains
Bourg-Madame : Guinguettois
Bourgoin-Jallieu : Berjalliens
Bourg-Saint-Andéol : Bourguesans
Bourg-Saint-Maurice : Borains
Bourgtheroulde-Infreville : Therouldebourgeois
Bouscat, Le : Bouscatais
Bouzonville : Bouzonvillois
Boves : Bovois
Bozouls : Bouzoulais
Braine : Brainois
Brantôme : Brantômais
Bray-Dunes : Bray-Dunois
Bray-sur-Seine : Braytois
Bréhat : Bréhatins
Bressuire : Bressuirais
Brest : Brestois
Breteuil : Bretoliens
Brétigny-sur-Orge : Brétignolais
Briançon : Briançonnais
Briare : Briarois
Bricquebec : Bricquebétais
Brides-les-Bains : Bridois
Briec : Briecois
Brie-Comte-Robert : Briards
Brienne-le-Château : Briennois
Briey : Briotins

Brignoles : Brignolais
Brionne : Brionnais
Brioude : Brivadois
Brive-la-Gaillarde : Brivistes
Bron : Brondillants
Brou : Broutains
Bruay-la-Buissière : Bruaysiens
Brunoy : Brunoyens
Bruyères : Bruyérois
Bruyères-le-Châtel : Bruyérois
Bruz : Bruzois
Buc : Bucois
Bugue, Le : Buguois
Buis-les-Baronnies : Buxois
Buisson-de-Cadouin : Buissonnais
Bully-les-Mines : Bullygeois
Bussang : Bussenets
Buzançais : Buzancéens
Cabestany : Cabestanyencs
Cabourg : Cabourgeais
Cachan : Cachanais
Cadillac : Cadillacais
Caen : Caennais
Cagnes-sur-Mer : Cagnois
Cahors : Cadurciens
Calais : Calaisiens
Callac : Callacois
Calvi : Calvais
Camaret-sur-Mer : Camarétois
Cambo-les-Bains : Camboars
Cambrai : Cambrésiens
Cancale : Cancalais
Candé : Candéens
Canet-en-Roussillon : Canétois
Cannes : Cannois
Cannet, Le : Cannettans
Canteleu : Cantiliens
Cany-Barville : Canycais
Capbreton : Capbretonnais
Cap-d'Ail : Cap-d'Aillois
Capdenac-Gare : Capdenacois
Capelle, La : Capellois
Capestang : Capestanais
Carbon-Blanc : Carbonblannais
Carbonne : Carbonnais
Carcassonne : Carcassonnais
Carentan : Carentanais
Carhaix(-Plouguer) : Carhaisiens
Carignan : Yvoisiens
Carmaux : Carmausins
Carnac : Carnacois
Carpentras : Carpentrassiens
Carquefou : Carquefolliens
Carrières-sous-Poissy : Carriérois

Carrières-sur-Seine : Carriérois
Carry-le-Rouet : Carryens
Carvin : Carvinois
Cassis : Cassidens
Castanet-Tolosan : Castanéens
Casteljaloux : Casteljalousains
Castellane : Castellanais
Castellet, Le : Castellans
Castelnaudary : Chauriens
Castelnau-de-Médoc : Castelnaudais
Castelsarrasin : Castelsarrasinois
Castillon-la-Bataille : Castillonnais
Castres : Castrais
Castries : Castriotes
Cateau-Cambrésis, Le : Catésiens
Cattenom : Cattenomois
Caudan : Caudanais
Caudebec-en-Caux : Caudebecquais
Caudebec-lès-Elbeuf : Caudebecquais
Caudry : Caudrésiens
Caulnes : Caulnais
Caussade : Caussadais
Cauterets : Cauterésiens
Cavaillon : Cavaillonnais
Cavalaire-sur-Mer : Cavalairois
Cayenne : Cayennais
Cayeux-sur-Mer : Cayolais
Caylus : Caylusiens
Cazères : Cazériens
Celle-Saint-Cloud, La : Cellois
Celles-sur-Belle : Cellois
Cerbère : Cerbériens
Cenon : Cenonnais
Céret : Céretans
Cergy : Cergyssois
Cernay : Cernéens
Cesson-Sévigné : Cessonnais
Chablis : Chablisiens
Chagny : Chagnotins
Chalais : Chalaisiens
Challans : Challandais
Challes-les-Eaux : Challésiens
Chalonnes-sur-Loire : Chalonnais
Châlons-en-Champagne : Châlonnais
Chalon-sur-Saône : Chalonnais
Châlus : Chalusiens
Chamalières : Chamaliérois
Chambéry : Chambériens
Chambon-Feugerolles : Chambonnaires
Chamonix-Mont-Blanc : Chamoniards
Champagnole : Champagnolais
Champigneulles : Champigneullais
Champigny-sur-Marne : Campinois
Champlitte : Chanitois

Chancelade : Chanceladais
Chantilly : Cantiliens
Chantonnay : Chantonnaisiens
Chapelle-sur-Erdre, La : Chapelains
Charenton-le-Pont : Charentonnais
Charité-sur-Loire : Charitois
Charleville-Mézières : Carolomacériens
Charlieu : Charliandins
Charmes : Carpiniens
Charolles : Charollais
Chartres : Chartrains
Château-Arnoux : Jarlandins
Châteaubriant : Castelbriantais
Château-Chinon : Château-Chinonais
Château-du-Loir : Castéloriens
Châteaudun : Dunois
Châteaugiron : Castelgironnais
Château-Gontier : Castrogontériens
Château-Landon : Châteaulandonnais
Châteaulin : Castellinois or Châteaulinois
Châteauneuf-en-Thymerais : Castelneuviens
Châteauneuf-les-Bains : Castelneuvois
Châteauneuf-sur-Charente : Castelnoviens
Châteauneuf-sur-Loire : Castelneuviens
Château-Renault : Renaudins
Châteauroux : Castelroussins
Château-Salins : Castelsalinois
Château-Thierry : Castelthéodoriciens or
    Castrothéodoriciens
Châtelaillon-Plage : Châtelaillonnais
Châtelguyon : Châtelguyonnais
Châtellerault : Châtelleraudais
Châtenay-Malabry : Châtenaisiens
Châtillon : Châtillonnais
Châtillon-sur-Chalaronne : Châtillonnais
Châtillon-sur-Indre : Châtillonnais
Châtillon-sur-Loire : Châtillonnais
Châtillon-sur-Seine : Châtillonnais
Chatou : Catoviens
Châtre, La : Castrais
Chaudes-Aigues : Caldaguès
Chauffailles : Chauffaillons
Chaumont : Chaumontais
Chaumont-en-Vexin : Chaumontois
Chauny : Chaunois
Chauvigny : Chauvinois
Chaville : Chavillois
Chazelles-sur-Lyon : Chazellois
Chelles : Chellois
Chennevières-sur-Marne : Canavérois
Chenôve : Cheneveliers
Cherbourg : Cherbourgeois
Chesnay, Le : Chesnaysiens
Chevreuse : Chevrotins

Chilly-Mazarin : Chiroquois
Chinon : Chinonais
Choisy-le-Roi : Choisyens
Cholet : Choletais
Chomérac : Choméracois
Chooz : Calcéens
Cintegabelle : Cintegabellois
Ciotat, La : Ciotadens
Clamart : Clamartois or Clamariots
Clamecy : Clamecycois
Claye-Souilly : Clayois
Clayes-sous-Bois : Clétiens
Clayette, La : Clayettois
Cléguérec : Cléguérecois
Clères : Clérois
Clermont : Clermontois
Clermont-Ferrand : Clermontois
Clermont-l'Hérault : Clermontais
Clichy : Clichois
Clichy-sous-Bois : Clichois
Clisson : Clissonnais
Cloyes-sur-le-Loir : Cloysiens
Cluny : Clunysois
Cluses : Clusiens
Cognac : Cognaçais
Cognin : Cognerauds
Cogolin : Cogolinois
Colle-sur-Loup : Collois
Collinée : Collinéens
Collioure : Colliourencs
Colmar : Colmariens
Colomiers : Columérins
Combourg : Combourgeois
Comines : Cominois
Commentry : Commentryens
Commercy : Commerciens
Compiègne : Compiégnois
Concarneau : Concarnois
Conches-en-Ouche : Conchois
Condé-sur-l'Escaut : Condéens
Condé-sur-Noireau : Condéens
Condom : Condomois
Condrieu : Condriots
Conflans-en-Jarnisy : Conflanais
Conflans-Sainte-Honorine : Conflanais
Confolens : Confolentais
Contamines-Montjoie, Les : Contaminards
Contes : Contois
Contres : Controis
Coquelles : Coquellois
Corbas : Corbasiens
Corbehem : Corbehemois
Corbeil-Essonnes : Corbeillessonnois
Corbie : Corbéens

Cordes-sur-Ciel : Cordais
Cormeilles-en-Parisis : Cormeillais
Cormelles-le-Royal : Cormellois
Cosne-Cours-sur-Loire : Cosnois
Cossé-le-Vivien : Cosséens
Côte-Saint-André, La : Côtois
Coudekerque-Branche : Coudekerquois
Coulommiers : Columériens
Coulonges-sur-l'Autize : Coulongeois
Courbevoie : Courbevoisiens
Courcouronnes : Courcouronnais
Courneuve, La : Courneuviens
Cournon-d'Auvergne : Cournonnais
Couronne, La : Couronnais
Coursan : Coursannais
Courseulles-sur-Mer : Courseullais
Courville-sur-Eure : Courvillois
Coutances : Coutançais
Coutras : Coutrasiens
Cran-Gevrier : Gévriens
Craon : Craonnais
Craponne-sur-Arzon : Craponnais
Crau, La : Craurois
Crécy-en-Ponthieu : Crécéens
Crécy-la-Chapelle : Créçois
Creil : Creillois
Crépy-en-Valois : Crépynois
Crest : Crestois
Créteil : Cristoliens
Creusot, Le : Creusotins
Crèvecœur-le-Grand : Crépicordiens
Criel-sur-Mer : Criellois
Croisic, Le : Croisicais
Croix : Croisiens
Crotoy, Le : Crotellois
Crozon : Crozonnais
Cuers : Cuersois
Cugnaux : Cugnalais
Cusset : Cussétois
Cysoing : Cysoniens
Dax : Dacquois
Decazeville : Decazevillois
Decize : Decizois
Delle : Dellois
Denain : Denaisiens
Descartes : Descartois
Desvres : Desvrois
Deuil-la-Barre : Deuillois
Die : Diois
Dieppe : Dieppois
Dieulefit : Dieulefitois
Dieulouard : Décustodiens
Digne-les-Bains : Dignois
Digoin : Digoinais

Dijon : Dijonnais
Dinan : Dinannais
Dinard : Dinardais
Dives-sur-Mer : Divais
Divion : Divionnais
Divonne-les-Bains : Divonnais
Dol-de-Bretagne : Dolois
Dole : Dolois
Dombasle-sur-Meurthe : Dombaslois
Domène : Doménois
Domfront : Domfrontais
Domont : Domontois
Donges : Dongeois
Donzenac : Donzenacois
Donzère : Donzérois
Dorat, Le : Dorachons
Douai : Douaisiens
Douarnenez : Douarnenistes
Doudeville : Doudevillais
Doué-la-Fontaine : Douessins
Doullens : Doullennais
Dourdan : Dourdannais
Douvaine : Douvainois
Douvres-la-Délivrande : Douvrais
Douvrin : Douvrinois
Draguignan : Dracénois
Drancy : Drancéens
Draveil : Draveillois
Dreux : Drouais
Ducey : Ducéens
Duclair : Duclairois
Dunkerque : Dunkerquois
Dun-sur-Auron : Dunois
Eaubonne : Eaubonnais
Eauze : Élusates
Échirolles : Échirollois
Écommoy : Écomméens
Écouen : Écouennais
Écully : Écullois
Égletons : Égletonnais
Élancourt : Élancourtois
Elbeuf : Elbeuviens
Elne : Illibériens
Elven : Elvinois
Embrun : Embrunais
Enghien-les-Bains : Enghiennois
Épernay : Sparnaciens
Épernon : Sparnoniens
Épinac : Épinacois
Épinal : Spinaliens
Épinay-sous-Sénart : Spinoliens
Équeurdreville-Hainneville : Équeurdrevillais
Éragny : Éragniens
Ermont : Ermontois

Ernée : Ernéens
Erquy : Réginéens
Erstein : Ersteinois
Escaudain : Escaudinois
Espalion : Espalionnais
Essarts, Les : Essartais
Essey-lès-Nancy : Ascyens or Ascéiens
Estrées-Saint-Denis : Dionysiens
Étables-sur-Mer : Tagarins
Étain : Stainois
Étampes : Étampois
Étaples : Étaplois
Étel : Étellois
Étréchy : Strépiniacois
Étrépagny : Sterpinaciens
Étretat : Étretatais
Eu : Eudois
Évaux-les-Bains : Évahoniens
Évian-les-Bains : Évianais
Évreux : Ébroïciens
Évron : Évronnais
Évry : Évryens
Eymet : Eymétois
Eysines : Eysinais
Èze : Ézasques
Falaise : Falaisiens
Fameck : Fameckois
Faouët, Le : Faouëtais
Faute-sur-Mer : Fautais
Faverges : Favergiens
Fayence : Fayençois
Fécamp : Fécampois
Felletin : Felletinois
Fère, La : Laférois
Fère-Champenoise : Fertons
Fère-en-Tardenois : Férois
Ferney-Voltaire : Ferneysiens
Ferrières : Ferriérois
Ferté-Alais, La : Fertois
Ferté-Bernard, La : Fertois
Ferté-Gaucher, La : Fertois
Ferté-Macé, La : Fertois
Ferté-Milon, La : Milonais
Ferté-Saint-Aubin, La : Fertésiens
Ferté-sous-Jouarre, La : Fertois
Feurs : Foréziens
Feyzin : Feyzinois
Figeac : Figeacois
Fismes : Fismois
Flèche, La : Fléchois
Flers : Flériens
Fleurance : Fleurantins
Fleurie : Fleuriatons
Fleury-les-Aubrais : Fleuryssois

Flins-sur-Seine : Flinois
Floirac : Floiracais
Florac : Floracois
Florange : Florangeois
Florensac : Florensacois
Foix : Fuxéens
Fontaine : Fontainois
Fontainebleau : Bellifontains
Fontenay-aux-Roses : Fontenaisiens
Fontenay-le-Comte : Fontenaisiens
Fontenay-le-Fleury : Fontenaysiens
Fontenay-sous-Bois : Fontenaysiens
Fontoy : Fonschois
Font-Romeu-Odeillo-Via : Romeufontains
Forbach : Forbachois
Forcalquier : Forcalquiérens
Forges-les-Eaux : Forgions
Formerie : Formions
Fouesnant : Fouesnantais
Fougères : Fougerais
Fougerolles : Fougerollais
Fourmies : Fourmisiens
Fraize : Fraxiniens
Francheville : Franchevillois
Franconville : Franconvillois
Fréjus : Fréjusiens
Fresnay-sur-Sarthe : Fresnois
Fresnes : Fresnois
Fresnoy-le-Grand : Fresnoysiens
Freyming-Merlebach : Freyming-Merlebachois
Friville-Escarbotin : Frivillois
Fronsac : Fronsadais
Frontignan : Frontignanais
Fronton : Frontonnais
Fruges : Frugeois
Fumay : Fumaciens
Fumel : Fumélois
Gacé : Gacéens
Gaillac : Gaillacois
Gaillard : Gaillardins
Gaillon : Gaillonnais
Gamaches : Gamachois
Gandrange : Gandrangeois
Ganges : Gangeois
Gannat : Gannatois
Gap : Gapençais
Garches : Garchois
Gardanne : Gardannais
Garenne-Colombes, La : Garennois
Garges-lès-Gonesse : Gargeois
Gargilesse-Dampierre : Gargilessois
Gérardmer : Géromois
Gerzat : Gerzatois
Gevrey-Chambertin : Gibriaçois

Gex : Gexois
Gien : Giennois
Gif-sur-Yvette : Giffois
Gignac : Gignacois
Gimont : Gimontois
Giromagny : Giromagniens
Gisors : Gisorsiens
Giverny : Givernois
Givet : Givetois
Givors : Givordins
Golbey : Golbéens
Gond-Pontouvre, Le : Gonpontolviens
Gonesse : Gonessiens
Gonfreville-l'Orcher : Gonfrevillais
Gordes : Gordiens
Gorron : Gorronnais
Gourdon : Gourdonnais
Goussainville : Goussainvillois
Gradignan : Gradignanais
Gramat : Gramatois
Grand-Bornand, Le : Bornandins
Grand-Champ : Grégamistes
Grand-Couronne : Couronnais
Grande-Synthe : Grand-Synthois
Grand-Pressigny, Le : Pressignois
Grand-Quevilly, Le : Grand-Quevillois
Grandvillars : Grandvellais
Granville : Granvillais
Grasse : Grassois
Grau-du-Roi, Le : Graulens
Graulhet : Graulhetois
Grave, La : Graverots
Gravelines : Gravelinois
Gray : Graylois
Grenoble : Grenoblois
Gréoux-les-Bains : Gryséliens
Grésy-sur-Aix : Grésyliens
Grigny : Grignois
Grimaud : Grimaudois
Grisolles : Grisollais
Guebwiller : Guebwillerois
Guérande : Guérandais
Guéret : Guérétois
Guéthary : Guethariars
Gueugnon : Gueugnonnais
Guilherand-Granges : Guilherandais-Grangeois
Guilvinec : Guilvinistes
Guînes : Guînois
Guingamp : Guingampais
Guipavas : Guipavasiens
Guise : Guisards
Hagondange : Hagondangeois
Haguenau : Haguenoviens
Halluin : Halluinois

Ham : Hamois
Harfleur : Harfleurais
Harnes : Harnésiens
Hasparren : Hazpandars
Haubourdin : Haubourdinois
Hautefort : Hautefortais
Hauteville-Lompnes : Hautevillois
Hautmont : Hautmontois
Havre, Le : Havrais
Hayange : Hayangeois
Hazebrouck : Hazebrouckois
Heillecourt : Heillecourtois
Hem : Hémois
Hendaye : Hendayais
Hénin-Beaumont : Héninois
Hennebont : Hennebontais
Herbiers, Les : Herbretais
Herblay : Herblaysiens
Héricourt : Héricourtois
Hérimoncourt : Hérimoncourtois
Hérouville-Saint-Clair : Hérouvillais
Hesdin : Hesdinois
Hirson : Hirsonnais
Hombourg-Haut : Hombourgeois
Honfleur : Honfleurais
Houches, Les : Houchards
Houdan : Houdanais
Houilles : Ovillois
Hourtin : Hourtinais
Huelgoat : Huelgoatais
Huningue : Huninguois
Hyères : Hyérois
Igny : Ignissois
Île-Rousse, L' : Isolani
Isbergues : Isberguois
Isle-Adam, L' : Adamois
Isle-d'Abeau, L' : Lilots
Isle-d'Espagnac, L' : Spaniaciens
Isle-Jourdain, L' : Lislois
Isle-sur-la-Sorgue, L' : L'Islois
Isle-sur-le-Doubs, L' : L'Islois
Issoire : Issoiriens
Issoudun : Issoldunois
Issy-les-Moulineaux : Isséens
Istres : Istréens
Ivry-la-Bataille : Ivryens
Ivry-sur-Seine : Ivryens
Janzé : Janzéens
Jargeau : Gergoliens
Jarnac : Jarnacais
Jarville-la-Malgrange : Jarvillois
Jeumont : Jeumontois
Joigny : Joviniens
Joinville : Joinvillois

Joinville-le-Pont : Joinvillais
Jonzac : Jonzacais
Josselin : Josselinais
Jouarre : Jotranciens
Joué-lès-Tours : Jocondiens
Jouy-en-Josas : Jovaciens
Jouy-le-Moutier : Jocassiens
Jumièges : Jumiégeois
Jurançon : Jurançonnais
Juvisy-sur-Orge : Juvisiens
Kremlin-Bicêtre, Le : Kremlinois
Lacaune : Lacaunais
Lacq : Lacquois
Lagny-sur-Marne : Latignaciens or Laniaques
Lalouvesc : Louvetous
Lamalou-les-Bains : Lamalousiens
Lamballe : Lamballais
Lambersart : Lambersartois
Landerneau : Landernéens
Landivisiau : Landivisiens
Lanester : Lanestériens
Laneuveville-devant-Nancy : Laneuvevillois
Langeac : Langeadois
Langeais : Langeaisiens
Langogne : Langonais
Langon : Langonais
Langres : Langrois
Lannion : Lannionnais
Laon : Laonnais
Lapalisse : Lapalissois
Largentière : Largentiérois
Larmor-Plage : Larmoriens
Lassigny : Lachenois
Lattes : Lattois
Lauterbourg : Lauterbourgeois
Laval : Lavallois
Lavandou, Le : Lavandourains
Lavaur : Vauréens
Lavelanet : Lavelanétiens
Laxou : Laxoviens
Lens : Lensois
Léognan : Léognanais
Lesneven : Lesneviens
Lesparre-Médoc : Lesparrains
Levallois-Perret : Levalloisiens
Lézignan-Corbières : Lézignanais
Libourne : Libournais
Liévin : Liévinois
Liffré : Liffréens
Ligny-en-Barrois : Linéens
Ligugé : Ligugéens
Lilas, Les : Lilasiens
Lille : Lillois
Lillebonne : Lillebonnais

Limoges : Limougeauds
Limours : Limouriens
Limoux : Limouxins
Lisieux : Lexoviens
Lisle-sur-Tarn : Lislois
Loches : Lochois
Loctudy : Loctudistes
Lodève : Lodévois
Lomme : Lommois
Longjumeau : Longjumellois
Longué-Jumelles : Longuéens or Jumellois
Longuenesse : Longuenessois
Longuyon : Longuyonnais
Longwy : Longoviciens
Lons-le-Saunier : Lédoniens
Loos : Loossois
Lorient : Lorientais
Loroux-Bottereau, Le : Lorousains
Lorris : Lorriçois
Loudéac : Loudéaciens
Loudun : Loudunais
Loué : Louésiens
Louhans : Louhannais
Lourdes : Lourdais
Louveciennes : Louveciennois or Luciennois
Louviers : Lovériens
Louvigné-du-Désert : Louvignéens
Louvres : Lupariens
Lucé : Lucéens
Luçon : Luçonnais
Lude, Le : Ludois
Lunel : Lunellois
Lunéville : Lunévillois
Lure : Lurons
Luxeuil-les-Bains : Luxoviens
Lyon : Lyonnais
Lys-lez-Lannoy : Lyssois
Mâcon : Mâconnais
Madeleine, La : Madeleinois
Magny-en-Vexin : Magnitois
Magny-les-Hameaux : Magnycois
Maillane : Maillanais
Maintenon : Maintenonnais
Maisons-Alfort : Maisonnais
Maisons-Laffitte : Mansonniens
Malakoff : Malakoffiots
Mamers : Mamertins
Manosque : Manosquins
Mans, Le : Manceaux
Mantes-la-Jolie : Mantais
Mantes-la-Ville : Mantevillois
Marignane : Marignanais
Marly-le-Roi : Markychois
Marmande : Marmandais

Marquise : Marquisiens
Marseille : Marseillais
Martigues : Martégaux
Marvejol : Marvejolais
Massiac : Massiacois
Massy : Massicois
Maubeuge : Maubeugeois
Mauguio : Melgoriens
Mayenne : Mayennais
Mazamet : Mazamétains
Meaux : Meldois
Mehun-sur-Yèvre : Mehunois
Melun : Melunais
Mende : Mendois
Menton : Mentonnais
Merdrignac : Merdrignaciens
Mers-les-Bains : Mersois
Méry-sur-Oise : Mérysiens
Metz : Messins
Meudon : Meudonnais
Meulan : Meulanais
Meung-sur-Loire : Magdunois
Meylan : Meylanais
Meymac : Meymacois
Mèze : Mézois
Mézidon-Canon : Mézidonnais
Migennes : Migennois
Millau : Millavois
Mimizan : Mimizannais
Miramas : Miramasséens
Mirande : Mirandais
Mirebeau : Mirbalais
Mirecourt : Mirecurtiens
Modane : Modanais
Moissac : Moissagais
Mondeville : Mondevillais
Mons-en-Barœul : Monsois
Montagne, La : Montagnards
Montargis : Montargois
Montataire : Montatairiens
Montauban : Montalbanais
Montauban-de-Bretagne : Montalbanais
Montbard : Montbardois
Montbéliard : Montbéliardais
Montbrison : Montbrisonnais
Montceau-les-Mines : Montcelliens
Montchanin : Montchaninois
Mont-Dauphin : Mont-Dauphinois
Mont-de-Marsan : Montois
Montdidier : Montdidériens
Montélimar : Montiliens
Montereau(-Fault-Yonne) : Monterelais
Montesson : Montessonnais
Montfermeil : Montfermeillois

Montfort : Montfortais
Montgeron : Montgeronnais
Montier-en-Der : Dervois
Mont-Louis : Montlouisiens
Montlouis-sur-Loire : Montlouisiens
Montluçon : Montluçonnais
Montmagny : Magnymontois
Montmartre : Montmartrois
Montmédy : Montmédiens
Montmorency : Montmorencéens
Montmorillon : Montmorillonnais
Montpellier : Montpelliérains
Montreuil(-sous-Bois) : Montreuillois
Montrouge : Montrougiens
Mont-Saint-Aignan : Montsaintaignanais
Morangis : Morangissois
Morlaàs : Morlanais
Morlaix : Morlaisiens
Mortagne-au-Perche : Mortagnais
Morteau : Mortuaciens
Motte-Servolex, La : Motterains
Moulins : Moulinois
Mouzon : Mouzonnais
Mulhouse : Mulhousiens
Mureaux, Les : Muriautins
Muret : Murétains
Nancy : Nancéiens
Nanterre : Nanterriens
Nantes : Nantais
Narbonne : Narbonnais
Nay-Bourdettes : Nayais
Nérac : Néracais
Neufchâteau : Néocastriens
Neuilly-Plaisance : Nocéens
Neuilly-sur-Marne : Nocéens
Neuilly-sur-Seine : Neuilléens
Neuves-Maisons : Néodomiens
Neuville-de-Poitou : Neuvillois
Nevers : Nivernais or Neversois
Nice : Niçois
Niederbronn-les-Bains : Niederbronnais
Nîmes : Nîmois
Niort : Niortais
Nogaro : Nogaroliens
Nogent-le-Rotrou : Nogentais
Nogent-sur-Marne : Nogentais
Nogent-sur-Oise : Nogentais
Nogent-sur-Seine : Nogentais
Nogent-sur-Vernisson : Nogentais
Noirmoutier-en-l'Île : Noirmoutrins
Noisy-le-Grand : Noiséens
Nontron : Nontronnais
Noyers : Nucériens
Noyon : Noyonnais

Nuits-Saint-Georges : Nuitons
Nyons : Nyonsais
Oignies : Oigninois
Olivet : Olivetains
Oloron-Sainte-Marie : Oloronais
Orange : Orangeois
Orchies : Orchésiens
Orléans : Orléanais
Ormesson-sur-Marne : Ormessonnais
Orsay : Orcéens
Orthez : Orthéziens
Oyonnax : Oyonnaxiens
Ozoir-la-Ferrière : Ozoiriens
Paimbœuf : Paimblotins
Paimpol : Paimpolais
Palais, Le : Palantins
Palaiseau : Palaisiens
Pamiers : Appaméens
Pantin : Pantinois
Paray-le-Monial : Parodiens
Paris : Parisiens
Parthenay : Parthenaisiens
Patay : Patichons
Pau : Palois
Périgueux : Périgourdins
Péronne : Péronnais
Perpignan : Perpignanais
Perros-Guirec : Perrosiens
Petit-Quevilly, Le : Quevillais
Pézenas : Piscénois
Pithiviers : Pithivériens
Plougastel-Daoulas : Plougastels
Poiré-sur-Vie : Genots
Poissy : Pisciacais
Poitiers : Poitevins
Pont-à-Mousson : Mussipontains
Pontarlier : Pontissaliens
Pont-Audemer : Pontaudemériens
Pontault-Combault : Pontellois-
   Combalusiens
Pontivy : Pontivyens
Pont-l'Abbé : Pont-l'Abbistes
Pont-l'Évêque : Pontépiscopiens
Pontoise : Pontoisiens
Pont-Sainte-Maxence : Pontois or Maxipontins
Pont-Saint-Esprit : Spiripontains
Pornic : Pornicais
Port-de-Bouc : Port-de-Boucains
Port-Saint-Louis-du-Rhône : Port-Saint-
   Louisiens
Prades : Pradéens
Privas : Privadois
Provins : Provinois
Puteaux : Putéoliens

Puy-en-Velay, Le : Aniciens or Ponots
Puy-Saint-Vincent : Traversouires
Quesnoy, Le : Quercitains
Quesnoy-sur-Deûle : Quesnoysiens
Quiberon : Quiberonnais
Quillan : Quillanais
Quimper : Quimpérois
Quimperlé : Quimperlois
Rambouillet : Rambolitains
Redon : Redonnais
Reims : Rémois
Relecq-Kerhuon, Le : Relecquois or Kerhorres
Remiremont : Romarimontains
Rennes : Rennais
Revel : Revélois
Reyrieux : Talançonnais
Rezé : Rezéens
Ribeauvillé : Ribeauvilléens
Ricamarie, La : Ricamandois
Riec-sur-Belon : Riécois or Rieccois
Rillieux-la-Pape : Rilliards
Riom : Riomois
Rive-de-Gier : Ripagériens
Roanne : Roannais
Rocamadour : Amadouriens
Rochechouart : Rochechouartais
Rochefort : Rochefortais
Rochefoucauld, La : Rupificaldiens
Rochelle, La : Rochelais
Roche-sur-Yon, La : Yonnais
Rochette, La : Rochettois
Rodez : Ruthénois
Romans-sur-Isère : Romanais
Romilly-sur-Seine : Romillons
Romorantin-Lanthenay : Romorantinais
Roquebrune-Cap-Martin : Roquebrunois
Roquecourbe : Roquecourbins
Roquemaure : Roquemaurois
Roquevaire : Roquevairois
Roscoff : Roscovites
Rosny-sous-Bois : Rosnéens
Rostrenen : Rostrenois
Roubaix : Roubaisiens
Rouen : Rouennais
Roussillon : Roussillonnais
Royan : Royannais
Roye : Royens
Ruitz : Ruitelots
Sables-d'Olonne, Les : Sablais
Sablé-sur-Sarthe : Saboliens
Sabres : Sabrais
Saillat-sur-Vienne : Saillatais
Saint-Amand-les-Eaux : Amandinois
Saint-Amand-Montrond : Saint-Amandois

Saint-Astier : Astériens
Saint-Avertin : Saint-Avertinois
Saint-Avold : Saint-Avoldiens or Naboriens
Saint-Berthevin : Berthevinois
Saint-Brieuc : Briochins
Saint-Céré : Saint-Céréens
Saint-Chamond : Saint-Chamonais or
 Couramiauds
Saint-Chély-d'Apcher : Barrabans
Saint-Claude : Sanclaudiens
Saint-Cloud : Clodoaldiens
Saint-Cyr-l'École : Saint-Cyriens
Saint-Cyr-sur-Loire : Saint-Cyriens
Saint-Denis : Dionysiens
Saint-Didier-en-Velay : Désidériens
Saint-Dié : Déodatiens
Saint-Dizier : Bragards
Saint-Doulchard : Dolchardiens
Sainte-Foy-la-Grande : Foyens
Sainte-Geneviève-des-Bois : Génovéfains
Sainte-Marie-aux-Mines : Sainte-Mariens
Sainte-Menehould : Ménehildiens
Saint-Émilion : Saint-Émilionnais
Saintes : Saintais
Saint-Étienne : Stéphanois
Saint-Étienne-du-Rouvray : Stéphanais
Saint-Flour : Sanflorains
Saint-Fons : Saint-Foniards
Saint-Gaudens : Saint-Gaudinois
Saint-Genest-Malifaux : Genésiens
Saint-Germain-en-Laye : Saint-Germanois
Saint-Gervais-les-Bains : Saint-Gervolains
 or Saint-Gervelains
Saint-Gilles(-du-Gard) : Saint-Gillois
Saint-Gilles-Croix-de-Vie : Gillocruciens
Saint-Girons : Saint-Gironnais
Saint-Gobain : Gobanais
Saint-Gratien : Gratiennois
Saint-Herblain : Herblinois
Saint-Jacut-de-la-Mer : Jaguens
Saint-James : Saint-Jamais
Saint-Jean-d'Angély : Angériens
Saint-Jean-de-Braye : Abraysiens
Saint-Jean-de-Losne : Saint-Jean-de-Losnais
Saint-Jean-de-Luz : Luziens
Saint-Jean-de-Maurienne : Saint-Jeannais
Saint-Julien-en-Genevois : Saint-Juliennois
Saint-Junien : Saint-Juniauds
Saint-Just-Saint-Rambert : Pontrambertois
Saint-Laurent-Blangy : Imercuriens
Saint-Léonard-de-Noblat : Miaulétous
Saint-Lô : Saint-Lois
Saint-Louis : Ludoviciens
Saint-Loup-sur-Semouse : Lupéens

Saint-Maixent-l'École : Saint-Maxentais
Saint-Malo : Malouins
Saint-Mandé : Saint-Mandéens
Saint-Marcellin : Saint-Marcellinois
Saint-Maur-des-Fossés : Saint-Mauriens
Saint-Maurice : Mauriciens
Saint-Méen-le-Grand : Mévennais
Saint-Mihiel : Sammiellois
Saint-Nazaire : Nazairiens
Saint-Nicolas-de-Port : Portois
Saint-Omer : Audomarois
Saint-Ouen : Audoniens
Saint-Palais : Saint-Palaisiens
Saint-Pierre-des-Corps : Corpopétrussiens
Saint-Pol-de-Léon : Saint-Politains or
    Léonards
Saint-Pourçoin-sur-Sioule : Saint-Pourcinois
Saint-Priest : San-Priots
Saint-Quay-Portrieux : Quinocéens
Saint-Quentin : Saint-Quentinois
Saint-Raphaël : Raphaëlois
Saint-Rémy-de-Provence : Saint-Rémois
Saint-Symphorien-sur-Coise : Pelauds
Saint-Tropez : Tropéziens
Saint-Yrieix-la-Perche : Arédiens
Salers : Sagraniers
Salies-de-Béarn : Salisiens
Salies-du-Salat : Salisiens
Salon-de-Provence : Salonais
Saran : Saranois
Sarcelles : Sarcellois
Sarlat-la-Canéda : Sarlat
Sarralbe : Sarralbigeois
Sarrebourg : Sarrebourgeois
Sarreguemines : Sarregueminois
Sartène : Sartenais
Sartrouville : Sartrouvillois
Sarzeau : Sarzeautins
Sassenage : Sassenageois
Saujon : Saujonnais
Saulieu : Sédélociens
Saulxures-sur-Moselotte : Saulxurons
Saumur : Saumurois
Savenay : Savenaisiens
Saverdun : Saverdunois
Saverne : Savernois
Savigny-sur-Braye : Saviniens
Savigny-sur-Orge : Saviniens
Sceaux : Scéens
Schiltigheim : Schilikois
Schirmeck : Schirmeckois
Seclin : Seclinois
Sedan : Sedanais
Sées : Sagiens

Segonzac : Segonzacais
Segré : Segréens
Seignosse : Seignossais
Sélestat : Sélestadiens
Selles-sur-Cher : Sellois
Selongey : Selongéens
Semur-en-Auxois : Semurois
Semur-en-Brionnais : Semurois
Senlis : Senlisiens
Senonches : Senonchois
Senones : Senonais
Sens : Sénonais
Septèmes-les-Vallons : Septémois
Sète : Sétois
Seurre : Seurrois
Sevran : Sevranais
Sèvres : Sévriens
Seyne-sur-Mer, La : Seynois
Seynod : Seynodiens
Seyssel : Seysselans
Sézanne : Sézannais
Sierre : Sierrois
Sigean : Sigeanais
Sillé-le-Guillaume : Silléens
Sisteron : Sisteronais
Six-Fours-les-Plages : Six-Fournais
Sochaux : Sochaliens
Soissons : Soissonnais
Soisy-sous-Montmorency : Soiséens
Solliès-Pont : Sollièspontois
Sommières : Sommiérois
Sorgues : Sorguais
Sotteville-lès-Rouen : Sottevillais
Souillac : Souillagais
Souterraine, La : Sostraniens
Soyaux : Sojaldiciens
Stains : Stanois
Stenay : Stenaisiens
Stiring-Wendel : Stiringeois
Strasbourg : Strasbourgeois
Suippes : Suippas
Suresnes : Suresnois
Tarare : Tarariens
Tarascon : Tarasconnais
Tarbes : Tarbais
Tartas : Tarusates
Tassin-la-Demi-Lune : Tassilunois
Taulé : Taulésiens
Taverny : Tabernaciens
Teyjat : Teyjatois
Tende : Tendasques
Thann : Thannois
Thaon-les-Vosges : Thaonnais
Thiais : Thiaisiens

Thiers : Thiernois
Thillot, Le : Thillotins
Thionville : Thionvillois
Thiviers : Thibériens
Thizy : Thizerois
Thônes : Thônains
Thonon-les-Bains : Thononais
Thouars : Thouarsais
Tignes : Tignards
Tinchebray : Tinchebrayens
Tinqueux : Aquatintiens
Tomblaine : Tomblainois
Tonnay-Charente : Tonnacquois
Tonneins : Tonneinquais
Tonnerre : Tonnerrois
Toucy : Toucycois
Toul : Toulois
Toulon : Toulonnais
Toulouse : Toulousains
Tourcoing : Tourquennois
Tour-du-Pin, La : Turripinois
Tournan-en-Brie : Tournanais
Tournon-sur-Rhône : Tournonais
Tournus : Tournusiens
Tours : Tourangeaux
Toussus-le-Noble : Nobeltussois
Tranche-sur-Mer, La : Tranchais
Trappes : Trappistes
Tréguier : Trégorois
Trélazé : Trélazéens
Trélon : Trélonais
Tremblade, La : Trembladais
Tremblay-en-France : Tremblaysiens
Trets : Tretsois
Trévoux : Trévoltiens
Triel-sur-Seine : Triellois]
Trinité, La : Trinitains
Trinité-sur-Mer, La : Trinitains
Trouville-sur-Mer : Trouvillais
Troyes : Troyens
Tulle : Tullistes
Ugine : Uginois
Ulis, Les : Ulissiens
Union, L' : Unionais
Ussel : Ussellois
Ustaritz : Uztariztar
Uzès : Uzétiens
Vaison-la-Romaine : Vaisonnais
Val-de-Reuil : Rolivalois
Val-d'Isère : Avalins
Valençay : Valencéens
Valence : Valentinois
Valence(-d'Agen) : Valenciens
Valenciennes : Valenciennois

Valentigney : Boroillots
Vallauris : Vallauriens
Vallet : Valletais
Vallon-Pont-d'Arc : Vallonnais
Valognes : Valognais
Valréas : Valréassiens
Vals-les-Bains : Valsois
Vandœuvre-lès-Nancy : Vandopériens
Vannes : Vannetais
Vans, Les : Vanséens
Varennes-sur-Allier : Varennois
Varilhes : Varilhois
Vatan : Vatanais
Vaucouleurs : Valcolorois
Vaugneray : Valnigrins
Vaulx-en-Velin : Vaudais
Vélizy-Villacoublay : Véliziens
Vence : Vençois
Vendeuvre-sur-Barse : Vendeuvrois
Vendôme : Vendômois
Vénissieux : Vénissians
Verdun : Verdunois
Verdun-sur-Garonne : Verdunois
Verfeil : Verfeillois
Verneuil-sur-Avre : Vernoliens
Vernon : Vernonnais
Versailles : Versaillais
Vertou : Vertaviens
Vertus : Vertusiens
Vervins : Vervinois
Vésinet, Le : Vésigondins
Vesoul : Vésuliens
Veynes : Veynois
Vézelay : Vézeliens
Vibraye : Vibraysiens
Vic-en-Bigorre : Vicquois
Vic-Fezensac : Vicois
Vichy : Vichyssois
Vic-le-Comte : Vicomtois
Vic-sur-Cère : Vicois
Vienne : Viennois
Vierzon : Vierzonnais
Vieux-Condé : Vixuex-Condéens
Vif : Vifois
Vigan, Le : Viganais
Vigneux-sur-Seine : Vigneusiens
Vihiers : Vihiersois
Villandry : Colombiens
Villard-de-Lans : Villardiens
Villars-les-Dombes : Villardois
Villecresnes : Villecresnois
Villefontaine : Villards
Villefranche-de-Lauragais : Villefranchois
Villefranche-de-Rouergue : Villefranchois

Villefranche-sur-Saône : Caladois
Villejuif : Villejuifois
Villemomble : Villemomblois
Villemur-sur-Tarn : Villemuriens
Villeneuve-la-Garenne : Villénogarennois
Villeneuve-le-Roi : Villeneuvois
Villeneuve-lès-Avignon : Villeneuvois
Villeneuve-Loubet : Villeneuvois
Villeneuve-Saint-Georges : Villeneuvois
Villeneuve-sur-Lot : Villeneuvois
Villeneuve-sur-Yonne : Villeneuviens
Villeparisis : Villeparisiens
Villepinte : Villepintois
Villers-Cotterêts : Cotteréziens
Villersexel : Villersexellois
Villers-le-Lac : Villeriers
Villerupt : Villeruptiens
Villeurbanne : Villeurbannais
Villiers-le-Bel : Beauvillésois
Vimoutiers : Vimonastériens
Vimy : Vimynois
Vinay : Vinois
Vincennes : Vincennois
Vineuil : Vinoliens
Vire : Virois
Viriat : Viriates
Viroflay : Viroflaysiens
Viry-Châtillon : Castelvirois

Vitré : Vitréens
Vitrolles : Vitrollais
Vitry-le-François : Vitryats
Vitry-sur-Seine : Vitriots
Vittel : Vittelois
Viviers : Vivarois
Vivonne : Vivonnois
Vizille : Vizillois
Voiron : Voironnais
Volvic : Volvicois
Vouillé : Vouglaisiens
Voulte-sur-Rhône, La : Voultains
Vouvray : Vouvrillons
Vouziers : Vouzinois
Wasquehal : Wasquehaliens
Wasselonne : Wasselonnais
Wassy : Wasseyens
Wattrelos : Wattrelosiens
Wimereux : Wimereusiens
Wingles : Winglois
Wissembourg : Wissembourgeois
Yenne : Yennois
Yerres : Yerrois
Yssingeaux : Yssingelais
Yvelines : Yvelinois
Yvetot : Yvetotais
Yzeure : Yzeuriens

Appendix 2: Revolutionary Renamings in France

The Revolution of 1789–1792 saw France in crisis: out with the monarchy, the aristocracy, and organized religion, in with egalitarianism and secularism. The new order affected all areas of society, not least the names of places. Names of royal, aristocratic, or religious origin were largely replaced by secular names, with the renaming process affecting both large towns and small villages. Following the establishment of the Directory in 1795 the former names were gradually restored, but for a time the republic was subjected to a wave of official renaming reminiscent of that imposed in the 20th century in Soviet Russia. In some cases, however, the revolutionary name has persisted, as with the poetically named village of *Bellevue-la-Montagne*, which originally bore the religious name *Saint-Just*.

Below is a broad selection of such renamings. The current name is given first, with the department name following the revolutionary name. Places with (1) and (2) have alternate names, in some cases chronologically. Some of the major renamings are explained in the appropriate Dictionary entry. Thus *Châteauroux* was renamed *Indreville*, while *Marseille* was rechristened *Ville-sans-Nom* ("Town Without a Name"). As can be seen, *Chapelle* ("Chapel"), *Château* ("Castle"), and *Saint(e)* ("Saint") names were ruthlessly eliminated, while *Libre* ("Free") was freely enlisted to replace an undesirable royal or religious element, as *Charlibre* for *Charleroi* ("King") and *Dun-Libre* for *Dunkerque* ("Church").

For similar renamings in Paris, see Appendix 4.

Abancourt: Abancourt-la-Montagne (Oise)
Abergement-Sainte-Colombe, L': L'Abergement-des-Bois (Saône-et-Loire)
Ablain-Saint-Nazaire: Ablain-la-Montagne (Pas-de-Calais)
Abzac: Gar-Dor-Isle (Gironde)
Aguts: Aguts-Rousseau (Tarn)
Aignay-le-Duc: (1) Aignay-Côte-d'Or; (2) Aignay (Côte-d'Or)
Aigueblanche: Blanches-Eaux (Savoie)
Aigues-Mortes: Fort-Peletier (Gard)

Aiguesvives-le-Roi: Aiguevive-la-République (Hérault)
Aime: Les Antiquités (Savoie)
Ainay-le-Château: Ainay-sur-Sologne (Allier)
Ainhoue: Mendiate (Pyrénées-Atlantiques)
Airon-Notre-Dame: Airon-les-Lois (Pas-de-Calais)
Airon-Saint-Vaast: Airon-la-République (Pas-de-Calais)
Aix-en-Gohelle: Aix-Noulette (Pas-de-Calais)
Aix-l'Évêque: Aix-en-Ergny (Pas-de-Calais)

Albertas: Bouc (Bouches-du-Rhône)

Alise-Sainte-Reine: Alise (Côte-d'Or)

Allainville: Franciade-Libre (Yvelines)

Allas-de-Berbiguières: Allas-l'Égalité
(Dordogne)

Allas-l'Évêque: Allas-la-Liberté (Dordogne)

Allues, Les: Valminéral (Savoie)

Alluets-le-Roi, Les: Les Alluets-la-Montagne
(Yvelines)

Ancy-le-Serveux: Ancy-le-Libre (Yonne)

Angerville-Bailleul: (1) La Plantée; (2) Saint-
Médard (Seine-Maritime)

Angerville-l'Orcher: L'Égalité (Seine-Maritime)

Anglès: Belle-Montagne (Tarn)

Anglesqueville-la-Bras-Long: Ang-
lesqueville-la-Réunie (Seine-Maritime)

Angoulême: Montagne-Charente (Charente)

Anguilcourt-le-Sart: (1) Séricourt; (2) Serre-
y-Court; (3) Serricourt (Aisne)

Anizy-le-Château: Anizy-la-Rivière (Aisne)

Antigny-la-Ville: Antigny-la-Montagne
(Côte-d'Or)

Antigny-le-Château: Antigny-sous-le-Mont
(Côte-d'Or)

Anzin-Saint-Aubin: Commune-des-Frères-
Unis (Pas-de-Calais)

Arblade-Brassal: Arblade-le-Bas (Gers)

Arblade-Comtal: Arblade-le-Haut (Gers)

Arbonne: Constante (Pyrénées-Atlantiques)

Arcy-Sainte-Restitue: Arcy (Aisne)

Argelès-de-Bigorre: La Montagne (Hautes-
Pyrénées)

Argenton-Château: Argenton-le-Peuple
(Deux-Sèvres)

Arnac-Pompadour: Arnac-la-Prairie (Corrèze)

Arnaud-Guilhem: Mont-Raisin (Haute-
Garonne)

Arnay-le-Duc: Arnay-sur-Arroux (Côte-d'Or)

Arpajon: Franc-Val (Yvelines)

Arrentès-de-Saint-Joseph: (1) Arrentès-de-
Corcieux; (2) Libre-Forge (Vosges)

Ars-en-Ré: La Concorde (Charente-Maritime)

Artiguedieu: Plaisance-de-Liberté (Gers)

Asfeld: (1) Écry-le-Franc; (2) Escry-le-Franc
(Ardennes)

Aspres-lès-Corps: Mont-Libre (Hautes-
Alpes)

Athesans-Saint-Georges: Athesans-et-les-
Forges (Haute-Saône)

Athie-lès-Moutier: Athie-sous-Réome
(Côte-d'Or)

Auberville-la-Renault: (1) La Réunion; (2)
Saint-Maclou-la-Montagne (Seine-
Maritime)

Aubin-Saint-Vaast: Aubin-Marat (Pas-de-
Calais)

Auchy-les-Moines: (1) Auchy-lès-Hesdin;
(2) Auchy-sur-Ternoise (Pas-de-Calais)

Augy-Bourbonnais: Augy (Allier)

Aumont: Aumont-la-Montagne (Oise)

Aumont: Isle (Aube)

Autels-Saint-Éloi, Les: Sonnettes (Eure-et-
Loir)

Autels-Tubœuf, Les: Commune-sur-Ozanne
(Eure-et-Loir)

Auteuil: Auteuil-Sans-Culottes (Oise)

Authieux-sur-le-Port-Saint-Ouen:
Authieux-sur-le-Port-des-Sans-Culottes
(Seine-Maritime)

Autun: Bibracte (Saône-et-Loire)

Auvers-le-Hamon: Auvers-l'Union (Sarthe)

Auxtot: Liberticole (Seine-Maritime)

Auxy-le-Château: Auxy-la-Réunion (Pas-
de-Calais)

Auzouville-Lesneval: (1) Auzouville-la-
Section; (2) Auzouville-sur-Motteville
(Seine-Maritime)

Auzouville-Lesneval: Auzouville-sur-
Motteville (Seine-Maritime)

Availles-Limousine: Availles-la-Montagne
(Vienne)

Avesne-le-Comte: Avesne-l'Égalité (Pas-de-
Calais)

Azat-le-Riz: Azat-l'Unité (Haute-Vienne)

Bagnac: Lacapelle-Bagnac (Loiret)

Baigneville: Les Trois-Moulins (Seine-
Maritime)

Bailleau-l'Évêque: Bailleau-les-Bois (Eure-
et-Loir)

Bailleul-Sire-Berthout: Bailleul-la-Liberté
(Pas-de-Calais)

Baladou: Creysse-et-Baladou (Loiret)

Balleroy: Bal-sur-Drôme (Calvados)

Balnot-le-Châtel: Balnot-sur-Laigues
(Aube)

Ban-le-Duc: Ban-sur-Meurthe (Vosges)

Banlieue-Haute: Haut-Lieu (Nord)

Baons-le-Comte: Baons (Seine-Maritime)

Bar-le-Duc: (1) Bar-sur-Meurthe; (2) Bar-
sur-Ornain (Meuse)

Barcelonnette: Val-Civique (Hautes-Alpes)

Baron: Bar-sur-Nonette (Oise)

Baron: Dère-la-Montagne (Gard)

Baron: La Montagne-des-Piques (Saône-et-
Loire)

Baron: Union (Gironde)

Barre (Château-Thierry): (1) Faubourg-du-
Puits-d'Amour; (2) Puits-d'Amour (Aisne)

Bassompierre: (1) Baudricourt; (2) Mengeval; (3) Saint-Menge (Vosges)

Bastide-d'Anjou, La: La Bastide-de-Fresquel (Aude)

Bastide-des-Feuillants, La: La Bastide-Clermont (Haute-Garonne)

Bastide-du-Temple, La: Labastide (Tarn-et-Garonne)

Bastide-Lévis, La: La Bastide-du-Tarn (Tarn)

Bastide-Saint-Pierre, La: Labastide-du-Tarn (Tarn-et-Garonne)

Bathie, La: Albine (Savoie)

Bâtie-d'Andaure, La: La Bâtie-du-Doux (Ardèche)

Batilly-en-Puisaye: Batilly-sur-Loire (Loiret)

Baume-de-Transit, La: La Baume-Marat (Drôme)

Baume-les-Dames: Baume-sur-le-Doubs (Doubs)

Baume-les-Messieurs: Baume-le-Jura (Jura)

Bazoches-en-Dunois: Bazoches-le-Plaisant (Eure-et-Loir)

Beaucaire: Pont-National (Gard)

Beaucamp: (1) Beau-Retranchement-sur-Mer; (2) Saint-Étienne (Seine-Maritime)

Beaufort: Mont-Grand (Savoie)

Beaulieu: Union-Bel-Air (Ardèche)

Beaumerie-Saint-Martin: Beaumerie (Pas-de-Calais)

Beaumont: Bourg-Montagne (Puy-de-Dôme)

Beaumont: Chabreilles (Ardèche)

Beaumont-le-Vicomte: Beaumont-sur-Sarthe (Sarthe)

Beaurain-Château: Beaurain-sur-Canche (Pas-de-Calais)

Bédouin: Bédouin-l'Anéanti (Vaucluse)

Beire-le-Châtel: Beire-le-Grand (Côte-d'Or)

Belle-Église: Belle-Montagne (Oise)

Belle-Isle-en-Mer: Île-de-l'Unité (Morbihan)

Bellecombe-en-Tarentaise: Le Torrent (Savoie)

Bellegarde (Fort): (1) Midi-Libre; (2) Sud-Libre (Pyrénées-Orientales)

Bellentre: Entrée-Belle (Savoie)

Belleville: Mont-Chalier (Paris)

Bellot: Bellot-la-Montagne (Seine-et-Marne)

Belluire-et-Saint-Seurin: Belluire (Charente-Maritime)

Berchères-l'Évêque: Berchères-les-Pierres (Eure-et-Loir)

Bergères-lès-Vertus: Mont-Aimé (Marne)

Bergues-Saint-Yinoc: Bergues-sur-Colme (Nord)

Bernard, Le: Bonfond (Vendée)

Bertincourt: Ossimont (Pas-de-Calais)

Bérulles: Séant-en-Othe (Aube)

Besace, La: Coteau-Libre (Ardennes)

Bessay-le-Monial: Bessay-sur-Allier (Allier)

Bessey-la-Cour: Bessey-la-Fontaine (Côte-d'Or)

Besseyre-Saint-Mary, La: La Besseyre-Nivôse (Haute-Loire)

Béthisy-Saint-Martin: Béthisy-sur-Autonne (Oise)

Béthisy-Saint-Pierre: Béthisy-la-Butte (Oise)

Beuzeville-la-Grenier: (1) L'Ingénue; (2) Saint-Martin-le-Généreux (Seine-Maritime)

Béville-le-Comte: Béville-la-Fontaine (Eure-et-Loir)

Bézu-Saint-Germain: Bézu-le-Grand (Aisne)

Biache-Saint-Vaast: Biache-sous-Scarpe (Pas-de-Calais)

Bièvres-le-Châtel: (1) Bièvre-la-Montagne; (2) Bièvre (Yvelines)

Biron: Mont-Rouge (Dordogne)

Blanc-Nez, Cap: Mont-la-Liberté (Pas-de-Calais)

Blay: Bellepente (Savoie)

Bléville: Saint-Jean-sur-Mer (Seine-Maritime)

Blosseville-Bonsecours: Blosseville-la-Montagne (Seine-Maritime)

Bockenheim: Sarre-Union (Bas-Rhin)

Boinet: Laussou (Lot-et-Garonne)

Boiry-Saint-Martin: Boiry-la-Montagne (Pas-de-Calais)

Boiry-Sainte-Rictrude: Boiry-l'Égalité (Pas-de-Calais)

Bois, Le: La Vérité (Charente-Maritime)

Bois-le-Roi: Bois-la-Nation (Seine-et-Marne)

Bois-les-Dames: Bois-Libre (Ardennes)

Bois-Normand-en-Ouche: Bois-Normand-près-Lyre (Eure)

Bois-Sainte-Marie, Le: Bois-Marie (Saône-et-Loire)

Boisleux-Saint-Marc: (1) Léanette; (2) Liauwette (Pas-de-Calais)

Boissise-le-Roi: Boissise-la-Nation (Seine-et-Marne)

Boissy-Saint-Léger: Boissy-la-Montagne (Yvelines)

Bonneval-en-Tarentaise: Bonnevallée (Savoie)

Bonneville: (1) Mont-Mole; (2) Mont-Molez (Haute-Savoie)

Bordeaux: Commune-Franklin (Gironde)

Bordeaux-Saint-Clair: La Trinité (Seine-Maritime)

Bornambusc: L'Union (Seine-Maritime)

Bosc-d'Avoiras, Le: Ruyernous (Hérault)

Bouchet-Saint-Nicolas: Bouchet-le-Lac (Haute-Loire)

Boucieu-le-Roi: Boucieu-le-Doux (Ardèche)

Bouillant: Bouillant-Germinal (Oise)

Bouin: Île-Marat (Vendée)

Bouin-Saint-Vaast: Bouin-Beaurepaire (Pas-de-Calais)

Boullay-les-Deux-Églises, Le: Boullay-la-Montagne (Eure-et-Loir)

Boullay-Mivoye, Le: Boullay-Brutus (Eure-et-Loir)

Boullay-Thierry, Le: Boullay-la-Société (Eure-et-Loir)

Boulogne-sur-Mer: Port-de-l'Union (Pas-de-Calais)

Bouquenom: Sarre-Union (Bas-Rhin)

Bourbon-Bourbon: (1) Boulbon-la-Montagne; (2) Bourg-Montagne (Bouches-du-Rhône)

Bourbon-l'Archambaud: Bourges-les-Bains (Allier)

Bourbon-Lancy: Bellevue-les-Bains (Saône-et-Loire)

Bourg-de-Visa: Bien-Avisat (Tarn-et-Garonne)

Bourg-des-Comptes: Bourg-la-Montagne (Ille-et-Vilaine)

Bourg-du-Péage: Unité-sur-Isère (Drôme)

Bourg-en-Bresse: (1) Bourg-Regénéré; (2) Épi-d'Ain; (3) Épi-d'Or (Ain)

Bourg-la-Reine: Bourg-Égalité (Paris)

Bourg-le-Comte: (1) Basses-Marches-du-Bourbonnais; (2) Bourg-le-Mont (Saône-et-Loire)

Bourg-le-Roi: Bourg-la-Loi (Sarthe)

Bourg-Saint-Andéol: (1) Bourg-sur-Rhône; (2) Commune-Libre (Ardèche)

Bourg-Saint-Bernard: Bourg-la-Loy (Haute-Garonne)

Bourg-Saint-Christophe: Bourg-sans-Fontaine (Ain)

Bourg-Saint-Maurice: Nargue-Sarde (Savoie)

Bourget, Le: Bourg-la-Montagne (Savoie)

Boussac: Boussac-la-Montagne (Creuse)

Boussac-les-Églises: Boussac-le-Bourg (Creuse)

Boussy-Saint-Antoine: Boussy-sous-Sénart (Yvelines)

Bouté, Le: Boutet (Gers)

Bouxières-aux-Dames: Bouxières-sur-Mont (Meurthe-et-Moselle)

Bozel: Fructidor (Savoie)

Braux-le-Comte: Braux-sur-Ravet (Aube)

Braux-Saint-Remy: (1) Braux-Cérès; (2) Braux-Val-Cérès (Marne)

Braux-Sainte-Cohière: (1) Braux-sous-Valmy; (2) Braux; (3) Mont-Braux (Marne)

Bréauté: Le Bourg-Libre (Seine-Maritime)

Bretteville: La Nativité (Seine-Maritime)

Brévainville: Brévain-Commune (Loir-et-Cher)

Briançon: Les Cols (Savoie)

Bridoré: (1) Bridoré-et-Martin; (2) Cerçay-Bridoré (Indre-et-Loire)

Brie-Comte-Robert: (1) Brie-la-Ville; (2) Brie-Libre; (3) Brie-sur-Hières (Seine-et-Marne)

Brie-sous-Chalais: Montlauzance (Charente)

Brienne-le-Château: Brienne-le-Bourg (Aube)

Brienon-l'Archévêque: (1) Brienon-d'Armançon; (2) Brienon-sur-Armançon (Yonne)

Brindas: Brindas-sur-Roches (Rhône)

Brinon-les-Allemands: Brinon-le-Franc (Nièvre)

Briscous: Hiribery (Pyrénées-Atlantiques)

Broglie: Chambrois (Eure)

Bruyères-le-Châtel: Bruyères-Libre (Yvelines)

Bucy-le-Roi: Bucy-la-République (Loiret)

Buglise: (1) Saint-Pierre-de-Bonsecours; (2) L'Unité-Nationale (Seine-Maritime)

Bussière-Poitevine: Bussière-l'Égalité (Haute-Vienne)

Bussière-Saint-Georges: Bussière-Nouvelle (Creuse)

Bussy-le-Château: Bussy-les-Mottes (Marne)

Bussy-Saint-Martin: Montagne (Seine-et-Marne)

Buxy-le-Royal: (1) Buxy-le-National; (2) Grand-Buxy (Saône-et-Loire)

Buzançais: La Fraternité-sur-Indre (Indre)

Caluire-et-Cuire: Scévola (Rhône)

Cambo: La Montagne (Pyrénées-Atlantiques)

Cambronne: Cambronne-le-Mont-Brutus
(Oise)

Candillargues: Côme-de-la-Palus (Hérault)

Capbreton: Capbrutus (Landes)

Capelles-les-Grands: Capelles-les-Patriotes
(Eure)

Carignan: Ivoy (Ardennes)

Carla-le-Comte: Carla-le-Peuple (Ariège)

Carlat-del-Conté: Carlat-le-Peuple (Ariège)

Carrouges: Carrouges-la-Montagne (Orne)

Casteljaloux: Rivière-Montagne (Gers)

Castelmoron-d'Albret: Castel-Marat
(Gironde)

Castelnau: Belhair-de-la-Garde (Gard)

Castelnau-Barbarens: Mont-d'Arrast (Gers)

Castelnau-d'Anglès: Montagnon (Gers)

Castelnau-de-Montratier: Castelnau-la-
Montagne (Lot)

Castelnau-Fimarcon: Castelnau-sur-
l'Auvignon (Gers)

Castelnau-Rivière-Basse: Mont-Louet
(Hautes-Pyrénées)

Castelsagrat: Chêne-Vert (Tarn-et-Garonne)

Castelsagrat: La Montagne-de-Traverse
(Tarn-et-Garonne)

Castelsarrasin: Mont-Sarrazin (Tarn-et-
Garonne)

Castets-des-Landes: (1) Cap-de-la-Côte-
Verte; (2) Rameau-Vert (Landes)

Castillon-de-Bats: Castillon-sur-Gélise
(Gers)

Cateau, Le: Fraternité-sur-Selle (Nord)

Catillon: Égalité-sur-Sambre (Nord)

Caumont-sur-Garonne: (1) Alout-sur-
Garonne; (2) Mont-Calvat (Lot-et-
Garonne)

Caux: Aron-la-Montagne (Nièvre)

Cavron-Saint-Martin: Cavron-l'Unité (Pas-
de-Calais)

Celle-Condé, La: La Celle-sur-Arnon
(Cher)

Celle-Guénand, La: (1) Lasselle-Remillon
(2) La Selle-Remillon (Indre-et-Loire)

Celle-Saint-Avant, La: (1) Lasselle-Avant;
(2) La Selle-Avant (Indre-et-Loire)

Celle-Saint-Cloud, La: La Celle-les-
Bruyères (Yvelines)

Celles-les-Condé: Vallon-Libre (Aisne)

Cercy-la-Tour: Cercy-sur-Aron (Nièvre)

Cerisy-l'Abbaye: Cerisy-la-Forêt (Manche)

Cervières: La Montagne-de-Cervières
(Loire)

Césancey: Val-d'Or (Jura)

Césarches: Cap-d'Arly (Savoie)

Cevins: La Roche (Savoie)

Ceyssac: Ceyssac-la-Roche (Haute-Loire)

Chaise-Dieu-du-Theil: Chaise-du-Theil
(Eure)

Chaize-le-Vicomte, La: Haute-Chaize
(Vendée)

Chalo-Saint-Mars: Chalo-la-Raison (Yvelines)

Chamarande: Bonne-Commune (Yvelines)

Chambord: Bordchamp (Loir-et-Cher)

Chambost: Beauchamp (Rhône)

Champ-au-Roi, Le: Champ-sur-Barse
(Aube)

Champ-le-Duc: Champ-sur-Lizerne
(Vosges)

Champ-Saint-Père, Le Champ-Perdu
(Vendée)

Champagnac-la-Noaille: Champagnac-la-
Montagne (Corrèze)

Champagne-la-Noaille: Champagne-le-
Doustre (Corrèze)

Champagné-Saint-Hilaire: Champagné-la-
Montagne (Vienne)

Champagny: Agreste (Savoie)

Champdeuil: Champlibre (Seine-et-Marne)

Champrond-en-Gatine: Champrond-Marat
(Eure-et-Loir)

Chantelle-le-Château: Chantelle (Allier)

Chantilly: Champ-Libre (Oise)

Chapelle, La: Bel-Air-aux-Bois (Ardennes)

Chapelle, La: Val-sur-Sonne (Isère)

Chapelle, La: Vaudragon (Rhône)

Chapelle-Achard, La: Belle-Chasse (Vendée)

Chapelle-Agnon: (1) Agnon; (2) Pierre-
Blanche (Puy-de-Dôme)

Chapelle-aux-Choux, La: Vallon-sur-Loir
(Sarthe)

Chapelle-aux-Lys, La: Bellevue (Vendée)

Chapelle-aux-Saints, La: (1) La Chapelle-
aux-Prés; (2) Les Prés (Corrèze)

Chapelle-Bâton, La: La Pique-Bâton
(Charente-Maritime)

Chapelle-de-Bragny, La: Bragny-sur-Grosne
(Saône-et-Loire)

Chapelle-des-Bois, La: La Poterie
(Charente-Maritime)

Chapelle-des-Marais, La: La Réunion
(Loire-Atlantique)

Chapelle-en-Serval, La: Rameuse (Oise)

Chapelle-Enchérie, La: Bois-Chéri (Loir-et-
Cher)

Chapelle-Espinasse, La: Le Doustre
(Corrèze)

Chapelle-et-Felcourt, La: Felcourt (Marne)

Chapelle-Gautier, La: La Chapelle-en-Brie (Seine-et-Marne)

Chapelle-Graillouse, La: Graillouze-sur-Loire (Ardèche)

Chapelle-Guillaume: Yerre (Eure-et-Loir)

Chapelle-Hermier, La: Josnay (Vendée)

Chapelle-Hortemale, La: Hortemale (Indre)

Chapelle-la-Reine, La: (1) La Chapelle-l'Égalité; (2) La Chapelle-Sainte-Geneviève (Seine-et-Marne)

Chapelle-Monthodon, La: Monthodon (Aisne)

Chapelle-Montlinard, La: Montlinard (Cher)

Chapelle-Montmartin, La: Montmartin (Loir-et-Cher)

Chapelle-Naude, La: Sâne-la-Morte (Saône-et-Loire)

Chapelle-Royale: Chapelle-sur-Yerre (Eure-et-Loir)

Chapelle-Saint-Denis, La: Chapelle-Franciade (Paris)

Chapelle-Saint-Hippolyte, La: Hypolite (Indre-et-Loire)

Chapelle-Saint-Jean, La: La Montagne (Dordogne)

Chapelle-Saint-Laud, La: La Montagne (Maine-et-Loire)

Chapelle-Saint-Laurian, La: La Menoterie (Indre)

Chapelle-Saint-Pierre, La: Pierre-la-Montagne (Oise)

Chapelle-Saint-Sauveur: Loréole (Loire-Atlantique)

Chapelle-Saint-Sauveur, La: Masselibre (Saône-et-Loire)

Chapelle-sous-Chanéac, La: Peledru (Ardèche)

Chapelle-sous-Orbais, La: Luceval (Marne)

Chapelle-sur-Loire, La: Les Trois-Volets (Indre-et-Loire)

Chapelle-Trècle, La: Sâne-la-Vive (Saône-et-Loire)

Chapelle-Vendômoise, La: Le Temple-Vendômois (Loir-et-Cher)

Chapelle-Villars, La: Villars-en-Montagne (Saône-et-Loire)

Chapelles, Les: Des-Sillons (Savoie)

Chapelles-Bourbons, Les: Les Chapelles-l'Union (Seine-et-Marne)

Chappes: Chapes (Allier)

Charbonnières: Charbonnières-les-Bains (Rhône)

Charenton-le-Pont: Le Républicain (Paris)

Charlemont: Fort-la-Montagne (Ardennes)

Charleroi: Charlibre (Ardennes)

Charleville: Libreville (Ardennes)

Charmontois-l'Abbé: (1) Charmontel; (2) Orme-sur-Aisne (Marne)

Charmontois-le-Roi: Charmontois-sur-Aisne (Marne)

Chassiers-Tauriers: Fanzove (Ardèche)

Chasteaux: La Fraternité (Corrèze)

Chastellux: Pont-sur-Cure (Yonne)

Château: La Combe (Saône-et-Loire)

Château, Le: Faubourg-la-Montagne (Ariège)

Château-Arnoux: La Roche-Arnoux (Alpes-de-Haute-Provence)

Château-Brehain: Brehain-Bas (Meurthe-et-Moselle)

Château-Chervix: Chervix-la-Chaumière (Haute-Vienne)

Château-Chinon: Chinon-la-Montagne (Nièvre)

Château-d'Oléron, Le: (1) Cité-de-l'Égalité; (2) Égalité (Charente-Maritime)

Château-d'Olonne: Beau-Séjour (Vendée)

Château-de-Londres: Mas-de-Londres (Hérault)

Château-du-Loir: (1) Mont-du-Loir; (2) Mont-sur-Loir; (3) Vau-du-Loir (Sarthe)

Château-Fouquet: Maison-des-Sans-Culottes (Morbihan)

Château-Fromage: Les Fromages (Vendée)

Château-Giron: Mont-Giron (Ille-et-Vilaine)

Château-Gontier: Mont-Hardi (Mayenne)

Château-Guibert: Fond-Guibert (Vendée)

Château-Guillaume: Guillaume-Tell (Indre)

Château-la-Beaume: La Haute-Beaume (Hautes-Alpes)

Château-la-Vallière: Val-Joyeux (Indre-et-Loire)

Château-Lambert: Mont-Lambert (Haute-Saône)

Château-Larcher: Le Rocher (Vienne)

Château-Ponsac: Ponsac-la-Montagne (Haute-Vienne)

Château-Porcien: (1) Marat-Fruvaine; (2) Marat-sur-Aisne (Ardennes)

Château-Renard: Mont-Renard (Bouches-du-Rhône)

Château-Renard: Réunion-sur-Ouanne (Loiret)

Château-Renaud: Beaulieu (Saône-et-Loire)

Château-Renault: Mont-Braine (Indre-et-Loire)

Château-Rouge: Rothdorf (Moselle)
Château-Salins: Saline-Libre (Meurthe-et-Moselle)
Château-sur-Allier: Montbel-sur-Allier (Allier)
Château-Thierry: (1) Château-Égalité; (2) Égalité-sur-Marne (Aisne)
Château-Verdun: Liberté-Verdun (Ariège)
Château-Voué: La Montagne (Meurthe-et-Moselle)
Châteaubourg: Rochebourg (Ardèche)
Châteaubriant: Montagne-sur-Chère (Loire-Atlantique)
Châteaudouble: Montdouble (Var)
Châteaudouble: Pont-Marette (Drôme)
Châteaudun: Dun-sur-Loir (Eure-et-Loir)
Châteaufort: Rochefort (Alpes-de-Haute-Provence)
Châteaufort-les-Moustiers: Sablons (Alpes-de-Haute-Provence)
Châteaugay: Bel-Air (Puy-de-Dôme)
Châteaulin: (1) Cité-sur-Aôn; (2) Montagne-sur-Aôn; (3) Ville-sur-Aône (Finistère)
Châteaumeillant: Tell-le-Grand (Cher)
Châteaumur: Libre-Mur (Vendée)
Châteauneuf: Mont-Franc (Côte-d'Or)
Châteauneuf: Pont-sur-Sornin (Saône-et-Loire)
Châteauneuf-d'Isère: Mivalon-d'Isère (Drôme)
Châteauneuf-d'Oze: Petit-Valon (Hautes-Alpes)
Châteauneuf-de-Chabre: Mont-Chabre (Hautes-Alpes)
Châteauneuf-de-Galaure: Mivalon-de-Galaure (Drôme)
Châteauneuf-de-Mazenc: Neuf-Mazenc (Drôme)
Châteauneuf-de-Rhône: Bourg-le-Rhône (Drôme)
Châteauneuf-du-Faou: Mont-sur-Aulne (Finistère)
Châteauneuf-en-Thimerais: Puits-la-Montagne (Eure-et-Loir)
Châteauneuf-et-Sainte-Marie: Mont-Combade (Haute-Vienne)
Châteauneuf-le-Rouge: (1) La Galinière; (2) Negrel (Bouches-du-Rhône)
Châteauneuf-Miravail: Auche-la-Garde (Alpes-de-Haute-Provence)
Châteauneuf-sur-Charente: Val-Charente (Charente)
Châteauneuf-sur-Cher: Montagne-sur-Cher (Cher)
Châteauneuf-sur-Sarthe: Mont-Sarthe (Maine-et-Loire)
Châteauneuf-Val-Saint-Donat: Beau-Vent-de-Lure (Alpes-de-Haute-Provence)
Châteauredon: Bel-Air (Alpes-de-Haute-Provence)
Châteauroux: (1) Indrelibre; (2) Indreville (Indre)
Châteauroux-les-Alpes: Mont-Roux (Hautes-Alpes)
Châteauvilain: (1) Commune-sur-Aujon; (2) Ville-sur-Aujon (Haute-Marne)
Châteauvillain: Franchison (Isère)
Châtel-Aillon: Les Sablons (Charente-Maritime)
Châtel-et-Chébéry: Mont-Redoutable (Ardennes)
Châtel-Montagne: Mont-sur-Bèbre (Allier)
Châtel-Moron: Moron-la-Montagne (Saône-et-Loire)
Châtel-sur-Moselle: Durbion-Moselle (Vosges)
Châtelard: Rocher-Sec (Alpes-de-Haute-Provence)
Châtelet-en-Berry, Le: Librefeuille (Cher)
Châtenay-lès-Bagneux: Châtenay-la-Montagne (Paris)
Châtenoy-le-Royal: Chatenoy-le-National (Saône-et-Loire)
Châtilllon-en-Bazois: Chatillon-sur-Aron (Nièvre)
Châtillon-le-Duc: Commune-du-Bellevue (Doubs)
Châtillon-les-Dombes: Châtillon-sur-Chalaronne (Ain)
Châtillon-sous-Bagneux: Montagne-l'Union (Paris)
Châtillon-sur-Indre: Indremont (Indre)
Châtillon-sur-Marne: Montagne-sur-Marne (Marne)
Chatrauvieux: Vieux-Logis (Loir-et-Cher)
Châtre-le-Vicomte, La: La Châtre-Langlin (Indre)
Chaudenay-la-Ville: Chaudenay-la-Montagne (Côte-d'Or)
Chaudenay-le-Château: Chaudenay-la-Roche (Côte-d'Or)
Chaumont-sur-Moselle: Neuviller-sur-Moselle (Meurthe-et-Moselle)
Chaussée-Saint-Victor, La: (1) Victoire; (2) Victor-la-Chaussée; (3) Victor (Loir-et-Cher)
Chauvé: Haxo-les-Landes (Loire-Atlantique)
Chazelles-sur-Lyon: Chazelles-la-Victoire (Loire)

Chères, Les: Les Échelles (Rhône)

Chesne-le-Populeux, Le: Le Chesne-la-Réunion (Ardennes)

Chevagnes: Chevagnes-l'Acolin (Allier)

Cheval-Blanc: Blanc-Montagne (Vaucluse)

Chevigny-Saint-Sauveur: Chevigny-Sauveur (Côte-d'Or)

Chézy-l'Abbaye: Chézy-sur-Marne (Aisne)

Chinon: Chinon-sur-Vienne (Indre-et-Loire)

Choisy-le-Roi: Choisy-sur-Seine (Paris)

Ciré-d'Aulnis: Tricolore (Charente-Maritime)

Cirey-le-Château: Cirey-sur-Blaise (Haute-Marne)

Clamart: Le Vignoble (Paris)

Clarens: Quinto-Rustan (Gers)

Clémence-d'Ambel: (1) Belauran; (2) Belaurent; (3) Belloran (Hautes-Alpes)

Clermont: Montclair (Dordogne)

Clermont-en-Argonne: Clermont-sur-Meuse (Meuse)

Clermont-Noble: (1) Benière; (2) Bourg-l'Égalité (Gers)

Clichy-en-l'Aunois: Clichy-sous-Bois (Yvelines)

Clichy-la-Garenne: Clichy-sur-Seine (Paris)

Coiffy-la-Ville: Coiffy-le-Bas (Haute-Marne)

Coiffy-le-Château: Coiffy-le-Haut (Haute-Marne)

Coligny: Nant-Coteau (Ain)

Colle-Saint-Michel, La: Colle-Froide (Alpes-de-Haute-Provence)

Colombey-les-Deux-Églises: Colombey-la-Montagne (Haute-Marne)

Colombier-le-Cardinal: Colombier-de-Déome (Ardèche)

Colroy-la-Grande: La Grande-Fave (Vosges)

Colroy-la-Roche: La Rochette (Vosges)

Compasseur, Le: Tarsul (Côte-d'Or)

Compiègne: Marat-sur-Oise (Oise)

Comps: Port-du-Gard (Gard)

Comté, La: Rochelle-sur-Lawe (Pas-de-Calais)

Conches-en-Ouche: La Montagne-de-Conches (Eure)

Conchil-le-Temple: Conchil-sur-Authie (Pas-de-Calais)

Concoules: Montagne-Concoules (Gard)

Condé: Libre-Puy (Cher)

Condé-en-Bommiers: Cosseron (Indre)

Condé-en-Brie: Vallon-Libre (Aisne)

Condé-le-Butor: (1) Liberté-sur-Orne; (2) Liberté (Orne)

Condé-les-Autry: La Montagne-aux-Bois (Ardennes)

Condé-les-Herpy: Nandin-sur-Aisne (Ardennes)

Condé-lès-Vouziers: Vieux-Pont (Ardennes)

Condé-Sainte-Libiaire: Condé-sur-Morin (Seine-et-Marne)

Condé-sur-Aisne: Scevole-sur-Aisne (Aisne)

Condé-sur-Iton: (1) Marat-sur-Iton; (2) Montagne-sur-Iton; (3) Pelletier-sur-Iton (Eure)

Condé-sur-l'Escault: Nord-Libre (Nord)

Condé-sur-Marne: Montagne-sur-Marne (Marne)

Condé-sur-Noireau: Noireau (Calvados)

Condé-sur-Suippe: Remy-sur-Suippe (Aisne)

Conflans: Roc-Libre (Savoie)

Conflans-Sainte-Honorine: Confluent-de-Seine-et-Oise (Yvelines)

Contes: Pointe-Libre (Alpes-Maritimes)

Corbeil: Corbeil-la-Montagne (Yvelines)

Corbeilles-en-Parisis: Corbeilles-la-Montagne (Loiret)

Corcelles-les-Citeaux: Corcelles-aux-Bois (Côte-d'Or)

Cordes: Cordes-la-Montagne (Tarn)

Corme-Royal: Corme-la-Forêt (Charente-Maritime)

Cormelles-le-Royal: Cormelles-le-Libre (Calvados)

Corquilleroy: Corquille-Libre (Loiret)

Corquoy: Corquoy-le-Libre (Cher)

Corvol-l'Orgueilleux: Corvol-le-Belliqueux (Nièvre)

Côte-Saint-André, La: (1) Côte-André; (2) Côte-Bonne-Eau; (3) Côte-Eau-Bonne (Isère)

Couarde, La: La Fraternité (Charente-Maritime)

Coucouron: Valmont (Ardèche)

Coucy-la-Ville: Coucy-la-Vallée (Aisne)

Coucy-le-Château: Coucy-la-Montagne (Aisne)

Coudray-Belle-Gueule, Le: Le Coudray-la-Montagne (Oise)

Coudray-Saint-Germer, Le: Le Coudray-en-Thelle (Oise)

Coulanges: Cou-Sans-Culottes (Loir-et-Cher)

Coulonges-les-Royaux: Coulonges-sur-l'Autise (Deux-Sèvres)

Courcelles-le-Comte: Courcelles-la-Liberté (Pas-de-Calais)

Courcelles-le-Roi: Courcelles-la-Rivière (Loiret)
Courceroy: La Motelle-sur-Seine (Aube)
Couronne, La: La Palud (Charente)
Coussac-Bonneval: Coussac-Sans-Culottes (Haute-Vienne)
Cram-le-Prieuré: Cram-Chaban (Charente-Maritime)
Craon: Haroué (Meurthe-et-Moselle)
Criquetot-Lesneval: La Hauteur (Seine-Maritime)
Croismare: Hudiviller (Meurthe-et-Moselle)
Croix-aux-Mines, La: Sadey-aux-Mines (Vosges)
Croix-Chapeau: Pique-Chapeau (Charente-Maritime)
Croix-Comtesse, La: La Liberté (Charente-Maritime)
Croix-Daurade: Prairial (Haute-Garonne)
Croix-de-Vie: Havre-de-Vie (Vendée)
Croix-en-Champagne, La: (1) Bel-Air; (2) Montbourg (Marne)
Croix-Rouge, La: Commune-Chalier (Rhône)
Croix-Saint-Ouen, La: Silvie (Oise)
Croixdalle: (1) Décadine; (2) Décadinière (Seine-Maritime)
Cros-de-Géorand, Le: Géorand (Ardèche)
Cruzy-le-Chastel: Cruzy-le-Sec (Yonne)
Culan: Arnon-Libre (Cher)
Curtil-Saint-Seine: Curtil (Côte-d'Or)
Cussy-le-Châtel: Cussy-sur-Arroux (Côte-d'Or)
Custines: Port-sur-Moselle (Meurthe-et-Moselle)
Damazan: Damazan-le-Républicain (Lot-et-Garonne)
Dammarie-les-Lys: Dammarie-les-Fontaines (Seine-et-Marne)
Dampierre-au-Temple: Mont-Dampierre (Marne)
Dampierre-le-Château: Dampierre-sur-Yèvre (Marne)
Dauphin: Mont-Roc (Alpes-de-Haute-Provence)
Decize: (1) Decize-le-Rocher; (2) Rocher-la-Montagne (Nièvre)
Déols: Céréale (Indre)
Derval: Montagne-sur-Kurel (Loire-Atlantique)
Deux-Villes, Les: Givercy (Ardennes)
Dierrey-Saint-Julien: Dierrey-Beaugué (Aube)
Dierrey-Saint-Pierre: Le Grand-Dierrey (Aube)

Dieulefit: Mont-Jabron (Drôme)
Dieulouart: Scarpone (Meurthe-et-Moselle)
Dolus: Sans-Culottes (Charente-Maritime)
Dommartin: Liberté (Pas-de-Calais)
Dommartin: Martin-Libre (Vosges)
Dompierre: Vallière-sur-Nièvre (Nièvre)
Dompierre-sur-Bèbre: Source-Libre (Allier)
Donjon, Le: Val-libre (Allier)
Donzac: Donzac-la-Montagne (Tarn-et-Garonne)
Donzy-le-Royal: Donzy-le-National (Saône-et-Loire)
Droup-Saint-Basle: Droup-le-Grand (Aube)
Droup-Sainte-Marie: Droup-le-Petit (Aube)
Duerne-et-Pitaval: Duerne (Rhône)
Dun-le-Roi: Dun-sur-Auron (Cher)
Dunkerque: (1) Dun-Libre; (2) Dune-Libre; (3) Dunes-Libres (Nord)
Écoust-Saint-Mein: Écoust-Lougastre (Pas-de-Calais)
Égliseneuve-près-Billom: Beauvallon (Puy-de-Dôme)
Églises-d'Argenteuil, Les: (1) Argenteuil; (2) Tricolore (Charente-Maritime)
Entrecasteaux: Entre-Montagnes (Var)
Ermenonville: Jean-Jacques-Rousseau (Oise)
Espaly-Saint-Marcel: Espaly-et-Marcel (Haute-Loire)
Essarts-le-Roi, Les: (1) Les Essarts-la-Montagne (2) Les Essarts-les-Bois (Yvelines)
Essarts-le-Vicomte, Les: Beaucessarts (Marne)
Estissac: (1) Lyébault-sur-Vanne; (2) Val-Libre (Aube)
Estrées-Saint-Denis: Estrées-Franciade (Oise)
Étang-la-Ville, L': L'Étang-les-Sources (Yvelines)
Étréchy: Étréchy-la-Montagne (Yvelines)
Évry-les-Châteaux: Évry-la-Montagne (Seine-et-Marne)
Faget-Abbatial: (1) Faget-Libre; (2) Faget-sur-l'Arrast (Gers)
Fain-lès-Moutier: Fain-lès-Réome (Côte-d'Or)
Faremoutiers: Mont-l'Égalité (Seine-et-Marne)
Faubourg-Montmartre: Faubourg-Mont-Marat (Paris)
Faubourg-Saint-Antoine: Faubourg-de-Gloire (Paris)
Faubourg-Saint-Denis: Faubourg-de-Franciade (Paris)
Faubourg-Saint-Jacques: Faubourg-de-l'Observatoire (Paris)

Faubourg-Saint-Laurent: Faubourg-du-Nord (Paris)

Feissons-sous-Briançon: Charmilles (Savoie)

Feissons-sur-Salins: Fessons (Savoie)

Fère-en-Tardenois: Fère-sur-Ourcq (Aisne)

Ferney: Ferney-Voltaire (Ain)

Ferté-Bernard, La: (1) La Ferté-les-Prés; (2) La Ferté-sur-Huisne (Sarthe)

Ferté-Gaucher, La: La Ferté-sur-Morin (Seine-et-Marne)

Ferté-Langeron, La: La Ferté (Nièvre)

Ferté-Milon, La: La Ferté-sur-Ourcq (Aisne)

Ferté-Saint-Aubin, La: La Ferté-Cosson (Loiret)

Ferté-Saint-Cyr, La: La Ferté-aux-Oignons (Loir-et-Cher)

Ferté-sous-Jouarre, La: La Ferté-sur-Marne (Seine-et-Marne)

Ferté-Vidame, La: La Ferté-les-Bois (Eure-et-Loir)

Feynoil, Le: Bel-Air (Rhône)

Fix-Saint-Genets: (1) Fix-d'Auvergne; (2) Fix-le-Haut; (3) Geneix-de-Fix (Haute-Loire)

Fleury: Pérignan (Aude)

Fleury-la-Tour: Fleury-sur-Canne (Nièvre)

Flines-l'Abbaye: Flines-lès-Raches (Nord)

Fontaine-le-Comte: Fontaine-l'Égalité (Vienne)

Fontaine-Notre-Dame: Cailloux-la-Montagne (Rhône)

Fontaine-Notre-Dame: Fontaine-la-Montagne (Nord)

Fontaine-Saint-Georges: Fontaine-les-Grès (Aube)

Fontainebleau: (1) Fontaine-la-Montagne; (2) Fontaine-le-Vallon (Seine-et-Marne)

Fontenay-le-Comte: Fontenay-le-Peuple (Vendée)

Fontenoy-le-Château: Fontenoy-en-Vosges (Vosges)

Foresaint-Saint-Julien: Foresaint-Républicain (Hautes-Alpes)

Forêt-de-Brotonne: (1) Forêt-de-l'Unité; (2) Forêt-Nationale (Seine-Maritime)

Forêt-du-Temple, La: La Forêt-la-Nation (Creuse)

Forêt-le-Roi, La: La Forêt-Bel-Air (Yvelines)

Fort-Louis: Fort-Vauban (Bas-Rhin)

Fort-Saint-Elme, Le: Fort-du-Rocher (Pyrénées-Orientales)

Fourvières: Quartier-de-la-Montagne (Rhône)

Françay: Gaulois (Loir-et-Cher)

Francheville: Franche-Commune (Rhône)

Franconville-la-Garenne: Franconville-la-Libre (Yvelines)

Fresnay-l'Évêque: Fresnay-le-Sec (Eure-et-Loir)

Fresnay-le-Comte: Fresnay-le-Peuple (Eure-et-Loir)

Fresnay-le-Gilbert: Fresnay-les-Cailloux (Eure-et-Loir)

Fresnay-le-Vicomte: Fresnay-sur-Sarthe (Sarthe)

Frolois: Acraigne (Meurthe-et-Moselle)

Frossay: Mont-Vineux (Loire-Atlantique)

Gaillac-Toulza: Gaillac-la-Montagne (Haute-Garonne)

Gaillon-Archévêque, L': Montagne-sur-Gaillon (Eure)

Gaujac: Cazaux-Républicain (Gers)

Gerberoy: Gerbe-la-Montagne (Oise)

Germigny-l'Évêque: Germigny-sur-Marne (Seine-et-Marne)

Gerville: Les Sans-Culottes-de-la-Manche (Seine-Maritime)

Ginestou: Nivôse (Haute-Garonne)

Gironde: Port-Libre (Gironde)

Gorniès: Renfort (Hérault)

Gournay: Consolation (Seine-Maritime)

Gouy-en-Artois: Gouy-la-Loi (Pas-de-Calais)

Grand-Couronne: La Réunion (Seine-Maritime)

Grand-Rozoy: (1) Les Oulchy; (2) Rozy-les-Oulchy (Aisne)

Grande-Rivière, La: L'Isle (Jura)

Granges-du-Cerf, Les: Les Granges-du-Gratteries (Doubs)

Granges-la-Ville: Granges-le-Bas (Haute-Saône)

Granges-le-Bourg: Granges-le-Haut (Haute-Saône)

Granges-Sainte-Marie, Les: Mont-des-Lacs (Doubs)

Granier: Du Grenier (Savoie)

Granville: Granville-la-Victoire (Manche)

Grau-du-Roi: Grau-le-Peletier (Gard)

Gravelines: Port-d'Aa (Nord)

Graville-Sainte-Honorine: Grasville-Lheure (Seine-Maritime)

Grézieu-la-Varenne: Grézieu-et-Craponne (Rhône)

Grézieu-Souvigny: Grézieu-le-Marché (Rhône)

Grignon: Brumaire (Savoie)

Grimaud: Athénople (Var)

Guerche-de-Bretagne, La: Montagne-de-la-Guerche (Ille-et-Vilaine)

Guiberville: Quiberville (Seine-Maritime)

Guibray: Guibray-la-Montagne (Calvados)

Guiche, La: Champvent (Saône-et-Loire)

Guignes-la-Putain: Guignes-Libre (Seine-et-Marne)

Guillaume-Peyrouse: (1) Mont-Cyra; (2) Mont-Sira (Hautes-Alpes)

Guise: (1) Beaupré; (2) Réunion-sur-Oise (Aisne)

Gurgy-la-Ville: Gurgy-la-Commune (Côte-d'Or)

Gurgy-le-Château: Gurgy-la-Pierre (Côte-d'Or)

Ham: Sparte (Somme)

Ham-les-Moines: Ham-Sans-Culottes (Ardennes)

Harcourt: Champ-Social (Eure)

Hautecour: Haut-Vallon (Savoie)

Hauteluce: Prime-Luce (Savoie)

Hauteville-Godon: Pente-Rude (Savoie)

Havre-de-Grâce, Le: Le Havre-Marat (Seine-Maritime)

Haye, La: La Haye-Descartes (Indre-et-Loire)

Haye-Pesnel, La: La Haye-Libre (Manche)

Heiltz-l'Évêque: Heiltz-Libre (Marne)

Hénin-Liétard: L'Humanité (Pas-de-Calais)

Henrichemont: Mont-Libre (Cher)

Hesdin: Le Pelletier-sur-Canche (Pas-de-Calais)

Hesdin-l'Abbé: Hesdin-au-Bois (Pas-de-Calais)

Hodenc-l'Évêque: Hodenc-les-Vignes (Oise)

Hombourg-l'Évêque: Hombourg-le-Haut (Moselle)

Homme, Le: Le Houlme (Seine-Maritime)

Hotois, Le: Clémery (Meurthe-et-Moselle)

Huby-Saint-Leu: Mont-Blanc (Pas-de-Calais)

Huviller: Jolivet (Meurthe-et-Moselle)

Ids-Saint-Roch: Ids-sur-Arnon (Cher)

Île-d'Oléron: Île-de-la-Liberté (Charente-Maritime)

Île-d'Yeu: Île-de-la-Réunion (Vendée)

Île-de-la-Cité: Île-de-la-Fraternité (Paris)

Île-de-Ré: Île-Républicaine (Charente-Maritime)

Illiers-l'Évêque: Illiers-sur-Condanne (Eure)

Irigny: L'Union-sur-Rhône (Rhône)

Isle-aux-Moines, L': Isle-du-Morbihan (Morbihan)

Isle-d'Albi, L': Lisle-du-Tarn (Tarn)

Isle-de-Noé, L': L'Isle-Bayse (Gers)

Isle-Saint-Denis, L': L'Isle-Franciade (Paris)

Issy: Union (Paris)

Issy-l'Évêque: Issy-la-Montagne (Saône-et-Loire)

Itsatsou: Union (Pyrénées-Atlantiques)

Ivry-la-Bataille: Ivry-la-Hauteur (Eure)

Jard: Jard-la-Montagne (Vendée)

Jarzé: Jarzé-Marat (Maine-et-Loire)

Jonquières-et-Saint-Vincent: Vincent-du-Gard (Gard)

Jouarre: Jouarre-la-Montagne (Seine-et-Marne)

Jouy-le-Comte: Jouy-le-Peuple (Yvelines)

Jully-le-Châtel: Jully-sur-Sarce (Aube)

Juvigny-les-Dames: Juvigny-sur-Loison (Meuse)

Kaysersberg: Mont-Libre (Haut-Rhin)

Kœnigsberg: Sarreinsberg (Moselle)

Kœnigsmacker: Freimacker (Moselle)

Labergement-le-Duc: Labergement-lès-Seurre (Côte-d'Or)

Labeyrie: Izaute (Gers)

Lacourt-Saint-Pierre: Lacourt (Tarn-et-Garonne)

Ladevèze-Ville: Ladevèze-Montagne (Gers)

Ladouze: Montagne-Ladouze (Dordogne)

Lagarde-Noble: Lagarde-Sousson (Gers)

Lagnieu: Fontaine-d'Or (Ain)

Lalleu-Saint-Jouin: Lalleu (Ille-et-Vilaine)

Lalœuf: Unité (Meurthe-et-Moselle)

Lamarche-en-Barrois: Lamarche (Vosges)

Lande, La: Floréal (Haute-Garonne)

Landeronde: Bonne-Lande (Vendée)

Lanloup: Lanmor (Côtes-d'Armor)

Lardenne: Vendémiaire (Haute-Garonne)

Laric: Chabestan (Hautes-Alpes)

Larroque-Maniban: Larroque-sur-l'Osse (Gers)

Lassouts: Montrouge (Aveyron)

Lavans-lès-Saint-Claude: Lavans-lès-Louvières (Jura)

Lavaudieu: L'Orme (Indre)

Laveline-du-Houx: Laveline-devant-Bruyères (Vosges)

Lembège: Garousset-Libre (Gers)

Lespéron: Luc-d'Allier (Ardèche)

Lessard-le-Royal: Lessard-le-National (Saône-et-Loire)

Levroux: Richelaine (Indre)

Lévy-Saint-Nom: L'Yvette (Yvelines)

Liancourt: (1) L'Unité-de-l'Oise; (2) Unité-sur-Oise (Oise)

Licy-les-Moines: Licy-Clignon (Aisne)
Lignières-Châtelain: Lignières-en-Chaussée (Somme)
Ligny-en-Barrois: Ligny (Meuse)
Livry-en-l'Aunois: Livry (Yvelines)
Loge-Mesgrigny, La: La Loge-aux-Chèvres (Aube)
Loiselière, La: La Fraternité (Seine-Maritime)
Longefoy: Cime-Belle (Savoie)
Longeville: Falerne (Vendée)
Longroy: (1) Gué-de-Voyse; (2) Val-Pelletier (Seine-Maritime)
Longueil-Annel: Longueil-sur-Oise (Oise)
Longueil-Sainte-Marie: Longueil-la-Montagne (Oise)
Lonlai-l'Abbaye: Lonlay-sur-Egrenne (Orne)
Lons-le-Saunier: Franciade (Jura)
Lormes: Lormes-la-Montagne (Nièvre)
Louhossoa: Montagne-sur-Nive (Pyrénées-Atlantiques)
Lourdoueix-Saint-Michel: Lourdoueix-Marat (Creuse)
Lourdoueix-Saint-Michel: Lourdoueix-Marat (Indre)
Louroux-Bourbonnais: Lourou-sur-Courget (Allier)
Luçay-le-Captif: Luçay-le-Libre (Indre)
Luçay-le-Chétif: Luçay-le-Libre (Indre)
Lucenay-le-Duc: Lucenay (Côte-d'Or)
Lucenay-les-Aix: Bourg-la-Réunion (Nièvre)
Lucy-les-Moines: Lucy-le-Bocage (Aisne)
Lurcy-le-Bourg: (1) Brutus-le-Bourg; (2) Lurcy-le-Sauvage (Nièvre)
Lurcy-le-Bourg: Lurcy-le-Sauvage (Nièvre)
Lussac-le-Château: Lussac-sur-Vienne (Vienne)
Lussac-les-Églises: (1) Lussac-la-Patrie; (2) La Patrie (Haute-Vienne)
Luynes: Roche-sur-Loire (Indre-et-Loire)
Lyon: Commune-Affranchie (Rhône)
Lyon quartier Bellecour: (1) Canton-de-la-Fédération; (2) Canton-Égalité (Rhône)
Lyon quartier Halle-aux-Blés: Canton-Chalier (Rhône)
Lyon quartier Hôtel-Dieu: Canton-Sans-Culotte (Rhône)
Lyon quartier La Montagne: Canton-le-Peletier (Rhône)
Lyon quartier Le Gourguillon: Canton-de-la-Montagne (Rhône)
Lyon quartier Maison-Commune: Canton-de-la-Liberté (Rhône)

Lyon quartier Métropole: Canton-de-la-Raison (Rhône)
Lyon quartier Nord-Est: Canton-de-la-Convention (Rhône)
Lyon quartier Nord-Ouest: Canton-de-Marat (Rhône)
Lys: Trois-Fontaines (Saône-et-Loire)
Lys-lès-Lannoy: Lannoy-du-Nord (Nord)
Lys-Saint-Georges, Le: Lys-le-Peletier (Indre)
Macot: Riant-Coteau (Savoie)
Magnac-Laval: Magnac-la-Montagne (Haute-Vienne)
Magny-Saint-Médard: Magny-sur-Albane (Côte-d'Or)
Mailly-l'Église: Mailly-le-Mont (Côte-d'Or)
Mailly-la-Ville: Mailly-le-Bas (Côte-d'Or)
Mailly-le-Château: Mailly-le-Vieux (Yonne)
Mailly-le-Château: Mailly-les-Ormeaux (Côte-d'Or)
Maisey-le-Duc: Maisey-sur-Ource (Côte-d'Or)
Maison-aux-Moines: Maison-Montagne (Côte-d'Or)
Maisoncelles-Pervey: Maisoncelles-sur-Seules (Calvados)
Malay-le-Roi: Malay-le-Républicain (Yonne)
Manneville-la-Goupil: Le Zèle-de-la-Patrie (Seine-Maritime)
Marchiennes-Hainault: Marchiennes-Campagne (Nord)
Marcilly-le-Châtel: Marcilly-le-Pavé (Loire)
Marcilly-sous-Mont-Saint-Jean: Marcilly-lès-Mont-Serein (Côte-d'Or)
Marconné: Fontaine-Libre (Pas-de-Calais)
Margouet: Montagne-la-Douze (Gers)
Marigny-l'Église: Marigny-la-Montagne (Nièvre)
Marisy-Sainte-Geneviève: Marizy-le-Grand (Aisne)
Marly-le-Roi: Marly-la-Machine (Yvelines)
Marquise: Beaupré (Pas-de-Calais)
Marseillan: La Barthe-Vallon-de-Losse (Hautes-Pyrénées)
Marseillan-Pardiac: (1) Labarthe-sur-l'Osse; (2) Labarthe-Vallon-de-l'Osse (Gers)
Marseille: (1) Sans-Nom; (2) Ville-sans-Nom (Bouches-du-Rhône)
Martigny-le-Comte: Martigny-le-Peuple (Saône-et-Loire)
Mas-Saintes-Puelles: Mas-l'Union (Aude)
Matton-et-Clémency: Mattonville (Ardennes)

Mauguio: Mont-Salaison (Hérault)

Mauperthuis: Mont-Aubetin (Seine-et-Marne)

Mayres: Sources-d'Ardèche (Ardèche)

Mazères-Campeils: Mont-Joly (Gers)

Melleroy: Melle-le-Peuple (Loiret)

Ménétréol-sous-le-Landais: Ménétréol (Indre)

Meslay-le-Vidame: Meslay-les-Bois (Eure-et-Loir)

Mesnil-au-Vicomte, Le: Mesnil-Forêt (Eure)

Mesnil-aux-Moines, Le: Mesnil-Follemprise (Seine-Maritime)

Mesnil-d'Heudreville: (1) Heudreville; (2) Mesnil-sur-l'Estrée (Eure)

Mesnil-la-Comtesse: Mesnil-la-Liberté (Aube)

Mesnil-le-Roi: Mesnil-Carrières (Yvelines)

Mesnil-Saint-Loup: Mesnil-Haut (Aube)

Mesnil-Saint-Père: Mesnil-sous-l'Orient (Aube)

Mets: Les Trois-Maisons (Meurthe-et-Moselle)

Metz-le-Comte: Metz-la-Montagne (Nièvre)

Meudon: Rabelais (Yvelines)

Meunet: Meunet-sur-Théols (Indre)

Meyrignac-l'Église: Meyrignac-la-Montagne (Corrèze)

Mézières-le-Mont: Mézières (Somme)

Miramont: Monte-Graciosa (Gers)

Moissy-Cramayel: Moissy-la-Plaine (Seine-et-Marne)

Monaco: Fort-d'Hercule (Alpes-Maritimes) [Monaco was annexed to France 1793-1814]

Monastère-sous-Rodez, Le: Bourg-la-Briane (Aveyron)

Monastier, Le: Mont-Breysse (Haute-Loire)

Moncé-en-Belin: Moncé-lès-Le Mans (Sarthe)

Monceaux-le-Comte: Monceaux-sur-Yonne (Nièvre)

Moncontour: Montagne-sur-Dive (Vienne)

Monestier-de-Clermont: Monestier-Libre (Isère)

Mons-en-Laonnois: Mons-les-Creuttes (Aisne)

Mont-aux-Malades, Le: Le Mont-Libre (Seine-Maritime)

Mont-d'Astarac: Montagnard (Gers)

Mont-d'Or, Le: Les Bains-du-Montdor (Puy-de-Dôme)

Mont-Dauphin: Mont-Lion (Hautes-Alpes)

Mont-Dauphin: Mont-Peletier (Seine-et-Marne)

Mont-de-Marsan: Mont-de-Marat (Landes)

Mont-de-Marsan: Mont-Marat (Landes)

Mont-l'Évêque: Mont-sur-Monette (Oise)

Mont-Louis: Monloire (Indre-et-Loire)

Mont-Louis: (1) Mont-de-la-Liberté; (2) Mont-Libre (Pyrénées-Orientales)

Mont-Louis: Mont-Loire (Indre-et-Loire)

Mont-Pardiac: Herrant (Gers)

Mont-Réal: Mont-Serein (Yonne)

Mont-Royal: Sarreinsberg (Moselle)

Mont-Saint-Eloi: Mont-la-Liberté (Pas-de-Calais)

Mont-Saint-Jean: Mont-Serein (Côte-d'Or)

Mont-Saint-Michel: (1) Mont-Libre; (2) Mont-Michel (Manche)

Mont-Saint-Père: (1) Mont-Bel-Air; (2) Mont-sur-Marne (Aisne)

Mont-Saint-Vincent: (1) Belvédère; (2) Mont-Belvédère (Saône-et-Loire)

Montagna-le-Templier: Montagna-la-Doie (Jura)

Montagne-les-Bois: Yzeron-et-Châteauvieux (Rhône)

Montagny: Mont-Noir (Savoie)

Montargis: Mont-Coulounies: (Loiret)

Montastruc-d'Astarac: (1) Montestruc-Égalité; (2) Montestruc-Libre (Gers)

Montaudran: Messidor (Haute-Garonne)

Montbéliard: Mont-Réuni (Doubs)

Montbrison: Montbrisé (Loire)

Montchamp: Montchamp-le-Grand (Calvados)

Montesquiou: Mont-Osse (Gers)

Montet-aux-Moines: Montet (Allier)

Montfort-l'Amaury: Montfort-le-Brutus (Yvelines)

Montfort-la-Cane: Montfort-la-Montagne (Ille-et-Vilaine)

Montfort-le-Rotrou: Montfort-sur-Huisne (Sarthe)

Monthion: Des-Chasseurs (Savoie)

Montigny-le-Roi: Montigny-la-Loi (Yonne)

Montigny-le-Roi: Montigny-Source-Meuse (Haute-Marne)

Montigny-sur-Barthélémy: Montigny-sur-Serein (Côte-d'Or)

Montivilliers: Brutus-Villiers (Seine-Maritime)

Montlezun: Mont-sur-le-Bouès (Gers)

Montmartre: Mont-Marat (Paris)

Montmirey-le-Château: Montmirey-les-Charmes (Jura)

Montmorency: (1) Émile; (2) Mont-Émile (Yvelines)

Montmorin: Mont-Libre (Puy-de-Dôme)

Montréal: Delilia-de-Crose (Ain)

Montréal: Mont-Franc (Gers)

Montréal: Mont-Libre (Ardèche)

Montreuil-aux-Lions: Montreuil-l'Union (Aisne)

Montreuil-Bellay: Montreuil-le-Thouet (Maine-et-Loire)

Montreuil-sur-Mer: Montagne-sur-Mer (Pas-de-Calais)

Montreux-Château: Montreux-Libre (Haut-Rhin)

Montrichard: Montégalité (Loir-et-Cher)

Montroman: Montroman-la-Combe (Rhône)

Montroy: (1) La Montagne (2) Montfaisceau (Charente-Maritime)

Montvalezan-sur-Bellentre: Cime-Bonne (Savoie)

Montvalezan-sur-Séez: Montvalezan (Savoie)

Morey: Trois-Montagnes (Meurthe-et-Moselle)

Morez: Morez-la-Montagne (Jura)

Mormant: Mormant-l'Égalité (Seine-et-Marne)

Mothe-Saint-Héraye, La: La Mothe-sur-Sèvre (Deux-Sèvres)

Motte-Saint-Berain, La: La Motte-sur-Dheune (Saône-et-Loire)

Motte-Saint-Jean, La: Montfleury (Saône-et-Loire)

Motte-Saint-Martin, La: La Motte-sur-Eaux (Isère)

Motteville-Lesneval: Motteville (Seine-Maritime)

Mouchy-le-Châtel: Mouchy-la-Réunion (Oise)

Mouilleron-le-Captif: Mouilleron-le-Libre (Vendée)

Mouleydier: Cybard-de-Mouleydier (Dordogne)

Moulins-Engilbert: Moulins-la-République (Nièvre)

Mourvilles-Hautes: La Montagne (Haute-Garonne)

Moussel: Montagne-du-Droit-de-l'Homme (Eure-et-Loir)

Moustier-Ventadour: Moustier-la-Luzège (Corrèze)

Moutier-Roseille, Le: La Raison (Creuse)

Moutier-Saint-Jean: Réome (Côte-d'Or)

Moutiers: Mont-Salins (Savoie)

Moutiers-en-Argonne: Yonval (Marne)

Moutiers-les-Maunfaits, Les: Les Moutiers-Fidèles (Vendée)

Mussy-l'Évêque: Mussy-sur-Seine (Aube)

Nampont-Saint-Martin: Nampont-l'Égalité (Somme)

Neauphle-le-Château: Neauphle-la-Montagne (Yvelines)

Nempont-Saint-Firmin: Nampont-la-Fraternité (Pas-de-Calais)

Neufchâteau: Mouzon-Meuse (Vosges)

Neuilly-le-Malherbe: Neuilly-sur-Odon (Calvados)

Neuilly-le-Noble: Neuilly-le-Brignon (Indre-et-Loire)

Neuilly-le-Réal: Neuilly-sur-Sanne (Allier)

Neuilly-Saint-Front: Neuilly-sur-Ourcq (Aisne)

Neuville-à-Maire, La: Libre-Maire (Ardennes)

Neuville-au-Pont, La: Pont-sur-Aisne (Marne)

Neuville-l'Archévêque: (1) Marat-sur-Saône; (2) Neuville-sur-Saône (Rhône)

Neuville-les-Dames: Neuville-sur-Renon (Ain)

Neuville-Roy, La: La Neuville-sur-Aronde (Oise)

Neuville-Saint-Vaast: Neuville-l'Égalité (Pas-de-Calais)

Neuville-Sire-Bernard, La: La Neuville-le-Vert (Somme)

Neuville-Vitasse: Neuville-la-Liberté (Pas-de-Calais)

Neuvy-Deux-Clochers: (1) Neuvy-la-Fontaine; (2) Neuvy-sur-Fontaine (Cher)

Neuvy-le-Roi: Neuvy-la-Loi (Indre-et-Loire)

Neuvy-Saint-Sépulcre: Neuvy-sur-Bouzanne (Indre)

Nézignan-l'Évêque: Nézignan-le-Libre (Hérault)

Nieul-lès-Saintes: Nieul-lès-Xantes (Charente-Maritime)

Nizy-le-Comte: Nizy-le-Marais (Aisne)

Noailles: Longvillers-Boncourt (Oise)

Noël-Saint-Martin: (1) Noël-les-Vallons; (2) Rouane (Oise)

Noël-Saint-Remy: Noël-Roberval (Oise)

Nogent-l'Abbesse: Mont-Nogent (Marne)

Nogent-l'Artaud: Nogent-la-Loi (Aisne)

Nogent-le-Roi: Nogent-Haute-Marne (Haute-Marne)

Nogent-le-Roi: Nogent-Roullebois (Eure-et-Loir)

Nogent-le-Rotrou: Nogent-le-Républicain (Eure-et-Loir)

Noirmoutier: Île-de-la-Montagne (Vendée)

Noroy: Mont-Libre (Aisne)

Noroy-l'Archevêque: Noroy-le-Bourg (Haute-Saône)

Notre-Dame-d'Épine: Épine (Eure)

Notre-Dame-d'Oé: Oë (Indre-et-Loire)

Notre-Dame-de-Cognehors: Proclamation (Charente-Maritime)

Notre-Dame-de-la-Mer: Commune-de-la-Mer (Bouches-du-Rhône)

Notre-Dame-de-la-Riche: (1) La Riche-Extra (2) La Varenne-de-la-Riche (Indre-et-Loire)

Notre-Dame-de-Pouligny: Bourg-des-Bois (Indre)

Notre-Dame-de-Val-Francèsque: Moissac (Lozère)

Notre-Dame-des-Millières: Les Étaux (Savoie)

Notre-Dame-du-Champ: Le Champ (Maine-et-Loire)

Notre-Dame-du-Cormier: Martainville-du-Cormier (Eure)

Notre-Dame-du-Pré: Hauts-Prés (Savoie)

Notre-Dame-du-Préaux: Préaux-la-Montagne (Eure)

Notre-Dame-du-Thil: Duthil-la-Montagne (Oise)

Nouvelle-Église: La Barrière (Pas-de-Calais)

Nouvion-l'Abbesse: Nouvion-le-Franc (Aisne)

Onet-le-Château: Onet-la-Montagne (Aveyron)

Oppy: Oppy-la-Liberté (Pas-de-Calais)

Oradour-Saint-Genest: Oradour-sur-Brame (Haute-Vienne)

Origny-en-Thiérache: Origny-sur-le-Thon (Aisne)

Origny-Sainte-Benoîte: Origny-sur-Oise (Aisne)

Ossun: Beauvais-de-Préau (Hautes-Pyrénées)

Ossun: Mardin (Hautes-Pyrénées)

Ouilly-le-Vicomte: (1) Ouilly-l'Union; (2) Ouilly-sur-la-Touques (Calvados)

Oulchy-le-Château: Oulchy-la-Montagne (Aisne)

Ourches: Huviller (Meurthe-et-Moselle)

Ozoir-la-Ferrière: Ozoir-la-Raison (Seine-et-Marne)

Pagny-la-Ville: Pagny-le-Peuple (Côte-d'Or)

Pagny-le-Château: Pagny-l'Égalité (Côte-d'Or)

Paillot: Thennelières (Aube)

Palais, Le: La Montagne (Morbihan)

Panthenor: Faubourg-des-Sans-Culottes (Nièvre)

Parey-Saint-Césaire: Parey-la-Montagne (Meurthe-et-Moselle)

Parigné-l'Évêque: Parigné-lès-Le Mans (Sarthe)

Paroisse-du-Vigan: (1) Commune-des-Monts; (2) Monts (Gard)

Passavant: Mont-sur-Aisne (Marne)

Péage-de-Roussillon, Le: (1) Franc-Passage; (2) Franc-Péage (Isère)

Peisey: Mont-d'Argent (Savoie)

Pellerin, Le: Port-Brutus (Loire-Atlantique)

Perrière, La: Petrée (Savoie)

Petit-Bourg-les-Herbiers, Le: Les Petits-Herbiers (Vendée)

Petit-Châtel, Le: Grenet (Jura)

Petit-Couronne: La Fraternité (Seine-Maritime)

Petit-Saint-Aigulin, Le: Le Petit-Aigulin (Charente-Maritime)

Petite-Sainte-Reine: Petite-Alise (Côte-d'Or)

Petite-Ville, La: La Petite-Commune (Marne)

Peyrat-de-Bellac: Peyrat-la-Montagne (Haute-Vienne)

Peyrat-la-Nonière: Peyrat-la-Montagne (Creuse)

Phalsbourg: (1) Fort-Français; (2) Roc-Ferme (Meurthe-et-Moselle)

Philippeville: La Vedette-Républicaine (Ardennes)

Plessis-de-Roye: Plessis-Belval (Oise)

Plessis-Piquet, Le: Le Plessis-Liberté (Paris)

Plouégat-Guérand: Plouégat-Gallon (Finistère)

Poiseul-l'Évêque: Poiseul (Haute-Marne)

Poivre-Sainte-Suzanne: Poivre (Aube)

Polignac: Mont-Danise (Haute-Loire)

Pommerit-le-Vicomte: Pommerit-les-Bois (Côtes-d'Armor)

Pompignan-le-Franc: Pompignan-Montagne (Tarn-et-Garonne)

Pont-aux-Moines: Pont-Peletier (Loiret)

Pont-Croix: Pont-Libre (Finistère)

Pont-du-Château: Pont-sur-Allier (Puy-de-Dôme)

Pont-en-Royans: Pont-sur-Bourne (Isère)

Pont-l'Abbé-d'Arnoult: Pont-Libre (Charente-Maritime)

Pont-l'Abbé-Lambour: Pont-Marat (Finistère)

Pont-l'Évêque: (1) Pont-Châlier; (2) Pont-Charlier; (3) Pont-Libre (Calvados)

Pont-l'Évêque: Pont-Port (Oise)

Pont-le-Roi: Pont-sur-Seine (Aube)

Pont-Saint-Esprit: Pont-sur-Rhône (Gard)

Pont-Saint-Mard: Pont-sur-Lette (Aisne)

Pont-Saint-Prix: Pont-Morin (Marne)

Pont-Saint-Vincent: Pont-la-Montagne (Meurthe-et-Moselle)

Pont-Sainte-Maxence: Pont-la-Montagne (Oise)

Pont-Sainte-Maxence: Pont-sur-Oise (Oise)

Ponts-de-Cé, Les: Ponts-Libres (Maine-et-Loire)

Port-à-l'Anglais: Port-de-Marat (Paris)

Port-Breton: Rocher-de-la-Sans-Culotterie (Vendée)

Port-Louis: (1) Port-de-l'Égalité; (2) Port-Liberté (Morbihan)

Port-Royal: Port-de-la-Montagne (Yvelines)

Port-Saint-Père, Le: Port-Boulay (Loire-Atlantique)

Port-Sainte-Marie: Port-de-la-Montagne-sur-Garonne (Lot-et-Garonne)

Port-Vendres: Port-de-la-Victoire (Pyrénées-Orientales)

Potherie, La: Châlain (Maine-et-Loire)

Pouilly-en-Auxois: Pouilly (Côte-d'Or)

Pouilly-le-Châtel: Pouilly-sur-Nizerand (Rhône)

Pouru-Saint-Remy: Pouru-sur-Chiers (Ardennes)

Pouvourville: Ventôse (Haute-Garonne)

Pouzauges: Pouzauges-la-Montagne (Vendée)

Pouzauges-le-Vieux: Pouzauges-la-Vallée (Vendée)

Prades: Charbomine (Ardèche)

Pradons: Pré-d'Ardèche (Ardèche)

Pralognan: La Vanoise (Savoie)

Prés-Saint-Gervais, Les: Les Prés-le-Peletier (Paris)

Presles-l'Évêque: Presles-et-Thierny (Aisne)

Pressgny-Orgueilleux, L': Pressagny-sous-Vernon (Eure)

Preuilly-la-Ville: Preuilly-les-Roches (Indre)

Pronleroy: Pron-l'Oise (Oise)

Puy-l'Évêque: (1) Puy-Libre; (2) Puy-sur-Lot (Lot)

Puy-Notre-Dame, Le: Puy-la-Montagne (Maine-et-Loire)

Puy-Saint-Eusèbe: Grand-Puy (Hautes-Alpes)

Puy-Saint-Martin: Puy-Montagne (Drôme)

Puycelci: Puicelcy-la-Montagne (Tarn)

Queige: Des-Ruisseaux (Savoie)

Querhoent: Montoire (Loir-et-Cher)

Queue-en-Brie, La: La Queue-le-Peletier (Yvelines)

Quimper: Montagne-sur-Odet (Finistère)

Quincy-le-Vicomte: Quincy-sur-Armançon (Côte-d'Or)

Ramefort: Rame-Libre (Haute-Garonne)

Réalmont: Montdadou (Tarn)

Réalville: Garde-Mont (Tarn-et-Garonne)

Reignac: Val-Indre (Indre-et-Loire)

Remalard: Remal-la-Montagne (Orne)

Remiremont: Libremont (Vosges)

Reuillon: La Montagne (Saône-et-Loire)

Richebourg-l'Avoué: Richebourg-l'Égalité (Pas-de-Calais)

Richebourg-Saint-Vaast: Richebourg-la-Fraternité (Pas-de-Calais)

Rieux-Mérinville: Rieux-Minervois (Aude)

Rilhac-Lastours: Rilhac-Chaumière (Haute-Vienne)

Rilly: Rilly-la-Montagne (Marne)

Rilly-Sainte-Syre: Rilly-la-Raison (Aube)

Ris-Orangis: Brutus (Yvelines)

Riverie, La: Beaurepaire (Rhône)

Rivière-Devant, La: Isle-Libre (Jura)

Roche-Bernard, La: La Roche-Sauveur (Morbihan)

Roche-en-Regnier: Roche-Marat (Haute-Loire)

Roche-Guyon: Roche-sur-Seine (Yvelines)

Roche-Pot, La: Roche-Fidèle (Côte-d'Or)

Roche-Saint-Cydroine, La: La Roche-sur-Yonne (Yonne)

Rochechouart: Roche-sur-Graine (Haute-Vienne)

Rochefort-en-Terre: (1) Roche-des-Trois; (2) Rochefort-des-Trois (Morbihan)

Rochefoucauld, La: La Roche-Tardoire (Charente)

Rochetaillée: Rochetaillée-sur-Saône (Rhône)

Rocles: Valbaume (Ardèche)

Rocroi: Roc-Libre (Ardennes)

Rognaix: Belle-Arête (Savoie)

Rohan-Rohan: Frontenay (Deux-Sèvres)

Roiffieux: Librefieux (Ardèche)

Roissy-en-Brie: Roissy-les-Friches (Seine-et-Marne)

Romilly-la-Puthenaye: Romilly-près-Bougy (Eure)

Romilly-sur-Seine: Romilly-Voltaire (Aube)

Rontalon: Rontalon-l'Union (Rhône)

Roquebrun: Roc-Libre (Hérault)
Roquebrussane: Roquelibre (Var)
Roquelaure: La Montagne (Gers)
Rouans: Barra-les-Marais (Loire-Atlantique)
Roy-Boissy: Choisy-Boissy (Oise)
Royaumeix: Libre-Meix (Meurthe-et-Moselle)
Roye: Avre-Libre (Somme)
Roye-sur-Matz: Source-du-Matz (Oise)
Royères-Saint-Léonard: Royères-la-Montagne (Haute-Vienne)
Royville: Peupleville (Seine-Maritime)
Rozet-Saint-Albin: (1) Les Mesnils; (2) Rozet-le-Mesnil (Aisne)
Rozier-Saint-Georges: Rozier-Combade (Haute-Vienne)
Rozières: Baubiac (Ardèche)
Rozières-Sommeycire: Baubiac (Haute-Marne)
Rozoy-Bellevalle: Rozoy-Gatebled (Aisne)
Rozoy-en-Brie: Rozoy-l'Unité (Seine-et-Marne)
Rumilly-le-Comte: Rumilly-Beaussart (Pas-de-Calais)
Saincaize: Caize-la-Vallée (Nièvre)
Sains-lès-Fressin: (1) Les Fressins-Pelletier; (2) L'Harmonie (Pas-de-Calais)
Saint-Acheul: Abladène (Somme)
Saint-Adrien: Montrieux (Côtes-d'Armor)
Saint-Affrique: La Montagne-sur-Sorgue (Aveyron)
Saint-Agathon: Bonvalon (Côtes-d'Armor)
Saint-Agnan: Aigna-Haute-Vue (Dordogne)
Saint-Agnan: Blandenant (Saône-et-Loire)
Saint-Agnan: Montagnan (Aisne)
Saint-Agnan-les-Marais: Mont-Agnan (Charente-Maritime)
Saint-Agnan-sur-Sarthe: Montagnan (Orne)
Saint-Agne: Germinal (Haute-Garonne)
Saint-Agrève: Mont-Chiniac (Ardèche)
Saint-Aignan: Aignan-sur-Roche (Tarn-et-Garonne)
Saint-Aignan: Carismont (Loir-et-Cher)
Saint-Aignan: Mont-Aignan (Ardennes)
Saint-Aignan: Scevola-Aignan (Sarthe)
Saint-Aignan-de-Chamesnil: Aignan-le-Propre (Calvados)
Saint-Aignan-le-Jaillard: Jaillard-sur-Sauge (Loiret)
Saint-Aignant-de-Versillat: Versillat-le-Marat (Creuse)
Saint-Aigny: Les Fontaines (Indre)
Saint-Aigulin: (1) Ami-des-Lois; (2) Le Grand-Aigulin (Charente-Maritime)

Saint-Albain: Mont-Marat (Saône-et-Loire)
Saint-Alban: Alban-sur-Cerdon (Ain)
Saint-Alban: Marat-de-Bruège (Gard)
Saint-Alban: Mont-Alban (Isère)
Saint-Alban: Monterminod (Savoie)
Saint-Alban: Ruberlac (Hérault)
Saint-Alban-d'Ay: Monban (Ardèche)
Saint-Alban-d'Hurtières: Cucheron (Savoie)
Saint-Alban-de-Montbel: Port-de-Montbel (Savoie)
Saint-Alban-des-Villards: Merlet (Savoie)
Saint-Alban-en-Montagne: (1) Alban-les-Baumes; (2) Luc-d'Alban (Ardèche)
Saint-Alban-sous-Sampzon: (1) Alban-le-Gras; (2) Chenevière-sur-Chassezac; (3) Trois-Eaux (Ardèche)
Saint-Alexandre: Roquebrune (Gard)
Saint-Alyre-ès-Montagne: Charlus (Puy-de-Dôme)
Saint-Amand: Amand-du-Fion (Marne)
Saint-Amand: Montlion (Marne)
Saint-Amand: Riche-Amand (Loir-et-Cher)
Saint-Amand: L'Union (Pas-de-Calais)
Saint-Amand-de-Coly: Amand-le-Vallon (Dordogne)
Saint-Amand-les-Eaux: Elnon-Libre (Nord)
Saint-Amand-Magnazeix: Amand-les-Montagnes (Haute-Vienne)
Saint-Amand-Montrond: Libreval (Cher)
Saint-Ambreuil: La Loi-sur-Grosne (Saône-et-Loire)
Saint-Ambroix: Pont-Cèze (Gard)
Saint-Amé: Nol-sur-Moselle (Vosges)
Saint-Amédée-de-la-Côte: (1) Côte-Belle-du-Granier; (2) Côte-Belle (Savoie)
Saint-Amour: Bellevue (Saône-et-Loire)
Saint-Amour: Franc-Amour (Jura)
Saint-Andéol-de-Fourchades: Fourchades (Ardèche)
Saint-Andéol-le-Château: Andéol-Libre (Rhône)
Saint-Andeux: Montribois (Côte-d'Or)
Saint-André: Montfort (Savoie)
Saint-André: Montmarat (Tarn)
Saint-André: Fort-Égalité (Jura)
Saint-André: Mont-Désert (Haute-Garonne)
Saint-André-aux-Bois: L'Union-aux-Bois (Pas-de-Calais)
Saint-André-d'Embrun: Mont-Aurel (Hautes-Alpes)
Saint-André-d'Olérargue: Oleyrargues (Gard)
Saint-André-d'Orsay: Les Minéraux (Vendée)

Saint-André-de-Chalançon: André-sur-Ance (Haute-Loire)

Saint-André-de-Cruzières: (1) Claisses; (2) Cruzières-Supérieur (Ardèche)

Saint-André-de-Cubzac: Montalon (Gironde)

Saint-André-de-Lancize: Côte-de-Lancize (Lozère)

Saint-André-de-Lidon: (1) Lidon; (2) Union-de-Lidon (Charente-Maritime)

Saint-André-de-Majencoules: (1) Majencoules-l'Hérault; (2) Majencoules (Gard)

Saint-André-de-Roquepertuis: Roquepertuis (Gard)

Saint-André-de-Rosans: (1) André-sur-Aigues; (2) André-sur-Coule (Hautes-Alpes)

Saint-André-de-Sangonis: Beaulieu (Hérault)

Saint-André-de-Seignaux: Haute-Montagne (Landes)

Saint-André-de-Valborgne: Valborgne-du-Gard (Gard)

Saint-André-des-Effengeas: Montvert (Ardèche)

Saint-André-en-Bochaine: La Faurie (Hautes-Alpes)

Saint-André-en-Bresse: Franc-Cœur (Saône-et-Loire)

Saint-André-en-Morvand: (1) La Montagne-André; (2) Pelletier-le-Rocher (Nièvre)

Saint-André-en-Terre-Pleine: Terre-Plaine (Yonne)

Saint-André-Goule-d'Oie: Goule-d'Oie (Vendée)

Saint-André-la-Côte: Haute-Montagne (Rhône)

Saint-André-Lachamp: (1) Allure; (2) Lachamp-du-Fer (Ardèche)

Saint-André-le-Château: (1) Bourg-Désert; (2) Bourg-le-Désert (Saône-et-Loire)

Saint-André-les-Alpes: Verdissole (Alpes-de-Haute-Provence)

Saint-André-sur-Mareuil: Vigneron (Vendée)

Saint-André-Treize-Voies: Treize-Voies (Vendée)

Saint-Andréol-de-Trouillas: Le Pradel (Gard)

Saint-Anthème: Pont-sur-Ance (Puy-de-Dôme)

Saint-Anthot: Anthot-la-Montagne (Côte-d'Or)

Saint-Antoine: La Motte-Feirand (Isère)

Saint-Antoine: Villenouvelle (Tarn-et-Garonne)

Saint-Antoine-du-Rocher: Le Rocher (Indre-et-Loire)

Saint-Antonin: Libre-Val (Tarn-et-Garonne)

Saint-Antonin-Lacalm: Haute-Montagne (Tarn)

Saint-Aoustrille Beau-Vinal (Indre)

Saint-Août: (1) Août-les-Bois; (2) Thermidor (Indre)

Saint-Apollinaire: (1) Apollinaire; (2) Apollon (Hautes-Alpes)

Saint-Apollinaire: (1) Fontaine-Soyer; (2) Fontaine-Soyeur (Côte-d'Or)

Saint-Apollinaire: Mont-Apollon (Hautes-Alpes)

Saint-Apollinaire-de-Rias: Riaspol (Ardèche)

Saint-Appolinard: Appolinard (Isère)

Saint-Apre: Barra-sur-Dronne (Dordogne)

Saint-Arailles (near Barcugnan): Marat (Gers)

Saint-Arailles (near Mirannes): Lamothe-sur-l'Osse (Gers)

Saint-Arcons-d'Allier: Arcons-sur-Allier (Haute-Loire)

Saint-Arcons-de-Barges: Arcons-Méjeanne (Haute-Loire)

Saint-Arnoult: Arnoult-les-Montagnes (Oise)

Saint-Arnoult: Arnoultval (Loir-et-Cher)

Saint-Arnoult: Montagne-sur-Seine (Seine-Maritime)

Saint-Arnoult-en-Yvelines: (1) La Méjeanne; (2) Montagne-sur-Remarde (Yvelines)

Saint-Arroman: Égalité-Sousson (Gers)

Saint-Arroman: Mont-Unité (Hautes-Pyrénées)

Saint-Astier: Astier-sur-l'Isle (Dordogne)

Saint-Aubert: Libreval (Nord)

Saint-Aubin: Aubin-la-Fontaine (Pas-de-Calais)

Saint-Aubin: Auroux-la-Montagne (Côte-d'Or)

Saint-Aubin: Corquelin (Aube)

Saint-Aubin: Franc-Cœur-la-Carrière (Aisne)

Saint-Aubin: Le Marcat (Allier)

Saint-Aubin: Mesnil-Marat (Yvelines)

Saint-Aubin: La Montagne (Eure)

Saint-Aubin: La Moule (Gers)

Saint-Aubin: Puits-Forêt (Indre)

Saint-Aubin-d'Appenai: Claire-Fontaine (Orne)

Saint-Aubin-d'Arquenay: (1) Aubin-Rousseau; (2) Aubin-sur-Orne (Calvados)

Saint-Aubin-d'Aubigné: Aubin-Philonome (Ille-et-Vilaine)

Saint-Aubin-d'Ecrosville: Ecrosville-la-Montagne (Eure)

Saint-Aubin-d'Eymet: Aubin-de-Cahuzac (Dordogne)

Saint-Aubin-de-Courteraie: Vallée-sur-Sarthe (Orne)

Saint-Aubin-de-Fontenay: (1) Fontenay-le-Pesnel; (2) Fontenay-sur-Seulles (Calvados)

Saint-Aubin-de-Luigné: Luigné-sur-le-Layon (Maine-et-Loire)

Saint-Aubin-des-Ormeaux: Aubin-la-Pierre (Vendée)

Saint-Aubin-du-Cormier: Montagne-la-Forêt (Ille-et-Vilaine)

Saint-Aubin-en-Charolais: Champ-Libre (Saône-et-Loire)

Saint-Aubin-le-Dépeint: Commune-du-Dépeint (Indre-et-Loire)

Saint-Aubin-sur-Loire: Bon-Air-sur-Loire (Saône-et-Loire)

Saint-Auclaire: L'Unité (Corrèze)

Saint-Augustin: Augustin-la-Monédière (Corrèze)

Saint-Augustin: La Forêt-sur-Mer (Charente-Maritime)

Saint-Augustin: Mont-l'Unité (Seine-et-Marne)

Saint-Augustin: Peu-de-Fonds (Maine-et-Loire)

Saint-Austremoine: Austremoine-d'Avène (Haute-Loire)

Saint-Avaugour-des-Landes: Les Palières (Vendée)

Saint-Avertin: (1) Vançay; (2) Vansay (Indre-et-Loire)

Saint-Avit: Montavit (Tarn)

Saint-Avold: (1) Rosselgène; (2) Trimouts (Moselle)

Saint-Avre: Antichambre (Savoie)

Saint-Ay: Ay-sur-Loire (Loiret)

Saint-Babel: Les Bois (Puy-de-Dôme)

Saint-Baldoph: L'Albanne (Savoie)

Saint-Barthélémy: Barthélémy-Préhaut (Seine-et-Marne)

Saint-Barthélémy: Beauvais (Lot-et-Garonne)

Saint-Barthélémy: Bon-Air (Maine-et-Loire)

Saint-Barthélémy: Montagne-le-Trieux (Dordogne)

Saint-Barthélémy: Val-de-Melisey (Haute-Saône)

Saint-Barthélémy-le-Meil: Mont-Meil (Ardèche)

Saint-Barthélémy-le-Pin: Pin-d'Issarles (Ardèche)

Saint-Barthélémy-le-Plein: Mont-Plein (Ardèche)

Saint-Basile: Basile-Maron (Ardèche)

Saint-Basile-de-Meyssac: Côte Montagnarde (Corrèze)

Saint-Baudel: Beau-Libre (Cher)

Saint-Bauld: Bault (Indre-et-Loire)

Saint-Baussant: Roche-sur-Mad (Meurthe-et-Moselle)

Saint-Bauzille-de-Putois: Bel-Hérault (Hérault)

Saint-Bazeille: Chalier (Lot-et-Garonne)

Saint-Béat: Entremons (Haute-Garonne)

Saint-Beauliz-d'Hirondel: L'Hirondel (Aveyron)

Saint-Beauzély: Libre-Muse (Aveyron)

Saint-Beauzire: Beauzire-l'Union (Haute-Loire)

Saint-Bel: Bel-les-Mines (Rhône)

Saint-Bénezet-de-Cheyran: Bellevue-la-Montagne (Gard)

Saint-Benin: Charnoux (Allier)

Saint-Benin-d'Azy: Azy-les-Amognes (Nièvre)

Saint-Benin-des-Bois: Source-de-la-Nièvre (Nièvre)

Saint-Benoît: Le Coulet (Alpes-de-Haute-Provence)

Saint-Benoît-de-Carmaux: La Montagne (Tarn)

Saint-Benoît-de-Frégefond: Agros (Tarn)

Saint-Benoît-de-la-Mort: Benoît-les-Bois (Indre-et-Loire)

Saint-Benoît-de-Quinçay: Quinçay-les-Plaisirs (Vienne)

Saint-Benoît-du-Sault: Mont-du-Sault (Indre)

Saint-Benoît-sur-Mer: Bon-Marais (Vendée)

Saint-Benoît-sur-Seine: Thurey (Aube)

Saint-Benoît-sur-Vanne: Courmorin (Aube)

Saint-Bérain: La Roche-Bérain (Haute-Loire)

Saint-Bérain-sur-Dheune: Bérain-la-Dheune (Saône-et-Loire)

Saint-Bernard: Brétigny-la-Rue (Côte-d'Or)

Saint-Beron: Gorges-de-Chailles (Savoie)

Saint-Berthevin-la-Tannière: Centranne (Mayenne)

Saint-Bertrand-de-Comminges: Hauteville (Haute-Garonne)

Saint-Beury: Bellevue-sur-Armançon (Côte-d'Or)

Saint-Blaise-la-Roche: La Roche-Blaise (Vosges)

Saint-Blaize: Montfroid (Haute-Savoie)

Saint-Blancard: Lasserre (Gers)

Saint-Bohaire: (1) Bienbohaire; (2) Bien-boire; (3) Bohaire (Loir-et-Cher)

Saint-Boil: Noizeret (Saône-et-Loire)

Saint-Bon: Bonval (Marne)

Saint-Bon: Prairial (Savoie)

Saint-Bonnet: Bonnet-du-Gard (Gard)

Saint-Bonnet: Bonnet-Rouge (Charente)

Saint-Bonnet: Bonnet-Rouge (Charente-Maritime)

Saint-Bonnet: Mont-sur-Belnave (Allier)

Saint-Bonnet: Montagne (Cantal)

Saint-Bonnet-de-Four: Bonnet-Libre (Allier)

Saint-Bonnet-de-Joux: Bonnet-Rouge (Saône-et-Loire)

Saint-Bonnet-de-Salendrenque: Mont-Bonnet (Gard)

Saint-Bonnet-Elvert: Liberté-Bonnet-Rouge (Corrèze)

Saint-Bonnet-en-Bresse: Bonnet-sur-Guyotte (Saône-et-Loire)

Saint-Bonnet-en-Champsaur: Bonnet-Libre (Hautes-Alpes)

Saint-Bonnet-la-Rivière: Bonnet-Rouge (Corrèze)

Saint-Bonnet-le-Château: Bonnet-la-Montagne (Loire)

Saint-Bonnet-le-Châtel: Bonnet-Libre (Puy-de-Dôme)

Saint-Bonnet-le-Désert: (1) Bonnet-sur-Sologne; (2) Le Désert (Allier)

Saint-Bonnet-le-Froid: Bonnet-Libre (Haute-Loire)

Saint-Bonnet-le-Port-Dieu: Bonnet-près-Bort (Corrèze)

Saint-Bonnet-les-Bruyères: Bonnet-les-Bruyères (Rhône)

Saint-Bouize: Les Jardins (Cher)

Saint-Brès: Mont-Usèze (Gard)

Saint-Bresson: (1) Mont-aux-Truffes; (2) Mont-Truffier (Gard)

Saint-Brevin: Union (Loire-Atlantique)

Saint-Briac: Port-Briac (Ille-et-Vilaine)

Saint-Brice: Fontenay-Brice (Seine-et-Marne)

Saint-Brice: (1) Liberté-sur-Vesle; (2) Montriqueux (Marne)

Saint-Brieuc: Port-Brieuc (Côtes-d'Armor)

Saint-Bris: Bris-le-Vineux (Yonne)

Saint-Brix-Saint-Mandé-des-Bois: Brix-Mandé (Charente-Maritime)

Saint-Broing-les-Moines: (1) Broing; (2) Fontaine-les-Roches (Côte-d'Or)

Saint-Calais: Calais-sur-Anille (Sarthe)

Saint-Calez-en-Saosnois: Calez-en-Saosnois (Sarthe)

Saint-Cannat: (1) Le Saizet; (2) Le Sauzet (Bouches-du-Rhône)

Saint-Caprais: Bruyère (Lot)

Saint-Caprais: Thémistocle (Allier)

Saint-Caradec: Caradec-sur-Oust (Côtes-d'Armor)

Saint-Cassin: Les Bocages (Savoie)

Saint-Cast: Havre-Cast (Côtes-d'Armor)

Saint-Céneri-le-Gérei: L'Isle-sur-Sarthe (Orne)

Saint-Céneri-près-Sées: Ventôse (Orne)

Saint-Céré: (1) Franc-Céré; (2) Seu-Céré (Lot)

Saint-Cernin-de-Larche: L'Union (Corrèze)

Saint-Cézert: Cézert-Libre (Haute-Garonne)

Saint-Chamans: La Fraternité (Corrèze)

Saint-Chamant: Basse-Bertrande (Cantal)

Saint-Chamarand: Beauchamp (Lot)

Saint-Chamas: Port-Chamas (Bouches-du-Rhône)

Saint-Chamond: (1) Mont-Rousseau; (2) Val-Rousseau; (3) Vallée-Rousseau (Loire)

Saint-Chapte: Beauregard (Gard)

Saint-Charles-de-Montchamp: Montchamp-le-Petit (Calvados)

Saint-Charles-de-Percy: Montchamp-le-Petit (Calvados)

Saint-Chartier: Vic-les-Eaux (Indre)

Saint-Chef: Francvallon (Isère)

Saint-Chély-d'Apcher: Roche-Libre (Lozère)

Saint-Chély-d'Aubrac: Vallée-Libre (Aveyron)

Saint-Cheron: Mont-Cheron (Marne)

Saint-Chinian: Vernodure (Hérault)

Saint-Christol: Auxon (Gard)

Saint-Christol: (1) Christolet; (2) Mont-Rond (Ardèche)

Saint-Christol: Pont-Auzon (Gard)

Saint-Christol-de-Rodières: Rodières (Gard)

Saint-Christophe: Beauvais (Charente-Maritime)

Saint-Christophe: La Grotte (Savoie)

Saint-Christophe-du-Ligneron: Le Ligneron (Vendée)

Saint-Christophe-du-Luat: Luat (Mayenne)

Saint-Christophe-en-Bazelle: Bazelle (Indre)

Saint-Christophe-en-Boucherie: (1)
Boucherie; (2) Bourg-Meuhers (Indre)

Saint-Christophe-en-Bresse: Hercule
(Saône-et-Loire)

Saint-Christophe-en-Brionnais: Bel-Air-les-
Foires (Saône-et-Loire)

Saint-Christophe-la-Chartreuse:
Christophe-près-la-Boulogne (Vendée)

Saint-Christophe-le-Chaudrier: Chaudry
(Cher)

Saint-Christophe-sur-Dolaison: (1)
Christophe-la-Montagne; (2) Christophe;
(3) Mont-Pelé (Haute-Loire)

Saint-Christophe-sur-le-Nais: (1) Val-Riam;
(2) Val-Riant (Indre-et-Loire)

Saint-Cierge: Cireval (Ardèche)

Saint-Ciers-Champagne: La Champagne
(Charente-Maritime)

Saint-Ciers-du-Taillon: Le Taillon (Charente-Maritime)

Saint-Cirgue: Mont-Aygou (Tarn)

Saint-Cirgues: Cirgue-l'Eyge (Corrèze)

Saint-Cirgues: Cirgues-d'Allier (Haute-
Loire)

Saint-Cirgues: Marcelie (Puy-de-Dôme)

Saint-Cirgues-en-Montagne: Bauzon-en-
Montagne (Ardèche)

Saint-Cirgues-en-Montagne: Bauzon-Luc
(Ardèche)

Saint-Civran: Civran-les-Coteaux (Indre)

Saint-Clair: Belle-Rivière (Lot)

Saint-Clair: Clair-Chalon (Ardèche)

Saint-Clair: Perrouzet-sur-Gallaure (Isère)

Saint-Clair-de-la-Tour: Mont-Clair (Isère)

Saint-Clamens: Perpignan-Bayse (Gers)

Saint-Clar: Mont-Arrast (Gers)

Saint-Clar-de-Rivière: Plaizance-d'Encataly
(Haute-Garonne)

Saint-Claud: Claud-la-Montagne (Charente)

Saint-Claude: Condat-Montagne (Jura)

Saint-Claude-de-Diray: (1) Claude; (2)
Diray-la-Montagne; (3) Diray-Moret; (4)
Moresaint-la-Montagne (Loir-et-Cher)

Saint-Claude-Froidmentel: Mont-Mentel
(Loir-et-Cher)

Saint-Clément: La Clémence (Charente-
Maritime)

Saint-Clément: Clément-Belle-Visite (Cantal)

Saint-Clément: Clémenval (Ardèche)

Saint-Clément: Mille-Vents (Hautes-Alpes)

Saint-Clément: Montagne-sur-Autonne
(Oise)

Saint-Clément: Plaisance (Yonne)

Saint-Clément-lès-Macon: Grosne-lès-
Macon (Saône-et-Loire)

Saint-Clément-les-Places: (1) Clément-
d'Argères; (2) Les Places (Rhône)

Saint-Clément-sous-Pradelles: Robertin
(Haute-Loire)

Saint-Clément-sur-Guye: Mont-sur-Guye
(Saône-et-Loire)

Saint-Clet: (1) Haut-Trieuc; (2) Léintréo
(Côtes-d'Armor)

Saint-Cloud: La Montagne-Chérie (Yvelines)

Saint-Cloud: Pont-la-Montagne (Yvelines)

Saint-Colomban-des-Villards: Glandon
(Savoie)

Saint-Colombe-la-Petite: Prairial (Orne)

Saint-Côme: La Montagne (Gironde)

Saint-Côme: Montagne-sur-Lot (Aveyron)

Saint-Côme-de-Marvejols: Cosme (Gard)

Saint-Connan: Roc-Conan (Côtes-d'Armor)

Saint-Cosme: (1) Côme-la-Montagne; (2)
La Montagne; (3) Montagne-lès-Chalon;
(4) Port-la-Montagne (Saône-et-Loire)

Saint-Cosme-du-Vair: Montrecipe (Sarthe)

Saint-Coulomb: Coulomb-Rocher (Ille-et-
Vilaine)

Saint-Coutant-le-Grand: Le Vallon (Charente-Maritime)

Saint-Crépin: Colles-sur-Boulou (Dordogne)

Saint-Crépin: Joug-Rompu (Charente-Maritime)

Saint-Crépin: Les Ravins (Hautes-Alpes)

Saint-Crépin-aux-Bois: Blanchérie (Oise)

Saint-Cristaud: Montagnac (Gers)

Saint-Cy-Fertrève: Saincy (Nièvre)

Saint-Cyprien: Cyprien-sur-Dordogne
(Dordogne)

Saint-Cyprien: La Gaîté (Haute-Garonne)

Saint-Cyprien: Petit-Bourg (Corrèze)

Saint-Cyr: Chazault (Saône-et-Loire)

Saint-Cyr: Ciran (Ardèche)

Saint-Cyr: La Constitution (Vienne)

Saint-Cyr: (1) Libreval; Vale-Libre (Yvelines)

Saint-Cyr-au-Mont-d'Or: Mont-Cindre
(Rhône)

Saint-Cyr-des-Gâts: Les Gâts (Vendée)

Saint-Cyr-du-Doret: (1) Le Doret; (2)
L'Union (Charente-Maritime)

Saint-Cyr-du-Gault: Cinq-Bougies (Loir-
et-Cher)

Saint-Cyr-du-Vaudreuil: Vaudreuil-les-
Ponts (Eure)

Saint-Cyr-en-Talmondais: Haute-Plaine (Vendée)

Saint-Cyr-la-Roche: Aubepart (Corrèze)

Saint-Cyr-Semblecy: (1) Cyr-en-Sologne; (2) Semblecy (Loir-et-Cher)

Saint-Cyr-sous-Dourdan: Franc-Cyr (Yvelines)

Saint-Cyr-sur-le-Rhône: Ovize-sur-le-Rhône (Rhône)

Saint-Cyr-sur-Loire: Belle-Côte (Indre-et-Loire)

Saint-Cyr-sur-Morin: La Fraternité (Seine-et-Marne)

Saint-Cyran-du-Jambot: Indre-Sable (Indre)

Saint-Dau (ou Do): Ceint-d'Eau (Lot)

Saint-Denis: Caramaule (Gard)

Saint-Denis: Celles-sur-Saudre (Loir-et-Cher)

Saint-Denis: Le Chosson-d'Albarine (Ain)

Saint-Denis: Franciade-sur-Yonne (Yonne)

Saint-Denis: Franciade (Paris)

Saint-Denis: Montplaisir-sur-Yonne (Yonne)

Saint-Denis-d'Anjou: (1) Bourg-la-Montagne-sur-Cogieux; (2) Bourg-la-Montagne; (3) Bourg-sur-Cogieux; (4) Mont-Vainqueur (Mayenne)

Saint-Denis-d'Oléron: (1) Cité-de-la-Réunion; (2) La Réunion-sur-Mer (Charente-Maritime)

Saint-Denis-de-Jouet: Jouhet-les-Marrons (Indre)

Saint-Denis-de-l'Hôtel: Marat-sur-Loire (Loiret)

Saint-Denis-de-Vaux: Roche-sur-Vaux (Saône-et-Loire)

Saint-Denis-des-Coudrais: Denis-des-Coudrais (Sarthe)

Saint-Denis-du-Pin: (1) Denis-du-Pin; (2) Le Pin (Charente-Maritime)

Saint-Denis-le-Héricourt: Héricourt-en-Caux (Seine-Maritime)

Saint-Denis-lès-Rebais: Mont-Libre (Seine-et-Marne)

Saint-Denis-près-Martel: Seu-Denis (Lot)

Saint-Denis-Saint-Florentin: Amboise-Extra-Muros (Indre-et-Loire)

Saint-Denis-sur-Loire: Franciade-sur-Loire (Loir-et-Cher)

Saint-Denis-sur-Sarthon: Sarthon-sous-Chaumont (Orne)

Saint-Deniscourt: Deniscourt-la-Montagne (Oise)

Saint-Denœux: Denœux-l'Inflexible (Pas-de-Calais)

Saint-Désert: Montbogre (Saône-et-Loire)

Saint-Désirat: Rochevine (Ardèche)

Saint-Dézéry: Font-d'Ezéry (Gard)

Saint-Didier: Le Désir (Orne)

Saint-Didier: Didival (Ardèche)

Saint-Didier: Marcenat-les-Levis (Allier)

Saint-Didier: Pierre-Blanche (Vaucluse)

Saint-Didier: (1) Port-Chanteau; (2) Val-d'Arenne (Côte-d'Or)

Saint-Didier-au-Mont-d'Or: Simoneau-au-Mont-d'Or (Rhône)

Saint-Didier-d'Allier: Le Chier-d'Allier (Haute-Loire)

Saint-Didier-de-Bizonnes: Marc (Isère)

Saint-Didier-en-Arroux: Mont-d'Arroux (Saône-et-Loire)

Saint-Didier-en-Donjon: Bois-Didier (Allier)

Saint-Didier-la-Séauve: Mont-Franc (Haute-Loire)

Saint-Didier-sous-Beaujeu: Montclair-la-Montagne (Rhône)

Saint-Didier-sous-Riverie: Basse-Montagne (Rhône)

Saint-Didier-sur-Doulon: Didier-des-Côtes (Haute-Loire)

Saint-Dié: Ormont (Vosges)

Saint-Dier-d'Auvergne: Pont-Libre (Puy-de-Dôme)

Saint-Diéry: Diéry-le-Franc (Puy-de-Dôme)

Saint-Dizant-du-Bois: (1) Dizant-du-Bois; (2) Essouvert (Charente-Maritime)

Saint-Dizier: Dixier-les-Pomaines (Creuse)

Saint-Dode: Montagne-sur-Bayse (Gers)

Saint-Donat: Jovincieux (Drôme)

Saint-Doulchard-en-Septaine: Unité-sur-Yèvre (Cher)

Saint-Dyé-sur-Loire: (1) Dié-sur-Loire; (2) Dié (Loir-et-Cher)

Saint-Eble: Coupet (Haute-Loire)

Saint-Égrève: Vence (Isère)

Saint-Élix: (1) Mont-Félix; (2) Plaisance (Haute-Garonne)

Saint-Élix: Mont-Marat (Gers)

Saint-Élix-Gimois: Mont-Gimois (Gers)

Saint-Ellier-les-Bois: Sarthon-Libre (Orne)

Saint-Éloi: Loi (Nièvre)

Saint-Éloy: (1) Mont-Glacière; (2) Montagne-Glacière (Puy-de-Dôme)

Saint-Émiland: Lux-Émiland (Saône-et-Loire)

Saint-Émilion: Émilion-la-Montagne (Gironde)

Saint-Ennemond: Labron (Allier)

Saint-Epvre: (1) Epvre-sur-Nied; (2) L'Ingressin (Meurthe-et-Moselle)

Saint-Esprit: Jean-Jacques-Rousseau (Pyrénées-Atlantiques)

Saint-Esprit-lès-Bayonne: Jean-Jacques-Rousseau (Landes)

Saint-Esteben: Garralde (Pyrénées-Atlantiques)

Saint-Estève: Larg-des-Duyes (Alpes-de-Haute-Provence)

Saint-Étienne: (1) Armes-Ville; (2) Canton-d'Armes; (3) Commune-d'Armes (Loire)

Saint-Étienne: Étienne-sur-Lié (Côtes-d'Armor)

Saint-Étienne: Libre-Ville (Loire)

Saint-Étienne: Rochers-Républicains (Cantal)

Saint-Étienne: Valmoselle (Vosges)

Saint-Étienne-au-Mont: Audisque (Pas-de-Calais)

Saint-Étienne-au-Temple: (1) Montvesle; (2) Temple-sur-Vesle (Marne)

Saint-Étienne-d'Albagnan: Terrebasse (Hérault)

Saint-Étienne-d'Avançon: Valon (Hautes-Alpes)

Saint-Étienne-d'Escate: Souvignargues-Escatte (Gard)

Saint-Étienne-de-Baigorry: Thermopile (Pyrénées-Atlantiques)

Saint-Étienne-de-Chigny: (1) Chigné-les-Bois; (2) Chigny-les-Bois (Indre-et-Loire)

Saint-Étienne-de-Cuines: Cuines (Savoie)

Saint-Étienne-de-Gourgas: Montbraize (Hérault)

Saint-Étienne-de-l'Olm: Étienne-de-Long (Gard)

Saint-Étienne-de-Lugdarès: Lugdarès (Ardèche)

Saint-Étienne-de-Mont-Luc: Messidor (Loire-Atlantique)

Saint-Étienne-de-Saint-Geoirs: Marathon (Isère)

Saint-Étienne-de-Valoux: Toranchon (Ardèche)

Saint-Étienne-des-Sorts: Sorts (Gard)

Saint-Étienne-du-Vigan: Vigan-d'Allier (Haute-Loire)

Saint-Étienne-en-Bresse: Niveau (Saône-et-Loire)

Saint-Étienne-Extra: (1) La Petite-Varenne; (2) La Petite-Varenne-du-Chardonnet (Indre-et-Loire)

Saint-Étienne-la-Varenne: La Varenne (Rhône)

Saint-Étienne-Lardeyrol: (1) Fraycelier; (2) Lardeyrol (Haute-Loire)

Saint-Étienne-les-Orgues: Mont-Lure (Alpes-de-Haute-Provence)

Saint-Étienne-lès-Pierrefonds: La Queue-du-Bois (Oise)

Saint-Étienne-près-Allègre: La Visade (Haute-Loire)

Saint-Étienne-près-Bonneville: Nant-du-Dard (Haute-Savoie)

Saint-Étienne-sur-Blesle: (1) Mont-Étienne; (2) Mont-Étienne-sur-Blesle (Haute-Loire)

Saint-Étienne-sur-Coise: Coise (Rhône)

Saint-Étienne-sur-Suippe: Fanecourt (Marne)

Saint-Étienne-sur-Usson: Puy-Chalin (Puy-de-Dôme)

Saint-Étienne-Vallée-Française: (1) Val-Libre; (2) Vallée-Libre (Lozère)

Saint-Eugène: L'Ingénuité (Charente-Maritime)

Saint-Eulien: Lieuval (Marne)

Saint-Eusèbe: Mont-Eusèbe (Hautes-Alpes)

Saint-Eusèbe: (1) Montfleury; (2) Sparte (Saône-et-Loire)

Saint-Eusèbe-de-Cœur: Petit-Cœur (Savoie)

Saint-Euzèbe: Cremont (Haute-Savoie)

Saint-Fargeau: Le Peletier (Yonne)

Saint-Félicien: Félisval (Ardèche)

Saint-Félix: La Félicité (Charente-Maritime)

Saint-Félix-de-Banières: Puy-du-Tour (Lot)

Saint-Félix-de-Bourdeille: Dujalieux (Dordogne)

Saint-Félix-de-Châteauneuf: Mont-Félix (Ardèche)

Saint-Félix-de-l'Héras: L'Héras (Hérault)

Saint-Félix-de-Lodèz: Lodès (Hérault)

Saint-Félix-de-Pallières: Mont-Félix-de-Pallières (Gard)

Saint-Félix-sur-Sorgues: Félix-de-Sorgues (Aveyron)

Saint-Féréol-d'Auroure: Mont-Sec (Haute-Loire)

Saint-Féréol-de-Cohade: Cohade (Haute-Loire)

Saint-Ferjeux: Gionges (Marne)

Saint-Ferjeux: Val-de-Grâmmont (Haute-Saône)

Saint-Ferjus: La Tronche (Isère)

Saint-Ferréol: Bellevue (Haute-Garonne)

Saint-Feyre: Feyre-la-Montagne (Creuse)

Saint-Fiacre: Boudonville (Meurthe-et-Moselle)

Saint-Fiacre: Fiacre-les-Bois (Côtes-d'Armor)

Saint-Firmin: La Chazelle-les-Graviers (Saône-et-Loire)

Saint-Firmin: Firmin-les-Uzés (Gard)

Saint-Firmin: Firmin-sur-Loire (Loiret)

Saint-Firmin: Montagne-sur-Nonette (Oise)

Saint-Firmin: Prés-Firmin (Loir-et-Cher)

Saint-Firmin-de-Bussy: Bussy-aux-Amognes (Nièvre)

Saint-Firmin-en-Valgaudemar: Firmin-Fort (Hautes-Alpes)

Saint-Florent-des-Bois: Bois-Milon (Vendée)

Saint-Florent-le-Vieil: Mont-Glone (Maine-et-Loire)

Saint-Florent-sur-Auzonnet: (1) Mont-Mayard; (2) Montmajord (Gard)

Saint-Florentin: Les Bruères (Indre)

Saint-Florentin: Mont-Armance (Yonne)

Saint-Florentin: Pont-Civique (Yonne)

Saint-Floret: Roche-la-Couze (Puy-de-Dôme)

Saint-Flour: (1) Fort-Cantal; (2) Fort-Libre; (3) Mont-Flour (Cantal)

Saint-Flour-du-Pompidou: Le Pompidou (Lozère)

Saint-Folquin: Le Bas-Morin (Pas-de-Calais)

Saint-Forgeot: Ferréol (Saône-et-Loire)

Saint-Fort: Dampierre (Charente-Maritime)

Saint-Fort-sur-Gironde: (1) Fort-Maubert; (2) Fort-sur-Gironde (Charente-Maritime)

Saint-Frajou: Belle-Serre (Haute-Garonne)

Saint-Franc: Bois-Franc (Savoie)

Saint-Franchy: Franchy-les-Fougères (Nièvre)

Saint-François-de-Sales: Charmillon (Savoie)

Saint-Frédéric (Villiers-Saint-Frédéric): Villiers-le-Voltaire (Yvelines)

Saint-Frézal-de-Ventalon: Paix-de-Ventalon (Lozère)

Saint-Frichoux: Combe-de-Cergues (Hérault)

Saint-Front: Ardenne-la-Montagne (Haute-Loire)

Saint-Froult: Le Peletier (Charente-Maritime)

Saint-Fulgent: Fulgent-les-Bois (Vendée)

Saint-Galmier: (1) Commune-Fond-Fort; (2) Ville-Fontfort (Loire)

Saint-Gaudens: Mont-d'Unité (Haute-Garonne)

Saint-Gaultier: Roche-Libre (Indre)

Saint-Gelais: Gelais-sur-Sèvre (Deux-Sèvres)

Saint-Genesaint-de-Bauzon: (1) Bauzon-sur-Salendre; (2) Salendre; (3) Val-Salendre (Ardèche)

Saint-Genesaint-Lachamp: (1) Champlein; (2) Ventôse (Ardèche)

Saint-Genesaint-Malifaux: Semeine-et-Furans (Loire)

Saint-Genest: Mont-Genest (Allier)

Saint-Genest: Sans-Préjugé (Haute-Vienne)

Saint-Genest (near Esternay): Montgenest (Marne)

Saint-Genest (near Saint-Remy-en-Bouzemont): Blaiseval (Marne)

Saint-Gengoux-de-Scissé: Bassy-de-Scissé (Saône-et-Loire)

Saint-Gengoux-le-Royal: (1) Gengoux-le-National; (2) Jouvence (Saône-et-Loire)

Saint-Geniès-de-Comolas: (1) Mont-Comolas; (2) Montclos (Gard)

Saint-Geniès-en-Malgoirès: (1) Mont-Esquielle; (2) Montesquielle (Gard)

Saint-Geniez: Dromont (Alpes-de-Haute-Provence)

Saint-Geniez: (1) Sans-Culottide; (2) Vallon-la-Montagne (Aveyron)

Saint-Geniez-ô-Merle: Geniès-las-Costas (Corrèze)

Saint-Genis: Mont-Plâtre (Hautes-Alpes)

Saint-Genis-l'Argentière: La Pique-sur-Brevenne (Rhône)

Saint-Genis-Laval: Genis-le-Patriote (Rhône)

Saint-Genis-lès-Ollières: Ollières (Rhône)

Saint-Genix: Entre-Rives (Savoie)

Saint-Genneys-près-Saint-Paulien: Peyramont (Haute-Loire)

Saint-Genou: Indreval (Indre)

Saint-Geoire: Val-d'Eynan (Isère)

Saint-Geoirs: Mont-Geoirs (Isère)

Saint-Georges: Fonds-Fort (Aveyron)

Saint-Georges: Georges-Fontaine (Ardennes)

Saint-Georges:(1) Georges-lès-Hesdin; (2) Georges-sur-Canche (Pas-de-Calais)

Saint-Georges: Georges-Libre (Nord)

Saint-Georges: La Meurthe (Meurthe-et-Moselle)

Saint-Georges: L'Unité (Charente-Maritime)

Saint-Georges-d'Aurac: Aurac-Chavagnac (Haute-Loire)

Saint-Georges-d'Auribat: Franc-Lous (Landes)

Saint-Georges-d'Espéranche: Espéranche (Isère)

Saint-Georges-d'Hurtières: Fer (Savoie)

Saint-Georges-de-Camboulas: Georges-Camboulas (Aveyron)

Saint-Georges-de-Cubillac: Cubillac (Charente-Maritime)

Saint-Georges-de-Dangeul: Dangeul (Sarthe)

Saint-Georges-de-Didonne: Didonne (Charente-Maritime)

Saint-Georges-de-Livoye: Le Grand-Livoye (Manche)

Saint-Georges-de-Longuepierre: (1) Indivisibilité; (2) Longuepierre (Charente-Maritime)

Saint-Georges-de-Mons: Mons-le-Libre (Puy-de-Dôme)

Saint-Georges-de-Pointidoux: Carrière-Grison (Vendée)

Saint-Georges-de-Reneins: Reneins-les-Sables (Rhône)

Saint-Georges-des-Agoûts: Les Agoûts (Charente-Maritime)

Saint-Georges-des-Coteaux: Les Coteaux (Charente-Maritime)

Saint-Georges-du-Plain: L'Unité-sur-Sarthe (Sarthe)

Saint-Georges-du-Theil: Le Gras-Theil (Eure)

Saint-Georges-les-Baillargeaux: La Montagne (Vienne)

Saint-Georges-sur-Arnon: Montagne-sur-Arnon (Indre)

Saint-Georges-sur-Cher: Albion-sur-Cher (Loir-et-Cher)

Saint-Georges-sur-Erve: Mauranne (Mayenne)

Saint-Georges-sur-la-Prée: (1) Égalité-sur-Prée; (2) Montagne-sur-la-Prée (Cher)

Saint-Georges-sur-Loire: Beau-Site (Maine-et-Loire)

Saint-Gérand-de-Vaux: Mont-Libre (Allier)

Saint-Gérand-le-Puy: Puy-Redan (Allier)

Saint-Germain: La Chambaute (Savoie)

Saint-Germain: Germain-Ferrugineux (Dordogne)

Saint-Germain: Lisle-du-Corbéis (Orne)

Saint-Germain: Le Mont-Germain (Haute-Saône)

Saint-Germain: Mont-Sec (Savoie)

Saint-Germain-Aiguiller, L': L'Aiguiller-sur-Maine (Vendée)

Saint-Germain-au-Mont-d'Or: Mont-Hydins (Rhône)

Saint-Germain-Beaupré: Germain-sur-Sédelle (Creuse)

Saint-Germain-d'Arcé: Arcé-sur-Fare (Sarthe)

Saint-Germain-d'Armagnac: Montagne-du-Jarras (Gers)

Saint-Germain-de-Calberte: (1) Calberte; (2) Côte-Libre (Lozère)

Saint-Germain-de-Coulamer: Colimer (Mayenne)

Saint-Germain-de-Joux: Joux-la-Montagne (Ain)

Saint-Germain-de-Lusignan: Germain-Lusignan (Charente-Maritime)

Saint-Germain-de-Marencennes: Germain-la-Rondée (Charente-Maritime)

Saint-Germain-de-Modéon: Modéon (Côte-d'Or)

Saint-Germain-de-Salles: Belair (Allier)

Saint-Germain-de-Seudre: La Seudre (Charente-Maritime)

Saint-Germain-de-Tallevende: Tallevende-le-Grand (Calvados)

Saint-Germain-de-Vibrac: Germain-Vibrac (Charente-Maritime)

Saint-Germain-des-Bois: Bellevue-les-Bois (Cher)

Saint-Germain-des-Bois: Grand-Bois (Saône-et-Loire)

Saint-Germain-des-Bois (near Buxy): Bois-Soleil (Saône-et-Loire)

Saint-Germain-des-Bois (near La Claye): Bellevue-des-Bois (Saône-et-Loire)

Saint-Germain-des-Fossés: Puymourgon (Allier)

Saint-Germain-des-Prés: Prés-Fleuris (Maine-et-Loire)

Saint-Germain-du-Bel-Air: (1) Belle-Plaine; (2) Seu-Libre (Lot)

Saint-Germain-du-Bois: Belle-Place (Saône-et-Loire)

Saint-Germain-du-Plain: (1) Le Pelletier-du-Plain; (2) Thorey-sur-Saône (Saône-et-Loire)

Saint-Germain-du-Puy: La Montagne-du-Puy (Cher)

Saint-Germain-en-Laye: Montagne-du-Bon-Air (Yvelines)

Saint-Germain-en-Montagne: Plaisance (Jura)

Saint-Germain-en-Vallière: Cercy-la-Dheune (Saône-et-Loire)

Saint-Germain-en-Viry: Viry-la-Montagne (Nièvre)

Saint-Germain-l'Herm: Germain-la-Montagne (Puy-de-Dôme)

Saint-Germain-la-Feuille: Source-Seine (Côte-d'Or)

Saint-Germain-la-Ville: (1) Germinal-sur-Marne; (2) Villemarne (Marne)

Saint-Germain-Laval: Gardeloup-sur-Seine (Seine-et-Marne)

Saint-Germain-Laval: (1) Chalier; (2) Montchalier-Laval (Loire)

Saint-Germain-le-Prinçay: Prinçay-le-Vineux (Vendée)

Saint-Germain-le-Rocheux: Montagne-en-Bellevue (Côte-d'Or)

Saint-Germain-le-Vicomte: Germain-sur-Sèvres (Manche)

Saint-Germain-le-Vieux: L'Unité-des-Grouas (Orne)

Saint-Germain-le-Vieux-Corbeil: Vieux-Corbeil (Yvelines)

Saint-Germain-Lembron: Liziniac-Lembron (Puy-de-Dôme)

Saint-Germain-lès-Arpajon: (1) Germain-lès-Châtres; (2) Germinal-sur-Orge (Yvelines)

Saint-Germain-les-Belles: Mont-les-Belles (Haute-Vienne)

Saint-Germain-lès-Senailly: Mont-sur-Armançon (Côte-d'Or)

Saint-Germain-les-Vergnes: Bruyères-les-Vergnes

Saint-Germain-sous-Doue: Bellefontaine (Seine-et-Marne)

Saint-Germain-sous-Usson: Varennes (Puy-de-Dôme)

Saint-Germain-sur-Aubois: La Canonière-sur-Aubois (Cher)

Saint-Germain-sur-Indre: Germain (Indre-et-Loire)

Saint-Germain-sur-l'Arbresle: Barras-sur-l'Arbresle (Rhône)

Saint-Germier: Jarras (Gers)

Saint-Géron: La Roche-Géron (Haute-Loire)

Saint-Gervais: Bonne-Crême (Loir-et-Cher)

Saint-Gervais: La Fraternité (Lot-et-Garonne)

Saint-Gervais: Gervais-lès-Bagnols (Gard)

Saint-Gervais: Gervais-sur-Cosson (Loir-et-Cher)

Saint-Gervais: Mont-Roubbion (Drôme)

Saint-Gervais: Mont-Taillis (Hérault)

Saint-Gervais-du-Perron: L'Unité-du-Perron (Orne)

Saint-Gervais-sous-Meymont: Gervais-May-mont (Puy-de-Dôme)

Saint-Gervasy: Belleviste (Gard)

Saint-Gervasy: Roche (Puy-de-Dôme)

Saint-Geyrac: Union (Dordogne)

Saint-Gibrien: (1) Jolibois; (2) Mont-Union (Marne)

Saint-Gildas: Gildas-du-Chaneau (Côtes-d'Armor)

Saint-Gildas-de-Ruis: Abélard (Morbihan)

Saint-Gilles: Mont-d'Abloux (Indre)

Saint-Gilles: Montardre (Marne)

Saint-Gilles-de-l'Isle: L'Unité-de-l'Isle-Bouchard (Indre-et-Loire)

Saint-Gilles-du-Gard: Héraclée (Gard)

Saint-Gilles-le-Vicomte: Saint-Gilles-les-Bois (Côtes-d'Armor)

Saint-Gilles-les-Bois: Bellevue (Côtes-d'Armor)

Saint-Gilles-les-Forêts: La Forêt-Bayée (Haute-Vienne)

Saint-Gilles-Pligeaux: Mont-Pligeaux (Côtes-d'Armor)

Saint-Gilles-sur-Vie: Port-Fidèle (Vendée)

Saint-Gingolph: Morgelibre (Haute-Savoie)

Saint-Girbelle: Danglars-de-Margices (Aveyron)

Saint-Girod: Les Vergers (Savoie)

Saint-Girons: Lunoque (Ariège)

Saint-Go: Lataboge (Gers)

Saint-Gobain: Mont-Libre (Aisne)

Saint-Gond-et-Oyes: Valmorin (Marne)

Saint-Gourgon: Gourgon-la-Plaine (Loir-et-Cher)

Saint-Grégoire-d'Ardennes: Ardennes (Charente-Maritime)

Saint-Griède: Planté (Gers)

Saint-Guilhem-le-Désert: Verdus-le-Désert (Hérault)

Saint-Guiraud: (1) Bel-Air; (2) Bellevue; (3) Guiraud (Hérault)

Saint-Guiraud: Mont-Franc (Gers)

Saint-Haon-le-Châtel: (1) Bel-Air; (2) Mont-Bel-Air (Loire)

Saint-Haond: La Parro (Haute-Loire)

Saint-Héand: Mont-Pailloux (Loire)

Saint-Hélène-d'Auberville: Dambarvalle (Seine-Maritime)

Saint-Hellier: Val-d'Oze (Côte-d'Or)

Saint-Herblon: Bellevue (Loire-Atlantique)

Saint-Hérent: Caribes (Puy-de-Dôme)

Saint-Héric: Décadi (Charente-Maritime)

Saint-Hermand: Hermand-le-Guerrier (Vendée)

Saint-Hervé: Hervé-le-Loup (Côtes-d'Armor)

Saint-Hilaire: Bon-Air (Nord)
Saint-Hilaire: Le Griffoul (Aveyron)
Saint-Hilaire: Le Mont-Hilaire (Haute-Saône)
Saint-Hilaire: Mont-Libre (Doubs)
Saint-Hilaire: Montfayet (Aube)
Saint-Hilaire: Le Morgon (Allier)
Saint-Hilaire: Roseille-la-Montagne (Creuse)
Saint-Hilaire: Saint-Hilaire-du-Rosier (Isère)
Saint-Hilaire-au-Temple: Veslecours (Marne)
Saint-Hilaire-de-Benaise: L'Union (Indre)
Saint-Hilaire-de-Brens: Mont-Bel-Air (Isère)
Saint-Hilaire-de-Brethmas: Brethmas-Avesnes (Gard)
Saint-Hilaire-de-Gondilly: Marat (Cher)
Saint-Hilaire-de-la-Côte: Hilaire-la-Montagne (Isère)
Saint-Hilaire-de-Lavit: La Combe (Lozère)
Saint-Hilaire-de-Riez: La Révolution (Vendée)
Saint-Hilaire-de-Talmont: Le Tanès (Vendée)
Saint-Hilaire-de-Villefranche: (1) Bélisaire; (2) L'Égalité (Charente-Maritime)
Saint-Hilaire-de-Voust: Le Pontreau (Vendée)
Saint-Hilaire-des-Landes: Landes-et-Landa (Mayenne)
Saint-Hilaire-du-Bois: La Courageuse (Vendée)
Saint-Hilaire-du-Harcouët: Hilaire-Harcouët (Manche)
Saint-Hilaire-en-Lignières: Vère-sur-Arnon (Cher)
Saint-Hilaire-Foissac: Foissac-la-Luzège (Corrèze)
Saint-Hilaire-la-Forêt: La Vineuse-en-Plaine (Vendée)
Saint-Hilaire-la-Gérard: Roulard (Orne)
Saint-Hilaire-la-Gravelle: Bois-Hilaire (Loir-et-Cher)
Saint-Hilaire-la-Palud: La Palud (Deux-Sèvres)
Saint-Hilaire-la-Perrière: La Ferrière-la-Montagne (Orne)
Saint-Hilaire-le-Grand: (1) Hilaire-le-Ménissier; (2) Montain (Marne)
Saint-Hilaire-le-Petit: Hautemont (Marne)
Saint-Hilaire-le-Peyroux: Le Peyrou-Marat (Corrèze)

Saint-Hilaire-le-Vouhis: La Vouray (Vendée)
Saint-Hilaire-Montgru: Hilaire-Montgru (Aisne)
Saint-Hilaire-sur-Auzon: Mont-Hilaire (Haute-Loire)
Saint-Hippolyte: Hippolyte-lès-Caromb (Vaucluse)
Saint-Hippolyte: Mont-Verrier (Saône-et-Loire)
Saint-Hippolyte-de-Biard: Biard (Charente-Maritime)
Saint-Hippolyte-de-Montaigu: Polithe-Montaigu (Gard)
Saint-Hippolyte-du-Fort: Mont-Polite (Gard)
Saint-Hippolyte-sur-le-Doubs: Doubs-Marat (Doubs)
Saint-Honoré: Honoré-la-Montagne (Nièvre)
Saint-Hostien: Mont-Pigier (Haute-Loire)
Saint-Hubert: Montagne-des-Essarts (Yvelines)
Saint-Huroge: La Rochette-sur-Guye (Saône-et-Loire)
Saint-Ignan: L'Union (Haute-Garonne)
Saint-Igny-de-Vers: Vers-la-Montagne (Rhône)
Saint-Ilpize: Roc-Libre (Haute-Loire)
Saint-Imoges: Longmont (Marne)
Saint-Ismier: Mansval (Isère)
Saint-Izaire: Rive-Libre (Aveyron)
Saint-Jacques: Jacques-les-Barrème (Alpes-de-Haute-Provence)
Saint-Jacques: Jacques-Républicain (Hautes-Alpes)
Saint-Jacques-d'Ambès: Ambès (Gironde)
Saint-Jacques-d'Atticieux: Atticieux (Ardèche)
Saint-Jacques-des-Guérets: Les Guérets (Loir-et-Cher)
Saint-Jacut-de-la-Mer: (1) Isle-Jacut; (2) Port-Jacut (Côtes-d'Armor)
Saint-Jal: Coq-Hardy (Corrèze)
Saint-James: Beuvron-les-Monts (Manche)
Saint-Jaymes: Unité (Gers)
Saint-Jaymes-de-Léon: Léon (Gers)
Saint-Jean: La Cavalerie (Meurthe-et-Moselle)
Saint-Jean Froidmentel: Aqua-Mentel (Loir-et-Cher)
Saint-Jean-aux-Bois: Libre-Bois (Ardennes)
Saint-Jean-aux-Bois: La Solitude (Oise)
Saint-Jean-Chambre: Val-Chambre (Ardèche)

Saint-Jean-d'Alcapiés: Alcapiés-et-Alcas (Aveyron)

Saint-Jean-d'Angély Angély-Boutonne (Charente-Maritime)

Saint-Jean-d'Angle: Arispe (Charente-Maritime)

Saint-Jean-d'Arves: Huilles-d'Arves (Savoie)

Saint-Jean-d'Arvey: Mont-d'Arvey (Savoie)

Saint-Jean-d'Aubrigoux: Ous-Brigoux (Haute-Loire)

Saint-Jean-d'Auph: Montmarat (Haute-Savoie)

Saint-Jean-d'Avelane: Mont-d'Avelane (Isère)

Saint-Jean-d'Ormont: Dormont (Vosges)

Saint-Jean-de-Belleville: Côte-Marat (Savoie)

Saint-Jean-de-Beugné: Beugné-en-Plaine (Vendée)

Saint-Jean-de-Bœuf: Bœuf (Côte-d'Or)

Saint-Jean-de-Bournay: Toile-à-Voiles (Isère)

Saint-Jean-de-Breuil: Breuil-du-Marais (Charente-Maritime)

Saint-Jean-de-Bruel: (1) Pont-Libre; (2) Sentinelle (Aveyron)

Saint-Jean-de-Buèges: (1) Roche-au-Midi; (2) Rochemidy; (3) La Sentinelle (Hérault)

Saint-Jean-de-Ceyrargues: Ceyrargues (Gard)

Saint-Jean-de-Chaussan: Chaussan-la-Montagne (Rhône)

Saint-Jean-de-Couz: Couz (Savoie)

Saint-Jean-de-Crieulon: Crieulon (Gard)

Saint-Jean-de-Fos: Fort-l'Hérault (Hérault)

Saint-Jean-de-Kyrie-Eleison: Lunion (Haute-Garonne)

Saint-Jean-de-la-Blaquière: La Blaquière (Hérault)

Saint-Jean-de-la-Chaize: Basse-Chaize (Vendée)

Saint-Jean-de-la-Croix: Île-Verte (Maine-et-Loire)

Saint-Jean-de-la-Porte: (1) Côte-Rouge; (2) La Porte (Savoie)

Saint-Jean-de-Linières: Linières (Maine-et-Loire)

Saint-Jean-de-Liversay: La Gerbe (Charente-Maritime)

Saint-Jean-de-Losne: Belle-Défense (Côte-d'Or)

Saint-Jean-de-Luz: Chauvin-le-Dragon (Pyrénées-Atlantiques)

Saint-Jean-de-Marcel: Marcel-Haut (Tarn)

Saint-Jean-de-Marsacq: Pelletier-de-Marsacq (Landes)

Saint-Jean-de-Maruéjols: Maruéjols-les-Anels (Gard)

Saint-Jean-de-Maurienne: Arc (Savoie)

Saint-Jean-de-Moirans: Moiraxis (Isère)

Saint-Jean-de-Monts: Grands-Monts (Vendée)

Saint-Jean-de-Muzols: Muzols (Ardèche)

Saint-Jean-de-Nay: (1) Nay-la-Montagne; (2) Nay (Haute-Loire)

Saint-Jean-de-Poucharramet: Égalité-de-la-Bure (Haute-Garonne)

Saint-Jean-de-Pourcharesse: (1) Mont-Pierre; (2) Pourcharesse-sous-Peyre (Ardèche)

Saint-Jean-de-Serres: Serres-la-Coste (Gard)

Saint-Jean-de-Toulas: Jean-à-Toulas (Rhône)

Saint-Jean-de-Toulas: Toulas (Rhône)

Saint-Jean-de-Valériscle: Valériscle (Gard)

Saint-Jean-de-Vaux: Vaux-la-Montagne (Saône-et-Loire)

Saint-Jean-des-Mauvrets: Les Mauvrets (Maine-et-Loire)

Saint-Jean-des-Ollières: Puy-la-Garde (Puy-de-Dôme)

Saint-Jean-des-Vignes: (1) Rochefort-des-Vignes; (2) Rochefort-la-Vigne (Saône-et-Loire)

Saint-Jean-des-Vignes: Vignat-la-Montagne (Rhône)

Saint-Jean-devant-Possesse: (1) Égure; (2) La Lobe; (3) Vierrecours (Marne)

Saint-Jean-du-Gard: Brion-du-Gard (Gard)

Saint-Jean-du-Pin: (1) Dupin; (2) Pin (Gard)

Saint-Jean-du-Roure: Val-Roure (Ardèche)

Saint-Jean-en-Royans: Lyonne (Drôme)

Saint-Jean-en-Val: Enval (Puy-de-Dôme)

Saint-Jean-Kérdaniel: Bois-Daniel (Côtes-d'Armor)

Saint-Jean-la-Chalm: Lachalm-la-Montagne (Haute-Loire)

Saint-Jean-le-Comtal: Vertu-sur-le-Sousson (Gers)

Saint-Jean-le-Priche: Roche-sur-Saône (Saône-et-Loire)

Saint-Jean-le-Vieux: Vieux-d'Oizellon (Ain)

Saint-Jean-Pied-de-Port: Nive-Franche (Pyrénées-Atlantiques)

Saint-Jean-Pierre-Fixte: Fontaine-Libre (Eure-et-Loir)

Saint-Jean-Saint-Gervais: Goulache (Puy-de-Dôme)

Saint-Jean-Saint-Nicolas: Montorcier (Hautes-Alpes)

Saint-Jean-sur-Indre: Jean (Indre-et-Loire)

Saint-Jean-sur-Mayenne: Boisse (Mayenne)

Saint-Jean-sur-Moivre: (1) Moivrecourt; (2) Moivremont (Marne)

Saint-Jean-sur-Tourbe: (1) Mont-sur-Tourbe; (2) Tourbemont (Marne)

Saint-Jeanvrin: Bord (Cher)

Saint-Jérôme: Vinnaveaux (Ain)

Saint-Jeure: Mounier (Haute-Loire)

Saint-Jeure-d'Andaure: Andauret (Ardèche)

Saint-Jeure-d'Ay: Fontaine-d'Ay (Ardèche)

Saint-Joachim: Les Îles (Loire-Atlantique)

Saint-Jorioz: Laudon (Haute-Savoie)

Saint-Jory-de-Chalais: Chalais-la-Montagne (Dordogne)

Saint-Joseph: Métairie-Chaude (Côte-d'Or)

Saint-Josse-sur-Mer: (1) Bois-Fontaine; (2) Fontaines-aux-Bois (Pas-de-Calais)

Saint-Jouin-des-Marnes: Jouin-lès-Marnes (Deux-Sèvres)

Saint-Juéry: Bellevue (Tarn)

Saint-Juire: La Smagne (Vendée)

Saint-Julia-de-Gras-Capou: (1) Mont-Civique; (2) Mont-Républicain (Haute-Garonne)

Saint-Julien: Doumergousse (Hérault)

Saint-Julien: Fontagneux (Savoie)

Saint-Julien: Val-Julien (Côte-d'Or)

Saint-Julien-aux-Bois: Julien-Quinsat (Corrèze)

Saint-Julien-Boutières: Bout-d'Érieu (Ardèche)

Saint-Julien-Chapteuil: Mont-Mégal (Haute-Loire)

Saint-Julien-d'Ance: Mont-d'Ance (Haute-Loire)

Saint-Julien-d'Asse: Julien-sur-Asse (Alpes-de-Haute-Provence)

Saint-Julien-de-Cassagnas: Cassagnas (Gard)

Saint-Julien-de-Chedon: Chien-de-Chedon (Loir-et-Cher)

Saint-Julien-de-Civry: Vertpré (Saône-et-Loire)

Saint-Julien-de-Coppel: Roche-Coppel (Puy-de-Dôme)

Saint-Julien-de-Cray: Julien-Bellevue (Saône-et-Loire)

Saint-Julien-de-Jonzy: Julien-de-Bel-Air (Saône-et-Loire)

Saint-Julien-de-l'Escap: (1) Pont-de-Surveillance; (2) Lescap (Charente-Maritime)

Saint-Julien-de-la-Nef: Mont-Julien (Gard)

Saint-Julien-de-Peyrolas: Peyrolas (Gard)

Saint-Julien-de-Thevet: Thevet-sur-Baudouin (Indre)

Saint-Julien-de-Valgague: Julien-les-Mines (Gard)

Saint-Julien-de-Vouvantes: Roche-Fontaine (Loire-Atlantique)

Saint-Julien-des-Chazes: Les Chazes-d'Allier (Haute-Loire)

Saint-Julien-des-Landes: Landes (Vendée)

Saint-Julien-du-Pinet: Mont-Alibert (Haute-Loire)

Saint-Julien-du-Verdon: Ille-Verdon (Alpes-de-Haute-Provence)

Saint-Julien-en-Bochaine: Durbon-sur-Buëch (Hautes-Alpes)

Saint-Julien-en-Champsaur: Julien-la-Montagne (Hautes-Alpes)

Saint-Julien-en-Quint: Ambel-en-Quint (Drôme)

Saint-Julien-en-Vercors: Julien-la-Montagne (Drôme)

Saint-Julien-Gaulène: Pradoux (Tarn)

Saint-Julien-l'Ars: La Réunion (Vienne)

Saint-Julien-la-Brousse: Brousseval (Ardèche)

Saint-Julien-le-Montagnier: Mont-Rocher (Var)

Saint-Julien-le-Pélerin: (1) La Bruyère; (2) Julien-la-Bruguière (Corrèze)

Saint-Julien-le-Roux: Le Roux (Ardèche)

Saint-Julien-Molhesabate: Molhesabate (Haute-Loire)

Saint-Julien-sur-Bibost: Le Fruitier-sur-Bibost (Rhône)

Saint-Julien-sur-Cher: Montjulien (Loir-et-Cher)

Saint-Julien-sur-le-Suran: Julien-le-Guerrier (Jura)

Saint-Julien-sur-Reyssouze: Unité-sur-Reyssouze (Ain)

Saint-Julien-Vocange: Vocancel (Ardèche)

Saint-Junien: Junien-la-Montagne (Haute-Vienne)

Saint-Jurs: Bellevue (Alpes-de-Haute-Provence)

Saint-Jusaint-de-Baffie: Bel-Air (Puy-de-Dôme)

Saint-Jusaint-des-Marais: La Chaussée-de-la-Montagne (Oise)

Saint-Jusaint-en-Chevalet: Mont-Marat (Loire)

Saint-Jusaint-et-Vacquières: (1) Bartanave; (2) Bertanave (Gard)

Saint-Jusaint-Malmont: Mont-Blanc
(Haute-Loire)

Saint-Jusaint-près-Brioude: Jusaint-l'Égalité
(Haute-Loire)

Saint-Jusaint-près-Chamolix: Bellevue-la-
Montagne (Haute-Loire)

Saint-Jusaint-Sauvage: Jusaint-en-Val
(Marne)

Saint-Just: Bellevue-sur-Réome (Côte-d'Or)

Saint-Just: Brutus (Charente-Maritime)

Saint-Justin: Bel-Endroit (Gers)

Saint-Juvin: Mont-sur-Agron (Ardennes)

Saint-Lactencin: Plaines-Libres (Indre)

Saint-Lager: Mont-Brouilly (Rhône)

Saint-Lambert: Lambert-les-Bois (Yvelines)

Saint-Lary: Mont-Ilaire (Haute-Garonne)

Saint-Lattier: Lattier (Isère)

Saint-Laud: Bonne-Terre (Maine-et-Loire)

Saint-Laurent: Barra (Landes)

Saint-Laurent: Beaulieu (Hautes-Pyrénées)

Saint-Laurent: Brolan (Côtes-d'Armor)

Saint-Laurent: Imercourt (Pas-de-Calais)

Saint-Laurent: (1) Laurent; (2) Saluber
(Alpes-de-Haute-Provence)

Saint-Laurent: Main-Libre (Jura)

Saint-Laurent: Seu-Laurent (Lot)

Saint-Laurent: Vautrincourt (Ardennes)

Saint-Laurent-Chabreuges: Chabreuges
(Haute-Loire)

Saint-Laurent-d'Agny: Dagny (Rhône)

Saint-Laurent-d'Algouze: Algouze (Gard)

Saint-Laurent-d'Andenay: Laurent-la-Garde
(Saône-et-Loire)

Saint-Laurent-de-Beaumesnil: Beaumesnil-
du-Perron (Orne)

Saint-Laurent-de-Carnols: Carnols (Gard)

Saint-Laurent-de-Chamousset: Chalier-la-
Montagne (Rhône)

Saint-Laurent-de-l'Ain: Ain-sur-Saône (Ain)

Saint-Laurent-de-l'Isle: Bellerive-sur-Save
(Haute-Garonne)

Saint-Laurent-de-la-Barrière: La Barrière
(Charente-Maritime)

Saint-Laurent-de-la-Côte: Des-Ravins
(Savoie)

Saint-Laurent-de-la-Salanque: Sentinelle-
de-l'Agly (Pyrénées-Orientales)

Saint-Laurent-de-la-Salle: La Salle (Vendée)

Saint-Laurent-de-Mure: Mure-la-Fontaine
(Isère)

Saint-Laurent-de-Vaux: Vaux-la-Garde
(Rhône)

Saint-Laurent-des-Eaux: Briou-sur-Ime
(Loir-et-Cher)

Saint-Laurent-du-Cros: Laurent-du-Serre
(Hautes-Alpes)

Saint-Laurent-du-Pont: (1) Laurent-Libre;
(2) Pont-la-Montagne (Isère)

Saint-Laurent-du-Tencement: Le
Tencement (Eure)

Saint-Laurent-en-Brionnais: L'Union
(Saône-et-Loire)

Saint-Laurent-en-Royans: Montagne-de-
Larps (Drôme)

Saint-Laurent-la-Roche: Bel-Air (Jura)

Saint-Laurent-le-Minier: Preslemont (Gard)

Saint-Laurent-les-Bains: (1) Bains-Chauds-
sur-Bornes; (2) Bains-Tanargues
(Ardèche)

Saint-Laurent-sur-Barenjon: Laurent-des-
Bois (Cher)

Saint-Léger: La Forêt (Charente-Maritime)

Saint-Léger: Grosne (Saône-et-Loire)

Saint-Léger: Léger-les-Côtes (Haute-Loire)

Saint-Léger: Léger-lès-Rebais (Seine-et-
Marne)

Saint-Léger: Léger (Charente-Maritime)

Saint-Léger: Rocaille (Savoie)

Saint-Léger-aux-Bois: La Chanvrière (Oise)

Saint-Léger-de-Fourches: Fourches (Côte-
d'Or)

Saint-Léger-des-Bois: Beauchêne (Maine-et-
Loire)

Saint-Léger-des-Bruyères: Les Bruyères (Allier)

Saint-Léger-du-Bois: Bois-Nègre (Saône-et-
Loire)

Saint-Léger-du-Bosc: Bosc-en-Auge (Calvados)

Saint-Léger-en-Yveliness: Marat-des-Bois
(Yvelines)

Saint-Léger-la-Bussière: La Bussière (Saône-
et-Loire)

Saint-Léger-la-Haye: La Haye (Orne)

Saint-Léger-le-Petit: La Pépinière (Cher)

Saint-Léger-lès-Paray: Bon-Léger (Saône-et-
Loire)

Saint-Léger-Magnazeix: Léger-le-Peuple
(Haute-Vienne)

Saint-Léger-sous-Beuvray: Beuvremont
(Saône-et-Loire)

Saint-Léger-sous-Margerie: Égalité-Bonne-
Nouvelle (Aube)

Saint-Léger-sur-Dheune: Léger-la-Dheune
(Saône-et-Loire)

Saint-Léger-sur-Sarthe: L'Union-sur-Sarthe
(Orne)

Saint-Léon: Mont-la-Hyse (Haute-Garonne)

Saint-Léon: Puy-la-Montagne (Allier)

Saint-Léonard: Fruits-Sucrés (Maine-et-Loire)

Saint-Léonard: Grainval-la-Montagne (Seine-Maritime)

Saint-Léonard: Herbidor (Orne)

Saint-Léonard: Léonardmont (Vosges)

Saint-Léonard: Louvesle (Marne)

Saint-Léonard: Pont-de-Brique (Pas-de-Calais)

Saint-Léonard-de-Noblat: (1) Léonard-sur-Vienne; (2) Tarn-Vienne (Haute-Vienne)

Saint-Léopardin-d'Augy: Vivier (Allier)

Saint-Leu-sur-Oise: Côte-de-la-Liberté-sur-Oise (Oise)

Saint-Leu-Taverny: Claire-Fontaine (Yvelines)

Saint-Lézer: Lézer-la-Côte (Hautes-Pyrénées)

Saint-Lhomer: Les Vallées (Orne)

Saint-Lieux-Lafenasse: Pied-Montagne (Tarn)

Saint-Lizier: Austrie-la-Montagne (Ariège)

Saint-Lô: Rocher-de-la-Liberté (Manche)

Saint-Loubouer: Castera (Landes)

Saint-Louet-sur-Lozon: Lozon (Manche)

Saint-Louis: Bourg-Libre (Haut-Rhin)

Saint-Louis: Montagne-Libre-sur-l'Isle-et-Beauronne (Dordogne)

Saint-Louis: Münsthal (Moselle)

Saint-Louis: Singly (Ardennes)

Saint-Louis-de-la-Petite-Flandre: La Petite-Flandre (Charente-Maritime)

Saint-Louis-de-Montferrand: Montferrand (Gironde)

Saint-Louis-près-Sarrebourg: (1) Commune-de-Montagne; (2) Keyersberg (Meurthe-et-Moselle)

Saint-Loup: Les Brosses (Allier)

Saint-Loup: Hautmont (Marne)

Saint-Loup: Montauloup (Loir-et-Cher)

Saint-Loup: Salut (Haute-Garonne)

Saint-Loup: Sans-Culottide (Charente-Maritime)

Saint-Loup: Vertu (Manche)

Saint-Loup: Voltaire-sur-le-Thouet (Deux-Sèvres)

Saint-Loup-de-Buffigny: Buffigny (Aube)

Saint-Loup-de-la-Salle: Arbre-Vert (Saône-et-Loire)

Saint-Loup-de-Varenne: Gras (Saône-et-Loire)

Saint-Loup-des-Chaumes: Les Chaumes-Bel-Air (Cher)

Saint-Loup-du-Dorat: Saint-Loup-du-Doigt (Mayenne)

Saint-Loup-Hors: Brunville (Calvados)

Saint-Louvent: Courdemont (Marne)

Saint-Lubin-de-Cinq-Fonds: Cinq-Fonds (Eure-et-Loir)

Saint-Lubin-des-Prés: Prés-Lubin (Loir-et-Cher)

Saint-Lubin-en-Vergonnois: Lubin (Loir-et-Cher)

Saint-Lumier-en-Champagne: (1) Fionval; (2) Lumier-le-Ruisseau (Marne)

Saint-Lumier-la-Populeuse: (1) Égalité-la-Populeuse; (2) Val-Populeuse (Marne)

Saint-Lunaire: Port-Lunaire (Ille-et-Vilaine)

Saint-Lupicin: Lauconne (Jura)

Saint-Lupien: Somme-Fontaine (Aube)

Saint-Lyons: Lyon-d'Asse (Alpes-de-Haute-Provence)

Saint-Lys: Eaubelle (Haute-Garonne)

Saint-Maclou-la-Brière: L'Unité (Seine-Maritime)

Saint-Maigrin: Le Bocage (Charente-Maritime)

Saint-Maime: Mont-Libre (Alpes-de-Haute-Provence)

Saint-Maixent: Maixent-sur-Quenne (Sarthe)

Saint-Maixent: Vauclair-sur-Sèvre (Deux-Sèvres)

Saint-Malo: (1) Commune-de-la-Victoire; (2) Mont-Mamet; (3) Port-Malo (Ille-et-Vilaine)

Saint-Mamert-de-Gard: (1) Mamert; (2) Mont-Mamert (Gard)

Saint-Mamet: Bonne-Garde (Haute-Garonne)

Saint-Mandé: La Révolution (Charente-Maritime)

Saint-Mansuy: (1) La Moselle; (2) La Paix (Meurthe-et-Moselle)

Saint-Marcel: Cote-Franche (Indre)

Saint-Marcel: Marcel-Libre (Haute-Saône)

Saint-Marcel: Mont-Marc (Savoie)

Saint-Marcel: Ubilac (Saône-et-Loire)

Saint-Marcel-de-Bel-Accueil: Mont-Marcel (Isère)

Saint-Marcel-de-Carreiret: Vione-Marcel (Gard)

Saint-Marcel-de-Fontfouillouse: Les Plantiers-de-Fontfouillouse (Gard)

Saint-Marcel-en-Murat: Venant (Allier)

Saint-Marcel-les-Annonay: Marcel-de-Déome (Ardèche)

Saint-Marcellin: (1) Donjon-la-Plaine; (2) Marcellin-la-Plaine (Loire)

Saint-Marcellin: Thermopyles (Isère)

Saint-Marcet: Mont-Rocher (Haute-Garonne)

Saint-Mard: Mard-sur-l'Isle (Charente-Maritime)

Saint-Mard-de-Vaux: Montabon (Saône-et-Loire)

Saint-Mard-lès-Rouffy: (1) Marat-lès-Rouffy; (2) Mont-Rouffy (Marne)

Saint-Mard-sur-Auve: (1) Montagne-sur-Auve; (2) Montauve (Marne)

Saint-Mard-sur-le-Mont: Montvierre (Marne)

Saint-Mards-en-Othe: Mards-la-Montagne (Aube)

Saint-Marien: Marat (Creuse)

Saint-Mars: Libreval (Seine-et-Marne)

Saint-Mars-de-la-Brière: Brière-de-l'Égalité (Sarthe)

Saint-Mars-des-Prés: La Prairiale (Vendée)

Saint-Mars-la-Réorthe: Le Val-la-Réorthe (Vendée)

Saint-Mars-sur-la-Futaie: Mont-Mars (Mayenne)

Saint-Martial: L'Industrie (Charente-Maritime)

Saint-Martial: (1) Mont-Liron; (2) Montliron (Gard)

Saint-Martial-de-Coculet: Coculet (Charente-Maritime)

Saint-Martial-de-Mirambeau: Martial-sous-Mirambeau (Charente-Maritime)

Saint-Martial-de-Valette: Valette-les-Eaux (Dordogne)

Saint-Martial-de-Vitaterne: (1) Martial-sur-Jonzac; (2) Martial-Vitaterne (Charente-Maritime)

Saint-Martial-Entraygues: Entraygues-Sans-Culottes (Corrèze)

Saint-Martin: Doussairolles (Hérault)

Saint-Martin (near Mirande): Marrasaint-du-Lizet (Gers)

Saint-Martin (near Nogaro): Lagobitz (Gers)

Saint-Martin l'Aiguillon: L'Aiguillon-Républicain (Orne)

Saint-Martin-aux-Champs: (1) Issouval; (2) Marat-aux-Champs (Marne)

Saint-Martin-Binagré: Justian (Gers)

Saint-Martin-Cantalès: Gilbert-Cantalès (Cantal)

Saint-Martin-Chocquel: Chocquel-lès-Menneville (Pas-de-Calais)

Saint-Martin-d'Ablois: Ablois (Marne)

Saint-Martin-d'Arc: Neufvachette (Savoie)

Saint-Martin-d'Ardentes: Ardentes-les-Bois (Indre)

Saint-Martin-d'Arrosa: Grand-Pont (Pyrénées-Atlantiques)

Saint-Martin-d'Ary: Ary (Charente-Maritime)

Saint-Martin-d'Auxy: Mont-d'Auxy (Saône-et-Loire)

Saint-Martin-d'Estreaux: Jars-la-Montagne (Loire)

Saint-Martin-d'Étableau: Étableau (Indre-et-Loire)

Saint-Martin-d'Hères: Hères-la-Montagne (Isère)

Saint-Martin-d'Ollières: Olière (Puy-de-Dôme)

Saint-Martin-d'Ouilly: Ouilly-la-Ribaude (Calvados)

Saint-Martin-de Goyne: Martin-Franc (Gers)

Saint-Martin-de-Belleville: Montalte (Savoie)

Saint-Martin-de-Boscherville: Boscherville (Seine-Maritime)

Saint-Martin-de-Boubeaux: Galeizon (Lozère)

Saint-Martin-de-Boulogne: (1) La Montagne; (2) Montagne-lès-Boulogne; (3) Section-de-la-Montagne (Pas-de-Calais)

Saint-Martin-de-Brem: Havre-Fidèle (Vendée)

Saint-Martin-de-Campselade: Bassurels (Lozère)

Saint-Martin-de-Castillon: Luberon-la-Montagne (Vaucluse)

Saint-Martin-de-Castillon: Paradou (Bouches-du-Rhône)

Saint-Martin-de-Connée: Connée (Mayenne)

Saint-Martin-de-Corconac: Corconac (Gard)

Saint-Martin-de-Cornas: Cornas-sur-Gier (Rhône)

Saint-Martin-de-Coux: Coux-Goulare (Charente-Maritime)

Saint-Martin-de-Croix: Burnand (Saône-et-Loire)

Saint-Martin-de-Fontaines: Brutus-la-Fontaine (Rhône)

Saint-Martin-de-Fresne: Mont-de-Fresne (Ain)

Saint-Martin-de-Hinx: Marat-de-Hinx (Landes)

Saint-Martin-de-Juillers: (1) Le Bonnet; (2) Juillers-l'Égalité (Charente-Maritime)

Saint-Martin-de-la-Brasque: Mont-Libre (Vaucluse)

Saint-Martin-de-la-Coudre: (1) La Coudre; (2) La Vigilance (Charente-Maritime)

Saint-Martin-de-la-Place: Unité-sur-Loire (Maine-et-Loire)

Saint-Martin-de-la-Porte: Lacossas (Savoie)

Saint-Martin-de-Laives: Laives (Saône-et-Loire)

Saint-Martin-de-Lamps: Choiseau (Indre)

Saint-Martin-de-Lerm: Montagne-sur-la-Dropt (Gironde)

Saint-Martin-de-Limouse: Limouse-la-Prade (Aveyron)

Saint-Martin-de-Lixy: Lixy (Saône-et-Loire)

Saint-Martin-de-Mont: Bellevue (Ain)

Saint-Martin-de-Montsurs: Hercule-Montsurs (Mayenne)

Saint-Martin-de-Pallières: Roc-Tarpéien (Var)

Saint-Martin-de-Pouligny: Pouligny-les-Brandes (Indre)

Saint-Martin-de-Queyrières: Roche-Forte (Hautes-Alpes)

Saint-Martin-de-Ré: Fort-de-la-Montagne (Charente-Maritime)

Saint-Martin-de-Ré: Île-de-la-République (Charente-Maritime)

Saint-Martin-de-Renacas: (1) Mont-Martin; (2) Mont-Renacas (Alpes-de-Haute-Provence)

Saint-Martin-de-Salencey: Salencey (Saône-et-Loire)

Saint-Martin-de-Saussenac: Saussenac (Gard)

Saint-Martin-de-Seignaux: Montagne-Seignaux (Landes)

Saint-Martin-de-Senozan: Belle-Roche (Saône-et-Loire)

Saint-Martin-de-Tallevende: Tallevende-le-Petit (Calvados)

Saint-Martin-de-Thevet: Thevet-les-Étangs (Indre)

Saint-Martin-de-Tournon: Tournon (Indre)

Saint-Martin-de-Valamas: Mas-d'Érieu (Ardèche)

Saint-Martin-de-Valgalgues: (1) Mont-Valgalgues; (2) Mont-Valgues (Gard)

Saint-Martin-de-Vican: Vican (Aveyron)

Saint-Martin-de-Villeneuve: La Bonne-Foy (Charente-Maritime)

Saint-Martin-de-Vinets: Vinets-sur-Marne (Marne)

Saint-Martin-des-Bois: Bois-Martin (Loir-et-Cher)

Saint-Martin-des-Champs: Champfleury (Saône-et-Loire)

Saint-Martin-des-Champs: Les Champs (Cher)

Saint-Martin-des-Champs: Montagne-sur-Morin (Seine-et-Marne)

Saint-Martin-des-Champs: Unité-des-Champs (Finistère)

Saint-Martin-des-Lais: Le Lais-sur-Loire (Allier)

Saint-Martin-des-Landes: Les Landes-de-Carrouges (Orne)

Saint-Martin-des-Noyers: Les Noyers (Vendée)

Saint-Martin-des-Vignes: Notre-Dame-des-Vignes (Saône-et-Loire)

Saint-Martin-du-Lac: Lac-sur-Loire (Saône-et-Loire)

Saint-Martin-du-Mont: Montagne-de-Mont (Saône-et-Loire)

Saint-Martin-du-Puits: Puits-l'Affranchi (Nièvre)

Saint-Martin-du-Tartre: (1) Martin-Bel-Air; (2) La Montagne-du-Plain (Saône-et-Loire)

Saint-Martin-du-Tertre: Martin-Bel-Air (Yonne)

Saint-Martin-du-Touch: Fructidor (Haute-Garonne)

Saint-Martin-en-Bresse: Tell-les-Bois (Saône-et-Loire)

Saint-Martin-en-Gâtinois: Gâtinois-sur-Dheune (Saône-et-Loire)

Saint-Martin-en-Haut: Martin-l'Espérance (Rhône)

Saint-Martin-l'Heureux: Montheureux (Marne)

Saint-Martin-la-Méanne: (1) Les Jacobins-de-la-Méanne; (2) Martin-Sans-Culottes (Corrèze)

Saint-Martin-la-Patrouille: Bragny-sur-Guye (Saône-et-Loire)

Saint-Martin-Lars-en-Sainte-Hermine: Lars-la-Valeur (Vendée)

Saint-Martin-le-Beau: Le Beau-sur-Cher (Indre-et-Loire)

Saint-Martin-le-Gaillard: Val-Gaillard (Seine-Maritime)

Saint-Martin-le-Mault: Martin-sur-Benaise (Haute-Vienne)

Saint-Martin-le-Pin: Le Chêne-Vert (Dordogne)

Saint-Martin-les-Bromes: Bromès (Alpes-de-Haute-Provence)

Saint-Martin-sous-Montaigu: Montaigu (Saône-et-Loire)

Saint-Martin-sur-la-Chambre: Bujon (Savoie)

Saint-Martin-sur-Oreuse: Franc-Oreuse (Yonne)

Saint-Martin d'Écublei: Écubley-sur-Rille (Orne)

Saint-Martory: Montagne-sur-Garonne (Haute-Garonne)

Saint-Masme: Fanémont (Marne)

Saint-Mathurin: Port-de-la-Vallée (Maine-et-Loire)

Saint-Maur: Beaupré (Indre)

Saint-Maur: Montagnarde (Gers)

Saint-Maur-Chaveroche: (1) Entrevilles; (2) Longbord (Cher)

Saint-Maur-en-Chaussée: Mor-la-Chaussée (Oise)

Saint-Maur-les-Fossés: Vivant-sur-Marne (Paris)

Saint-Maurice: Anglas-la-Montagne (Lot-et-Garonne)

Saint-Maurice: Charenton-Républicain (Paris)

Saint-Maurice: La Côte (Charente-Maritime)

Saint-Maurice: Fontenille-de-Vis (Hérault)

Saint-Maurice: Maurice-Belle-Fontaine (Drôme)

Saint-Maurice: Maurice-la-Montagne (Jura)

Saint-Maurice: Maurice-les-Fontaines (Nièvre)

Saint-Maurice: Mont-Romain (Puy-de-Dôme)

Saint-Maurice: Montfleuri (Jura)

Saint-Maurice: Montgravier (Yvelines)

Saint-Maurice: Val-Maurice (Hautes-Alpes)

Saint-Maurice-aux-Riches-Hommes: Maurice-les-Sans-Culottes (Yonne)

Saint-Maurice-d'Etelan: Maurice-sur-Seine (Seine-Maritime)

Saint-Maurice-de-Beynost: La Fontaine (Ain)

Saint-Maurice-de-Casevieilles: Maurice-de-Rocher (Gard)

Saint-Maurice-de-Laurençanne: Laurençanne (Charente-Maritime)

Saint-Maurice-de-Lignon: Lignon (Haute-Loire)

Saint-Maurice-de-Reyment: Reyment (Ain)

Saint-Maurice-de-Roche: Maurice-de-Roche-Marat (Haute-Loire)

Saint-Maurice-de-Rotherens: Roc-de-Rotherens (Savoie)

Saint-Maurice-de-Savonnay: Mauris-des-Prés-et-Champagne (Saône-et-Loire)

Saint-Maurice-de-Tavernolle: Maurice-Tavernolle (Charente-Maritime)

Saint-Maurice-de-Ventalon: Montjoye-de-Ventalon (Lozère)

Saint-Maurice-des-Champs: Champ-des-Bois (Saône-et-Loire)

Saint-Maurice-des-Noues: Les Noues (Vendée)

Saint-Maurice-en-Chalançon: Rimaure (Ardèche)

Saint-Maurice-en-Rivière: Fort-Chevrey (Saône-et-Loire)

Saint-Maurice-le-Girard: Vaugirard (Vendée)

Saint-Maurice-lès-Charencey: Bon-Air (Orne)

Saint-Maurice-lès-Châteauneuf: Sornin (Saône-et-Loire)

Saint-Maurice-sur-Dargoire: Désille-sur-Dargoire (Rhône)

Saint-Maurice-sur-Vingeanne: Avallon-sur-Vingeanne (Côte-d'Or)

Saint-Max: Max-la-Montagne (Meurthe-et-Moselle)

Saint-Maximin: (1)Marathon; (2) Maximin-la-Coste (Gard)

Saint-Maximin: Marathon (Var)

Saint-Maximin: Maximum (Oise)

Saint-Mayme: Lanterne-sous-Rodez (Aveyron)

Saint-Mayme-de-Pereyrol: Pereyrol-la-Montagne (Dordogne)

Saint-Médard: (1) Beaurepaire; (2) Médard; (2) Val-Pastour (Charente-Maritime)

Saint-Médard: Les Bois (Indre)

Saint-Médard: Haute-Vue (Haute-Garonne)

Saint-Médard: Médard-Libre (Meurthe-et-Moselle)

Saint-Médard: Mont-Médard (Gers)

Saint-Médard-d'Excideuil: Médard-sur-la-Loup (Dordogne)

Saint-Médard-de-la-Barde: La Barde (Charente-Maritime)

Saint-Médard-en-Jalles: Fulminant (Gironde)

Saint-Médier: Vivacité (Gard)

Saint-Méen: (1) Méen-la-Forêt; (2) Méen-Libre (Ille-et-Vilaine)

Saint-Mélaine: Aubance (Maine-et-Loire)

Saint-Mélany: La Gardète (Ardèche)

Saint-Méloir-des-Bois: Méloir-Richaux (Côtes-d'Armor)

Saint-Méloir-des-Ondes: Méloir-Richeux (Ille-et-Vilaine)

Saint-Mémin: Mont-Mémin (Dordogne)

Saint-Mengès: Union (Ardennes)

Saint-Menoux: Maillé-sur-Rese (Allier)

Saint-Merd-en-Gimel: Gimel-Dordogne (Corrèze)

Saint-Mesmin: Beauvallon-sur-Sèvre (Vendée)

Saint-Mesmin: Rochefontaine (Côte-d'Or)

Saint-Mézard: Augas-Libre (Gers)

Saint-Micaud: (1) Mancerre; (2) Mancert (Saône-et-Loire)

Saint-Michel: Barra (Bouches-du-Rhône)

Saint-Michel: Belmont (Vosges)

Saint-Michel: Bois-au-Mont (Pas-de-Calais)

Saint-Michel: Grâces (Côtes-d'Armor)

Saint-Michel: Mont-Michel (Alpes-de-Haute-Provence)

Saint-Michel: Nive-Montagne (Pyrénées-Atlantiques)

Saint-Michel: La Nuelle (Charente-Maritime)

Saint-Michel: Pas-du-Roc (Savoie)

Saint-Michel: Seu-Michel (Lot)

Saint-Michel: Taran (Gers)

Saint-Michel-d'Euzet: Euzet (Gard)

Saint-Michel-de-Chaillol: (1) Chaillol-la-Montagne; (2) Montorcier-de-Chaillol (Hautes-Alpes)

Saint-Michel-de-Chavaigne: Chavaigne-sur-Nogue (Sarthe)

Saint-Michel-de-Dèze: Rivière-de-Gardon (Lozère)

Saint-Michel-du-Puech-d'Aubaignes: Le Puech (Hérault)

Saint-Michel-en-Brenne: Michel-le-Peletier (Indre)

Saint-Michel-en-Herm: L'Union-sur-Mer (Vendée)

Saint-Michel-Ferrery: Thermidor (Haute-Garonne)

Saint-Michel-Labadié: Montagnarde (Tarn)

Saint-Michel-le-Rance: Rancevallon (Ardèche)

Saint-Michel-Mont-Mercure: Le Mont-Mercure (Vendée)

Saint-Michel-sur-Loire: Mont-sur-Loire (Indre-et-Loire)

Saint-Miniel: Roche-sur-Meuse (Meuse)

Saint-Mitre: Bellefont (Bouches-du-Rhône)

Saint-Mont: Mont-d'Adour (Gers)

Saint-Montant: Rouanesse (Ardèche)

Saint-Moré: Moré-sur-Cure (Yonne)

Saint-Nabord: Roche-Libre (Vosges)

Saint-Nazaire: Boisbrion (Indre)

Saint-Nazaire: (1) Marat; (2) Port-Nazaire (Charente-Maritime)

Saint-Nazaire: Senary-Beau-Port (Var)

Saint-Nazaire-en-Royans: Nazaire (Drôme)

Saint-Nazaire-sur-Loire: Port-Nazaire (Loire-Atlantique)

Saint-Nicolas: Châlier (Alpes-Maritimes)

Saint-Nicolas: Champ-Libre (Manche)

Saint-Nicolas: Lugrand (Aube)

Saint-Nicolas: La République (Haute-Garonne)

Saint-Nicolas-au-Bois: La Vallée-aux-Bois (Aisne)

Saint-Nicolas-de-Brem: Bellevue (Vendée)

Saint-Nicolas-de-l'Aa: Libre-sur-Aa (Pas-de-Calais)

Saint-Nicolas-de-la-Grave: (1) La Grave-Bec-du-Tarn; (2) La Grave-du-Bec (Tarn-et-Garonne)

Saint-Nicolas-de-Pierrepont: Pierrepont (Manche)

Saint-Nicolas-de-Port: Port-sur-Meurthe (Meurthe-et-Moselle)

Saint-Nicolas-de-Redon: Union-sur-Vilaine (Loire-Atlantique)

Saint-Nicolas-de-Vérosse: Vérosse (Haute-Savoie)

Saint-Nicolas-des-Bois: Bellevue-la-Montagne (Orne)

Saint-Nicolas-du-Bosc-Asselin: Bosc-Asselin (Eure)

Saint-Nicolas-en-Méaulens: La Fraternité (Pas-de-Calais)

Saint-Nicolas-lès-Cîteaux: Unité (Côte-d'Or)

Saint-Nizier-le-Bouchoux: Nizier-la-Liberté (Ain)

Saint-Nizier-sous-Charmoy: Scaevola (Saône-et-Loire)

Saint-Nom-la-Bretêche: Union-la-Montagne (Yvelines)

Saint-Norvez: Prajou (Côtes-d'Armor)

Saint-Offenge-Dessous: Les Avanchers-Dessous (Savoie)

Saint-Offenge-Dessus: Les Avanchers-Dessus (Savoie)

Saint-Ombre: Chambéry-le-Vieux (Savoie)

Saint-Omer: Morin-la-Montagne (Pas-de-Calais)

Saint-Omer-Capelle: La Barrière (Pas-de-Calais)

Saint-Orse: Orse-le-Pierreux (Dordogne)

Saint-Ost: (1) Bayzole; (2) Breton (Gers)

Saint-Ouen: Bon-Accord (Seine-et-Marne)

Saint-Ouen: Fondouen (Loir-et-Cher)

Saint-Ouen: (1) La Ramberge; (2) La Remberge (Indre-et-Loire)

Saint-Ouen (now Saint-Ouen-d'Aunis): (1) Marat; (2) La Société (Charente-Maritime)

Saint-Ouen (near Matha): Châlier (Charente-Maritime)

Saint-Ouen l'Aumône: (1) L'Aumône-la-Montagne; (2) Montagne-sur-Oise (Yvelines)

Saint-Ouen-des-Gâts: Les Gâts (Vendée)

Saint-Ouen-des-Vallons: Saint-Ouen-des-Oyes (Mayenne)

Saint-Ouen-et-Saint-Étienne-aux-Ormes: (1) Ormont; (2) Vinon-sur-Oiselet (Marne)

Saint-Ouen-la-Rouërie: Ouen-la-Montagne (Ille-et-Vilaine)

Saint-Ouen-le-Brisoult: Le Brisoult-Regénéré (Orne)

Saint-Ouen-Marchefroy: L'Abolition (Eure-et-Loir)

Saint-Ouen-sur-Seine: Bain-sur-Seine (Paris)

Saint-Ours: Forêt-d'Ours (Savoie)

Saint-Oyen: Prime-Jour (Savoie)

Saint-Pair: Pair-Libre (Manche)

Saint-Pal-de-Chalançon: Montalet (Haute-Loire)

Saint-Pal-de-Murs: Pal-Sénouire (Haute-Loire)

Saint-Palais: Mont-Bidouze (Pyrénées-Atlantiques)

Saint-Palais-de-Négrignac: Négrignac (Charente-Maritime)

Saint-Palais-de-Phiolin: Phiolin-Chaumière (Charente-Maritime)

Saint-Palais-sur-Mer: Chaumière-sur-Mer (Charente-Maritime)

Saint-Pancrace: Colonnes (Savoie)

Saint-Pantaléon: Communes-Réunies (Saône-et-Loire)

Saint-Pantaléon: Pantaly (Vaucluse)

Saint-Pantaléon-de-Larche: La Fraternité (Corrèze)

Saint-Pantaly-d'Ans: Pantaléon-le-Bon-Vin (Dordogne)

Saint-Pantaly-d'Excideuil: Pantaly-Albarède (Dordogne)

Saint-Pardoult: La Bienfaisance (Charente-Maritime)

Saint-Pardoux: Commune-sur-Rocher (Dordogne)

Saint-Pardoux: La Viette (Deux-Sèvres)

Saint-Pardoux-Corbier: Pardoux-et-Corbier (Corrèze)

Saint-Pardoux-la-Croizille: Bellone (Corrèze)

Saint-Pargoire: Pargoire-l'Hérault (Hérault)

Saint-Parizé-en-Viry: Montvert (Nièvre)

Saint-Parizé-le-Châtel: Brennery (Nièvre)

Saint-Paterne: Les Bains (Indre-et-Loire)

Saint-Patrice-du-Désert: Le Désert (Orne)

Saint-Paul: Du Passage (Savoie)

Saint-Paul: Mont-Liberté (Hautes-Pyrénées)

Saint-Paul: Monts (Alpes-de-Haute-Provence)

Saint-Paul-aux-Bois: Vignette-aux-Bois (Aisne)

Saint-Paul-Cap-de-Joux: Agout-Rousseau (Tarn)

Saint-Paul-d'Iseaux: Bellevue (Isère)

Saint-Paul-d'Oueil: Maylin-d'Oueil (Haute-Garonne)

Saint-Paul-de-Tartas: (1) Mont-de-Tartas; (2) Tartas (Haute-Loire)

Saint-Paul-de-Varax: Varax (Ain)

Saint-Paul-de-Varces: (1) Ancoin; (2) Paul-d'Ancoin (Isère)

Saint-Paul-de-Vence: Paul-du-Var (Alpes-Maritimes)

Saint-Paul-du-Mont-Carmel: Paul-le-Montagnard (Hérault)

Saint-Paul-en-Jarret: Valdorley (Loire)

Saint-Paul-en-Pareds: La Regénérée (Vendée)

Saint-Paul-Lacoste: La Cosainte-la-Montagne (Gard)

Saint-Paul-le-Vicomte: Saint-Paul-sur-Sarthe (Sarthe)

Saint-Paul-lès-Dax: Bonnet-Rouge (Landes)

Saint-Paul-lès-Romans: Paul-la-Joyeuse (Drôme)

Saint-Paul-sur-Yenne: Des Bovines (Savoie)

Saint-Paul-Trois-Châteaux: Paul-les-Fontaines (Drôme)

Saint-Paulet: La Réunion (Aude)

Saint-Paulet-de-Caisson: Caisson (Gard)

Saint-Paulien: Velaune (Haute-Loire)

Saint-Pée-sur-Nivelle: Beaugard (Pyrénées-Atlantiques)

Saint-Pellerin: Isle-sur-Yerre (Eure-et-Loir)

Saint-Peray: Peray-Vin-Blanc (Ardèche)

Saint-Père-en-Retz: Fraternité (Loire-Atlantique)

Saint-Pern: Pern-les-Rochers (Ille-et-Vilaine)

Saint-Péver: Péver-la-Lande (Côtes-d'Armor)

Saint-Pey-de-Langon: Mont-Marat (Gironde)

Saint-Pey-de-Langon: Pont (Gironde)

Saint-Phal: (1) Bel-Air; (2) Belle-Vue; (3) Bon-Air (Aube)

Saint-Phalier: La Fontaine (Indre)

Saint-Phalier: La Liberté (Cher)

Saint-Philbert-du-Pont-Charrault: La Résolue (Vendée)

Saint-Philbert-sous-Gevrey: Velle-sous-Gevrey (Côte-d'Or)

Saint-Philibert: Paty (Côte-d'Or)

Saint-Piat: Martel-les-Vaux (Eure-et-Loir)

Saint-Pience: Sapience (Manche)

Saint-Pierre: La Constitution (Meurthe-et-Moselle)

Saint-Pierre: Niveau-près-Surgères (Charente-Maritime)

Saint-Pierre: Oberstossen (Bas-Rhin)

Saint-Pierre: Puget-Figette (Alpes-de-Haute-Provence)

Saint-Pierre: Séloiché (Côte-d'Or)

Saint-Pierre-aux-Oies: (1) Fontaine-aux-Oies; (2) Valbourg (Marne)

Saint-Pierre-Avez: Mont-Avez (Hautes-Alpes)

Saint-Pierre-Brouck: (1) Brouck-Libre; (2) Marais-Libre (Nord)

Saint-Pierre-d'Albigny: Albigny (Savoie)

Saint-Pierre-d'Alvey: Val-d'Avey (Savoie)

Saint-Pierre-d'Amilly: Amilly (Charente-Maritime)

Saint-Pierre-d'Archiac: Archiac (Charente-Maritime)

Saint-Pierre-d'Aurillac: Aurillac-sur-Garonne (Gironde)

Saint-Pierre-d'Entremont: Entremont-le-Jeune (Savoie)

Saint-Pierre-d'Oléron: L'Unité (Charente-Maritime)

Saint-Pierre-de-Bailleul: L'Unité (Eure)

Saint-Pierre-de-Belleville: Arbaretan (Savoie)

Saint-Pierre-de-Bœuf: Bœuf (Loire)

Saint-Pierre-de-Buzet: Bois-des-Vignes (Lot-et-Garonne)

Saint-Pierre-de-Chandieu: Chandieu-la-Montagne (Isère)

Saint-Pierre-de-Colamine: Colamine-la-Montagne (Puy-de-Dôme)

Saint-Pierre-de-Colombier: Pruneirolle (Ardèche)

Saint-Pierre-de-Curtille: Val-de-Crème (Savoie)

Saint-Pierre-de-Genebroz: Genebros (Savoie)

Saint-Pierre-de-Jards: L'Herbon (Indre)

Saint-Pierre-de-Juicq: La Cocarde (Charente-Maritime)

Saint-Pierre-de-Juillers: (1) Juillers-l'Unité; (2) L'Union (Charente-Maritime)

Saint-Pierre-de-l'Isle: L'Isle-Boutonne (Charente-Maritime)

Saint-Pierre-de-Lamps: Lamps-la-Colline (Indre)

Saint-Pierre-de-Palais: (1) La Chaumière; (2) La Fraternité (Charente-Maritime)

Saint-Pierre-de-Soucy: Les Rocs (Savoie)

Saint-Pierre-des-Corps: La Clarté-Républicaine (Indre-et-Loire)

Saint-Pierre-des-Machabées: Macheloup (Ardèche)

Saint-Pierre-du-Bois: Bois-Pierre (Loir-et-Cher)

Saint-Pierre-du-Châtel: Pierre-la-Montagne (Eure)

Saint-Pierre-du-Chemin: Chemin-sur-le-Lay (Vendée)

Saint-Pierre-Église: Pierre-Ferme (Manche)

Saint-Pierre-en-Grandvaux: Roche-Pierre (Jura)

Saint-Pierre-Eynac: (1) Eynac; (2) Montplo (Haute-Loire)

Saint-Pierre-la-Cour: Bourg-l'Union (Mayenne)

Saint-Pierre-la-Vieille: Vieille-sous-le-Mont (Calvados)

Saint-Pierre-le-Bost: Les Bois (Creuse)

Saint-Pierre-le-Dechausselat: Decaussetat (Ardèche)

Saint-Pierre-le-Moutier: (1) Brutus-la-Vallée; (2) Brutus-le-Magnanime; (3) Brutus-le-Moutier (Nièvre)

Saint-Pierre-le-Vieux: Pierre-Neuve (Saône-et-Loire)

Saint-Pierre-lès-Bitry: Les Gorges-de-Bitry (Oise)

Saint-Pierre-les-Bois: Les Bois (Cher)

Saint-Pierre-lès-Calais: Dampierre-les-Dunes (Pas-de-Calais)

Saint-Pierre-lez-Étieux: Beauval (Cher)

Saint-Pierre-Oursin: Pierre-du-Marais (Calvados)

Saint-Pierre-Saint-Martin-d'Argençon: (1)

Argenson; (2) Rives-de-Choranne (Hautes-Alpes)

Saint-Pierremont: Libremont (Ardennes)

Saint-Pierreville: La Montagne (Ardèche)

Saint-Pilard-la-Palud: (1) Palud-la-Montagne; (2) Pelletier-la-Palud (Rhône)

Saint-Pizard-de-Senozan: Senosan (Saône-et-Loire)

Saint-Plaisir: La Bieudre (Allier)

Saint-Plancard: Vallon-Libre (Haute-Garonne)

Saint-Plantaire: Plantaire-le-Bouzantin (Indre)

Saint-Point: Mont-Brillant (Saône-et-Loire)

Saint-Pol-de-Léon: (1) Mont-Frimaire; (2) Port-Pol (Finistère)

Saint-Pol-sur-Ternoise: Pol (Pas-de-Calais)

Saint-Polgues: Roche-Libre (Loire)

Saint-Pons: Jolival (Alpes-de-Haute-Provence)

Saint-Pons: Thomières (Hérault)

Saint-Pons-de-Mauchiens: Mont-Ventôse (Hérault)

Saint-Pons-de-Thomières: Thomières (Hérault)

Saint-Pons-la-Calm: Pont-sur-Tave (Gard)

Saint-Pont: Mont-sur-Chalon (Allier)

Saint-Porchaire: L'Épine (Charente-Maritime)

Saint-Porquier: Mont-Porquier (Tarn-et-Garonne)

Saint-Port: Seine-Port (Seine-et-Marne)

Saint-Pourçain: Mont-sur-Sioule (Allier)

Saint-Pourçain-Mauchère: Dorvalet (Allier)

Saint-Pourçain-sur-Bebre: Bebre-la-Montagne (Allier)

Saint-Préjet-Armandon: Mont-Pregeix (Haute-Loire)

Saint-Préjet-d'Allier: Rive-d'Ance (Haute-Loire)

Saint-Preuil: Preuil-Champagne (Charente)

Saint-Priesaint-de-Gimel: La Montagne (Corrèze)

Saint-Priest: (1) Beau-Priest; (2) Zélé-Patriote (Isère)

Saint-Priest: Font-Indre (Cher)

Saint-Priest: Val-d'Or (Ardèche)

Saint-Privat: Maro (Hérault)

Saint-Privat: (1) Privat-Haute-Montagne; (2) Privat-le-Centre (Corrèze)

Saint-Privat-d'Allier: Privat-la-Roche (Haute-Loire)

Saint-Privat-de-Champclos: Champclos (Gard)

Saint-Privat-de-Vallongue: (1) Bellegarde-de-Vallongue; (2) Bellegarde-Raudon (Lozère)

Saint-Privat-des-Vieux: La Font-le-Vieux (Gard)

Saint-Privat-du-Dragon: Coteau-Libre (Haute-Loire)

Saint-Privé: (1) Libre; (2) Mont-Libre (Saône-et-Loire)

Saint-Prix: Bellevue-la-Forêt (Yvelines)

Saint-Prix: Commune-de-la-Marne (Marne)

Saint-Prix: Prix-sous-Beuvray (Saône-et-Loire)

Saint-Projet: Bertrande (Cantal)

Saint-Projet: Mont-Libre (Lot)

Saint-Prouant: La Draperie (Vendée)

Saint-Puy: Puy-la-Montagne (Gers)

Saint-Quentin: (1) Égalité-sur-Somme; (2) Linon-sur-Somme; (3) Somme-Libre (Aisne)

Saint-Quentin: Grand-Châlier (Isère)

Saint-Quentin: (1) Mont-Quentin; (2) La Réunion (Marne)

Saint-Quentin: Prés-Quentin (Loir-et-Cher)

Saint-Quentin: Quentin-la-Poterie (Gard)

Saint-Quentin: Roche-Quentin (Puy-de-Dôme)

Saint-Quentin-Chaspiniac: Mont-Quentin (Haute-Loire)

Saint-Quentin-de-Rançanne: Quantin-Rançanne (Charente-Maritime)

Saint-Quentin-le-Petit: L'Unité (Ardennes)

Saint-Quentin-le-Petit: Unité (Orne)

Saint-Quentin-Motte-Croix-au-Bailly: Croix-au-Bailly (Somme)

Saint-Quentin-sur-Coole: (1) Égalité-sur-Coole; (2) Hautcoole (Marne)

Saint-Quentin-sur-Fion: Fioncourt (Marne)

Saint-Quentin-sur-Indrois: (1) Quantin; (2) Quentin (Indre-et-Loire)

Saint-Quirin: (1) Cœurs-Francs; (2) Vérité (Meurthe-et-Moselle)

Saint-Racho: Dun-la-Montagne (Saône-et-Loire)

Saint-Rambert: Mont-Ferme (Ain)

Saint-Rambert: Rambert-Loire (Loire)

Saint-Rambert-l'Île-Barbe: Beauvais-l'Isle-Barbe (Rhône)

Saint-Raphaël: Barraton (Var)

Saint-Raphaël: Monchemin (Dordogne)

Saint-Règle: (1) Règle-l'Amasse; (2) Règle-sur-Amasse (Indre-et-Loire)

Saint-Rémi: Arpingon (Savoie)

Saint-Rémy: Bellevue-sur-Saône (Saône-et-Loire)

Saint-Rémy: Chêne-Libre (Vosges)
Saint-Rémy: Mont-sur-Brenne (Côte-d'Or)
Saint-Rémy: Montpignon (Haute-Loire)
Saint-Rémy: Somanges (Marne)
Saint-Rémy-au-Bois: (1) L'Ami-de-la-Vertu;
    (2) L'Amie-de-la-Vertu (Pas-de-Calais)
Saint-Rémy-Blanzy: (1) Blanzy; (2) Rémy-
    Blanzy; (3) Rémy-Ivry (Aisne)
Saint-Rémy-de-Blot: Blot-le-Rocher (Puy-
    de-Dôme)
Saint-Rémy-de-la-Vanne: Vaux-de-la-Vanne
    (Seine-et-Marne)
Saint-Rémy-de-Provence: Glanum
    (Bouches-du-Rhône)
Saint-Remy-en-Bouzemont: (1) Bouzemont;
    (2) La Fraternité (Marne)
Saint-Rémy-en-Rollat: Servagnon (Allier)
Saint-Rémy-la-Varenne: Varennes-sur-Loire
    (Maine-et-Loire)
Saint-Remy-sur-Bussy: (1) Somme-Bussy;
    (2) Somme-Remy-sur-Bussy-les-Mottes;
    (3) Somremy-sur-Bussy (Marne)
Saint-Rémy-sur-Durolle: Montoncel (Puy-
    de-Dôme)
Saint-Restitut: Restitut-la-Montagne (Drôme)
Saint-Révérien: Brutus-le-Bourg (Nièvre)
Saint-Rimay: Fond-Rimay (Loir-et-Cher)
Saint-Riquer-ès-Plains: Es-Plains-sur-Mer
    (Seine-Maritime)
Saint-Robert: (1) Bel-Air; (2) Mont-Bel-Air
    (Corrèze)
Saint-Roch: La Montagne (Indre-et-Loire)
Saint-Rogatien: L'Égalité (Charente-Mar-
    itime)
Saint-Rogatien: Prompt-Secours (Charente-
    Maritime)
Saint-Romain: Belle-Roche (Côte-d'Or)
Saint-Romain: Brutus (Loir-et-Cher)
Saint-Romain: Romain-de-Colbosc (Seine-
    Maritime)
Saint-Romain: Romain-Libre-du-Mont-
    d'Or (Puy-de-Dôme)
Saint-Romain-d'Ay: Roche-d'Ay (Ardèche)
Saint-Romain-de-Benet: Romain-la-
    Fontaine (Charente-Maritime)
Saint-Romain-de-Lerp: Mont-Lerp
    (Ardèche)
Saint-Romain-de-Malegarde: (1) Romain-
    Montagnard; (2) Romain-sur-Aigues
    (Vaucluse)
Saint-Romain-de-Roche: Baume-la-Roche
    (Jura)
Saint-Romain-des-Îles: Île-sur-Saône
    (Saône-et-Loire)

Saint-Romain-en-Gal: Romain-les-Roches
    (Rhône)
Saint-Romain-en-Gier: Sautemouche-en-
    Gier (Rhône)
Saint-Romain-en-Jarret: Romain-les-Vergers
    (Loire)
Saint-Romain-en-Viennois: Romain-sur-
    Lauzon (Vaucluse)
Saint-Romain-le-Couzon: Romain-Libre
    (Rhône)
Saint-Romain-le-Désert: Mont-Désert
    (Ardèche)
Saint-Romain-sous-Versigny: Raveau-sur-
    Arrière (Saône-et-Loire)
Saint-Roman-de-Codière: Mont-de-
    Vidourle (Gard)
Saint-Romans: Romans-Libre (Isère)
Saint-Rome-de-Cernon: Fort-Cernon
    (Aveyron)
Saint-Rome-de-Tarn: Pont-Libre (Aveyron)
Saint-Saëns: Saëns-la-Forêt (Seine-
    Maritime)
Saint-Salvadour: Salvador (Corrèze)
Saint-Samson: Gaie-Vallée (Maine-et-Loire)
Saint-Samson-la-Poterie: Samson-sur-
    Thérain (Oise)
Saint-Sanin-d'Escanecrabe: Escanecrabe
    (Haute-Garonne)
Saint-Satur: Thibault-la-Fontaine (Cher)
Saint-Saturnin: Bombardon (Cher)
Saint-Saturnin: Lucian (Hérault)
Saint-Saturnin: Mont-Rude (Maine-et-
    Loire)
Saint-Saturnin: Montauges (Marne)
Saint-Saturnin-d'Avignon: Mont-Saturnin
    (Vaucluse)
Saint-Saturnin-de-Séchaud: Port-d'Envaux
    (Charente-Maritime)
Saint-Saud-la-Coussière: La Coussière-sur-
    Dronne (Dordogne)
Saint-Saulge: Marat-les-Forêts (Nièvre)
Saint-Sauvant: Silvain-la-Roche (Charente-
    Maritime)
Saint-Sauve: Sauve-Libre (Puy-de-Dôme)
Saint-Sauvent: Sauvent-la-Plaine (Vienne)
Saint-Sauveur: Alpha (Côte-d'Or)
Saint-Sauveur: Méalle (Hautes-Alpes)
Saint-Sauveur: Mont-Méale (Hautes-Alpes)
Saint-Sauveur: La Réunion (Pas-de-Calais)
Saint-Sauveur: La Rivière (Calvados)
Saint-Sauveur: Sauveur-Géroménil (Oise)
Saint-Sauveur-de-Carrouges: Bel-Air (Orne)
Saint-Sauveur-de-Cruzières: Cruzières-
    Inférieur (Ardèche)

Saint-Sauveur-de-Givre-en-Mai: Givre-en-Mai (Deux-Sèvres)

Saint-Sauveur-de-Nuaillé: La Concorde (Charente-Maritime)

Saint-Sauveur-des-Bornes: Borne (Ardèche)

Saint-Sauveur-des-Poursils: Plan-des-Pourcils (Gard)

Saint-Sauveur-en-Puisaye: (1) Montagne-sur-Loing; (2) Sauveur-sur-Loing (Yonne)

Saint-Sauveur-la-Vallée: Puyvalon (Lot)

Saint-Sauveur-le-Vicomte: Sauveur-sur-Douve (Manche)

Saint-Sauvy: Montagne-de-l'Arrats (Gers)

Saint-Savin-de-Blaye: Mont-des-Landes (Gironde)

Saint-Savin-du-Port: (1) Mont-Savin; (2) La Montagne (Charente-Maritime)

Saint-Savin-sur-Gartempe: Pont-sur-Gartempe (Vienne)

Saint-Savinien: (1) Carrière-Charente; (2) La Roche-sur-Charente (Charente-Maritime)

Saint-Sébastien-d'Aigrefeuille: (1) Sébastien-la-Montagne; (2) Sébastien-Montagneux (Gard)

Saint-Secondin: Molineuf (Loir-et-Cher)

Saint-Senoch: Senoch-et-Barbeneuve (Indre-et-Loire)

Saint-Sernain-du-Plain: La Montagne-en-Plain (Saône-et-Loire)

Saint-Sernin-lès-Mailhoc: (1) Bon-Air; (2) Roc-la-Montagne (Tarn)

Saint-Sernin-sur-Rance: Roc-Montagne (Aveyron)

Saint-Servan: Port-Solidor (Ille-et-Vilaine)

Saint-Seurin-d'Uzet: Uzet-sur-Gironde (Charente-Maritime)

Saint-Seurin-de-Palenne: (1) Palenne; (2) Seurin (Charente-Maritime)

Saint-Sever: Rostaing (Hautes-Pyrénées)

Saint-Sever: Toudourg (Aveyron)

Saint-Sever-sur-l'Adour: Mont-Adour (Landes)

Saint-Severin: (1) Belluire; (2) Brumaire (Charente-Maritime)

Saint-Siffret: Pomeyrole (Gard)

Saint-Sigismond: Sigismond-les-Marais (Vendée)

Saint-Sigismond: Val-d'Auxance (Maine-et-Loire)

Saint-Sigismond: Valbeau (Savoie)

Saint-Sigismond-de-Clermont: La Tenaille (Charente-Maritime)

Saint-Silvain: (1) L'Égalité; (2) Union (Corrèze)

Saint-Silvain: Les Mazenottes (Côte-d'Or)

Saint-Silvain: Union (Maine-et-Loire)

Saint-Silvain-Bas-le-Roc: Bas-le-Roc (Creuse)

Saint-Silvain-sous-Toulx: Sous-Toulx (Creuse)

Saint-Siméon: Union (Seine-et-Marne)

Saint-Simon: Brumaire (Haute-Garonne)

Saint-Simon-de-Bordes: Simon-Bordes (Charente-Maritime)

Saint-Simon-de-Pellouaille: Pellouaille (Charente-Maritime)

Saint-Solve: (1) Air-Salutaire; (2) Ère-Salutaire (Corrèze)

Saint-Sorlin: Bonne-Fontaine (Ain)

Saint-Sorlin: La Bruyère (Rhône)

Saint-Sorlin: Roche-Vineuse (Saône-et-Loire)

Saint-Sorlin-d'Arves: Col-d'Aule (Savoie)

Saint-Sorlin-de-Conac: Conac-la-Vallée (Charente-Maritime)

Saint-Sorlin-Montmélas: Bonnet-la-Montagne (Rhône)

Saint-Sornin: Les Bois (Vendée)

Saint-Sornin: La Bretêche (Charente-Maritime)

Saint-Sornin-Lavolps: Sornin-Lavaux (Corrèze)

Saint-Sornin-le-Lac: Sornin-le-Pont (Haute-Vienne)

Saint-Souplet-sur-Py: Mont-Souplet (Marne)

Saint-Stanislas: Toul (Meurthe-et-Moselle)

Saint-Suliac: Port-Suliac (Ille-et-Vilaine)

Saint-Sulpice: Les Forêts (Savoie)

Saint-Sulpice: Les Gorges-Sableuses (Maine-et-Loire)

Saint-Sulpice: Libre-Lèse (Haute-Garonne)

Saint-Sulpice: Roche-la-Montagne (Nièvre)

Saint-Sulpice: Le Val-de-Scey (Haute-Saône)

Saint-Sulpice-d'Arnoult: (1) Arnoult; (2) Les Montagnards (Charente-Maritime)

Saint-Sulpice-d'Excideuil: Sulpice-le-Calvaire (Dordogne)

Saint-Sulpice-de-Favières: Favières-Défanatisé (Yvelines)

Saint-Sulpice-de-Pommeray: Sulpice (Loir-et-Cher)

Saint-Sulpice-en-Pareds: La Fertile (Vendée)

Saint-Sulpice-sur-Rille: (1) Sulpice-la-Montagne; (2) Vendémiaire (Orne)

Saint-Sylvestre: Duson (Ardèche)

Saint-Symphorien: Bellevue-sur-Saône (Côte-d'Or)

Saint-Symphorien: Grand-Air (Lozère)
Saint-Symphorien: La Hure (Gironde)
Saint-Symphorien: Marat (Haute-Vienne)
Saint-Symphorien: Phorien-sur-Sèvre
  (Deux-Sèvres)
Saint-Symphorien: Pont-de-Vanson (Alpes-
  de-Haute-Provence)
Saint-Symphorien: La Réunion-du-Nord
  (Indre-et-Loire)
Saint-Symphorien: La Révolution (Char-
  ente-Maritime)
Saint-Symphorien-d'Ancelles: Fougère-
  d'Ancelles (Saône-et-Loire)
Saint-Symphorien-d'Ozon: Ozon (Isère)
Saint-Symphorien-de-Lay: (1) Lay; (2)
  Symphorien-Lay (Loire)
Saint-Symphorien-de-Mahun: Mahun-Libre
  (Ardèche)
Saint-Symphorien-de-Marmagne: Le
  Pelletier (Saône-et-Loire)
Saint-Symphorien-le-Château: Chausse-
  Armée (Rhône)
Saint-Symphorien-lès-Charolles: Phorien-
  lès-Charolles (Saône-et-Loire)
Saint-Thélo: Thélo-sur-Oust (Côtes-
  d'Armor)
Saint-Théodorit: Théodorite (Gard)
Saint-Thibaud-de-Couz: La Cascade
  (Savoie)
Saint-Thibault: Fontaine-sur-Armançon
  (Côte-d'Or)
Saint-Thibault-des-Vignes: La Côte-des-
  Vignes (Seine-et-Marne)
Saint-Thibault-en-Chaussée: L'Union (Oise)
Saint-Thiébaud: Fontenelle (Jura)
Saint-Thierry: Montdor (Marne)
Saint-Thomas: (1) Bel-Air-sur-Aisne; (2)
  Mont-Aisne (Marne)
Saint-Thomas: Le Désert (Haute-Garonne)
Saint-Thomas: Les Esserts (Savoie)
Saint-Thomas-de-Cœur: Grand-Cœur
  (Savoie)
Saint-Thomas-de-Conac: Conac (Charente-
  Maritime)
Saint-Thomas-du-Bois: Les Brandes (Char-
  ente-Maritime)
Saint-Thual: Motay-Thual (Ille-et-Vilaine)
Saint-Trivier-de-Courtes: Val-Libre (Ain)
Saint-Trivier-sur-Moignans: Pont-Moignans
  (Ain)
Saint-Trojan: La Montagne (Charente-Mar-
  itime)
Saint-Tropez: Héraclée (Var)
Saint-Usage: Bon-Usage (Côte-d'Or)

Saint-Usuge: Chalon-sur-Seille (Saône-et-
  Loire)
Saint-Utin: Lignoncourt (Marne)
Saint-Uze: Mont-Bertheud (Drôme)
Saint-Vaasaint-de-la-Hougue: (1) La
  Hougue; (2) Port-la-Hougue (Manche)
Saint-Vaasaint-de-Longmont: Longmont
  (Oise)
Saint-Vaize: Vaize-Charente (Charente-Mar-
  itime)
Saint-Valbert: Val-d'Héricourt (Haute-
  Saône)
Saint-Valentin: La Cadoue (Indre)
Saint-Valéry-en-Caux: Port-le-Pelletier
  (Seine-Maritime)
Saint-Valéry-lès-Aumale: (1) La Montagne-
  sur-Bresle; (2) Valéry-la-Montagne; (3)
  Vallée-la-Montagne (Oise)
Saint-Valéry-sur-Somme: (1) La Montagne-
  sur-Somme; (2) Port-Somme (Somme)
Saint-Vallerin: (1) Chinte-sous-Roche; (2)
  Vallerin-Rochefort (Saône-et-Loire)
Saint-Vallier: Vallier-les-Bois (Saône-et-
  Loire)
Saint-Vallier-sur-Rhône: Val-Libre (Drôme)
Saint-Venant: Pot-Vert (Pas-de-Calais)
Saint-Vénérand: Vénérand-la-Garde
  (Haute-Loire)
Saint-Véran: Blanche-Froide (Hautes-Alpes)
Saint-Vérand: Arlois (Saône-et-Loire)
Saint-Vert: Vert-les-Eaux (Haute-Loire)
Saint-Viance: (1) Avelque-Courte; (2) Belle-
  Rive (Corrèze)
Saint-Victor: Victor-sur-Ouche (Côte-d'Or)
Saint-Victor: Victoral (Ardèche)
Saint-Victor-de-Morestel: Mont-Vallon
  (Isère)
Saint-Victor-la-Coste: Serre-la-Coste
  (Gard)
Saint-Victor-Malescours: Victor (Haute-
  Loire)
Saint-Victor-sur-Arlanc: Victor-la-Mon-
  tagne (Haute-Loire)
Saint-Vidal: La Pénide (Haute-Loire)
Saint-Vigor-d'Ymonville: Beauvais-sur-
  Seine (Seine-Maritime)
Saint-Vincent: Lassaigne (Puy-de-Dôme)
Saint-Vincent: Mars (Cantal)
Saint-Vincent: Mont-Clergot (Haute-Loire)
Saint-Vincent-d'Olargues: (1) Collines-et-
  Rochers; (2) Vincent-de-Collines-et-
  Rochers (Hérault)
Saint-Vincent-de-Cosse: Montagne-
  Regénérée (Dordogne)

Saint-Vincent-de-Lauzet: Mont-Clocher (Alpes-de-Haute-Provence)

Saint-Vincent-de-Noyers: Vincent-la-Lauze (Alpes-de-Haute-Provence)

Saint-Vincent-de-Xaintes: Lepelletier (Landes)

Saint-Vincent-des-Prés: Gande (Saône-et-Loire)

Saint-Vincent-du-Fort-du-Lay: Fort-du-Lay (Vendée)

Saint-Vincent-en-Bresse: Vincent-des-Bois (Saône-et-Loire)

Saint-Vincent-Sterlanges: Le Gravereau (Vendée)

Saint-Vincent-sur-Graon: Le Graon (Vendée)

Saint-Vincent-sur-Jard: Le Goulet (Vendée)

Saint-Vinnemer: Vinnemer-l'Armançon (Yonne)

Saint-Vital: Côtes-Rives (Savoie)

Saint-Vitte-le-Fleuriel: (1) Fleuriel-sur-Poncignon; (2) Fleuriel-sur-Queune (Cher)

Saint-Vivien: Franklin (Charente-Maritime)

Saint-Vivien: (1) Sans-Culottes; (2) Vivien-le-Mont (Charente-Maritime)

Saint-Voy-de-Bonas: Mont-Lizieu (Haute-Loire)

Saint-Vrain: (1) Olcomval; (2) Vrain-la-Fertilité (Marne)

Saint-Vulbas: Claires-Fontaines (Ain)

Saint-Witt: Égalité-sur-Doubs (Doubs)

Saint-Xandre: Gemmapes (Charente-Maritime)

Saint-Yan: Yan-l'Arconce (Saône-et-Loire)

Saint-Ybard: L'Union-sur-Vézère (Corrèze)

Saint-Ybars: (1) Mont-Sauveterre; (2) Mont-Ybars (Ariège)

Saint-Yon: Boissy-la-Montagne (Yvelines)

Saint-Yors: La Fougère (Gers)

Saint-Yrieix-la-Perche: Yrieix-la-Montagne (Haute-Vienne)

Saint-Ythaire: (1) Mont-Ainard; (2) Monteynard (Saône-et-Loire)

Saint-Yvoine: Roche-sur-Allier (Puy-de-Dôme)

Saint-Zacharie: Théoulen (Var)

Sainte-Adresse: (1) Cap-d'Antifer; (2) Cap-de-la-Hève (Seine-Maritime)

Sainte-Anastasie: Montauri (Gard)

Sainte-Assise: Seine-Assise (Seine-Maritime)

Sainte-Aurence-Cazaux: Dargelles (Gers)

Sainte-Austreberthe: (1) L'Égalité-sur-Canche (2) Montagne-sur-Canche (Pas-de-Calais)

Sainte-Brigitte: La Source (Hérault)

Sainte-Catherine: Les Tanneries (Meurthe-et-Moselle)

Sainte-Catherine-lès-Arras: (1) Faubourg-l'Unité; (2) L'Unité (Pas-de-Calais)

Sainte-Catherine-sous-Riverie: Riard-sous-Riverie (Rhône)

Sainte-Cécile: Cécile-les-Monts (Manche)

Sainte-Cécile: Cécile-Montagnarde (Vaucluse)

Sainte-Cécile: Petit-Lay (Vendée)

Sainte-Cécile: Pont-sur-Crosne (Saône-et-Loire)

Sainte-Cécile: Renon-Libre (Indre)

Sainte-Cécile-d'Andorge: Andorge-le-Gardon (Gard)

Sainte-Cerotte: Cerotte-en-Bel-Air (Sarthe)

Sainte-Christie: (1) Mont-Vineux; (2) Vineux (Gers)

Sainte-Colombe: Bas-Franc (Landes)

Sainte-Colombe: Belle-Roche (Côte-d'Or)

Sainte-Colombe: La Colombe (Charente-Maritime)

Sainte-Colombe: Colombe-lès-Vienne (Rhône)

Sainte-Colombe: Colombe-sur-Chabre (Hautes-Alpes)

Sainte-Colombe: Fonds-Cœur (Indre)

Sainte-Colombe: Montrouge (Sarthe)

Sainte-Colombe-en-Auxois: Rochefontaine (Côte-d'Or)

Sainte-Colombe-en-Morvand: Colombe-la-Montagne (Yonne)

Sainte-Colombe-en-Puisaye: Loing-la-Source (Yonne)

Sainte-Consorce: Les Marrons (Rhône)

Sainte-Croix: Centre-de-Vallée-Française (Lozère)

Sainte-Croix: Croix-Gazonfière (Sarthe)

Sainte-Croix: Solnan (Saône-et-Loire)

Sainte-Croix: L'Union-sur-Belle (Dordogne)

Sainte-Croix-à-Lauze: La Lauze (Alpes-de-Haute-Provence)

Sainte-Croix-de-Caderle: Mont-Bize (Gard)

Sainte-Croix-de-Verdon: Peiron-Sans-Culottes (Alpes-de-Haute-Provence)

Sainte-Enimie: Puy-Roc (Lozère)

Sainte-Eulalie: Basse-Maronne (Cantal)

Sainte-Eulalie: (1) Le Bleynet; (2) Source-de-Loire (Ardèche)

Sainte-Eulalie: Canteperdrix (Gard)

Sainte-Eulalie: Faubourg-Égalité (Corrèze)

Sainte-Eulalie-de-Larzac: Source-Libre (Aveyron)

Sainte-Euphrasie: Ardrecours (Marne)

Sainte-Euphrone: Choisy-lès-Semur (Côte-d'Or)

Sainte-Fauste: La Ferté-les-Bois (Indre)

Sainte-Ferréole: (1) Montagne-Frimaire; (2) Montfrimaire (Corrèze)

Sainte-Flaive-des-Loups: Louvetière (Vendée)

Sainte-Florence: L'Hébergement-Idreau (Vendée)

Sainte-Florine: Florine-le-Charbon (Haute-Loire)

Sainte-Foy: Le Désert (Vendée)

Sainte-Foy: Valamont (Savoie)

Sainte-Foy-d'Aigrefeuille: L'Unité (Haute-Garonne)

Sainte-Foy-de-Peyrolières: Peyroulières (Haute-Garonne)

Sainte-Foy-l'Argentière: Foy-sur-Brevenne (Rhône)

Sainte-Foy-la-Grande: Bonne-Foy (Gironde)

Sainte-Foy-lès-Lyon: (1) Bonnefey; (2) Mont-Chalier (Rhône)

Sainte-Gemme: Bel-Air (Cher)

Sainte-Gemme: Gemme-la-Rivière (Charente-Maritime)

Sainte-Gemme: (1) Marinville-Libreville; (2) Montagron (Marne)

Sainte-Gemme-des-Bruyères: Les Bruyères (Vendée)

Sainte-Gemme-du-Sablon: Les Sablons (Indre)

Sainte-Gemmes: Gentlibre (Loir-et-Cher)

Sainte-Gemmes: Mont-Joli (Maine-et-Loire)

Sainte-Gemmes-le-Robert: (1) Jeune; (2) Jouanne; (3) Mont-Rochard (Mayenne)

Sainte-Geneviève: Mont-Bon-Air (Meurthe-et-Moselle)

Sainte-Geneviève: Montcailloux (Oise)

Sainte-Geneviève-des-Bois: Colbert-la-Réunion (Yvelines)

Sainte-Hélène: (1) Phorien-sur-Guye; (2) Sources-de-Guye (Saône-et-Loire)

Sainte-Hélène-du-Lac: Commune-du-Lac (Savoie)

Sainte-Hélène-sur-Isère: Les Forges (Savoie)

Sainte-Hermine: Hermine-sur-Smagne (Vendée)

Sainte-Julie: Falerne (Ain)

Sainte-Lheurine: Lheurine-la-Montagne (Charente-Maritime)

Sainte-Livière: (1) Belle-Prairie; (1) Montlivière (Marne)

Sainte-Lizaigne: Vin-Bon (Indre)

Sainte-Magnance: Magnance-le-Rocher (Yonne)

Sainte-Marguerite: Marguerite-la-Mer (Manche)

Sainte-Marguerite: Meurthe-Fave (Vosges)

Sainte-Marguerite: Phare-de-l'Ailly (Seine-Maritime)

Sainte-Marguerite-de-Carrouges: Carrouges (Orne)

Sainte-Marguerite-Lafigère: Valborne (Ardèche)

Sainte-Marie: Maratide (Pyrénées-Atlantiques)

Sainte-Marie: Val-d'Oule (Hautes-Alpes)

Sainte-Marie-à-Py: (1) Montagne-à-Py; (2) Valaumont (Marne)

Sainte-Marie-au-Bosc: Unité (Seine-Maritime)

Sainte-Marie-aux-Mines: Val-aux-Mines (Haut-Rhin)

Sainte-Marie-d'Alloix: Alloix (Isère)

Sainte-Marie-d'Alvey: Des-Fontaines (Savoie)

Sainte-Marie-de-Bickenholtz: Bickenholtz (Meurthe-et-Moselle)

Sainte-Marie-de-Cuines: Mont (Savoie)

Sainte-Marie-de-Gosse: Barra (Landes)

Sainte-Marie-de-la-Mer: (1) Redoute-de-l'Agly; (2) Redoute-Maritime (Pyrénées-Orientales)

Sainte-Marie-de-Ré: (1) La Pointe; (2) Union (Charente-Maritime)

Sainte-Marie-des-Chazes: Marie-Pénible (Haute-Loire)

Sainte-Marie-la-Blanche: Montagne-Unie (Côte-d'Or)

Sainte-Marie-la-Robert: Pommidor-sur-le-Don (Orne)

Sainte-Marie-Pornic: Roche-Peltier (Loire-Atlantique)

Sainte-Marie-sur-Ouche: (1) Bain-sur-Ouche; (2) Coyon; (3) République-sur-Ouche (Côte-d'Or)

Sainte-Maure: Mont-Bel-Air (Aube)

Sainte-Maure-de-Touraine: Maure-Libre (Indre-et-Loire)

Sainte-Maxime: Cassius (Var)

Sainte-Même: L'Harmonie (Charente-Maritime)

Sainte-Memmie: Brutus (Marne)

Sainte-Menehould: Montagne-sur-Aisne (Marne)

Sainte-Mère-l'Église: Mère-Libre (Manche)

Sainte-Mesme: Bruyères-les-Fontaines (Yvelines)

Sainte-Osmane: Osmane-la-Fontaine (Sarthe)

Sainte-Outrille: L'Égalité (Cher)

Sainte-Paule: Roche-Guillon (Rhône)

Sainte-Pazanne: Franchère (Loire-Atlantique)

Sainte-Pexine: Les Deux-Rives (Vendée)

Sainte-Quitterie: Marat (Bouches-du-Rhône)

Sainte-Radegonde: Bel-Air (Aveyron)

Sainte-Radegonde: Chassigny (Saône-et-Loire)

Sainte-Radegonde: Varanzay (Charente-Maritime)

Sainte-Ramée: La Ramée (Charente-Maritime)

Sainte-Reine: Baux-Prés (Savoie)

Sainte-Ruffine: Anthoine-le-Mont (Moselle)

Sainte-Sabine: Sabine-le-Plein (Côte-d'Or)

Sainte-Scolasse: Plaine-sur-Sarthe (Orne)

Sainte-Seine-en-Bache: Beau-Séjour (Côte-d'Or)

Sainte-Seine-l'Abbaye: Seine-en-Montagne (Côte-d'Or)

Sainte-Sévère-sur-Indre: Indre-Source (Indre)

Sainte-Sigolène: Segolaine-les-Bois (Haute-Loire)

Sainte-Soulle: (1) Roche-Libre; (2) Rousseau (Charente-Maritime)

Sainte-Suzanne: Mont-d'Erve (Mayenne)

Sainte-Thérèse: Neuville (Allier)

Sainte-Trie: Trie-Argileux (Dordogne)

Sainte-Tulle Tulle-les-Durance (Alpes-de-Haute-Provence)

Sainte-Valière: Mont-Floréal (Aude)

Saintes: Xantes (Charente-Maritime)

Saints-en-Puisaye: Cousay-en-Puisaye (Yonne)

Salles-Comtaux: Salles-la-Source (Aveyron)

Sanssac-l'Église: Sanssac-la-Montagne (Haute-Loire)

Sarrelouis: Sarre-Libre (Moselle)

Sarrians: Marat (Vaucluse)

Saugues: Saugues-la-Montagne (Haute-Loire)

Saulon-la-Chapelle: Saulon-Sanfond (Côte-d'Or)

Saulx-le-Duc: (1) Saulx-en-Montagne; (2) Saulx-la-Ville; (3) Saux-la-Ville (Côte-d'Or)

Saulx-les-Chartreux: Saulx-le-Rocher (Yvelines)

Saumane: Union-la-Montagne (Gard)

Savigné-l'Évêque: Savigné-lès-Le Mans (Sarthe)

Savigny-en-Terre-Pleine: Savigny-les-Forges (Yonne)

Savigny-le-Temple: (1) Savigny-le-Port; (2) Savigny-sur-Balory (Seine-et-Marne)

Sceaux: Sceaux-l'Unité (Paris)

Séez: Val-Joli (Savoie)

Selles-Saint-Denis: Celles-sur-Saudre (Loir-et-Cher)

Semur-en-Auxois: Semur (Côte-d'Or)

Semur-en-Brionnais: Semur-la-Montagne (Saône-et-Loire)

Sennecey-le-Château: Grand-Sennecey (Saône-et-Loire)

Serrières-lès-Saint-Sornin: Port-du-Mézenc (Ardèche)

Sévérac-l'Église: Sévérac-l'Union (Aveyron)

Siaugues-Saint-Romain: Siaugues-le-Romain (Haute-Loire)

Signy-l'Abbaye: Signy-Librecy (Ardennes)

Sillé-le-Guillaume: Sillé-la-Montagne (Sarthe)

Simiane-les-Aix: Collongue (Bouches-du-Rhône)

Sin-le-Noble: Sin-lès-Douai (Nord)

Soisy-sous-Étiolles: Soisy-Marat (Yvelines)

Solre-le-Château: Solre-Libre (Nord)

Soubise: La Regénération (Charente-Maritime)

Soudé-Notre-Dame: (1) Soudé-la-Petite; (2) Soudé-le-Petit (Marne)

Soudé-Sainte-Croix: (1) Soudé-la-Grande; (2) Soudé-le-Grand (Marne)

Souillac: Trente-un-Mai (Lot)

Souraïde: Mendialte (Pyrénées-Atlantiques)

Soursac: Soursac-Moustier (Corrèze)

Sully-la-Chapelle: Sully-le-Peletier (Loiret)

Sury-le-Comtal: Sury-la-Chaux (Loire)

Sylvanès: Union (Aveyron)

Tabanac: Coteau-Libre (Gironde)

Temple-Rivière, Le: Huitrepin (Pas-de-Calais)

Tercillat-Saint-Paul: Tercillat-Pelletier (Creuse)

Tertre-Saint-Denis, Le: Le Tertre-la-Montagne (Yvelines)

Tessens: Mont-Vineux (Savoie)

Thun-l'Évêque: Thun-l'Escault (Nord)

Thurins: Thurins-le-Français (Rhône)

Thury-Harcourt: Thury (Calvados)

Til-Châtel: Mont-sur-Tille (Côte-d'Or)

Tilloy-lès-Mofflaines: Tilloy-aux-Fosses (Pas-de-Calais)

Tilly-d'Orceau: Tilly-sur-Seulles (Calvados)

Tonneins: Tonneins-la-Montagne (Lot-et-Garonne)

Toulon: Bel-Air (Marne)

Toulon: Mont-la-Loi (Allier)

Toulon: Port-la-Montagne (Var)

Toulon-sur-Arroux: Bel-Air-sur-Arroux (Saône-et-Loire)

Tour-de-Salvigny, La: Salvagny (Rhône)

Tour-de-Sçay, La: Sçay-la-Montagne (Doubs)

Tour-du-Pin, La: Val-du-Pin (Isère)

Tour-en-Sologne: Baraque (Loir-et-Cher)

Tournan: Tournan-l'Union (Seine-et-Marne)

Tournon-d'Agenais: Tournon-la-Montagne (Lot-et-Garonne)

Tours: Cérisanne (Savoie)

Toussus-le-Noble: Toussus (Yvelines)

Treignac: Treignac-la-Montagne (Corrèze)

Tremblade, La: Réunion-sur-Seudre (Charente-Maritime)

Tremblay-le-Vicomte: Tremblay-Sans-Culottes (Eure-et-Loir)

Tremblay-le-Vicomte: Tremblay-Sans-Culottes (Yvelines)

Trenal: Pré-Fleur (Jura)

Trinité-du-Mont, La: Le Mont (Seine-Maritime)

Trois-Cocus, Les: Frimaire (Haute-Garonne)

Trois-Fontaines-la-Ville: Troisfontaines (Haute-Marne)

Trye-Château: Trye-sur-Troesne (Oise)

Turenne: Mont-Franc (Corrèze)

Urcuit: Le Laurier (Pyrénées-Atlantiques)

Urt: Liberté (Pyrénées-Atlantiques)

Ustaritz: Marat-sur-Nive (Pyrénées-Atlantiques)

Uzer: Lande (Ardèche)

Uzès: Uzès-la-Montagne (Gard)

Val-Benoîte: Val-d'Armes (Loire)

Val-d'Isère: Laval (Savoie)

Val-de-Bon-Moutier: Val-et-Châtillon (Meurthe-et-Moselle)

Val-du-Roy, Le: Le Val-Marat (Seine-Maritime)

Val-Saint-Germain: Val-Libre (Yvelines)

Val-Saint-Pair: Le Val-Père (Manche)

Valigny-le-Monial: Valigny (Allier)

Vallant-Saint-Georges: Vallant-les-Fontaines (Aube)

Valleroy: Val-de-Loi (Moselle)

Valleroy: Val-le-Libre (Doubs)

Vallon: Vallibre (Ardèche)

Vallouise: Val-Libre (Hautes-Alpes)

Vanault-le-Châtel: (1) Mont-Vanault; (2) Vanault-près-la-Montagne (Marne)

Vanault-les-Dames: (1) Vanault-les-Frères; (2) Vanault (Marne)

Varennes-Saint-Honorat: Varenne-la-Raison (Haute-Loire)

Varennes-Saint-Sauveur: Varennes-sur-Sevron (Saône-et-Loire)

Varennes-sous-Montsoreau: Varennes-sur-Loire (Maine-et-Loire)

Vau-Sainte-Anne, La: La Vau-sur-Cher (Allier)

Vaugirard: Jean-Jacques-Rousseau (Paris)

Vauréal: Lieux (Yvelines)

Vavray-le-Grand-et-le-Petit: Vavrais (Marne)

Vendée (the department): Vengé (Vendée)

Vendôme: Vendôme-Regénéré (Loir-et-Cher)

Venthon: Ventôse (Savoie)

Verlhac-Saint-Jean: Verlhaguet (Tarn-et-Garonne)

Verrière-la-Grande: Verrière-sur-Gienne (Saône-et-Loire)

Versailles: Berceau-de-la-Liberté (Yvelines)

Versoix: Versoix-la-Raison (Ain)

Veuve, La: La Voix-du-Peuple (Marne)

Vic-en-Carladès: Vic-sur-Cère (Cantal)

Vic-Fezensac: Vic-sur-l'Osse (Gers)

Vic-le-Comte: Vic-sur-Allier (Puy-de-Dôme)

Vic-Saint-Chartier: Vic-la-Montagne (Indre)

Vicherey: Bourg-de-l'Unité (Vosges)

Vie, La: Chabestan (Hautes-Alpes)

Vieil-Moutier: Prairie-la-Calique (Pas-de-Calais)

Vieille-Église: L'Indivisible (Pas-de-Calais)

Vienne: Vienne-la-Patriote (Isère)

Vienne-la-Ville: Vienne-sur-Aisne (Marne)

Vienne-le-Château: (1) Vienne-le-Bourg; (2) Vienne-sur-Biesme (Marne)

Vieux-Château: Laure-sur-Serein (Côte-d'Or)

Vieux-Condé: Vieux-Nord-Libre (Nord)

Vieux-lès-Asfeld: Vieux-lès-Écry (Ardennes)

Vilatte, La: Sapette (Ardèche)

Villard-sur-Doron: Fertiline (Savoie)

Villargerel: Sur-Vignes (Savoie)

Villaroger: Roc-Vert (Savoie)

Villars-Saint-Georges: Bonfruit (Doubs)

Villavard: Commune-Avare (Loir-et-Cher)

Ville-aux-Dames, La: Les Sables (Indre-et-Loire)

Ville-Bourbon: Rive-Civique (Tarn-et-Garonne)

Ville-Comte: Bellefontaine (Côte-d'Or)

Ville-Dieu: Côte-Libre (Vaucluse)

Ville-l'Évêque, La: (1) Rougemont; (2) Ville-la-Côte (Eure-et-Loir)

Ville-Moisan: Mont-de-l'Étang (Maine-et-Loire)

Ville-sur-Tourbe: Val-sur-Tourbe (Marne)

Villebarou: Commune-Barou (Loir-et-Cher)

Villecomtal: Dordon (Aveyron)

Villecomtal: Pont-Libre (Gers)

Villedieu: Vérité (Indre)

Villedieu, La: La Carmagnole (Charente-Maritime)

Villedieu-en-Beauce: Commune-Être-Suprème (Loir-et-Cher)

Villefranche: (1) Commune-Franche; (2) Ville-Libre-sur-Saône (Rhône)

Villefrancœur: Commune-Francœur (Loir-et-Cher)

Villefranque: Tricolore (Pyrénées-Atlantiques)

Villemardy: Commune-Duodi (Loir-et-Cher)

Villemontry: Villé-le-Libre (Ardennes)

Villeneuve-l'Archévêque: (1) Villeneuve-la-Montagne; (2) Villeneuve-sur-Vanne (Yonne)

Villeneuve-la-Comtesse: Villeneuve-le-Mont (Charente-Maritime)

Villeneuve-la-Guyard: Villeneuve-la-Guerre (Yonne)

Villeneuve-le-Comte (near Donnemarie-Dontilly): Villeneuve-les-Bordes (Seine-et-Marne)

Villeneuve-le-Comte (near Rozoy-en-Brie): Villeneuve-le-Peuple (Seine-et-Marne)

Villeneuve-le-Roi: Villeneuve-la-Montagne (Paris)

Villeneuve-le-Roi: Villeneuve-les-Sablons (Oise)

Villeneuve-le-Roy: Villeneuve-sur-Seine (Yvelines)

Villeneuve-le-Roy: Villeneuve-sur-Yonne (Yonne)

Villeneuve-les-Chanoines: Villeneuve-Minervois (Aude)

Villeneuve-Mesgrigny, La: La Villeneuve-au-Chêne (Aube)

Villeneuve-Saint-Denis: (1) Villeneuve-Franciade; (2) Villeneuve-l'Union (Seine-et-Marne)

Villeneuve-Saint-Georges: Villeneuve-la-Montagne (Yvelines)

Villeneuve-Saint-Vistre: Villeval (Marne)

Villenouvelle: (1) La Fraternité; (2) L'Unité (Charente-Maritime)

Villerable: Commune-Rable (Loir-et-Cher)

Villerbon: Bonne-Commune (Loir-et-Cher)

Villermain: Bonnemain (Loir-et-Cher)

Villeroy: Ville-Loi (Meuse)

Villeroy: Villemare (Yonne)

Villers-Chambellan: Villers-sous-Barentin (Seine-Maritime)

Villers-en-Argonne: Villers-sur-Aisne (Marne)

Villers-la-Ville: Villers-sur-l'Oignon (Haute-Saône)

Villers-lès-Moivron: Villers-et-Rupt (Meurthe-et-Moselle)

Villers-Saint-Frambourg: Villers-la-Forêt (Oise)

Villers-Saint-Sépulcre: Villers-Coteaux (Oise)

Villers-Sire-Nicole: Villers-sur-Nicole (Nord)

Villers-Sire-Simon: Villers-la-Montagne (Pas-de-Calais)

Villers-sous-Saint-Leu: Villers-sur-Oise (Oise)

Villers-Vicomte: Villers-Marat (Oise)

Villette: Marmorine (Savoie)

Villevêque: Port-du-Loir (Maine-et-Loire)

Villey-le-Sec: Villey-la-Montagne (Meurthe-et-Moselle)

Villey-Saint-Étienne: Villey-sur-Moselle (Meurthe-et-Moselle)

Villiers-Faux: Fauxvilliers (Loir-et-Cher)

Villiers-le-Duc: Villiers-la-Forêt (Côte-d'Or)

Villiers-le-Mathieu: Villiers-le-Voltaire (Yvelines)

Villiers-Louis: Villiers-Libre (Yonne)

Villiers-Saint-Benoît: Villiers-sur-Ouanne (Yonne)

Villiers-sous-Praslin: Villiers-le-Merlet (Aube)

Villiers-sur-Marne: Villers-aux-Pierres (Aisne)

Vineuil: Les Sans-Culottes-sur-Nonette (Oise)

Vitry-en-Perthois-et-Saint-Étienne: Vitry-sur-Saulx (Marne)

Vitry-le-François: Vitry-sur-Marne (Marne)

Vitz-Villeroy: Vitz-sur-l'Authie (Somme)

Viviers-les-Montagnes: Viviers-la-Montagne (Tarn)

Voillecomte: Voille-sur-Héronne (Haute-Marne)

Voisins: Pezens (Aude)

Vollore-Ville: Vollore-Chignore (Puy-de-Dôme)

Vourles: Vourles-le-Courageux (Rhône)

Voûte-de-Polignac, La: Lavoûte-sur-Loire (Haute-Loire)

Yèvre-le-Châtel: Yèvre-la-Patriote (Loiret)

Yvetot: Yvetot-la-Montagne (Seine-Maritime)

Yvré-l'Évêque: Yvré-sur-l'Huisne (Sarthe)

Appendix 3: Paris Métro Stations

The Paris Métro (in full *Chemin de Fer Métropolitain*, "Metropolitan Railway"), originally planned in 1855, opened its first line, from Porte de Vincennes to Port Maillot, on the occasion of the 1900 Exposition Universelle.

There are now 14 lines, complemented by the five lines of the RER (*Réseau Express Regional*, "Regional Express Network"), a sort of "supermetro" extending further into the suburbs. (RER station names do not appear below unless they coincide with Métro names.)

The earliest names of Métro stations were those of important buildings along the line in question, or those of a street or square (*place*) at right angles to the line. At the end of the line, at the city boundary, the name was prefixed by *Porte*, "Gate," although the original fortifications of Paris have long been dismantled.

Many names reflect the history of France, and are mostly those of generals and battles of the Napoleonic era. A glance through the list below will soon find examples.

Inevitably, names have been changed for various reasons. *Berlin*, for example, was closed in 1914 and later reopened as *Liège*, while that same year *Allemagne* ("Germany") was renamed *Jaurès* (see below). After World War II, *Franklin D. Roosevelt* gave his name to a station in 1946 and some stations were renamed for Resistance heroes, such as the two *Corentins* and *Colonel Fabien*.

Compound names, such as *Champs-Élysées Clemenceau*, either denote a street that changes its name as it crosses the line or combine a street name with some other kind of name, such as that of a square, a bridge, or a former village. Some names have an addition in brackets.

In practice, unwieldy names of this type do not bother passengers familiar with the system, since there is a flat fare for each travel zone (Zone 1 covers most of central Paris) and there is no need to ask for a specific destination when buying a ticket.

French-speaking readers interested in Métro names will enjoy Marc Augé's little book *Un ethnologue dans le métro* (Paris: Hachette, 1986). Readers with little or no French should turn to Tom Conley's translation, *In the Métro* (University of Minnesota Press, 2002).

Station names below give line numbers and are notated "see Dictionary" or "see Appendix 4" where a name is treated in the main text or that appendix. (Cross-references are in **bold**, either to one of these sources, as indicated, or to an entry in this appendix.)

Abbesses (12) : The "abbesses" were the *Dames de Montmartre*, or nuns of the Benedictine convent here, founded in 1133 by Queen Adelaide, wife of Louis VI.

Alésia (4) : The name is that of the Gaulish *oppidum*, today **Alise-Sainte-Reine** (see Dictionary), where Caesar captured the Gaulish leader Vercingetorix in 52 BC.

Alexandre Dumas (2) : The name honors the French writer *Alexandre Dumas*, also known as Dumas *père* (1802-1870).

Alma Marceau (9) : The first part of the name commemorates the Crimean War battle of September 20, 1854, in which Franco-British forces defeated the Russians at the mouth of the *Alma* River, southwestern Crimea. The second honors the French general François Séverin *Marceau*-Desgraviers (1769-1796).

Anatole France (3) : The name honors the French writer *Anatole France*, original name Anatole François Thibault (1844-1924).

Anvers (2) : The name is French for the Belgian city of *Antwerp*, captured by the French in 1832.

Argentine (1) : The name commemorates the aid offered by *Argentina* to France in World War II.

Arts et Métiers (3, 11) : The name is that of the *Conservatoire National des Arts et Métiers*, "Conservatory of Arts and Crafts," founded in 1794.

Assemblée Nationale (12) : See **Bourbon, Palais** in Appendix 4.

Aubervilliers Pantin Quatre Chemins (7) : See the names of the first two northeastern suburbs in the Dictionary. *Les Quatre Chemins*, "The Four Ways," is the suburb where the road from Saint-Denis to Nogent-sur-Marne crosses that from Le Bourget to Paris.

Avenue Émile Zola (10) : The name honors the French writer *Émile Zola* (1840-1902).

Avron (2) : See Dictionary.

Balard (8) : The name honors the French chemist Antoine-Jérôme *Balard* (1802-1876).

Barbès Rochechouart (2, 4) : The first part of the name commemorates the French politician Armand *Barbès* (1809-1870). The second honors Marguerite de *Rochechouart* de Montpipeau (1665-1727), abbess of the convent of the *Dames de Montmartre* (see **Abbessess**).

Basilique de St. Denis (13) : The name is that of the abbey church (now cathedral) in the suburb of **Saint-Denis** (see Dictionary) where many French kings are buried.

Bastille (1, 5, 8) : See Appendix 4.

Bel-Air (6) : The name commemorates those who fell in the Franco-Prussian War battle of December 16, 1870, at *Bel-Air*, Maine-et-Loire. The surrender of Paris followed on January 28, 1871. The name is as for the latter half of **Bouc-Bel-Air** (see Dictionary).

Belleville (2, 11) : The northeastern district has a name as for **Belleville** (see Dictionary).

Bérault (1) : The name honors Michel *Bérault*, deputy mayor of Vincennes and a deputy in the French Parliament in 1787.

Bercy (6, 14) : The name is that of a southeastern district of the city.

Bibliothèque François Mitterrand (14) : See **Bibliothèque Nationale** in Appendix 4.

Billancourt (9) : See **Boulogne-Billancourt** in Dictionary.

Bir-Hakeim (Grenelle) (6) : The bridge *pont de Bir-Hakeim* here takes its name from the World War II battle of 1942 in which the French were surrounded by German and Italian forces at *Bir Hakeim*, in the Libyan desert, resisted for 16 days under General Koenig, then managed to rejoin the British lines. The boulevard de *Grenelle*, in the southwest of the city, takes its name from a former village here, its own name perhaps from Low Latin *warenna*, "warren," "game reserve."

Blanche (2) : The name is that of the rue *Blanche* ("White Street"), itself so called from the white dust of the gypsum (plaster of Paris) mined here in Montmartre.

Bobigny Pablo Picasso (5) : For the first name, see Dictionary. The second honors *Pablo Picasso* (1881-1973), the Spanish artist who worked in Paris from 1904. (The station is not near the Picasso Museum.)

Bobigny Pantin Raymond Queneau (5) : For the names of the first two suburbs, see the Dictionary. The second part of the name commemorates the French writer *Raymond Queneau* (1903-1986), author of *Zazie dans le métro* (1959).

Boissière (6) : The name is that of the rue *Boissière* ("Boxwood Street").

Bolivar (7b) : The name honors the Venezuelan general and politician Simón *Bolívar* (1783-1830), nicknamed "The Liberator" and regarded as a hero in the Third Republic

Bonne Nouvelle (8, 9) : The name is that of the church of *Notre-Dame-de-Bonne-Nou-*

velle, "Our Lady of Good News," referring to the Annunciation of the Blessed Virgin Mary.

Botzaris (7b) : The name honors Markos *Botzaris* (1786-1823), a hero of the Greek War of Independence and a defender of Missolonghi in 1822-3.

Boucicaut (8) : The name commemorates Aristide *Boucicaut* (1810-1877), the founder of **Bon Marché** (see Appendix 4).

Boulogne Jean Jaurès (10) : For the first name, see **Boulogne-Billancourt** in Dictionary. For the second, see **Jaurès.**

Boulogne Pont de St. Cloud (Rhin et Danube) (10) : For the first name, see **Boulogne-Billancourt** in Dictionary. The second name is that of a bridge (*pont*) over the Seine at **Saint-Cloud** (see Dictionary). The addition commemorates the First French Army, who fought on the Rhine and the Danube in World War II under General Jean-Marie de Lattre de Tassigny (see **Porte Dauphine**).

Bourse (3) : See Appendix 4.

Bréguet Sabin (5) : The first part of the name commemorates the French watchmaker Abraham Louis *Bréguet* (1747-1823). The second names Charles de *Saint-Sabin,* a municipal magistrate in Paris in 1777.

Brochant (13) : The name commemorates the French geologist and mineralogist André François Marie *Brochant* de Villiers (1772-1840).

Buttes Chaumont (7b) : The names are those of two hills in **Belleville,** from *butte,* "height," and Latin *calvus mons,* "bald hill."

Buzenval (9) : The name is that of the Siege of Paris battle of January 19, 1871, at *Buzenval,* now a district of the suburb of Rueil-Malmaison, Hauts-de-Seine.

Cadet (7) : The name is that of the rue *Cadet* here, commemorating a family of gardeners.

Cambronne (6) : The name honors Vicomte Pierre *Cambronne* (1770-1842), commander of the Light Infantry of the Guard at the battle of Waterloo (1815).

Campo Formio (5) : The name commemorates the peace treaty of October 17, 1797, signed between France and Austria at *Campo Formio* (now Campoformido), Italy, following the defeat of Austria by Napoleon.

Cardinal Lemoine (10) : The name honors Cardinal Jean *Lemoine* (1250-1313), founder of a college near the Sorbonne.

Carrefour Pleyel (13) : The name of the crossroads (*carrefour*) here commemorates the Austrian composer Ignaz *Pleyel* (1757-1831), founder in 1817 of a piano factory in Paris.

Censier Daubenton (Arènes de Lutèce) (7) : The rue *Censier* here appears to derive its name from *censier,* a historical term for a register of tenants and their tenancies. But according to one account it is a form of *sans-chef,* "without head," denoting a cul-de-sac. The second word honors the French naturalist Louis *Daubenton* (1716-1800). For the addition, see Appendix 4.

Champs-Élysées Clemenceau (1, 13) : For the first part of the name, see Appendix 4. The second part honors French prime minister Georges *Clemenceau* (1841-1929).

Chardon-Lagache (10) : The name honors the French merchant Alfred Chardon (1807-1879), who with his wife, Pauline Lagache, founded the retirement home Maison de Retraite Chardon-Lagache

Charenton Écoles (Place Aristide Briand) (8) : For the first part of the name, see **Charenton-le-Pont** in Dictionary. The *Écoles* ("schools") are the *École Vétérinaire de Maisons-Alfort* (see below) and the *École d'Architecture.* French politician *Aristide Briand* (1862-1932), not to be confused with music-hall artist Aristide Bruant (1851-1925), was 11 times prime minister of France.

Charles de Gaulle Étoile (1, 2, 6) : See **Charles-de-Gaulle, Place de** in Appendix 4.

Charles Michels (10) : The name honors the French Communist deputy *Charles Michels* (1903-1941), killed by the Germans on October 22, 1941.

Charonne (9) : The rue de *Charonne* takes its name from that of a former estate here, in the eastern part of the city.

Château d'Eau (4) : The *Château d'Eau* ("Water Castle") on the present place de la République was not a castle but a huge fountain erected in 1811 to bring fresh water to the district. Its tall, three-tier construction earned it its nickname.

Château de Vincennes (1) : The name derives from the 14th-century castle (*château*) in the eastern suburb of **Vincennes** (see Dictionary).

Château-Landon (7) : The rue du *Château-Landon* is named for a family from **Château-Landon** (see Dictionary) who owned property here in the 17th century.

Château Rouge (4) : The *Château Rouge* ("Red Castle") here was a dance hall, demolished in 1882.

Châtelet (Pont au Change) (11, 14) : The name of the 12th-century fortress here means "small castle," as at **Châtelet-en-Brie** (see Dictionary). The *Grand Châtelet*, on the north bank of the Seine, was a tribunal and prison where the *Prévôt de Paris* (see **Le Peletier**) exercised the royal jurisdiction over the viscounty and provosty of Paris. It was demolished in 1802. The *Petit Châtelet*, on the south bank of the Seine, was the official residence of the *Prévôt*. It was demolished in 1782. The *Pont au Change*, over the Seine, has preserved the name of a medieval bridge where money-changers (*changeurs*) traded.

Châtelet Les Halles (1, 4, 7) : For the first part of the name, see **Châtelet**. For the second, see **Halles, Les** in Appendix 4.

Châtillon Montrouge (13) : See the name of each southern suburb in the Dictionary.

Chaussée d'Antin (La Fayette) (7, 9) : The *rue de la Chaussée-d'Antin* here takes its name from the *chaussée* (pathway) at the Porte Gaillon, near the city's edge, where Louis de Pardaillan de Gondrin, duc *d'Antin* (1665-1736), superintendent of buildings under Louis XIV, had bought a large residence. The addition names the French general Marie Joseph Gilbert Motier, marquis de *La Fayette* (1757-1834), who fought against the British in the American Revolution.

Chemin Vert (8) : The *Chemin Vert* ("Green Path") here wound its way through gardens.

Chevaleret (6) : The name is the word for a tool (from *cheval*, "horse") used by tanners here.

Cité (4) : The station is on the **Île de la Cité** (see Appendix 4), the oldest part of Paris.

Cluny La Sorbonne (10) : See **Cluny, Hôtel de** and **Sorbonne** in Appendix 4.

Colonel Fabien (2) : The name commemorates *Colonel Fabien*, code name of the Resistance worker Pierre Georges (1920-1944), killed by the Germans.

Commerce (8) : The rue du *Commerce* here has long been noted for its many businesses.

Concorde (1, 8, 12) : See **Concorde, Place de la** in Appendix 4.

Convention (12) : The name commemorates the *Convention Nationale* ("National Convention"), which governed France under

Robespierre from September 21, 1792 through October 26, 1795.

Corentin Cariou (7) : The name honors the municipal counselor *Corentin Cario* (1898-1942), killed by the Germans.

Corentin Celton (12) : The name honors the Resistance worker *Corentin Celton* (1901-1943), killed by the Germans.

Corvisart (6) : The name commemorates Jean, baron *Corvisart* (1755-1821), physician to Napoleon.

Cour St. Émilion (14) : The courtyard (*cour*) here is named for the *St. Émilion* wine (see **Saint-Émilion** in Dictionary) and stands within an area of former wine warehouses.

Courcelles (2) : The boulevard de *Courcelles* takes its name from the former hamlet here, its own name as for **Courcelles-lès-Lens** (see Dictionary).

Couronnes (2) : The full name of this hilly eastern district is *Couronnes-sous-Savies*, with *Couronnes* probably from Latin *corona*, "height," and *Savies* a former name of **Belleville**.

Créteil L'Échat (8) : For the first name, see Dictionary. The second name comes from the former *chemin de l'Échat* here.

Créteil Préfecture (8) : For the first name, see Dictionary. The second name refers to the *Préfecture de Police* here, the Paris police headquarters.

Créteil Université (8) : For the first name, see Dictionary. The second name refers to a branch of the University of Paris here.

Crimée (7) : The rue de la *Crimée* here is named for the *Crimea*, referring to the Crimean War, which ended in 1856 with the Treaty of Paris.

Croix de Chavaux (Jacques Duclos) (9) : The name is apparently a form of *croix de chevaux*, "horses' cross," perhaps denoting a real cross or a point where coaches stopped. The addition commemorates the French Communist leader *Jacques Duclos* (1896-1975).

Danube (7b) : See **Boulogne Pont de St. Cloud**.

Daumesnil (Félix Éboué) (6, 8) : The name commemorates the French general Pierre *Daumesnil* (1776-1832), who defended Vincennes against the allies in 1814. The addition names the French colonial administrator *Félix Éboué* (1884-1944).

Denfert-Rochereau (4, 6) : The name

commemorates the French colonel Pierre Philippe *Denfert-Rochereau* (1823-1878), who took part in the defense of Belfort in 1870-1.

Dugommier (6) : The name commemorates the French general of Creole origin, Jacques François *Dugommier*, original name Jacques François Coquille (*c.*1736-1794), who led the army in the siege of Toulon in 1793 and who was killed in battle in the Pyrenees.

Dupleix (6) : The name commemorates the French administrator and governor-general of French India, Joseph François *Dupleix* (1696-1793).

Duroc (10, 13) : The name commemorates the French general Géraud Christophe Michel *Duroc*, duc de Frioul (1772-1813), grand marshal of the palace, who took part in campaigns in Austria, Prussia, and Poland and was killed in the battle of Bautzen (1813).

École Militaire (8) : See Appendix 4.

École Vétérinaire de Maisons-Alfort (8) : The name is that of the *École Vétérinaire* ("Veterinary School") in the suburb of **Maisons-Alfort** (see Dictionary).

Edgar Quinet (6) : The name honors the French historian *Edgar Quinet* (1803-1875), a professor at the Collège de France.

Église d'Auteuil (10) : The name is that of the church of *Notre Dame d'Auteuil* ("Our Lady of Auteuil"), built in 1877. See **Auteuil** in Dictionary.

Église de Pantin (5) : The church in **Pantin** (see Dictionary) referred to is that of St. Germain-l'Auxerrois ("of Auxerre").

Esplanade de la Défense (1) : The name refers to the esplanade here with the sculpture *La Défense de Paris* (1871), representing the defense of the capital against German invasion in the Siege of Paris (1870) during the Franco-Prussian War (1870-1).

Étienne Marcel (4) : The name commemorates the French cloth merchant *Étienne Marcel* (*c.*1316-1358), who led opposition to the Dauphin (the future Charles V) and for a time was master of Paris. He was assassinated by a royalist partisan.

Europe (3) : The place de l'*Europe* here was created in 1826 in response to the wish of Parisians to be part of Europe.

Exelmans (9) : The name commemorates Marshal of France Remy Isidore, comte *Exelmans* (1775-1852), who fought in the battles of Austerlitz (see **Gare d'Austerlitz**) and Eylau.

Faidherbe Chaligny (8) : The first part of the name commemorates the French general Louis *Faidherbe* (1818-1889), governor of Senegal. The second honors the French sculptor Jean *Chaligny* (1529-1613).

Falguière (12) : The name commemorates the French painter and sculptor Jean Alexandre Joseph *Falguière* (1831-1900).

Félix Faure (8) : The name honors French president *Félix Faure* (1841-1899).

Filles du Calvaire (8) : In 1617 a convent of Benedictine nuns, *Notre-Dame-du-Calvaire* ("Our Lady of Calvary") was founded in Poitiers. In 1622 they opened a convent in Paris as the *Filles du Calvaire*, "Daughters of Calvary."

Fort d'Aubervilliers (7) : The fort at **Aubervilliers** (see Dictionary) was part of Napoleon's defense line during the battle of Paris (1814).

Franklin D. Roosevelt (1, 9) : The name honors US president *Franklin D. Roosevelt* (1882-1945), who supported Britain and France against Germany and Italy in World War II.

Gabriel Péri (Asnières-Gennevilliers) (13) : The name commemorates the French Communist leader and Resistance member *Gabriel Péri* (1902-1941), killed by the Germans. The addition names the northwestern suburbs of **Asnières-sur-Seine** and **Gennevilliers** (see Dictionary).

Gaîté (13) : The rue de la *Gaîté* ("gaiety") is famed for its dance halls, theaters, and nightlife.

Gallieni (Parc de Bagnolet) (3) : The name honors Marshal of France Joseph *Gallieni* (1849-1916), appointed governor of Paris in 1914. He helped win Franco-British victory in the battle of the Marne (1914) and was minister of war in 1915-16. The addition names the park in the eastern suburb of **Bagnolet** (see Dictionary).

Gambetta (3, 3b) : The name commemorates the French lawyer and politician Léon *Gambetta* (1838-1882), who proclaimed the Third Republic in 1870.

Gare d'Austerlitz (5, 10) : The railroad station (*gare*) commemorates the battle of *Austerlitz* (1805), in which Napoleon defeated the emperors of Austria and Russia.

Gare de l'Est (Verdun) (4, 5, 7) : The railroad station (*gare*) was built to serve lines running out of Paris to the east (*est*). The addition commemorates the battle of **Verdun** (see Dictionary) in 1916, in which the French successfully resisted the Germans.

Gare de Lyon (1, 14) : The railroad station (*gare*) was built to serve the line between Paris and **Lyon**.

Gare du Nord (4, 5) : The railroad station (*gare*) was built to serve lines running to the north (*nord*) and into Belgium and the Netherlands.

Gare St.-Lazare (3, 12, 13) : The railroad station (*gare*) takes its name from the 12th-century asylum for lepers here (later a women's prison) dedicated to *St. Lazarus*, the biblical brother of Martha and Mary who was raised from the dead by Jesus (John 11). (St. Lazarus was equated with the biblical beggar Lazarus "full of sores" in Christ's parable of Dives and Lazarus recounted in Luke 16. Hence the adoption of his name for the asylum.)

Garibaldi (13) : The name honors the Italian patriot Giuseppe *Garibaldi* (1807-1882), who joined the French in the fight against Bismarck in 1870.

George V (1) : The name honors the English king *George V* (1865-1936), who often visited the French front in World War I to encourage the troops in the trenches.

Glacière (6) : The name ("Glacier") refers to the Bièvre River here, where skating was possible and from which ice was formerly taken to preserve food in warm weather.

Goncourt (Hôpital St. Louis) (11) : The name honors the French writer brothers Edmond Huot de *Goncourt* (1822-1896) and Jules Huot de *Goncourt* (1830-1870), founders of the *Académie des Goncourt* literary society, which instituted the *Prix Goncourt* in 1903. The addition names the *Hôpital St. Louis*, founded as a plague hospital in 1616 and named for Louis IX (1214-170), otherwise *St. Louis*, who died of plague in North Africa.

Grande Arche de la Défense (1) : The "Grand Arch of the Defense" was completed in 1989 adjacent to the **Esplanade de la Défense** with its sculpture *La Défense de Paris*. The name *La Défense* is that of the whole business district here, beyond the western edge of Paris.

Grands Boulevards (8, 9) : The centrally located station takes its name from the "great boulevards" carved out in the 1860s by Baron Haussmann, especially those that run from the place de la République to the Madeleine.

Guy Môquet (13) : The name honors the anti-Nazi and anti-Vichy activist *Guy Môquet* (1924-1941), killed by the Germans aged 17.

Havre Caumartin (3, 9) : The rue du *Havre* lies at the Paris end of the route between the capital and *Le Havre* (see **Havre, Le** in Dictionary). The second part of the name commemorates the Paris magistrate Antoine Louis François Le Fèvre de *Caumartin* (1725-1803), who cleared the way for new streets, including the one he named after himself. (His official title was *Prévôt des marchands*. See **Le Peletier**.)

Hoche (5) : The name commemorates the French general and Revolutionary leader Lazare *Hoche* (1768-1797), who with **Kléber** annihilated the Breton royalists seeking to escape to England from Quiberon in 1795 and who pacified the Vendée in 1796.

Hôtel de Ville (1, 11) : See Appendix 4.

Iéna (9) : The name commemorates the Napoleonic Wars battle of *Jena*, Germany, on October 14, 1806, when Napoleon defeated the Prussian and Saxon armies on the same day as the French victory at Auerstedt.

Invalides (8, 13) : See **Invalides, Les** in Appendix 4.

Jacques Bonsergent (5) : The name honors *Jacques Bonsergent* (1912-1940), the first civilian Parisian to be executed by the Germans during the Occupation.

Jasmin (9) : The name commemorates the French Gascon poet *Jasmin*, original name Jacques Boé (1798-1864).

Jaurès (2, 5, 7b) : The name commemorates Jean *Jaurès* (1859-1914), a founder of the Communist daily *L'Humanité* (1904) and effective head of the French socialists. He was assassinated on the eve of World War I.

Javel (André Citroën) (10) : The name is that of a former hamlet south of the Seine, where *eau de Javel* was produced. The addition commemorates the French engineer *André Citroën* (1878-1935), a munitions manufacturer in World War I who then turned to making cars on the first automobile assembly line in France.

Jourdain (11) : The rue *Jourdain* here is named after the *Jordan* River of biblical fame.

Jules Joffrin (12) : The name commemorates the French politician François Alexandre *Jules Joffrin* (1846-1890), a member of the Chamber of Deputies.

Jussieu (7, 10) : The name commemorates

a noted French family of botanists: the three brothers Antoine de *Jussieu* (1686-1758), Bernard de *Jussieu* (1699-1777), and Joseph de *Jussieu* (1704-1779), Bernard's nephew, Antoine Laurent de *Jussieu* (1748-1836), and Antoine Laurent's son, Adrien de *Jussieu* (1797-1853).

Kléber (6) : The name honors the French general Jean-Baptiste *Kléber* (1753-1800), who commanded the campaign in the Vendée, led the Army of the Rhine, and succeeded Napoleon in Egypt, where he was assassinated.

La Chapelle (2) : The district of *La Chapelle* ("The Chapel") is in the north of the capital.

La Courneuve 8 Mai 1945 (7) : For the first part of the name, see **Courneuve, La** in Dictionary. The second part commemorates *May 8, 1945*, the date of the capitulation of Germany at the end of World War II.

La Fourche (13) : The name ("The Fork") is that of the point here where the avenue de Clichy divides, one branch leading to Clichy, the other to Saint-Ouen. Metro Line 13 also divides here, one branch going to **Gabriel Péri (Asnières-Gennevilliers)**, the other to **Saint-Denis Université**.

La Motte Picquet (Grenelle) (6, 8, 10) : The name commemorates Comte Picquet de La Motte, known as *La Motte-Picquet* (1720-1791), the French naval officer who fought against the British during the American Revolution. For the addition, see **Bir-Hakeim**.

La Muette (9) : The name is that of the Château *La Muette* built by Charles IX in the 16th century as a hunting lodge. The castle name itself is from Latin *movita*, "hunting lodge."

La Tour Maubourg (8) : The name commemorates the French general Marie Victor Nicolas de Fay, marquis de *La Tour Maubourg* (1768-1850), aide-de-camp to **Kléber** in Egypt, and minister of war under Louis XVIII (1819-21).

Lamarck Caulaincourt (12) : The first part of the name commemorates the French naturalist Jean Baptiste de Monet, chevalier de *Lamarck* (1744-1829), a professor at the National Museum of Natural History from 1793 to his death. The second part names the French general Armand, marquis de *Caulaincourt*, duc de Vicence (1773-1827), French ambassador in Russia from 1807 to 1811, and minister for foreign affairs subsequently.

Laumière (5) : The name commemorates the French general Xavier Jean Marie Clément Vernhet de *Laumière* (1812-1863), killed in battle during the French campaign in Mexico.

Le Kremlin Bicêtre (7) : See Dictionary.

Le Peletier (7) : The name commemorates Paris magistrate Louis *Le Peletier* de Mortefontaine, killed when the Bastille was stormed in 1789. (He was *Prévôt des marchands*, "Provost of the Merchants," as the senior magistrate of the royal government of the City of Paris. His title was not the same as that of the *Prévôt de Paris*, who was a royal officer charged with representing the sovereign in the viscounty and provosty of Paris, otherwise the supreme officer of the **Châtelet**, who collected the taxes due to the king in the city. Both offices existed from the 13th century to the Revolution.)

Ledru-Rollin (8) : The name commemorates the French politician Alexandre Auguste Ledru (*Ledru-Rollin*) (1807-1874), Republican deputy from 1841 to 1848. Together with **Louis Blanc** he founded the radical socialist journal *La Réforme* in 1843 and ran unsuccessfully for president in 1848.

Les Gobelins (7) : The name commemorates the noted *Gobelin* family of dyers and tapestry makers, sponsored by Henry IV in the early 17th century. They were given the title of *Manufacture Royale des Meubles de la Couronne* ("Royal Manufacturers of Furniture for the Crown") and their royal (later, state) factory still exists.

Les Halles (4) : See **Halles, Les** in Appendix 4.

Les Sablons (Jardin d'Acclimatation) (1) : The name of the district derives from Latin *sabulum*, French *sable*, "sand." The *Jardin d'Acclimatation* (literally "Garden of Acclimatization") is an amusement park in the Bois de Boulogne. A zoo was established here in 1860, but there are now only a few farm animals, such as donkeys, cows, and goats.

Liberté (8) : The avenue de la *Liberté* here was so named in 1889 on the centennial of the Revolution.

Liège (13) : The rue de *Liège* here was originally the rue de *Berlin*, but in World War I this undesirable German name was changed to the friendly Belgian one. It is one of the six streets radiating from the place de l'Europe that were named for European capitals, the others being the rue de *Londres*, rue de *Vienne*, rue de *St.-Pétersbourg*, rue de *Madrid*, and rue de *Constantinople*.

Louis Blanc (7, 7b) : The name commemorates the French historian and socialist politician *Louis Blanc* (1811-1882), who was largely responsible for the overthrow of Louis-Philippe in 1848.

Louise Michel (3) : The name honors the French anarchist *Louise Michel* (1830-1905), a key figure in the insurrections that led to the forming of the Paris Commune in 1871.

Lourmel (8) : The name commemorates the French general Frédéric Henri Lenormand de *Lourmel* (1811-1854), killed in the battle of Inkerman (1854).

Louvre Rivoli (1) : For the first name, see Appendix 4. The second name is that of the rue de *Rivoli* here, named for the battle of *Rivoli* on 14 January, 1797, in which Napoleon defeated the Austrians on the Adige River, Venice, at the start of his Italian campaign.

Mabillon (10) : The name honors the French Benedictine monk and scholar Jean *Mabillon* (1632-1707).

Madeleine (8, 12, 14) : See Appendix 4.

Mairie d'Issy (12) : The name is that of the town hall (*mairie*) of *Issy* (see **Issy-les-Moulineaux** in Dictionary).

Mairie d'Ivry (7) : The name is that of the town hall (*mairie*) of *Ivry* (see **Ivry-sur-Seine** in Dictionary).

Mairie de Clichy (13) : The name is that of the town hall (*mairie*) of **Clichy** (see Dictionary).

Mairie de Montreuil (9) : The name is that of the town hall (*mairie*) of **Montreuil** (see Dictionary).

Mairie de Saint-Ouen (13) : The name is that of the town hall (*mairie*) of **Saint-Ouen** (see Dictionary).

Mairie des Lilas (11) : The name is that of the town hall (*mairie*) of *Les Lilas* (see **Porte des Lilas**).

Maison Blanche (7) : The district of *Maison Blanche* ("White House") apparently takes its name from an inn here.

Maisons-Alfort Les Juilliottes (8) : See the first part of the name in Dictionary. *Les Juilliottes* is the name of a former village here.

Maisons-Alfort Stade (8) : See the first part of the name in Dictionary. The second part names the sports stadium (*stade*) here.

Malakoff Plateau de Vanves (13) : See the first part of the name in Dictionary. The second part names the plain (*plateau*) of **Vanves** (see Dictionary).

Malakoff Rue Étienne Dolet (13) : See the first part of the name in Dictionary. The second part commemorates the French printer and humanist *Étienne Dolet* (1509-1546). Accused of heresy and atheism, he was tortured and burned at the stake.

Malesherbes (3) : The name honors the French magistrate and statesman Chrétien Guillaume de Lamoignon de *Malesherbes* (1721-1794), who defended Louis XVI at his trial and was guillotined.

Maraîchers (9) : The name is from *jardin maraîcher*, "market garden," referring to the fruit and vegetables grown here for the market at Les Halles (see **Halles, Les** in Appendix 4).

Marcadet Poissonniers (4, 12) : The first part of the name is that of the rue *Marcadet*, with a name related to French *marché*, "market," English *merchandise*. The second part means "fishermen." The road was one along which fish from the English Channel came to Paris.

Marcel Sembat (9) : The name honors the French socialist *Marcel Sembat* (1862-1921).

Marx Dormoy (12) : The name commemorates the French socialist *Marx Dormoy* (1888-1941), killed by the Germans.

Maubert Mutualité (10) : The name of the place *Maubert* here probably derives from the German Dominican theologian St. *Albert* le Grand (*c.*1200-1280), who taught in Paris and lectured on Aristotle. The *Mutualité* building nearby was built in 1931 to host congresses and demonstrations. Its name is connected with the "mutualist" movement, a type of union providing benefits for members of different professions.

Ménilmontant (2) : The eastern district derives its name from Latin *mansionile*, "peasant dwelling," and *montant*, "ascending," denoting rising ground.

Michel Bizot (8) : The name commemorates *Michel Bizot* (1795-1855), director of the École Polytechnique. He planned the siege of Sébastopol (see **Réaumur Sébastopol**) and died during the assault there.

Michel-Ange Auteuil (9, 10) : The first part of the name is that of the Italian Renaissance sculptor and painter *Michelangelo* (1475-1564), honored when Napoleon III renovated

Paris in the 19th century. For the second part, see **Auteuil** in Dictionary.

Michel-Ange Molitor (9, 10) : The first part of the name commemorates *Michelangelo* (see **Michel-Ange Auteuil**). The second part honors Marshal of France Gabriel Jean Joseph, comte *Molitor* (1770-1849), who fought for the First Empire and commanded the troops in Spain.

Mirabeau (10) : The name commemorates the French politician and orator Honoré Gabriel Riqueti, comte de *Mirabeau* (1749-1791), who although a nobleman represented the Third Estate at Aix-en-Provence and was privately counselor to Louis XVI.

Miromesnil (9, 13) : The name commemorates the French statesman Armand Thomas Hue de *Miromesnil* (1723-1796), Garde des Sceaux (Attorney General) under Louis XVI, who humanized the French justice system.

Monceau (2) : The northwestern district derives its name from Latin *monticellum*, a diminutive form of *mons, montis*, "mountain."

Montgallet (8) : The name is that of the rue *Montgallet* here.

Montparnasse Bienvenüe (4, 6, 12, 13) : For the first part of the name, see Appendix 4. The second part commemorates the French engineer Fulgence *Bienvenüe* (1852-1936), who planned and supervised the construction of the Métro. (Work on Line 1 began in 1898.)

Mouton-Duvernet (4) : The name commemorates the French general Régis Barthélemy, baron *Mouton-Duvernet* (1769-1816), who supported Napoleon during the Hundred Days (the period March 20–June 22, 1815, during which the emperor was again in power) and also during his subsequent exile, for which he was imprisoned and shot.

Nation (Place des Antilles) (1, 2, 6, 9) : The name is that of the place de la *Nation* here. It was originally the place du Trône ("Throne Square"), so named when Louis XIV entered Paris on being crowned king of France in 1643. During the the Terror it became the *Place du Trône renversé* ("Square of the Overthrown Throne") and was a noted guillotine site. It gained its present name in 1880 in honor of the French national holiday, Bastille Day (July 14). The addition names the French *Antilles* (the French West Indies), i.e. the overseas departments of Guadeloupe and Martinique.

Nationale (6) : The name is that of the rue *Nationale*, named in 1848 to honor the *Garde Nationale* ("National Guard"), which sided with the Republicans in the 1848 Revolution.

Notre-Dame-de-Lorette (12) : The church of "Our Lady of Loretto" here was built in 1823.

Notre-Dame-des-Champs (12) : The chapel dedicated to "Our Lady of the Fields" here was that of the Carmelite convent of the Incarnation, established in 1603. It was rebuilt in the 19th century in the style of a 12th-century church.

Oberkampf (5, 9) : The name commemorates the German-born French industrialist Christophe Philippe *Oberkampf* (1738-1815), inventor of a wallpaper-making machine and founder of a wallpaper factory in 1758 at Jouy-en-Josas, in the southwest of the city.

Odéon (4, 10) : See Appendix 4.

Opéra (3, 7, 8) : See Appendix 4.

Ourcq (5) : The name is that of a river. The canal de l'Ourcq, in northeastern Paris and its suburbs, was built in 1808 to bring fresh water to Parisians from the Marne.

Palais Royal Musée du Louvre (1, 7) : See **Palais-Royal** and **Louvre** in Appendix 4.

Parmentier (3) : The name commemorates the French military pharmacist Antoine Augustin *Parmentier* (1737-1813), popularizer of the potato. (Hence *Parmentier* as a culinary term for a dish made or served with potatoes.)

Passy (6) : See Appendix 4.

Pasteur (6, 12) : The name commemorates the French chemist and biologist Louis *Pasteur* (1822-1895), originator of the process known as pasteurization.

Pelleport (3b) : The name commemorates the French general Vicomte Pierre de *Pelleport* (1773-1855), involved in many major military campaigns.

Père Lachaise (2, 3) : See Appendix 4.

Pereire (Maréchal Juin) (3) : The name commemorates the French banker and politician Jacob Émile *Pereire* (1800-1875), who promoted the railroads and with his brother and associate, Isaac *Pereire* (1806-1880), founded the Crédit Mobilier (1852), giving loans to industrialists. The addition commemorates Marshal of France Alphonse *Juin* (1888-1967), distinguished in World War II as commander of the French Expeditionary Forces in Italy, whom he led to victory at Garigliano in 1944.

Pernety (13) : The name commemorates the

French general Vicomte Joseph Marie de *Pernety* (1766-1856), who fought in many noted battles, including Marengo (1800), Austerlitz (see **Gare d'Austerlitz**), Jena (see **Iéna**), and **Wagram**.

Philippe Auguste (2) : The name honors *Philippe II Auguste* (1165-1223), the first proper "king of France" (unlike the earlier kings of the Franks).

Picpus (Courteline) (6) : The rue de *Picpus* here is the site of a cemetery with the common grave of the 1,308 people guillotined at the nearby place de la **Nation**, as it now is. The addition commemorates the French writer George *Courteline*, original name Georges Moinaux (1858-1929).

Pierre Curie (7) : The name commemorates the French physicist *Pierre Curie* (1859-1906), who with his wife, Marie, discovered radioactivity in 1898 and isolated radium in 1905.

Pigalle (2, 12) : The French sculptor Jean-Baptiste *Pigalle* (1714-1785) lived in the rue *Pigalle* here.

Place d'Italie (5, 6, 7) : The name is that of the square laid out in 1760 on the road from Paris to *Italy*. It had various earlier names before settling to the present one in 1864, when Napoleon III had his eyes on Italy.

Place de Clichy (2, 13) : The square here lies at the intersection of the boulevard de *Clichy* and the avenue de *Clichy*. The latter branches off at **La Fourche** to lead to **Clichy** (see Dictionary).

Place des Fêtes (7b, 11) : The square here was laid out in 1836 for festivals (*fêtes*) in Belleville, especially the annual Mardi Gras.

Place Monge (Jardin des Plantes) (7) : The name of the square commemorates the French mathematician Gaspard *Monge*, comte de Péluse (1746-1818), the creator of descriptive geometry, who accompanied Napoleon to Egypt. For the addition, see Appendix 4.

Plaisance (13) : The name of the former village of *Plaisance* here presumably has the same origin as that of **Neuilly-Plaisance** (see Dictionary).

Poissonière (7) : The rue *Poissonière* here has a name of the same origin as that of the rue des *Poissonniers* (see **Marcadet-Poissonniers**).

Pont de Levallois-Bécon (3) : The bridge (*pont*) here is named commemoratively for the French businessman Nicolas Eugène *Levallois*

(1816-1879), who in 1845 developed the site to make automobile parts. See also **Levallois-Perret** in Dictionary. *Bécon*, with a Gaulish name of uncertain origin, lies across the Seine.

Pont de Neuilly (Avenue de Madrid) (1) : The bridge (*pont*) here leads over the Seine to **Neuilly-sur-Seine** (see Dictionary). The addition refers to the avenue de *Madrid* here, named for the Spanish capital.

Pont de Sèvres (9) : The bridge (*pont*) here leads over the Seine to **Sèvres** (see Dictionary).

Pont Marie (7) : The bridge over the Seine here was built in 1635 and designed by Christophe *Marie*.

Pont Neuf (La Monnaie) (7) : See Appendix 4. For the addition, see **Monnaie, Hôtel de la** in Appendix 4.

Porte d'Auteuil (10) : The gate (*porte*) here leads out of Paris to **Auteuil** (see Dictionary).

Porte d'Italie (7) : The gate (*porte*) here leads out of Paris in the direction of *Italy*.

Porte d'Ivry (7) : The gate (*porte*) here leads out of Paris to **Ivry-sur-Seine** (see Dictionary).

Porte d'Orléans (Général Leclerc) (4) : The gate (*porte*) here leads out of Paris to **Orléans** (see Dictionary). The addition commemorates the French general Philippe de *Leclerc* (originally Philippe de Hautecloque) (1902-1947), who took part in the allied invasion of Normandy 1944 and accepted the German surrender of Paris. He was killed in an airplane accident over Algeria.

Porte Dauphine (Maréchal de Lattre de Tassigny) (2) : The gate (*porte*) here was royal property and named for the *Dauphine*, i.e. Marie-Antoinette, who was given this title while awaiting marriage to the *Dauphin*, the future Louis XVI. See **Dauphiné** in Dictionary. The addition commemorates Marshal of France Jean-Marie *de Lattre de Tassigny* (1889-1952), commander of the First French Army, which he led from Provence to the Rhine and the Danube (see **Boulogne Pont de St. Cloud**) in World War II. He was one of the signatories of the Act of Capitulation of the Third Reich at Berlin on May 8, 1945.

Porte de Bagnolet (3) : The gate (*porte*) here led out of Paris to **Bagnolet** (see Dictionary).

Porte de Champerret (3) : The gate (*porte*) here led to the district of *Champerret*.

Porte de Charenton (8) : The gate (*porte*) here led out of Paris to **Charenton-le-Pont** (see Dictionary).

Porte de Choisy (7) : The gate *(porte)* here led out of Paris to **Choisy-le-Roi** (see Dictionary).

Porte de Clichy (13) : The gate *(porte)* here led out of Paris to **Clichy** (see Dictionary).

Porte de Clignancourt (4) : The gate *(porte)* here led out of Paris to the village of *Clignancourt.*

Porte de la Chapelle (12) : The gate *(porte)* here led out of Paris to **La Chapelle.**

Porte de la Villette (7) : The gate *(porte)* here led out of Paris to *La Villette* (see **Villette, La** in Dictionary).

Porte de Montreuil (9) : The gate *(porte)* here led out of Paris to **Montreuil** (see Dictionary).

Porte de Pantin (5) : The gate *(porte)* here led out of Paris to **Pantin** (see Dictionary).

Porte de Saint-Cloud (9) : The gate *(porte)* here led out of Paris to **Saint-Cloud** (see Dictionary).

Porte de Saint-Ouen (13) : The gate *(porte)* here led out of Paris to **Saint-Ouen** (see Dictionary).

Porte de Vanves (13) : The gate *(porte)* here led out of Paris to **Vanves** (see Dictionary).

Porte de Versailles (12) : The gate *(porte)* here led out of Paris to **Versailles** (see Dictionary).

Porte de Vincennes (1) : The gate *(porte)* here led out of Paris to **Vincennes** (see Dictionary).

Porte des Lilas (3b, 11) : The gate *(porte)* here led out of Paris to *Les Lilas* ("The Lilacs"), a district where the many outdoor cafés had lilac gardens.

Porte Dorée (8) : The name, apparently meaning "Golden Gate," is said to have originally been *Porte d'Orée du Bois de Vincennes*, "Gate at the Edge of the Vincennes Wood" (see **Bois de Vincennes** in Appendix 4).

Porte Maillot (1) : The gate *(porte)* formerly here has a name of uncertain origin.

Pré St.-Gervais (7b) : The station is near the *Porte du Pré St.-Gervais*, where a gate *(porte)* led out of Paris to *Le Pré-Saint-Gervais* (see **Pré-Saint-Gervais, Le** in Dictionary).

Pyramides (7, 14) : The name commemorates the battle of the *Pyramids* on July 21, 1798, in which Napoleon defeated the Mamelukes near the pyramids of Giza, Egypt.

Pyrénées (11) : The rue des *Pyrénées* is named for the **Pyrenees** (see Dictionary), perhaps partly because it is hilly.

Quai de la Gare (6) : The embankment *(quai)* here takes its name from the *gare de l'eau*, "water station," an 18th-century boat harbor on the Seine.

Quai de la Rapée (5) : The embankment *(quai)* here is named commemoratively for Jean-Baptiste *La Rapée*, general superintendent of armies under Louis XIV, who owned a mansion here by the Seine.

Quatre Septembre (3) : The name refers to *September 4*, 1870, when the end of the Second Empire under Napoleon III was declared following the emperor's capture at the battle of Sedan and the formation of the Third Republic was proclaimed.

Rambuteau (11) : The name commemorates the French administrator Claude Philibert Barthelot, comte de *Rambuteau* (1781-1869), who did much to improve the Paris streets, replacing the oil lamps with gas.

Ranelagh (9) : The name is that of the dance hall and theater built in 1774 in the grounds of the Château **La Muette** in imitation of the *Ranelagh* Gardens, London, themselves laid out in 1741 by the purchasers of the Chelsea home of Lord *Ranelagh* (1636-1712).

Raspail (4, 6) : The name commemorates the French chemist and socialist politician François *Raspail* (1794-1878), who ran unsuccessfully for president while imprisoned for sedition.

Réaumur Sébastopol (3, 4) : The first part of the name honors the French physicist and naturalist René Antoine Ferchault de *Réaumur* (1683-1757), inventor of an alcohol thermometer and authority on insects. The second commemorates the battle of *Sebastopol* in 1855, a key engagement of the Crimean War, in which the town was eventually taken by Franco-British forces.

Rennes (12) : The rue de *Rennes* here was built in 1853 with the aim of connecting the Seineside quays with the railroad station (now the Gare Montparnasse) from which trains left for **Rennes** (see Dictionary), but the street was unfinished and never reached the river.

République (3, 5, 8, 9, 11) : The place de la *République*, built in 1811 in the district of the **Château d'Eau**, took its present name in 1883 in honor of the Third Republic

Reuilly Diderot (1, 8) : The first part of the name is that of the former village of *Reuilly*, from the Roman personal name *Rullius* and the associative suffix *-acum*. The second part commemorates the French writer and philosopher Denis *Diderot* (1713-1784).

Richard-Lenoir (5) : The name commemorates François *Richard* (1765-1839) and Joseph *Lenoir*-Dufresne (1768-1806), who built the first cotton factory in Paris in 1802, adopting the joint name *Richard-Lenoir*.

Richelieu Drouot (8, 9) : The first part of the name commemorates the French prelate Armand Jean Du Plessis, cardinal de *Richelieu* (1585-1642), prime minister of Louis XIII. The second part honors Marshal of France Antoine, comte *Drouot* (1774-1847), who accompanied Napoleon to the island of Elba. The Hôtel *Drouot* on the rue *Drouot* is a famous auction house.

Riquet (7) : The name commemorates the French engineer Pierre Paul de *Riquet* (1604-1680), who built the canal du Midi in 1666-81.

Robespierre (9) : The name commemorates the Jacobin leader Maximilien de *Robespierre* (1758-1794), who inaugurated the Terror with its many executions. He was guillotined for his excesses.

Rome (2) : The rue de *Rome* here, named for the Italian capital, leads from the place de l'Europe. See **Liège**.

Rue de la Pompe (9) : The *rue de la Pompe* ("Pump Street") here is so named for its proximity to the pump that fed water to the Château **La Muette**.

Rue des Boulets (Rue de Montreuil) (9) : The *rue des Boulets* ("Canonball Street)" owes its name to the occasion when Henry IV bombarded Paris from the hills here when its citizens refused to accept him as Protestant king of France in 1589. The station is also near the *rue de Montreuil* (see **Montreuil** in Dictionary).

Rue du Bac (12) : The *rue du Bac* ("Barge Street") leads to the Seine at the Pont Royal, where barges ferried stone blocks across the river to build the **Tuileries** (see Appendix 4).

Rue Saint-Maur (3) : The street here is named for the 6th-century abbot *St. Maurus*. The Benedictine Congregation of St. Maur took his name in the 17th century.

Saint François Xavier (13) : The name honors the French missionary of Basque Spanish origin *St. Francis Xavier* (1506-1551), an early member of the Society of Jesus (Jesuits), who evangelized Portuguese India and China.

Saint Marcel (5) : The name honors *St. Marcellus*, 5th-century bishop of Paris.

Saint-Ambroise (9) : The name honors *St. Ambrose*, 4th-century bishop of Milan, who baptized St. Augustine. The church dedicated to him is on the street here.

Saint-Augustin (9) : The name honors *St. Augustine*, 4th-century Father of the Church, bishop of Hippo, theologian and philosopher. The church dedicated to him is nearby.

Saint-Denis Porte de Paris (13) : For the first part of the name, see **Saint-Denis** in Dictionary. The gate (*porte*) here is not one of the main gates leading out of Paris but a "gateway" to the **Basilique de St. Denis**.

Saint-Denis Université (13) : For the first part of the name, see **Saint-Denis** in Dictionary. The second part refers to a branch of the *University* of Paris here.

Saint-Fargeau (3b) : The name commemorates the French politician Louis Michel Lepeletier de *Saint-Fargeau* (1760-1793). He voted for the execution of Louis XVI, for which he was assassinated.

Saint-Georges (12) : The name honors the 4th-century martyr *St. George*.

Saint-Germain-des-Prés (4) : See Appendix 4.

Saint-Jacques (6) : The boulevard *Saint-Jacques* here, named for the apostle *St. James*, marks the site of an old street leading south from the Seine on the pilgrimage route to Santiago de Compostela. See also **Tour Saint-Jacques** in Appendix 4.

Saint-Lazare (3, 12, 13) : The station is named for the **Gare St.-Lazare** here.

Saint-Mandé Tourelle (1) : See the first part of the name in Dictionary. The second part refers to the former route de la *Tourelle* ("Turret") here, so named because it lay alongside one of the turrets on the Château de Vincennes.

Saint-Philippe-du-Roule (9) : The name refers to a chapel here dedicated to *St. Philip* in the former village of *Le Roule*.

Saint-Sulpice (4) : The name refers to the church here dedicated to *St. Sulpicius*, 7th-century bishop of Bourges.

Ségur (10) : The name commemorates the French general and historian Philippe Paul, comte de *Ségur* (1780-1873).

Sentier (3) : The name is that of the rue du Sentier, "Footpath Street," which led to the fortifications that surrounded Paris.

Sèvres Babylone (10, 12) : See the first name in Dictionary. The rue *Babylone* here was so named in 1673 for the priest Bernard de Sainte-Thérèse, known as *l'évêque de Babylone*, "the bishop of Babylon," who started a seminary here in the 1660s to train missionaries for Persia, a country in a region for which Babylon was long the capital.

Sèvres Lecourbe (6) : See the first name in Dictionary. The second name commemorates the French general Claude, comte *Lecourbe* (1758-1815), who fought in Germany with General Moreau in 1796, then in Switzerland against General Suvorov in 1799.

Simplon (4) : The name is that of the *Simplon* Pass, between Switzerland and Italy, made a carriage road by Napoleon in 1800-7.

Solférino (12) : The name commemorates the battle of *Solferino*, Italy, on June 24, 1859, in which the French under Napoleon III defeated the Austrians under Emperor Franz-Joseph.

St. Michel (4) : The place *Saint-Michel* here takes its name from *St. Michael* the Archangel, adopted as a guardian saint more powerful than St. Denis, the patron saint of France, after the English captured the cathedral of St. Denis in the Hundred Years' War. (See **Saint-Denis** in Dictionary.)

St. Paul (Le Marais) (1) : The name is that the former parish church of *St. Paul* here. For the addition, see **Marais, Le** in Appendix 4.

St. Placide (4) : The name honors *St. Placid*, a 6th-century Benedictine monk.

St. Sébastien Froissart (8) : The first part of the name honors the 3d-century martyr *St. Sebastian*, who had given the name of a tavern here. The second part commemorates the French chronicler Jean *Froissart* (c.1337-c.1404).

Stalingrad (2, 5, 7) : The name commemorates the World War II battle of *Stalingrad* (September 1942-February 1943), in which Soviet forces defeated the German 6th Army, marking a turning point in the war on the Russian front.

Strasbourg Saint-Denis (4, 8, 9) : The first part of the name symbolizes Franco-German rivalry, since the city of **Strasbourg** (see Dictionary) has changed hands many times. See the second part of the name in Dictionary.

Sully Morland (7) : The first part of the name commemorates the French statesman Maximilien de Béthune, baron de Rosny, duc de *Sully* (1559-1641), superintendent of finance to Henry IV, noted for his encouragement of

agriculture and trade. The second part names the French colonel François Louis *Morland* (1771-1805), killed at Austerlitz (see **Gare d'Austerlitz**).

Télégraphe (11) : The station is near the site in **Belleville** where the first telegraph was set up by Claude Clappe in 1794 to link Paris and Lille.

Temple (3) : The station is near the former fortified monastery of the Knights Templars, built in the 13th century. It was razed by Napoleon in 1808 to prevent its becoming a site of royalist pilgrimage following the imprisonment of Marie-Antoinette and her children here during the Revolution.

Ternes (2) : The name is that of a former hamlet here that grew up around the château built on the site of the 15th-century country house of the bishop of Paris, itself named *Villa externa prope Rotulum*, "Outer estate near Le Roule" (see **Saint-Philippe-du-Roule**). *Ternes* thus represents the second (Latin) word of this full name.

Tolbiac (7) : The name is that of *Tolbiac*, now Zülpich in Germany, the Gaulish village where the Franks defeated the Germanic Alemanni tribe in 496.

Trinité (d'Estienne d'Orves) (12) : The name is that of the church here, built in 1863 and dedicated to the Holy *Trinity*. The addition commemorates the French naval officer and Resistance worker Henri Honoré *d'Estienne d'Orves* (1901-1941), charged with espionage by the Germans and shot.

Trocadéro (6, 9) : See Appendix 4.

Tuileries (1) : See Appendix 4.

Vaneau (10) : The name commemorates a student called *Vaneau*, killed at the barricades in 1830 when a mob attacked the Swiss Guard on the rue Babylone.

Varenne (13) : The rue de *Varenne* here has a name of the same origin as **Varennes-en-Argonne** (see Dictionary).

Vaugirard (12) : The former village of *Vaugirard* derives its name from Latin *vallis Gerardi*, "Gérard's valley," for *Gérard* de Moret, who built a priests' home here in 1256.

Vavin (4) : The name commemorates the French notary and politician Aléxis *Vavin* (1792-1863), who laid out the street here in 1831 and called it after himself.

Victor Hugo (2) : The name commemorates the French writer *Victor Hugo* (1802-1885).

Villejuif Léo Lagrange (7) : For the first part of the name, see Dictionary. The second part commemorates the French politician *Léo Lagrange* (1900-1940), a promoter of sports facilities, who was killed in World War II.

Villejuif Louis Aragon (7) : For the first part of the name, see Dictionary. The second part comemorates the French Communist writer *Louis Aragon* (1897-1982), a founder of surrealism.

Villejuif Paul Vaillant-Couturier (7) : For the first word of the name, see Dictionary. The second part commemorates the French Communist journalist Paul *Vaillant-Couturier* (1892-1937), chief editor of the Communist daily *L'Humanité* from 1928 to his death.

Villiers (2, 3) : The road here led to *Villiers-la-Garenne*, with a name as for **Villiers-le-Bel** (see Dictionary) and *Clichy-la-Garenne* (see **Saint-Ouen** in Dictionary).

Volontaires (12) : The rue des *Volontaires* here has a name honoring the volunteer soldiers of the Revolution who sought to defend the Republic.

Voltaire (9) : The name commemorates the French writer, philosopher, and social critic *Voltaire*, original name François Marie Arouet (1694-1778).

Wagram (3) : The name commemorates the battle of *Wagram* on July 6, 1809, when Napoleon defeated the Austrians under Archduke Charles Louis at Wagram, Austria.

Appendix 4: Major Placenames in Paris

Below are the origins of the names of most of the familiar places or sites in Paris, from streets and statues to parks and palaces. Places best known by English names, as the *Eiffel Tower*, are cross-referred to their French name, as *Tour Eiffel, La.* (The French article in such cases follows the name in its entry.) Some of the entries are a little more discursive than strictly necessary for the explanation of the name, but the added information is always relevant to the place itself. A separate listing at the end of this appendix shows revolutionary renamings in Paris. (It has its own preamble, but see also the more general preamble to Appendix 2.)

Arc de Triomphe. There are two "triumphal arches" in Paris. The larger, and more famous, is the *Arc de Triomphe de l'Étoile*, at the end of the **Champs-Élysées** in the center of the circular place Charles de Gaulle (see **Charles de Gaulle, Place**). It commemorates the victories of Napoleon, under whose decree it was built (1806-36). Beneath it lies the Tomb of the Unknown Soldier (see **Tombe du Soldat Inconnu**.) The smaller, erected in 1806, is the *Arc de Triomphe du Carrousel* (see **Carrousel, Place du**) at the eastern end of the **Tuileries** gardens. It also commemorates Napoleon's military achievements. A third arch, not triumphal, is the **Grande Arche de la Défense** (see Appendix 3).

Arènes de Lutèce. The "Lutetia Amphitheater," on the rue Monge, displays the remains of the 2d-century amphitheater from the Roman settlement of *Lutetia* (see **Paris** in Dictionary).

Assemblée Nationale *see* **Bourbon, Palais**

Bastille. The notorious fortress, built by Charles V in 1370-82 to defend the eastern edge of the city, soon became a jail for political prisoners. It was stormed on July 14, 1789 by angry citizens incensed by the excesses of the monarchy, and destroyed the following year. Its site is marked by the **Colonne de Juillet**. Its name is an altered form of *bastide*, "walled town," itself from Provençal *bastida*, "built (place)."

Batignolles, Les. The name of the northwestern district is an altered form of *Bastilloles*, recorded in the 16th century as a quarter of Clichy, itself a diminutive of French *bastille*, "fortress," "castle" (as for the **Bastille**).

Bibliothèque Nationale. The *Bibliothèque Nationale de France* ("National Library of France") (BNF) was formed in 1994 through a merger of the *Bibliothèque Nationale* (BN), in the rue de Richelieu, and the *Bibliothèque de France* (BF), in the quartier de Tolbiac. In 1996 the Tolbiac BNF, renamed *Bibliothèque François-Mitterrand* for president *François Mitterrand* (1916-1996), opened in new premises on the quai François-Mauriac by the Seine, and was joined by the Richelieu BNF in 1998.

Bois de Boulogne. The "Boulogne Wood," a large park at the city's western edge, is named for *Boulogne* (see **Boulogne-Billancourt** in Dictionary), which borders it to the south. It was laid out under Napoleon and contains the racecourses of Auteuil and Longchamps and the **Jardin d'Acclimatation** (see Appendix 3).

Bois de Vincennes. The "Vincennes Wood," a rival in appearance (but not size) to the **Bois de Boulogne**, lies at the city's southeastern edge, where it is bordered to the north by **Vincennes** (see Dictionary).

Bon Marché. The city's oldest department store, on the left bank, was founded in 1852 by Aristide Boucicaut (1810-1877). At that time, many Paris stores had names such as *Le Diable Boîteux* ("The Lame Devil"), *Les Deux Magots* ("The Two Magots"), or *La Belle Jardinière* ("The Beautiful Lady Gardener"). But Boucicaut and his wife called their enterprise *Au Bon Marché* ("The Bargain"), referring to their wide range of inexpensive goods.

Bourbon, Palais. The "Bourbon Palace," on the left bank, opposite the place de la Concorde, was built in 1722 for the duchess of *Bourbon* (see **Bourbonnais** in Dictionary), daughter of Louis XIV. It is now occupied by the *Assemblée Nationale* ("National Assembly"), which with the *Sénat* ("Senate") has formed the French parliament since 1946.

Bourse. The building which houses the *Bourse de Commerce* ("Commercial Exchange") on the rue de Viarmes was erected as a grain market in 1767 and remodeled in the early 19th century. French *bourse* happens to mean "purse," appropriately enough for a stock exchange, but the Bourse, founded in 1719 by the Scottish financier John Law, took its name from a Flemish family of Venetian origin called *Van der Burse* (Italian *della Borsa*), who set up the first such exchange in Bruges, Belgium, in 1549.

Butte, La *see* **Montmartre**.

Carnavalet, Musée de. The museum, devoted to the history of Paris, is housed in the *Carnavalet* mansion, the home of the letter-writer Madame de Sévigné. Built in 1548, the mansion was acquired in 1578 by Françoise de Balsam-Montrevel, widow of the Breton nobleman François Kernevenoc'h (or Kernevenoy), and his name was turned by Parisians into *Carnavalet*, probably under the influence of *carnaval*, "carnival."

Carrousel, Place du. French *carrousel* means "carousel," a historical term for a kind of tournament in which variously dressed companies of knights engaged in games and contests. The French court first showed interest in such carousels in the 17th century, and on June 5, 1663, Louis XIV organized a spectacular one on the site of the present square to celebrate the birth of the Dauphin (see **Dauphiné** in Dictionary).

Cernuschi, Musée de. The museum of oriental art was set up in the Parc Monceau mansion which the Italian banker and collector Ernico *Cernuschi* (1821-1896) bequeathed to the city.

Centre Pompidou. The *Centre National d'Art et de Culture Georges-Pompidou*, as it is formally known, is named for president Georges Pompidou (1911-1974) and opened in 1977. It stands between the rues Beaubourg and Saint-Martin and houses the *Musée National d'Art Moderne* ("National Museum of Modern Art") and the *Bibliothèque Publique d'Information* ("Public Information Library").

Chaillot, Palais de. The public building, built for the 1937 Universal Exhibition on the site of the former **Trocadéro**, is named for the former village of *Chaillot* here, from Old French *chail* (modern *caillou*), "stone," "pebble." It houses the *Musée de l'Homme* ("Museum of Man"), *Musée de la Marine* ("Museum of the Navy"), and the *Musée du Patrimoine et de l'Architecture* ("Museum of Heritage and Architecture"), the latter being the former *Musée des Monuments Français* ("Museum of French Monuments").

Champ-de-Mars. The "Field of Mars" (the Roman god of war) is a former vast parade ground laid out in 1765-7 between the **École Militaire** and the Seine. On July 14, 1790, Louis XIV took an oath here to uphold the new revolutionary constitution, and Napoleon celebrated his battle victories here. The Eiffel Tour (see **Tour Eiffel**) was built here in 1889. The name itself was adopted from the *Campus Martius* in Rome, the exercise ground of Roman armies, so called from an altar to Mars erected there. It later became a park open to the Roman public, just as its French equivalent did for Parisians and visitors to the capital.

Champs-Élysées. The broad avenue, between the Place de la Concorde (see **Concorde, Place de la**) and the **Arc de Triomphe**, came into being in 1667 when the royal gardener André Le Nôtre planted an arbor of trees beyond the **Tuileries** Gardens. It was at first called the *Grand Cours*, "Great Way," but was later renamed the *Champs-Élysées*,

"Elysian Fields," after the dwelling place of mortals made immortal by favor of the gods in Greek mythology.

Charles-de-Gaulle, Place. The great square in western Paris, with the **Arc de Triomphe** at its center, was built from 1768 to 1784 and originally called *Place de l'Étoile*, "Star Square," for the five (now 12) that radiate from it. It was named as now in 1970 in honor of president *Charles de Gaulle* (1890-1970), who walked at the head of a triumphal procession from here down the **Champs-Élysées** on August 26, 1944, following the liberation of Paris.

Cité *see* **Île de la Cité**

Cluny, Hôtel de. The Cluny mansion stands on the site where the Benedictine abbey of **Cluny** (see Dictionary) purchased Gallo-Roman remains in 1334. The monks of Cluny built a mansion here in the late 15th century as a residence for visiting abbots, and the museum that now occupies it displays the remains. Its full title is *Musée National du Moyen Âge–Thermes de Cluny* ("National Museum of the Middle Ages–Thermal Baths of Cluny").

Collège de France. The "College of France" is an educational and research establishment founded in 1529 by François I to provide courses in subjects not offered by the university.

Colonne de Juillet. The "July Column" was inaugurated on July 28, 1840, on the site of the **Bastille**, in memory of the combatants who lost their lives in the uprising against Charles X on July 27-29, 1830 (the *Trois Glorieuses*, "Three Days of Glory"), when the victorious insurgents set up a provisional government at the **Hôtel de Ville.**

Conciergerie. The Conciergerie is the medieval part of the **Palais de Justice** on the **Île de la Cité**. It was originally the residence of the governor of the king's palace (hence its name, literally "caretaker's lodge"), and in 1392 became a prison with the concierge as chief jailer.

Concorde, Place de la. "Harmony Square," between the **Tuileries** gardens and the **Champs-Élysées**, was laid out between 1735 and 1755 as the *Place Louis-XV*, for *Louis XV* (1710-1774). During the Revolution it became the *Place de la Révolution*, and was the scene of over a thousand executions, including those of Louis XVI and Marie-Antoinette. The present name was given symbolically in 1795. The

central obelisk, a gift from Egypt erected in 1836, is from a 3,300-year-old Luxor temple.

Défense, La *see* **Grande Arche de la Défense** in Appendix 3.

Deux Magots, Les. The noted literary café, on the Boulevard Saint-Germain, was founded in 1881 and named after the wooden statues of two Chinese dignitaries (*magots*) who sit atop boxes of money inside. The word itself, originally meaning "monkey," derives from *Magog*, a biblical name associated with *Gog*, and in Revelation 20:8 that of one of the nations assembled by Satan for an assault on the saints.

Dôme. The Église du Dôme ("Church of the Dome"), so named for its golden dome, stands in the **Invalides** complex, where it was built as a chapel for the resident soldiers in 1680.

École Militaire. The "Military School" (Royal Military Academy), at the edge of the **Champ-de-Mars**, was built in 1752-74 on the orders of Louis XV with the aim of educating the sons of impoverished officers.

Égouts, Les. The present sewers (*égouts*) of Paris, now an unlikely tourist attraction, were built by Baron Haussmann in the mid-19th century. They bear no comparison with the sewers that existed earlier, graphically described by Victor Hugo in *Les Misérables* (1862).

Eiffel Tower see **Tour Eiffel**

Élysée, Palais de l'. The Élysée Palace, on the corner of the rue du Faubourg-Saint-Honoré and the avenue de Marigny, not far from the **Champs-Élysées**, was built in 1718 for the comte d'Évreux. It was occupied by a succession of famous historical figures until 1873, when it became the presidential residence.

Étoile, Place de l' see **Charles-de-Gaulle, Place**

Folies-Bergère. Paris's first "purpose-built" music hall opened in 1869 on the corner of the rue Richer and rue de Trévise and was originally to have been called the *Folies-Trévise*. The duc de Trévise objected to the name, however, so the theater instead adopted the name of the nearby rue *Bergère*. *Folies* means "revue," as for the Ziegfeld Follies.

Forum des Halles see **Halles, Les**

Goutte d'Or. The name of the northern district means "golden drop," from the medieval vineyard formerly here.

Grand Palais. The "Great Palace" and *Petit*

Palais ("Little Palace") exhibition halls, either side of the Pont Alexandre III, were built for the 1900 Universal Exhibition.

Grande Arche *see* **Grande Arche de la Défense** in Appendix 3

Grevin, Musée. The waxworks gallery, on the boulevard Montmartre, was founded in 1882 by the journalist Arthur Meyer (1844-1924) and the draftsman Alfred *Grévin* (1827-1892).

Guimet, Musée de. The museum of Asiatic art, on the avenue d'Iéna, was founded at Lyon in 1879 by Émile *Guimet* (1836-1918). It was transferred to Paris in 1885.

Halles, Les. The district of central Paris known as *Les Halles* ("The Halls") stands on the old site of the city's covered food market, set up here in 1183. In 1969 it moved to Rungis, south of Paris, and in 1977 the *Forum des Halles* opened on the former site as a commercial and shopping center.

Homme, Musée de l' *see* **Chaillot, Palais de.**

Hôtel de Ville. The original Paris city hall was the Maison aux Piliers ("House of Pillars"), in use from 1357 to 1533. The second was in use from the 16th century until it was burned down by insurrectionary Communards in 1871. The present building, which contains the apartments of the mayor of Paris, dates from 1874. *Hôtel* here, now the standard word for "hotel," means in effect "public building."

Hôtel-Dieu. The name, literally "hostel of God," came to be used in medieval times for a hospital. The Paris Hôtel-Dieu, on the Île de la Cité, now the hospital for the city center, was built in 1866-78 on the site of a foundling home dating from the 12th century.

Île de la Cité. The "City Island," in the Seine, is the site where the present city of Paris arose in pre-Roman times.

Île Saint-Louis. The "Island of St. Louis," upstream on the Seine from the Île de la Cité, was originally known as the Île Notre-Dame, "Island of Our Lady." In 1614 it was joined to the small neighboring Île aux Vaches ("Island of Cows") and renamed as now for *Saint Louis*, otherwise Louis IX (1214-1270), king of France from 1226 (aged 12) to his death.

Institut de France. The "Institute of France," on the left bank of the Seine, is the home of the Académie Française ("French Academy"), founded in 1666, and four other academies.

Invalides. The Hôtel des Invalides ("Hospital of the Disabled") dates from 1670, when Louis XIV built a convalescent home for wounded soldiers. It is still home to war veterans, but is now primarily a memorial to the battles and campaigns of French history. (French *invalide* does not mean "invalid" in the general sense but specifically means "disabled person.")

Jardin d'Acclimatation *see* Appendix 3

Jardin des Plantes. The "Garden of Plants" is a great public park laid out around the buildings of the *Muséum national d'histoire naturel* ("National Natural History Museum") beside the Seine. It has evolved from a royal herb garden established in 1626 and first opened to the public in 1640.

Jeu de Paume. The art gallery and exhibition center is housed in a former real tennis court, the name of the game being *jeu de paume*, literally "game of (the) palm." (Real tennis, the precursor of lawn tennis, although now a racket game, was originally played by using the palm of the hand to strike the ball over the net.) The Paris court, built in 1862, was the last major building devoted to the sport.

Latin Quarter *see* **Quartier Latin**

Left Bank *see* **Rive Gauche**

Louvre. The celebrated art gallery was originally the *Palais du Louvre*, a royal residence that began as a hunting lodge built in the 12th century by Philippe Auguste. It was improved and enlarged under successive kings until the time of Napoleon III in the 19th century. The art collection evolved from a set of 12 paintings displayed by François I in the 16th century. The Louvre was first opened to the public in 1793, and it is now the *Musée du Louvre*. The name was recorded in the 12th century as *Louvrea*, probably from Latin *lupus*, "wolf," and the suffix *-ara*, denoting a place frequented by wolves.

Luxembourg, Palais du. The palace, on the rue de Vaugirard, was built in 1615-20 for Marie de Médicis, widow of Henri IV, on the site of a former palace belonging to the duke of Piney-*Luxembourg*, which Marie had bought in 1612. It is now home to the French Senate.

Madeleine. Construction of the church began in 1764, when Napoleon commissioned it as a *Temple de Gloire* ("Temple of Glory") to his armies. In 1845, however, it was dedicated to *Marie-Madeleine*, "Mary Magdalene," a name associated with three biblical women: the anonymous sinner who washed the feet of Jesus with her tears during a meal at Simon's house (Luke 7), Mary of Magdala who was the first to see Jesus alive after the Crucifixion (Matthew 28), and Mary of Bethany, the sister of Lazarus and Martha (John 11). (At one stage the Madeleine nearly became a railroad station, serving the new Paris to Saint-Germain-en-Laye line. Hence the student pun, "C'est magnifique, mais ce n'est pas la gare.")

Marais, Le. The name of the right-bank district means "the swamp," referring to a formerly uninhabitable stretch of marshy ground by the Seine here used for market gardening.

Marché aux Fleurs. The "Flower Market" on the Île de la Cité is the oldest in Paris, dating from 1898.

Marché aux Oiseaux. The "Bird Market" joins the **Marché aux Fleurs** on Sundays as a relic of the numerous bird markets that existed in Paris from medieval times.

Marché aux Puces. The "Flea Market" lies just outside the city perimeter at Saint-Ouen, where it has evolved from the stalls set up by rag merchants in the late 19th century to avoid paying taxes levied within the city. The cloths and clothing that they sold often contained fleas. Hence the name of the present antiques market, said to be the largest in the world.

Marmottan, Musée. The *Musée Marmottan Claude Monet*, on the rue Louis-Boilly, contains the world's largest collection of paintings by the named Impressionist artist. The collection is housed in the mansion of the art collector Paul *Marmottan* (1856-1932).

Matignon, Hôtel. The mansion in the rue de Varenne, now the official residence of the French prime minister, was built in 1722-25 and bought soon after by the comte de *Matignon* who offered it to his son, the duc de Valentinois.

Métro *see* Appendix 3

Monnaie, Hôtel de la. The left-bank mansion, built in 1768-77, is the administrative base of the French Mint. (French *monnaie*, directly related to English *money*, is the normal word for "change" but more narrowly means "coin," "currency.")

Montmartre. The Roman name of this northern district was *Mons martyrum*, "martyrs' mount," the martyrs in question being St. Denis (see **Saint-Denis** in Dictionary) and his two companions, Rusticus and Eleutherius.

The name replaced the earlier *Mons Mercurii*, "mount of Mercury," for the Roman god. The slight hill here (the "mount" of the name) is known as *La Butte*, "The Mound," a name synonymous with Montmartre itself.

Montparnasse. The former hill (*mont*) of this left-bank district was leveled when the Boulevard *Montparnasse* was laid out in the 18th century. The name is French for *Mount Parnassus*, the mountain in central Greece that was sacred to Apollo and the Muses. The quarter has long been a focal point for Parisian writers and artists.

Moulin de la Galette. The windmill, on the rue Tholozé, is one of just two remaining in **Montmartre**. It was built in 1622 and was formerly the venue for an open-air cabaret. It is named after the *galettes* made using flour ground in the mill. (The *galette*, a flat, round cookie made of puff pastry, takes its name from *galet*, "pebble," referring to its shape.)

Moulin Rouge. The "Red Windmill" opened in **Montmartre** as a music hall in 1889, taking its name from an old dance hall and restaurant on the avenue d'Antin (the present avenue Franklin D. Roosevelt). The name soon became synonymous with the cancan danced there.

Musée *see* the next main word, e.g. for *Musée d'Orsay* see **Orsay, Musée d'**.

Notre-Dame. *Notre-Dame de Paris*, "Our Lady of Paris," on the Île de la Cité, is the metropolitan church or cathedral of the French capital. Its foundation stone was laid in 1163 on the instigation of Maurice de Sully, bishop of Paris, and it was essentially completed by the mid-13th century.

Observatoire. The *Observatoire de Paris*, "Paris Observatory," is a center of astronomical research founded in 1667. The original building, on the avenue de l'Observatoire, now houses offices, a science museum, a library, and a speaking clock.

Odéon. The theater of this name is housed in the building constructed for the Comédie Française on the left bank of the Seine in 1782. The theater itself, founded in 1797, takes its name from Greek *ōideion*, a building for musical performances.

Opéra. The major opera house, on the place de l'Opéra, was built in 1862-74 and is also known as the *Palais Garnier*, after the building's architect, Charles *Garnier* (1825-1898). The first opera was performed there in

1875 but it has staged only ballets since the opening in 1989 of the *Opéra-Bastille* on the place de la **Bastille**. The two operas, together with the École de Danse de Nanterre ("Nanterre Ballet School"), combined in 1994 to form the *Opéra National de Paris*.

Orangerie. The present art museum was originally the greenhouse (literally "orangery") of the **Tuileries** gardens. The collection of mainly Impressionist and early 20th-century paintings was donated to the state by Domenica Walter, widow of the art dealer Jean Walter.

Orly *see* Dictionary

Orsay, Musée d'. The noted museum, with a collection covering a variety of art forms from the 1848-1914 period, is housed in the former *d'Orsay* railroad station on the left bank of the Seine. The station, named for its location on the quay d'Orsay, was built for the 1900 Paris Exhibition. It was in use until 1939, when it was closed and largely ignored, although later used as a theater and as auction rooms. In 1977 the Paris authorities decided to convert it into a link between the **Louvre** and the Musée National d'Art Moderne (see **Centre Pompidou**), as which it finally opened in 1986. The quai d'Orsay itself, formerly the longest Seineside quay, was built in 1708 by the mayor of Paris, Charles Boucher *d'Orsay*.

Palais de Justice. The "Palace of Justice," on the **Île de la Cité**, contains the city's law courts. It originated in the 13th century as the home of French kings on the site of the palace of the Roman rulers. When the French royal family abandoned the palace for the **Louvre**, it was taken over by Parliament. It acquired its present name during the Revolution.

Palais-Royal. The "Royal Palace," on the square of the same name, was built for Cardinal Richelieu in 1633 and was originally called the *Palais-Cardinal*. On his death in 1642 it passed to the king and gained its present name. The ducs d'Orléans acquired it in 1661 and it now houses the Council of State and the Ministry of Culture.

Panthéon. The resting place for the famous was based on the *Pantheon* in Rome. Hence its name, meaning "(temple of) all gods," from the Greek. It was built in 1764-90 and was originally a church, dedicated to St. Genevieve, the patron saint of Paris. During the Revolution it became a mausoleum for the city's notables, but Napoleon gave it back to

the Church in 1806. It was later desecularized, returned once more to the Church, and finally became a public building in 1885, when the ashes of Victor Hugo were transferred here.

Passy. *District, Paris*. The western quarter has a name of the same origin as **Passy** (1) (see Dictionary).

Père Lachaise. The *Cimetière du Père-Lachaise*, "Cemetery of Father Lachaise," containing many famous tombs, was laid out in 1804 at **Menilmontant** (see Appendix 3) on the site of the former estate of François d'Aix de *La Chaise* (1624-1709), confessor to Louis XIV.

Petit Palais *see* **Grand Palais**

Pont Neuf. The "New Bridge" is Paris's oldest surviving bridge. The name seems incongruous, but the bridge was new by comparison with the four already existing when Henri III laid the first stone in 1578. The Wars of Religion delayed completion until 1604.

Pyramide. The "Pyramid" is the modern glass pyramid erected as the main entrance to the **Louvre** in 1988. It was created by the Chinese-American architect Ieoh Ming Pei.

Quartier Latin. The "Latin Quarter," on the left bank of the Seine, takes its name from the Latin spoken by students of the **Sorbonne** here from the Middle Ages until the Revolution. The name first occurs in the writings of Rabelais (*c*.1494-1553).

Quatre-Nations, Collège des. The "College of Four Nations" was founded in 1661 by Cardinal Mazarin. It was designed to take 60 "scholars" from the four "nations" that had recently been reunited with France: Alsace, the Netherlands, Roussillon, and the province of Pignerol. It was suppressed in 1793 and its premises passed to the **Institut de France**.

Quinze-Vingts. *Les Quinze-Vingts*, "The Fifteen Twenties" was a hospital founded between 1254 and 1261 by Louis IX to take 300 blind patients. Its modern equivalent provides ophthalmic services for hospitals.

RER *see* Appendix 3

Right Bank *see* **Rive Droite**

Rive Droite. The "Right Bank" of the Seine (the northern bank, facing downriver to the west) is traditionally regarded as the "mainstream" part of Paris, as against the **Rive Gauche**.

Rive Gauche. The "Left Bank" of the Seine (the southern bank, facing upriver to the east) is traditionally regarded as the intellectual, literary, and artistic quarter, with the **Sorbonne** and the **Quartier Latin**. It is on the Rive Gauche that the *bouquinistes* have their booths, full of secondhand and antiquarian books.

Rodin, Musée. The museum devoted to the works of the sculptor Auguste *Rodin* (1840-1917) is in the Hôtel Biron, on the rue de Varenne, where he spent the last years of his life.

Roissy Charles-de-Gaulle. The Roissy Charles de Gaulle airport is Paris's main airport, 20 miles northeast of the city center. It opened in 1974 and is named after its location near **Roissy-en-France** (see Dictionary) and for president *Charles de Gaulle* (1890-1970).

Sacré-Cœur. The *Basilique du Sacré-Cœur*, "Basilica of the Sacred Heart," was built on the *butte* (hill) of **Montmartre** from 1876 to 1912 to atone for the humiliating defeat of France in the Franco-Prussian War (1870). Devotion to the Sacred Heart of Jesus holds a special significance for Catholics, especially in acts of reparation and consecration.

Saint-Eustache. The second largest church in Paris (after **Notre-Dame**) was built from 1532 to 1637 for the congregation of Les Halles (see **Halles, Les**) and dedicated to the Roman martyr *St. Eustace*.

Saint-Germain-des-Prés. The left-bank district takes its name from the Benedictine abbey "St. Germanus of the Meadows," founded here in 558 at what was then the edge of the city and dedicated to *St. Germanus*, 6th-century bishop of Paris. It was a powerful ecclesiastical complex throughout the Middle Ages, but today, following the Revolution, only the church survives. It is the oldest in Paris, dating from the 11th and 12th centuries.

Sainte-Chapelle. The "Holy Chapel," within the complex of the **Palais de Justice**, was built next to the royal palace in 1248 by Louis IX (St. Louis) to house a fragment of the True Cross and the entire Crown of Thorns.

Salpêtrière. *La Salpêtrière*, on the boulevard de l'Hôpital, was founded by royal edict in 1656 as a hospital and almshouse for infirm, insane, and indigent women on the site of an arsenal and saltpetre (*salpêtre*) works dating from the time of Louis XIII. It remains a leading women's hospital today.

Samaritaine. The department store of this name was founded in 1870 by Ernest Cognacq (1839-1928), It was so called from a pump

under the **Pont Neuf** which drew water from the Seine to supply the **Louvre** until 1813 and which was decorated with a figure of the biblical woman of Samaria (*la Samaritaine*) giving Jesus water at the well (John 4:7).

Seine *see* Dictionary

Sorbonne. The city's university, between the **Panthéon** and the place Saint-Michel, was founded in 1257 by Robert de *Sorbon* (1201-1274), confessor to Louis IX, as a college for 16 poor students to study theology. It soon grew into a major European center of learning and was the core of the University of Paris, itself founded in 1215.

Soubise, Hôtel de. The mansion, in the **Marais**, today houses the Archives Nationales ("National Archives") and the Musée de l'Histoire de France ("Museum of the History of France"). It was built in the early 18th century as a residence for François de Rohan, prince of Soubise (1630-1712).

Tertre, Place du. The square of this name (*tertre*, "hillock") is in the heart of **Montmartre**.

Tomb of the Unknown Soldier see **Tombe du Soldat Inconnu**

Tombe du Soldat Inconnu. The "Tomb of the Unknown Soldier" dates from 1921, when an unidentified French soldier, killed in World War I, was buried beneath the **Arc de Triomphe**.

Tour Eiffel. The "Eiffel Tower" takes its name from the French engineer Gustave *Eiffel* (1832-1923), who erected it on the **Champ-de-Mars** to mark the 1889 Universal Exhibition.

Tour Saint-Jacques. The "St. James Tower," on the place du Châtelet, dates from 1523. It is all that remains of the church of St.-Jacques-de-la-Boucherie, once the largest medieval church in Paris and the point of departure for pilgrims to Santiago de Compostela (named after St. James) in Spain. See also **Saint-Jacques** in Appendix 3.

Trocadéro. The name commemorates the battle of *Trocadero*, on August 31, 1823, when Louis XVIII invaded Spain and defeated the Spanish at this fort near Cádiz. The fort itself took its name from Spanish *trocar*, "to barter," denoting a market site. In 1827 the king organized a reenactment of the battle at the Butte Chaillot, by the Seine, and the area became known by the battle name, which in turn passed to the ornate palace built here as part of the Universal Exhibition of 1878. It was largely demolished in 1936, but its two curving wings were retained and incorporated into the Palais de Chaillot (see **Chaillot, Palais de**), built for the Universal Exhibition of 1938. The name caught on elsewhere in Europe for various places of popular entertainment, such as the Trocadero Palace of Varieties in London, England, known as "the Troc," which opened as a music hall in 1882: "*We* had a rag at Monico's. *We* had a rag at the Troc." (John Betjeman, "The Varsity Students' Rag," 1927).

Tuileries. The former *Palais des Tuileries*, to the west of the **Louvre**, was built in 1564 for Catherine de Médicis, widow of Henri II, taking its name from the tileworks (*tuileries*) over which it was erected. It was partly burned down in 1871 and finally demolished in 1882. What remains are the gardens (*Jardin des Tuileries*), first created by Catherine herself, but formally redesigned in 1664 by André Le Nôtre, gardener to Louis XIV.

Val-de-Grâce. The Benedictine abbey of Notre-Dame-du-Val-de-Grâce ("Our Lady of the Vale of Grace") was founded as a convent on the rue Saint-Jacques in 1621. It became a military hospital in 1793 and is now a teaching hospital and army medical school.

Vendôme, Place. The central square so called, originally planned in 1685, was laid out in 1698 as the *Place Louis-le-Grand*, after *Louis* XIV, who commissioned it from François Mansart. It was built on the site of the razed mansion of the duc de **Vendôme** (see Dictionary). Hence its name, acquired when Napoleon came to power in 1804. Meanwhile the original equestrian statue of Louix XIV had been demolished during the Revolution, when the square was renamed *Place des Piques*, for the heads of executed aristocrats paraded here on pikes (*piques*). In 1806 the *Colonne Vendôme* ("Vendôme Column") was erected on the site of the king's statue to commemorate Napoleon's victories. It was based on Trajan's Column in Rome and made from the bronze of Austrian guns captured at Austerlitz (1805), with a statue of Napoleon over all. The column was destroyed in 1871 but reerected in 1875.

Victoires, Place des. "Victory Square," adjacent to the **Palais-Royal**, was laid out in the 17th century and commemorates the victories of Louis XIV, whose equestrian statue stands at the center.

Villette, La. The name of the northeastern quarter derives from Latin *villa*, "estate," "village," and the diminutive suffix -*itta*.

Voie Triomphale. The "Triumphal Way" or *Grande Axe* ("Great Axis") is a name sometimes used for the grand perspective or line of sight that runs northwest from the Arc de Triomphe du Carrousel, through the Tuileries Gardens to the obelisk in the Place de la Concorde, on up the Champs-Élysees to the Arc de Triomphe, and finally to the Grande Arche de la Défense, a distance of 5 miles.

Revolutionary Renamings in Paris

Below are some of the main Revolutionary renamings in Paris for (a) streets, (b) squares, (c) riverside roads (embankments), and (d) buildings. The original name is given first. In (a), (b), and (c), the generic word is omitted, so "Angoulême, d' : de l'Union" = "Rue d'Angoulême : Rue de l'Union," and "Vendôme : des Piques" = "Place Vendôme : Place des Piques."

The Bonnet Rouge ("Red Cap") which replaced the Croix Rouge ("Red Cross") at the crossroads (*carrefour*) of this name represents the distinctive headgear of the Sans-Culottes ("Breechless"), so called as they wore trousers, not aristocratic knee breeches. Both terms were synonymous for revolutionaries. Other keynotes selected for renaming include Marat's revolutionary daily *L'Ami du Peuple* ("Friend of the People"), Rousseau's *Du contrat social* ("A Treatise on the Social Contract") (1762), the *Droits de l'homme* ("Rights of Man") declaration, promulgated by the National Assembly in 1789, and one or other of the three watchwords *Liberté*, *Égalité*, *Fraternité* ("Liberty, Equality, Fraternity"), the slogan of the Revolution itself. The date May 31, substituted for the royalist name of the rue du Petit-Bourbon, is that of the day in 1793 when the Sans-Culottes invaded the Convention to demand the arrest of the Girondins following their refusal to provide for the economic demands of Parisian workers.

As with the town and village renamings listed in Appendix 2, some of the names remain today, among them the rues de Lille, de l'Université, de l'Observatoire, d'Hauteville, de Jean-Jacques-Rousseau, the place des Vosges, and the quai Voltaire.

Street (*Rue*)

Angoulême, d' : de l'Union
Antin, Chaussée d' : du Mont-Blanc
Artois, d' : de Cérutti
Bourbon, de : de Lille
Bourbon-le-Château : de la Chaumière
Bourbon-Villeneuve : Neuve-de-l'Égalité
Colonne, de, or de La Fayette : Contrat-Social, du
Comtesse-d'Artois : Mont-Orgueil
Condé, de : de l'Égalité
Cordeliers, des : de Marat
Cour au Vilain, or de Montmorency : de la Réunion
Croix-Rouge, Carrefour de la : du Bonnet-Rouge
Dauphin, du : de la Convention
Dauphine : de Thionville
Fontaine-au-Roi : de la Fontaine
Fossés-Monsieur le Prince, des : de la Liberté
Fossés-Saint-Victor, des : de Loustalot
Francs-Bourgeois, des : des Francs-Citoyens
Gros-Caillou, du : de l'Université
Guisarde : des Sans-Culottes
Honoré-Chevalier : Honoré-Liberté
Hôpital Saint-Louis, de l' : de l'Hospice-du-Nord
Jardin-du-Roi, du : du Jardin-des-Plantes
Louis-le-Grand : des Piques
Martin : du Faubourg-du-Nord
Michel-le-Comte : Michel Le Pelettier
Michodière (now d'Hauteville) : d'Hauteville
Montmartre : Mont-Marat
Montmorency : de la Réunion
Neuve-de-Richelieu : Petite Rue Chalier
Neuve-Notre-Dame : de la Raison
Neuve-Saint-Roch : de la Montagne
Observance, de l' : de l'Ami-du-Peuple
Parc-Royal, du : du Parc-National

Petit-Bourbon, du : du 31 mai
Platrière : de Jean-Jacques Rousseau
Richelieu, de : de la Loi
Roi-de-Sicile, du : des Droits-de-l'Homme
Roi-Doré, du : Dorée
Royale (in Barrière-Blanche) : de la République
Royale (now de Birague) : Nationale (or du Parc-d'Artillerie)
Royale (now des Moulins) : des Moulins
Royale (now Royale) : de la Révolution
Saint-Denis : de Franciade
Saint-Jacques : de l'Observatoire
Saint-Laurent : du Faubourg-du-Nord
Saint-Louis (on the Quai des Orfèvres) : Révolutionnaire
Saint-Louis (on the Île Saint-Louis) : de la Fraternité
Sainte-Anne : Helvetius

Square (*Place*)

Carrousel : de la Réunion
Cimetière Saint-Jean : des Droits-de-l'Homme
Dauphine : de Thionville
Grève, de : de la Maison-Commune
Henry IV, de : Parc-d'Artillerie
Louis XV, de : de la Révolution
Parvis-Notre-Dame : de la Raison
Royale (now des Vosges) : des Fédérés, or Parc d'Artillerie
Sorbonne : de Chalier
Vendôme : des Piques
Victoires, des : de la Victoire-Nationale

Riverside Roads (embankments) (*Quai*)

Anjou, or d'Alençon : de l'Union
Balcons, des, or Dauphin : de la Liberté

Bourbon, de : de la République
Horloge-du-Palais, de l' : du Nord
Orfèvres, des : du Midi
Orléans, d' : de l'Égalité
Théatins, des : de Voltaire

Buildings

Anciens Juges-Consuls : Tribunal de Commerce
Bibliothèque du Roi : Bibliothèque Nationale
Collège de Louis-le-Grand : Collège de l'Égalité
Collège Royal de France : Collège de France
Église de Sainte-Geneviève : le Panthéon-Français

Hôpital de la Charité : Hospice de l'Unité
Hôpital de Notre-Dame-de-la-Pitié : Maison des Élèves de la Patrie
Hôpital des Enfants-Trouvés : Maison des Enfants de la Patrie
Hôpital Saint-Louis : Hospice du Nord
Hôtel Royal des Invalides : Hôtel National des Militaires Invalides
Hôtel-Dieu : Grand Hospice d'Humanité
Jardin du Palais-Royal : Jardin Égalité
Jardin du Roi : Jardin des Plantes
Palais de Bourbon : Maison de la Révolution
Pont de Louis XVI : Pont de la Révolution
Pont Notre-Dame : Pont de la Raison
Pont-Royal : Pont-National
Porte Saint-Denis : Porte de Franciade

Appendix 5: Common Words and Elements in French Placenames

Mention was made in the Introduction of the general composition and characteristics of French placenames. The information given there is supplemented here by a more detailed listing of the most commonly found words and elements, with their meaning, language of origin, and examples of names in the Dictionary containing them.

aqua, "water" (Latin) : The origin of French *eau*, "water," and a word often denoting thermal springs or baths. It sometimes occurs as *aquis*, the ablative (locative) plural form. Examples: **Aigues-Mortes, Aix-en-Provence, Ax-les-Thermes, Condezaygues, Entraygues, Outreau, Tramezaïgues.**

arcus, "arch" (Latin) : The word usually refers to the arch of a bridge. Examples: **Arc, Arcueil, Ars-sur-Moselle.**

balneolum, "small bath" (Latin) : The word, a derivative of *balneum*, "bath," usually denotes a bathing place in a river, or refers to former Roman baths. Examples: **Bagneux, Bagnolet, Banyuls-sur-Mer.**

barr, "height" (pre-Celtic) : The word refers to an elevated site or summit. Examples: **Bar-le-Duc, Barr, Barrois.**

basilica, "church" (Latin) : Originally meant "market," then "church." Example: **Bazeilles.**

bastita, "built (place)" (Latin) : Grammatically a feminine past participle used as a noun. It originally denoted a fortified place, then (13th and 14th centuries) a small town built around such a fort, especially one where the inhabitants were exempt from feudal dues (see **Villefranche**). It later meant a country cottage, especially in the region around Marseille. Any addition is usually the name of the place where the fort was built. Example: **Bastia.**

boscus, "wood" (Low Latin) : The source of French *bois*, "wood," often accompanied by the personal name of the owner of the wood. Examples: **Bois-Colombes, Bois-Guillaume, Verrières-le-Buisson.**

briga, "height" (Gaulish) : The word, indirectly related to *burgus*, refers to an elevated locality, and in some cases to a fortress, often built on a raised site. Examples: **Briançon, Brie, Escaudœuvres, Moyeuvre-Grande.**

briua, "bridge" (Gaulish) : Most places named with this word (akin to English *bridge*) are on or near a river. In some instances the original name has been replaced by a new one, as with **Amiens, Pontoise.** Examples: **Bléré, Briare, Brides-les-Bains, Chabris, Salbris, Verberie.**

burgus, "fortified place" (Low Latin) : A word of Germanic origin. Examples: **Bourg, Bourgueil, Villarodin-Bourget.**

cambo-, "curve" (Gaulish) : The word can refer to a bend in a river or a curve in a hill, and when applied to a natural feature that is usually straight, can mean "crooked." Examples: **Chambéry, Chambord, Kembs.**

campus, "field" (Latin) : The source of French *champ*, "field," and a word denoting cultivated land, as distinct from uncultivated terrain. Its derivative *campania*, "plain," also occurs. Examples: **Camembert, Champagne, Champs-sur-Marne.**

caput, "head" (Latin) : The source of both

French *cap*, "cape," and *chef*, "head (person),"and a word usually translated "head" or "end." A headland or promontory is the end of a piece of land. The word may also refer to an important or chief place, as a main estate. Examples: **Cabestany, Capbreton, Chabeuil, Chef-Boutonne.**

casa, "house" (Latin) : The original sense was "hovel," then "country cottage," then "estate." See also *chez*. Examples: **Cazouls-lès-Béziers, Chazelles-sur-Lyon, Deux-Chaises.**

castellum, "castle" (Latin) : A diminutive of *castrum*, "fortified place," and the source of French *château*. In its earliest sense the word denoted a fortification or stronghold of any kind, from the dungeon of a castle to a walled town or city. It then gained a more specialized sense as the French *château fort*, or fortified castle, and finally passed to the more recent *château*, as a large country house like an English manor. It is thus somewhat misleading to refer to a *château* as a "castle," and the famous *châteaux* of the Loire, noted for their architectural grandeur and formal gardens, are hardly castles in the English historical sense. Such *châteaux* are usually named either for the location where they were built or with a more or less fanciful name given by the owner. Examples: **Cassel, Casteljaloux, Châteaubriant.**

chapelle, "chapel" (French) : A word often meaning "church" rather than simply "chapel." For the history of the word, see **Chapelle-aux-Saints, La.** Examples: **Cappelle-la-Grande, Crécy-la-Chapelle, Lacapelle-Marival.**

chez, "at the house of" (French) : A word prefixed to a personal name to designate a country estate or a hamlet. Such names are found in a broad band across central France, from Poitou in the west to Savoy in the east. The personal name is that of the former owner of the estate. Thus in Haute-Savoie, to the south of Lake Geneva, are *Chez-Bochet, Chez-Cachat, Chez-Crosson, Chez-Thiollay*, and a plural *Chez-les-Girards*, this last perhaps as the name of a tenant family. The word itself ultimately derives from Latin *casa*.

condate, "confluence" (Gaulish) : A preceltic word denoting the place where one river joins another. In some cases a name with this word has been superseded by a newer name, as with **Rennes, Saint-Claude.** Examples: **Candé, Condé-sur-Vire, Cosne-d'Allier.**

cors, "court" (Latin) : The name, with genitive form *cortis*, is the Vulgar Latin equivalent of Classical Latin *cohors, cohortis*, "courtyard." It was originally used for the main buildings of a farm, then for an estate, and finally for an entire village. It is frequently accompanied by a Germanic personal name. Examples: **Achicourt, Cousoire, Élancourt, Nonancourt.**

dominus, "lord" (Latin) : This word amounts to "saint" in names dating from around the 6th to the 10th century. Most such names are in the north and east of France and usually begin with *Dom-* or *Dam-*. The most common are *Dompierre* and *Dampierre* (honoring St. Peter), *Dommartin* and *Dammartin* (St. Martin), and *Dommarie, Dammarie, Dannemarie* and *Donnemarie* (St. Mary). Examples: **Damparis, Domrémy-la-Pucelle.**

dunon, "fort" (Gaulish) : The word originally meant "hill" before it gained the sense "fort," and both the natural and the manmade object are suitable for defense, the latter often being built on the former. Names with *dunon* are often those of an *oppidum* (a Roman fortress town) by a main route, which needs to be guarded. In some cases the current name has replaced an earlier name with the word, as with **Nevers, Rodez, Tours.** Examples: **Autun, Châteaudun, Dun-sur-Auron, Embrun, Issoudun, Laon, Lyon, Verdun.**

duron, "gate" (Gaulish) : The word has the primary meaning "gate," then by extension, "enclosed market," "fortified town." (It is unrelated to Latin *durus*, "hard," but akin to English *door*.) The word is invariably accompanied by a qualifier, often a personal name, and sometimes appears in the earlier name of a place, as with **Bayeux, Metz, Reims.** Examples: **Auxerre, Bressuire, Duclair, Issoire, Jouarre, Meudon, Nanterre, Tarare, Tonnerre.**

fontana, "fountain" (Latin) : A derivative of *fons, fontis*, "spring," with the suffix *-ana*, used in a collective sense. It is usually accompanied by the name of a river, a village, a local lord, or an adjective, and can itself add the collective suffix *-etum*. Examples: **Fontaine, Fontainebleau, Fontenay-le-Comte.**

fraxinum, "ash tree" (Latin) : One of the more common tree names, others being *alnus*, "alder," *buxus*, "box," *castaneum*, "chestnut," *fagus*, "beech," *pinus*, "pine," *robur*, "oak," *salix*, "willow," *tilia*, "lime," *ulmus*, "elm." Examples: **Fraisses, Freneuse, Fresnes.**

ialon, "clearing" (Gaulish) : The word is usually rendered "clearing" or "field," but sometimes "village," implying a site that has been cleared or prepared for purposes of settlement. It can combine with either another Gaulish word or a Latin one, the former being much more common. Examples: **Arcueil, Argenteuil, Bailleul, Creil, Deuil, Jargeau, Moreuil, Rambouillet, Villenoy**. (American footnote: Gaulish *ialon* is related to Welsh *iâl*, "hill country," which gave the name of *Iâl* near Wrexham, Wales, which gave the name of both Elihu *Yale*, benefactor of Yale University, and Linus *Yale*, inventor of the Yale lock.)

insula, "island" (Latin) : The source of French *île*, "island," and a word often used of a location on higher ground by water such as a river. Examples: **Isle, Isle-Aumont**.

kal, "rock" (pre-Indoeuropean) : The word (more precisely element) is believed to have a sense development "rock," "shelter," "habitation," "fortress." Examples: **Calais, Calvi, Challans, Chelles, Lascaux**.

kêr, "town" (Breton) : The word, related to Welsh *caer*, "castle," "city," originally meant "house." Examples: **Carhaix, Kervignac, Locmariaquer, Tréguier**.

lann, "territory" (Breton) : The word, related to Welsh *llan*, "church," and ultimately English *land*, is common in Brittany placenames. It usually refers to a church, or a church site, and is normally accompanied by the name of the saint to whom the church is dedicated. Examples: **Landerneau, Landivisiau, Lannion**.

loch, "church site" (Breton) : The word, from Latin *locus*, "place," is common in Brittany placenames, where at first it often designated a church or monastery. It later came to apply to a parish or village, and (as *Loc-*) is almost always followed by the name of the patron saint. Examples: **Locmariaquer, Locminé, Locronan, Loctudy**.

magos, "market" (Gaulish) : The word first meant "field," then "market," and is sometimes found for an original name superseded by the current one, as with **Angers, Beauvais, Senlis**. Examples: **Billom, Caen, Carentan, Condom, Gien, Mouzon, Noyon, Riom, Rouen**.

mansus, "staying (place)" (Latin) : The indirect source of French *maison*, "house," and a feudal term for a small farm held by a single tenant. Examples: **Masseube, Mazamet, Mézidon-Canon**.

monasteriolum, "religious house" (Latin) : A diminutive form of *monasterium*, "monastery." Examples: **Monéteau, Monistrol-sur-Loire, Montreuil**.

mons, "mountain" (Latin) : A word, with genitive *montis*, that often does not denote a mountain in the usual sense but simply a hill in an otherwise flat region. It is usually accompanied by a personal name, placename, or descriptive. Examples: **Beaumont, Cornimont, Hautmont, Lormont, Montaigu, Montcenis, Offemont, Réalmont**.

murus, "wall" (Latin) : The reference is usually to a fortification, especially a Roman or pre-Roman one. Examples: **Meursault, Moret-sur-Loing, Murat**.

nanto-, "valley" (Gaulish) : The word can mean "stream" as well as "valley." Examples: **Dinan, Mornant, Nantua**.

petra, "stone" (Latin) : The word can mean "stone," "rock," or "mountain," and in some cases denotes ancient ruins. Examples: **Pérols, Pierre-Bénite, Pierrefonds**.

plebs, "the common people" (Latin) : Found mainly in Breton names, where its original meaning was "church providing baptism," then "parish" (Welsh *plwyf*). It is usually represented by initial *Plé-*, *Pleu-*, *Plou-*, or simply *Pl-*, depending on the following letter or syllable. Names based on *plebs* are always old parishes, and *plebs* is always followed by a defining word. Example: **Plabennec**.

podium, "raised place" (Latin) : The word denotes a height of some kind, typically a rounded hill. It frequently appears in the French form *puy*, as for *Le Puy* (see **Puy, Le**). Examples: **Peypin, Piolenc, Pujols**.

pons, "bridge" (Latin) : The source of French *pont*, "bridge," and a word (genitive *pontis*) often accompanied by a placename or personal name, and typically by the name of the river crossed by the bridge. In the case of **Pontoise**, the word translates Gaulish *briua*. Examples: **Escautpont, Paimpont, Pontarlier, Pont-Aven**.

pratum, "meadow" (Latin) : The source of French *pré*, "meadow," and a word usually occuring in its plural form of *prata*. Examples: **Pardies, Prades, Presles**.

puteus, "well" (Latin) : The source of French *puits*, "well," and a word found with various suffixes. Examples: **Pouzauges, Puiseaux**.

ritu-, "ford" (Gaulish) : The word can

occur in names that have now been superseded, as with **Limoges, Vannes**. Examples: **Bort-les-Orgues, Chambord, Javols, Niort**.

rocca, "rock" (pre-Latin) : The word, the source of French *roche*, "rock," is used of any rocky eminence, from a small hill to a full-blown mountain. By extension it can also denote a fortress built on a rocky rise or even the fortress itself. It is usually found with a qualifier. Examples: **Rochechouart, Rochefort, Roquefort**.

sanctus, "saint" (Latin) : The word, the source of French *saint*, "holy," is found as the source of the many names derived from a patron saint, usually the one to whom a parish church is dedicated. It is normally followed by a personal name (the saint in question) or less often by an inanimate or abstract object. In some instances it can denote a sanctuary or place where holy relics are preserved, as at **Sains-du-Nord**. Examples: **Saint-Affrique, Saint-Cloud, Saint-Léonard, Saint-Lys, Samer, Sancerre**.

vallis, "valley" (Latin) : The Latin word was originally feminine, so that names with masculine French *le* came later. Examples: **Bonneval, Clairvaux, Entrevaux, Laval, Valbonne**.

vicus, "village" (Latin) : The Roman *vicus* was contrasted for tax purposes with *municip-*

ium, a village of Roman citizens, and *colonia*, a village of colonizers, but itself had no legal status. Examples: **Blévy, Longwy, Neuvic, Vibraye, Vichy, Vivonne**.

villa, "village" (Latin) : The usual meaning of the very common word, the source of French *ville*, "town," is "estate," "village." The former meaning was current for a country estate from the 4th through 11th centuries, after which the sense "village" gradually evolved. The word is almost always qualified, and an accompanying personal name is usually that of a local lord. In several instances the personal name appears in a Latin feminine adjectival form, with *villa* understood, as for **Comines, Éguilles, Lisses, Vergèze**. Examples: **Abbeville, Chaville, Eppeville, Lunéville, Offranville, Tancarville, Villandraut**.

villare, "farmstead" (Latin) : A derivative of *villa*, typically found in the form *Villard* or *Villers* followed by a placename, personal name, or descriptive. The word originally denoted a separate part of an estate, such as a farm and its buildings or an isolated group of houses. Germanic names ending in *-viller* or *-willer* also contain it. Examples: **Abreschwiller, Dettwiller, Folschviller, Mertzwiller, Villard-de-Lans, Villers-Bocage**.

Bibliography

AA Road Book of France. London: The Automobile Association/Charles Letts, 3d ed, 1972.

Baillie, Kate, and Tim Salmon. *The Rough Guide to France.* London: Rough Guides, 7th ed., 2001.

Cherpillod, André. *Dictionnaire étymologique des noms géographiques* [Etymological Dictionary of Geographical Names]. Paris: Masson, 2d ed., 1991.

Cohen, Saul B., ed. *The Columbia Gazetteer of the World.* New York: Columbia University Press, 1998. 3 vols.

Dauzat, Albert, and Charles Rostaing. *Dictionnaire étymologique des noms de lieux en France* [Etymological Dictionary of Placenames in France], revised and completed by Charles Rostaing. Paris: Librairie Guénégaud, 2d ed., 1978.

Delamarre, Xavier. *Dictionnaire de la langue gauloise* [Dictionary of the Gaulish Language]. Paris, Éditions Errance, 2d ed., 2003.

Delaney, John J. *Dictionary of Saints.* New York: Doubleday, 1980.

Farmer, David Hugh. *The Oxford Dictionary of Saints.* Oxford: Oxford University Press, 5th ed., 2003.

Fierro, Alfred. *Histoire et Dictionnaire de Paris* [History and Dictionary of Paris]. Paris: Robert Laffont, 1996.

Graesse, Johann Gustav Theodor, and Friedrich Benedict. *Orbis latinus, oder Verzeichnis der wichtigsten lateinischen Orts- und Ländernamen* [The Latin World, or Index of the Most Important Latin Place and Province Names]. Berlin: transpress VEB Verlag für Verkehrswesen, 1980. (A reprint of the 2d edition of 1909, published in Berlin by Richard Carl Schmidt & Co.)

Hardy, Brian. *Paris Metro Handbook.* Harrow Weald: Capital Transport, 2d ed., 1993.

Harvey, Sir Paul, and J.E. Heseltine, comps. and eds. *The Oxford Companion to French Literature.* Oxford: Clarendon Press, 1959.

Illustrated Guide to France. Windsor: AA Publishing, 2003.

Losique, Serge. *Dictionnaire étymologique des noms de pays et de peuples* [Etymological Dictionary of the Names of Countries and Peoples]. Paris: Éditions Klincksieck, 1971.

Merriam-Webster's Geographical Dictionary. Springfield, MA: Merriam-Webster, 3d ed., 1997.

Michaud, Guy, et Alain Kimmel. *Le Nouveau Guide France.* Paris: Hachette, 1996.

Morlet, Marie-Thérèse. *Dictionnaire étymologique des noms de famille* [Etymological Dictionary of Family Names]. Paris: Perrin, 1991.

Nègre, Ernest. *Toponymie générale de France* [The Placenames of France]. Geneva: Droz, 1990–91. 3 vols.

Le Petit Larousse Illustré [Little Illustrated Larousse]. Paris: Larousse, 1997.

Plotkin, Susan L. *The Paris Metro: A Ticket to French History.* Philadelphia, PA: Xlibris, 2000.

Prigmore, B.J. *On Rails under Paris.* London: Light Railway Transport League, 1970.

Rostaing, Charles. *Les noms de lieux* [Placenames]. Paris: Presses Universitaires de France, 12th ed., 1997.

Touring Atlas France. Windsor: AA Publishing, 3d ed., 2003.

Wallace-Hadrill, J.M., and John McManners, eds. *France: Government and Society.* London: Methuen, 2d ed., 1970.

Watkins, Dom Basil, ed. *The Book of Saints.* London: A & C Black, 7th ed., 2002.

Young, Edward, ed. *The Shell Guide to France.* London: Michael Joseph, 1983.

The revolutionary placenames in Appendix 2 are based on those listed at two Internet sites: *Villes révolutionnaires par ordre alphabétique* ("Revolutionary towns in alphabetical order") at http://www.chez.com/memorial/doc-vil-rev, and *Liste de noms révolutionnaires de certaines communes de France, ainsi que des noms originaux, avec indication du département* ("List of revolutionary names of certain towns and villages in France, as well as their original names, together with their departments") at http://mapage/noos.fr/echolalie. Further such names may be found at http://www.geneaguide.com/onomastique/revolution.

For a wry Russian view of French revolutionary renamings, see Chapter 2, *Pereimenovaniye ulits i seleniy* ("The renaming of streets and settlements"), in O. Kabanes and L. Nass, *Revolyutsionnyj nevroz* ("Revolutionary neurosis"), St. Petersburg: D.F. Komorsky, 1906.